Kurile Is.
(U.S.S.R.)

HOKKAIDO

AN

na

Bonin Is.

OCEAN

MARIANA IS.

Saipan

Guam
(U.S.)

(U.S. Occupied)

Samar
Panay   Leyte
Palawan
Negros

CAROLINE IS.

MINDANAO

(Br.)   North
Brunei   Borneo   (Br.)

SARAWAK
(Br.)

CELEBES SEA

HALMAHERA

EQUATOR

BORNEO

CELEBES

REPUBLIC OF INDONESIA   Ceram

DUTCH
NEW GUINEA

NORTH-EAST
NEW GUINEA   Rabaul

arta   BANDA SEA

Madura

AVA   Bali   Sumbawa Flores   (Port.)   PAPUA

Sumba   Timor   Arafura Sea

AUSTRALIA

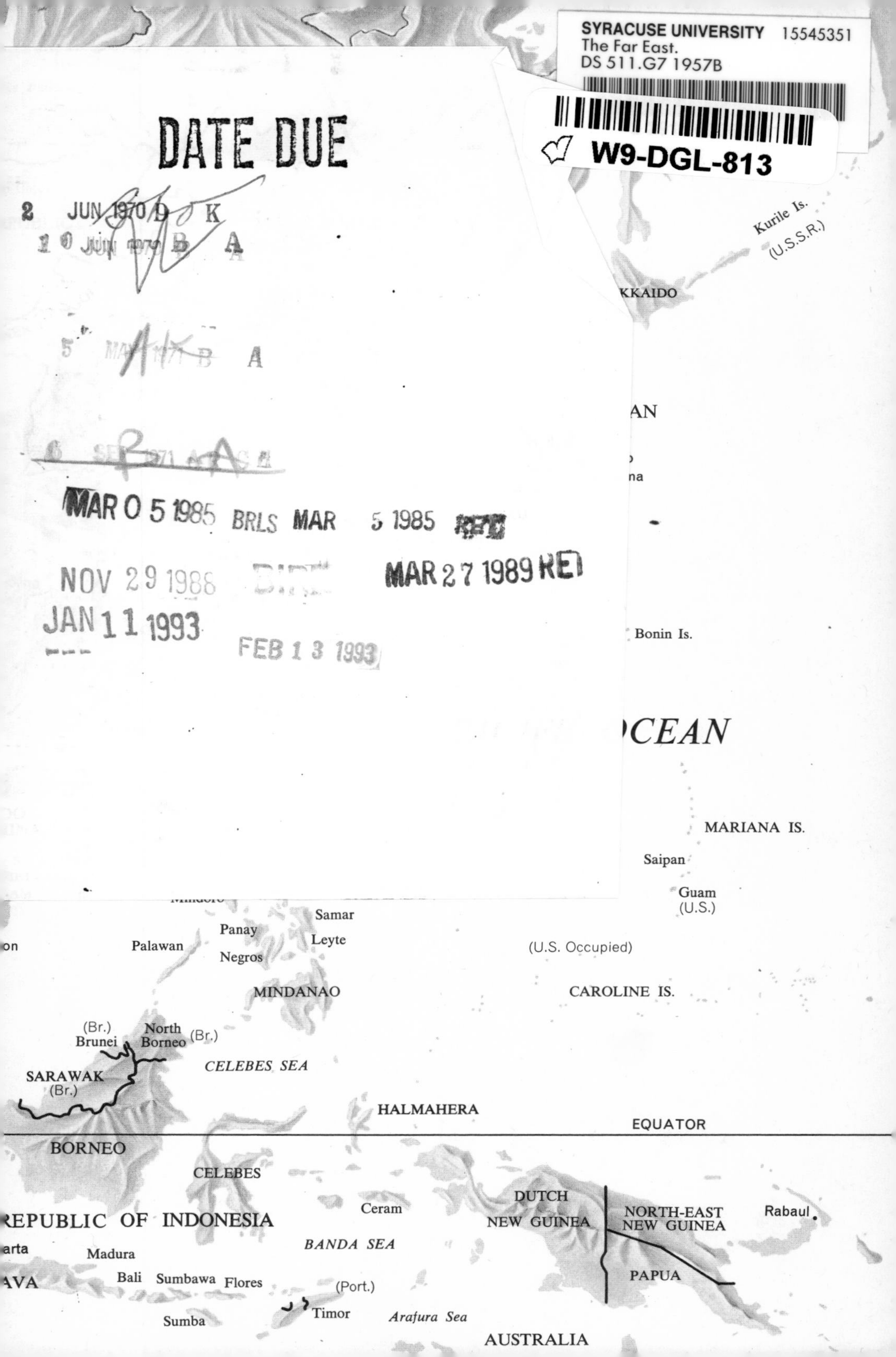

The Far East

The
Far
East

Fred Greene
Williams College

Holt, Rinehart and Winston

NEW YORK – CHICAGO
SAN FRANCISCO – TORONTO
LONDON

For Lynn

with love, honor, and remembrance

Preface

This century has witnessed extraordinary political changes and revolutions. The countries of Eastern Asia have experienced political, economic, and social upheavals that have occurred with unbelievable speed since 1945. The purpose of this study is to describe the nature and strength of the major political forces in the area in the hope of clarifying this complex picture. From the viewpoint of historical development, a threefold subdivision emerges: (1) the political traditions and historical evolutions of the member states of this area, (2) the impact of the West and its profound influences on an already changing political order, (3) and the issues that have come to the fore in today's revolutionary and fluid situation.

In narrating these events, I have sought to draw attention to the political characteristics dominating the scene prior to the rise of European influence. These differed markedly in content, stature, and appeal throughout the Orient, a factor that led to sharply varied responses to the Western challenge. The ebbing away of this foreign power is a forceful reminder that the period of Occidental political domination was merely one phase in Asian history.

The states extending from Japan to Pakistan are grouped together because happenings in any one sector today affect the rest of the region. In world politics, these countries appear more closely knit than before, both as storm centers in the Cold War and as leading exponents of insurgent nationalism. Their importance to the international balance of power—in the racial and ideological sense as well as in political-military affairs—becomes increasingly evident with each passing year.

India plays a significant role in this drama. Formerly there was a real political separation between the affairs of colonial India and those of China and Japan. This permitted us to compartmentalize the study of these countries. Today the entire region's economic and social development, and the outcome of its painful effort to come to terms with modern political ideologies, are heavily dependent on the performance of India. It is no exaggeration to place India's role on a level of importance with that of China. The issues of democracy *versus* communism and the question of political balance and stability may hinge on the outcome of a contest between these two regional powers.

The ideological and power aspects of this struggle will persist for some time.

However, Indian and Chinese efforts at economic development may prove even more significant. The "underdeveloped" lands have placed such heavy stress on modernization that they have allocated a great part of their scarce capital and many of their public administrative services to this problem. Since the outcome of these efforts will do much to determine the political future of each country and the region as a whole, the question of economic growth has been given extensive consideration on the pages that follow.

The book is introduced with two chapters on the political and economic characteristics existing, in varying degrees, in the region as a whole. China, Japan, and the Indian subcontinent, as the major powers of this region, are at the core of this study. However, instead of following a chronological narrative, the book considers each country in turn. In this way, I hope, the political evolution of these divergent cultures will emerge more clearly. This introduction to the three major powers is supplemented by a brief survey of the six states of Southeast Asia, an area whose future is closely tied to the attitudes of both the great Asian and the great Western powers. A final section is concerned with the problem of regional international relations, in which the United States, Soviet Russia, and Great Britain play vital roles as outside powers.

This type of presentation necessarily means that certain significant events (for example, Chinese affairs in the 1940's) must be touched on in different parts of the book. Such an approach serves to highlight the variety of motives and the differing, often conflicting, viewpoints held by the central participants in these dramas. It is hoped that the reader, observing these developments from varying perspectives, may gain a clearer view of the crosscurrents of East Asian politics.

I am grateful to my colleagues at Williams College for encouragement and helpful advice, and especially to Professors Vincent M. Barnett, Frederick L. Schuman, and Edwin Drexel Godfrey, Jr. of the Political Science Department, and Emile Despres and William B. Gates, Jr. of the Economics Department. Valuable suggestions were made by Professors Wesley R. Fishel of Michigan State University, Francis H. Heller of the University of Kansas, and Amos A. Jordan, Jr. of the United States Military Academy, all of whom reviewed the manuscript at various stages in its development. All maps including the endpapers were prepared with great professional skill by Vincent Kotschar.

FRED GREENE

Williamstown, Massachusetts
March, 1957

Contents

Maps and Charts

Photographs

Tables

PART ONE **Introduction**

1 _The Political Setting_

Eastern Asia became an active participant in world politics when the Japanese empire embarked on its career of expansion in 1894. The tempo of violence and change accelerated during this century and reached a peak at the end of the Second World War. Japan and China acquired new forms of government, while the colonial lands emerged as new states. This complex situation became ominous because the nationalist struggle for self-rule triumphed in the Far East just as the ideological and power struggle called the Cold War broke out in full fury. The countries of Southern and Eastern Asia, possessing great historic cultures, are free to determine their own political course. The ingredients that combined to create this maelstrom—nationalism, communism, democracy, and modern war—all stem from the West. How these elements operate in their Asian setting comprises one of the greatest problems of our time. And it is the specter of communism that has given a sharp edge to existing American interests in this area.

The region extending from Pakistan to Japan appears so vast and is so full of divergent cultures that one analyst has observed that "there is no Asia." Others have noted that each major culture is a civilization unto itself. Additional variations arise from differences in size, population, and strategic location. Contact with the West brought further divergences, according to the time it occurred, its political consequences, and the identity of the foreign power. Any attempt to generalize about Asia must therefore be cautious and tentative.

The Traditional Heritage

Similarities and Diversities

Despite many subtle differences in its manifestation, contact with the West was nevertheless a common experience shared by all of Southern and Eastern Asia. Several centuries of constant pressure from the West, often resulting in conquest and rule, have left an indelible mark. Local responses involved more than a political struggle over self-determination. They reflected the painful experience that an advanced culture undergoes when confronted with a foreign civilization powerful enough to upset its social and political traditions. The Asian nations were compelled to reassess and often to discard traditional values.

3

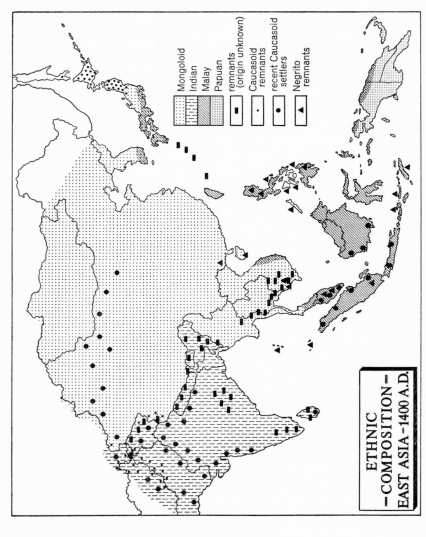

**ETHNIC
—COMPOSITION—
EAST ASIA—1400 A.D.**

Mongoloid

Indian

Malay

Papuan

remnants
(origin unknown)

Caucasoid
remnants

recent Caucasoid
settlers

Negrito
remnants

Adapted from J. E. Spencer, *Asia, East by South* (New York: John Wiley & Sons, Inc., 1954). © 1954.

They had to learn to think in terms of a Western-paced environment, featuring constant innovation and change.

Unlike much of Africa or the New World, Eastern Asia had developed an advanced civilization when it was confronted by the West in the sixteenth century. By then it had evolved its own high religions, political orders, complex social hierarchies, and intensive agrarian economies. Jawaharlal Nehru has claimed that until modern times it lay at the center of human history. These cultures, moreover, developed a number of common features that gave this region its own distinctive characteristics.

One reason for stressing the importance of South and East Asia is the large population of the region. It has contained far more people than any other segment of the globe since ancient times. India and China today contain more than 350 and 550 million people, respectively. On a less massive scale, Japan, Indonesia, and Pakistan each has over 80 million, and Korea and Indochina are among the fifteen most populous states. All these countries have low standards of living and, except for Japan, depend overwhelmingly on agriculture for their livelihood. In all of these "underdeveloped" areas there is a belief in the possibility of improvement, a new concept in the Orient, and one that has been adopted with fervor.

The two emerging great powers of Asia, India and China, have been the sources from which higher civilization has radiated over Eastern Asia during the past 2,000 years. The recipients modified and molded these cultural benefits to their own traditions, but the original imprint remains. The two states themselves, though touching each other on their mountainous interior frontiers, had little intimate contact and no close political relations for millennia. Cultural exchanges, especially in the realm of religion, were significant, but even these activities were gravely hampered by terrain, distance, and fear of warring nomads. China's great Confucian tradition and its concept of society penetrated to the east and south—to Japan, Korea, and Vietnam. The interior border regions of Mongolia, Manchuria, and Tibet were also affected. India's art and its Buddhist religion spread eastward to Burma, Thailand, Laos, Cambodia, and parts of the East Indies. A different interpretation of Buddhism penetrated northward to Tibet and Mongolia and for a long time held sway in China and Japan.[1] In modern times immigrants from the southern Chinese coastal regions have settled in all the lands of Southeast Asia. On a smaller scale, Indians from around Madras moved to Burma, Malaya, and the western portions of Indochina.

India never established a significant overseas empire, and the political control China exercised abroad was highly sporadic. China's neighbors enjoyed sufficient freedom to develop their own cultural patterns, a sense of identity, and cherished historical experiences. These attitudes are clearly visible in the southern border state of Vietnam. Japan was greatly influenced by Chinese culture

[1] For descriptions of Buddhism, see pages 307 and 425.

for over a millennium, yet remained politically independent and reacted much more vigorously and quickly to the modern challenges of the West. Today, Japan stands apart from other Asian states in its physical development—from rural electrification and use of artificial fertilizer to industrial development and urbanization—and has been grappling for some time with the difficult problem of cultural adjustment to these changes.

Administrative Difficulties

It is significant that the new states of Asia experienced considerable difficulty in establishing stable constitutional orders after 1945. Indonesia and Pakistan are handicapped by geographic difficulties, but they face other basic problems that exist throughout the area. Many countries lack an efficient administrative apparatus and directing center whose physical presence and authority can be felt throughout the land. It is difficult for a new state to assure itself of popular support without the existence of such basic services as police control and protection, sanitation and health facilities, road and rail maintenance and construction, irrigation and flood control, and public education. In turn, a government experiences great difficulties in gaining enough strength to undertake these vital projects without an adequate underpinning of popular support. What makes urgent problems of these difficulties is that in Asia, even more than in the West, the state has traditionally been responsible for many functions, even though these were essentially rudimentary by modern standards. In modern times people have come to expect social services from their government. Yet these new functions, born of the industrial era, are altogether novel to the Asian pattern of administration.

Thus the Chinese empires with their great bureaucracies had duties involving hydraulic engineering,[2] tax collection, and grain storage, but little else. When the modern era arrived, even allowing for decay and disruption caused by revolution, China's administrative apparatus was totally unprepared to handle the new functions required of the state. The Nationalist and Communist revolutions both reflected this deficiency, which they strove vigorously to repair. And no other Asian state before the nineteenth century reached the traditional Chinese level of government. Even in this century, Korea under Japan, independent Siam, Dutch Indonesia, French Indochina, Burma under Britain, and the American colony of the Philippines did not develop an adequate apparatus of government.

Only in British India and Japan was the basis of a modern state firmly established in the past century. Britain gave its colony an efficient bureaucracy and eventually trained a sufficient number of Indians to staff this "steel frame" after independence. Japan, by its own effort, has made the greatest progress along

[2] Canals, irrigation works, reservoirs, and other forms of storage, dams, flood control, and the like.

administrative lines and by 1900 was the only sovereign Asian state with a truly modern government.

In Southeast Asia the state has not been a focal point of primary loyalty, a condition still evident on the vast Indian subcontinent. The overwhelming majority of people reside in villages, work the land, or labor in an occupation dependent on agriculture. Life is therefore oriented around the self-sufficient village and its environs, and it is at this level that political activity, economic power, and the social order are most decisively controlled. The East Asians must undertake a sweeping modernization of their physical environment, create efficient systems of state services, and effect a profound revolution in popular attitudes if they are to benefit from their new freedom. Otherwise any change will simply be a veneer laid over the traditional village order.

A Tradition of Social Integration

What were the characteristics of the traditional village-oriented society that persisted into the modern era? Two features stand out in contrast to the West: stability and a high degree of social integration. Absence of change in social affairs or in physical conditions of life was accompanied by an almost total submergence of the individual as a social unit. An independent role for the individual or for any group was inconceivable, since society was an entity whose units and persons were inseparably integrated. As the focal point of authority, the state played a pivotal role in this society, though in practice it had to share popular loyalty with other institutions. Nevertheless, there were no independent entities (towns, guilds, or other corporate bodies) protected by charter or custom from the state or the society as a whole. A tradition of individual initiative and a sense of independence could not develop and thrive as in the West.

The Oriental political system, early cast in an authoritarian mold, evolved steadily toward absolutism with the passing centuries. The arrival of the Mongols in China (1279) and the Mogul rulers in India (after 1500) brought this tendency to a climax. These periods of rule gave specific form to the belief, which had been gradually gaining acceptance, that a monarch's powers were absolute. This concept was tempered by bureaucratic inefficiency and decentralization as well as the lack of technical means to exercise complete authority. Custom, religious ethics, and, at times, law still had restraining influences so that rulers were often hedged in the practical application of power. But as a social and political concept, this version of the state reinforced the view that the individual was subjected to the requirements of larger social units. He was bound by strong family commitments and, in the larger order of things, was obliged to serve the interests of his feudal leader, his caste or other social unit, or the central authority. In this type of society, cities never developed as centers of political fermentation or cultural change. They served as strongholds of the central bureaucracy, local aristocracy, and landed gentry, rather like provincial command posts manned by those who dominated the countryside.

Diffusion of Authority

Political power in practical affairs, in contrast to theory, was highly diffused. The customary and physical limits to central power provided for a wide dispersal of authority along territorial and social lines. Regional or provincial officials, lesser princes, and a variety of feudal leaders all enjoyed considerable autonomy in directing local affairs; often these satrapies of power paid only nominal allegiance to the center. Even when central authority asserted itself and was respected, considerable leeway was given to officials on the scene. The villages themselves handled many affairs, ranging from local law enforcement and rudimentary self-defense to the settlement of legal disputes and provision of some social services.

The social unit to which a person belonged established strict rules or ethical codes for social intercourse and even personal habits, the extreme example being India's caste system. Economic functions were fixed by a person's station in life, and rules of operations were prescribed by groups organized along guild lines. Finally, a large share of control remained with the family, which often regulated the vocation, marriage, and personal life of its members. Sanctions were generally supported by religious precept, a fact that made obedience to the family a sacred duty. It is true that obligations to the family could conflict with one's duties to the state and other groups. Different balances among these values were found throughout Asia. But in all cases the source of family authority was held to be divine.

This diffusion of power may appear superficially to encourage the development of democracy. Yet, even with competing groups, overlapping authorities, and a wide degree of autonomy, it is a serious misreading of Asian politics to describe it as a breeding ground for democratic pluralism. There was no idea of popular responsibility, rooted in individual initiative and decision making. Instead, each group had its assigned duties, to be carried out under the direction of its traditional leaders. There was no democratic check on such officials as the village elder, the family head, the local gentry, the feudal leader, or the agent of the ruler. The rights and obligations of all were established on customary foundations and were rarely modified. The legal process of change through democratic impulses and voting processes had no place here.

However, it is also unwise to consider this pattern a suitable basis for modern totalitarian ideologies, under which the state and its rulers take absolute precedence over all other considerations. Under the Oriental tradition of authoritarian controls, the state in practice did not weigh as heavily on the people as does the contemporary police state. The exercise of authority by other institutions and individual obligations to these groups were very real factors, and did not fit into a totalitarian pattern. Then, too, there was a belief in China and elsewhere in the harmony of nature and all its parts, and excesses were deplored no matter how often they recurred. This is not to say that totalitarian communism cannot make serious inroads in Asia. But the doctrine has many aspects alien to Asian traditions, portending a clash of values that can well cause violent resistance.

Stability of Classes

Each individual then had his place within a group, and the status of all groups in the society as a whole was carefully defined. The Asian communities possessed social structures featuring elaborate pyramids of authority. The position of any one class in these settings varied from country to country. Ethical justifications for this structure also differed, and the degree of individual mobility from class to class was still another variant. But it is striking that fixed gradations of class rank were established and retained in each society for enormously long periods of time, without undergoing radical changes or devastating social upheavals. Thus China placed the scholar-official at the top of its social order, in contrast to India's Brahmin priest and Japan's warrior-noble. As to social mobility, India evolved a rigid caste system and Japan developed an hereditary feudal order with some flexibility for individual advances. China enjoyed a theoretically egalitarian tradition that became seriously restrictive in practice over the centuries.

In general, a close correlation existed between economic well-being and high social position in all lands, with alliances among ruling groups quite common. The peasantry formed the wide base of this structure even when, as in Japan, it was nominally superior to another group (the merchants). Farmers were generally kept under strict rule, suffered high taxes, and led a most difficult life. Their condition was tempered only by certain customary restraints and the fact that excessive exploitation would lead to desperation and rebellion. Actually, many peasant uprisings occurred in China and elsewhere, but even when dynasties were overthrown, the social order and the basic political institutions survived. This social stability persisted through countless feudal wars, dynastic struggles, and invasions down to modern times.

Not everything remained static, however. Some technical progress was made, land frontiers were expanded, and frequent changes occurred in political leadership. Yet the basic social pattern proved capable of absorbing such novel developments. Religion and philosophy played important roles in reinforcing beliefs in the value and inevitability of a stable order. These ideals further bound the individual to the group by providing moral and ethical motives for performing prescribed duties. Oriental religions encouraged indifference to physical science. There was not the urgent compulsion felt in the West to investigate the physical basis of nature in order to harness it or refashion man's economic pursuits.

Hinduism prescribed a rigid social order with elaborately set duties for all. Confucian ideals were more flexible, but even they emphasized an orderly society, specific tasks, and obedience to acknowledged superiors. Buddhism was

9

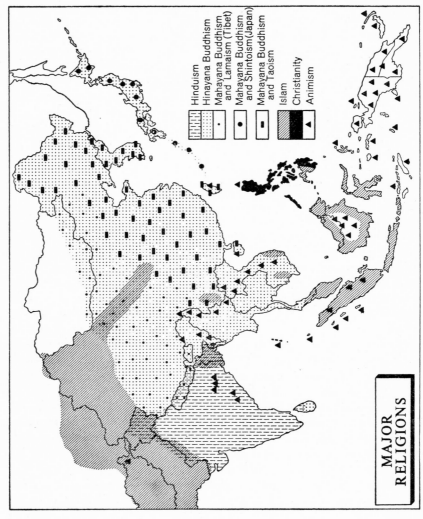

MAJOR RELIGIONS

Hinduism

Hinayana Buddhism

Mahayana Buddhism and Lamaism (Tibet)

Mahayana Buddhism and Shintoism (Japan)

Mahayana Buddhism and Taoism

Islam

Christianity

Animism

Adapted from J. E. Spencer, *Asia, East by South* (New York: John Wiley & Sons, Inc., 1954). © 1954.

a pessimistic, renunciatory religion whose major purpose was to teach people how to break the life cycle of desire and rebirth. Taoism, a second major Chinese philosophy, revealed important strains of superstition, mysticism, and a passive belief in the harmony of nature. Shintoism was native to Japan, a primitive animistic faith that stressed blood relations to the throne and so sanctioned the maintenance of a hereditary aristocracy. Leading Christian philosophers have contrasted these beliefs with their own faith, which, they hold, has dignified the individual and stimulated man's interest in nature and the scientific order.

In sum, political, economic, and ethical aspects of Asia's culture were closely interdependent supports of a particular type of social order. The very firmness of this interrelationship meant that changes anywhere could not help having serious repercussions in other areas. Without ascribing primary importance to any one of these fundamental characteristics, we can conclude that changes begun anywhere set off a chain reaction of doubt, criticism, and further change that eventually engulfed the entire order.

The Tides of Imperialism and Nationalism

Though Asian social orders remained relatively stable, war and conquest were constant phenomena that repeatedly modified local balances of power. Japan was plagued by feudal struggles and civil wars until the seventeenth century. China engaged in an endless series of defensive and offensive operations against inland barbarians, as well as many dynastic struggles. India was host to virtually all types of conflict—invasion, struggles among petty princes, and occasional wars for unification. In Southeast Asia, the lesser states enjoyed brief moments of glory and expansion, only to fall rapidly. When the Western explorers and conquerors reached this region after 1498, they found it in a normal state of political turmoil. Western political rule eventually covered a great part of South Asia, but it never extended to China and Japan in the distant northeast. A major characteristic of European expansion was the fact that large rewards followed from fairly small-scale efforts.

This European incursion came on the heels of widespread Islamic conversions that extended to India, Malaya, Indonesia, and the southern Philippines before checked by the West. The Portuguese, traditional foes of Islam, swept the prosperous and powerful Arab ships out of South Asian waters in the sixteenth century and established their own naval bases from Arabia to the China coast. Macao, Timor, and Goa are contemporary remnants of this period. The Spaniards meanwhile occupied the Philippines in the sixteenth century, stayed until 1898, and converted the colony to Catholicism. In the following century the Dutch and English rose to naval prominence. Since the Dutch were temporarily stronger, they were able to hold the East Indies, whose eastern islands were highly prized for their spices. The British were forced to seek their reward in India, in competition with France. In the eighteenth century, Britain eliminated this rival from India and took both Ceylon and Malaya from Holland in the course of the Napoleonic Wars. During the nineteenth century, British rule was extended over all India and Burma, while the French conquered Indochina after 1875. Only Siam retained its freedom as a small buffer state between these imperial rivals.

North of India, British and Russian imperial interests clashed repeatedly, but agreements were reached that avoided war. Afghanistan remained an independent buffer, and Tibet was recognized as an autonomous area still under the suzerainty of a decaying Chinese empire. Russian pressure extended eastward after vast conquests in central Asia until it reached the Chinese border regions of Sinkiang, Mongolia, and Manchuria, as well as Korea. The Russians managed to detach Outer Mongolia from China early in this century but lost out to Japan in the struggle for Korea. By 1914 these two rivals carved Manchuria into zones of economic influence. China itself was divided into similar spheres by all the powers and after 1911 faced a double menace of revolution and foreign conquest.

Yet, within two generations the imperial tide receded, slowly at first and then at an astonishing rate. By 1955 Malaya was the only important territory under foreign rule, and it was promised self-government before 1960. Today imperialism is decried as a morally wrong policy that thwarts self-rule. The modern era has witnessed an air of inevitability concerning its decline, in Africa as well as Asia; self-determination is considered a just and practicable right for all peoples still under colonial rule. Only backwardness in political and economic development is tolerated by world public opinion as a cause for retaining Western rule in colonial lands. This is a complete reversal of the historical acceptance of Western domination that marked the early days of imperial expansion and contributed to the successful rise of European rule.

The Strength of Imperialism

The forces that motivated European expansion are accurately summarized by the words "glory, gold, and God." The maritime powers of the Atlantic and the North Sea drew strength from the valuable skills and inventions that followed the Renaissance. During this era men dreamt of conquering nature and undertaking great individualistic adventures. The technological supremacy of the West, especially in the military realm, was a factor of decisive importance in establishing Western primacy. By the nineteenth century this material advantage was so great that the Japanese, despite their intense hatred of foreigners, could alertly perceive that security lay only in learning Western ways. Yet technical superiority cannot be the entire key to this remarkable development. The West's margin of technical superiority was actually smallest when the most difficult tasks of conquest and consolidation were achieved. Its greatest advantage in weapons came in this century, just when the whole political process underwent a stunning reversal.

In the early days of imperialism, weapons, armor, ships, and the technique of supply were at their crudest levels. The manpower in these expeditions was composed of impressed troops and riffraff. Viewed in absolute terms, the

Europeans hardly presented forces whose quality, size, and equipment made them unbeatable. Moreover, the conquests were spun out over a few centuries, giving the Asians ample opportunity to acquire Western artillery and other weapons. Since the Europeans were fighting each other for these colonies, the native rulers could have used diplomacy as a means of survival. But instead of

Territorial Changes and Acquisitions

Liaotung Peninsula—Russian Leasehold (1898-1905); to Japan (1905)
Wei-Hai-Wei—British Leasehold (1898)
Kiaochow—German Leasehold (1898)
Yangtse Valley—British Concession (1898)
Kwang Chow—French Leasehold (1898)
Southern Sakhalin—Ceded to Japan by Russia (1905)
Korea—Russian withdrawal (1905); Japanese annexation (1910)

American
British
Dutch
French
German
Japanese
Russian

IMPERIALISM IN THE FAR EAST AND WESTERN PACIFIC
——— (1842-1914) ———

From Richard M. Brace, *The Making of the Modern World* (New York: Rinehart & Company, Inc., 1955). © 1955.

playing off the foreigners against one another, the Asians were used as pawns by the invaders. The determined resistance by the ruler of Mysore in India at the start of the nineteenth century and the disaster that befell the British in the First Afghan War (1839-1842) were rare examples of the potential strength available to Asian rulers.

The European powers also followed the theory of mercantilism in the early stages of imperialism. Under mercantilist principles, no more than 1 per cent of a national economy could be devoted to military affairs. Since economic power was not too advanced and considerable effort went into European wars, little energy was left for colonial expansion. It is most significant that 250,000 American troops were required to defend a portion of the narrow Korean peninsula after 1950, whereas less than 2,000 troops were involved on each side of the great Anglo-French rivalry in India before 1750. Britain conquered Burma with only 10,000 men, and the French took Indochina at a moderate cost despite some reverses. A defeat in the 1880's nevertheless overturned a French cabinet just as the great military debacle at Dienbienphu did in 1954. The Europeans were not willing to expend great energy on colonization in the past, but they were able to achieve great success with limited means.

Imperial conquests have been called unequal struggles between the hunter and the elephant; the hunter had a gun but also the ability to organize. The West was superior to its opponents at all levels of social discipline, an advantage not restricted to public affairs. At the political level, most Asians were unconcerned with the concept of the state, were not nationalists in the modern sense, and did not believe that the political sovereignty of their culture had to be protected at all costs. The ruler was a vital factor in this society, but it mattered little who he was as long as traditional functions—such as the support of temples and other religious structures—were carried out. Beyond this, Asian society was not disciplined or cohesive enough to bring about effective organized activity. In economic affairs, factory discipline, corporate organization, and differentiation and specialization of labor were beyond this region's social capacity. Military demands proved but one significant aspect of this over-all pattern. Disciplined regimental units, adequate supply lines, rational staff and command functions were European advantages that proved too great for their disorganized rivals. Asiatic troops were inherently as competent as Europeans and proved their worth many times when trained and organized by Western rulers. But Asian political societies lacked the nationalist urge, political competence, and social cohesion to make effective use of their larger numbers, and thus could offer no effective opposition to European conquests in South and Southeast Asia. The ability of Japan to ward off foreign rule illustrated a rare capacity to muster these intangible forces and prove their worth.

The Decline of Imperial Rule

It is evident that the challenge to imperialism was rooted in the changed social and political attitudes of the colonial peoples. Under Western rule, the European concept of nationalism diffused rapidly throughout Asia and gave its Western-educated leaders a focal point around which to rally popular support. As Western patterns of activity permeated all aspects of life, advanced types of group discipline and corporate organization became more common, and could be harnessed to nationalist movements.

The imperial powers played a vital role in committing themselves to the ideology of democratic self-rule and even permitting nationalist sentiments and political consciousness to develop. Britain, France, Holland, and the United States all preached this democratic creed to Asian subjects and so encouraged them to seek self-determination. The Western rulers had to agree in principle with such demands and were thrown morally on the defensive when confronted by independence movements. Their only argument was one of timing—that the colonial peoples were still unprepared for self-rule and required further training. This in turn put a burden on the Western rulers to proceed with such programs or be accused of hypocrisy and incompetence. When it came to a showdown and a question of force, the people of the Western democracies had little heart for a long and costly fight, especially where the colonial peoples had been oriented toward democratic self-government.

A third related consideration was the drastic change in Europe's power position during this century. There is a direct connection between the collapse of European political authority overseas and the two devastating wars of 1914-1918 and 1939-1945. Western imperialism reached its high-water mark in China at the turn of the twentieth century, after which it began to ebb under the pressure of Europe's internal troubles, the rise of Japanese imperialism, and the sudden emergence of Chinese nationalism. The climax of European imperial expansion came after Japan's victory over China in their first modern war (1894-1895), but it is significant that China was divided only into economic spheres. It was as though the delicate world balance of power was projected into China and prevented any one power from attaining political dominance. The war of 1914 marked the end of European influence in China, and left Japan as the main imperial threat there. The second holocaust of 1939 enabled this new power to drive the West out of all its colonial possessions east of India and so undermine the power basis of imperial rule. Japan's effort to fill the vacuum created by these "divine winds" of Western self-destruction were resisted by Asian nationalists. When the Japanese empire was smashed by the American-led Western counteroffensive, national self-determination emerged as the dominant force in Asian politics.

Political change occurred in East Asia with bewildering rapidity after 1945. The Philippines won their long-promised freedom in 1946, Britain granted India and Pakistan their independence in 1947, and Burma was freed in 1948. Indonesia had to fight the Netherlands for four years, but Holland was handicapped by adverse world and domestic opinion and finally capitulated in 1949-1950. China was cleared of its Japanese tormenters in 1945, but its long-standing internal struggle produced a communist victory in 1949 and a Nationalist refugee government on Formosa. Korea emerged from thirty-five years of Japanese rule in 1945 divided between a communist north and a quasi-democratic south, and endured a bitter war (1950-1953) that simply ratified the partition. Japan itself was occupied by American forces in 1945, but this foreign rule was considered temporary and ended after six years of reformist efforts. Indochina, like Indonesia, rebelled against its imperial masters, but in this instance the independence movement was dominated by the Communists. A truce in 1954 left the Communists in control of Vietnam above latitude 17° and a Nationalist regime in the south, with the French on their way out. Finally, the British made concessions toward Malayan nationalist sentiments in 1955 by yielding certain rights to self-government and promising freedom in 1957.

The Modern Era of Nationalism

It is clear that political considerations dominate the Eastern Asian scene. Nationalism has been the major driving force but, as the communization of China and some of its borderlands reveals, it gives no guarantees concerning the form of self-determination. Will the political revolution for self-rule become a gateway for a communist sweep? Can democracy strengthen its roots in India, Pakistan, the Philippines, Indonesia, Burma, and Japan in the face of internal difficulties and foreign pressures? What role will these states play in the new international order, itself a revolutionary outcome of a generation of warfare? Further, do the new states of Asia possess the administrative capacity to provide the minimum services required of a government by its society, let alone undertake reform programs considered essential for political stability?

The Western impact on Asia went far beyond the political realm, where it contributed Marxism, in its socialist and communist forms, as well as democracy and nationalism. The urge for economic betterment, the expansion of individual rights against the oppressive demands of society, the challenge to religion, and the attraction of scientific rationalism all made a lasting impression on the modern Asian intellectual. However, these urban political leaders are far removed from the peasant masses who have remained in their farming villages, relatively unaffected by these new currents. The importance of the nationalist credo lies in its exceptional power to gain mass support. Thus the intellectual leaders were able to form an alliance with the peasants and lead them in a common cause. Nationalism proved to be an unfailing source of power that projected these native leaders into public prominence and political responsibility. The task confronting the new governors now is to use this opportunity to consolidate their position and maintain their authority.

Although these intellectuals are a small minority whose modernistic outlook may be rare in their own lands, they are the key figures in this drama. Their political philosophy, social outlook, and position on economic reform will do much to determine the course of Asian affairs in the near future. The peasant masses are still sufficiently passive and committed to their nationalist leaders to allow them fairly wide latitude. However, the fate of Nationalist China clearly reveals that this leadership is not given a completely free hand. It can lose the support and respect of its own people and prove unable to cope with a threat from a competing communist elite. Since the Leninist tactical quest for power does not call for a numerically large party, the present dependence on a small body of leaders in Asian politics is a point of danger.

Imperial Japan, war-scarred China, the India of British rule and Gandhian nationalism, and the new states of southeast Asia have all experienced profound

16

crises. Nationalism provides no blueprint for the future; its greatest construc-tive role is simply to create an atmosphere in which changes can occur. It is one of the most bewildering and dynamic elements in world politics, releasing tremendous social energy, and nowhere is it more strident than in East Asia. One of its sharpest critics, a former Indian Communist, M. N. Roy, denounced nationalism as a fundamentally evil and undemocratic force because it teaches each nation to consider itself apart from others and preaches the doctrine of mass solidarity at the expense of individualism. These, Roy noted, simply rein-force antidemocratic patterns already entrenched in Asian political cultures and expose these lands to rule by demagogic leaders. It is also true that a nation-alist movement cannot easily cope with the problem of social and economic reform. Since its strength lies in uniting native elements in a common cause, upper-class landowners and reformist elements often confront each other once the foreign ruler is gone. The Chinese Nationalist, or Kuomintang party, is an example of a group that contained these rival components. It was a revolution-ary party, struggling against great odds to establish a modern government free of foreign rule, but it proved unable to devise a coherent reformist program.

Yet to the nationalist in search of political freedom, these criticisms are of secondary importance. Social conflicts and the danger to democracy would exist in any event. Only through nationalism can all native forces be grouped to-gether under a single banner that leads to self-rule and a very real opportunity to resolve problems of political ideology and reform. In Japan and, to a lesser degree, in China, where a sense of political or cultural identity already existed, the threat of foreign rule and the presence of alien forces fanned nationalist sentiment. Elsewhere the traditional state had not played a major role in history and its administrative organization was rudimentary. Moreover, the lands of southern Asia contained a formidable array of different peoples, tongues, and cultures. In this situation, the foreign ruler served as a target against which nationalist antagonism could be focused. Beyond this, it was the Westerner who created the modern state, giving it geographic form, political structure, and a modern bureaucratic apparatus. The imperial power created a governing ap-paratus that eventually included a certain amount of native representation. It was the foreigner who formed the modern Asian state around which nationalist sentiment could rally. Finally, the racial and cultural differences between West and East and the claim to moral superiority, put forth by Europeans in the late stages of the imperialist era, aroused Asian interest in native traditions and intensified demands for freedom.

The Ideological Struggle

The Western Democratic Heritage

Independent Asia may be confronted with a choice between some form of democracy and communism. The democratic alternative made an auspicious start but must inevitably encounter many difficulties. In part this stems from the basic pattern of Asian political traditions: rule from above, emphasis on the group rather than the individual, and dependence on the state to direct a much wider segment of human activities than is usually deemed wise in a free society. This theme of "incompatibility" was complemented by the lack of faith and air of suspicion with which Asians viewed their Western mentors. The imperial powers set bad examples even while fostering democratic beliefs and installing governmental systems to put their principles into operation. The rulers of imperial Japan after 1932 followed these lines of criticism in challenging the applicability of democracy in Asia, with a modest degree of success.

However, much of this suspicion of the West has been directed primarily against Western capitalism, rather than against democracy itself. Capitalism was bitterly condemned as an economic system that had to exploit hapless colonies in order to survive. Moreover, its philosophy, especially the doctrine of laissez faire, was essentially alien to Asian concepts. The notion of a capitalist who benefits society as a whole by the tireless pursuit of his own interests was difficult to grasp in a region where unproductive merchants and businessmen thought only in terms of expanding their share of a fixed amount of wealth. Finally, the new intellectuals who sought sweeping reforms in agriculture and wanted to industrialize their economies turned to socialist doctrines and state leadership for guidance.

Antipathy to capitalism inflamed nationalist feeling against the West and was reinforced by Marxian and other socialist critiques emanating from Europe. Socialism in general and Marxism in particular gained widespread following in Asia in this century. These doctrines offered a severe ethical criticism of the West at a time when Asian intellectuals were infuriated by the white man's air of moral superiority. Lenin popularized this aspect of Marxism with the claim that imperialism was the final stage of a disintegrating capitalistic system, in which colonies serve as a last desperate area of exploitative investment. Without imperialism, it was argued, the entire economic structure would crumble. Although this theory has been proved grossly inaccurate, it fostered an Asian intellectual and moral offensive against the West.

Socialism in general was attractive also because it maintained that careful planning and central direction would enable the state to reshape a nation's entire economic system. To people seeking radical changes and long accustomed to state controls, this doctrine had far greater appeal than the model of limited government idealized by laissez-faire capitalism. On the other hand, resort to Marxist and Leninist arguments, and even open admiration of Russian economic advances, do not signify a rejection of democracy, for socialism, including its Marxian variety, can operate within a democratic framework. In fact, the leading states of western Europe—the former imperial powers themselves—all have democratic socialist parties that have held office and shaped government policy and doctrine. The advent of Britain's Labor party to power in 1945 was the most dramatic indication that socialism could thrive in a democracy. As long

18

as democratic government is not exclusively identified with capitalism, it may retain the vigor and flexibility required to maintain its hold in Eastern Asia.

Democracy, Reform, and Paternalism

The other fundamental problem is the difference between the traditional pattern of Asian political rule and the public attitude required for the operation of an open democratic society. The habits of passivity and acceptance of authoritarian direction are reinforced by the absence of an individual or corporate spirit, free from political direction and with an independent purpose of its own. To illustrate the nature of this problem we need only consider the dilemma posed by the need for social and economic reform. It is generally agreed that free Asia must undertake a vigorous program of democratizing social relationships. Governments must win peasant support through changes in land tenure and by legislation that gives the farmer technical competence and financial security. Moreover, the state is expected to bring about industrialization while advancing the cause of democracy itself. Without this dynamic policy, it is doubtful that democracy can survive in its new Asian environment. Yet such large-scale programs can cause an excessive centralization of power and bring political issues into everyday affairs. Nor can we, in the light of Japan's disastrous record after 1931, complacently equate material progress with the creation of a peaceful, democratic society. Thus there is reason to fear that widespread government supervision of a modernization program may injure Asia's vulnerable democratic forces and reinforce traditional dependence on an all-powerful paternalistic government whose word is law. This is a perplexing and tangled problem because the region desperately needs centrally directed changes and efficient modern bureaucracies.

An illustration of the heavy dependence of Asian society on governmental leadership is found in the evolution of the labor union movement, which also concerns the key role of the intellectuals. It is remarkable that unions do play a vigorous role in Asian affairs and possess so highly organized a membership, since the region is relatively unindustrialized. This paradox is partly due to the leadership of Western-trained intellectuals who could not gain public office under colonial administrations and turned to union leadership as a fruitful substitute in their search for prestige and power. The wide gulf between the union leaders and the mass membership persisted, and the average laborer remained a passive follower who wanted his leaders to make decisions for him even in his personal affairs. As was true of the peasantry, nationalism united the native political leaders, the politically-minded union leaders, and the working population in a common cause.

After independence the new governments sought to use the unions as disciplined agencies in the service of their new economic reform programs. Union leaders often sought to use their positions as entrees to political careers. They maintained close relations with the government and often fostered policies, like fixed wage rates in public enterprises, not in harmony with union objectives.

The governments, in turn, have been prudent enough to protect the unions and meet their demands, in return for continued political support. Educated union leaders have much more in common with public officials than with the working class, itself newly formed from the peasantry. Many high union officials even hold important civil service positions. In all, the union movements are susceptible to political manipulation and even to authoritarian techniques of leadership. This situation can endanger political democracy even when the purpose is to further the nation's economic well-being. It can be argued that democracy in Asia will be secure when politically independent groups in a pluralistic society will be strong enough to act in their own interests. For organized labor this means an independent union movement with its own bureaucracy, sense of identity, and strength to pursue chosen objectives.

The Western-trained leader who resorts to authoritarian techniques to further what he considers to be the national interest presents a broader political problem. His sense of superiority over the peasant masses may induce him to use nondemocratic means to foster economic reform or, more dangerously, to suppress political opponents. On various occasions, in the decade after 1945, Premiers Yoshida of Japan, Nehru of India, and U Nu of Burma, Presidents Sukarno of Indonesia, and Quirino of the Philippines have been accused of such arbitrary political behavior. The problem is doubly serious in these lands where democratic processes and institutions have not yet taken firm root; for here the governmental system comes to be identified with certain outstanding individuals, always a frailer base for stability than faith in a political structure or ideology. Should these leaders prove high-handed or demagogic, the entire system may be endangered.

The Growth and Appeal of Democracy

Popular ignorance, peasant apathy, oppressive action by the ruling class, and a weak bureaucratic structure are serious challenges to the future of democracy in Southern and Eastern Asia. Certainly the political evolution of the area's three independent states—China, Japan, and Thailand—during this century is not heartening. Must we therefore agree with one disheartened observer who concluded that the West's major contributions to Asia are limited to nationalism, communism, and jazz?

The prerequisites normally considered essential for the growth of democracy would be drawn from the following: a firm liberal tradition, capitalism or the independence of economics from strict political control, industrialization and a high standard of living, public education and a literate populace, and a competent civil service. Above all, a middle class is deemed essential because it embodies most of the above characteristics and has been most concerned with the individual's rights and his protection against arbitrary rule. Complete reliance on these criteria leads to the conclusion that democracy can develop and operate successfully only in its natural habitat, a Western society. Yet we are confronted by conflicting evidence. Democracy failed to maintain itself before

1945 in a society like Germany, with its industry, education, middle class, and respect for law. This failure is in contrast to an amazing *initial* success in its application in exotic Asian cultures. The novel fact about Asia has been the injection of democratic ideals and forms by imperial rulers who then sustained and developed them, partly out of pride and habit, in their colonies. Equally significant was Japan's attempt, on its own initiative, to develop a democratic order before 1931. Even without an American occupation, one of the consequences of defeat may well have been the resurgence of a constitutional order in Tokyo.

Study in Western lands and limited experience at home under imperial rule further contributed to an intellectual appreciation of this democratic ideology. The creed was strengthened because it proved an effective and successful weapon in the struggle for self-rule. Despite inherent drawbacks and animosity toward the Western powers, democracy has become, outside of China, the dominant form of government. The first decade following the Second World War reveals that it has fared at least as well in Asia as it did in Eastern Europe during the ten years after 1918. After 1928 authoritarian rule dominated the Central and Eastern European scene. Training and interest in democratic ways apparently must be weighed as heavily as political and social considerations in studying this problem. Democratic self-rule has been accepted in the former British and American colonies, where the transfer of power was peaceful, and in Indonesia despite an anti-Dutch war. To some extent the battered states of Indochina (Southern Vietnam, Cambodia, and Laos) have revealed a similar preference, even though the Communists gained immeasurable prestige and won northern Vietnam in the war against French colonialism. In South Korea, free elections were held and a democratic order was developing in the few years between the attainment of self-rule and the North Korean assault of 1950. In the last really free election there, just prior to the invasion, President Syngman Rhee's party suffered a severe defeat. It has been only in a period of national crisis that the president has asserted an authoritarian leadership, which may pass should military stability endure.

It is now evident that the Asians turned to the West for political ideologies as well as for new industrial, military, and administrative techniques. On the basis of available evidence, democracy is sufficiently attractive to satisfy Asia's deep need for guidance. Had there been an intellectual vacuum in this field, it would have immediately been filled by communism. This is, after all, a revolutionary political era in which violence, hostility to colonialism, and utopian economic aspirations are dominant themes. Since the communists thrive in such an environment, and are the party of conspiracy and disciplined action, their containment in Southern Asia and Japan during this era of disorder is an important testament to the ideological appeal of democracy.

A major attraction to Asian intellectuals has been the concept of political liberalism, with its emphasis on limited government and the dignity of the individual. These points must be stressed because they are such novelties in

Asian culture, a fact that is a source of democracy's attraction and vulnerability. Limited government meant that political power was restricted by law and practice as a result of a self-imposed policy by the government itself. Democracy's elaborate precautions against unlimited or tyrannical authority amounted to a sharp reversal of the trend of Asian political development in the pre-Western period. The rule of law was one of the most significant manifestations of this philosophy and took firm root in colonial lands. It was used by nationalist agitators as a protective device, a phenomenon that would have been impossible under German, Russian, or Japanese imperial rule.

The belief in the dignity and equality of all human beings struck at the root of Asia's status-oriented societies, marked as they were by caste, hierarchy, and even involuntary servitude down to the present era. Ironically, the air of moral superiority adopted by the foreign rulers who introduced this egalitarian doctrine often served to make this new concept more attractive. Old patterns of deference, social privilege, and servitude cannot be changed immediately by legislation, but it is significant that political action and agitation are pointed in this direction. The old order has become morally indefensible. Such reforms reflect and stimulate the development of mass democracy, making political leaders more sensitive to mass interests. The peasantry is still not alert enough to its political rights, but since it holds the balance of power in the free states of Asia, progress in this field is of major significance.

Finally, representative government has been adopted in Japan and all the former colonies. The British parliamentary-party form has been followed in all countries save the Philippines, which patterned itself on the American model. All these lands have conducted at least one major election, in which the party in power has been willing to stake its rule in a free vote. On the whole, contests since 1950 have been fair ones and election results have been respected, despite unpleasant surprises for the parties in power. The most outstanding technical achievement was the Indian national election of 1951-1952, in which more than 100 million voters participated despite widespread illiteracy. Admittedly, the adoption of formal democratic processes is only one factor to be considered, but the experience of electing rulers who can be voted out of office makes the system more meaningful and sharpens the popular appetite for responsible government.

Party Patterns

The system of party rule has been transplanted to the Orient together with the formal structure of government, but, as in Europe, no single pattern has emerged. Only in Japan and the Philippines has anything resembling a two-party system developed, and both countries also possess small Communist parties. India has a multiparty system dominated by the National Congress party. Rightist groups have proved weak, and left-wing opposition comes primarily from Communists and democratic socialists. In Pakistan, the Moslem League has lost a comparable position of supremacy and is confronted by a Republican opponent, the United Front (Bengal), and the Awami League. Indonesia has a wide variety of parties with two Moslem groups, the Nationalists, and the Communists the four leading elements. In Burma, most democratic elements are found in an Anti-Fascist Peoples Freedom League dominated by a well-knit Socialist party. The Communists have been in rebellion since 1948 and have refused to take part in peaceful political contests. The emerging government of Malaya also has an outlawed Communist party, a majority party consisting of a Malay-Chinese conservative alliance and an equally conservative opposition that espouses Malay nationalism.

One or two elections and a brief decade of democratic self-rule admittedly form an inadequate basis for prediction, but a few tentative generalizations can be made. In the first place, with the exception of Burma, popular support in each state goes to parties that are conservative, democratic, and nationalist in nature. In a sense this is to be expected, since the bulk of the voters are peasants. But the desire for reform is quite strong in the countryside as well as among intellectuals. These parties of the right are compelled to adopt reformist programs, execute their tasks of government with some degree of efficiency, and present popular candidates for office if they are to retain their advantage.

Yet it must be acknowledged that party lines are by no means firm. Politicians change camps, splinter groups emerge and disappear, and party machines lack the personnel and cohesion of their Western counterparts in the performance of their functions. In addition, a tendency to follow personal leaders has plagued both Japan and the Philippines during their extended experience with party government. The foreign observer, forgetful of the painful and long evolution of party rule in the West, is disconcerted and alarmed by the confusion and instability of Asian politics. Pakistan and Indonesia have appeared unstable in their party alignments and have had difficulties in establishing acceptable constitutions. Ideally, each land should have a two-party system, with a conservative right and a socialist left vying with each other within a mutually acceptable democratic framework. Such a situation would ensure political stability, remind the conservative right of its need to sponsor reform, and give the populace a democratic socialist alternative to the communists if it chose to vote for radical changes. An Asian might reply that there are European lands, such as France and Italy, where such a development would be equally welcome and surprising.

At present socialist opposition to the dominant conservatives has had a spotty record. Though a significant force in India, it is challenged by the communists and has yet to display the dynamism and cohesion that will attract a mass following. It is strongest in Burma as the party in power, and in Japan, where it has emerged in the postwar period as the major alternative to the conservatives. The Singapore elections of 1955 revealed that community to be in a radical mood; a party of socialist persuasion took office and faced its greatest challenge from the extreme left. However, the socialists have not been able to break into the Philippine two-party system. They have proved exceptionally weak also in Indonesia, where they barely polled 5 per cent of the vote in 1955, despite their fine revolutionary effort against the Dutch, and their highly qualified intellectual leadership.

The Communists

The strength of the socialists and their conservative opponents takes on vital significance in the light of the objectives of their common opponent, the communists, who seek to gain power and destroy the new democratic order in Asia. The communists utilize all channels that may lead to power, and they operate on many levels. They appear as a parliamentary party, an underground conspiracy planning a coup or a war, a revolutionary movement fomenting social strife, and a military force actually engaged in campaigns against a government. In any one country, the party might be operating on two or more of these levels simultaneously, or switch suddenly from one tactic to another as the situation changes.

Communist political fortunes differ markedly according to locale, but all remain conspiracies to win political power along the general lines developed by Lenin early this century. Each national party remains affiliated to all others as part of a common group, and all depend on Russian and Chinese support— psychological as well as material. By endeavoring to prove themselves the foremost nationalists and reformers, they exploit the anti-Western, anticapitalist spirit that has permeated modern Asia. Democratic nationalist or socialist parties are therefore their most serious enemies and are so treated, regardless of any temporary appeal for cooperation or coalition with such groups.

In countries dominated by democratic governments, the postwar period has been somewhat frustrating for the communists. In 1945 communist parties enjoyed legal status throughout most of this area, since they had been wartime allies of the nationalists or the Western powers. However, in 1948-1950, a policy of social strife and revolutionary warfare was adopted, with disastrous results. In Burma and Malaya, military combat ensued, with the Communists holding out for a long time. After 1952 they no longer posed a threat to either government, even though they were not completely stamped out. In Japan, India, and Indonesia, the Communist uprisings were quickly suppressed and appeals to violence lost the party considerable popular support. Since then these parties have promised to work within the constitutional framework, compete peacefully in elections, and take their place in the parliamentary system. However, they have continued to maintain and expand their underground military apparatus and at no time have given up their ultimate purpose of gaining dictatorial control of the state. They have thus far had little success in Japan and only slightly better results in India. Only in Indonesia, where the Nationalist party has cooperated with it for tactical political purposes, has the Communist party made serious inroads in the labor unions or gained an appreciable share (20+ per cent) of the popular vote.

The two main tactics in the communist quest for power are operations through legitimate parties and resort to force in the hope of gaining a territorial base. The first method is followed when the state is too well organized to permit the creation of "a state within a state." In this case, by vigorous campaigning, the party tries to build its own popular support or form coalitions, which it hopes to dominate, with any other group that proves amenable. In federal India this technique has been followed in an effort to control a state government and thereby gain a territorial base through political means. The second technique was brilliantly executed by the Chinese Communist party, whose success encouraged parties in other lands to establish themselves in inaccessible areas and build their strength from these sources. However, the level of native communist leadership in India, Japan, and other lands has not been as competent as in China. Moreover, it must be remembered that China's administrative and military unity was shattered by the total collapse of the monarchial system, a generation of provincial autonomy and warlordism, civil war, and repeated Japanese assaults. Nowhere else did such chaotic conditions prevail for so long a period of time. Only in northern Indochina has communism made further gains. Here the Communists were considered national heroes in a war against French colonialism, and the Chinese Communists arrived at a crucial moment to support and sustain the rebellion.

Two observations appear justified at this time. The first is that communism, regardless of past failures, poses a serious threat to democracy in South Asia. The second is that democracy, where it is in power, holds the initiative but must remain highly efficient to survive. A summary of communist assets makes formidable reading but must be considered in the light of gains already made by democracy in South Asia and Japan. The communist movement retains a tightly knit, fanatical organization that derives much of its strength and belief in ultimate success from its foreign affiliations. As the political opposition, the Communists can harp on the existence of poverty and the need for reform. Since distance lends enchantment, they contrast these realities with Russian successes and alleged industrial and welfare progress in China. They can also blame "foreign elements" and their "native lackeys" for the failure to improve conditions rapidly enough. Flexible tactics and cynical opportunism enable communists to prepare secretly for revolt and resort to violence at will. As parliamentary parties, they appeal to the "nationalist middle class" for support or call on their "socialist brothers" to join in campaigns to gain political power and so foster reforms. Meanwhile, disciplined full-time party members can extend the communist apparatus to the villages, where they strengthen their influence. This tactic gives them a reservoir of power to be tapped in a crisis or when the opportunity arises to establish a territorial base of power. Should a communist party rise to power, it can secure its position by coercive rule and police-state methods; its use of force contrasts sharply with the permissive type of control exercised in a democratic order. Finally, once in office, the communists seeks to aggrandize the power of the state, creating a military machine that can be used to further the cause elsewhere.

25

Yet the communist achievement has been limited, especially when measured in terms of Lenin's criteria for success: a revolutionary environment and a small, well-knit minority with enough discipline and strength to seize power. At a glance, the 1940's appeared to present an ideal opportunity, with a world war, nationalist revolts, weak governments, rudimentary administrations, and a general air of uncertainty. In addition, economic dislocations followed on a general condition of poverty and squalor. Yet in free elections in at least ten Asian states, the people have rejected authoritarian solutions and have thus far expressed their support for the open political society of a democracy.

Conclusion

The preceding statement does not mean, however, that these political cultures are at all firmly wedded to the democratic way. Japan and the newer governments of free Asia must still be able to handle the very difficult political-administrative tasks and act vigorously in the field of social and economic reform. Democracy may fail, not because people consciously turn to communism, but because they become apathetic and indifferent to the fate of a system that fails to bring results. When they do, should the holders of public office also lack vigor in defending their regime, a more competent revolutionary communist group might win power by default.

Clearly, the competence and devotion of the Western-trained leaders of Asia play a vital role in this drama, and, with the triumph of nationalism, the ultimate responsibility rests with them. Yet we should recall that in the era of colonialism the West did far less than was within its power to foster democracy in this region. In the political sphere, the introduction of parliamentary rule, the development of a native bureaucracy, and the final transfer of power often left much to be desired. Social reform, education, economic modernization, and agrarian reform were even less adequate in the light of present problems. However, in this imperfect world we must pass judgment sparingly. The rise of democracy in colonial Asia and Japan is an impressive historical event. It remains a major task of the democratic West, in its cultural relations, foreign policy, and economic programs, to assist Asian democrats in the strengthening of this recent heritage. The quest for economic progress and reform has acquired such political significance in this context that we must examine the problems and the difficulties that it raises for both Asia and the West.

2 *The Economic Setting*

The economic organization of Asia traditionally had been that of a peasant economy, based on the activity of farmers working small plots of land. This agrarian society was a logical complement to the authoritarian-bureaucratic political community that rested upon it. The characteristic feature, so heavily emphasized in all analyses, was the grinding poverty of the area. This condition preceded the arrival of Western influence and control and has remained, despite two centuries of extensive contact with the West.

A political study must evaluate this basic pattern of economic life, for it has been one of the persistent and dominant factors in Far Eastern affairs. With this background, other economic issues—the impact of the West and the problem of improvement of conditions through industrialization—can be discussed in their proper perspective. Also, these economic considerations have a vital bearing on the political future of Asia. The survival of democratic government will depend very heavily on an understanding and resolution of the economic problems faced by the mass of the people there. Responsibility in this regard rests both in the West and in Asia itself. Thus a study of Asia's economy of poverty and the attempts to improve it bear directly on some of the most important political problems of our time: the political stability of the Far East and the chances of establishing a democratic tradition on a firm footing.

An Agrarian Economy of Poverty

A study of Asia's economic ills cannot be limited to current problems or even to the effects of colonial rule. It requires a survey of Asia's traditional economy, which has served as the base for these later developments. In terms of man's general economic condition, the low Asian standard of life, unchanged over the years, was not far out of line with the way most people have lived through recorded time. It was only with the development of the industrial revolution in Europe, and its diffusion over the past two centuries, that an essentially different and materially superior way of life emerged, making Asia a very depressed area by comparison.

People and the Land

A unique historical feature of Asia's economy was its ability, well before close contact was made with the West, to support very large populations. Almost

INCOME DISTRIBUTION BY GEOGRAPHIC SUBDIVISIONS

Area	Population (1,000's)	World Total Population (%)	Income (In Billions U.S. Dollars)	World Total Income (%)	Per Capita Income (In U.S. Dollars)
Africa	197,881	8.3	14.0	2.6	75
N. America	213,316	9.0	237.0	43.6	1,100
S. America	107,519	4.5	18.0	3.5	170
Asia	1,253,514	53.0	58.0	10.5	50
Europe	392,789	16.6	148.5	27.3	380
U.S.S.R.	193,000	8.1	59.5	11.1	310
Oceania	12,434	0.5	7.0	1.5	560

SOURCE: *National Income and Its Distribution in Underdeveloped Areas* (Statistical Papers Series E, No. 3; New York: UN Department of Economic Affairs, 1951), p. 3.

PER CAPITA NATIONAL INCOME FOR 1949

(IN U.S. DOLLARS)

Australia	679	Japan	100
Burma	36	S. Korea	35
Ceylon	67	New Zealand	856
China	27	Pakistan	51
India	57	Philippines	44
Indonesia	25	Thailand	36

SOURCE: *National and Per Capita Incomes Seventy Countries—1949* (Statistical Papers Series E, No. 1; New York: UN Department of Economic Affairs, 1950), pp. 14-16.

all arable land, except disease-infested regions, became densely settled. For the most part, the farms developed as family-size units of from two to five acres, powered either by men alone or with the aid of cattle or water buffalo. Modern implements, techniques, and fertilizers were lacking, but the skill and ability of Asian farmers were traditionally of a very high order; before the modern period they were perhaps the most proficient in the world. Unfortunately, these complex endeavors served merely to sustain a large number of people at a relatively meager level of existence. Limited as he was by hand farming, the peasant could not hope to operate a plot of land larger than his family could handle. With the land fully occupied under such methods of cultivation, the standard of living was bound to reflect the low return from the soil. As the number of people rose, not only did the peasant's lack of tools prevent him from undertaking large-scale farming, but the population pressure on the land kept the farming unit below the size at which it could operate most efficiently even with the equipment on hand.

Although this was a fairly stable economy of small self-sufficient units, the constant growth of population kept it from becoming static. The immediate solution was that of migration in steady waves toward unused land. But this expansion of acreage under cultivation did not result in larger farms using new methods in the pioneering regions; rather, the new settler, usually a poor man driven to find new means of self-support, tended to use the techniques of farming common to the area he left. Although in most instances the principal areas of settlement have been fully occupied, the migratory tendency continues, either autonomously or under governmental sponsorship. Examples in this century are the movement of the Chinese people into Sinkiang, Mongolia, and Manchuria, and official efforts to get Indonesians to shift from Java to the outer islands and Filipinos from Luzon to Mindanao. Thus the land frontier is closing, with no leveling off of the population in prospect.

In spite of his most intensive efforts, a majority of the cultivator's crop has to be kept for the support of his family. An economy with so little surplus food can support only a small nonfarm population. In this subsistence economy, few goods and services can be produced by the nonfarming elements. If poor people spend the bulk of their income on food and a small fraction on other products, the consumer market for goods other than food is extremely limited. Thus, unless agricultural output is raised, the society will not become a good market, because it cannot afford to yield food in return for other commodities. It is true that Asia is poor because it is not industrialized, but in this important sense it is equally valid to note that Asia is unindustrialized because it is poor. Here a balanced program of increased agricultural output as well as improved transportation and the development of industry is essential for efficient modernization.

For a combination of reasons, including religious objections to the taking of life and the relatively high cost of sustaining animals, Asia has never developed a livestock economy. An exception is the nomadic people in sparsely settled fringe areas like Mongolia. The chief source of food has been cereal—mostly rice and wheat; and the production of grains has been the main focal point of activity, not only for food but also for housing, fuel, and even clothing. Cash crops have been produced in increased quantities since the arrival of the West, especially in the smaller countries of Southeast Asia. However, the main efforts in many of these lands and in the Far East as a whole have still centered around a subsistence level of grain cultivation.

With no modern hand tools, little or no capital to invest in improvements, and ignorance of modern methods and skills, the peasant came to depend on human labor as his main source of strength to draw more sustenance out of his small plot of land. The result was very intensive farming with production per acre rising as the number of people working each acre increased. Thus Asia had a respectable rate of production per acre compared with the rest of the world, but it did nothing to better its very low rating with regard to production per person. In fact, a vicious circle was created: a greater dependence on labor for agricultural production meant that the increased number of workers on the land absorbed the increments in production. With no other solution available, the peasantry continued to fall back on an increased labor supply, thereby reducing further the ratio of available land per worker.

The life of a peasant, based as it was on the rhythm of cereal production,

AGRICULTURAL PRODUCTIVITY BY CONTINENTS
(Wheat Equivalents in Metric Tons)

	Prod. per Person		Prod. per Hectare	
	Prewar	1947-1948	Prewar	1947-1948
Africa	0.12	0.12	0.77	0.73
N. America	1.80	2.57	1.07	1.50
S. America	0.58	0.48	1.28	1.39
Asia	0.24	0.22	1.26	1.20
Europe	1.04	0.88	1.51	1.34
Oceania	1.94	2.38	1.06	1.20

Source: F.A.O. Monthly Bulletin, *Food and Agricultural Statistics*, II, No. 9 (September, 1949), 4.

varied between two types of activity. When work was required, it approached a feverish intensity, with hands never in sufficient number at harvest time. For a good part of the year however, in some places over half the time, there was literally nothing to do; given the peasant's level of knowledge and outlook on life, he underwent what would be called in the West enforced idleness. The Asian enjoyed the luxury of his holidays and did not consider himself unemployed; yet, in a direct sense, the price for this was a lower standard of living.

No substantial savings could be amassed in a world of small production after the payment of taxes, rents, and debts, and the purchase of a few necessities. What was saved often went into ceremonial affairs, religious obligations, or the purchase of a new animal, or was absorbed in meeting some ever-present urgent requirement. In fact, the peasant's main concern was getting enough money together to pay for his operational or routine costs. The very low monetary income an Asian makes per year emphasizes further his inability to save any money.

Near-Bankruptcy

Thus we are confronted with a unique and precarious Far Eastern economy, which was potentially unstable before Western influence was felt. There was very little chance of industrialization coming to pass as matters stood. Considering this economic base, the population was attaining an alarmingly high level. India and China were already in the vicinity of 150 million by 1750, and Japan had about 25 million inhabitants by 1800. These figures are astonishing when one considers that around 1700 France, with a population of 20 million, was the largest country in Europe.

It can be plausibly argued that conditions of life in Asia would have continued to decline slowly, as the land gave out, had the Far East been left to its own devices. If such had been the case, there would have been an inevitable increase in economic and social hardships, which would probably have been reflected in debt, tenancy, human bondage, and landlessness. It can further be maintained that Asia can cure its impoverished condition only with techniques learned from the West and, probably, with Western assistance. Yet in a very important way the West is a responsible element in intensifying Asia's economic troubles.

The West upset Asia's dangerously balanced survival economy by unleashing a tremendous upsurge in population. At the same time there was no Western-inspired effort to alter fundamentally the Asian economic structure by encouraging the industrialization and urbanization necessary for stability. Some assistance along these lines was given, but there was no plan or intent to undertake a systematic effort. The prevalent attitude was one of laissez-faire and, on certain important occasions, hostility.

The history of China reveals several instances of economic hardship and temporary overpopulation, which often led to rebellions. When these problems arose in the past century they were far from novel occurrences; yet their incidence became so widespread—in the form of mounting debt, increased tenancy, and landlessness—that peasants throughout Monsoon Asia were on the verge of bankruptcy.

There was no one way in which the peasant fell into tenancy and debt; an unforeseen emergency could bring this about, since he always lived on the brink of disaster. Any personal or community hardship could cause grave discomfort and even starvation. Also, the lack of flexibility inherent in the economic structure made it impossible to absorb the latest rise in population without serious dislocations. A famine, the inability to make ends meet with more mouths to feed, and the growing temptation to spend wastefully—all led to debt at the hands of the moneylender. Interest rates were extremely high, since rural credit facilities were primitive and little capital was available. In most regions the rate of interest ranged from 20 to 200 per cent per year—the average being 30 to 50 per cent—and the incidence of debt among the farmers ran from more than 50 to as high as 75 to 90 per cent. With land becoming more valuable as the number of people depending on it rose, the moneylenders stopped at nothing to use this entering wedge to gain possession of farms.

RATE OF TENANCY IN ASIA IN THE 1940's
IN TERMS OF THE PERCENTAGE OF ARABLE LAND WORKED BY

	Year	Tenants	Part Owners	Owners
Burma	1940	33		67
Lower Burma	1940	50		50
China	1946	35	25	40
British India	1946	55		45
Japan	1947	27	37	36
Korea	1944	55	25	20
Philippines	1946	35	16	49

SOURCES: Economic Commission for Asia and the Far East (ECAFE), *Economic Survey of Asia and the Far East, 1950* (New York: UN Department of Economic Affairs, 1951), pp. 183-190; Maurice Zinkin, *Asia and the West* (London: Chatto & Windus, 1951), p. 48.

Debt, dispossession, and tenancy became common features in many vital areas that were densely settled and heavily populated. Tenancy compounded the difficulty, since rental costs ranged from one third to two thirds of production. Under these conditions the cultivator could not work his way out of debt and regain ownership of his land. He was often reduced to a very small holding or suffered complete loss of land. Either circumstance was likely to bring about a sense of rootlessness, or alienation from the land, which threatened the entire system. Because all plots were small and landlords generally operated on a small scale, avarice and oppressiveness became most extreme. The landlord was not concerned with improving his property because he was interested only in profit on his investment and was certain that tenants would apply for almost any plot of land. Since the insecure tenant lacked the means and incentive to improve his holdings, the productivity of the soil suffered.

The question of land reform and its role in the economic reconstruction of Asia will be discussed below. At this point it should be observed that only a thorough modernization of the Asian economy can reverse this unfortunate trend. It was a grave misfortune that more progress toward this goal was not made during the long period of Western rule, when the task was technically easier and disruptive political forces were far less evident.

The Role of the West

The activities of the Westerner who arrived in this basically unhealthy economy have been subjected to heated, emotionally charged debates. The political implications of colonial rule and the drive for independence have become tightly linked to the economic issues. Although much attention has centered about the question of imperial exploitation, the unpremeditated effects of Western influence seem, from the vantage point of contemporary observations, to have had more vital consequences.

Since the acquisition of wealth was a prime motive of the Westerner's activity, he adopted the easiest, most efficient, and least risky means at his command. This statement does not necessarily mean that his efforts were exploitative in the sense that the natives became economically depressed, for the question of profit-through-investments is difficult to appraise in terms of drawing a balance of economic effects. Although colonial rulers drew profits from their possessions, the new activity they stimulated added to the total wealth of these communities.

Yet the West did interfere with life in Asia with little or no consideration for the repercussions that would follow from its profit-making activities. Its influence was essentially unconstructive, bringing about considerable changes in the Asian scene without any positive effort to give the area a better balanced and more stable economy. This attitude stands out more sharply when contrasted with the conscientious and positive endeavors of the Japanese government to industrialize its economy after 1868.

Production of Commodities for Export

The West developed those unique resources of the colonial possessions that would win strong positions in world markets. The result was a series of flourishing enterprises based on cash crops, extractive industries, and the processing of primary commodities. As these efforts met with success, a considerable amount of economic activity became geared almost exclusively to the needs of the European and American industrial markets. This situation occurred largely in Southeast Asia, where a great deal of energy was devoted to the production of commodities for export. Although the peasant of course did not stop growing his own food—for the bulk of the people of Asia were still engaged primarily in this type of activity—in some areas of Malaya and Ceylon the raising of grain crops became a secondary occupation.

Production for overseas markets attained considerable volume; because incomes were so small to begin with, this further source of pay was of the utmost importance. The export trade became very significant in the economies of the Southeast Asian states, ranging from 20 per cent of the national income in the Philippines to over 40 per cent in Ceylon. Even India and China, with a smaller ratio of 4 to 6 per cent, were influenced in their economic stability by foreign trade. The products most heavily relied on were tea, rubber, and coconuts in Ceylon; rubber and tin in Malaya; rubber, tea, sugar, copra, and tobacco in Indonesia; sugar cane, tobacco, coconuts, and abaca in the Philippines; rice, petroleum, and teak in Burma; rice, tin, rubber, and teak in Thailand; and rice and rubber in Indochina. Since two thirds of the cultivated area in Ceylon, an even larger proportion in Malaya, and one quarter of the land in the densely settled Dutch Indies, were not devoted to food production, these areas as well as the Philippines became food importers. They were supplied by the three great rice-growing states of Thailand, Burma, and Indochina, which also serviced the food-import needs of India and China; these huge communities were not able to grow the food needed to sustain their growing populations.

In all this economic activity the emphasis remained agrarian—either subsistence farming or cash-crop production for a foreign market. The area remained dependent on one type of economic activity because there was little or no industrial development. Many of the states lacked diversity even within their agricultural efforts. Others, like China and India, if diversified, were no longer self-sufficient. This degree of economic specialization had serious consequences. In the first place, the peasant was brought into the world market as a primary supplier of the industrial world's needs. In this position he was always at a disadvantage in establishing the value of his commodities as against that of manufactured articles. That is, his "terms of trade" were generally unfavorable.

The marketing of goods was in Western hands, so that even when export prices rose European companies absorbed most of the benefits. This trend was made possible because agricultural overpopulation insured an abundant labor market. Wages did not rise with profits, for when prices rose and production increased, more employees could be hired from this elastic labor supply. Native producers were also severely handicapped because they faced a monopoly of European traders, at least until the Japanese entered the world market on an appreciable scale.

Asian "prosperity" therefore came to hinge on Western demands. The value of primary export products was highly unstable, capable of changing at times with a sixfold magnitude. The basically unfavorable ratio these commodities had in Western markets stemmed in good part from the wide dispersion of the sources of production. When the primary product was in demand, there was a vigorous response on the part of a series of disunited, uncontrolled producers. As demand became satisfied, the product began to glut the market and its value fell even during prosperous times. It took a greater quantity of the Asian product to buy a set amount of European output. The reverse side of the "terms-of-trade" picture was the relatively strong purchasing power of industrial commodities in the raw-materials market. This basic relationship was most important because it regulated a considerable portion of world trade during the past century.[1]

More dramatic in their effect on Asian price levels and well-being have been depressions in the West. In these more extreme cases of dislocation, demands for raw material products underwent precipitous declines. These developed from the traditional tendency of industrial communities in a depression to undergo substantial deflation by cutting production sharply and keeping the level of prices as high as possible. Thus there was a sickening decline in the price level of raw-material commodities, as well as a rapid fall in the cost of food grains. As this source of income fell, the Asian producer's reaction was to increase his output in order to sell a maximum quantity of goods at the low price available. Where cash-crop exports were used to import food, the repercussions could be most serious. These crises occurred in varying degrees of intensity during the half dozen major industrial depressions that have occurred since 1850.

From the Western point of view, depressions might almost be considered an historic weapon, although not utilized consciously or intentionally, to keep primary products in a position of price inferiority. The Westerner might suffer from the deflationary spiral of low production and unemployment, but the fall in his standard of life was cushioned by the decline in the cost of raw material and food. To the Asian, a sudden fall in income meant the loss of money to pay debts or keep up rentals, and often signified bankruptcy and loss of land. Sharp economic reversals were suffered by the peasant silk cultivator in Japan and the cotton and jute growers of India, as well as by the cash-crop producers of Southeast Asia.

This precarious cash-crop system existed alongside the old subsistence economy, but the entire structure remained unstable because it was not complemented by native industry. In other words, there was no reliable source of

---

[1] Underlying this cyclical condition is the added difficulty, from the Asian viewpoint, that the supply of primary products has generally been plentiful, whereas that of manufactured goods is relatively scarce with regard to demand.

demand at home for raw materials to counterbalance Western market pressures. The fact that many nations depended on one or two commodities in their export activities increased the difficulty. Thus, if anything happened to the market of one or two particular products, national well-being was seriously affected. This point is especially relevant, since a major commodity may fall victim to scientific advances (as in the case of silk, rubber, and quinine), changes in consumer taste and demand, or a depression in one activity (like a slump in the textile industry).

PERCENTAGE OF INCOME BY SOURCE

Originating in	Burma 1946–47	Ceylon 1948	China 1946	India 1948–49	Japan 1949	Paki- stan 1945–46	Philip- pines 1948	Thai- land 1948
Agriculture	39	56	62.7	47.5	28.4	60	62.2	63.1
Mining			0.4	0.7	2.2		1.0	0.6
Manufacturers		7	7.2	16.5	27.1		3.5	12.8
Transport & Communication	61	5	3.8	2.6	11.1	40	4.9	23.5
Commerce		8	13.5	16.8	16.0		14.6	
Dwellings			3.6	5.2	0.9			
Other		24	8.8	10.7	14.3		13.8	

Since agricultural commodities and labor are valued lower than industrial output and effort, the proportion of people involved in agricultural and related pursuits is higher than an income table would indicate. For example,

PERCENTAGE OF ECONOMICALLY ACTIVE POPULATION

Engaged in	India 1948–49	France 1949	United States 1949
Agriculture	68.2	36.5	14.3
Mining	0.5	1.7	1.6
Manufacture	13.6	22.7	24.1
Transportation & Communication	1.8	11.6	11.3
Commerce	6.2	8.6	23.5
Other	9.7	18.9	25.2

Note the statistics for India in both tables, especially the emphasis on agriculture in the second listing.

SOURCES: Statistical Papers Series E, No. 3, p. 4; ECAFE, *Economic Survey, 1950*, p. 120.

To make matters worse, the people of backward areas have been prevented, for political reasons, from migrating to industrial states. Therefore economic diversification at home is looked on as an essential step toward greater well-being.

The European attitude toward industrial development was what could be expected, given the profit-making orientation with which the problem was faced. There was no incentive for the colonial powers to foster the establishment of native industries. On the contrary, the pressure that did exist was exerted toward the destruction of such establishments, which were mostly of the artisan and cottage variety. During the eighteenth century, in the waning days of mercantilism, both economic theory and the political efforts of home manufacturers led the new rulers, in such places as India, to discourage and eliminate native enterprise. Indian products not only were driven out of the South Asian markets but lost their hold over their home territories. As the nineteenth century progressed, it was easy to argue within the framework of the law of comparative economic advantage that the mother countries, now well along the road to industrial proficiency, should handle manufacturing, while the colonies best served as producers of raw material. The system could then be perpetuated without any drastic recourse to political and military pressure.

The colonial areas were not the only sectors affected by competition with the industrial West. Native industry suffered sharp blows also in independent states like China, Japan, and Thailand. And it should not be inferred that Western hostility and later disinterest formed the sole obstacle in Asia's failure to industrialize. Equally important was the failure of the Oriental economic groups, which could have led an industrial revolution, to grasp the essentials involved. There was also a failure of political leadership throughout Asia, with the brilliant exception of Japan, to understand the absolute importance of modernizing the economy with utmost vigor. The evident hostility displayed by the ruling elements of China during most of the nineteenth century—the most outstanding example of hostility to the new dispensation in Asia—was a major barrier to that country's progress. The difficulties encountered by Thailand in its still painfully slow effort to build a modern economy also illustrate the complexity of the task, even given the will to act.

Nor was there any understanding of the price to be paid in work and effort, greater social and economic discipline, and the acceptance of a different set of values if the new mode of production was to be earnestly adopted. Moreover, the commercial classes of Asia suffered from a sense of political inferiority as well as a lack of appreciation of the dynamics of expansive production. According to their notion of an economy, wealth was a static quantity, with the task being to increase one's share of the pie through shrewd commercial manipulation. There was no thought of increasing the amount of wealth in the community through greater investment and productivity, either by means of industrial activity or by better agricultural techniques. Improvements that were undertaken usually stemmed from governmental initiative.

The passive outlook on life of the merchant class was closely tied to its political subservience before bureaucrats and soldiers. Lacking any sense of the freedom or power developed in the West, the business elements also felt their position to be one of inferiority in the sociopolitical hierarchy of the authoritarian state. Thus, in Japan, the initiative for modernization, its inspiration and guidance for over half a century, came not from the merchant class, though it had accumulated considerable economic power, but from its political and social superiors, the nobles and the soldiers. On the other hand, the motivation behind Japan's enormous politically inspired endeavor was that of power and not primarily the well-being of the people.

Asian business operatives continued their age-old habits of concentrating their activity in commercial ventures and speculation in commodities. They invested their profits in "safe" purchases of land, placed them in bonds, converted them into jewelry, or indulged in conspicuous consumption. Leadership in economic modernization therefore had to come from political sources, but the colonial rulers did not undertake such activity. It is understandable that the private European businessmen would show little interest in a costly and risky transplantation of Western economic techniques to a society that was lukewarm to the new processes and ignorant of their mode of operation.

NET FOOD SUPPLY PER CAPITA
(IN KILOGRAMS PER YEAR)

	Cereal	Potatoes	Sugar	Pulses	Meat	Milk	Fats & Oils	Total Calories per Day
Burma 1947–48	154	8	6	10	6	8	3	1,990
Ceylon 1951–52	123	35	16	6	3	16	4	1,950
India 1948–49	110	6	12	17	2	46	3	1,620
1952–53	118		11	19	1	45	3	1,685
Indochina 1947–48	152	58	6	7	4		2	2,040
Japan 1949–50	149	60	3	1	2	4	1	2,100
1953–54	149	56	11	5	3	10	2	2,165
Pakistan 1948–49	153	5	12	11	4	73	2	2,030
1952–53	149	5	12	8	5	82	4	2,025
France 1952–53	127	136	24	4	53	150	14	2,830
Italy 1952–53	160	36	14	5	18	95	12	2,580
Sweden 1952–53	83	114	39	2	50	300	20	3,000
United Kingdom 1952–53	98	105	38	3	53	202	20	3,060

SOURCES: *Statistical Yearbook, 1951* and *1954* (New York: UN Department of Economic Affairs), Table 124; *Statistical Yearbook, 1955,* Table 123.

It is doubtful that Asia suffered an over-all decline in its living standards because its economy was compelled to rely squarely on primary production.

Yet much of the increase in total wealth accruing to the area was absorbed by the rapidly rising population. Since the economy was not altered fundamentally in its productive capacity, it could barely keep pace. The net result was that for all the increased economic activity in the area, and the undoubted rise in the value and quantity of its produce, the real income of the peasant and his standard of living showed little or no increase.

It must be admitted that only by withholding of the fruits of production, and keeping the native population from spending the economy's earnings on immediate needs, can capital be accumulated to finance a program of industrialization. In fact, a great deal of these forced "savings" was drained off either to Europe or to foreign Asian states, and the portions that were reinvested went for the most part into an expansion of extractive and cash-crop enterprises. From the Asian point of view, the only justification for the peasant's economic plight would have been a determined effort to use the profits of these primary producing enterprises to build a modern industrial plant. Neither the foreign nor the domestic business element operated with such an undertaking in mind.

Western Indifference

There were some developments along modern lines. Port and shipping facilities expanded, and, as trading centers developed, various commercial and financial services came into being. There gradually arose a few home industries, but most of these were concerned with the processing of raw material, and their impact on the standard of living was infinitesimal. In fact, as roads, railroads, and canals penetrated the interiors of several lands, a result was the destruction of the domestic manufactures that had persisted inland after those along the coast had disappeared. Again, this condition occurred in independent as well as in colonial states.

Aside from Japan, the progress that did take place could be described only as fitful and slow. Little positive encouragement was given to the development of sound native banking, shipping, land transportation, and various forms of corporate organization. Little attention was paid to the development of modern native institutions and skills although the training of local personnel was essential if Asians were to assume positions of responsibility and form a cadre to spread knowledge of Western skills, techniques, and standards among their fellow countrymen. However, since Western individuals and organizations could do jobs better and do them more cheaply, such a training program was never adopted. The dissemination of modern skills is a costly and painful exercise that can bear productive results in an alien environment only after careful nurturing; but European interest in efficiency served as an effective deterrent to such an undertaking. Although there was no open economic discrimination against natives—except, ironically, in Japanese-dominated Korea—no positive help was extended and no government protection given. By contrast, the Western governments and in more recent times the Japanese had encouraged and protected the development of skills and services in their own lands.

What political intervention there was operated to the detriment of industrial development. Both China and India found themselves without adequate tariff protection. China was restricted to a 5 per cent rate by international agreement until 1928 and India was compelled to admit foreign manufactures duty free until after the First World War. Moreover, no efforts were made to aid native industry through such devices as government purchases. For example, the British continued to buy rail equipment and locomotives for the Indian rail service in England even after Indian production along these lines, though less efficient, had begun.

DEGREE OF URBANIZATION
PERCENTAGE OF RURAL AND URBAN POPULATIONS

	Rural	Urban
Ceylon (1955)	84.6	15.4
India (1955)	82.7	17.3
Indochina (1930's)	90–95	5–10
Indonesia (1930's)	92.5	7.5
Japan (1935)	35.5	64.5
Korea (1930's)	88.3	11.7
S. Korea (1955)	80.4	19.6
Malaya (1930's)	70.5	29.5
Malaya (1955)	73.5	26.5
Manchuria (1930's)	80	20
Pakistan (1955)	88.6	11.4
Philippines (1930's)	90	10
Philippines (1955)	75.9	24.1
Thailand (1930's)	89	11
Thailand (1955)	90.1	9.9

SOURCES: Zinkin, *Asia and the West*, pp. 23–24; Karl Pelzer, *An Economic Survey of the Pacific Area* (New York: Institute of Pacific Relations, 1941), pp. 13–15; *Demographic Yearbook, 1955* (New York: UN Department of Economic Affairs), Table 7.

Industrialization is a slow and costly process that requires the application of considerable energy and wealth, and a long passage of time, before it can bring results. The enormous scope of the area's requirements can be measured from the argument that, to raise its standard of living, an Oriental economy would have to remove almost half its laboring population from the land. The remaining agrarian labor force would have to maintain or even increase the level of production for the increased urban population to be adequately fed. The manpower transplanted to the cities would have to be housed, and employed in industry, trade, transportation, and other productive activities. The task of carrying out this project is so great that only a sustained, long-term effort under positive governmental guidance or direction could eventually guarantee results.

Consider the case of Japan, the only Asian state that has carried on a successful industrial revolution. In 1868 about 80 per cent of the people depended on agriculture, and only 5 per cent lived in cities of 50,000 or more. By 1930 only

47 per cent of the population was engaged in agriculture. From 1920 to 1940 the rural population was almost stationary. About 16 million people, a number equal to the increase in population, were added to the urban areas. In this shift to the cities the Japanese left an agricultural subsistence economy for a much higher industrial standard of living. Moreover, this new type of economy and lowered fertility rates began to be diffused in the countryside. The economic revolution thus made possible a better life for all and presented the likelihood of a relatively stable population in the future. Had Japan not launched its campaign of expansion, its standard of living would now be even higher. What Japan accomplished relatively early became progressively more difficult for the other states to achieve as their populations rose sharply.

The Population Problem

One of the most important achievements of the Western powers was the restoration or establishment of law and order in the countries of South Asia. Internal banditry, local political wars, and other forms of chaos were terminated as the ruling power became far superior in strength to any rebel force. Before the rise of nationalism created the physical and psychological climate for mass unrest, outbursts against the colonial powers tended to be sporadic and limited. Meanwhile a long period of international peace, based on British power, characterized the South Pacific and Indian Ocean areas. In Northeast Asia, Japan presented an internally secure state, and brought about conditions of police order in Korea after subjugating that hapless land in 1910.

Only China stood out in marked contrast, suffering civil strife, foreign incursions, and wars of various sorts in modern times. Untold hardships followed from the partial disintegration of vast agricultural operations, especially flood control, irrigation, and storage. There was therefore a "natural check" on the rise of population, which was slowed down but not halted. Because of this physical damage and slight increase in population, the standard of living in China showed no improvement; in fact, in many areas it declined.

Elsewhere in Asia, government meant more stability and peace, for the colonial powers began to spend money on important community services. At first the motivation was primarily to facilitate economic activity, but gradually there arose the belief that such services were important ends in themselves. In a large country like India, the establishment of law and order and the development of sea and overland transportation facilities were very important achievements. The dreaded possibility of famine no longer plagued the country, despite the fact that the population gradually outstripped the food supply grown at home. Famines had been local, affecting one or two provinces; now a stricken area could make its need known and receive aid quickly. The great exception was the Bengal famine of 1943, when a poor crop, Japanese control over the rice areas to the east, and an energy-consuming war occurred simultaneously. The improvement in health and sanitation services, plus the development of medical care, however rudimentary at first, further facilitated a rise in population.

To obtain an adequate supply of food, India has to increase its own production and develop its export power so that it can make purchases abroad. Some slight industrialization and growth of modern business facilities occurred under the British, especially in the Bombay and Calcutta areas, but, compared with India's needs, this was most inadequate. Since it was not Britain's ambition to alter the Indian economy drastically, the bulk of the people remained subsistence agrarian workers. Moreover, because the peasantry demonstrated no apprehension of new farming techniques, even agricultural production remained relatively static.

The number of inhabitants in the countries of Southeast Asia increased during the past century from three to ten times. The great population pockets were located in Tonkin along the Red River of North Indochina, the plains of central Luzon, and the fantastically crowded island of Java. Malaya and the adjacent city of Singapore underwent a tenfold increase in population. The rice-exporting regions of Thailand, lower Burma, and Cochinchina also experienced rapid population growth. The old structure of a peasant economy remained, though considerably weakened by the intense pressure on the land.

The Population Cycle

The establishment of law and order, linkage to the world market, the development of transport facilities, and the creation of health and social services all operated together to accelerate this trend toward increased population. In a sense, Asia experienced an intense version of the pattern of population growth common to preindustrial states. In this type of society, the point of departure is a fairly stable population whose equilibrium is maintained by a high birth rate balanced by a high death rate. What happened in England, continental Europe, and now Asia, was a considerable decline in the death rate before the industrial revolution was fully under way. Europeans during this time had an escape route open, since they were able to migrate abroad in large numbers. The industrial revolution, where it did occur, created the wealth required for a large number of people to enjoy a constantly rising standard of living—no small achievement in any era.

A program of industrialization is slow to bring rewards to the consumer. Physical dislocations and discomforts occur in the early stages, especially with regard to housing conditions, and deprivations characterize the extended period required for intensive savings and investment. A qualifying condition is the amount of information, skills, and techniques already available when a nation begins to industrialize. The late-comers can take advantage of the progress made in pioneer states and save vast amounts of time and effort by adopting lines of operation successfully developed elsewhere through the painful method of trial and error. A savings of what can amount to generations in terms of time can be achieved, and from this point of view the Asian states stood to benefit.

Meanwhile the population pattern became alarmingly clear. The gap of time between the fall in the death rate and the decline in the birth rate is usually quite long. The fertility rate begins to fall as the standard of living rises, but this is accompanied by a continued decline in the death rate. Thus it is some time before the gap between the two rates starts to close, usually in the form of a tapered-off death rate accompanied by an ever-diminishing birth rate. The

POPULATION TRENDS IN ASIA, 1920–1954
(IN MILLIONS)

Area	1920	1930	1940	1954
Asia (except U.S.S.R.)	967	1,073	1,213	1,451
South West	44	48	54	67
South Central	326	362	410	489
South East	110	128	155	183
Japan	56	64	71	88
Rest of Far East	431	471	523	634

SOURCES: *Demographic Yearbook, 1955,* Table 2; and *Statistical Yearbook, 1955,* Table 1.

1947 BIRTH AND DEATH RATES IN ASIA

Area	Rate per 1,000 People Birth	Death	Approximate Number per Year in Millions Birth	Death
Near East	40–45	30–35	2.6– 3.0	2.0– 2.3
South Central	40–45	30–35	15.1–17.0	11.3–13.2
Japan	28	17	2.0	1.2
Rest of Far East	40–45	30–35	25.1–28.2	18.8–21.9
Compare with the following:				
U.S. and Canada	17	11	2.4	1.5
North West Central Europe	17	13	3.3	2.5
South Europe	23	16	1.9	1.3
East Europe	30–34	17–21	8.5– 9.6	4.8– 5.9

ASIA: POPULATION BY AGE GROUPS, 1947

Area	By Percentage Under 15	15–59	60 and over	By Millions Under 15	15–59	60 and over
Near East	40	54	6	30	40	4
South Central	40	56	4	170	239	17
Japan	37	55	8	29	44	6
Rest of Far East	40	55	5	264	362	33
Compare with the following:						
U.S. and Canada	25	64	11			
North West Central Europe	24	62	14			
South Europe	30	59	11			
East Europe	34	59	7			

SOURCE: The two tables above are from *World Population Trends, 1920–1947* (New York: UN Department of Social Affairs, December, 1949), pp. 3, 6, 10, 15, 16.

NATIONAL POPULATIONS

Country	1950	1953	1954	1955	People per Square Kilometer 1953–54
Burma	18,489		19,242		28
Cambodia		3,860			28
Ceylon	7,550	8,155		8,588	124
China*	463,500	582,603			60
Formosa	7,477			8,907	240
India	358,000	372,000			113
Indonesia	73,500		81,110		54
Japan	82,900		88,900		238
Korea	29,500	30,000			136
Laos		1,260			5
Malaya	5,227			6,059	45
Singapore	1,018			1,213	1,547
Mongolian Peoples Republic	885	910			1
Pakistan	75,040				79
Philippines	19,557		21,440		70
Thailand	18,313			20,300	39
Vietnam			26,000		79

* According to census published by Peking in 1955.

SOURCES: *Demographic Yearbook, 1951*, pp. 97-99; *1954*, pp. 102-105; *1955*, pp. 120-124.

social forces behind these developments seem to operate autonomously, with political intervention possessing only limited power to guide the course of events. A reduction in the rate of fertility stems from such interrelated factors as urbanization, greater industrialization, desire or need to educate children, desire for leisure time, and a rising standard of living. But it must be emphasized that the arrival at a new level of equilibrium, with lower fertility and mortality rates, does not occur until a rapid increase in population has taken place. When, as in Asia, industrialization proceeds at a snail's pace, a grave difficulty arises. The increase in population means that a greater magnitude of industrialization is required. Unless the alien concept of "planned parenthood" is adopted, population increases can be checked only through an adequate degree of industrialization.

Thus the level of industrial production now required by India to raise its standard of living is far greater than that originally required by Japan. Even two generations ago this effort could have been more modest in scope. The contrasting case of Japan is again instructive. Starting with a population of about 30 million after 1850, the Japanese undertook a policy of complete modernization. They began to show results after the turn of the century, after a long period of what amounted to national training. Aided by the First World War, the economy finally assumed the characteristics of an industrial society as the population reached the level of about 70 million in 1930. Thereafter, though temporarily checked by a disastrous war, Japanese industrial development has proceeded at a rapid rate. Its population is now over 85 million and it is estimated that the tapering-off process will have its effect when the population approximates the 100 million mark. Although the Japanese cannot claim to be living as well as the more developed Western communities, they are far ahead of their Asian neighbors and are on a level with the less advanced Western European states. Yet it is worth noting that, with this heroic effort and its satisfactory degree of achievement, Japan's population will have more than tripled during the course of a century before attaining stability.

THE STRUCTURE OF MANUFACTURING

	Year	Number of Establishments	Wage Earners (1,000's)	Salaried (1,000's)
Burma	1938	1,019	86.4	
	1947	473	46.5	
	1953	1,982	86.2	4.35
India	1949	6,257	1,529	163
	1951	6,392	1,478	154
	1952	6,470	1,496	153
Japan	1949	106,854	2,728	577
	1952	168,109	——4,319——	
	1953	172,613	——4,667——	
Korea	1937	6,298	170.1	37
S. Korea	1947	3,246	156.3	44.5
Pakistan	1953	1,230	—— 125.8——	
Philippines	1948	29,463	77.5	12.6
United Kingdom	1948	54,847	5,492	1,095

SOURCES: *Statistical Yearbook, 1951*, Table 165; *1954*, Table 66; *1955*, Table 67.

ELECTRIC ENERGY PRODUCTION
(IN MILLION KWH.)

	1950	1953	1954
Ceylon	81.0	144.4	162.4
Formosa	1,040	1,564	1,805
Hong Kong	294	436	492
India	5,103	6,627	7,522
Indonesia	362 (1948)	733	
Japan	44,890	55,698	59,605
S. Korea	337	736	898
Malaya	600	780	873
Pakistan	181.5	402.7	488
Philippines	820 (1951)	1,111	1,140
Singapore	187	281	318
Thailand	68.6	102	156.8
Vietnam	181	295	
Asia—Total	56,100	71,500	

SOURCES: *Statistical Yearbook, 1951* and *1954*, Table 121; *1955*, Table 120.

INDUSTRIAL PRODUCTION*

(In 1,000 Metric Tons)

Country	Coal	Cement	Cotton Yarn	Sulphuric Acid	Pig Iron and Ferro Alloy	Steel Ingots	Finished Steel	Aluminum	Nitrogenous Fertilizer
Ceylon		63.9	0.90						
		65.9	1.06						
China	28,289‡	749							
	25,627‡								
Manchuria					36	16			
					2,352‡	1,412‡			
Formosa	799	332.0						1.76	3.5
	897	519.7						4.90	15.3
Hong Kong		68.1	24.25						
		63.7	32.63						
India	32,506	2,655	534.3	106	1,708	1,461	1.018	3.65	8.4
	36,422	3,841	669.5§	110.8	1,804	1,531		3.82	61.5
Indonesia									10.3
Japan	38,461	4,462	238.3	2,030	4,308†	6,844†	3,471	24.8	396.9
	46,531	8,768	414.5	2,685	2,299	4,839		45.5	560.0
					4,653	7,662			
S. Korea	1,066	10	9.8		607‡ (All Korea)	112‡ (All Korea)			
	866	44	13.27						
Pakistan	444	431	9.65						
	588	604	53.74						
Philippines	123	298	0.32						
	154.9	319	0.80						
Thailand		165							
		288							
Vietnam	499	144							
	832	290							

*For each country the upper row of figures indicates 1949–1950; the lower line, 1953.
†1941; ‡1944; §1952.

Sources: *Statistical Yearbook, 1951,* Tables 78, 89, 104, 107, 108, 114, 130, 131; *1954,* Tables 38, 81, 94, 105, 108, 109, 115.

RICE, RUBBER, AND TIN PRODUCTION IN 1,000 METRIC TONS

	Rubber			Tin Concentrates			Rice		
	1938	1948	1953	1938	1948	1953	1934–38	1948	1953
Burma	6.8	9.2	10.5	4,612	1,165	1,383	6,971	5,153	5,616
Ceylon	50.8	96.5	100.2						
China				13,400	4,900	6,400	50,065	48,134	49,000
Formosa							1,642	1,329	2,042
India	12.7	15.7	21.5				32,308	34,439	42,004
Indonesia	322.3	439.3	705.7	30,205	29,499	34,365			10,970
Japan				2,106	120	745	11,501	11,993	10,298
Korea							3,699	3,052	4,100
Malaya	365.3	709.4	583.6	44,071	45,534	57,157	513	495	658
Pakistan							11,169	12,814	13,946
Philippines							2,179	2,491	3,105
Thailand	42.3	97.4	97.1	15,058	4,308	10,288	4,357	6,835	8,239
Indochina	61.0	44.6	75.7	1,625	32	268	6,498	4,350	4,466

SOURCE: *Statistical Yearbook, 1955*, Tables 13, 17, 48.

What of China and India with their enormous populations of 300 million and 200 million in 1850? What small modernization has occurred in these lands does not even measure up to Japan's accomplishments in absolute terms. The task ahead of Indonesia and Pakistan is of an intermediate magnitude, since their populations are about 80 million. The smaller states of Thailand, Burma, and the Philippines, each around the 20-million mark, are theoretically capable of making substantial advances, given rational policies, internal stability, staying power, and adequate foreign assistance. Indochina and Korea, with their brutal civil wars, internal divisions, and populations of 30 million, present more difficult problems within this general grouping.

Economic Reform and Modernization

The economic situation became more explosive than ever when people in impoverished lands realized that a better life could be attained in this world. There had been peasant revolts and other disturbances in the past, indicating that Western concepts of Asian lassitude have been exaggerated. Yet never before had the notion of a decent living appealed so vividly to the mass of people. So attractive is the example of the West today that Asians are impatient when told that such an achievement is both novel and difficult. It also does little good to observe that the Asian standard of life today is not too different from that of the preindustrial West. Economic improvement in the West may be relatively recent, but it has brought advanced Western states to a point at least eight or nine times above the Asian level.

Whatever contentment has existed in the Orient is being eaten away by the corrosive impact of comparisons with the more tolerable conditions prevailing in distant lands. The discrepancy between what is wanted and what is immediately attainable is so great that there is a danger that disillusion with the new democratic governments may come to a head as the chances of immediate success fade. Such a situation may lead to the growth in popularity of extremist movements, ultranationalist and xenophobic on the right and communist on the left.

Land Reform: Value and Consequences

With this sword over their heads the new democratic governments of Asia are faced with grave difficulties. These are compounded by their own optimistic arguments, during the era of colonial administration, that the elimination of alien rule would lead directly to great material progress. Even as the hopes of the people were being aroused, independence arrived under adverse conditions: the chaotic postwar situation with its accompanying political and psychological instability, the lack of administrative experience, and the rather low level of industrialization. The new governments must demonstrate considerable tact and keen political skill in instituting certain necessary reforms that will bring immediate, if short-range, results in terms of economic benefits and popular confidence.

Intelligent reform requires a high degree of political stability and orderly government, for the inevitable slowness of economic improvement and development must be widely explained. The new governments have an important asset on their side—the willingness of their peoples to support them as long as some constructive effort is undertaken. It is up to the new leaders in Asia to take advantage of the situation and channelize the newly released nationalist energy into constructive endeavors.

A most useful tactic in this context is land reform. Its results may be marginal and short-range in the light of Asia's basic needs, for conditions will not begin to improve sufficiently until dependence on the land by an overwhelming proportion of the population is drastically reduced by industrialization. Reform will not necessarily assure an improvement in agricultural production, because its basic plank is to secure for the peasant control over the land he operates. This effort may promote an equalization in the size of holdings, making for small plots, which are comparatively inefficient in their yields. Then, too, the peasant will be unable to retain all the produce that formerly went to the landlord and moneylender. The nonagrarian elements in the community have to be fed, and some pressure, perhaps in the form of taxes, must be substituted for the need to pay interest and rent. The substantial tax on the farming community in Japan late in the nineteenth century is a case in point. Of course, a foreign aid program can ease the pressure in this regard considerably.

Nevertheless, land reform must be pursued vigorously because it will remain a central political issue. Cultivators require security of tenure, simple procedures for the purchase of land, protection against alienation of land, and extension of credit. These measures would give the peasant a sense of belonging and check the alarming incidence of landlessness. Unless the drift toward

47

rootlessness is checked, the peasant will continue to be thrown to the mercy of the elements for his livelihood, stripped of pride and prestige. Without land he becomes helpless prey to various forces at work in the community, very apt to be jailed at little or no provocation. Land reform will play the vital role of arresting the disintegration of the peasantry and stabilize the base on which to build a modern society.

The owners who have to be dispossessed are naturally fiercely opposed to the entire program because they wish to retain their valuable property. They fear that the cash compensation usually provided may become almost valueless under inflationary conditions. Landowners are more often than not fellow nationals and not easily coerced foreigners, and their political influence is bound to be quite powerful. Yet their acquiescence is essential, for overt hostility would be a sharp blow to the political stability of the nation. As a matter of fact, landowners and the economy as a whole would benefit greatly if the attention of this class were diverted from agrarian real-estate activities toward more productive types of investment in industrial and financial enterprises.

This latter point bears directly on the unproductive economic bent of the wealthier elements in the Asian community, and their general lack of initiative. Compensation for the expropriation of farmland can serve to revolutionize the outlook of the landholders if this class can be linked to the government-sponsored drive for modernization. This solution will not lead immediately to a middle class that is independent in its political outlook, since such a revolution in attitude cannot occur so abruptly. But by drawing these elements out of their shell, admittedly through government sponsorship, the groundwork can be laid for the emergence of a new business class as the modernization program advances. The urgency of such an undertaking is intensified by the existence of a small foreign, though Oriental, middle class in many of the small countries. This phenomenon makes for considerable antagonism and suspicion between nationalist governments and the alien middle-class elements with whom some cooperation is essential. That Thailand, the only state in Southeast Asia that was never a colony, should be so embroiled in a struggle with its Chinese business element is an indication of how dangerous this obstacle can become. That nation expended so great a part of its limited resources in an effort to supplant the Chinese business community that modernization was impeded.

Difficulty of Industrializing

Before going on to discuss the problems involved in the actual process of industrialization, we should note certain psychological hazards and other dangers involved. The difficulty in adopting a new mode of economic life stems from its extreme novelty. It should not be surprising that ruling classes— feudal leaders, aristocratic warriors, or Chinese classical scholars—were unwilling and unable to make the necessary adjustments. Both potential management and labor groups display a negative attitude toward the harsher and more rigorous requirements of business and industrial life. The early years of industrialization bring changes that unhinge the traditional structure of a community. The anonymous causes of delay in progress and the irritants that arise during the era of transition can contribute to a dangerous sense of frustration. Only publicity and clarification, if not given in a condescending or hectoring manner, can help alleviate such tensions.

Perhaps the waste, dislocations, and economic hardships involved can be more clearly understood if we observe the difficulties encountered by Argentina and Australia in their effort to industrialize. These two countries are far more favorably endowed than the average Asian state, with modest-sized populations that are oriented in Western traditions and techniques. If anything, they may have too few people to maintain their primary producing activities while undertaking a program of industrialization. Neither state has a low standard of life, both fared quite well during the war, and both have dealt in exports that were in high demand during the postwar period. Presumably these factors made the availability of foreign currencies and capital a less formidable problem than it is in Asia. Nonetheless, though one country is a democracy and the other operated as a dictatorship until 1955, both encountered difficulties in their efforts. Trouble arose in the form of inflationary pressures and lowered agricultural production, which led to shortages in commodities that used to be important exports. It was only in the mid-1950's that Australia, at least, made progress in modernizing its economy. The trouble can be traced to several sources, such as ineptness in economic theory, failure to go slowly enough, miscalculation of economic trends, and political pressures and errors. It is sufficient to note that even where nature's endowments, historical developments, and economic conditions created at least a mildly favorable situation, the going still proved rough. In Asia, where benefits are meager and difficulties more pronounced, the chances of error, unexpected obstacles, and repeated setbacks are that much greater.

At this stage the main incentive to develop a modern industrial economy lies in the possibility of increasing the total wealth of Asia. Although the distribution of income is always a serious issue, the alarmingly low standards of the Orient reflect fundamental problems that resemble those dealt with by nineteenth-century classical economists like Ricardo. The primary tasks are basic improvements in the means of production and a rapid accumulation of wealth. If this produces a rise in the standard of living at a gradually increasing rate, the mass of people will experience a considerable improvement in their condition even without a drastic alteration in the distribution of income. Japan is an example of how all levels of society can benefit when modernization is maintained at a steady tempo. If, in addition, extreme inequality is avoided, important psychological benefits can accrue to the government. Most important is the need to prevent capital, as it accumulates, from being utilized in the traditionally unconstructive manner.

How to Industrialize

The all-important question of deciding how to industrialize and the self-discipline required to carry out a program are of crucial importance once plans reach the stage of maturity. It is at this juncture that other motives in addition to those of popular well-being play an influential role. The urge to acquire prestige, build one's power, provide for an adequate national defense, and, perhaps unfortunately, to lay the groundwork for future expansionist policies may be among the important motivating forces in any specific case. In such instances a powerful bias would develop in the direction of a rapid buildup of capital goods and other heavy industries.

Desires to establish a heavy industry plant are legitimately rooted in the realization that until this is achieved the drive to pull the economy up by its own bootstraps can hardly be considered under way. Moreover, as long as one is dependent on foreign sources for heavy equipment, the possibility of economic and even political subservience remains at issue in former colonial lands. Without full control over these elements of production, the governments that are planning industrialization projects are somewhat restricted in their choice of alternatives. Their freedom of maneuver may be sorely curtailed by dependence on uncontrollable and even unreliable foreign sources.

The creation of heavy industry became an obsession with the planners of the immediate postwar period. As the Cold War developed in intensity, the urge to produce one's own military equipment gained ground. If heavy industry is expensive, modern combat elements like jet planes, warships, and tanks appear to be extravagances. Yet some sense of security and prestige may be important prerequisites for the successful conduct of a long and arduous economic rehabilitation program.

The advocates of a rapid build-up of heavy industry have argued that concentration on consumer enterprises will not bring long-term improvements, even if an immediate rise in the standard of living occurs. National savings, it is claimed, should be devoted to this politically less palatable heavy investment program. The success of the Soviet Union in this regard is often cited by such advocates, who add that they wish to emulate Russia only in the economic sense, without resorting to its oppressive political policies. Yet considerable discontent is generated by a belt-tightening process, especially when the level of wealth is low to begin with. Political uncertainty, the painfulness of industrial development, and the already depressed conditions pose a real dilemma for the advocates of heavy industry in an Asian democracy.

The new states reflected this dilemma in their programs. Before and immediately after attaining independence they pressed for the development of heavy industry. However, they came to realize the limitations of the skills that were available, the extraordinary physical difficulties involved, and the political risks such a procedure would entail. The ultimate goal—a heavy industrial plant complemented by light consumer-goods production—has not changed, but

short-range ambitions were moderated. Gradually and reluctantly it was realized that emphasis on heavy industry must come later in a program of
modernization.

Meanwhile the school of thought which held that backward areas ought to
move from the familiar to the difficult elaborated a comprehensive approach.
It follows the line of least resistance and seeks a rapid increase in the standard
of living and available wealth, while establishing the basis for more complex
operations later. Emphasis is placed on agricultural improvement, transportation, sanitation, better education, electrification, and the expansion of processing and consumer-goods industries. Many of these activities are closely related,
as in the case of agricultural improvement, which involves the following:
improved seeds; better farming methods and land utilization; controlled water
supply by means of wells, irrigation, and flood control; rural electrification on
the successful Japanese model; better storage facilities; improved light-farming
implements; adequate marketing and credit facilities; pest control; and artificial fertilizer.

The most important enterprises that can be undertaken in this regard are
multipurpose dams of the type now being constructed in India. These can be
modeled in part after the Tennessee Valley projects. It is hoped that the over-all
program will raise the output of food by as much as 50 per cent. Since the
peasant's political support is essential and his food production must be improved
in order to feed the people involved in the construction of new industries, this
type of program seems unavoidable.

Electrification and road and rail transportation, to further the production
and marketing of commodities, also play important roles in the development
of light consumer and processing industries. Furthermore, these facilities are
vital prerequisites for future industrial progress. The processing industries can
serve as a transitional step on the road to industrialization. The skills and
machinery required, while not too complex, are good points of departure for
more complex operations in terms of operational discipline, business management, and maintenance and repair work. These efforts may lead to a temporary
rise in sales to foreign markets, or at least to a curtailment in foreign purchases.
The foreign currency thus gained can be used to speed acquisition of essential
capital goods from abroad.

Some analysts argue that it would be wise to develop light industries when
the more basic projects appear under way. The process of capital investment
can be significantly encouraged at the same time that additional skills and
techniques are developed. The capital required for such enterprises should be
obtainable from domestic sources, because the amount required is relatively
moderate. The chances of making a profit are excellent if production becomes
centered in items high in public demand. In this way the people have some
concrete manifestation of progress—in such forms as cosmetics, cloth, household equipment—and the process of capital accumulation is strengthened. That
is, the light industries that can make a large profit could be encouraged as pain-

ROAD AND RAIL FACILITIES

	Railway Lines in Km. (1949)	No. of Locomotives (1949)	Km. of Highways (1949)	1000's of Motor Vehicles—1950	
				Commercial	Passenger
N. Borneo	187	16		0.34	0.51
Burma	2,850	284	41,209 (1938)	22.02	10.056‡
Ceylon	1,444	236	10,699	14.30	34.21
China	18,391	2,477	203,414‡	39.87	16.16*
India	54,494	8,228	384,753	87.81	157.23
Indochina	1,353	122	20,377	7.61	13.28†
Indonesia	4,607	681	3,844	18.70	16,62‡
Korea	2,568	289	29,223‡	12.3	3.4‡
Malaya	1,400	188	72,596	14.4	25.2
Pakistan	11,256	1,276	9,117*	11.1	16.6‡
Philippines	900	80	23,851	49.8	43.0
Thailand	3,272	388	5,758	6.5	8.5
Japan	19,760	5,973	919,621	132.1	25.1

*1947, †1948, ‡1949.

NUMBER OF PERSONS PER

	Route Km. of Railways (1948)	Registered Motor Vehicle (1947)
United States	390	3.8
Western Europe	980	43.4
Japan	4,200	665.0
Rest of East Asia	9,700	2,440.0

SOURCES: ECAFE, *Economic Survey, 1949*, p. 69; *1950*, pp. 254, 256, 259, 263.

less devices for drawing money from the populace in order to finance more costly and less immediately remunerative capital enterprises.

This pleasant and profitable activity must be kept sternly in check lest the entire program of industrialization become distorted. Private interests will be especially persuasive in attempting to avoid projects that are slow to bring profitable returns. However, the strong urge in Asia to create modern industrial complexes seems to afford sufficient protection against this eventuality. In fact, suggestions by Western experts that full-blown industrialization be delayed are met with the suspicion that such advice is motivated by a desire to keep Asia in a state of economic subjugation, with continued emphasis on food production, agricultural exports, light industries, and the extraction, production, and processing of raw materials. Yet the fact remains that most modernization programs, including that of Japan before 1930, did not plunge exclusively into large-scale industrial projects.

In view of the mental outlook in Asia, especially with the Russian example as a goad, it is inevitable that the effort to modernize Oriental economies must come sooner than a technical expert would prefer on the grounds of economic soundness and efficiency. Provided this endeavor is kept within bounds, the "price" will be worth while if it results in appreciable psychological satisfaction. A healthy sign is the soberness with which Asian states are approaching the problem. The largest portion of funds the Asian democracies devoted to improvements in the first decade after 1945 were centered on agriculture, transportation, and power. Investment in industry, especially by the state, was relatively small, but a sharp increase in this sector was expected by 1960. Each nation has varied its effort within this framework in accordance with its most pressing needs. India has concentrated on raising its food and raw-material production, improving its transport facilities, and utilizing its current industrial

CAPITAL EXPENDITURES: PROPOSED GOVERNMENT OUTLAYS
(In Millions of U.S. Dollars)

	Period Covered	Agriculture; Fisheries; Forestry; Livestock; Irrigation	Transport; Communication	Electric Power	Industry
Ceylon	1951–57	106.4	61.6	22.4	16.8
Hong Kong		1.4		3.5	
India	1951–57	1,276.8	1,475.6	120.4	378.0
Indochina	1st 5 yrs.	141.0	137.9	35.0	47.5
Malaya	1951–57	36.4	59.1	56.3	.6
Nepal	1st 5 yrs.	2.7	3.1	5.9	6.7
Pakistan	1951–57	246.4	159.6	142.8	148.4
Philippines	1950–54	14.8	18.9	2.5	5.6
Thailand				14.0	125.0

Source: ECAFE, *Economic Survey, 1950*, p. 161.

GOVERNMENT DEVELOPMENT EXPENDITURE, 1955
(In Millions of U.S. Dollars)

	Total Allocated	Agriculture; Community Development; Resettlement	Irrigation; Power	Transportation; Communication	Industry; Mining	Social Welfare and Other
Burma	175	24	34	35	43	39
Ceylon	84	11	32	20	2	19
China	7,660	—— 1,765 ——		911	2,712	2,272
India	1,492	243	441	396	88	324
Indonesia	85	6	17	32	12	18
Japan	1,555	455	178	518	282	124
Malaya & British Borneo	119	7	27	26	0.2	59
Pakistan	337	16	122	82	53	63
Thailand	64	3	9	29	3	20

Source: ECAFE, *Economic Survey, 1955*, p. 49.

capacity. Pakistan is now stressing basic development of power and the further strengthening of its profitable cash-crop and agricultural activities. Other examples are food production, transportation and power development in the Philippines; irrigation and profitable consumer activity in Indonesia; improvement of transport, port, and irrigation facilities in Thailand; and expanded welfare and cash-crop production in Malaya. In all states, long-range efforts must be made in the fields of education and medicine, transportation, electric power, mining, and technical training.

Unemployment in Asia has assumed forms different from those in the West. A large portion of the labor force could be removed from agricultural work without reducing output. Such "disguised unemployment" could be relieved by transferring this labor to the production of industrial capital. However, there would be a problem of getting food to these people while they were being productively employed, a difficulty not faced in subsistence farming. This might be met by the establishment of small workshops and processing plants in rural areas. Rural industrialization would also enable farmers to be gainfully employed in off-seasons and so alleviate a second major type of unemployment, seasonal idleness.

Foreign Aid

The shortage of private domestic capital and the costliness of most projects have involved the native governments deeply in these economic development programs. The accessibility of foreign capital will significantly influence the content, rate of progress, and degree of success of these programs. Loans can be translated into goods and services to build new industries, feed and house the people so employed, and help carry them through the critical transitional years. Without foreign loans capital accumulation may require some depression of living standards. Domestic funds, even if augmented through the active cooperation of wealthy native classes, a doubtful assumption at best, would still be inadequate for the task at hand. Foreign aid may well be an essential factor in the economic transformation of Asia, since its availability can ensure early, modest successes. However, a project of this magnitude is often characterized by the snowball effect of early results. Once advances are under way, the entire mutually supporting structure of economic development tends to gather momentum at an ever-accelerating rate. Thus the success of small steps at the start becomes considerably magnified as time progresses. Yet even the moderate beginning to which the Asian states have adjusted themselves may be too great a burden for native capital resources, in view of the nature of private investment and the limited funds that a government can accumulate through taxes.

Unfortunately, the issue of international loans has become increasingly delicate during the course of this century, and since 1945 has appeared more vexing than ever. It became emotionally charged because of the anti-Western, anticapitalist orientation of many of the new governments of Asia. As their need for aid became apparent, the Asians vacillated between critical comments (for example, that America had to invest in Asia in order to avoid a depression) and plaintive remarks (for example, that Europe was receiving attention, whereas Asia was being neglected). Any foreign investment in Asia was suspected as a foot in the door that could lead to alien control over many aspects of the economy and perhaps give the West a chance to reassert its political authority. Counterarguments that foreign investment has occurred in many independent states without such effects could not make an immediate impression in the psychological climate prevailing in Asia. Nor could Asians be easily persuaded by the argument that many nations were helped by foreign investors even when the latter were former rulers. For example, British investments contributed greatly to the economic development of the United States in the nineteenth century.

The most hostile reaction to Western aid comes from the Communist bloc. Soviet Russia has frequently denounced the concept of outside help in its program of industrialization, though this made matters much more difficult for its own people. The negative attitude of Communist China toward all gestures of "economic coexistence," such as those extended by Great Britain in 1949-1950, will undoubtedly add enormously to the hardships that nation will undergo during its economic transformation.

The other states of Asia do not display such a doctrinaire hatred of the West, but their suspicions have remained vigorous. Concern over possible American political dominance is lessening, but there is fear that assistance will commit Asia to support American foreign policy. More conventionally, it is argued that the money will be so manipulated that exploitation, in the form of heavy profits to foreign investors, will result; ideological prejudices and past experience serve to strengthen this view.

On the other side of the fence, the private foreign investor sees no broad field of operations opening, and in fact has been systematically discouraged from investing abroad. Americans have been especially cautious since the failure of their extravagant foreign-loan activities after the First World War. The risks currently appear so great that attractive inducements, in the form of high return on investments, must be presented to encourage participation. This condition, which the Asian decries as exploitative, is what the investor calls his fair return in view of the political and economic risks run and the scarcity of available capital today.

The American has a fine opportunity to invest at home in comparative security, and can obtain a good rate of return for his effort. Abroad he runs the risk that international violence will destroy his investment. The uncertainty of internal political stability in Eastern Asia is another source of concern. Moreover, the foreign investors regard the anti-Western nationalistic and ideological bias a rationalization for obtaining foreign capital and skills without payment. He fears such devices as tight profit restrictions, curtailment of the percentage of property to be owned by aliens, restrictive regulations on the use of foreign technicians, and a ceiling on the convertibility of profits into his own currency. This ceiling would make it difficult to withdraw money from the land in which capital was invested. Some of these regulations obviously are justified from the viewpoint of those who want to develop their economies. But their paralyzing effect on potential private capital is nonetheless real.

There is also the fear of expropriation. The original hostility displayed in the new states, the most extreme case being Burma, was most discouraging. Modified positions, like promises not to expropriate for ten or twenty-five years, and then only with adequate compensation, will hardly inspire confidence. Control of the native government may change hands, either by revolutionary or democratic processes, and bring to power political forces committed to immediate expropriation with inadequate or no compensation. Finally, much of the money is needed for "public works" types of projects, which are ill-suited to private investment because returns are nonexistent or delayed, and close government supervision is unavoidable.

It is therefore evident that intergovernment loans must be the chief method of getting foreign aid to Asia and perhaps establishing the conditions to facilitate the flow of private capital. Even here, there are important political undercurrents. It has been maintained that assistance given through the auspices of the United Nations would prove more effective than direct American aid. The latter seems to be even more difficult to accept than British and Commonwealth help in certain parts of Asia. Nevertheless, considerable activity in the form of capital loans and technical aid and advice has taken place, and more assistance is planned for the future.

These aids have come in the form of technical assistance through the American Point Four program and United Nations activity; group planning and financial aid such as the (British) Commonwealth Colombo Plan and the release of British sterling balances, which accumulated as credit to former Asian colonies during the Second World War; loans by the International Bank for Reconstruction and Development; and capital assistance from the United States through the Import-Export Bank and the Mutual Security Administration. In the mid-1950's the Russians entered the scene, offering technical and financial aid to the underdeveloped areas. The scope and objectives of these endeavors will be studied in more detail when we examine the area's international relations.

At this stage the tendency in Asia is to look less suspiciously on foreign help, ease regulations somewhat in order to encourage private investment, and welcome more warmly intergovernment assistance programs. However, conditions remain far from satisfactory, and the aid tendered is far from sufficient. Governmental aid has the drawback of being under heavy restrictive pressure by political opposition forces in the Western democracies, where the tax burden is already quite large. In this context, the extension of American economic assistance to Asia has ranked behind aid to Europe and the military rearmament program in degree of urgency.

Even with an adequate supply of capital, it must be understood that Asia's ascent to a wealthier economic level will be a lengthy and arduous task. Many setbacks can occur to slow the process to a halt and endanger the survival of the new democratic regimes. If immediate success is politically necessary in order to satisfy high popular expectations, the pressure thus created may make the difficult task of economic modernization even more complicated.

Finally, even success in raising the level of existence in India and China (the latter, of course, being beyond the pale of Western influence) and, to a lesser extent, in Indonesia and Pakistan, bears within itself grave dangers. As a consequence of improved conditions there may occur a further decline in the death rate while the birth rate remains stationary or falls very slowly. The increased gap between fertility and mortality and the leisurely pace at which the birth rate falls give ample time for a steady rise in the population. Even an unspectacular increase of from 10 to 15 per cent means enormous increases in the number of inhabitants. This contingency might again create those conditions of hardship that Malthusian economists claim are the only effective check in such situations. Certainly the problem of population control becomes more acute as industrial progress moves through its early stages. Since our concern is with the preservation of democracy in Asia, solutions other than the costly and painful "natural checks" must be sought. Solutions to this complex and grave problem are not yet in sight.

Bibliography

INTRODUCTION

Regional Surveys

CRESSEY, G. B., *Asia's Lands and Peoples.* 2nd ed.; New York: McGraw-Hill, 1951.

STAMP, A. D., *Asia: A Regional and Economic Geography.* 8th ed.; London: Dutton, 1950.

BERGSMARK, D. R., *Economic Geography of Asia.* New York: Prentice-Hall, 1935.

EAST, W. G., *and* O. H. K. SPATE, *The Changing Map of Asia: A Political Geography.* New York: Dutton, 1951.

LASKER, B., *Asia on the Move.* New York: Holt, 1945.

SPENCER, J. E., *Asia: East by South.* New York: Wiley, 1954.

THOMPSON, W. S., *Population and Peace in the Pacific.* Chicago: Univ. of Chicago Press, 1946.

BUXTON, L. D., *The Peoples of Asia.* New York: Knopf, 1925.

WOYTINSKY, W. S., and E. S. WOYTINSKY, *World Population and Production.* New York: Twentieth Century Fund, 1953.

The Western Impact

ZINKIN, M., *Asia and the West.* London: Chatto & Windus, 1951.

PANIKKAR, K. M., *Asia and Western Dominance.* New York: John Day, 1954.

CLYDE, P., *The Far East.* New York: Prentice-Hall, 1948.

ECKEL, P., *The Far East since 1500,* New York: Harcourt, Brace, 1948.

LANGER, W. L., *The Diplomacy of Imperialism.* New York: Knopf, 1935.

LATOURETTE, K. S., *A History of the Expansion of Christianity.* New York: Harper, 1944, Volume 6.

Economic Conditions and Problems

WICKIZER, V. P., and M. K. BENNETT, *The Rice Economy of Monsoon Asia.* Stanford: Stanford Univ. Press, 1941.

STAMP, L. D., *Land for Tomorrow: The Underdeveloped World.* Bloomington: Ind. Univ. Press, 1952.

CHANDRASEKHAR, S., *Hungry People and Empty Lands.* London: Allen & Unwin, 1954.

STALEY, E., *The Future of Underdeveloped Countries.* New York: Harper, 1954.

HOSELITZ, B. (ed.), *The Progress of Underdeveloped Areas.* Chicago: Univ. of Chicago Press, 1952.

MASON, E. S., *Promoting Economic Development.* Claremont: Claremont College, 1955.

MACK, R. T., *Raising the World's Standard of Living.* New York: Citadel, 1953.

RUSSELL, E. J., *World Population and World Food Supplies.* London: Allen & Unwin, 1954.

BUCHANAN, N. S., and H. S. ELLIS, *Approaches to Economic Development.* New York: Twentieth Century Fund, 1955.

FRANKEL, S. H., *The Economic Impact on Underdeveloped Societies.* Cambridge: Harvard Univ. Press, 1953.

NURSKE, R., *Problems of Capital Formation in Underdeveloped Countries.* New York: Oxford, 1953.

LEWIS, W. S., *The Theory of Economic Growth.* Homewood, Ill.: Irwin, 1955.

GADGIL, D. R., *Economic Policy and Development.* New York: Inst. of Pacific Relations, 1955.

KUZNETS, S., and others, *Economic Growth; Brazil, India, Japan.* Durham: Duke Univ. Press, 1955.

SINGH, B., *Federal Finance and Underdeveloped Economy.* New York: Heinman, 1952.

MADAN, B. K. (ed.), *Economic Problems of Underdeveloped Countries in Asia.* Bombay: Oxford Univ. Press, 1953.

GOUROU, P., G. E. SPENCER, and G. TREWARTHA, *The Development of Upland Areas in the Far East.* New York: Inst. of Pacific Relations, 1947.

ALLEN, G. R., and A. C. DONNITHORNE, *Western Enterprise in Far Eastern Economic Development: China and Japan.* New York: Macmillan, 1954.

UNITED NATIONS ECONOMIC COMMISSION FOR ASIA AND THE FAR EAST (ECAFE), Quarterly *Bulletins* and annual *Economic Survey of Asia and the Far East.*

UN ECAFE, *Mobilization of Domestic Capital: Reports and Documents of the First and Second Working Parties,* 1952 and 1953.

UN ECAFE, *Coal and Iron Resources of Asia and the Far East,* 1952.

UN, DEPARTMENT OF ECONOMIC AND SOCIAL AFFAIRS, *Processes and Problems of Industrialization in Underdeveloped Countries,* 1955.

PART TWO **China**

3 *The Chinese*

Political Tradition

Since 1839 the great civilization of China has undergone a series of wars and revolutions on a truly colossal scale. All the great powers were drawn into this area, with interest and sympathy especially keen in the United States. The abrupt rise of communism after 1945 provided a surprising climax to this century of violence. The search for an understanding of these modern events must be carried into the roots of Chinese history, if superficial conclusions are to be avoided.

On the international scene, during the nineteenth century, China fell from the rank of a great power whose influence permeated the Orient, to the position of a legally inferior state beset by foreign menaces of all sorts. These ranged from slights to Chinese pride and prestige to a series of pecks and bites at Chinese territory that grew alarmingly larger each decade. Finally, Japan undertook a long-range effort of conquest (1894-1945) and almost succeeded in wrecking this badly battered giant. Suddenly, under communism, China emerged in 1950 as a major aggressive military power for the first time since the West came in force to the Far East.

Internally, this century has witnessed the last desperate years of Manchu rule, the rise of a great revolutionary movement that too often lacked coherent guidance, and a chaotic fragmentation of power during a period of warlord domination. There followed the attempt of Chiang Kai-shek and the Kuomintang party to reunify the country. During this time, the impact of Western ideologies and economic techniques on a tradition-bound people continued unabated. A bitter, long-term civil war and the Japanese invasion kept matters in a state of turmoil until the unexpected end of the struggle, the Japanese falling in 1945, and the Kuomintang in 1947-1949.

So much has happened, with foreign interventions playing a dominant role —by their absences as well as appearances—that the main factor, China itself, is often overlooked when explanations of these events are put forth.

It is primarily from the viewpoint of China's "accommodation" to the strange and terrible happenings of modern times that its history must be studied;

otherwise foreign influence and activities tend to receive a disproportionately heavy stress, often being erroneously considered as the sole determinant of China's internal developments. Moreover, this country, a civilization unto itself, has such a rich history and tradition that even an analysis of the past hundred years would not present an adequate portrayal of its content. While the foreign influence cannot be minimized, attention must constantly be focused on the internal problems and conflicts reflecting political and economic issues peculiar to China. It is therefore important to keep in mind the institutional, political, and ideological baggage, as well as the pattern of political behavior that the Chinese possessed when the modern world descended so brusquely on them. These values may reassert themselves quite vigorously, undoubtedly in highly modified form, in the near future.

The Middle Kingdom

It must be remembered that China not only had a unique culture but was the center—the Middle Kingdom—of a civilization that included bordering states. In this area of the world the influential effect of Chinese ideology and political leadership was unmistakable. The Chinese way of life served as a source of inspiration because it was an excellent one, considered by its practitioners to be far superior to all others, known or unknown. So certain were the Chinese of the grandeur of their own achievements, and so impressed were they by the continuous stability of their culture, that they became contemptuous of the achievements of other peoples, an attitude which was to cost them dearly after 1800.

Their behavior and the uniqueness of this magnificent culture can be traced in part to China's relative isolation from the rest of the world. Although far from being completely cut off—many significant concepts and inventions were imported—China was distant enough to avoid the persistent and direct impact of another advanced civilization, either in a cultural or military-political sense. That is, China did not encounter a neighbor whose material and ideological development could present a serious challenge. Even the powerful nomads of the northwest, who persistently conducted raids or even conquered the land, lacked the degree of organization required to influence or alter fundamentally the Chinese way of life.

This subworld, with its center in China, was bounded on the east by the Pacific Ocean, which served as a barrier to extensive foreign influence, for China rarely developed its naval power or an interest in maritime affairs. The country was, in fact, oriented westward, and until the nineteenth century it was across its land frontier that China's major contacts with the outside world were made. Japan was troublesome at times but was not a formidable threat; rather, China looked down upon Japan as a semibarbaric nation that had acquired its civilization from China, and was thus a cultural if not a political dependent.

China's nearness to India, by land or sea, is most deceptive. The two nations have had very little contact, if we consider their size and the advanced levels of their respective cultures. The sea was never developed as a broad avenue of communication around the Southeast Asian mainland and through the East Indies; and the land barrier, as American military forces learned after 1941, is most formidable and does not encourage easy, large-scale direct contacts. Nevertheless, the extremely long route running across Central Asia, strange as it may seem at first, was heavily utilized as an avenue of commerce and intercourse with other nations. This may have been the way early achievements of the Mediterranean civilizations were transmitted to China during the latter's late preliterary period. It is known that Hellenic and powerful Buddhist influences made their way eastward through this route and that China developed a considerable trade with lands to the west in such items as silk and paper. The great trade routes, known as the Silk Route, became China's means of contact with the Roman and Arab-Moslem worlds. As has been noted, this channel of communications enabled China to deal with the outside world without coming under intensive pressure of these distant Western societies.

Therefore it is of great importance to examine the essence of this unique civilization that the Chinese developed almost alone in their corner of the world —that so influenced lesser powers coming under its magnetic influence. To understand it requires an appreciation of the fundamental concepts and institutions that made it unmistakably Chinese. These elements then must be examined in chronological perspective in order to illustrate their evolution and operation.

Unity and Empire

As might be expected in such a self-centered, self-contained culture, its philosophical outlook was based on a belief in the wholeness of the universe and the oneness of mankind. This faith encompassed acceptance of the harmony of nature and the unity of all culture; to the Chinese there could be no separation of the natural from the supernatural or the condition of man from either. Man was just one vital element in this pattern of life, with everything considered as part of one indivisible whole.

From this belief there derived the wish to bring man's behavior into harmony with nature by adopting the high standards—called Tao, or Way—of the great cosmic principles of the universe. Such "other-worldliness" is similar to other notable Oriental religions in its effort to achieve unity with the universe and so free man from human travail and emotion. This outlook did not embody the central Chinese ethical or religious beliefs, since it became a secondary strain to the great theme of Confucianism. However, the Tao is worth noting at this stage for its emphasis on the existence of unity and harmony.

The wholeness of the universe led quite logically to the thought that civilization had to be homogeneous, in its political institutions as well as its cultural conceptions. It followed that in China the highest type, on both counts, had been attained. The notion of Chinese unity, implied in this sense of superiority, was of considerable service in keeping the ideal of a single state alive through many dark and prolonged periods of civil strife and seemingly hopeless political fractionalization. The Chinese were constantly motivated by a drive to reassert their unity over the huge geographical area in which this sway was theoretically to prevail. The power of this ideal and its eventual triumph gave rise to a historical pattern quite different from that which occurred in post-Roman Europe.

This high estimate of themselves led the Chinese to disdain all outsiders, be they neighbors or complete strangers. All who were not versed in the niceties of Chinese civilization were called barbarians, just as the Greeks identified outsiders. Such low esteem was not simply the result of racial or ethnic bias; rather, the attitude was based on cultural achievement. This approach made the cultural assimilation of others not only feasible but even desirable.

The belief that China was superior to all other nations led to the formulation of a doctrine of inequality in international relations, although China was never considered to be a state in the Western sense of the term—not even a country that was ahead of all the rest. Since there could only be one true civilization, there could be only one rule—the Chinese—all other peoples being subordinate. China did not conceive of the diplomatic relations and the status of equality that theoretically prevail in the Western world of sovereign states. All others had to be tribute-paying inferiors, acknowledging Chinese suzerainty. There was but one deserving civilization, whose political and ethical precepts were based on the philosophic tenets of the great scholar-teacher Confucius (551-479 B.C.), but other cultures were tolerated unless they threatened the unique Chinese institutions. Moreover, the Chinese never felt a compulsion to remake the entire world in their own image by embarking on an expedition of limitless conquest. Actually, their world consisted of the Middle Kingdom— China—at the center; political satellites surrounded it and invariably adopted some modified version of the Chinese structure of society, though the fringe areas were less consistently dominated and so developed more independently; finally, there was the outside world of barbarians, beyond the pale and of little interest or importance to the Chinese.

Chinese stress on culture accounts for the remarkable degree of racial, social, and religious homogeneity of this people. This achievement stands out in marked contrast to developments in India, where races and peoples have been kept apart by religion and caste stratification. As the Chinese spread over what is now China Proper, their advancing civilization was able to assimilate to a remarkable degree, though not completely, the diverse races it encountered. These peoples were willing to adopt the Chinese way of life, an act that was sufficient to win them acceptance in the community as Chinese. In other words, conformity to certain ethical and cultural standards was enough to gain one acceptance as a member of China's highly esteemed civilization.

This remarkable community originated in North China in the region of the Yellow River; the more powerful political forces were generally located inland to the west in the valley of the Wei River, near its point of juncture with the

Yellow. In spite of incursions by nearby desert raiders, the Chinese took root and flourished with a culture that seems to have developed some time after those of Egypt and Mesopotamia. Migrations to the south followed, the advances coinciding with periods of strong central rule. In the 1,000-year period of 300 B.C.–700 A.D. the Chinese populated the Yangtze River basin at its mouth and lower reaches, moved up this river into Szechuan Province and pushed southward into the Canton region and beyond. As barbarian incursions from the northeast mounted in intensity and duration, the center of gravity of China's civilization shifted southward from the Yellow to the more centrally located Yangtze River. Nevertheless, the political nerve center of China has been located in the northern region whenever possible.

The preservation of political and cultural unity over this vast subcontinent, during and after the period of settlement, and without modern techniques, is a strong tribute to the attraction of Chinese civilization. Not only were there northern nomads to ward off or absorb and southern natives to assimilate, but the Chinese also had to maintain their own political cohesion while spreading over a wide expanse. Differences between the north and the south in cultural outlook and shadings of interest were bound to develop; at times the considerable friction that was generated led to political struggles from these territorial bases. The astonishing fact is that through it all the concept of unity was never submerged.

Beyond its borders China's influence expanded and retracted in accordance with its domestic political fortunes. For the most part, the strength of its central government was the controlling feature in foreign affairs, although on occasion powerful outside forces would remove matters from Chinese control. Invariably, strong monarchies kept the frontier secure and extended Chinese domination well beyond the borders. During a period of weak leadership, dynastic troubles and the like, China would suffer incursions from without and often face serious threats to its political regimes. Although alien rule was established on two occasions over all of China—by the Mongols and the Manchus—China was able to bear this burden, since these dynasties accepted the Confucian way of life. Yet a certain restiveness remained because foreign rulers never fully identified themselves with China. What the conquests reveal about the strength of China's civilization must be examined later.

The Emperor

The political structure of government held the empire together and fostered and maintained cultural homogeneity. The position of the emperor in this setting was of central importance, for he was the personification of the unity of men and indeed was his people's representative on earth. There never was an organized priesthood among the Chinese, of the sort that developed in Europe; rather, the emperor was the nation's spokesman, the intermediary between the affairs of heaven and earth. Thus, he was the personal embodiment of the concept of a single rule over mankind.

The political powers of this all-important office had a most unique and thoroughly Confucian Chinese ethical base. The emperor was deemed to hold his position by means of a *mandate of heaven*—an authorization from the deity to establish or maintain his rule. Furthermore, it was held that the emperor ruled by means of his virtue. In this context, virtue had a double meaning: it had a moral and ethical content, but it also implied control over a force adequate enough to maintain and protect a stable regime.

Thus the emperor's mandate depended on the twin bases of moral leadership and adequate staying power. To the Chinese these two tests appeared to be naturally interrelated. Since the people had certain moral beliefs firmly in mind, they could differentiate between good and evil behavior; it was up to the ruler to demonstrate his moral virtue and set an example of high moral standards.

The virtuous leader was one of the essential features of the Confucian philosophy of society. Be he the emperor or simply the head of a family, he was obliged to govern by precept, example, persuasion, and moral exhortation. The use of reason to maintain one's power was preferred, with force considered a measure of last resort. Resort to force was often considered a sign of weakness, of the ruler's inadequacy to govern under the professed Confucian ideals. In theory, then, it was a sign that the ruler might be losing his mandate of heaven. In reality, many dynasties used force successfully to crush rebellions and continue in power for considerable lengths of time.

Nevertheless, the concept of the *loss* of a mandate of heaven was of fundamental importance, for it amounted to theoretical acceptance, and even approval under such conditions, of the right of revolution. Although a crude and bloody method of governmental reform, revolution permitted that degree of flexibility required for the over-all stability of the system as a whole. There was also the germ of a responsible government here, since the regime had to maintain certain standards in order to retain its right to rule.

The mandate might be lost because of moral turpitude, inefficient and weak government, oppression and trying conditions at the local level, plus natural calamities or foreign invasions. If such phenomena as droughts, earthquakes, or floods occurred during the reign of a ruler who was not known for his virtue or ability, it was safe to say that his mandate was in danger. Pragmatically speaking, it was not fully lost until the regime was overthrown; thus only a successful revolt, usually precipitated in very difficult times, could show that the mandate was clearly lost.

This theory of government therefore permitted revolts to occur but did not guarantee their success. The subordinate officials were obliged to obey the ruler, who was, in turn, supposed to govern virtuously. Both the emperor's moral ineptitude and his failure to maintain a strong regime operated corrosively, in a cumulative manner, on the loyalty of these officials. If a revolt was successful, the people and the bureaucrats were morally required to give their allegiance to the new ruler on the grounds that he obtained a new mandate by his success. The new emperor at times rose from the peasant class to his position of eminence, as there was no obstacle of class stratification to block one's attainment of supreme power.

Chinese history reveals a succession of dynastic lines, varying in duration, usually established by a successful rebel or warrior at the end of a period of civil strife. Explanations of these dynastic cycles have included several related factors. For one thing, the vigorous rulers were usually found at the beginning of a dynasty; as the quality of leadership fell off precipitously after a few generations, disastrous consequences were inevitable. There occurred a mounting oppressiveness in terms of taxes extorted from the peasantry at the local level, insufficient services rendered by corrupt regional officials, inadequate protection from invaders, and lack of assistance in times of economic stress. Then, too, the earlier achievements of the dynasty probably increased stability and heightened agrarian efficiency, thereby causing a rise in population. This factor eventually increased pressure on the land and led to a rise in debt, loss of land, and widespread unrest. With reforms rarely attempted, inasmuch as the government generally adopted a conservative hands-off policy, peasant uprisings increased in frequency and intensity until widespread revolts developed.

Concepts and Institutions

The Confucian Philosophy

The durable concepts of the empire and the position of emperor were rooted intellectually in the Confucian philosophy of society. Its ideology became the foundation of the Chinese ethic of civilization and the basis for the regulation of its social order. This moral philosophy of conduct and not a formal organized religion provided the spiritual basis of Chinese culture. Confucius undoubtedly found previous studies and teachings a source of content and inspiration for his ideas, and each passing generation later added its modifications to this doctrine. Reverence for ancestors probably caused Confucius to minimize unduly the creative role he himself played. Be that as it may, this philosophy was not quickly and easily accepted as the norm of Chinese life, and for a while its fortune ebbed and flowed with the attitudes of a succession of rulers. In time, its evident popularity and deep hold on the mass of the people won it official support, especially when it became apparent that the Confucian advocacy of stability and of knowing one's place could be of great service to the ruling house. When it became the accepted doctrine of Chinese political and social life, orthodox interpretations became standardized and Confucianism became more conservative in tone. It certainly had a different connotation in later years from that which the master's more radical followers had in mind.

We have already observed two aspects of Confucian socio-political organization: the ruler of a group must conduct his affairs in a moral and conscientious manner, while subordinate officials and subjects comply with and obey his commands. Clearly, the issues Confucius dealt with revolved around the salvation of society rather than the fate of the individual in the universe. Seeking the way to stable human relationships, Confucius adopted a realistic and pragmatic approach that rejected metaphysical speculations of the sort found in Hinduism.

As an ex-official, Confucius hoped that the state and the ruling class could be the agencies through which a maximum degree of harmony could be brought into the social order. The state was considered an enlargement of the family unit—the national family with the emperor considered the parent of the people. The essence of the Confucian pattern lay in the belief that each person was to assume a specific place in society and that there were specific duties and modes of conduct for each position. Those rules of conduct had to be observed by each individual for the good of his group and so, indirectly, for the community as a whole. Emphasis was placed on the well-being of the social unit, large or small, and the individual's activities had to be geared to the group's desires and welfare.

Confucianism was a paternalistic system, presupposing an aristocracy or ruling class, with stress on superior-inferior relations. Theoretically, the state was not to be run for the benefit of the ruling group, which was to lead the way to the ideal society by setting a worthy example for the masses to follow. In this way all persons would behave in an exemplary manner, and the ruler, reinforced by this upright ruling class, would be able to govern by means of his virtue, supplemented by reason and moral exhortations.

This aristocratic concept fitted the actual pattern of how China was governed. In prescribing benevolent moral rule by all superiors, Confucius was attempting to strengthen this system. Hence stress was laid on knowing one's place in society and performing duties morally and efficiently. Significantly, of the five relationships Confucius expounded (prince-subject, father-son, husband-wife, elder brother-younger brother, friend-friend), four represented relations between people of unequal rank. Partly to reinforce the acceptance of established relationships, Confucius placed great emphasis on ceremony and the formalities of behavior, and favored orderly and reverent continuation of sacrifices and other rituals inherited from antiquity. These were considered indispensable measures for the maintenance of civilization.

On some questions Confucius did not state his position clearly, either purposely or otherwise. These involved the inherent goodness or badness of man and the problem of life after death. Yet implicit in the Confucian system was a belief that the universe was on the side of righteousness, governed by a being who protects the good.

The Family

The family played a central role in Chinese society, as its involvement in three of the five Confucian relations attested. In China's agrarian community the family became the major social-economic unit to absorb and direct human activity. It protected and aided the individual in time of need and was the agency through which relations assisted each other. The individual's interest and rights ran secondary to the family's, so closely knit was this social structure; one's marriage, earnings, and the like were handled by the family. Filial piety was deemed a major obligation, and the importance of duty and obedience was heavily emphasized. The wife occupied a subordinate position, but her depressed status should not be exaggerated; on bearing children and reaching an advanced age, she was bound to experience a considerable rise in prestige. Only when the ideas of the West made themselves felt, did the traditional concept of family life come under heavy criticism and lose its position of invulnerability. Nevertheless, whatever the future of the family may be in the Chinese order of things, we must keep in mind that it was one of the keystones of the country's civilization.

In addition to caring for the aged and rearing the young, the family was also the center of the practice of ancestor reverence, which, from the early days of Chinese civilization, was the most vital and sincere expression of religious feeling. The dead were venerated, with copious family records kept; many families kept tablets and ancestral rolls. Ceremonies in honor of ancestors were performed regularly, in good Confucian tradition. These practices were of the utmost significance; religious appeals could be directed only to the individual family concerned, since there was no national faith with a central hierarchy. Thus veneration of ancestors strengthened the authority of the family but weakened the binding ties of the national political structure. Not only was religious attention turned away from the state, but the absence of a national priesthood meant that an important additional prop was unavailable to the central government. The family-state problem was further complicated by the individual's belief that his first allegiance and primary duty was to the family. This feeling was carried to such an extent that he condoned or even supported the practice of defrauding the state for the benefit of the family. Under such conditions, practices like nepotism were not considered morally repugnant.

In a sense this allegiance to the family and the dispersal of loyalty in small packets minimized the extent to which the spirit of nationalism and the sense of political solidarity were developed. On the other hand, the more extreme kinds of individual identification with the nation did not occur, though the pride in China's cultural achievements was maintained. The family performed a unifying service as the most important repository of the culture's norms and ideals, and it served as an agency of transmission from generation to generation. During prolonged periods of political turmoil the family was the sturdy vessel that protected and kept alive the main tenets of this civilization. It thus contributed greatly to the continuity of Chinese development because of its own staying powers.

Decentralized Empire

At the same time, the family was a competitor with the state for popular support and weakened the latter's ability to act as a dominant factor in everyday affairs. This condition reinforced a tendency of the Chinese to maintain a rather decentralized empire, quite limited in its practical authority. Paradoxically, in view of what has been said earlier about the nature of the empire and the role of the emperor, the central government was limited in its actual power. The tradition of decentralized administration was so strong that the country was extremely vulnerable to military attacks from beyond the frontier. The imperial structure was adequate in performing its task of holding the vast area of China together under one political rule, but it was apparently too decentralized to ward off powerful aggressors. The Chinese repeatedly found themselves fighting on their own soil before an organized defensive effort could be made.

Decentralization stemmed from physical-technical handicaps and the development of a traditional outlook in this direction. In fact, before the development of modern inventions, the physical handicaps facing anyone who tried to conduct a strict rule from a central source were enormous. Just as the great Roman Empire was, in comparison with modern standards, a decentralized organization based on indirect rule from the capital, so China, with its environmental and cultural diversities, also depended on relaxed rule from the center, though it never abandoned its minimal degree of political unity.

Cultural tendencies reinforced the physical handicaps confronting strong central rule. It became customary to leave as much control as possible in the hands of local self-governing units, like the family, the guilds, and the village and its elders. The imperial machinery gave the national structure its necessary degree of cohesion, but it interfered as little as possible in the affairs of the individuals and the smaller units that made up the national community. The Taoist philosophy gave doctrinal support to this tendency with its extreme assertion that a governmental policy of laissez faire was ethically imperative.

This school of philosophy was reputedly founded by Lao-tzu, a fellow northerner and elder contemporary of Confucius. However, since the great *Classic of Tao* places great stress on naturalism and reflects an antisocial outlook, its authorship is believed by some scholars to have stemmed from the more southerly Yangtze region. Naturalism of this sort, unlike the romantic Western kind, was a stern call to man to lift himself to a high standard of behavior in conformity with the Tao. The Taoists stressed the Unknown and the Unknowable as factors permeating and controlling the universe and desired nothing that was not in conformity with nature. To society and the state this philosophy was an admonition to keep organization and regulation of activity at a minimum. The ideal society was considered to be a series of self-sufficient villages so located as to avoid intimate contact with each other. Commerce and trade were frowned on; laws, elaborate codes of ethics, and ceremonies were also opposed, since these could lead only to violations. Politically, this outlook was tantamount to a plea for the absence of government.

Lao-tzu also considered hollowness and nonexistence as factors of great importance. In a similar vein he argued that softness and weakness would overcome hardness and strength. Therefore humility and passivity were presented as high Taoist virtues, and human institutions and regulations as faults—as harmful, for they kept man from operating according to the goodliness and simplicity of his original nature. Even culture and knowledge were viewed with great suspicion, since man's hope lay in pursuing *Tao*—the unchanging law underlying the universe, which follows the way of nature.

This belief was obviously contrary to the Confucian attitude toward ethics, statecraft, ceremony, and economic activity—a down-to-earth theme that had greater appeal to the pragmatic Chinese. Yet there was room for both systems once the Taoist's extreme social precepts were rejected; Taoism then concerned itself primarily with the fate or salvation of the individual. In fact, Chinese and other Oriental religious systems are as a rule unlike those of the West in that they are not mutually exclusive. Tolerance is carried to the extent of accepting parts of two or more beliefs. And with the advent of Buddhism, the Chinese could and did adhere to aspects of three religious-ethical systems. In the field of statecraft, the Confucian stress on political rule remained a strong antidote to the disintegrative tendencies of Taoism. However, the latter was not without influence, especially when its philosophy coincided with the drift toward autonomy at the provincial and local levels.

China may have solved its problem of reconciling unity and diversity by giving considerable autonomy to the lesser political and social agencies. Nevertheless, the central regime was more than just a capital city and its environs. The skeletal structure that held the empire together was a centrally controlled bureaucracy stationed in the provinces. The government had a system of nationwide taxation, though it did not have absolute control over collection. It also directed considerable large-scale activity in the field of agricultural operations, and managed an intricate system of irrigation networks; China's system of water control was, in fact, one of the most comprehensive ever designed by man. These improvements led to increased levels of production, which sustained the nation's ever-expanding population. Supplementary activities included the storage of grain and its distribution in time of shortage. Then, too, the government had the important function, inadequately performed all too often, of maintaining internal security and protecting the country from foreign attack.

The bureaucracy that performed these tasks was quite large and even gave rise to the term "Oriental Society," to describe the great role officials played in the nation's political and economic affairs. Cities especially were developed as focal points of bureaucratic activity in the provincial areas. In these respects, the central government had considerable powers, far beyond those of any neighboring state; yet by modern standards the Chinese empire must be described as a decentralized one. Trouble between the provinces and the central government over traditional lines of jurisdiction and power has been a recurrent problem throughout Chinese history. It was made more complex by the incidence of "warlordism," a particularly extreme type of autonomy that came close to establishing independent centers of power, based on provincial units. In modern times this issue has repeatedly plagued efforts at economic reform and political reorganization.

The Ruling Class

Officials and Scholars

The bureaucracy that administered the government was still another unique feature. The empire often threatened to degenerate into hereditary feudal principalities, especially in its early days, for a high degree of independence from the central government was inevitable when the empire failed to perform its administrative and security functions adequately. The central bureaucracy was developed as the major check to this tendency, and implemented the policies of a strong monarch throughout China. The civil service, then, was the cement of the empire and was an invaluable contributor to its long and stable existence.

The imperial government controlled all key appointments, such as the offices of provincial governors, viceroys (over two provinces), and heads of lesser territorial subdivisions, like the *hsien* (similar to a county). In order to keep officials from "taking root" in localities, no one was appointed to his home province, personnel was constantly shifted to different posts, and other safeguards in the nature of checks and balances were adopted. The central administration itself was of considerable importance, as it was composed of the standard governmental ministries, a censorate (under the Manchus) to watch over and criticize other officials, and an office to supervise the administration of criminal law. Both the civilian and military wings of the bureaucracy were appointive, nonhereditary offices, but the former had far greater prestige and power. A place in the civil service became so highly prized that the most capable men in the land often competed vigorously for these posts. This custom was closely related to the practice of making rigorous and fair civil service examinations the basis of appointment. It proved to be a most satisfactory alternative to filling the rank of officialdom by means of hereditary transferral of office and power.

High regard for office and a merit system of appointment comprised the basis of the famed official service, which lasted until this century. Its existence, however, had important consequences for China beyond the adequate operation of the large empire's machinery of government. Choice of candidates through competitive examinations encouraged the Chinese inclination to avoid a stratification of society on rigid, inherited class lines. Inasmuch as the official and scholar classes ranked high in this society, it was of the utmost importance that a person could, theoretically at least, reach this level on the basis of his own ability, regardless of the position into which he was born. The fluidity of Chinese society, with its nonhereditary "aristocracy of merit" was sharply differentiated from the feudal-aristocratic Japanese and the caste-bound Indian communities. In practice, of course, the Chinese were far from having equal opportunity for all, for the person who starts from a low station in life is handicapped even in a "classless society." Yet the concrete difficulties involved did not diminish the positive, supporting effect which this theory had on the egalitarian outlook of Chinese society.

Another effect stemmed from the nature of the examinations and the standards they set. The tests and the competition were so severe that only a few of the many who tried could attain the signal honor of success. Inevitably the Confucian classics formed a greater part of the examination as time went on. This was in part due to the vested interest of existing scholars and officials to propagate their own field of knowledge. It was also due to the fact that these works were the source of morality, for, to the Chinese, wisdom was the moral comprehension of right and wrong. The cumulative effect was to strengthen the prestige of both the official class and Confucian scholarship in the eyes of the people.

Since the Confucian concept of society was impressed on all aspirants, the method of recruiting the civil service proved to be an excellent vehicle to advance a common Chinese culture. The successful candidates who became bureaucrats were immersed in Confucianism, as were the others who entered scholarly, pedagogical, and related fields. Thus the Confucian tradition was maintained, and transmitted to succeeding generations of scholars and officials, by means of the Chinese merit system. In later times, when a rudimentary national educational system was established in order to assist candidates in preparing for their examinations, the diffusion of Confucian ideals was further encouraged.

The Manchu era was the last one governed under the traditional Confucian precepts as interpreted by the ruling element of officials, scholars, and gentry. During the nineteenth century, this elite group numbered between 1,100,000 and 1,500,000; with its families it totaled between 5,500,000 and 7,500,000, or from 1½ to 2 per cent of the total population. As the cultural and ideological leader of China, this class was socially and legally above the rest. It was identified by its superior education and, more specifically, by the academic degrees held by its members.

There were only 40,000 official positions in the civil services at this time; therefore very few of this gentry held public office. Yet China was in fact governed only through the close cooperation existing between the gentry and the numerically restricted public bureaucracy. The gentry proved indispensable managers of important public works and of various economic controls undertaken by the administration. Significantly, the boundaries within which they operated were the political-administrative ones of the district or province. Maintenance and construction of water control and transportation facilities formed the core of these activities, which also included charity work, food distribution, and local arbitration and order. During periods of internal stress, this class had to organize and lead military formations and exercise control over public tax sources in order to finance these operations. Its power therefore increased markedly during such crises as the great T'ai P'ing Rebellion of the 1850's.

The authority of the gentry was rooted in its superior education. This class believed that education prepared them for positions of rule and responsibility, and the community as a whole respected this interpretation. As a reward, the gentry enjoyed a preferred legal position. There were also social privileges in matters of comportment and dress. Moreover, the gentry were exempt from the public labor (*corvée*) required of other subjects and in general carried a relatively light money-tax burden.

Most important was the income that the gentry obtained from its performance of public functions. It is estimated that the class as a whole received 23 per cent of the national income. Almost half of this could be traced to payments for public functions, teaching and other intellectual activity, and improper income based on squeeze and graft. By contrast, land ownership accounted for less than one third of the income and business activities contributed the remaining fifth. Since the upper gentry (the 14 per cent of this class holding official rank or higher examination degrees) received three quarters of the rental income from land, it is clear that the bulk of the gentry derived well over half its income from public functions and services.

The conclusion reached by Franz Michael was that China at this time was

> a society in which an educated elite, as officials of the state and as the leading social group, managed vital public functions . . . and derived its dominant position from this monopoly of management.[1]

One school of philosophy—the Legalists—tried to extend the power and activity of the bureaucrats by advocating a positive and active national policy that would mean dynamic control over public affairs. In an important sense Legalism was anti-Confucian, since it took a strong position against pinning its hopes on mere moral example set by the rulers. Agreeing with Confucius that the state was the only means through which the society of man could be adequately regulated, the Legalists saw the key to success in the establishment and firm enforcement of a detailed legal code. Strangely enough, while proposing the very opposite of the Taoist hands-off policy, this view held that the laws which were adopted had to conform to the Tao, the ruling principle of the universe, and had authority only on this condition.

It must not be concluded that law was a new concept developed by the Legalists. They simply formulated a plan, in the late Chou dynasty, of giving law new and heavier stress. They sought to increase the ruler's grip on the daily activities of government and broaden, far beyond the concept envisioned in Taoism or even Confucianism, the role that law and government could play. While their ideology remained a subordinate strain in Chinese philosophy, the

---

[1] Franz Michael, "State and Society in Nineteenth-Century China," *World Politics*, VII (April, 1955), 427.

Legalists set a precedent for comprehensive reform programs based on direct government action. Some reformers tried to link the Confucian concept of a good ruler with the Legalist notion of an active reform program. The infrequent appearances and very limited successes of these reformers indicate that such a judicious combination did not take hold in any significant fashion.

That Legalist views never became dominant in China, even among officials, is easy to understand. They were considered too rigid and harsh, and they demanded more governmental activities than the culture was willing to accept. In contrast, according to the best Confucian tradition, moral suasion and not legal compulsion was the main rule. Confucianism attained a balance by upholding the prestige of the ruling class while not giving it what was considered an excess amount of work to do. This relatively easy-going system, much more satisfactory to the Chinese, placed greater stress on virtue (*li*) than it did on the law itself. Moreover, the Confucian system, unlike the Western-style governmental and legal systems, did not stress impartial justice. When existing laws were applied in China, they were made dependent on the interpretation and judgment of the official. His experience and high moral standards were relied on to lead to a better decision than one would get solely by referring to the law itself.

The two Confucian pillars, the bureaucrats and the scholars, became important molders of public opinion. With their highly developed standards of right and wrong, they were extremely influential in determining the public's attitude toward an imperial regime, especially with regard to the ruler's mandate of heaven and the degree to which his behavior indicated whether he was successful in retaining it. The intelligentsia—including the students during this century—has taken its function quite seriously and its attitudes have often had great influence.

An insight into Chinese civilization may be obtained from a review of the major strengths and weaknesses of the intellectual classes. The Chinese developed a strong sense of history, as would be expected from a people who revered ancestors and held precedent and achievements of the past in high esteem. For this reason, and also because it had the moral purpose of aiding people to decide how to conduct themselves in the present and the future on the basis of past experience, history was considered to be too important to be left in private hands. Historical events were therefore organized and clarified to a remarkably scientific degree under a series of dynastic sponsorships; each new line commissioned a historical chronicle of the events that occurred in the dynasty just displaced. The records so compiled, especially the early ones, were of course not necessarily entirely accurate or without bias, but on the whole the field of historical writing, stressed so heavily in Chinese scholarship, yielded creditable results. A similar degree of efficiency and achievement crowned scholarly efforts along such lines as the organization of encyclopedic studies and the compilation of dictionaries (a difficult task in a language whose writing is based on ideographs rather than an alphabet).

The Chinese record in the natural sciences was somewhat uneven, but it is a common misconception in the West that China produced very little in this field. Chinese scholarship itself contributed to this error by failing to realize that the culture had registered noteworthy achievements. One chief reason for this failure was that traditional scholarship emphasized literary studies above all others. Yet there is a great deal of scientific information in Taoist studies and in books labeled "miscellaneous" by Confucian scholars.

It was characteristic of Chinese science that it remained on an empirical level; observation, use of manual operations, and resort to experimentation to improve techniques were its strong points. Actually, China's early scientific initiative and technical achievement rose above the Hellenistic and Medieval European levels; in fact, down to 1500 the Middle Kingdom was well in advance of the West in technical discoveries and general fund of scientific knowledge. This was the land that produced, among a host of other discoveries, paper and printing, gunpowder, the magnet, piston bellows, cast-iron metallurgy, deep-drilling techniques, the crossbow, various types of bridges, porcelain, and water-tight compartments for boats. It must be remembered, however, that these activities were interpreted in terms of primitive theories and hypotheses, and that the country's weakness in theory and systemization constantly retarded the scope and value of its scientific activity. As a consequence, no modern science arose in East Asia as it did in the West after 1500. It was, in fact, partly their comparison with the scientific tradition of contemporary Europe that led the Chinese to conclude that they lacked a scientific tradition of their own.

Weaknesses in the Chinese System

Inadequacy in scientific theory was not the sole deficiency in the Chinese system of training. Other weaknesses were evident in the general field of scholarship, the civil service system, and even beyond these realms. As has been noted, the absence of social or political barriers to entrance into governmental service had an important egalitarian influence on Chinese society over the long run. But the advantages were all with the well-to-do, and the tendency arose—never legalized or formalized—for a scholar class to perpetuate itself. The heavy investment that had to be made in scholarship, in terms of time lost from productive manual work and the positive costs of education, weighed heavily on the poorer elements in the community. Their chances of getting a bright young man into the civil service were much weaker, all other things being equal, than a wealthy family would have. The desire to become an official burned intensely, and there are model examples of a village pooling its resources to finance a worthy aspirant from its midst. Although the procedure was admirable, it reflected the difficulties facing the ambitious poor.

The successful bureaucratic candidate was beset by other problems in the execution of his official duties. Although discouraged from attempting to assert political control over the areas they administered, officials could and did operate to benefit the position of their families. Such allegiance was so highly prized that it is doubtful whether by Chinese standards a government official was morally in the wrong if he used his position to benefit his family by direct accumulation of wealth or through his powers of appointment. In any event, two conflicting sets of loyalties were fostered, one to the state and one to the family, with the latter evidently having priority. Since salaries were very low, an almost unbearable temptation was placed before the bureaucrat to indulge in corrupt practices once he had successfully covered the arduous road to officialdom.

Corruption, however, was not a uniquely Chinese vice and was not ordinarily flagrant enough to disrupt administrative services. Corrupt monetary practices, called "squeeze," such as graft and the pocketing of tax money, came to be accepted as an integral part of the scene. Only in times of economic unrest or grave political stress could these bureaucratic failings, especially if they became intensified, serve appreciably to undermine a regime. For the most part the central machinery was more than adequate and many high-minded men performed their public service honorably.

Another handicap lay in the type of preparation the officials and scholars received for their careers as administrators or alert enlightened intellectuals. Their training, of course, emphasized the study of the Confucian classics and Chinese history. Unfortunately, the very success of the effort to achieve cultural unity through a like-minded civil service meant that the pattern of education, the civil service criteria, and the examinations became rigid and stereotyped, with primary emphasis placed on conformity to accepted standards. Such preparation had a bad effect on the Chinese powers of creativity and contributed to what many analysts have called the cultural stagnation of the last thousand years. Moreover, the context of the material learned became less and less helpful. Emphasis on ancient texts and classics went far beyond the limits required to inculcate the desired moral standards and cultural homogeneity. In fact, as study of these older works assumed an overwhelming proportion of the material to be mastered, they came to be treated as ends in themselves. Exaggerated importance was given to achievements of rote memory, the ability to write in acceptable literary style, and even to one's calligraphy or style of writing.

Very little of the practical matters of running a state, either administratively or in field operations like irrigation and grain storage, was learned through this educational system. As a consequence, efficiency was sharply curtailed. Yet the educated Chinese placed unwarranted confidence in such teachings. They persistently defeated efforts to modernize the educational requirements for civil service trainees, and so, indirectly, for the intellectual class as a whole. Apparently no change in the standards of educational values would be permitted if it threatened to depress the level of prestige of subjects in which the educated classes were proficient. Since the reformers often challenged the position of the economically privileged as well, the latter became powerful allies of the officials and scholars. The conservative position was successfully defended even during shifts in dynasties, since new regimes, in their effort to gain a firm hold over China, vigorously adopted the basic values of the traditional culture. In this way the new rulers allied themselves with the powerful classes and so were not a source of support for any reform movements. Such attempts at change, therefore, proved rare and abortive.

It was in character for the Chinese to look down on the techniques and achievements of the West when they made contact with this alien culture. A leadership that scorned changes proposed by its own educational reformers naturally did not view with favor an attempt to introduce new ideas stemming from a foreign source. Even if the new facts of life were accepted, their application would have required a revamped central governmental structure, a new concept of the functions of government, and a drastic revision of the relationship between the center and the provinces. Even with the intellectuals' enthusiastic support of change, the task would have been enormous. In the face of their determined opposition in the nineteenth century, the difficulties became insurmountable.

At base, much of the trouble lay in the shortcomings of the Confucian system itself. As might be expected, the theory of rule by a benevolent and virtuous emperor, aided by a devoted class of subordinate officials, was rarely approximated in real life. As the Legalist critics noted, efficient government or a high level of morality cannot be attained simply by declaiming its value and importance, or even its inevitability. There was too much preaching of lofty doctrine, with insufficient concern for the problem of its practical realization. Corruption in the official class in the sale of literary degrees and noncompetitive offices, extortionary behavior, and the like caused the peasants, especially in hard times, to look on the preachment of virtue by their superiors as hypocrisy.

Ideally, scholars were held in higher esteem than soldiers, in contrast to aristocratic inclinations in Europe and Japan. However, fighting was not beneath the dignity of a gentleman when the need arose. Actually, political warfare was as frequent in China as in the military-aristocratic societies, causing considerable waste and destruction in the land. Many of the struggles arose as civil wars because the emperor was deemed to have lost his mandate; in this connection, the ability of a ruler to demonstrate a forceful grip on the situation was important for the nation's internal peace. In practice, "loss of virtue" by the ruler recurred frequently; in fact, all dynasties were founded by military endeavor, as was permitted under the Confucian doctrine.

It must be remembered, however, that the ideal of model, virtuous leadership retained its hold over the Chinese mind. Such an attitude placed considerable pressure on governing officials, who knew their actions would be measured against these ideal standards. Many political leaders conscientiously tried to reach these levels. In fact, it is important to note that the Confucian ideal, effective rule through virtuous example by the rulers, was not abused to the extent that the mass of people became disillusioned with it. After all, the Chinese considered the Confucian code an adequate one to live by for more than 2,000 years.

Nevertheless, the Chinese system was becoming culturally and ideologically more rigid with each passing century, despite the right of revolution implicit in the doctrine of the mandate of heaven. It is of great significance that no new political philosophy developed from Chinese thinking after the downfall of the Chou dynasty in the third century B.C. Also, little originality was displayed in the fields of administration and governmental organization after the Han dynasty in the third century A.D.; activity thereafter was mainly a refinement of earlier devices and concepts. These developments were closely related to the increasingly stereotyped and impractical nature of the civil service examinations.

As Chinese history progressed, the culture produced fewer new techniques and ideas, and creativity diminished in an alarming manner. Yet its basic stability and the repeated appearances of new, vigorous dynasties led to a remarkable increase in wealth and population, with great areas coming under intensive irrigated cultivation. Adjustments contributing to this growth were adequate though uninspiring. Thus, under the Manchus in the eighteenth century the population doubled, probably reaching 300 million by the next century. The establishment of peace and order and the importation of new types of food plants from America were the chief causes of this increase. However, deforestation proceeded apace and upland or hillside terracing increased, demonstrating the mounting pressure of people on the land.

The spirit of originality and creativity, in general, is considered to have lost most of its strength after the Sung dynasty, which fell about 700 years ago. The Confucian pattern that served China so well was also a major cause of this society's constricted intellectual progress. For the price of having one dominant, unchallenged social philosophy was the absence of a political-philosophical ferment that could stimulate a high degree of originality and experimentation. The country became bound in what can be described as an intellectual strait jacket.

Closely related to this tendency were the rising frequency and duration of foreign conquests and the ascension of alien dynasties. The native Sung regime was unable to hold all of China and was driven from the northern sector after 1000 A.D. In the thirteenth century it was overthrown by the Mongols, who lasted less than a century. The Manchus conquered China in the seventeenth century and remained in power for about 250 years, until 1911. Scholarship under the Manchus became increasingly unimaginative. One school of analysis, concerned over this lack of vitality and the presence of foreign rulers, sought without success a revitalization of thought. It challenged classical doctrine as developed by the neo-Confucian thinkers of the twelfth and thirteenth centuries and sought to return to the original classics in their primary form. This early, tentative move to escape from intellectual decay and sterility suggested how difficult such endeavors were to be.

The impact of the West was decisive in breaking this strait jacket. Intellectual and even moral chaos ensued as the Chinese made a slow and painful adjustment to the new situation, within an uncertain political environment. The convulsions that have shaken China during the modern era reflect the enormous intellectual dislocation and the cost of long centuries of stagnation. The endeavor to free itself from self-imposed and foreign shackles was made enormously difficult by the predatory behavior of the major powers adopting an "active" China policy. China did not emerge from its critical period with a democratic peaceful government and society. But before condemnation is expressed, the West would do well to appreciate the problems China faced and to ask itself whether during the past sixty years, it sought to ease China's burden.

Chinese Buddhist Temple in Singapore

Summer palace built by the Mongol dynasty at Peking

A section of the Great Wall of China

Communist troops outside the northwest gate of captured Peking, January, 1949

(From *Peking Diary* by Derk Bodde, 1950. Courtesy Abelard-Schuman, Inc., New York)

Mao Tse-tung and Chu Teh, Chairman and Vice-Chairman of the Central People's Government under the constitutional revision of 1954

Chou En-lai, Premier and Foreign Minister, conferring with Premier Kotelewala of Ceylon at the Bandung Conference in 1955

A Communist "liberation parade" in Shanghai, July, 1949

Nationalist troops training on Formosa

Nationalist rally in Shanghai, February, 1946,
welcoming Chiang Kai-shek on his first visit
since 1937

*The Horyuji Temple at Nara, reputed to be
the oldest wooden structure in the world*

The Great Buddha statue at Kamakura

A rice field south of Yokohama at cutting time. The rail and electric lines, uncommon elsewhere in Asia, reflect the extent of Japan's modernization.

The industrial center of Yawata, in northern Kyushu, site of Japan's first major government-sponsored steel plant

The point of the Hiroshima atomic explosion has since been rebuilt as a war memorial hall

The second Konoye cabinet, August, 1941, facing the Diet. Premier Konoye is at the extreme right in the front row. Seated to the right of War Minister Tojo (in uniform) is Foreign Minister Matsuoka.

A rally of the Government Workers Union and affiliated organizations held on the Imperial Palace Plaza in 1948 to protest working conditions

The investiture of Crown Prince Akihito

4 China:

an Historical Perspective

A discussion of the problem China has faced in modern times must be prefaced by a review of its political evolution. In this way an adequate perspective of the contemporary situation can be attained. A survey of China's dynastic cycles may also serve to reinforce our earlier study of political culture traits by presenting these features in their order of chronological development.

The Setting

The center of the stage, China Proper, is surrounded by the outlying provinces and dependencies of Manchuria, Mongolia, Sinkiang, and Tibet, to move counterclockwise from north to south. The geography of China itself is admirably suited to the cultural evolution that occurred, for the country is composed of plains and fertile valleys (especially the Yellow and Yangtze), which make for ease of communications and a favorable climate. The western mountains are the source of many rivers and form a rugged terrain; to the northwest lie the desert edges of the great Asian land mass. Agriculturally, North China has relatively sparse rainfalls and features dry-cropping. It has alternate fears of drought and a flooded overflow of the unpredictable Yellow River, "China's sorrow." To the south, from the coast inland to the rich and populous Szechuan Province up the Yangtze, heavier rains and warmer climate favor the rice economy so prevalent in Monsoon Asia.

The north, where Chinese civilization began, served as the political nerve center of the empire, and, whenever it was militarily possible, the capital has been located there. This region was of great political and strategic importance, for the northwest frontier remained the most sensitive boundary area until the advent of the West in the nineteenth century. It is interesting to note that, whereas the southern and central coastal regions rose in importance during the past century, the field of decision in the great civil war terminating after 1945 proved to be North China. The present Communist regime, turning its back on friendly intercourse with the West, has thus far re-established the importance of both the northern region and the inland frontiers.

MAJOR ERAS IN CHINA'S POLITICAL HISTORY

Shang	to *ca.* 1122 or 1050 B.C.
Chou	1122 (or 1050) to 221 B.C.
	(*Confucius 551–479* B.C.)
Ch'in	221–207 B.C.
Early or Western Han	207 B.C.–8 A.D.
Wang Mang	8–23 A.D.
Later or Eastern Han	23–221
Decline of Central Rule	221–589
	(*Buddhism introduced*)
Sui	589–618
T'ang	618–907
Five dynasties (weak center)	907–960
North Sung	960–1127
South Sung	1127–1279
Mongol (Yuan)	1279–1368
Ming	1368–1644
Manchu (Ch'ing)	1644–1912
Nationalist Republic	1912–1949
Communist Republic	1949——

The Imperial Dynasties

Early Dynasties: Shang and Chou

The first dynasty that can be positively identified is the Shang, though it comes second in the traditional narration of history. It was a rich bronze culture and followed three Neolithic societies. Though a harsh era, with stratification of society, the Shang practiced the Chinese style of writing and ancestor reverence, and in general revealed a relatively sophisticated level of political development.

The Shang realm was located along the trade routes crossing Asia, with neighbors who also governed territories in North China. It is uncertain whether the Shang dynasty was a supreme monarchy or whether it was simply another small ruling line. Although its exact tenure of reign is not known, it is traditionally said to have been from 1765 to 1122 B.C., though some place its downfall around 1050 B.C. Since this civilization developed later than those in the Mediterranean region, it may be assumed that many inventions and discoveries utilized by the Shang derived from Western sources. However, the basic culture traits indicate strong indigenous influence; the culture itself was definitely a local development.

The Chou dynasty that followed was the longest in Chinese history, lasting until 221 B.C., though its period of rule was by no means a serene one. It came from the western frontier region, in the Wei Valley, and was culturally backward. Yet there was no sudden break in tradition, for it appears that Shang scholars tutored the Chou. This practice may have established a precedent and reflected the tendency of later conquerors to adopt and continue the culture of their victims. To bolster its own honor and prestige, the Chou account of its rise to power held that the Shang tyrant was overthrown in righteous indigna-

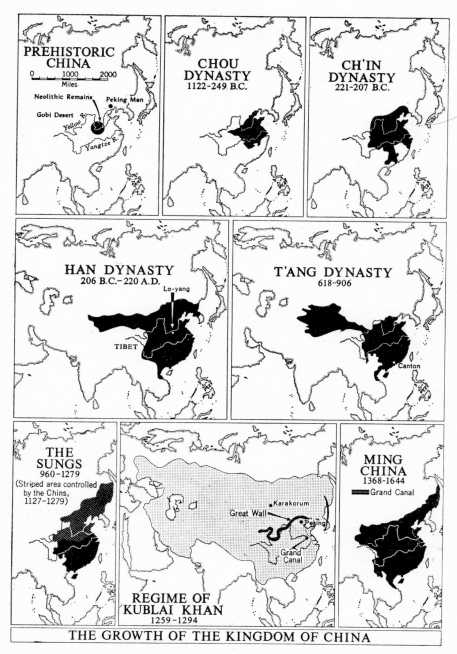

THE GROWTH OF THE KINGDOM OF CHINA

From Stewart C. Easton, *The Heritage of the Past* (New York: Rinehart & Company, Inc., 1955). © 1955.

83

tion. Regardless of its doubtful validity, this argument reveals the existence of a moral sense in public affairs that had to be appeased in explaining the transfer of dynastic power. It also indicates that there already existed the theory that a monarch had to govern righteously, or be faced with justifiable revolution led by those who would rule according to moral principles.

Under Chou rule, Chinese culture expanded from the north central plain and the Wei Valley into the Shensi and Shansi highlands and down into Szechuan Province. Other peoples were encountered during these migrations, some of whom had advanced cultures themselves. Chinese traits were modified by these contacts but retained their basic form and prevailed as the dominant force. In political affairs, this was not a period of powerful central rule. In fact, centralized authority was considerably weakened as the country became divided into many states. The Chou leaders held ritualistic and theoretical predominance, but they wielded little actual power, as the various states became the real centers of authority. These political entities were bound by a common culture; many of them even formed a league that lasted for more than two centuries, with investiture received from the Chou. There was a superior-inferior relationship among these rulers somewhat akin to feudalism.

Warfare was chronic and political chaos the rule, but the savagery of fighting was restricted by custom. In spite of anarchy in the late Chou period, considerable progress was made in the arts and in economic activity. Most important of all was the development of the three major schools of thought in this, the classical period of Chinese philosophy. Confucian, Taoist, and Legalist concepts flourished and developed during this era, for there was no stable government with its philosophical orthodoxy to stifle independent thought. The Period of the Warring States (481–221 B.C.) also aroused the interest of scholars and philosophers in politics; concern over the fate of society and not mere abstract speculation led to an acceleration of thought and a competition of ideas that had most stimulating effects.

Although Confucius (551–479 B.C.), like the Legalists, turned to government as a source of salvation, he still held to a moderate position, even in such troubled times. He disliked an intense rule bearing down on the people in a direct and impersonal way, but he accepted the necessity of government. In his travels from one princedom to another, he failed to get any rulers to adopt his major precepts, such as rule by virtuous example. His following, however, was widespread, and his ideas took hold, even though they were to undergo a long wait before attaining undisputed supremacy.

A leading Confucian scholar in this age was Mencius (373–288 B.C.) who, like Confucius, came from the province of Lu. He, too, traveled from state to state in an effort to get the principles of worthy government and rule by example put into practice. Setting less store in ceremony than Confucius did, and emphatically arguing that man is good by nature, Mencius devoted considerable attention to the right of rebellion against an unjust prince. He maintained that heaven withdrew its sanction from a ruler against whom the governed had serious cause for complaint. Although Mencius continued to stress the class distinction between the rulers and the ruled his progressive philosophy contained the elements of a more liberal approach to society.

The Ch'in and the Han

As warfare became more intense, two states on the periphery—Ch'in from the Wei Valley and Ch'u in the Yangtze region—fought a struggle that resembled a contest between two empires of related but different cultures. Fighting increased in ferocity, the league of states disappeared, and by 221 B.C. the Ch'in, which had violated all the rules of courteous warfare, triumphed and took over the territory and symbols of rule of the Chou dynasty.

The new ruler systematically tried to establish an empire based on Legalist principles. His efforts accounted for the dynasty's immediate success but also contributed to its short duration. A major achievement was the abolition of separate states and hereditary rulers; thus the Chinese equivalent of feudalism came to an end. Private ownership of land, common in Ch'in, was extended over the empire. The realm was divided into provinces and these into hsien, each administered by a member of the bureaucracy, which was established at this time under the control of the emperor. This new officialdom was tied to the Legalist school of socio-political thought, for the central administrative system generally reflected one official theory of society. One body of law was promptly established throughout the empire.

Important changes were made after the Ch'in, especially in the replacement of Legalism by the milder Confucian doctrine as the government's philosophical guide. Still, the contribution of this dynasty to China's cultural and political unity remained substantial. However, a conflict was already apparent between freedom of thought and the strain of keeping the empire united culturally as well as politically. Efforts were made by the Ch'in to stifle free discussion and many books of non-Legalist outlook were burned.

Although the dynasty lasted only a few years after its founder's death in 210 B.C., it fully deserved to be the source of the name China. Not only was China united by this forceful regime, but its area was extended along the coast below the Yangtze and as far southward as the Indochina border region. Migration in this direction and toward Szechuan was encouraged as a means of consolidating China's hold on these areas. Advances were also made to the northwest, but the Yellow River remained the core region of Chinese power and cultural achievement.

Popular resentment against the Ch'in rule, which had ended the old order so abruptly, an incompetent successor to the throne, heavy taxes, and numerous harsh laws led to a rebellion in which the capital was plundered. The disorder soon ended, as the throne was won by a capable farmer, turned bandit and then rebel leader in the prevailing hard times. This new Han dynasty kept the administrative machine built by the Ch'in leaders and introduced a great period in Chinese history. The Early, or Western, Han (207 B.C.–8 A.D.) and the late, or Eastern, Han (23–220 A.D.) were divided by an interesting revolutionary breach of fifteen years.

At first the Han rulers seemed intent on undoing the work of the Ch'in, but they could not make much progress in this direction. An attempt to restore hereditary principalities within the Ch'in administrative divisions had to be given up because of the evident peril they posed to imperial supremacy and security. The harsh legal and tax systems were eased, and the Han emperor was more inclined to take advice from his subordinates than was the autocratic Ch'in ruler. The original Han ruler did not favor Confucianism, feeling it to be too pompous and fussy, but its popularity insured its eventual acceptance nonetheless. The decision to retain Confucianism, plus the retention of an appointed bureaucracy and a modified legal code, assured the continuity of a culturally and politically united kingdom. It was also during the Han dynasty that the examination system was developed as a means of recruiting government officials. Even at this early stage the tests were based primarily on Confucian classics. The state and private schools that were later established developed uniform characteristics under the pressure of preparing candidates for these tests.

During this great dynasty, China not only strengthened its political culture but at the end of the second century B.C. literally expanded in all directions. The barbarians to the northwest were pushed back, and the Great Wall, begun earlier, was considerably extended. A move into Central Asia went beyond Sinkiang and touched the fringe of the Middle Eastern world. Parts of South Manchuria and Korea were invested. The Ch'in boundaries to the south were surpassed as the Canton area became more fully settled. Hainan Island and Annam came under Chinese influence. Though South China was not brought fully under control, almost all China Proper was occupied. And it was at this time that the great Historical Records, chronicles of the previous dynasties, were begun.

Around the beginning of the Christian era the Han regime was experiencing a period of decline. This occurred despite the regime's rather extensive irrigation and flood-control works and considerable activity in regulating commerce, especially food staples. An official named Wang Mang, who maintained that the emperor lost his mandate of heaven, succeeded in displacing him (8–23 A.D.). Wang Mang tried to be a model ruler in the Confucian tradition, though his concept of an active government policy carried him beyond moderate Confucian bounds. The powerful gentry and other entrenched classes were considerably antagonized by such reform activities as his attempt to nationalize the land and break up large estates. The subsequent unrest and rebellion culminated in a restoration of the Han dynasty. But Wang Mang's attempted reforms are of significance because they reflected the persistent and basic agrarian troubles besetting China. The similarity of this situation to that of China in the twentieth century is quite striking.

The intellectual atmosphere of the Later Han period became less suitable to original thinking. Confucianism was now firmly entrenched as the basis of society, standard texts of these classics were developed, and the Confucian school became a sort of intellectual ruling clique knit together by inter-marriage. This attitude affected other schools of thought adversely, as it discouraged the development of new precepts. Taoism retained its existence by dropping its emphasis on the issue of man in society and concentrating on more personal and religious questions, such as the meaning of life itself and the means to personal immortality. As a further sign of increasing rigidity, and as a portent for the future, the scholar class concentrated primarily on the collection and edition of literature of the past. Similarly, in later centuries, efforts were to be directed toward interpreting and reinterpreting earlier classical writings.

Sui and T'ang

Following the fall of the Han dynasty, China had no unified rule for more than 350 years (221–589). Its territory shrank to the size of China Proper, and invaders occupied parts of the north from time to time. Though anarchy prevailed, Chinese culture was not adversely affected; in fact, most invaders became culturally assimilated. One important result of the invasion was that the civilization gained strength in the Yangtze Valley under the pressure of population movements to the south. Thus the great ideal of a unified empire, developed in the Chou period, was now powerful enough to be a motivating factor in Chinese political life, aided as it was by the maintenance of the administrative system. Yet, even with new concepts and material inventions being introduced from abroad, this age of turmoil was quite different from its Chou predecessor in that no great intellectual achievements were recorded.

The material innovations, such as tea, the wheelbarrow, the water wheel, and the use of coal, stemmed from the growth of foreign commerce, from migrations, and from generally broader contacts with foreign cultures. Also imported, probably by both land and sea routes, was the Buddhist religion from India. It was the most important alien contribution to Chinese culture before modern times, and its favorable reception demonstrated that the Chinese were still flexible enough to accept outside ideas. In fact, Buddhism remained an important popular religion for at least 1,000 years and served as a transmitting vehicle for other cultural innovations, from India and elsewhere, in art and medicine. Perhaps even more would have come of this fluid, potentially revolutionary era if Buddhism were more aggressive or positive in its views on political and social affairs. Being essentially an Indian philosophical and spiritual effort to escape from the world, it could not seriously challenge or displace the more positive Confucian ideals.

The brief Sui dynasty (589–618) revealed China's powers of political recuperation. Not as dramatic as its Ch'in prototype, it nonetheless succeeded in largely reunifying China. The main Sui contributions were an improvement of the administration and a modification of the civil service examinations. In addition, operations were undertaken on the canal linking the Yellow and Yangtze rivers. This project furthered the empire's political and economic unity and served to facilitate the northward flow of southern rice produce.

The great T'ang dynasty (618–907) completed the reunification of China and was of a stature equal to that of the Han. Some Chinese call themselves the Sons of Han, and others in the south use the name of Sons of T'ang. The magnificence of the T'ang period led the Japanese to borrow consciously and heavily from China, though China's influence had been felt earlier. Foreign expansion was carried to new lengths—to the Moslem lands of the west, well into Manchuria and Mongolia, and across Tibet and the upper reaches of the Indus River. Trade and contact with foreigners was maintained on a flourishing level. Buddhism still had a wide following but was already beginning to lose its vigor in the face of a Confucianist revival. Confucian temples bearing the names of leading Confucian scholars were built throughout China, and officials and scholars were obliged to make sacrifices there. No basic changes were made in governmental administration, but it was more tightly centralized, especially in the matter of appointments.

Sung, Mongol, and Ming

The end of the T'ang dynasty led to a brief period of political turmoil (907-960). Cultural stability was again maintained, but various invaders appeared more frequently and occupied parts of North China. This worrisome development continued during the next dynasty, that of Sung (960–1279). The new ruling family was not up to the level of its predecessors, its authority was not recognized on the borderlands, and it ruled over only part of China Proper. Eventually ousted from the north, the Sung regime moved southward in 1123 and set up a new capital near the present site of Hangchow, thereby ushering in the period of the Southern Sung. The Sung dynasty engaged in balance-of-power politics, which eventually backfired; it dealt with the distant Mongols of Genghis Khan, allying with his forces in order to combat alien armies pressing more closely on the northern frontier region. The great Mongol warriors subdued most of West and Central Asia, then turned on Sung China, which proved to be their toughest opponent. It finally fell to Kublai Khan in 1279, and for the first time China came under a foreign dynasty.

The Sung era witnessed a flourishing of the arts and a thorough exposition of the major religious-philosophical tenets. Confucian ideas were reinterpreted and expanded into a coherent explanation of the universe. The leading scholar of this neo-Confucian school was Chu Hsi (1130–1200), who synthesized his philosophy on the basis of his own and contemporary ideas, the Confucian texts, the Buddhist concept of meditation and sudden enlightenment, and the Taoist belief that some principle underlies the workings of the universe. For the next 700 years, the interpretation of Chu Hsi remained the accepted orthodox approach to Confucianism.

During the Sung era occurred the second great attempt in China to undertake widespread socio-economic reform from above; it was apparent that such a program was better than suffering a revolution or a peasant rebellion. This endeavor to break through the ever-stiffening strait jacket of thought and tradition was motivated by a desire to alleviate or remove some of the more flagrant injustices in Chinese life. It was also an attempt to put the empire in a stronger position to meet the growing menace from the north. It was conducted by Wang An-shih (1021–1086), a high-ranking statesman who envisaged those reforms so familiarly associated with China's present needs: a budget to control state finances and effect savings; state monopoly of commerce, including control and storage of surplus food staples; credit expansion to needy farmers; equal division of land; taxes on all property; an end to conscript labor, with payment for services rendered by means of graduated taxes; a reorganized military establishment to include compulsory service; and a revised civil service examination that would stress more practical problems. Again, opposition was bitter and powerful. The reform program did not last after Wang's death, save for the adoption of a grain-storage system.

The Sung period, then, featured some reformist endeavors and vigorous, if unorganized, intellectual activity. The Mongol conquerors, on the other hand, though religiously and socially tolerant, really caused an interruption in Chinese life and produced little that was new. In their desire to adapt themselves to the new culture, they behaved in such a cautious way that their uneasiness precluded any constructive alterations in the pattern of Chinese life. Such was the situation in spite of a considerable influx of foreigners from all parts of the Mongol empire and beyond. This was the era of Marco Polo and Franciscan missionary work; the Moslem religion also gained in prominence at this time. But Mongol foreign policy was not successful. There was an inconclusive move into Annam, and the great, disastrous expedition against Japan, in which Chinese forces took part. That this foreign rule was unpopular in China is evidenced by the fact that as soon as the dynasty gave signs of diminished vigor, rebellions broke out and the Mongols were overthrown after a relatively brief period of rule (1279–1368).

The Ming dynasty that followed was of native stock, and its reign (1368–1644) was long and prosperous. It was not as brilliant as the great Han and T'ang eras, and continued to demonstrate the lack of inventiveness that was becoming so alarmingly characteristic of the Chinese. The civil service tests were stereotyped, officials were accordingly mediocre, and political organization was no more than a refinement of inherited techniques. Philosophical works were uninspired, and so low was the level of Chinese receptiveness to new thought that the most creative Chinese thinker of the time enjoyed a greater popularity in Japan than at home. This passive attitude was complemented by a defensive posture in relation to the surrounding areas. Nor was this empire as large as earlier ones, since it did not encompass Sinkiang. Fortifications were built in a manner that emphasized them as defenses rather than as outposts of an expansive empire. Finally, the coastal regions were open to numerous Japanese pirate raids, the consequences of China's inadequately developed seapower.

As opposition to the Ming dynasty rose, a rebellion broke out over heavy taxes. This led to an insurgent capture of Peking, the magnificent capital city built by the Ming rulers. The Manchus from the north, aided by a Ming general, then took the city and drove the Ming emperor to the southwest. Since the emperor had lost his mandate, it was quite permissible for the Chinese to support the new rulers, even if they were of alien origin.

The Manchus

The Manchus sought to cement their hold by behaving like Chinese emperors and ruling through native officials and institutions. Yet they tried to remain apart and keep their own identity as conquerors, maintaining their own custom and dress, and keeping Manchu garrisons strategically located throughout China. Chinese males had to copy Manchu customs, shave their heads, and wear a queue. When certain trusted Chinese officials in the south, who had been given high offices after they helped the Manchus ascend to power, used their position of trust to launch an unsuccessful rebellion, the Manchus adopted precautionary measures to control the bureaucracy and keep it from becoming a source of unrest.

A series of very capable early rulers enabled the Manchus to stay in power for about as long a period of time (1644–1912) as the Ming dynasty. The empire reached its peak in the eighteenth century, when it was probably the wealthiest and most prosperous in the world. China's territorial limits reached new heights under these alien rulers, who pushed northward from their Manchurian homeland as far as the northern watershed of the Amur River. Mongolia was entered, and Sinkiang (New Dominion) was incorporated into China. Tibet and Nepal came under Manchu authority, and Burma, after it was invaded, sent periodic tribute. At sea, Formosa was taken and the Ryukyus sent vassalary payments to China. Korea recognized Chinese overlordship and likewise sent monetary tribute.

By the start of the nineteenth century the rulers had lost their vigor, and a decline set in. Unrest grew under the trying conditions of inefficient rule, high taxes, corruption, mounting population pressure on the land, and the increased concentration of land ownership in fewer hands. To this scene of dynastic decline and periodic peasant revolts came the stunning impact of the West. China was already approaching an era of turmoil, of the kind that erupted periodically in its history, when it was assaulted by a culture that was its equal in many ways and its superior in military and organizational matters. Despite the unrest prevailing throughout China, the ruling class and the scholars considered their civilization far superior to that of the Western barbarians. They therefore treated the foreigners with a contempt that proved unwarranted from the viewpoint of China's weakened power position—and this was an immediate cause of trouble. But they also suffered from intellectual inbreeding and a smug sense of superiority to the extent that they would not observe the Westerners carefully and rationally to see what could be learned from them. This lack of wisdom cost China undue and almost unbelievable hardships in its later adjustment to the modern era.

The Modern Era Begins

The Display of Western Power

The primary motivation behind the heightened interest of the West in China was the expansion of trade and, for this purpose, the establishment of "normal" diplomatic relations. Commercial intercourse before 1839 was confined to the port of Canton and had to be conducted through an officially designated group of Chinese merchants, called the Co-hong. This group was given a monopoly of all legal trade so that it would act as a screen to protect the rest of China from contamination with the barbarians. The Westerners were restricted to a crowded, guarded area in the Canton port region, and the Co-hong itself was kept under close observation. The Chinese may have been so accustomed to having dangers arise from the landlocked western region that they underestimated the threat that could come from the usually quiescent southern and eastern coastal area. In any event, European efforts to establish diplomatic ties were incessantly thwarted; the Chinese treated European emissaries as barbaric tribute-bearing vassals. The West was therefore given ample motivation to adopt a more forceful position.

In the pre-1839 period the Westerners accepted Chinese insults at a cost of "face," and this probably increased Chinese contempt for them. Undoubtedly the successful show of force after 1839 brought considerable rewards. Yet it cannot be concluded from this and similar incidents that a show of force always suffices to win the day in Oriental power politics. Success was achieved only when superior power was available to the Westerners. If the Chinese felt that they could match this effort, or emerge victorious, they did not flinch from a fight. Moreover, they generally were willing to go to war and yielded only after a defeat or in the face of overwhelming odds. Such victories did not necessarily increase "respect" for the West. In fact, these contacts merely intensified China's anti-Western, antiforeign bias. Eventually the Chinese were compelled to seek the means to attain equality with the West and, if possible, to reassert their superiority or even hegemony over the region formerly dominated by the Middle Kingdom. Without discussing the question of motivation for the moment, the behavior of the present Communist government can be considered a fulfillment of a century-old desire for revenge, the reassertion of self-respect, and the re-establishment of power predominance in this area.

In the middle of the nineteenth century, China was ready for an internal change and desperately needed a renovation of its national defense. However, it then lacked the institutions, leadership, and mental attitude required to undertake the large-scale transformation required. The Opium War of 1839 was the slow start of China's accelerating downward spiral in the face of formidable military opponents. The conflict arose out of many causes—China's attempt to forbid any authorized British opium trade, while corrupt officials made lucrative profits from illegal smuggling activities; the irksome air of Chinese superiority; and the Chinese sense of justice that held the group (in this case the foreign settlement) responsible for the activities of individuals.

This Anglo-Chinese War of 1839–1842, begun in the south, ended with the rupture of China's north-south lines of communications and a British threat to Nanking. Matters were not actually settled by the Treaty of Nanking (1842), as each side felt it could have won a more favorable agreement. The treaty's provisions included: the end of the Co-hong, the opening of five ports to British travel and residence, intercourse on a basis of equality, and fair and regular Chinese publications of tariff rates. In addition, Hong Kong Island was ceded to the British, who built a large modern city on this site. The following year, a regular tariff schedule was fixed, commercial regulations were promulgated, and the principle of extraterritoriality[1] was adopted. Other nations, including the United States, obtained similar treaties, and under the "most-favored-nation clause" all states received the most beneficial concessions China made to any one foreign power.

A second war, conducted by the British and French from 1856 to 1860, with sporadic starts and stops, led to further concessions. Symptomatic of China's attitude is the fact that in 1859, after sustaining defeats in battle, it still treated foreign envoys as inferiors, and so precipitated a resumption of combat and the loss of Peking, the capital city. In accordance with treaties signed by 1860, eleven more treaty ports were opened, Western merchant ships were able to sail on the Yangtze (the beginning of the growth of Shanghai), diplomatic representation at Peking was established, foreigners with passports could trade anywhere in China, Christian missionary activity was permitted, French (and later other) missionaries could buy land outside the treaty-port regions and build on the property, Kowloon on the mainland opposite Hong Kong was ceded to Britain, and the opium trade was legalized.

These treaties are significant because they formed the legal basis of China's relations with the outside world for nearly a century. China was to suffer through more wars, losses of territory, and near dismemberment. Nevertheless, the status created by these particular agreements rankled, and they were called the "unequal treaties," since they bestowed upon the foreigner in China rights that were not matched by special Chinese rights abroad. Especially painful were the extraterritorial privileges and the establishment of a fixed tariff rate that left the Chinese government powerless to control customs duties. Since the rate of 5 per cent was imposed for a long period of time, the Chinese lost an important source of revenue as well as a means of protecting nascent industries. These serious infringements on Chinese sovereignty further intensified the

---

[1] Defined in Chapter 7, page 195.

animosity China bore toward people who were not even accepted as equals in the first place. Unfortunately, as in most such cases, the privileged foreigner was used as a convenient scapegoat by the succeeding rulers of China, to be blamed for the deep-rooted and varied troubles that afflicted the nation.

Nor did Western behavior ease this alarming situation. The Westerners in their way felt superior to the Chinese and had the power and wealth to give expression to this attitude. There were special areas—concessions—set aside in treaty ports for the aliens, the most famous being the International Concession at Shanghai, and those at Tientsin and Hankow. These foreign enclaves with their exotic way of life, in the midst of China's great commercial centers, were a material embodiment of China's new position of inferiority. The foreigners also took over the collection of China's tariff during a period of internal unrest and continued this activity after order was restored, so that the Imperial Maritime Customs remained an efficient but foreign-dominated organization. Overseas trade and finance were handled by foreign firms because this arrangement meant greater savings and efficiency; such a policy did little to speed the modernization of China's economy or help Chinese learn the techniques of modern financial, shipping, or insurance operations.

The T'ai P'ing Rebellion

Western stress on the international aspects of Chinese history may have been carried to an extreme and unprofitable degree, but there is something to be said for such an orientation. China's response to the stimulus of the West was very sluggish and it became questionable whether China would reform in time to avoid destruction. The very enormity of the menace posed by the outside world gave the problem of foreign affairs highest priority.

Yet domestic affairs were of the utmost significance, in the nineteenth century as well as after the overthrow of the Manchus. The dynasty's decline was now sharply accelerated by its inability to cope with the foreign barbarians; this obvious indication that its mandate was endangered gave rise to considerable rebellious activity. Several outbursts had occurred before 1850, and some time later there were revolts in the outlying Moslem regions in the west. The most formidable assault broke out in South China in 1850 and lasted until 1865; this protracted war cost about 20 million lives in the fighting and in the flood, famine, and disease that accompanied it.

The leader of the rebellion was Hung Hsiu-ch'üan, a teacher who had been an unsuccessful aspirant to the civil service. His inspiration stemmed from a recently acquired rudimentary Christian faith that gave him a satisfactory explanation of visions he had seen during a recent illness. He organized a socio-religious movement in Kwangsi Province (the location of Mao Tse-tung's Soviet State in the early 1930's) to study the Bible and certain Christian beliefs and customs. At best this nascent faith was half-understood and represented merely a crude and dimly grasped effort to bring China into the main stream of modern affairs. At first converts were found among descendants of South

China's aboriginal peoples, who had been only partly assimilated into the Chinese culture. However, political ambition and the depressed socio-economic conditions in South China led the leaders of this movement to think of overthrowing the Manchu regime and establishing their own T'ai P'ing (Great Peace) dynasty.

The revolt gained the support of impoverished farmers who were impressed by the promises that land would go to the cultivator, distributed according to need, and that all people would be treated equally. There was an air of unrest in the region because residents had been armed to fight the British in 1839 and many still possessed their weapons; armed bands that had been roving the area also joined the movement. Powered by a new religious creed, strengthened by popular animosity to an alien dynasty that had just lost face, and excited by the prospect of social and economic reform, the rebel forces swept northward to the Yangtze, took Nanking in 1853, and proclaimed it the capital of a new dynasty.

A similarity existed between the T'ai P'ing and the later Communist movement, in that both had a new creed and set forth concrete promises of economic reform. The main differences lay in the level of political understanding and sophistication attained and the degree of political discipline maintained by the rebellious commands. T'ai P'ing leadership was slipshod and dissension in the top ranks was all too common. The religious creed was not capable of inspiring adequate administrative and governmental activity, a situation exacerbated by the necessity of giving top priority to military considerations rather than civil rule. The area held by the T'ai P'ing forces was never brought under order and could not serve as a powerful territorial base for the new state. Promised reforms were not carried out, and the disappointed peasantry refused to support the movement. Finally, the disciplined behavior of the rebel troops in the early period gave way to less orderly activities, with looting becoming more pronounced.

The T'ai P'ing movement was basically a peasant revolt that had accepted a foreign ideological doctrine, but without an adequate understanding of the West and its impact on China. The Westerners, for their part, became increasingly alarmed at the rebellion, which they considered to be a caricature of Christianity, since it produced grave uncertainties, turmoil, and a threat to the status quo in general. The foreigners therefore supported the old order, even though it would not compromise with Western ideological concepts at the time.

The Manchu regime was so decrepit that it could not crush this disorganized revolt until 1865. Moreover, the government's defense was spearheaded by Chinese officials and gentry who chose the lesser of two evils in upholding the foreign dynasty in Peking. Both the land reform program and the ideological tenets of the rebellion were repugnant to the scholars, bureaucrats, and landowners; military forces were willingly organized by these elements on a provisional basis in order to cope with the enemy. Such action was necessary because of the incompetence of Manchu garrison (banner) armies and their

Chinese militia, which often existed only on paper. Thus the government had to give considerable powers to Chinese viceroys and governors in the war areas. The newly organized combat forces, composed mainly of well-to-do peasants, carried on successful campaigns against the rebels. But this development cast an ominous shadow on the future strength of the Manchu and subsequent central governments. Decentralization, always an alarming reality in China, was now fortified by the great freedom and authority given to the viceroys. Still more important, these leaders were beginning to train armies whose loyalties were provincially oriented. The descent to "warlordism" was greatly facilitated by this turn of events.

There was also a small but efficient foreign-led force, the Ever-Victorious Army, which operated against the rebels in the Shanghai area. It was led by an American, Ward, and then by a Briton, General "Chinese" Gordon. While this army was of considerable help to the government, foreign interference was not directed solely against the rebels; for the French and British attacks in the north against the Manchu government from 1857 to 1860 culminated in the humiliating capture of Peking by the invaders. Had the T'ai P'ing forces been alert or capable, they might have swept victoriously northward against the discredited dynasty. Their failure can be traced to their own ineptitude and basic inferiority to the traditional political order. After 1863, the rebels were so badly mauled that the foreign-led army was disbanded and Chinese forces finished the war alone. Those T'ai P'ing leaders who escaped abroad continued to agitate for the revolution, which finally occurred after the turn of the century.

The Lull before the Storm (1865-1894)

The thirty years between the end of the rebellion and the Sino-Japanese war of 1894–1895 were tragic ones for China, even though they were relatively peaceful. Little was done to modernize China or prepare it to cope with dangers from abroad. By contrast, its major nemesis, Japan, used these very thirty years to overhaul its economic and political apparatus in preparation for defensive-offensive military activities. China wasted its last opportunity to lay the groundwork for a modern state that could meet the complex political and military requirements of the twentieth century.

China's scholar and official classes refused to appreciate the intense necessity of drastic change, at least materially and institutionally, if not in basic ideology and outlook on life. There were efforts at reform before 1894, but these were grossly inadequate in view of the needs of the time. Reformers had to struggle against powerful elements who argued that China could be saved if it dismissed and then ignored the foreigners, and returned to the old ways. The proponents of this policy were entrenched in the government, and thus presented a reverse picture of what occurred in Japan. There the reactionary forces were driven to an unsuccessful revolt against a government controlled by reformers, who kept forcing the pace toward modernization.

The spirit of Chinese resentment against the West was mirrored in the

Dowager Empress Tz'u Hsi, who was the real ruler of China during most of this period until her death in 1908. Her regency was perpetuated by the device of placing minors on the throne. This custom upset the Chinese, for they suspected Tz'u Hsi of acts of violence and, in her juggling the succession to the throne, of an irreverent attitude toward family rights. Her skill at the game of palace intrigue enabled her to recapture control of the throne in 1898, after one minor ruler came of age and undertook a short-lived reform program.

This strong-willed ruler had the support of the officials, who helped check the great rebellion and who remained loyal because of tradition and for fear of a chaotic alternative. Though the dowager empress understood Chinese literature and culture, she was also superstitious and miserly. Moreover, her misunderstanding of the West led her into many costly errors of decision. The educated classes supported her because they opposed any change in the empire's static social and philosophical foundations that might weaken their vested interests. They also regarded the West's use of force as crude and barbaric behavior, and considered its culture unworthy of emulation.

The bureaucracy, the intellectuals, and the throne itself placed formidable restrictions on the activity of reformers. For example, an educational mission of Chinese scholars studying in the United States (1872–1881) was terminated because the students were reported to have veered too far from Confucian principles. However, a few improvements were made in river navigation, and railroad construction was begun, though severely hampered by local resistance and prejudices. Telegraphic communications, modern coal-mining methods, and Western-style arsenals were introduced, with the arsenals receiving most attention, although even here interest slackened off after a while. Efforts that later proved inadequate were made to modernize the army and the navy. The navy was hurt by a diversion of funds to build the empress a marble palace, and its technically competent forces were riven with dissension and poor organization to the extent that the Southern Squadron sat out the Japanese war while the Northern Squadron was being mauled by the enemy's navy.

Also, a few light industries were launched in the Canton area and on Formosa. Activity was especially marked in the Wuhan cities (Wuchang, Hankow, and Hanyang) in the Yangtze Valley, where textile factories, the great Hanyehping iron and steel works, and other establishments were constructed. But without vigorous central direction and support China could not progress at an adequate rate. With a larger area and population than Japan's to manage, the Chinese had to move even more rapidly in order to obtain satisfactory results. Yet life went on basically very much the same in 1894 as it had before the Opium War of 1839—the government, the system of education, and the civil service examinations remained unchanged. The drift toward provincial autonomy continued, weakening the fabric of government even further. Provincial officials used the grave problem of adjustment to the outside world and the distressing floods, droughts, and locust plagues of the 1870's to strengthen their independence from the Peking regime.

China's intellectual response to the challenge of the West took several forms. The ultraconservatives desired to return to the old ways and adopt no Western innovations; they counted on a strong moral resurgence and adherence to traditional customs to carry the country through the crisis. This outlook lost a great deal of support as many faithful adherents of Confucianism came to feel that industrial and military techniques of the West had to be adopted as "armor" to protect the Confucian way of life. Naturally, they wanted to retain the basic ethical beliefs and social relationships as the foundations of Chinese culture. This attitude of compromise was most popular, but a school of thought even further to the left maintained that social change was also essential. Significantly, even these advocates adopted the traditional tactic of appealing to precedent. They argued that Confucius himself had been a reformer, and would have supported radical change at this time. A leader of this school of thought was K'ang Yu-wei. He sought sweeping social and political reforms, and developed ideas that played a vital role in the abortive reform effort of 1898.

In terms of domestic change the questions were, how far would reform have to be carried out, and to what extent would it come from above or through revolution? The low level of Manchu prestige and the rise of secret societies, especially in South China, did not augur well for the future of reform-from-above. In 1898, a young emperor came of age and made an effort to lead the reform movement; he was advised by K'ang Yu-wei and other reformers, who, it must be remembered, were a minority group in scholar-official circles. Unfortunately, the reform-reaction conflict came to hinge on the antagonism that the antiforeign, antireformist dowager empress harbored against the young ruler. His edicts, so mild in retrospect, were violently opposed when promulgated during the summer of 1898—the Hundred Days of reform. He envisaged reform in office holding, which angered the officials; revision of educational practices, to the dismay of the traditionalists; modification in the examination for government service; the fostering of railroad construction; and further reforms in the military service.

Tz'u Hsi, wiser and more cunning than the emperor and his sincere advisers, succeeded in regaining power. A military official, Yüan Shih-k'ai, for reasons never clarified, failed to carry out his emperor's orders to provide the palace with adequate security forces. This enabled the dowager empress to call on other military units, loyal to her, to execute her palace coup. The emperor's orders were rescinded, the reform movement was smashed, and progress toward change was temporarily halted.

Carving the Chinese Melon

The reform activity of 1898 was given considerable impetus by the disastrous war with Japan. The year 1898 also witnessed an intense foreign effort to carve out spheres of influence in China, following decades of nibbling at its territorial peripheries. During the Second Opium War Czarist Russia had succeeded in acquiring from China the territories north of the Amur (1858) and east of the

Ussuri River between Manchuria and the sea (1860). Later, the Russians won part of Ili on China's western frontier. The British detached Upper Burma, and the French conquered Indochina, two areas in which Chinese predominance had already disappeared. Portugal had long held the island of Macao, which it formally obtained in 1877.

These frontier losses made the Peking government determined to retain its suzerainty over Korea. However, the Japanese, who had not been political satellites of China, also claimed control over this land. A double claim of suzerainty also existed with regard to the Ryukyu Islands, but the issue had been decided in favor of the Japanese when the islands were incorporated into their kingdom by 1878. The immediate cause of the Sino-Japanese War lay in the intervention of these two powers in internal Korean politics, but the underlying issue was the collision of Japan's expansionist ambitions with China's endeavor to reassert and stabilize its prestige and power. Defeat in 1894–1895 at the hands of a barbaric island people, who had imitated China's culture and had been held in contempt, rocked the Chinese to their heels. Still worse, the war had a disintegrative effect on China's international position, in view of its display of inadequate military power. The foreign powers, amazed at China's incredible weakness in a war with "little" Japan, began moving in with halting, uncertain steps, to divide up the Chinese melon.

Once the scramble started, it was difficult to check, as each power feared that the others would deprive it of an adequate share. Specific leaseholds and spheres of influence less exactly defined were therefore obtained by the major powers. In the north, the Russians concluded a secret alliance with the Chinese against Japan and willingly loaned China money needed to pay its peace-treaty indemnity to Japan.[2] In return, Russia was given the right to construct a railroad across Manchuria—the Chinese Eastern Railway. In 1898 the territory forbidden to Japan in 1895—Dairen and Port Arthur at the tip of the Liaotung Peninsula in South Manchuria—was leased to Russia. The latter also won the right to build a railroad northward from Dairen to join the Chinese Eastern, and to construct a naval base at Port Arthur.

Shortly before Russia obtained these concessions in 1898, the Germans had seized the opportunity afforded by the murder of two German missionaries to obtain a lease at Kiaochow Bay on Shantung Peninsula. There the port of Tsingtao was built and plans were laid to run a railroad into the interior of the peninsula to Tsinan, as part of an ambitious project to exploit the region's resources.

Britain's center of interest was the Yangtze Valley. As the world's leading commercial and industrial power, England stood to gain from completely unrestricted economic activity. The Russian threat southward, with its "closed-door" policy, alarmed the British and led to considerable agitation in England for the "open door" (equality of economic opportunity) in China. However,

[2] For the Japanese perspective during this period, see Chapter 8, pages 211–216.

the Chinese seemed bent on making sweeping concessions to Russia in Manchuria in order to assure themselves of a counterweight to Japan. The British therefore became reconciled to having their own "unofficial" sphere in the Yangtze area, although they did establish a naval base to the north at Weihaiwei, to be held as long as the Russians were in Port Arthur.

Finally, the French asserted their interest in the three southern provinces of Yunnan, Kwangsi, and Kwangtung near their Indochinese possession, after obtaining a "favorable rectification" of the Chinese-Annam frontier. The French received priority rights in mining, railroad, and trading activities in the three Chinese provinces.

This activity created an ugly situation, for it appeared not too difficult for the powers to use their vague status in the allotted spheres to detach these areas politically from China. China agreed not to alienate land in a sphere of influence to a power other than the one which was dominant in that region. (The Japanese wanted Fukien Province, opposite their newly acquired island of Formosa, but the Chinese stated that they would not alienate this area to anyone, including Japan.) More concrete manifestations of the danger to China were the railway concession schemes, which could have served as the basis for territorial claims if conditions in China had deteriorated further. In this light, financial loans and economic assistance appeared to be other entering wedges.

It was at this juncture in 1899 that the first Open Door Note of United States Secretary of State Hay was circularized. The long-range significance of this pronouncement will be discussed elsewhere in an analysis of America's role in the Pacific drama. In this context, it may be observed that the note dealt only with equal economic opportunity; but even here spheres of interest were accepted and no opposition was voiced against preferential treatment to nationals in matters of investment capital. Hay merely asked the powers not to interfere with treaty ports or foreign vested interests within their spheres, and to avoid discrimination on the basis of nationality in questions of tariffs, harbor dues, and railroad rates.

Between 1899 and 1914 the foreign spheres of influence remained stabilized, save for a modification in the north resulting from the Japanese victory over Russia in 1904–1905. Yet American pressure cannot be given major credit for preserving the status quo, for the Hay note was given lukewarm reception at best, and was ignored more often than observed. By this time even the British proponents of the Open Door no longer believed that this objective was attainable. The answer lay in good part in the balance of foreign power in China. The Chinese seemed to be playing the game of "divide and *not* be conquered" successfully, even at the cost of yielding spheres. That the Chinese did not relish simply handing them out was indicated by their refusal to grant one to Italy at Chekiang in 1899. Then, too, the mounting tension in Europe was beginning to have its effect at this juncture; in time, the intra-European struggles were to diminish the West's political power and influence in the Orient almost to the vanishing point.

The uneasy balance of forces in Europe before 1914 was reflected in the nervous equilibrium that prevailed in China. Japan was a powerful force in the Far East but was unable to act until the First World War presented an opportune occasion; meanwhile it was content to hold the gains earned in checking the expansionist Russian forces. The Chinese scene, therefore, was one in which tension was high between 1900 and 1914, but China was fortunate enough to be confronted by a disunited pack of wolves.

The greatest threat to China during this era occurred at the time of the violent antiforeign Boxer "Rebellion" in 1900. The uprising resulted from an attempt by the ultraconservative forces to drive out foreign ideas and destroy the foreign concession program. Although not inspired by Tz'u Hsi, it certainly received her encouragement and support and so cannot be considered a rebellion against the state. Spearheaded by fanatical antiforeign societies and backed by many officials and some militia forces, the uprisings broke out in the northeast—Shantung (until suppressed by Yüan Shih-k'ai), Chilhi, Shansi, Manchuria, and Inner Mongolia. Foreign rail construction, missionary work, and leaseholds were most prominent in these areas.

The center of the crisis was Peking, where foreign legations and religious houses were besieged until relieved by an international force that marched to the rescue. Many Christian Chinese were saved in this locale, but others were massacred elsewhere in the northeastern region. The great viceroys in other provinces kept the situation under control, since they realized the danger that would follow if the violence spread. On the other hand, they insisted that foreign forces stay out of their sectors, that the affair be treated as a rebellion, and that the imperial family was not to be penalized. The Westerners felt they had no alternative and so accepted the fiction of a rebellion.

Various humiliations were imposed on the Chinese, including the razing of forts on the river at Tientsin, in order to clear the route to Peking, the maintenance of foreign troops along the Tientsin-Peking Railway, and the levying of a large indemnity. The Western attitude, that of conquerors, further angered the Chinese. The uprising gave the powers an excuse to tighten controls over their spheres of influence, and for a moment raised the specter of partition. Among the factors that prevented such serious consequences was the balance of forces noted above, supplemented by an American circular in 1900 that upheld the administrative entity and territorial integrity of China.

The Russians took advantage of the confusion to occupy all Manchuria, a move which led to the struggle over Korea and eventual war with Japan four years later. The moderate attitude of the United States was underscored by a decision to use its portion of the indemnity to finance Chinese student missions to America. This won for the Americans an esteemed place in Chinese eyes, apart from and above other foreigners.

The dowager empress, unaffectionately called "Old Buddha," was able to ride out the storm. The lesson was clearly grasped: China had to modernize itself if it was to rise above the level of impotence. The argument was clinched by the humiliating inability to prevent a war between Russia and Japan from taking place on the very homeland of the Manchus. Finally, the Treaty of Portsmouth was made without Chinese participation; moreover, it involved the transfer of rights in Manchuria from one foreign power to another. China's acquiescence was obtained by Japan later in the Treaty of Peking of December, 1905. This was the first of a series of efforts to widen the scope of Japan's legal rights in China. The treaty provided for China's acceptance of the transfer of Russian holdings to Japan, opened more towns in Manchuria to foreign residence, and permitted Japan to build rail lines connecting its Korean holdings with the newly won South Manchurian (Changchun–Port Arthur) Railway. Japan later claimed that this treaty included secret Chinese promises, such as an agreement not to build lines to compete with the South Manchurian Railway, which gave Japan special privileges in the area of Manchuria. Alleged Chinese violations of these agreements served as pretexts for Japanese military activity after 1930.

Failure of Belated Reform

The pressure of wars and the exchange of notes among the foreign barbarians arranging to "respect" Chinese integrity aroused the Manchus to make efforts at reform. It was a case of "too little and too late," for the foreigners were now pressing heavily on China. Tz'u Hsi and her more capable viceroys were in their late years, and no adequate administrative successors arose to tide over the delicate transferral of power in the offing. The change in China thus came late, and was introduced grudgingly by a passing regime in the name of a dying dynasty.

The reform effort in effect touched off a tremendous political revolution, behind which lay a deep transformation of China's ethical concepts, social structure, and economic activity. The basic ingredients in the great revolution that has shaken the Chinese world can be said to include the sudden unmooring of political institutions, the impact of Western ideas on Chinese thought and custom, the terrible catalyst that was Japanese militarism, and the attempts to transform the means of production. Changes in each of these facets of life, once begun, seriously affected the course of development in the others. Take, for example, the Western emphasis on modern industrial methods and the need for efficiency in both business and industry. What of the traditional concept that the family comes first, even if it means a corrupted bureaucracy or an inefficient business? Extended emphasis on efficiency would reduce obligations to the family and so contribute to an atomistic, individualistic type of society; but by removing the family as a center of loyalty, the culture brings the individual, shorn of traditional loyalties, more directly into contact with the state. That communism would also favor such a modification in the fundamentals of Confucianism is all too clear.

Ironically, the Manchu reform effort that sparked one of the greatest upheavals of this century was an attempt to emulate the conservative achievement of Meiji Japan. There was no intention to yield any important power to a democratic government, since the people were to have only the right of being consulted. The basic Chinese social structure and political philosophy were to be maintained, even as Japan's new rulers modernized their country and guided all reform efforts while preserving and strengthening the basic elements of the social structure they held dear. In a reversal of tradition, China had become the imitator but was to fail miserably in this novel role. The Chinese government lacked the vigorous and far-sighted leadership required to control the country, minimize violence, and institute the changes deemed necessary. Once the traditional rulers lost control over events, and once traditional institutions likewise became discredited, China had to grope for new leadership and a new institutional pattern and philosophy of rule under most trying domestic and international conditions. Even with a favorable environment, this adjustment would have been an extremely painful endeavor; given the prevailing conditions, a cataclysm was almost inevitable.

The reforms instituted by Tz'u Hsi were more drastic than those of 1898. The most successful was to curtail the production and importation of opium, the consumption of which was sharply reduced after 1900. The army, though not the navy, underwent considerable reorganization, with General Yüan Shih-k'ai the leading modernizer. This military careerist was a symbol of the changing times, for he rose to prominence despite the low esteem in which his profession was traditionally held. Yüan developed a modern army that owed its primary allegiance to him; such "personal" military forces were henceforth to be important sources of power to those seeking control of the government. The military reorganization program therefore became an unstabilizing factor rather than a contribution to greater government security. Such fractionalization of loyalty was to break down to the warlord level before the central government could again assert its authority. In 1907 a Board of War was supposed to take command of the various forces trained and led by provincial officials. But these armies were not capable or loyal enough to protect China from foreign attack or even, as events proved, to save the Manchu dynasty itself.

The attempt to modernize education was of great ideological importance. The formal civil service examination system based on the Confucian classics was abolished in 1905, and a Ministry of Education was set up to direct the establishment of governmental schools that would stress modern subjects. Actually, there was no strong guidance from the center, and little was accomplished in the provinces, where lack of money, inertia, and incomprehension were supplemented by the natural resistance to such a sweeping change. A fundamental reform like this clearly could not be achieved immediately or simply by means of a mere decree. Some progress was made as new schools were created, although unfamiliarity with the novel subject matter on the part of teachers and pupils alike made for an uneven rate of development. Supplementary efforts were made to have Chinese students study abroad. Whatever the eventual benefit of these educational programs, the net immediate effect was to make the students politically conscious; those who returned from abroad were quick to agitate for reform and to develop a revolutionary state of mind.

It may be that this educational reform, with its implicit denial that Confucianism was the core of learning, contributed further to the rejection of the very principles that gave the Chinese a sense of social order. Although Confucianism was taught to the young through other social institutions, like the family, these reforms could not help undermining the stability of the old sociopolitical system.

A direct path to revolution can be traced from the political reforms cautiously proposed after 1900. At that time the major ideological import from the West was the democratic form of government, at least in its surface manifestations. Italy had become a limited monarchy, and Germany, copied by Japan, had introduced the superficial apparatus of representative government in its new constitution. Even Czarist Russia was to acquire a legislature of some sort during the decade after 1900. China was also to try its hand at making a similar adjustment to the times. There is no telling the extent to which this global effort to establish some sort of representative government would have progressed had it not been so sharply and tragically curtailed by the great wars that began in 1914.

Some of the Chinese political and institutional customs that have already been noted contained elements contributing to democracy within their framework. For example, at the local level, there was a high degree of autonomy in decision making possessed by families, clans, guilds, and village leaders. On the national level, the ruler was accountable for his actions, in that he had to merit his office and rule virtuously to retain his mandate. Although no peaceful electoral process existed, there was an acceptable violent way to oust a ruler who had aroused popular discontent. This method permitted a crude display of the popular will, since a manifestation of the mandate of heaven was the degree of popular support and lack of internal strife that a regime enjoyed. Moreover, there was a healthy assumption that no line of rule was inviolate. Finally, the civil service system and the "aristocracy of merit" gave the society a more egalitarian tone than did a government that awarded high social stations simply on the basis of birth.

Nevertheless, the central factor remained China's complete inexperience with the concept of peaceful democratic procedures and modern, liberal constitutional systems. Authority prevailed even at the village and family level; the leaders made the decisions and there was little stress on aiding the individual to work things out for himself. No machinery existed through which an individual could peacefully and effectively express his will, and, if there had been, it would have taken many years for him to learn how to utilize it. For such self-expression, both peace and stability were required, plus an active, competent government to train the populace and carry out the transitional reforms essential to the growth of popular rule. In addition, the governing officials would have had to learn to yield power and be willing to compete for control of the state under the democratic process.

It is obvious that such requirements are rarely fulfilled, and it should come as no surprise that China's political leaders lacked the skill and determination to carry out such a monumental assignment. The Chinese were doubly unfortunate in that they received no aid or comfort from the democratic powers on a significant and meaningful scale, either in the shape of technical help to carry out their political reforms, or in the form of assistance in the cruel and exacting task of warding off the Japanese.

The incapacity of the Manchus made it certain that they would be unable to lead and control the reform movement. As matters developed, no other dynasty could arise, although the attempt was made to continue this traditional device of transferring power. Political reform was begun in 1906, when the government decided to bring about a constitutional form of government in slow stages. Progressive stages were necessary, since there was educating to be done among the populace and the officials as well. After some study of foreign systems, the Japanese model was chosen because it would enable the aristocratic reformers to hold the levers of power and maintain direction over the modernization of the state.

The training process was to be in the form of provincial assemblies whose members would gain the experience needed for adequate participation in a later *consultative* national assembly. These assemblies, which were dignified debating societies, were to convene in 1909, and a constitution was to be adopted by the national assembly in 1917. The procedure and time sequence were roughly the same as those used by the Japanese a generation earlier. Perhaps this loss of a generation was the most significant cause of the failure that followed, for during this interim Manchu prestige collapsed under foreign blows, while the pressure for reform reached new heights.

In 1908, both Tz'u Hsi and the emperor, who had been kept prisoner for a decade, died. There followed the convening of provincial assemblies in 1909 under the reactionary and weak regent, Prince Ch'un. These assemblies agitated for the transferral of more power to the provincial governments and demanded that the national assembly be called soon. The government responded by accelerating its reform program; the national assembly convened in 1910 in order to push through reforms in three years, with a constitution to be provided in 1913. While the government was thus on the defensive and under unexpected verbal assaults from these varied assemblies, it suddenly became involved in a jurisdictional dispute with the provinces over the control of railway finances. It was accused of abjectly surrendering China's rights to foreign financial interests. An incident then touched off a rebellion in 1911 that ended in the overthrow of the dynasty and the unexpected birth of the Chinese Republic. The fate of this novel political entity occupied the center of attention during the next generation. The tragic and turbulent life of this republic must be examined in scrupulous detail, for it held a primary place on the stage of world politics even during this dramatic century.

5 *The Chinese Revolution:*

Nationalist Phase

The uprising of 1911 was at first a spontaneous assertion of regional autonomy, a series of unplanned and uncoordinated revolts throughout southern China. The participants did not at first realize that they were delivering the final blow to a political culture so seriously undermined that its brittle structure was ready to snap. In the ensuing chaos, the old order seemed to dissolve on all fronts. The Confucian ethic had been challenged by Western ideals, as the civil service reform of 1905 indicated. Now the historic political system associated with this concept disintegrated and further weakened the confidence in old beliefs.

Disillusionment with the existing ideology left the country completely at a loss, without institutional or ideological signposts to replace the old. The tasks confronting revolutionary China therefore assumed a scope without precedent. The nation desperately needed a modern, efficient government that could protect and enhance the people's well-being. Its international position had deteriorated to the point where national security could be recovered only by radical political changes. In the economic sphere the attractive Western creed of the good life on earth seemed to depend on proper political organization. The Chinese avidly sought a modern ideology that would give them a rational and inspirational guide in establishing a government best suited to achieve these ambitions. This intellectual quest was doubly important in a land where scholars, officials, and now students—the nation's intellectuals—held a vital position in the cultural and political scheme of things.

Yet old traditions could not be shaken off overnight in the search for a new order. A painful effort was made to link the new with basic Chinese traditions. The revolution, as it unfolded, became a bitter struggle for power, and the question of territorial control and governmental stability often seemed uppermost in mind. Yet the ideological issue of what kind of China was to emerge constantly guided the rival contestants. The Kuomintang and the Communists eventually emerged as the major contestants for power. The outcome of their struggle was in good part determined by the manner in which they sought to remold Chinese society.

This search for survival and order became an almost insuperable task because of China's incredibly vulnerable international situation. Western political ideologies—such as nationalism, democracy, and communism—had a profound effect on China, but their ultimate fate was intimately connected with the attitudes of nations representing these beliefs. There was rarely any constructive intervention by the West to foster the growth of democracy or to strengthen its political roots in a new environment. There was little or no positive assistance in the form of financial or technical aid, or guidance in the practical operations of a free political society. At best, Westerners remained indifferent, or looked on the effort at modernization as a hopelessly difficult task for this disintegrating Oriental state.

Still worse, China was not left alone to work out its own destiny; thus the internal course of the revolution became heavily dependent on the policies of the great powers. The West was distrusted for its sphere-of-influence policy in the late imperial period and its persistent retention of the hated unequal treaties. It also gained the unfortunate reputation of being openly hostile to democratic native revolutionaries, favoring instead old-fashioned "strong men." But it was the rapacious policy of Japan after 1936 that really played havoc with the delicate internal balance of Chinese affairs and fatally undercut the achievements of the nationalist revolutionaries; the sledgehammer blows of the implacable Japanese invaders, bent on carving an empire in China, were primary catalysts of the stunning events of the late 1940's.

In 1949, the revolution was climaxed by the sweeping victory of communism on the Chinese mainland and the retreat of the former rulers, the Nationalist Kuomintang, to the island of Formosa. Up to this point, it had appeared that China was moving, however hesitantly, in the direction of Western principles of nationalism and democracy. China had also broadened its cultural and economic connections with the West until the Japanese invasion of 1937. With the success of communism, it can be argued, this temporary trend has been reversed, as China reverted to type—the land is closed to the West, and its historic western frontiers in the heart of Asia are again its main roads to foreign contacts. Ideologically, it is again an authoritarian community with a new universalist creed, communism, replacing the old, and with the scholar-official class now believers in the orthodoxy of Marxism.

Much of this parallel is striking, and superficial similarities between the Confucian tradition and communism may have helped determine the outcome of the revolution. Yet the success of the Communists was not inevitable; in fact, it astounded the world. Central emphasis must be placed on the *change* in China's political and social structures, the role and scope of government, and economic philosophy and activity, as well as the pattern of foreign policy. Since communism is a radically new authoritarian mold, we must concern ourselves with the revolution and the competing forces that strove to master it. The total collapse of the old order cleared away the traditional obstacles to political power. Yet the very grandeur of the opportunity open to those who could direct the revolution made the prize of power so valuable.

A Decade of Turmoil (1911–1920)

The Revolution Unfolds

The decade following the fall of the Manchu dynasty faithfully reflected the interplay of competing elements: revolutionary nationalists, reactionaries, military leaders, and warlords. To these were added the Bolshevik Revolution, the creation of a Chinese Communist party; in the background was mounting unrest among peasants suffering from the dislocation of civil war and the exactions of regional warlords.

The revolution was touched off by an accidental explosion in a bomb factory located in the Russian concession in Hankow. The garrison at Wuchang across the Yangtze River, already implicated in revolutionary activity, then rebelled on October 10 ("Double Ten"), 1911, and compelled the commander, Colonel Li Yüan-hung, to lead them. The insurrection spread rapidly over south China in an uncoordinated manner, with the massacre of hapless Manchu garrisons providing the major form of violence. Representatives of various provincial governments under rebel control then met in Shanghai and Hankow to proclaim a republic and issue a new constitution on December 2, 1911. Political leadership was exercised by a Cantonese group, whose authority Colonel Li agreed to recognize. Canton had long been a center of republican and separatist intrigue. The republican leader-in-exile, Sun Yat-sen, hurried back from the United States, arriving later in December.

A Christian by faith, Sun had studied medicine abroad in Hawaii and Hong Kong. As he matured, Sun became a sharp critic of the Manchu dynasty and of the traditions that kept China so weak. His prime objective became the establishment of a modern republican nation-state, and he strove to develop a progressive philosophy on which to base a renovated, democratic community. Many of his concepts and aspirations were mirrored in the secret societies and organizations in south China with which he was associated after 1894. These nationalist bodies were constantly regrouping; the name of one of these, the National People's party (Kuomintang) of 1912–1914 was finally assumed by Sun's group. There were other reformists and rebels who opposed Sun because of regional or ideological differences, among whom a leading figure was Liang Ch'i-ch'ao. However, as the acknowledged leader of the revolutionary tradition, Sun was elected provisional president of the Republic at Nanking at the end of 1911 and took office January 1, 1912.

But the revolutionary movement still lacked coherent organization and the people as a whole were not ready for so radical a concept as republicanism, which even Sun came to espouse only after long years in exile. North of the Yangtze, the amorphous rebellion lacked fervent support, and revolts in Shantung, Chilhi, and Shensi provinces were crushed in the name of the imperial authority. In fact, a determined regime might have subdued this disorganized rebellion, but the Manchu dynasty proved incapable of decisive action. It was obliged to recall to active service its best general, Yüan Shih-k'ai, who had been dismissed from office in 1908. His support was so essential that Yüan was able to gain the position of premier, with broad powers, before taking the field to preserve the dynasty. Even then, he moved slowly, with the limited objective of securing only the northern provinces.

The Manchu position was further weakened when the government reconvened the National Assembly in October, 1911, just after the Wuchang revolt. The Assembly demanded, and was promised, immediate constitutional reform. However, the incapacity of the monarchy was clear to all, and the six-year-old boy emperor abdicated in February, 1912; in return, he retained his palace, an annuity, and his title. The ominous sequel was the inability of the Republic to muster the leadership, power, or popular support to fill this vacuum. Sun Yat-sen was a great revolutionary leader whose intellectual and inspirational achievements were of a high order, but he lacked the organizing genius the immediate situation required. In the decade of bitter disappointmnt that followed for the Nationalists, Sun proved a consistently poor political tactician.

The transition from monarchy to republic, then, was relatively peaceful, but it was carried through with a smoothness that gave rise to false hopes. For the sake of harmony and stability, Sun yielded his office as provisional president to Yüan Shih-k'ai in March, 1912, in the belief that he would thus consolidate the revolutionary cause. This amalgam of traditionalism and militarism with revolutionary nationalism was an alliance of incompatible forces. Yüan was playing his own game of double-crossing all other elements: he had had the imperial decree of abdication authorize him to organize a republic, and he had assured the revolutionaries that the republic would be maintained if he were chosen its president. In fact, he despised the revolutionary leaders and their cause, and saw only an easy path to power. However, the revolutionary group had promulgated a democratic Provisional Constitution of 1912 as a counterbalance to hold Yüan in check. It restricted the president's executive power by sharing it with a premier and giving the legislature important restrictive authority. Yüan and the northern reactionary militarists dominated the executive, while the southern revolutionary-liberal group controlled the new parliament, which was convoked in April, 1913. The Kuomintang was the strongest party in the legislature, and hoped to maintain its position of revolutionary leadership.

As a governmental document the constitution suffered from several technical imperfections, but these were completely overshadowed by the basic difficulty that the entire system of parliamentary democracy was too novel to be appreciated by the country as a whole. A few decades of underground revolutionary agitation and some abortive Manchu reforms provided a totally inadequate basis for self-rule.

The Influence of Foreign Affairs

The main potential sources of support for the central government lay outside its constitutional framework: the military power of Yüan and his supporters and the appeal of revolutionary ideals. But this unstable central government did not control the whole country. Provincial military leaders in the outlying regions had been steadily augmenting their own power; with the end of the empire they were freed from obligations to obey the government. Yüan's cynical behavior toward the monarchy could serve to rationalize a refusal to transfer allegiance to the new regime. The new government was also plagued by near-bankruptcy and desperately needed foreign financial aid. The foreign powers had organized an international banking consortium to reduce their own rivalries and deal with China's needs in an orderly manner. They did not wish to aid the dying Manchu regime; nor were they impressed by China's democratic reforms, whose sweeping extremes suggested chaos rather than stability. Like the other powers, the Japanese government concluded that China could not be reorganized along modern lines; it therefore abetted revolutionary efforts in the hope of weakening the country further. There were some Japanese, it is true, who sincerely aided Sun Yat-sen during his exile in the island kingdom (1913–1917) when the fortunes of revolution turned against him; these idealists actually strove for a China and an Asia free of Western domination. The official Japanese position, though, was much narrower in outlook and sought to take advantage of China's troubles.

Still, the emergence of Yüan gave the Western powers the "strong man" who seemed able to maintain China's political traditions, although in modern garb, and stabilize the situation. He was granted the required financial aid, with the salt tax as security, in return for a promise not to seek tighter control over outlying territories. He was also obliged to respect foreign spheres of influence, especially in Manchuria. This proved a costly concession, for Tibet, Outer Mongolia, and the province of Sinkiang were already in danger of being lost.

The Mongols had recently become apprehensive over the migration of Chinese settlers to the north and west. This latest phase of the centuries-old population movement took the form of rapid expansion into Manchuria at the turn of the century, when the Manchus ended the policy of keeping their homeland an imperial reserve. The removal of restrictions led the people of Shantung and other northern provinces to colonize the area. To the northwest, Chinese agrarian settlers were moving into Mongolia, threatening to outnumber the Mongols and endangering the grazing land these nomadic cattle raisers required for a livelihood. The restive Mongols in the outlying sectors declared their independence in December, 1911. They were encouraged in their separatist inclinations by Russia, which sought to bring this politically weak region within its own orbit. When China tried to reassert its authority, Russia recognized the new state in 1912. The next year, Yüan Shih-k'ai agreed to consider Outer Mongolia as autonomous but not independent, a status ratified by the three parties concerned in 1915. The Chinese have as yet been unable to reverse this trend.

Tibet had been declared a neutral buffer by the British and Russians in their settlement of 1907. This area, conquered in the early days of Manchu expansion, also took advantage of the revolution to oust a Chinese garrison and declare its independence. The British thwarted Yüan's efforts to reassert Chinese authority, and again a compromise was reached by the three interested parties. Western Tibet was recognized as autonomous, with a Chinese resident and a small force stationed at Lhasa, and Chinese authority was retained in the east. However, China never ratified this treaty of 1914; though the political situation faithfully reflected this arrangement, China awaited favorable international developments to reassert its legal claim to sovereign authority.

The Fall of Yüan Shih-k'ai

The consortium loan of 1913 was regarded with dismay by the Kuomintang and other revolutionary elements. Joint foreign operations aroused suspicions of further intervention, and strict alien control over governmental expenditures supported this fear. The loan also gave Yüan financial strength independent of the new constitutional order that, added to his formidable military power, placed him in a position of dominance. Impelled by a combination of personal and patriotic motives, Yüan attempted to turn the revolutionary effort toward a constitutional monarchy somewhat along the lines of the abortive reform of 1898. He believed that this would satisfy China's need for imperial continuity and progressive reform without the excesses of incomprehensible republicanism. In this scheme he was opposed by the regional militarists, republicans, and the Japanese who fought any strong Chinese state.

Yüan approached the problem of political and military integration under central rule cautiously because his military force was essentially a northern army. Elsewhere provincial forces were independent and, in the general disorder, military control meant political rule. He sought to make allies of the southern militarists by appointing these commanders to the posts of provincial governors, eventually hoping to establish a unified civil and military administration. Yet there was no way to bring these local warlords under central authority, for Yüan lacked the strength required for such a drastic step. There was, in effect, no modern Chinese state that could boast of an administrative service, organized along national lines and directed from Peking. What little apparatus the old empire possessed began to deteriorate after 1911.

Under these difficult circumstances, Yüan's effort to dominate the central government weakened the Peking regime further. He clashed with the first National Assembly in 1913 and crushed a revolt in the southern provinces undertaken by the Kuomintang that summer. In 1914 he suspended the surviving rump Assembly, rejected a liberal draft for a permanent constitution, and put through his own reform. This version established a presidential dictatorship reflecting Yüan's dominant position; as Sun had fled to Japan in 1913, the revolutionary coalition was shattered. But Yüan overreached himself by proclaiming a constitutional monarchy in December, 1915. The response was open rebellion in the south, and he was promptly compelled to renounce this ambition. Five southern provinces successfully declared their independence of Peking in April, 1916, and, when Yüan died two months later, the political disunity that threatened the country became a devastating reality.

Yüan's failure may be attributed in part to his own unsavory record of double-dealing, the implacable hostility to monarchism among revolutionaries, the rising tide of regional power at the center's expense, and the fact that he had no ideological appeal which could rally popular support around his own banner. In addition, the international situation worked against his government, already weakened by earlier territorial concessions. The European war of 1914 offered China a great opportunity, considered in long-range terms, for it signified the recession of the Western tide and the destruction of Western power on French and Russian battlefields. But, in the immediate sense, it opened the field to Japan and placed China, desperately trying to preserve itself against Japan's financial and political-military encroachments, in mortal danger. Yüan's government had to suffer the indignity of a Japanese-German war in Shantung during 1914. The following year, despite stubborn diplomatic resistance, China had to accept Tokyo's Twenty-one Demands. Even in modified form, this agreement would have made China into a puppet state of Japan. By 1916, Yüan's foreign policy was a failure insofar as Japan held Germany's Shantung concession, gained priority investment rights in Fukien Province, and had its Kwantung leasehold and other rights in Manchuria extended to 99 years.

Government Impotence and Warlord Rule

The decade after Yüan's death in 1916 saw central political authority collapse in the north as well as the south. The Peking regime soon became the impotent puppet of whichever warlord in the region happened to be in momentary control. A constitutional struggle within this shadow government led to a new break in the revolutionary camp, and Sun Yat-sen and his followers established a rival government at Canton in 1917. They too were at the mercy of local militarists and exercised no firm control over any sizable portion of South China. Peking remained China's capital and, to the despair of the southern revolutionaries, continued to receive diplomatic recognition and financial aid from abroad. Yet its government proved ideologically and politically bankrupt and was bypassed by the main stream of events.

In 1917 the new president was the moderate revolutionary leader Li Yüan-hung. He reconvened the parliament, which had been disbanded in 1914, and restored the Provisional Constitution of 1912. But the government was again split by hostility between the premier, Tuan Ch'i-jui, a northern militarist of the Anhwei Clique, and the Kuomintang dominated parliament. To establish his authority, Tuan sought to use the issue of whether China should enter the First World War. For China, belligerency would bring an Allied loan and reinforce the prestige of the Peking regime; but there was little popular support for the move, and Tuan's adamant position led President Li to dismiss him. Tuan's military allies then declared their provinces independent. Li was compelled to call in still another warlord for support, but made the error of turning to a monarchist, Chang Hsun, who had the parliament dissolved and then restored Emperor P'u Yi in July, 1917. Tuan and his allies quickly swept the monarchists out of Peking. As premier, he declared war on Germany and turned to the interminable task of redrafting a parliamentary constitution. By 1917, however, the Peking government's dignity had been destroyed, with Sun's regime established in Canton under the banner of the original revolution.

China was reduced to near-chaos, with powerless rival governments at the extremes and the country, in fact, ruled by provincial warlords, or *tuchuns*. This situation had a disastrous effect on the welfare of the peasantry. Under the Manchus there had been at least a semblance of order and security; taxes or squeeze could be pushed only so far by officials. Excessive exploitation would lead to unrest, which would precipitate an investigation and punishment for the offender. Now there was no central check on local and regional military rulers who used their power for gain. The old civil servants had no choice except to cooperate in the collection and sharing of "revenue." The militarists also had to feed their armies, usually composed of bankrupt peasants who also sought to profit from plunder. The leaders could amass wealth by taxing the peasantry to the limit and, should the tide of fortune turn against them, then retire to the protective shelter of a foreign concession in a large city. The absence of central authority was also an inducement for these ill-trained marauding armies to engage in fighting that, however desultory, caused further destruction. Still worse, there was no one to maintain the rudimentary maintenance services required for flood control, irrigation, and transportation. Even local marketing systems broke down, fields fell into disrepair, and the plight of the peasantry in the decade after 1915 became so wretched that a truly revolutionary atmosphere was developing in the countryside.

Even under these conditions, however, the peasants did not look with favor on the revolution of 1911, for it was to them ideologically meaningless and proved materially unrewarding. Taxes were not removed with the new order, as many farmers naively expected, and conditions continued to deteriorate. The peasants were ripe for another change—one which would bring order to the countryside, restore efficient government, and establish just economic relations between the peasant and his landlords and tax collectors.

The era of the *tuchuns* is dated from 1917 to 1927, but it lasted to an important extent beyond this period. Though there is some justification in arguing that the warlords have been used as a convenient scapegoat to be blamed for all of China's failures and inadequacies, *tuchun* rule was destructive to the social order. They can be considered a consequence of the times, given the collapse of central authority and the loss of a unifying political ideal. They actually were provincial rulers who maintained their territorially limited authority during a period of national convulsion. Some warlords held fast to the territories they controlled and ruled with some degree of order and stability. Yet even in the few good examples, they rarely exerted competent or reformist rule to meet the needs of the times. All in all, their lack of constructive efforts and their contribution to the disintegration of the old order made the later process of rebuilding much more difficult. The shock and dislocation of this period did much to intensify the radical nature of the Chinese revolution.

Effects of the First World War

China's main contribution to the Allied war effort—large-scale coolie labor in France—was made before 1917; its declaration of war was of little military consequence. It is difficult to draw a balance sheet on the value of belligerency to China. Boxer indemnity payments were temporarily suspended, Germany and Austria-Hungary lost their concessions in Tientsin and Hankow, and China participated in the Allied control of Russian Manchurian railways after the Bolshevik Revolution of 1917. Against these gains was the ascendancy of Japanese influence over the Peking regime of Tuan Ch'i-jui. Japan placed military advisers there, gained arms contracts, and granted loans that could not be repaid and for which public utilities, mineral resources, and taxes were set aside as security. While this appeared to give Japan the influence it sought in 1915, the island empire at this time did not seek absolute political control. With the end of the German war in 1918, American and European pressure could be relied on to hold Japan in check, and China itself was represented at the peace conference with the other victorious Allies.

The rival Chinese regimes were able to agree on a single delegation to the Paris Peace Conference, where China's position was admirably stated, with good propaganda effect. The foreign affairs of the country in general were competently handled in comparison with the other functions of government. However, China could not reassert its rule over Shantung—its main objective at Paris. Only at Washington in 1922 did China regain control over the province, in return for acknowledging Japanese economic privileges. This settlement reflected Japan's moderate attitude during the 1920's, a policy that gave China a breathing spell in which to deal with its acute political crisis.

One important consequence of the Paris Conference was China's decision to walk out—to refuse to sign the Treaty of Versailles when it could not recover Shantung. The Chinese representatives there, especially C. T. Wang and Wellington Koo, presented a stirring case for a modern progressive China, a movement that was still not a governing force back home. Their performance and the allied "betrayal" aroused Chinese national spirit and led to antiforeign demonstrations in 1919, in which the students played a leading role. Their volatile and extremist attitude reflected the new dynamic and explosive mood of the country. Because China was a weak military power, its action took the negative form of a boycott against Japanese goods. This phenomenon, called the May Fourth Movement, reflected the opening of a new era. The ideology behind this demonstration, the willingness of the business community to make economic sacrifices, and the ability of the people to cooperate for political action on such a grand scale revealed the rise of popular feelings and the growth of national political cohesion. China was ready to support a modern government, not necessarily democratic, that would satisfy national aspirations and give the country order and dignity in domestic and international affairs.

The Triumph of the Kuomintang

The Struggle for Order

This quest was made more urgent by the rapid deterioration of political conditions. The ranks of the provincial armies were swelled by peasants who could not make ends meet during this chaotic era. These poorly trained, undisciplined forces appeared to the farmers to be merely armed bandits rather than the military component of a provincial government. Such devices as collecting twenty years' "revenue in advance" emphasized this point. The Peking government, meanwhile, deteriorated completely with the expulsion of Tuan by the Manchurian warlord, Chang Tso-lin, in 1920. Thereafter control varied among Chang, Tuan, Wu P'ei-fu, and Fêng Yü-hsiang, the so-called Christian general who kept his troops better disciplined than most. There was one attempt by Wu to restore Li Yüan-hung and revive the government of 1913, but this effort of 1923 to restore the prestige of the revolution proved a failure.

The political response to China's needs came from the south, where Sun Yat-sen and his followers in Canton remained the most attractive and dynamic force in Chinese politics. Yet their political fortunes also sank to a low ebb, for the revolutionaries remained without an effective army and at the mercy of the southern warlords of Kwangtung and Kwangsi. The local rulers of the three southwestern provinces of Szechuan, Yunnan, and Kweichow remained free of effective government control, a position they maintained with some success even after the Kuomintang rose to power. The years 1918–1923 were marked by such political instability that Sun had to flee from Canton twice, in 1919 and 1922. It was in 1922 at Shanghai that Sun met Adolf Joffe, the Soviet diplomat, and under Russian guidance revised his tactics for gaining power.

Despite repeated defeats, Sun remained his country's most popular revolutionary leader. The Chinese saw in him the embodiment of their belief that a strong central government could be re-established, and that it would be rooted in ethical principles and a modern ideology. Many warlords saw in Sun and his teachings the answer to the political vacuum in China and often gave him aid and protection. It is a political fiction to argue that there was an unbroken thread of continuity between the revolutionary government of 1912 and the Kuomintang effort of the 1920's, but Sun Yat-sen still personified the revolution and its quest for a democratic and modern China.

Sun considered himself a democrat imbued with Western concepts of government, although in developing his plan for a new Chinese structure he was to modify these liberal tenets considerably. Elected president of the government in Canton in 1921, he continuously appealed to the United States and other Western powers for the financial and technical support needed to carry out his plans for an orderly government conceived along modern democratic lines. He was unsuccessful in this approach because of American isolationism, Western disbelief in the chances for this effort to succeed, and a general air of bemusement with the chaotic affairs in China. This very attitude had led the West first to accept and support Yüan Shih-k'ai and then to recognize the Peking regime instead of Sun's revolutionary efforts. In desperation, Sun turned to the new government of Soviet Russia for assistance, with consequences that were most significant in ideology as well as political tactics. In this political context it was inevitable that a Chinese Communist party should develop into a major political force. Furthermore, Sun became more favorably inclined toward Soviet Russia, though not toward communism, in his last years. But it was also inevitable that under Bolshevik tutalege the Kuomintang would take on an organizational structure and ideological perspective considerably different from that usually conceived of in conventional democratic circles. The course of the revolution might have been different had the West taken a more active and sympathetic interest in China's internal affairs.

The Value of Soviet Assistance

The motivation behind the decision of the new Russian government to aid the Kuomintang is a complex amalgam of Communist ideology, international political calculations, and domestic Soviet political considerations. For most of the 1920's it became a steadfast Soviet objective to develop a stable nationalist government in China. In Marxian terms, this would drive the Europeans out of the Chinese "semicolonial" markets and undermine their vulnerable economics at home; moreover, it would set China on the path to modernization and ultimately to a later proletarian revolution. Without precluding the chances of a communist uprising in the indeterminate future, the Soviet government ordered the new Chinese Communist party to join forces with the Kuomintang in order to achieve a unified government under Kuomintang control. The discipline of international communism, exercised through the Communist International, was already sufficient to compel grudging obedience from the protesting Chinese Communists. They proceeded to work with the Kuomintang, but not all joined Sun's party, and those who did entered only as "individuals" who still owed primary allegiance to the Communist party. The Chinese

Communists were determined to gain control of the revolution at the earliest possible moment, and used this period of induced cooperation to infiltrate and undermine the nationalist movement.

Ironically, the Russians did such an efficient job of overhauling the Kuomintang organization and tactical political program that the Chinese Communists found this goal beyond their reach. The basis of Russian aid was an agreement reached in January, 1923, between Sun and the Soviet envoy Joffe, stating that Soviet communism was not suitable for China and that the immediate objective was the realization of political unity and independence. A Russian mission under Michael Borodin was then dispatched to create an efficient government structure based on the Soviet model, centering about a powerful party machine. Sun's old party was in a state of disintegration, and many members of the Cantonese government did not even belong to the Kuomintang. Thus the party was not even tightly linked to the political power that the weak southern government possessed. Jockeying for authority within the party was almost like operating in a political vacuum, for the Kuomintang had only slight contact with the mass of the people. Its efforts to build a military machine were only partially successful, since the army was not given intensive indoctrination and differed little in comportment or competence from that of nearby warlords.

Borodin and his staff of military and political advisers set to work to tighten the organization and effectiveness of the Kuomintang, while simultaneously broadening its base of popular support. A new Kuomintang constitution based the party's structure on a network of local cells that were to attract members, further the revolution, and maintain party discipline. At a higher level there were district and provincial organizations. Ultimate authority theoretically lay with the National Party Congress, which established policy at its annual meeting. The permanent central bodies, the Central Executive Committee (C.E.C.) and a Supervisory Committee, were to carry out Congress directives. Actually, the C.E.C. became the center of authority and responsibility, for the democratic ideal of control exercised from below proved impracticable at this time. Russian influence, then, fostered the creation of a single party as the sole repository of power, with control exercised by the central directors of this political machine. However, the Kuomintang itself did not become a monolithic, tightly-knit organization like its Communist prototype in Moscow. Sun still espoused a democratic philosophy and he prided himself on being able to manage a coalition of widely divergent views within the reorganized Kuomintang framework. These included right-wing nationalists whose main interest lay in political nationalism and a strong state, moderate liberals, the Left Kuomintang, which espoused social and economic reform, and the Communist party. Despite Sun's efforts, fractionalism could not be avoided, and a crisis became inevitable on his death in 1925.

Under Borodin's guidance in 1923–1925, the party's operational activities were also revamped. Military formations were reorganized and the troops became indoctrinated with nationalist ideology. The army thus became a loyal and efficient arm of the government, though here too the differences in the Kuomintang top command pointed to future difficulties. The Whampoa Military Academy was established under the vigorous leadership of Chiang Kai-shek. Considerable success was attained in this effort to develop a modern and loyal officer corps that would not become involved in political intrigue.

In the field of active political propaganda, Kuomintang and Communist agents moved northward, preaching the gospels of nationalism and economic reform. Unions were started in central and southern China with a claimed membership of 12,000,000 peasants and 2,500,000 workers by 1926–1927. The peasantry especially was eager for a government that would bring positive reforms in credit and land tenure, as the agitators promised. Student and youth groups fervently participated in this revolutionary effort, and their ideals were then primarily nationalist rather than communist. Canton's field agents were given their training both in China and at the new Sun Yat-sen University in Moscow after 1925. The Chinese Communists, seeing the success of reformist propaganda in the country, felt that they could capture the revolution in alliance with the Left Kuomintang and eventually create a purely communist regime. But the Russians continued to pursue their tactic of supporting the nationalist objectives first and therefore held their impatient Chinese colleagues in check.

The Revolution Triumphs; The Coalition Collapses

The power of the revolutionary Canton government continued to grow as the Overseas Chinese, long supporters of Sun Yat-sen, increased their financial aid. Soldiers from warlord armies deserted to the Kuomintang, and the southern and central provinces became ripe for revolutionary conquest. Early in 1925 Sun made a futile effort to reach some agreement with the Peking regime, but at this critical juncture he died while in the northern capital. One of his last speeches, delivered en route at Shanghai, stressed Pan-Asian sentiment and a strong pro-Soviet diplomatic orientation. With Sun's death, his political limitations as tactician and administrator were quickly forgotten and he was enshrined and revered as the great founder of the modern Chinese state. For more than a generation his person and principles were the dominant symbols of the Chinese Republic. A mausoleum was constructed at Nanking after the nationalist triumph, and his portrait was circulated and honored all over China.

His passing threw into sharp focus the deep cleavages within the Canton coalition government. On one side were the Communists and the Left Kuomintang, whose influence grew as revolutionary fervor mounted in the provinces and as agitation among peasants and workers, preparatory to military campaigns, brought appreciable results. The Left Kuomintang, however, was not under Communist control; in fact, it dominated many unions in its own right. On the other side were the more moderate leaders, the nationalists and most of the high military command. Chiang Kai-shek emerged as the leader of these elements, as he was already suspicious of Communist motives. However, the year he had spent in Moscow for training and his association with the revolutionary cause led the conservative business community to dub him a "Red general."

Before undertaking the drive northward, the revolutionary leaders reorganized their government by establishing an Administrative Council as the directing agency of the executive departments, and a Political Council composed of Kuomintang leaders. Wang Ching-wei, a left-wing follower of Sun Yat-sen, was elected the party's official leader, but in March, 1926, Chiang struck at the left, arresting some of its leaders and causing Wang to flee in exile. Chiang and Borodin then reached a temporary compromise in which the Russian was retained as Chiang's adviser, with Chiang becoming acting party leader and chairman of the important Standing Committee of the Kuomintang's Central Executive Committee. This uneasy balance could not stand the strain of the military successes of 1926–1927.

The campaign itself was preceded by intensive nationalist agitation against the foreign powers, especially Britain. The effect of the agitation against unequal treaty privileges was most acutely felt on the coastal and river-port cities, when the foreign powers proved reluctant to make any substantial concessions. Deep antiforeign sentiment became a powerful aspect of the Kuomintang creed, expressed even two decades later in Chiang's political tract, *China's Destiny*. The crisis came to a head in May, 1925, when a crowd agitated against working conditions in a Japanese cotton mill in Shanghai's International Settlement; a British officer ordered the police to fire, and nine persons were killed. This episode climaxed a long series of incidents and strikes and led to an infuriated Chinese reaction. Commercial activity in the great city of Shanghai was brought to a standstill all summer, and outbreaks against the foreigners spread along the coast and up the Yangtze as far inland as Chungking. In Canton, British goods were boycotted, and the nearby British island of Hong Kong was paralyzed by a general strike. The right-wing Kuomintang accounted for many fervent supporters of this effort in the revolutionary capital region.

After considerable negotiation, an international convention was held in Peking in 1926, but no serious modifications of the unequal treaties were forthcoming. The Chinese became convinced that the Peking regime was helpless and that the Western countries were hostile. This attitude strengthened the position of the revolutionaries and enhanced the prestige of the Soviet Union, which had already renounced extraterritoriality and other "Czarist imperial privileges." In the summer of 1926, the Kuomintang launched its great northern expedition under Chiang's over-all direction. The nationalist armies quickly rolled to the Yangtze region of Central China over the old route of the T'ai P'ings, for these disciplined forces had overwhelming popular support. By the end of 1926, the inland industrial centers of Hankow and Wuchang were taken; Nanking and Shanghai to the east appeared ready to fall. Half of China came under Kuomintang control, and the revolutionary armies were poised to continue northward.

At this point the left revolutionaries made a bid for power. The armies that had taken Hankow, 600 miles up the Yangtze, were under their influence. The Wuhan region (Hankow, Wuchang and Hanyang) was a leading industrial center whose workers had been successfully unionized; and support in the peasant hinterland had been gained through certain agricultural reforms. The left wing succeeded in moving the government from Canton to Hankow and, encouraged by its success in this friendly environment, deprived Chiang Kai-shek of his committee chairmanship. The reason given was his refusal to leave his armies to the east and attend a Central Executive Committee session called at Hankow. Instead, Chiang took Nanking on March 24, 1927, and two days later occupied Shanghai with only 3,000 troops. There had been a Communist-led strike and insurrection in Shanghai in February which had been suppressed by a local commander. When Chiang arrived, the Communists did not offer resistance, for they had not yet reorganized their forces. More significantly, the Comintern still adhered to the policy of maintaining the revolutionary coalition at all costs. Only after success was achieved would a break be permitted, at which time the right wing was to be discarded like a "squeezed-out lemon." The Shanghai insurrectionists were therefore ordered to hide their arms and not oppose Chiang.

But the nationalist leader was misunderstood and underestimated by all. He effected a coup in April that led to the arrest and execution of almost all Shanghai's Red leaders, crushing the potential resistance movement thoroughly. Many moderates in the Kuomintang were apprehensive over the rising Communist influence in the Hankow government and threw their support to Chiang. Conservative leaders and the business element in Shanghai were also disturbed. They overcame what doubts they still harbored about this revolutionary general and gave Chiang much needed financial and political support. He then established his own Kuomintang regime at Nanking. When the anti-Russian Peking regime raided the Soviet Embassy and revealed captured documents that bared communist duplicity, the Hankow regime was doomed. Borodin and his fellow advisers then left Hankow and returned to Moscow in mid-1927. Mme Sun Yat-sen returned with them, claiming that her husband's revolutionary concepts were betrayed.

The Kuomintang Position

The Kuomintang regime had only one decade of relative peace, 1927–1937, in which to establish a stable political order. The tasks confronting it were enormous, and what accomplishments it could boast were seriously undermined during the frightful Japanese invasion and war of 1937–1945.

The Nanking government in 1927 was the leading element among several competitors for power; its task was to attain complete dominance and sovereignty over China Proper. This meant subordinating influential provincial leaders to Nanking and reducing the Communist rebels, now battered and defeated, but still a force in Kiangsi and nearby provinces. A parallel requirement was the creation of a modern administrative system, already begun at Canton, out of the rubble of a disintegrated imperial service and fifteen years of political strife. In addition, the country was in great need of economic reforms that would ameliorate and repair the damage caused during the recent period of turmoil. Industrialization and a higher standard of living were related objectives that brought in their train further problems of social and cultural dislocations. Finally, there was the vexing issue of treaty relations with the foreign powers, especially Japan.

Some of these objectives proved to be literally beyond China's grasp at this time; the others could not be attained simultaneously, and some order of priority had to be established. Chiang and his government eventually failed in their program, but it should be noted at the outset that the difficulties were so enormous that probably only political genius of the first magnitude could have succeeded. The Nationalist level of competence, while on a high plane in contrast to previous performances, was not of this caliber; nor, as events were to prove, was it equal to that of the Chinese Communists under the leadership of Mao Tse-tung. In all justice, however, the tragic history of the Chiang regime must be soberly evaluated in the light of its own ideology and the notable successes, as well as the drawbacks, that marked its career.

Kuomintang Ideological Dilemmas

The Nationalist government was fashioned after the teachings of Sun Yat-sen, since it was led by his disciples. These principles in turn were modified by the lessons of political experience and by Chiang Kai-shek's views on the tasks and purposes of government. Late in life Sun formulated his Three Principles of the People (*San Min Chu I*)—nationalism, democracy, and the people's livelihood—which formed the essence of his appeal and the revolutionary legacy to which the Kuomintang was committed. This was a major source of Kuomintang power, for it gave the regime an ethic and dignity that were respected by the intellectuals. This philosophy was a synthesis of Sun's earlier political beliefs and the lessons he drew from the bitter failure to transform politics in the decade after 1912. None was easy to apply, and in the end they proved beyond the Kuomintang's grasp.

Greatest success was achieved with regard to *nationalism*, the very heart of the Kuomintang cause. It is the most universally appealing of Western political doctrines and could not fail to win a response from the beleaguered Chinese. Sun recognized it as the basis of the political cohesion enjoyed by the powerful and wealthy Western states and he sought to infuse this ideology into the Chinese scene in order to accelerate his country's revival. It was directed against the Manchus and the imperialist powers, with great emphasis placed on the significance of Chinese traditions and ethical values. Sun also gave his argument a racist coloration by claiming that his nation was unique in that it embraced an entire race.

However, the creation of a nation-state directed by a central government remained a formidable task. Even within China Proper, the Kuomintang never enjoyed the legal monopoly of violence that all sovereign states claim as their right. The most important challenges were posed by the Communists, the Japanese, and the autonomous provincial governors. A deeper issue was the persistence of traditional loyalties in such lesser units as the family, the village, and the region. The transfer of allegiance to a distant central government was thus a slow but essential process. Though Sun's contribution was of great significance, the reorientation of values, despite great strides made by 1937, was far from completed. The Communist regime after 1949 was able to make more rapid progress, largely because it built on earlier Nationalist efforts.

This type of nationalist appeal created a delicate issue with regard to ethnically different peoples along China's perimeter. Sun wanted these elements—Tibetans, Mongols, Moslems—to be loyal to the Chinese state, and he promised to recognize their cultural rights. Many of these groups pressed for a federal system which would recognize their autonomy, but Sun would not go this far for fear that, in the light of China's weakness, this solution would hasten political disintegration. The Nationalist regime at Nanking tried to assert its authority over these regions with a vigor that showed little respect for the desires of these minority groups. Since this policy could not be enforced, it led the Tibetans and Mongols to reassert their independence, Outer Mongolia becoming a full-fledged Soviet satellite.

The *people's livelihood* was akin to socialism in that it turned to the state to foster improved living conditions and provide all people with their basic needs. Though impressed by the writings of Karl Marx, Sun was not a Marxist; the class struggle and the economic interpretation of history were contrary to his beliefs. He advocated vigorous social reforms, and a mixed economy of state enterprise and private capitalism. He did favor nationalization of transportation and communications, development of consumer cooperatives, improved working conditions, and expanded educational facilities. On the whole, though, his ideas on this topic of people's livelihood seem somewhat vague, for a good part of his written work was lost. Yet this principle was placed on a level with the other two, and its application was a source of grave concern during the Kuomintang era.

The Kuomintang proved incapable of fostering the social and economic reforms that could have cemented its hold over the peasantry and perhaps given it the political strength required to achieve its nationalist ambitions. Policies like agrarian reform were associated with the Left Kuomintang and the bitter legacy of 1927, which weakened this platform within the party. Many Kuomintang leaders came from the old official and gentry classes and were not really interested in a drastic implementation of Sun's economic plank.

Then, too, as in the case of democracy, the regime became obsessed with creating an orderly, stable government before undertaking any program that meant sweeping changes and uncertainty. Reformers, with equal sincerity, pointed out that failure to act played into the Communists' hands, giving them the initiative and the ability to take credit for what improvement eventually took place. The government failed to carry through an intensive reform program in such vital matters as rent control, better terms for rural credit, improved storage and marketing facilities, technical aid in the form of better seed and planting techniques, and the more popular issue of land ownership. Even when protective legislation was enacted, as in the rent law establishing the landlord's share at 37.5 per cent, it was honored more in the breach than in practice. As a result, the peasantry gauged that this government, despite its revolutionary and nationalist heritage, was not its ally. The disaffection and disinterest which followed were of vital importance as the three-way struggle for China—Nationalist, Communist, and Japanese—became more violent.

The principle of *democracy* provided an issue of equal significance. It was the basis of a prolonged debate over the degree and timing of constitutional reform in China. Sun considered democracy another key to the successful modernization of China, since he came of age during its golden era of development in all major states. However, his own bitter experiences, the obvious need to harmonize these new concepts with Chinese traditions, and the effects of the First World War and its aftermath all contributed to a sharp modification of his views. Chinese democracy, as envisaged by Sun, was therefore a peculiar mixture of views. It incorporated the people's four rights—suffrage, initiative, referendum, and recall—so reminiscent of Western reform movements around 1900. But, while accepting ultimate popular control, Sun did not believe that the mass of the people understood questions of public policy, let alone the complex operations of state affairs. He therefore sought to protect the state from exposure to direct public pressure and to keep the bureaucratic machinery free from popular influence. The concept of an elite ruling class was a major element in this philosophy, but the people retained the right to vote on keeping or changing its leaders. In this limited interpretation of democracy, the state was not a mere instrument of the people. Rather, it was a separate institution above all others, with a justification of its own.

For its part, the government was to enjoy five powers over the people—a system dutifully established by the Nationalists after 1927. Three of these branches (Yuan) were executive, legislative, and judicial; the other two, examination and control, were rooted in Chinese tradition. Examination was a modern version of the historic system of recruitment for the civil service, now to be organized along Western lines. Control, which came to include the power of impeachment, auditing, and criticism of officials, was related to the Manchu Dynasty Censorate—an agency that policed and criticized the administrative machinery. The Censorate had sought to keep the public service efficient, but it had also served to exercise political control over government servants. The Nationalists found it difficult to maintain a competent, imaginative administration that was not directly exposed to popular pressures. The examinaion and control branches were therefore designed to keep governmental operations at a high level of efficiency. On the whole, Sun's concept of government retained the traditional pattern of a self-perpetuating bureaucracy, save that now it was to be governed and changed by popular vote instead of an emperor exercising the mandate of heaven.

Tutelary Rule

Sun realized that this indirect democracy and complex administrative system could be reached only by gradual stages. First there was the period of revolution and military command, with the objective of controlling all China. Then the country was to enter on a period of tutelage under Kuomintang dictatorship. This regime was to construct a sound economic foundation, perfect the bureaucracy, and prepare the people for their future role in public affairs. When conditions warranted, the final stage of democracy, as defined by Sun, was to begin.

The Kuomintang has been criticized for its retention of controls during a long period of tutelary rule, and for the limited type of democracy that it promised at the end of this era. Yet as Chiang viewed his mandate, he was to perfect the new order and then move from dictatorship to democracy. On the other hand, it is quite difficult though not impossible (as the example of modern Turkey shows) for a party to maintain a dictatorship for a long time and still adhere to the principles of eventual democratization. The concept of tutelage has its own built-in tensions: the government is obliged to yield power in the future and yet does not create the conditions under which a responsible opposition can flourish. The easy way out lay in perpetuation of Kuomintang power, especially since the country lacked a meaningful democratic tradition and possessed a party-government structure organized by the Russians along authoritarian lines. Then, too, Chiang himself was a perfectionist who honestly believed that a modern state structure had to be completed before Kuomintang paternal ist rule could be ended.

Chiang's regime was soon caught in a vicious circle: democracy had to wait until the state was perfected, but the Kuomintang suffered a loss in its sense of dedication and capacity to govern because the realization of its ideals seemed so distant. The obligation of tutelage placed a tremendous burden on the party, adding new tasks of administrative and political education to the difficult duty of developing a modern state. The Kuomintang thus set itself an almost impossible standard by which the whole country could judge its performance and decide whether it earned the mandate to rule. By 1937, despite serious defects in the area of economic reform and democratization, the government was still in control of the situation and had enjoyed moderate success in creating a modern political system within the framework of the revolutionary credo. It may well have maintained its equilibrium and persisted in its slow but progressive work had the Japanese invasion not occurred.

Kuomintang Rule (1927–1937)

Organization of the State

The government made its greatest progress in establishing a pre-democratic constitutional order and developing an adequate system of public administration. To begin with, Organic Laws were formulated in 1927 and a provisional constitution adopted in 1931. Thus the transitional tutelary period began even before military unity was achieved, for the Communists, warlords, and Japanese continued to plague the Nanking regime's efforts to unify the country.

The Constitution of 1931, though considered provisional, lasted until the post-1945 era. The Kuomintang was identified in this basic document as different from and above all other parties. Its resolutions were given the force of law by the constitution, and the party could change or cancel a law by this method—a most graphic implementation of the concept of tutelary dictatorship. The official party agencies armed with this legal power were to be the Party Congress and the Central Executive Committee, but the Congress met only five times between 1925 and 1945.

The Central Executive Committee, with over 100 members, was large enough to reflect shifts of policy and power within the Kuomintang. It therefore served as the key point of authority in Nationalist China. Also, a Central Control Committee was created to maintain honesty, efficiency, and obedience within the party. However, as was symbolic of Kuomintang rule, the committee proved inadequate in this supervisory and disciplinary assignment. The party agency which saw to it that the Kuomintang's will was effectively exercised over the government was the Central Political Council, reorganized under the pressure of war in 1938 as the Supreme National Defense Council. Its tasks were to decide basic principles of legislation, carry through governmental policy, and appoint or dismiss governmental agencies.

The formal structure of government was headed by a Council of State; its chairman was the titular head of the Chinese state, but this position lacked importance until assumed by Chiang in 1943. There were five branches of government, as prescribed by Sun Yat-sen, but the only important one was the Executive Yuan. It can be likened to a cabinet only in the sense that it was the executive and administrative center of the new government's modern bureaucracy. It lacked the political power of policy direction enjoyed by Western parliamentary cabinets. The Executive Yuan could not dissolve itself or challenge the superior Kuomintang agencies that directed its operations. It had thirteen ministries and, when in full session, was the unifying agency for all

NATIONAL GOVERNMENT OF CHINA (1941): STATE COUNCIL

Military Affairs Commission	President of the National Government				
	Executive Yuan	Judicial Yuan	Examination Yuan	Control Yuan	Legislative Yuan
Generalissimo General Staff Armed Forces	Ministries of Foreign Affairs Interior Finance Economic Affairs Social Affairs Education Communications Agriculture and Forestry Commissions on Overseas Chinese Affairs Mongolian and Tibetan Affairs National Relief	Ministry of Justice Supreme Court Administrative Court	Examination Commission Ministry of Personnel	Ministry of Audit Office of Regional Control Commissions	

SOURCE: Based on a chart by P. M. A. Linebarger, *The China of Chiang Kai-shek* (Boston: World Peace Foundation, 1941).

governmental activity. Chiang also presided over this body during the war. Since the Executive Yuan issued ordinances, the Legislative Yuan was reduced to an organ that merely drafted and codified administrative law. It also had the more important task of drawing up a permanent democratic constitution. The Judicial Yuan was the staff agency for prosecuting and judiciary offices, and worked on standardizing judicial procedures and interpretations. A really independent judiciary, free of party control, could not be expected at this stage.

It should be noted that the Ministry of War was not placed under the Executive Yuan. A Military Affairs Commission was created in the 1920's to direct the great northern campaigns. It was supposed to be absorbed by a war ministry, but the reverse occurred. When war began again in 1937, the Commission grew in size and importance and was in effect a sixth Yuan, with the highest post held by Chiang.

Despite his direction of all the key party and state agencies, Chiang was not an all-powerful dictator. Like Sun before him, he held key positons in order to harmonize and coordinate the different branches of his administration and to settle policy differences that arose. Despite the five-yuan concept, three centers of authority emerged—the military, the party, and the bureaucracy. There was no clear-cut line of distinction because many leaders in the other two fields were party members and the Kuomintang theoretically was supreme. Yet the government developed into a loose oligarchy of army, governmental, and party officials who, moreover, shared power with independent military

125

chiefs and nonofficial professional or economic leaders in the community at large. Chiang served as the final authority and balancer who made this cumbersome machine operate.

Within this complex framework, a workable administrative system was created. The periods of rule at Canton and briefly at Hankow in the 1920's gave the Nationalists practical experience. In the decade after 1927, field services as well as a central bureaucratic apparatus were fashioned, so that China reached a level of organization which was at least comparable to that of other states. An intellectual renaissance, called the New Tide, was featured by vigorous student activity. A standard vernacular form of writing was developed through the initiative of Hu Shih, a modern intellectual. Chinese students had been studying Western techniques for a sufficient length of time to give the country at least a skeletal force of modern administrators. This intellectual and bureaucratic growth formed a firm basis for the development of a modern state.

A major Kuomintang achievement was the creation of a modern treasury and fiscal system. The government sought to regularize a tax program, expand transport facilities, and create the conditions required to encourage industrialization and business skills. To make progress in this direction, the Nanking regime felt it essential to regain tariff autonomy, as foreign-controlled ceilings on duties had curtailed revenue and hampered efforts to protect and develop native industries. Nanking's relations with foreign powers continued on an uneasy footing, with nationalist oratory directed against the treaty powers. Antiforeign strikes and demonstrations had occurred at Hankow in 1926, continuing the pattern set the previous year in Canton; and when Nanking fell in 1927, violence against foreigners was checked only by fire from American and British gunboats. However, when the new regime was recognized in 1927, the foreign powers continued their negotiations with Chiang. Starting with the United States, China reached a series of agreements in 1928–1930, whereby it regained tariff autonomy. China could not, however, eliminate extraterritoriality because its judicial reforms were considered inadequate. Nanking then unilaterally abrogated this concession but agreed to negotiate; a compromise was reached whereby the foreign powers admitted the end of such rights in principle but retained them in practice for more than a decade.

Economic Development

To encourage the growth of a modern economy the Kuomintang tried to improve China's primitive communications network and system of distribution. Telegraphic lines, railways, highways, and air transportation were developed. The government also implemented Sun's concept of a mixed economy by fostering state enterprises, an activity intensified after 1937 by the needs of war. The process of industrialization had been under way only since the 1890's and had followed the common pattern of early emphasis on consumer industries, such as cotton textiles, flour mills, and cigarette factories. Light engineering works to service these plants and other factories related to foreign trade also developed. By 1937 domestic and Japanese capital were supplanting Western investments in this field.

In all, Chinese mainland industry, at its prewar peak, had about 3 million employees and produced a bit under 10 per cent of the national output. But these figures include the Manchurian industrial complex, which was under Japanese direction in the 1930's. In China Proper, development did not move at the energetic rate sought and despite government efforts, remained concentrated in the coastal regions without making adequate uses of resources in the interior. Presumably, the Western legal system and modern institutions developed in the Treaty Ports attracted investment at these centers. Since both Western and Chinese capital were invested for maximum profit, emphasis was placed on machinery that could use China's cheap labor advantageously, and not with long-range economic development in mind. There was also a tendency for native and foreign enterprises to compete with each other rather than enter different fields or seek different locales. In any event, though industry did grow, it remained outside the main stream of Chinese economic life. It was adjusted to foreign trade, and was too small to serve as a basis for a thorough program of modernization.

No revolutionary changes occurred in the field of agriculture, but conditions improved substantially simply because a stable order had been established. The government undertook some work on the dangerously run-down flood control and irrigation systems which, though modest by absolute standards, led to a peak in farm production in 1936. Peak yields (in thousand million tons) were: rice—48,000; wheat—24,000; and soybeans—10,000 in mainland China. The economic burden of overpopulation, inefficient small farms, and old farming methods kept the peasantry at the edge of disaster. The Japanese invasion increased peasant disaffection, for it destroyed public works and reduced productivity. It also led to intensified exploitation by landlords, without governmental restraint. Production fell precipitously between 1937 and 1945. It is no coincidence that the lack of agrarian reforms was matched by a rapid decline of Kuomintang popularity in the countryside. The government could not escape being charged with responsibility for soil erosion, widespread sharecropping, usury, and landlord despotism. Though these agrarian evils existed long before the Kuomintang era, the regime was eventually judged by its failure to ease the mounting burden of China's peasant masses.

Military Organization and Control

The theme of partial success characterized the military reform program. The disciplined core of the Nationalist army that had swept northward in 1926–1927 again proved its superiority in victorious campaigns against warlords in 1930–1931. It symbolized the regime's position as the strongest power in China, but it nevertheless lacked the strength to bring all of China under Nationalist political control. The government's power was centered on Nanking and the surrounding provinces, but it diminished in strength and authority as it radiated out toward the peripheral regions. It may eventually have mastered the problem of bringing the distant warlords to heel and disposing of the Communist menace had not the Japanese threat hung over its head.

The army improved steadily as its officer corps, trained in Kuomintang military academies, developed into a sizable nucleus of loyal, competent men. Many units were conditioned by German military specialists who had been with the army for some time. As the government grew in stature, the army likewise gained prestige, for its pay, allowances, and mode of conduct became comparable with foreign forces. It became partially mechanized, had China's only air force, and acquired some modern artillery. It thereby became a modern field army, not up to the Japanese level, but superior to any other Chinese force in recent times. Indoctrination of the troops ensured political loyalty. This professional force remained the dominant military component in China as long as there was peace.

Unfortunately, the slow political-military process of integrating the provincial forces with the national army required more time than the regime was to have. In the 1930's, the *tuchuns* were willing to link their forces to the national army because the latter's competence, equipment, and pay scale all improved markedly. They were obliged to accept the government's plans to establish an integrated command, but this had not been realized by 1937. The warlord armies therefore were still semi-independent and poorly prepared for the tasks that lay ahead. They reduced the nation's capacity for combat and were unreliable politically, so that Chiang's freedom of action against the Communists and Japanese was seriously restricted.

The Communists proved difficult to control even though the coup of 1927 seriously crippled the party, which then had about 50,000 members. Yet within two years, this outlawed movement established its own state in the rugged terrain of Kiangsi and portions of the neighboring provinces of Anhwei and Hunan. A "soviet" state, with a program of sweeping agrarian reform, was established there with its own government, ideology, and army. The army had a hard professional core, augmented by guerilla and peasant militia formations, but as a whole it could not compare with the Nanking army and was essentially a defensive force. The balance of power between the two sides was graphically illustrated by the unsuccessful annual campaigns of extermination of 1930–1934 undertaken by Chiang. The larger government forces, trained for field operations, lacked the flexibility required to match the Red Army's guerilla tactics. In each campaign, the invaders approached deep into communist territory in separate columns. When widely separated and fully extended, one of the columns would be successfully attacked by the defenders, who concentrated for a quick assault. The Kuomintang forces then retreated, losing men and equipment.

Finally, in 1934, a strategic siege operation was launched on the Kiangsi redoubt under German guidance, compelling the Communists to evacuate. Again the Red forces proved elusive, for they slipped through the encircling cordon, disengaged themselves militarily, and began a long retreat to the northwest. This painful Long March of 10,000 miles brought them to Shensi Province and the surrounding regions; in 1936 they placed their capital at Yenan and re-established a soviet state. This record reveals the tremendous resiliency of the Communist party and the military inadequacies of the Nationalists, which were later to prove fatal. But it also emphasized the dominance of the Nationalists, for their enemies had to stay in inaccessible regions with second-rate field or guerilla armies.

The Issue of Political Reform

By 1937 constitutional reform was being vociferously advocated by both the democratic and communist critics of the Kuomintang regime. They disagreed with both the timing and the scope of the changes planned, arguing that Chiang was moving too slowly and did not plan a sufficiently broad reform program. Defenders of the regime's structure argued that it passed the test of pragmatic operations; in fact, it continued to do so under the burden of war after 1937. Admittedly, the organization of the government was awkward and elaborate, but it proved far sounder than the half dozen constitutional systems advanced by democratic reformers after 1911. Here at least there was no unbridgeable gap between the legal sources of authority and the holders of real political power.

Still, opposition mounted against the provisional constitution of 1931, which was supposed to last only five years. For one thing, factional struggles for power within the government produced considerable friction and loss of strength. Clashes over personality are inevitable, but in this self-styled dictatorship they took the form of "palace intrigues" and proved difficult to direct into constructive channels. The dilemma of operating a government along Moscow-inspired theory and lines of organization while preparing the country for democratic reform became more apparent daily. With an elitist concept of government efficiency and a mistrust of popular rule, the Kuomintang left its task of tutoring the country in democratic practices largely unfulfilled.

As the discrepancy between ideology and reality became pronounced, the Kuomintang lost much of its original revolutionary fire and purpose. The model administration that was to precede reform became more difficult to attain because adequate economic and constitutional reforms were not undertaken. This state of affairs in turn reduced the popularity of the government further and made change more difficult. Chiang Kai-shek appreciated this problem and, as a Christian with a strong Confucian background, tried to apply the precept of rule by example. Theoretically this fitted admirably into the Kuomintang tutelary scheme. Chiang fostered a New Life Movement in 1934 to revive the moral fiber of the bureaucracy by stressing the inherent human basis of proper behavior. The movement sought to inculcate the principles of ethics, justice, integrity, and honor in official life. But this vigorous effort at national reconstruction could not long be sustained without fundamental reforms. Failure to inspire the nation in this way made Chiang's effort appear somewhat quixotic. A revolutionary situation continued to exist, and with all its dangerous energy uncontrolled, it was now threatening to bypass the Kuomintang regime.

It is still possible to argue, however, that the government had the flexibility and will to meet popular demands. For example, Chiang proposed a constitutional reform in 1936. However modest its scope, this draft of May 5 ("Double Five"), 1936, was a literal interpretation of Sun's ideas on democracy as well as a Kuomintang effort to adhere to its pledge to end tutelary rule. Popular control was to be exercised through a National Congress that was to meet only once every three years. As against this limited type of representative participation, there was to be a strong president with broad powers in military and foreign affairs and in the field of personnel control. He was to be elected for six years by the National Congress and be responsible only to it. At a lower level, the five yuan were to have powers roughly similar to that of the past, although there now seemed to be enough leeway for some type of parliamentary responsibility to develop between the Executive and Legislative Yuan. In any event, a National Constituent Congress to approve this mild reform was not called before 1937, after which war and bombings led to several postponements.

Instead, a People's Political Council was created in 1938 to give the government a deliberative body reflecting varying political opinions. It was well attended in its early years and was a center of genuinely useful discussions. It had power to deliberate, present proposals to the government, demand reports from the Executive Yuan, and interpellate state officials. The major participating groups were the Kuomintang and its supporters, the Youth party, the National Socialists, a popular front group of intellectuals and National Salvationists, and the Communists.[1] This step toward popular government was not adequately exploited, for, as Chiang told the People's Political Council in 1939, the people were still unprepared for democratic rule, even of the type proposed in the 1936 Constitution. He pointed out that the country was accustomed to anarchy, disorganization, and the pursuit of particularist rather than national interests. Chiang concluded that China had to win the war, recover its territory, and restore order before reform could be undertaken. According to Chiang, democracy could work only when there was respect for law and when freedom did not conflict with the public welfare.

Proponents of reform agreed that self-rule meant some dislocation but held that a democratic framework would compensate for this by giving the government a firm base of popular support. They challenged the limited nature of the 1936 proposals and were especially opposed to the provision limiting political privileges and civil rights "in accordance with the law." The people of China were pictured as eager for self-government and better prepared than in 1911, because the spirit of nationalism had fostered a new sense of group action and

[1] Though outlawed, the Communists were allowed to participate in this body following agreements reached with the government in 1936–1937.

political awareness. Antiforeign boycotts, economic and political strikes, and the formation of peasant associations and labor unions had all occurred since the Manchus fell. Reform, it was argued, would revitalize China by tapping reservoirs of loyalty and energy and so make the government more vigorous and efficient in pursuing its war effort. To Chiang, however, popular rule and democracy were gambles to be entered upon cautiously in time of peace; they seemed completely out of place during a war for survival.

The Japanese Onslaught

The rise of a strong government in China posed a threat to Japan's special economic position in 1930. Thus the assault on Manchuria in 1931 could be considered an effort to preserve control over a sector that was coming under Nanking's influence. The tangled story of military expansionism, economic need, and domestic Japanese politics leading to the assault of 1937 is recounted elsewhere.[2] This eventuality was the one thing Chiang had desperately sought to avoid, for he correctly reasoned that a war with Japan before the country was politically or militarily prepared would be a disaster for China and the Kuomintang.

Attempts at Political Unity

This was the rationale for the cautious policy adopted in 1931–1932 by Chiang Kai-shek when Japan conquered Manchuria and adjacent Jehol Province. These were areas where effective Kuomintang rule had not yet been established. In order to appease the Japanese Kwantung army, he accepted a cease-fire, known as the Tangku Truce, in May, 1933, which established a demilitarized zone a bit north of Peking and Tientsin. China maintained a correct and conciliatory attitude in this sensitive region, especially in Hopei Province. Chiang adhered to this tactic despite strong nationalist opposition from students and other pressure groups. He was determined to protect his northern front by diplomacy while endeavoring to crush the Kiangsi Soviet. Campaigns against the Communists were continued after the Long March, as the Nationalists blockaded and prepared to assault the Red Army in Shensi Province during 1936.

Japanese threats to North China intensified in 1935–1936 and included a so-called popular Mongolian revolt, which was crushed by the Nationalist forces. Despite governmental suppression, popular demonstrations occurred in the major Chinese cities against yielding to Tokyo's efforts to detach these northern regions from Chinese control.

The Communists had already "declared war" on Japan in 1932 while isolated in Kiangsi Province. They now appealed to the Kuomintang to halt the civil war and unite in resisting Japan. A crisis developed in December, 1936, when Chiang Kai-shek went to Sian, an important base on the upper Yellow River,

[2] See Chapter 9, pages 234–242.

officially to direct further operations against the Mongolian uprising. It was rumored that his real purpose was to order an all-out offensive against the Communists. He was captured and held prisoner by his own subordinates, who wanted China to unite and confront the Japanese. For a while his life was endangered, but early in 1937 a compromise settlement was arranged with the Communists and a united national front was formed.

The Communist party promised to abandon its objective of overthrowing the Kuomintang by force and establishing a Soviet system; it also agreed to end confiscation of land in its zone of rule. Finally, it expressed a willingness to bring its autonomous regime and army under control of the national government. For its part, the Nanking government agreed to undertake a full-scale effort against Japan; it also promised constitutional changes, the establishment of a democratic system, and social and economic reforms. This settlement gave China two years of political unity in the face of its greatest danger and enabled it to withstand the first shocks of war. When the struggle for survival became stalemated in 1939–1944, the pact disintegrated under the pressure of violations and bad faith. Above all there remained a basic incompatibility in the objectives sought by the two rival groups.

The War (1937–1939)

Chiang adhered to his obligation to confront the Japanese and resist further encroachments. When Japan attacked in the summer of 1937, the invaders moved swiftly through northern China but met strong Nationalist resistance at Shanghai, Soochow, and Hankow. Here the pride of Chiang's army, the Eighteenth Army Corps, well-trained by German tutors, fought a bitter but futile battle from positional defenses. Its army shattered, the government had to retreat up the Yangtze, finally settling at Chungking in Szechuan Province; from there, Free China continued its resistance. A stable front was established, largely because the Japanese army decided against an all-out effort, but the Chinese lacked offensive power and were effectively pushed back toward the southwestern portion of China Proper. Japan methodically occupied the important maritime and rail centers, though its actual occupation power did not extend beyond the lines of communication. Chinese resistance did not waver, and only one key Kuomintang official, Wang Ching-wei, deserted to the Japanese. He headed an ineffectual puppet government, established at Nanking in 1940, and modeled along Kuomintang lines. Japan used this regime primarily as a diplomatic bargaining counter to reach a satisfactory peace treaty with Chiang Kai-shek. Wang's death in 1944 destroyed even this limited role of the puppet Nanking regime.

The Japanese invasion smashed the Nationalists' fragile administrative and power structures. The important start in creating health and educational facilities was disrupted, and transport lines were either destroyed or used by the invader. The new fiscal system, with its modern budgetary and accounting methods, national banking and currency, was seriously impaired, and the economy suffered what was to be a devastating inflation. Less apparent than these setbacks was a steady loss of political strength, which ultimately had tragic consequences.

In the decade before 1937, the liberal elements had lacked real power within the party and military hierarchies, but they did exert some influence, especially in the Executive Yuan. These moderate groups were not effectively organized. One faction, the Political Science clique, had a limited influence on policy and concentrated on introducing modern methods of administration into government. There were also individuals with high prestige, like H. H. Kung, a financial expert and one-time president of the Executive Yuan, and his more liberal relation, T. V. Soong, related to Chiang by marriage. In addition, many truly liberal and devoted officials appeared within the Kuomintang and gained some middle-class following. The wealthy business community in the coastal cities was anxious to restrain the authoritarian elements within the party. An important party liberal was Sun Fo, son of the great leader. Though unsuccessful in getting changes in the party command, he and his colleagues did seek to democratize the party, extend civil liberties, and develop social reforms. The pressure of events in the 1930's was slowly pushing the Kuomintang toward this orientation as progressive civil servants, capable professionals, and middle-class leaders influenced the tone and policy of the government. The National Salvation Movement of 1936–1937, though directed mainly against appeasing Japan, had such support and reflected the improved political organization of this liberal element. The constitutional reform program of 1936 and the creation of the People's Political Council in 1938, with its freedom of political expression and debate, further reflected this trend.

The defeats of 1937–1939 reversed this process and upset China's internal political balance. Loss of the modern coastal regions and the retreat into the interior meant the disappearance of this liberal base of support. Chiang now depended heavily on the anti-Western, antidemocratic leaders of these conservative regions. Reliance on a reactionary landed gentry and its provincial political associates added an insuperable obstacle to an effective agrarian reform program. Within the Kuomintang the dominant right wing was now practically unrestrained. Admittedly, the struggle for survival was the poorest imaginable setting for the pursuit of constitutional reform. But the right-wing leaders, under the guise of adopting essential security measures, undertook a policy of political suppression against all opponents, thereby alienating many elements and reducing the government's power to attract supporters.

The control of the Kuomintang lay in the hands of Nationalist conservatives after the 1927 coup. Among these were the Chen brothers, Li-fu and Kuo-fu, leaders of the powerful Chen (CC) clique. Their concentration on the vital matters of party discipline, loyalty, and organizational strength kept them close to Chiang. They dominated the party machine and its finances, and were closely associated with the secret police. Their influence in the governmental bureaucracy did much to foster ultranationalist and authoritarian views.

KUOMINTANG PARTY ORGANIZATION (1941)

Under the Central Executive Committee were the following: Training Committee, Party Affairs Committee, and the *San Min Chu I* Youth Corps.

Also directed by the Central Executive Committee were the Central Secretariat and the following party ministries: Organization, Publicity, Women's Affairs, Social Affairs, Overseas Chinese, and sundry special committees.

SOURCE: Based on P. M. A. Linebarger, *The China of Chiang Kai-shek* (Boston: World Peace Foundation, 1941).

A similar set of values permeated the military command: order before reform, retention of exclusive Kuomintang leadership of the armed forces, and adherence to the status quo. The field officers—called the Whampoa clique after the first academy of the Canton era—were conservative, but here at least there was a strong pressure for military reform. The main objectives were the elimination of dishonesty and favoritism, and the use of more advanced organizational and training systems. The reformers here enjoyed only sporadic success in combating the entrenched army bureaucracy, typified by such officials as War Minister General Ho Ying-chen.

The liberals bitterly criticized the trend toward authoritarianism after 1939 that led to the suppression of freedom of speech and assembly and the terrorizing of moderates and reformers by the secret police. Freedom of inquiry in education was sharply curtailed, and a Youth Corps was sponsored by the Chen clique to thwart liberal movements. The government's critics were quick to link the failure to foster democracy and reform during the war with the corruption and incompetence that now threatened to overwhelm China's administrative and military structures. Demands for the end of Kuomintang dictatorship in turn led to further suppression, often through violence. Yet such groups as the Democratic League, which later sided with the Communists, continued to press for the end of one-party rule, and for administrative reform, civil liberties, and a changed tax structure that would give some relief to the poor.

The Absence of Social Reform

The Kuomintang right wing was justified in arguing that the Nationalist cause was threatened by the Communists as well as the Japanese. The Nationalists never did expect the Communists to place themselves under Kuomintang political and military jurisdiction. The 1937 agreement established the Red Army's sector to the north of the Yangtze, where it operated as the Eighth Route Army, nominally under Nationalist orders. However, the Communists organized a separate force below the Yangtze, and it was here that friction developed in 1940–1941. A fire fight climaxed the mounting tension, the coalition was shattered, and sporadic fighting continued between the two Chinese forces. Chiang dispatched some of his best troops to blockade the Communist sector and to prevent it from expanding further into Free China during the war. These Nationalist contingents were estimated at over 200,000 in 1943 and as high as 400,000 later in the war.

The reality of the Communist menace intensified the Kuomintang's dilemma further. Subversion had to be rooted out, since the Nationalists were engaged in what amounted to a two-front war. But authoritarian excesses, the absence of political and social reform, and the intensified party dictatorship were ingredients for potential disaster. The devoted and crusading spirit that pervaded the city of Chungking during its early days as China's provisional capital evaporated as the war dragged on. It was replaced with a lethargy born in good part from disillusionment with the government's ability to cope with the social and economic dangers besetting the besieged Republic of China. The lot of the peasantry grew still harder and it became more willing to follow the lead of other groups, Communists included, which preached sweeping reform and economic justice. Equally significant was the gradual alienation of the middle class, which began to lose interest in the Nationalist government. Inflation became more intense, causing considerable hardship among teachers, officials, and others who lived on fixed salaries. Heavy-handed official controls over the economy brought no relief in this matter but served to outrage the small merchants. Oppressive political measures angered the intellectuals and students who were still devoted to the course of democratic reform. These trends became more apparent in the late stages of the war and were to accelerate with incredible speed after 1945. The result was a failure of political leadership and executive administration, the very skills that Chiang strove so hard to develop. Toward the end of the war the bureaucracy was almost benumbed into inactivity and was desperately short of technicians, scientists, and administrators. Yet this was the hour of critical importance, for the Nationalists hoped to regain all the territories, including the great urban centers, lost to Japan since 1937. In fact, the Cairo Declaration of December, 1943, also promised to return to China the well-developed territories of Manchuria and Formosa. The gap between need and performance in the realm of governmental efficiency was an ominous sign of future danger.

The Kuomintang still retained some important advantages. It remained the spearhead of a determined, popular resistance effort against Japan. Its chief, Chiang Kai-shek, had gained international prestige and had won for China a place in the councils of the major powers. The despised unequal treaties that gave the West the right of extraterritoriality were finally terminated in January,

1943. And the Nationalist armies were still the strongest military component among the Chinese forces. But these diplomatic and military advantages no longer rested on a firm base of popular support for the Kuomintang; instead, they had become the mainstay of Nationalist strength. The question could be raised even before Japan was defeated: What would become of the Kuomintang should the uncertainties of combat reduce the government's military ascendancy over its Communist rival?

Military Difficulties (1940–1945)

The Nationalist army remained Japan's primary opponent, and from 1939 to 1944 proved competent enough to withstand limited assaults. But it was woefully weak in equipment and training, and was greatly taxed by its assignments to confront both the invader and the Communists. Its ramshackle organization of 327 divisions was criticized by American military advisers who believed that a compact force of ninety divisions, properly trained and indoctrinated, would better suit China's needs. Such a complete reorganization required a dangerous transitional period in which the army might be unable to fulfill its commitments. A greater difficulty involved the political balance within China, especially acute after the defeats suffered by "Chiang's own" troops in 1937–1939. These had reduced the Kuomintang's relative military strength and made the party acutely conscious of the attitudes of the semi-independent provincial leaders, who opposed a reform so dangerous to their independence. Chiang did not want to upset the balance between the units under central control and those over which the government's power was less direct. As in other matters, he hesitated to experiment with reforms that promised eventual benefits for fear of the more immediate consequences.

The army succumbed to the inertness, lack of *élan*, and inefficiency that had permeated the government and the party. Embezzlement of funds, supplies, and food by officers and brutal treatment of the soldiers made conscription a terrifying experience to be avoided, instead of a patriotic duty to the state in its hour of need. Even in the forces under central control, military service was no longer a useful channel through which the government could propagate Kuomintang doctrine and loyalty to the state. This divorce of the army from the function of political education was a further reflection of the atrophy of purpose in the Nationalist camp.

A policy of caution hampered Nationalist military activity late in the war. All Chinese parties, in fact, estimated that the Americans were going to defeat Japan, and the Chungking government wanted to husband its strength for a future conflict with the Communists. Hence Chiang was reluctant to go along with an American plan to break the Japanese siege of China by a joint Allied effort to clear northern Burma of the enemy. This proposed campaign was linked to the American policy of retraining the Chinese army in three successive waves of thirty divisions each. Only partial progress on these matters was achieved. A Burma campaign was begun but not until 1944, when it got bogged down in the monsoon before effective use could be made of the supply route. The Chinese finally got thirty-nine divisions trained and equipped by the United States, but even this limited task was not completed by the end of the war.

Another approach, sponsored by General Claire Chenault, was to use China as an air base from which to assault the Japanese home islands and the enemy's field armies on the mainland. This promised to affect China's military organization only indirectly and was favored by Chiang over the American army plan, whose author, General Joseph Stilwell, did not get along with the Chinese leader. The air program was attempted with support from Washington, but the results were disappointing, and led to mutual recriminations and fault-finding. The overriding difficulty remained the inability to give the Chinese theater of operation sufficient military support for the air and the land campaigns. Transport difficulties and the prior claims of other theaters kept the China front permanently in short supply.

The American army had warned that the creation of effective air bases would incite the Japanese to undertake a preventive campaign. In 1944, the Japanese undertook a vigorous offensive, climaxed that fall by the destruction of the strategic air bases built to accommodate B-29 bombers. Its major effect was to cripple and scatter the Chinese army, though it did not capture the ultimate objectives of Chungking and Kunming, the terminal of the air lift from India. Allied pressure on other fronts prevented Japan from continuing this assault in 1945; thus the Chinese were given a breathing space. Under General Wedemeyer's direction, the Nationalist armies recovered their cohesion and improved considerably in 1945. Nevertheless, they suffered from the defeat, for they had been pushed further back into the southwestern corner of China.

Despite marked improvement, the Chinese were militarily unprepared for the sudden end to the war in 1945. Neither their troop strength nor territorial position had been adequately recovered for the tremendous task that lay ahead. The Nationalist government now was confronted with the awesome task of asserting military rule over all of China, establishing a stable political authority, and introducing effective administration in a country ravaged by almost a decade of war. Given the military situation, the destruction of transport facilities, and the level of competence in the party and the administration, this would not have been possible without American help. It was to prove a difficult and tragic undertaking even with this assistance.

At its most dramatic triumph, the Kuomintang had entered upon its moment of greatest peril. Peace presented new opportunities to the Communists in the north and northwest. The final test revolved around the Kuomintang's ability to deal with this major rival now that Japan was defeated. A closer study of the composition and strength of the Communist movement is essential for an appreciation of the amazing turn of events during the years 1945–1949.

6 *Communist*

Victory and Rule

The intellectual environment of China after 1911 was most suitable for the foundation and growth of a communist movement. The total collapse of the old order, the ensuing political vacuum, and the Bolshevik Revolution of 1917 led to the establishment of a Chinese Communist party in 1921. This movement offered a new universalist creed with a firm political order, and promised a dynamic assault against the country's economic backwardness. The party suffered a series of dismal failures during its first decade, but demonstrated the strength and stability required for survival. Mao Tse-tung became its undisputed leader in the course of the difficult years 1931–1935. He maintained unswerving allegiance to Soviet Russia and the international Communist movement but freed the party from Moscow's complete tactical direction. It took another fifteen years, Kuomintang inertia, and the havoc caused by Japan's invasion to enable a serious Communist bid for power. In the light of this long frustrating history, the complete triumph of the Chinese Communist party came as a complete surprise to the world.

The First Two Decades

Early Difficulties

The Chinese Communists faced two difficult problems from the very outset. One was to determine what tactics and policies would enable them to dominate the Chinese Revolution. The other was an ideological issue of great importance to these doctrinaire, theory-conscious revolutionaries: how to develop their strategy and concepts in an almost totally unindustrialized country whose economy lacked all the prerequisites cited by Marx as essential for a proletarian uprising. The proletariat still played an important role in the Russian Revolution, even though Lenin had inverted Marxism by creating a disciplined Communist party that directed the uprising and took control of the state. Lenin had

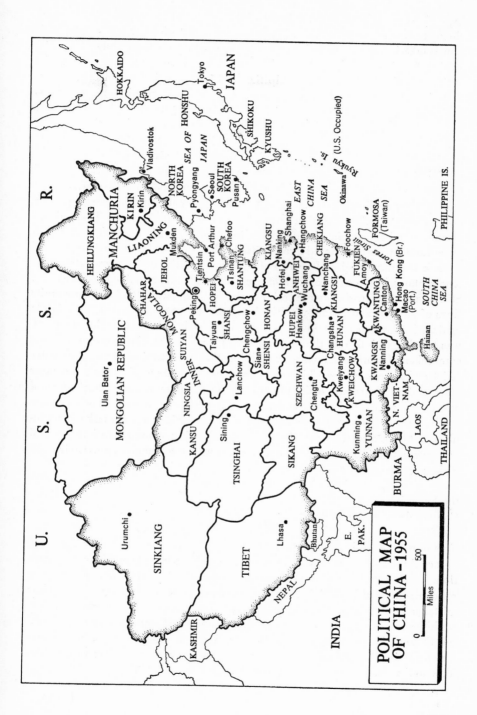

POLITICAL MAP
OF CHINA – 1955

139

recognized as early as 1905 the importance of the peasantry as the "bourgeois" element that had to be allied with the workers, but the proletariat and their Communist leaders remained the paramount factors in the revolution.

These tactical and doctrinal problems were made more acute by the Soviet decision in the early 1920's to help the Nationalists gain control over China. The Kuomintang was dubbed a representative of all revolutionary classes, proletarian as well as peasant and middle class, and it was with this dubious justification that the Russians ordered the Chinese Communists to cooperate with the Nationalists in 1923. Party leadership was still in the hands of its idealistic founders, led by Ch'ên Tu-hsiu, a Peking University intellectual and participant in the May Fourth Movement. The years before 1923 were devoted to training this ex-democrat and his fellow Communists in the lore of Leninist party strategy—tight party discipline, complete devotion to the cause, and the acceptance of policy direction from the Comintern in Moscow. The Chinese Communists had associated different political parties with different classes and, since classes were considered irreconcilable, they reasoned that parties were too. It took communist discipline to enforce the directive to cooperate with the Kuomintang, because this order appeared both tactically and doctrinally wrong. Still worse, the Russians were training the Nationalist party along communist lines of party organization, with the inevitable effect of perfecting its defenses against infiltration and subversion. An alert, tightly knit Kuomintang party was tougher to infiltrate than a diffusely organized liberal group that did not comprehend Communist tactics. In addition, the Russian mission operated under strict orders to keep the Chinese Communists from tampering with the army command and troops, in order to maintain Kuomintang military efficiency and ensure the success of its military campaign.

The years of collaboration (1923–1927) were bitter ones for the Communists, who succeeded in creating a mass following among the workers and peasants but remained under orders to work with the Kuomintang. Their complaints to the Comintern evoked contradictory directives to adhere to the coalition and yet undermine it in preparation for a seizure of power. Not only were the Kuomintang center and right wings, under Chiang Kai-shek, wary of the Communists, but the Left Kuomintang leaders were determined to retain their political position after they established a government at Hankow in 1926. The Communist party therefore had an ultimate objective that proved unattainable —it could not overturn the Nationalists after the latter had mastered the revolution. Russian advice to the Communists to follow this line was either a weak rationalization of its decision to sacrifice the Communists or was rooted in the mistaken belief that a noncommunist party, even if trained in Leninist methods, could be overthrown by true believers. The colossal failure of 1927, which saw the Communist party in Shanghai smashed, the Kuomintang reunited under Chiang Kai-shek, and the Russian advisers ousted from China, was a shattering blow to the party's prestige and strength.

Further Defeats (1928–1930)

The Soviet government promptly placed responsibility for the discredited policy of collaboration on Chinese leaders and forced the ouster of Ch'ên Tu-hsiu. Moscow retained effective control over policy direction, but its instructions proved erratic and were not conceived in the light of Chinese conditions. This strategy was partly due to the great distance involved, but it also reflected the influence of the Stalin-Trotsky struggle for power. Until 1928, Trotsky called for immediate revolutionary action, and Stalin took an opposite view. Now that Trotsky was defeated, Stalin could order a more vigorous program for the Chinese Communists, but the party was in no condition to wage such campaigns. Events after the break with the Kuomintang took the form of a dreary succession of changes in party leadership, rapid shifts in tactics, and the use of the remaining support in laboring centers for political purposes. The result of this opportunism, foreign control, and shuffling commands was a deterioration of morale among Chinese Communist leaders and a disintegration of popular support.

During the years 1928–1930, the now-isolated Communist party undertook a series of insurrections that ended in total failure. There was an abortive army mutiny at Nanchang in August, 1928, followed by a peasant revolt in Hunan Province planned by Mao Tse-tung, an agrarian organizer. After the failure of this Autumn Crop Uprising, Mao withdrew to an old inaccessible bandit area in Kiangsi, to hold out and build a peasant army. Meanwhile an assault was made on Canton, with the uprising linked to the countryside in an effort to create a base of power in this revolutionary stronghold. The revolt was accompanied by slogans reminiscent of the Bolshevik coup of 1917, but it was thoroughly crushed by Kuomintang forces and anti-Communist labor unions that aided mopping-up operations in the city. Further efforts were made to link the peasantry with urban revolts, for the Communists appreciated the value of agrarian support, but only in a secondary role. A final major uprising occurred at Changsha in July and August, 1930, and again proved a total failure.

During this time party leadership had moved from Ch'ên to Ch'u Ch'iu-pai in 1927, and then to Li Li-san in 1928. Li was replaced after the Changsha fiasco, though he had operated under the policy directives of the Comintern. The new leader was Wang Ming, one of the Returned Students—a group of young Communists who had recently completed their revolutionary education in Russia. Their youth and foreign background prevented Wang and his colleagues from exercising effective leadership. The party was at the crossroads in 1930 because Russian-dominated policy had failed and Chinese leadership was discredited.

The Rise of Mao Tse-tung

It was at this juncture that Mao Tse-tung and his associates in the Kiangsi countryside rose to power within the party. This group was called the Real Power Faction, since it was now far stronger than the formal party leadership.

When Mao retreated to Kiangsi, other military elements, including those led by Chu Teh, joined him; in 1928 Mao was recognized as party commissar, with Chu Teh as military commander. Thus began a fruitful partnership between the two Communist leaders that removed possible tension regarding party control over the military arm. A Red army was gradually formed, and, wherever it went in Hunan and Kiangsi, a soviet administration was established. Mao's policy had two main aspects—the development of political power through agrarian reform, including land distribution, and the constant increase in Communist military power.

Mao was a young library assistant at Peking University when he joined the party in 1921. His organizing activities among the peasants, especially in Hunan in 1926, gave him a nondoctrinaire understanding of their value in the revolution. His report of 1926 stressed the acuteness of their grievances and their vigorous revolutionary frame of mind. He claimed that, in a revolution, the peasantry would sweep all before it, crushing all forces of government that were considered oppressive. Mao later tempered these views, adjusting them to communist doctrine, and decided to use this peasant force to generate power for the party. He also determined to develop a regular military force as an engine for revolution; the result was the Red army that ultimately captured China after a full field campaign. Nevertheless, the foundation of Chinese Communist strength rested squarely on the peasantry. This tactic is different in doctrine from the Leninist philosophy of using the countryside as a supplementary source of support. Mao left the cities alone, built his strength in the countryside, and eventually captured the cities with armies fashioned out of the Chinese peasantry.

Despite this unorthodox approach, Mao remained a staunch communist who sought to establish a party dictatorship over China, in order to industrialize and modernize it as an ally of Soviet Russia. Communist ardor was not dampened by the obvious discrepancy between the Marxian prediction of proletarian revolutions in highly industrialized countries and Mao's effort to use peasant unrest as a means to gain power and modernize China. Always flexible and realistic in his tactics, Mao realized that the agrarian uprising of 1927 did not spark the hoped-for national rebellion because China was still divided into self-contained regions. A chain reaction of uprisings was made impossible by the nation's economic backwardness and poor communications.

The more cautious policy of creating a territorial base of power—the Kiangsi Soviet—was adopted, on the model attempted in the early 1920s by P'eng Pai at Haifeng and Lufeng. In order to avoid capture, Mao and his colleagues chose a difficult terrain for their area of operations and perfected evasive and guerilla combat tactics. These precautions were in recognition of Communist military weakness and of the party's inability to sweep the country by a revolutionary coup. But the strategy's realism and modesty of scope enabled the Communists to stabilize their position and ward off the total collapse of their effort in China.

In 1932 party headquarters was moved from Shanghai to Kiangsi Province, as Moscow grudgingly acknowledged Mao's leadership.

Communist Expansion in the North

From this point forward, the decision-making power over Chinese Communist policy remained in Mao's hands. His tactical competence and ability to construct a loyal and efficient party machine bolstered the movement's prestige. It now had a working doctrine: to form agrarian soviets and, on these territorial bases, build a Red army. The party's competence and discipline stood it in good stead when Kuomintang assaults forced it to move from Kiangsi in 1934 to Shensi Province in Northwest China. It re-created an agrarian base there in 1936 and was in a position to take swift advantage of the revolutionary opportunity afforded by the Japanese invasion of 1937; for the invader drove back the Nationalists but proved unable to govern the rural hinterlands of North China. The Communists showed great skill and energy in expanding into this power vacuum and establishing an underground government in areas whose cities and rail lines were controlled by Japan.

Popular antagonism to the Japanese was strong enough to induce the peasants to form pockets of military and political resistance on their own. Since the Communists possessed a superior organization, greater ability in clandestine operations, and a doctrine of reform, they were soon able to dominate the resistance movement. At the end of the war they claimed control over more than a fifth of the country, with a population of 90 million. They applied the principles developed in Kiangsi by fostering agrarian reform, mobilizing peasant political support, developing the Red army, and creating a rudimentary form of government.

Moderate Rule from Yenan

The reform program instituted in the north was less stringent than that of the Kiangsi period, when landlords were harshly treated and lost their property. Anxious to avoid creating irreconcilable opponents, the Communists adopted a program of progressive taxation and rent and credit controls, instead of undertaking widespread expropriation of land. Only those who collaborated with Japan lost their land, which was then redistributed through village organizations trained by party cadres. This program of protection to the individual farmer ensured mass support, which is ironic because an ultimate purpose of communism is the socialization of landed property and the collective operation of agriculture. By contrast, the Kuomintang became so dependent on the support of the gentry that it failed to effect land-reform programs, which were actually in closer harmony with Nationalist ideology.

Political activity was also geared for maximum popular support. The Communist-controlled territories, called Liberated Areas, were divided into five provincial areas with governmental structures organized up to the *hsien* levels. The core of each sector remained a defensible mountain base, since the entire region was under the shadow of the Japanese army. Still, assemblies elected by popular vote were established in the villages. In order to extend their reputation for moderation, the Communists restricted their share of seats in all governing bodies to one third. Their superior organization and power actually gave the Communists full control over affairs, but this tactic strengthened their argument that, on a national scale, Kuomintang tutelage should give way to a multiparty coalition government.

The "New Democracy"

From this wartime base in Shensi, Mao developed his concept of how the Communists would govern China. As detailed in his *New Democracy* (1941), it added further to the Communist reputation for moderation. Mao started from the premise that China was not economically advanced enough for communist or even socialist rule but would first have to pass through a period of "controlled capitalist" development. Land was to be redistributed, with equal shares the ideal; private capitalism would be allowed under state guidance in all except the very large industries, utilities, and financial institutions. If China was to work itself up from a semifeudal, semicolonial status, cooperation among labor, peasantry, capitalists, and the government was deemed essential.

In political terms, this was to be a coalition government of the party, proletariat, peasantry, and "national bourgeoisie"—in other words, all elements who were not Japanese puppets, ardent supporters of the Kuomintang, or subservient to foreign interests. It was perfectly clear from Mao's analysis, however, that this coalition government would serve only during a transitional period of undefined duration, that the ultimate goal remained communism, and that he was following the most rational approach to this objective. Yet this short-range picture was made very attractive and had the advantage of diminishing the concern of the middle class and even the landlords over the possible advent of communist rule. Kuomintang failures had already alienated much of the business community, and Communist promises of moderation added to its indifference over the outcome of the civil war.

Communist Discipline and Purpose

The Communists were able to dominate Northwest China by judiciously combining popular reform programs with an inflexibility of purpose and a disciplined party command. Party doctrine under Mao's leadership, which allowed for many policies that could be interpreted as departures from strictly orthodox dogma, led many foreign observers to assume that the Chinese Communists were merely agrarian reformers. Josef Stalin himself encouraged Westerners to believe this myth by "laughingly" referring to them as margarine or radish Communists in 1944–1945. It was therefore with considerable care that Mao and other leaders emphatically stressed the need for party members to adhere fully to communist ideology, and not to mistake democratic-reformist tactics for a fundamental change in party purpose. In 1942–1944, even while moderate policies were being practiced, the entire party membership underwent an intensive refresher program of study in the ideals and purposes of communism. Basic works of the masters were repeatedly read, soul searching and confessions of error in thought were undertaken in great profusion, and the party's revolutionary purity and zeal were reaffirmed.

The Communists also retained control over their military formations throughout the Japanese war, as the Red army continued to grow and perfect its tactics under Chu Teh's leadership. The Communists claimed to have pinned down strong Japanese forces and to have inflicted heavy casualties on the enemy. Though their guerilla activity may have been widespread, their assertions of great military achievements are suspect because they lacked the force and equipment to undertake significant campaigns. It must also be remembered that their major objective was to conserve strength for the postwar period and not have their forces decimated in large-scale battles with the Japanese.

The army received intensive political indoctrination and was divided into three parts for maximum flexibility and efficiency. These were the regular troops, guerilla forces who were well-disciplined second-line troops, and looser formations of peasant militia used only in their home regions. At the end of the war, when the Red units moved to Northeast China and Manchuria, they were able to organize new formations quickly around the core of regulars and guerillas. Peasant support for this effort was directly linked to the rapid implementation of an economic reform program and popular participation in local government.

Climax of the Civil War (1945–1949)

The Situation in 1945

The end of the Japanese war found civil affairs and the military situation in a precarious state. The nation's economy was in an extreme stage of disruption. Production in rural areas suffered from deterioration of China's irrigation facilities, and acute shortages of fertilizer, tools, and labor. The decline in food production and the breakdown of transport facilities turned the inflation into one of runaway proportions. Despite all its exhortations, the Nationalist regime failed to arrest this calamitous trend. When it regained territories from the Japanese, the government tried to restore order by placing the industrial economy under state control, and directed such enterprises as steel, textiles, milling, and chemicals, but this action further alienated the business community and, through inefficiency, retarded economic recovery.

Public administration of the liberated areas was equally disappointing. Health facilities and other necessary equipment were desperately lacking, and there was a serious shortage of key personnel, such as engineers, industrial managers, and trained civil servants. The bureaucracy seemed unable to shake off its wartime lethargy and give China the efficient administrative system to sustain a national-recovery effort. In addition, Nationalist officials often proved no better than carpetbaggers, whose corruption and exploitation quickly turned the warmth with which the liberators were greeted to hostility and resentment against these "aliens" from the south. Thus the fruits of victory over Japan, after a brief moment of glory, served to undermine further the prestige of the Kuomintang.

The military picture, meanwhile, had become confused, and Nationalist superiority over the Communists was threatened for the first time. The center of gravity shifted to North China, close to the Communist wartime base of operations. Since this region and Manchuria were well beyond Nationalist lines of supply, a fight in this area would neutralize the government's numerical advantage. The Communists, moreover, had infiltrated Manchuria as well as northeastern China at the end of the war and, with clandestine Russian help, captured Japanese field equipment. Possession of artillery meant that the Red Army could, for the first time, engage in field operations as well as defensive guerilla activities. The Nationalists, who also had acquired Japanese equipment in addition to American military aid, continued to enjoy a clear advantage in men and matériel during 1945–1946. But the overwhelming advantage of the past was gone because the Communists now possessed the power to deal the foe crippling blows should the military opportunity arise.

The thirty-nine American-trained divisions, though not fully organized, were a formidable nucleus for a modern Nationalist army. However, the rest of the Kuomintang forces were not yet properly reorganized and the army as a whole could move only by sea and air in the fall of 1945, so widespread was the destruction of communication facilities. The United States carried three Nationalist armies by air lift to Shanghai and Nanking, and then flew some of these forces by relay to Peking in the north. In addition, the Nationalists required the assistance of a corps of United States Marines and Japanese forces to keep the Communists from flooding across all of North China. The Americans occupied four ports in North China, while the Japanese followed orders to guard cities and rail centers and to surrender only to the Nationalists.

Communist military units could not be kept from the countryside around Peking and from Shantung Province. They did not move south of the Yangtze in the fall of 1945, but an uneven combat line was formed across North China. Wherever they went, the Communists destroyed communication facilities and sought to arouse the populace against the government. With a full-scale civil war about to explode, the American General Wedemeyer recognized the Kuomintang's military weakness and counseled against a thrust into Manchuria. He advised the Nationalists to consolidate their hold on China Proper, arguing that the task of clearing even North China of Communists would be difficult. At a critical juncture in February, 1946, a truce was reached, and an effort was made to reach a political settlement that would prevent a civil war.

The Truce of 1946: Background and Effect

All American efforts to bring about a truce during the war had failed because of intense Nationalist-Communist antagonism. However, Chiang Kai-shek did commit himself in 1943, in the face of right-wing Kuomintang opposition, to seek a political solution to the civil war. His terms included the assimilation of the Red Army, an end to the Communist separate state, and treatment of the Communists as an ordinary party. In return he promised a democratic constitution guaranteeing fundamental civil and political rights and an end to Kuomintang tutelary rule. The Communists, on the other hand, wanted a coalition government and the right to keep the Red Army and a territorial base. Neither side would yield, out of fear of eventual destruction by its opponent.

The Soviet position appeared somewhat ambiguous. In 1937–1941 Russia assisted the Nationalists because the China war reduced military pressure on Siberia's vulnerable frontiers. The Nazi assault on Russia in 1941 ended this flow of aid, and, with the German retreat of 1943, Moscow took a more hostile line and supported Chinese Communist claims for a coalition. Chiang in turn sought a Russian promise of nonintervention in Chinese affairs. It was for this purpose and to get Russia into the Far Eastern war that the United States made the famous Yalta Agreement of February, 1945. The Chinese were not present there and it was with great reluctance that Foreign Minister T. V. Soong signed the Sino-Soviet Treaty of August, 1945. Based on the Yalta settlement, it gave Russia rail and port concessions in Manchuria. In return, Stalin promised to respect China's territorial integrity and sovereignty, refrain from interfering in China's domestic affairs, and give moral and material support only to the Nationalists. Russia was to occupy Manchuria for a brief period, respect China's sovereignty there, and permit the Nationalists to establish a civil administration during the Soviet occupation.

Actually, the Russians looted Manchurian industries, allowed the Communists to enter the region, and connived in blocking the entry of Nationalist forces by sea. Thus the great industrial base in the north, on which the Kuomintang placed its hopes of rapid economic recovery, turned into an enemy bastion. Nevertheless, the Soviet government was skeptical about Chinese Communist chances and seems to have expected them to hold out in northern Manchuria, in a buffer region that could both protect and gain strength from its Russian neighbor. Stalin apparently advised Mao to make peace with the Nationalists and enter a coalition government; the treaty of August, 1945, did place pressure on the Communists to reach a peaceful settlement.

Persistent American efforts led to a meeting of Chiang and Mao, their first since 1927, and negotiations were conducted by an American mediator, General George Marshall. The political terms of the truce called for a constitutional convention to establish the legal framework of a democratic coalition government. Militarily, the Chinese army was to be reduced to ninety divisions, of which eighteen were to be Communist, but fully integrated into the regular army. Finally, cease-fire teams were sent to enforce the truce in the field.

It would have been most difficult to effect this political-military settlement under the most favorable conditions. The cease-fire broke down under the strain of mutual suspicion, constant truce violations, and the unresolved struggle for Manchuria. When the Russians prepared to leave that area in January, 1946, the Nationalists were unprepared to take over the large cities of Changchun and Mukden. They therefore arranged for a brief delay, but even then the Chinese Communists occupied Changchun until forced out by Nationalist units arriving by air. These cities and their rail lines from Peking were held only with the greatest difficulty, and the Nationalist occupation of Manchuria, which employed many American-trained divisions, amounted to a restricted penetration of enemy-held territory. In fact, the rail network between Peking and the south had not even been cleared, and Communist strength in North China increased. A new cease-fire was arranged, but by mid-1946 it was again broken and civil war appeared imminent.

Nationalist Political Reform

The question of constitutional reform also reached an impasse. The Kuomintang had already decided, in May, 1945, to promulgate a permanent constitution by convening the national convention in November. Protests by Communists and other groups that this prewar assembly was unrepresentative brought a one-year postponement. Meanwhile, the People's Consultative Council, an all-party group established during the Marshall mission, agreed to liberalize the restrictive 1936 draft constitution. Chiang accepted these modifications despite opposition from the right but, when the convention met in November, 1946, the civil war was again under way. The Communists and their lesser allies boycotted the meeting, labeled it unrepresentative, and claimed that it was illegally convened by the government before a coalition was established. The constituent assembly proceeded with its work under Chiang's direction and passed the new document in December, 1946.

Like the 1936 draft, it provided for a powerful president who was responsible only to an assembly that met every three years. However, the Executive Yuan shared power with the president and, under this version, the Legislative Yuan could request a change of policy and legislation. If the Legislative Yuan adhered to this view by a two-thirds vote, the Executive Yuan had to yield or resign. Thus the constitutional system was somewhat vague: it could have developed along the lines of a semidictatorial presidential system, but there was an alternative possibility of evolving into a cabinet-parliamentary type of government. However, the system never received a fair trial. It went into effect in December, 1947, with elections to the triennial National Assembly occurring that year and the choice of the Legislative Yuan following in 1948. In neither case did any party other than the Kuomintang fare well; the Communists and the fellow-traveling Democratic League, strongest of the lesser parties, were outlawed, and the other groups proved entirely ineffectual. The National Assembly elected Chiang president in March, 1948, and in the light of the civil war then raging, authorized him to take emergency measures free of constitutional restrictions. The Assembly did elect General Li Tsung-jen over Chiang's candidate, Sun Fo, to the vice-presidency, but hopes for immediate social reform were not realized. Even with a civil war endangering its very survival, the right wing of the Kuomintang would not make the concessions sought by reformist elements in an effort to check the party's loss of popular support.

Civil War

Late in 1946, when Chiang finally decided to proceed with the moderate constitutional reform program, he also had to decide on a military policy toward the Communists. The cease-fire and negotiations had broken down, but the initiative still lay with the Nationalists, as the stronger military force. Chiang decided to undertake an all-out offensive instead of consolidating his position in Central and North China. Undoubtedly he was encouraged by the favorable diplomatic situation, in which Russia was committed to neutrality and the United States was an ally. Nationalist forces totaled more than three times the million men in the Communist camp, of whom less than half were regulars. The government enjoyed a superiority in equipment, possessed a small modern air force, and was encouraged by results of recent small skirmishes. The Nationalists probably still retained the image of an enemy capable only of adroit guerila and defensive activities. When the opening phases of the all-out assault at the end of 1946 appeared successful, remaining doubts about the wisdom of this decision were cast aside.

At the start of 1947 the Nationalists reached their peak in territorial control, having swept through the northwest and the old Red capital of Yenan without encountering resistance. The Communists retreated intact, but the government's military position and lines of communication became increasingly vulnerable. As the year wore on, the Communists retained control of the countryside in Manchuria and parts of North China, and continued their harassing operations. The Kuomintang forces in the urban rail centers of Manchuria lacked the strength to sweep out and wrest control of the surrounding regions. During 1947–1948 the Communists took the offensive and captured several enemy units. Morale even among the best Nationalist formations in Manchuria began to crack. Their government lacked a spirit of dedication and appeared riddled with corruption and inefficiency; Kuomintang administrators had compiled so poor a governing record that the population became hostile. The Communists, by contrast, appeared to have a strong sense of solidarity and purpose. Dropping their wartime moderation, the Communists immediately instituted sweeping land reforms in Manchuria in order to rally the people to their side and swell their military ranks with peasant militia formations.

The Nationalist northern garrison commanders fell back on a traditional Chinese defensive technique of retreating to the cities and holding out there.

Thus isolated and incapable of mounting offensive counterthrusts, they permitted the enemy to surround entire Nationalist armies at will. Cut off by rail, these forces had to be supported by an air lift, which seriously drained Nationalist strength. During 1948 the Communists captured a considerable quantity of American equipment that had been sent to the government forces. In the last four months of the year they struck hard and achieved four decisive successes in southern Manchuria and North China. The Kuomintang was reported to have lost 300,000 men (thirty-three divisions) in these battles and an overall total of 1 million men, including seventeen American-trained divisions, during 1948. The loss of Mukden in October, 1948, was most disastrous because its highly trained garrison had defected to the enemy without a fight.

Peking and Tientsin fell at the start of 1949, but the Nationalists still controlled most of China Proper and possessed armies at least equal to the Communist force. Chiang Kai-shek had fought against the Japanese under military and territorial conditions that superficially appeared far worse. However, he now concluded that the fight was lost, resigned as president in January, 1949, and prepared to hold out on Formosa. He removed much of his treasury to the island and eventually gathered about 500,000 troops there. Meanwhile Vice-President Li assumed authority on the mainland and tried unsuccessfully to negotiate a settlement with the Communists, who reached the Yangtze that spring. General David Barr, the American military adviser, stated that the Nationalists could have held this river front had they possessed the will to resist. But the Nationalist defenses crumbled, and the Communists crossed the Yangtze without encountering effective opposition.

Military disaster in the north had destroyed the government's prestige and capacity to resist. The people stood passively by, for this regime had clearly lost the mandate to rule. Ethically, the new rulers could be accepted without qualm, since allegiance can be transferred to a successful rebellious government.

The Communists swept across the country at will, taking Canton in October, 1949. That month they proclaimed the People's Republic of China, with its capital in the imperial city of Peking. The civil war that ended in such a dramatic fashion brought a new era to China and the entire Far East.

Consolidation of Communist Control

At first the Communists put their recent moderate theories into practice. This was, however, an act of prudence taken to consolidate power. Once power was achieved, China was to enter on a truly new era—that of the totalitarian state dedicated to the difficult program of industrialization through state control and coercion. The main issues—structure of government, relations of the social classes, agrarian reform, and development of the economy—are closely interwoven in communist theory. In the first stage, the government tried to restore orderly political conditions, curtail inflation, and reconstruct the economy. Hence it adhered to "coalition rule," furthered agrarian reforms, and tolerated the national bourgeoisie and lesser Kuomintang officials. These policies did much to enhance the government's prestige and so, ironically, paved the way for the most ruthless program to follow.

Once firmly entrenched in power, with a police-state apparatus behind them, the Communists began their program of collective farming and large-scale industrialization. According to communist doctrine, these "objective" changes —carried through by coercive governmental measures—alter the political functions and rights of the various social classes. This alteration, in turn, enables the form of government to be modified further on the long road to "socialism." In other words, Communist rule meant coercive economic reform, the eventual elimination of capitalists and old bureaucrats, and the strengthening of totalitarianism.

Agrarian Reform

Though Mao consistently described the peasantry as the key to power, he was orthodox enough to believe that the future lay with industry and its proletariat—even a state-created one. Chinese history is now restated in more orthodox terms, giving the proletariat "due credit" for its role in the communist triumph. Nevertheless, agrarian reforms held top priority and were applied to all of China by 1953. The program was modified in order to diminish the dislocations that change of ownership would have on an economy. The Communists had adopted a harsh reform policy in Manchuria after 1945 in order to win immediate peasant support. Landlords often lost all their property, though some were allowed a unit of land. However, many Japanese collaborators and others, unjustly accused, were deprived of their possessions and executed. By October, 1947, a more lenient law was applied to the rest of Manchuria and North China. Landlords lost their legal rights, all agrarian debts were canceled, and the peasants and the landlords shared the latter's property and possessions. The northern and northeastern regions, containing about 150 million people, were affected by this law. At that time equal distribution of property, not collectivization, was the objective.

After 1949 the Communists shifted away from equal ownership to a still more moderate law that would maximize production. In central China during 1949–1950, the well-to-do peasant was protected from loss of property. Only landlords had to yield their possessions, and even they could retain land that they or their hired hands cultivated. The poor peasant's plot of land was smaller by comparison and often he remained a tenant. The government sought to appease him by establishing and enforcing low rents and reduced interest rates on debts. Landlords were allowed to retain their hidden wealth if they invested it in productive agrarian or industrial enterprises. In 1951, this program was completed in central and southeastern China, affecting 130 million people. In 1952–1953, reforms were carried out in the south and southwest, thereby completing this program. A hastily trained cadre of 100,000 political workers was organized to administer the reforms, but the program was so massive that excesses and errors were bound to occur. The geographic unit was the *hsiang*, or group of villages. Peasant Associations, formed to implement these policies, later served as institutions through which the government would introduce agrarian education and further changes in the system of ownership. Even before this program was completed, new forms had been developed: collectives had been introduced on the large tracts taken over from the Japanese in Manchuria, and producer cooperatives had been started in parts of North China.

In order to increase production, the government also intensified its efforts to improve rural credit, storage facilities, and transportation. It vigorously fostered all reform in agrarian techniques developed in Nationalist China under American auspices. An efficient method of tax collection was introduced, for the government replaced the landlord as grain collector. Agriculture provided 40 per cent of the revenue collected from taxes in the 1950 budget. As expected, the tax schedule that September established a progressive rate of from 8 per cent for poor peasants to 30 to 50 per cent for landlords. Production, which fell to a low of 109 million metric tons in 1949, compared to the annual average of 140 million during 1931–1937, rose to 130 million in 1951. Agrarian reform, then, has continued to serve the Communists after playing an instrumental role in their rise to power. It has enabled the Peking government to gain direct control over farm produce through the tax mechanism. By eliminating the landlord and bringing the peasant in direct contact with the regime through the Communist-dominated Peasant Associations, it has enabled the regime to consolidate its position in the countryside.

Economic Rehabilitation

In the field of economic reform, the government had three immediate objectives—to restore market stability, revive industrial production to the pre-1949 peaks, and gain control of the major activities of the economy. When these were achieved in 1949–1952, the regime proceeded with long-range plans for industrialization.

The new government's most dazzling success was in checking the inflation that had all but paralyzed the economy in the last years of Nationalist rule. It checked deficit financing and the printing of paper currency, collected heavier taxes in the cities, held bank credit to a minimum, and undertook a series of bond sales to reduce purchasing power. With order restored in the countryside and transportation facilities repaired, town-country trade became more normal. Monetary controls were centralized and government expenses were sharply cut, so that a balanced budget was achieved by 1951. In order to maintain popular faith in the new currency, the government guaranteed the purchasing power of wages and salaries by linking them with fixed quantities of basic commodities—rice, vegetables, oil, cloth, and coal. Similar assurances covered bank deposits and government bond issues. Intensive efforts were made to improve rail transportation, so essential to immediate stability and long-range developments; all pre-1949 lines were restored in 1951 and new construction was vigorously pushed. The government, on the whole, wisely avoided the Nationalist policy of trying to check inflation by direct means, and adhered to indirect controls, market forces, and fiscal policy. Aided by three excellent crops in 1950–1952, it succeeded in stabilizing market prices.

By this time, however, the government's military expenditures in Korea, the cost of an army of 3 to 4 million men, and the new investment program under conditions of full employment led to a new suppressed inflation. Consumer-goods production did not keep pace with consumer income, and prices began to rise again, from 40 to 100 per cent according to various foreign estimates. In 1953–1954 bad harvests and floods added to the difficulty. The worst damage was in the Hwai River area between the Yellow and Yangtze basins, where a new dam was constructed in 1951 to prevent such disasters. As a result, extraordinary taxes were levied to keep purchasing power down, and in 1953 rationing had to be introduced.

It proved far simpler to maintain control over industrial production, partly because of the government's political power but also because the Nationalists had already created an important nationalized sector. Thus the government, which directed 44 per cent of the nation's industrial production in 1949, raised this sector to 67 per cent by 1952. It controlled all railways, 80 per cent of the heavy and 60 per cent of the light industries, 90 per cent of all loans and deposits through the People's Bank, and about half the wholesale and 30 per cent of the retail trade. In addition, the government regulated the flow of raw materials, controlled cash and credit holdings, monopolized trade in key commodities of all types, had supreme tax powers, and could resort to bulk purchases to control prices.

The mixed economy, then, was hardly more than a slogan even at the start of Communist rule. Nevertheless, there was a place for the individual owner and "national capitalist" in Mao's scheme of political economy. There were five sectors of the economy—peasant and handicraft units, and capitalist, mixed state-capitalist, cooperative, and nationalized enterprises. The national capitalists, after all, were one of the four classes (together with the workers, peasants, and petty bourgeoisie) to be led by the Communists under the doctrine of coalition rule. Private concerns were therefore encouraged to conduct their affairs, in cooperation with the state, for the mutual benefit of both. In practice, this doctrine meant that capitalists were reduced to managerial bureaucrats who ran their own concerns under state direction. Yet, even with their skills so sorely needed, capitalists were constantly harassed and often squeezed out by methods short of direct expropriation—taxes, credit controls, special levies, and union demands. All that was left of the great promises of the *New Democracy* was an undertaking to allow capitalists to survive as persons provided that they followed the dictates of the state and permitted themselves to be "educated and reformed."

Industrial production showed marked recovery by 1952, despite the reduced contribution of Manchurian industry, which had been looted by Soviet Russia in 1945–1946. Japan had built up this region to a production level of 1 million tons of steel and 25 million tons of coal per year; the Communists themselves noted in 1949 that Manchurian heavy industries were 35 per cent below these levels. Yet, instead of criticizing the Russians for this act of despoilation, the Chinese praised them unstintingly and looked forward to obtaining all their economic help from Moscow.

On the whole, industrial recovery was rapid, though it did not reach new heights, as the government claimed. Progress was greatest in steel, cotton cloth, flour, and cigarette production, as prewar peaks were surpassed in 1952. However, in pig iron, coal, electric power, wheat, soybean, and sugar production the pre-1949 peaks were not yet reached. Cotton cloth was a high priority item because it was highly valued in the countryside and so served as an incentive to economic activity there. In general, the government greatly exaggerated its industrial progress, resorting to false statistics and comparisons. It even tried to fool an Indian delegation with a display of machinery that was of Russian and Japanese origin. The propaganda value of rapid economic progress in the Orient is enormous, and the Chinese will make even greater efforts to broadcast their achievements once these are more firmly rooted in reality.

The Communist State

Communist Political Concepts

In a communist society, political institutions are merely agencies for carrying out the will of the party, which is actually above the constitution and the state. To a Western observer, the Chinese Communist apparatus of government is significant primarily as an administrative exercise of power by a totalitarian party, which alone makes all major decisions. To the Chinese Communists, the "governmental form" is but a reflection of the "state form," which is the class structure of society and its economic functions. This is orthodox Marxism, which roots all political order in the economic system and its class structure. Hence to communists the basic changes occur in the economy and class composition of society; a political structure follows and must be studied in the light of these other developments.

Therefore the constitutional order of September 1954, which followed the provisional structure of 1949–1954, is only a transitional form that will be modified once an industrial, collective society is achieved. With the country still far from socialism, all classes are permitted to participate in the creation of a New China. The 1954 constitution states that the new order is "led by the working class and based on an alliance of workers and peasants." This implies the continuation of a coalition that can make use of the skilled intellectuals, Kuomintang officials, and the lower middle class, as well as the capitalists.

Unlike the Russians, the Chinese Communists undertook many experiments in coalition politics before coming to power, including two united fronts with the Kuomintang (1924–1927 and 1937–1941), and one in 1946–1948 with various splinter parties. The government can claim a link with past practices, save that now the United Front is dominated by the left.

Yet the foreign observer is still confronted by the fact that the present regime is thoroughly totalitarian, completely dominated by the central command of the Communist party. The lower middle class, the capitalists, and the old Kuomintang bureaucrats are being squeezed out far more rapidly than economic changes warrant, while the "leading" classes of workers and peasants are under total Communist domination. The proletariat, numbering only 3 million industrial laborers and 10 million in service fields, has been organized into a Federation of Labor, but it is forbidden to strike, exhorted to work efficiently for the socialist state, and cannot engage in unofficial ("black") meetings of any kind. For the peasantry, compulsory grain deliveries above the tax quota were ordered in 1953, and full collectivization was planned for the future.

The Political System

On October 1, 1949, the new People's Republic of China was proclaimed, with a new flag of five stars standing for the Communist party and the four social classes in the coalition. At that time, the constitutional basis was established by three documents: the Organic Law of the Chinese People's Political Consultative Conference (CPPCC), the Organic Law of the Central People's Government, and the Common Program of the CPPCC.

The CPPCC, with a slight non-Communist majority, was supposed to be the supreme source of authority until a National People's Congress could be chosen. However, as in all totalitarian states, this legislative agency was simply a rubber stamp, giving its approval to all policies determined by the ruling group. The government itself had a rambling structure that vaguely resembled the elaborate Nationalist regime in complexity of organization and division of tasks. At the top was the Central People's Government Council, under Chairman Mao, with wide powers over policy and personnel. Under it was the State Administrative Council, with Chou En-lai as premier, which resembled the old Executive Yuan in that it was the administrative arm that carried out state policy. The People's Revolutionary Military Council, with Mao chairman and Chu Teh vice-chairman, was another subordinate body, placed outside the administrative scheme as in the Kuomintang system. Other agencies were the Supreme People's Court and the People's Procurator General's Office.

The new constitution was adopted on September 1, 1954, by the first National People's Congress, with all 1,197 deputies unanimously voting for the government's draft in secret ballot. The National People's Congress is called the "highest organ of state power," but its broad authority over legislation, appointments, and amendments is not exercised in the Western parliamentary sense. Its 1,226 members are elected indirectly, by people's congresses at the provincial level. The National People's Congress is to have a Standing Committee to exercise its full powers between the larger body's annual sessions. The Standing Committee theoretically is the constitutional watchdog of the government's authority, supervising the administrative and legal agencies of the state, and exercising the principal powers of the legislature. Its chairman in 1955 was a high Communist official, Liu Shao-ch'i.

This position, however, is subordinate to a new one created by the constitution, that of the Chairman of the Chinese People's Republic, elected for a four-year term (and removable) by the National People's Congress. Mao Tse-tung was the first to hold this post, a constitutionally stronger position than that he held as Chairman under the 1949 statute. He has specific powers in foreign and defense affairs, free from legislative control, enjoys wide appointive powers, and presides over policy-making agencies. His strong position hardly squares with the supremacy of the legislature, but it bears striking resemblance to the power of the president as envisaged by Chiang Kai-shek in his draft of a permanent constitution. The office of Vice-Chairman was created in order to insure a constitutional line of succession, and election to this position is made separately. That Chu Teh was chosen in 1954 shows that the veteran leaders of Chinese communism still dominated the government.

A State Council replaced the Government Administration Council as the highest administrative organ of the state, with Chou En-lai still premier. It has the added task of developing the nation's defense forces, but a new National Defense Council, elected by the Congress on nomination by the Chairman of the Republic, may be in charge of formulating military policy.

Finally, a new State Supreme Conference may be called and presided over by the Chairman of the Republic. Its permanent members are the Chairman and the Vice-Chairman of the Republic, the Chairman of the Standing Committee of the National People's Congress, and the Premier of the State Council. Other officials may also be called in. The Conference may submit its views to other agencies for "consideration." The four permanent members of this Conference, holders of the key posts in the government, are also the four leading members of the Communist Party Politburo. Hence control over party and government can be closely coordinated through the Supreme State Conference.

Mao Tse-tung has remained the undisputed leader of the new state, although the "cult of personality" became discredited elsewhere in the communist world after Stalin's death in 1953. Mao's infallibility was stressed in the party claim that no errors in policy were made after 1935 and he is spoken of in the most adulatory manner. The new western communist concept of "collective leadership" was blandly dealt with by the observation that Mao embodies the party's collective will.

Regional and local administration has also been brought under firm central control. Provinces and autonomous regions are subdivided into *chou* (districts), counties, and municipalities, with the counties broken down into groups of villages and towns. Each unit is ruled by a people's council and a people's congress chosen by the representative bodies at the next lower administrative level. Each regional body has the right to revise or amend orders issued at a lower level.

The Communist Party

The extraordinary position of the Communist party is reflected in the Preamble to the Constitution, which refers to the party as the leader of the people in their revolution and of the broad "democratic" coalition. It is not mentioned elsewhere in the constitution and in fact stands above and beyond it, as did the Kuomintang during its period of rule. The constitution is a creation of the Communists to guide the action of the state and the ordinary citizen. The party is the driving force of state rule and as such enjoys its own constitution and administrative structure.

Like Communist parties everywhere, the central apparatus is theoretically responsible to a National Party Congress, which in turn vests power between its sessions in a Central Committee. The Central Committee chooses a Political Bureau (Politburo) and a Central Secretariat. Actually, the chain of command is reversed, with the Politburo the country's highest authority. Mao Tse-tung controls the formal party mechanism as chairman of the National Congress, Politburo, and Central Secretariat. The party's field forces are organized at every administrative level, from the provinces down to cells in the village, city block, or factory. There are about 6 million party members, many of whom are recent replacements of those considered to be unfit. The party is making a determined effort to get recruits from the proletariat and poorer peasantry, though most of its thirteen Politburo leaders come from the bureaucracy and the landlord class. Members are supposed to lead incorruptible Spartan lives, respect party discipline, and work all their lives for the cause. The party leadership periodically exhorts its rank and file to purify its doctrinal understanding of Marxism-Leninism-Maoism. It requires self-examination sessions and purges in order to combat soft living and corruption within the party.

The main party duties are to execute tactical decisions made by the leadership, follow its doctrinal line rigidly, carry out party policy regarding relations with or activities of the people, keep in close contact with nonparty elements whose cooperation is deemed essential, and see that the basic policies of the state are effected by responsible government agencies. Often leading party members hold key government posts and carry out their tasks from this strategic position. The party also has its own agencies to deal with research and propaganda, party finances, organization and membership, cadre training, and united-front activities.

An engine as powerful as the Communist party requires disciplined obedience to central direction in order to avoid internal strife and sustain a maximum impact on Chinese society. It brooks no internal opposition and permits no outside interference with its control over the state bureaucracy, the development of policy, and direction of military affairs. The Communists have thus far avoided internal factionalism of the kind that weakened the Kuomintang, and, unlike its predecessor, this regime has extended its rule over all China.

Totalitarian Control

The Communist party has gone to unprecedented extremes in organizing the populace and indoctrinating it with a new ideology. It is a logical extension of totalitarian thought that the actions and the thoughts of the people must be fully controlled and directed. No intermediary groups or other loyalties can be permitted to check the power of the state over the individual. Mass organization under close party direction has been a characteristic of the new regime. Its primary purpose is to instill in the people devotion to the regime and an appreciation of the transformation communism seeks to bring to China. As early as 1950 the party claimed no less than 84 million members in the Peasant Associations, 7 million in its various youth movements (Federation of Democratic Youth, Young Pioneers, and Students' Federation), 30 million in the Democratic Women's Federations and more than 4 million in the Federation of Labor. In addition, there are 6 million party members and 10 million working for the government. Indoctrination programs, innumerable meetings, and seemingly endless parades with demonstrations and banners are among the techniques used.

The educational system was quickly geared to the country's political and technical needs. Intensive training in communist principles was given, schools that were ideologically suspect were quickly nationalized, and all educators were made to follow the new ideological line. The main emphasis at the college level was placed on technical training, with the number of students in each field regulated by quota. Thus of 70,000 students chosen in one year, over 40 per cent were in engineering and another 25 per cent were in teachers' colleges.

The government is also revolutionizing the Chinese system of writing. The historical system of ideographs is a cumbersome obstacle to modern means of communication and technical development. It has also been extremely difficult for the Chinese to master and is considered a hindrance to the regime's program of mass education. The government moved cautiously at first, with its Written Language Reform Committee, established in 1952, concentrating on the simplification or elimination of many ideographs. However, the ultimate objective, according to Mao Tse-tung, is to adopt a completely phonetic alphabet system.

The press is fully controlled and faithfully follows the party line. People are encouraged to read newspapers or listen to radio broadcasts, also fully controlled by the government. In addition, state-owned publishing houses turn out large numbers of books and journals, far surpassing Kuomintang efforts in this field.

It is, however, still questionable whether the new order has been able to revolutionize Chinese society as rapidly as surface changes indicate. The old system of values and beliefs was deteriorating under the pressure of modernization well before 1949, but this influence has by no means disappeared. The Communists condemn the old liberal philosophies, castigate Confucianism as an outdated system of feudal beliefs, and seek to replace loyalty to the family with devotion to the state. It is true that the Chinese people are more accustomed to an authoritarian system than a democratic one, but their ideal of the state is that of a distant, benevolent despot which keeps peace and order. The thoroughness of state controls, the intensely intimate relation between state and individual, and the drastic changes in Chinese society make Communist totalitarianism a harsh system foreign to Chinese understanding. The Chinese people in the past have shown a genius for resisting overbearing regimes, and it is possible that this "new dynasty" will encounter severe opposition. This statement does not mean that Communist efforts to maintain their rule and carry forward their program will fail. But there is no reason to conclude that their vast popular organizations are cohesive units whose members are loyal supporters of the regime. Nor is it clear that the people either believe they are living under a democratic coalition government or are indifferent about the absence of real democracy after more than a generation of agitation for liberal reforms.

The Police State

The Communist police state has made frequent use of terror and violence, in marked contrast to the rights guaranteed in the Constitution of 1954. This coercion is a far cry from the tactics of moderation displayed toward the end of the civil war. It was a result of the will to maintain power, fear of counter-revolutionary activity, and the decision to modernize the country at an extremely rapid rate. A secret police was organized, and the Ministry of Public Security was made responsible for the security of the regime. The country was covered by a vast espionage network. Peasant associations, village militia, residents' committees, and neighborhood associations were given the duty of taking care of security risks or aiding the police in such matters. There was no protection from house search or arrest, permits were required for any meeting of five or more persons, and the police had to be notified should a person spend even one night away from home.

A series of slogans and campaigns was designed to whip the populace into a frenzy. The refugee Kuomintang government on Formosa and the United States were depicted as the enemies of the state who support counterrevolutionaries. Actually, guerilla resistance was almost completely suppressed and the powerful army of 3 million regulars, 700,000 security troops, and about 12 million militia men was more than a match for any rebellion. Still, rallies were held at which some people were angrily denounced, while others made confessions and self-accusations of various sorts. Mass trials were another feature of the new order, and by 1955 the people's courts decided over 1 million cases, with death the penalty for treason, and compulsory labor and "re-educa-

159

tion" the punishment for lesser crimes. The American government has accused the Communist regime of eliminating no less than 15 million people. Peking arrogantly publicizes these activities in order to indoctrinate the people, keep the public in a submissive frame of mind, and maintain an unflagging vigilance against alleged enemies of the regime.

The Three-Anti (*San Fan*) and Five-Anti (*Wu Fan*) Movements of 1951–1952 illustrate the method and purpose of the regime's terrorist policies. These started with a series of scandals involving minor party and government officials in the provinces during 1951. Liu Shao-ch'i and the tough Manchurian party leader Kao Kang stressed the need for a purge to restore party purity. In October, Mao Tse-tung called for increased production as well as ideological reforms and blamed the capitalists for infiltrating and corrupting the party with bribes. It was at Mao's "suggestion" that the party underwent a vigorous program of self-criticism and education, resembling on a grand scale the self-examinations of 1942–1944.

The Three-Anti Movement, then, was aimed at the sins of the officials—corruption, waste, and bureaucracy (that is, red tape, "bourgeois" conduct, indifference to work, high living). For four months, all officials volunteered self-criticism and confessions, and faced the accusations of others. Even Mao and Chou En-lai admitted and criticized their own mistakes. By early 1952, the drive netted 1,670 corrupt officials, most of whom confessed and received light punishment. Public trials were held as one means of bringing the general public into this brain-washing campaign. Its ultimate purpose was to strengthen thought control over the officials and the people as a whole by establishing a recognized authoritative mold of the absolute truth. Heresy was stamped out and uniformity of thought assured.

In February, 1952, this campaign merged into the Five-Anti Movement, directed against the business community. At first merchants took the intitiative in weeding out corrupt or undesirable elements, but the government still launched a savage attack. The five sins were bribery, stealing government property, cheating the government, using economic information for speculation, and tax evasion. Every private economic enterprise went through the ordeal of confession, self-criticism, and accusations. Severe economic penalties amounted to a virtual confiscation of movable property. In the professions, committees were formed to examine their members. Scholars and teachers denounced past knowledge and beliefs and accepted the official version of history and society as the absolute truth.

What happened to the landlords and to "Kuomintang reactionaries" before 1950 is apparently to be the fate of the bourgeois elements under the new regime. But the warning that "heads will nod, then shake, then roll" may also be applied to the peasantry as the government presses forward with its effort to collectivize the farms. Thus in 1956 the Chinese Communist party boasted that it had converted capitalists to socialism and induced middle peasants to join cooperatives, by using legal pressures, "practical" education, and discriminatory economic practices.

160

Even the ruling group has not escaped the purges that plague communism. Kao Kang, once the fifth-ranking leader, fell from grace and was reported a suicide in the spring of 1955. This incident is constantly cited as an example and warning to all party members who might be tempted to challenge the present leaders. A distinguished literary critic and party sympathizer, Hu Feng, was ousted from various cultural groups and branded "anti-Socialist" in July, 1955. The party also promised to smash his clique in a campaign to exploit the arts for the "advance to Socialism." The sophisticated Chinese culture is thus being brought to heel by the crude demands of "socialist realism."

Western observers who held that muted complaints at the lack of democracy persisted in China found some evidence to support this view in 1956. In June, criticism was voiced in the national legislature for the first time, though of course it followed the line already established in party organs. Chou En-lai promised that the National People's Congress would meet more often and engage in criticism and self-criticism. When the Eighth Communist Party Congress, the first since 1945, was held in September, a new party constitution was adopted. It contained a provision that congresses at the local and national level be held at least once a year. Chou also pledged greater authority to the provincial governments with regard to planning, capital construction, and political-legal affairs. In light of the firm grip exercised by the government on the country's economic and political structure, these tentative reforms appear comparatively insignificant. The individual gained no protection against the state and, as the head of the Chinese Supreme Court observed, the country still lacked sorely needed civil, criminal, and labor codes.

Plans for Modernization

The ability to industrialize a society rapidly has become, especially in the Orient, communism's strongest appeal. The terror and rigidity of the new era have enabled the government to force from the people any sacrifices held necessary for the country's economic programs. China is following the Russian pattern of firm state control and direction, little investment in consumer goods or even essential agricultural enterprises, and concentration on heavy manufacturing and extractive industries. Western capital will be suspect or avoided altogether, but the Soviet government is committed to give China technical and financial aid for an extended period of time. However, the Bolsheviks of 1917 inherited a partly modernized economy and never ruled a population whose very size was a handicap. Communist China has a small industrial base and a population of more than 550 million (600 million claimed in the 1955 census), which threatens to increase rapidly.

Industrialization

The government adopted a relatively modest first five-year plan (1953-1957) but, when the results proved highly satisfactory, it established more ambitious targets for the period 1958-1962. Kuomintang rule followed centuries of relative stagnation, and its efforts at economic progress were partial and erratic at best. The country's economy at mid-century was typical of an underdeveloped region, save for the high government share of the gross national product.

GROSS NATIONAL PRODUCT	Percentage	EXPENDITURES	Percentage
Agriculture	40	Household consumption	73
Small industry	15	Communal services	4
Factory, industry, and mining	7	Government administration	4
Trade-transportation	24	Military outlay	7
Dwellings	4	Investment	12
Government	10		

SOURCE: Alexander Eckstein, "Conditions and Prospects for Economic Growth in Communist China," *World Politics*, VII, No. 3 (April, 1955), 435.

The rate of investment is high, compared to India's 8 per cent, and it is significant that almost half of it is going into industry. Agriculture received only 10 per cent, transportation 15 per cent, trade and banking 11 per cent, and the rest, including the military, 15 per cent. Four fifths of the investment in industry (or 40 per cent of the total investment) is going into heavy or producer goods items, with light industry getting the rest.

The emphasis on modern industry, heavy producers' goods, and state control brought notable results by 1954. At that date the output value of private industry had fallen from 63.3 per cent of all industrial output to a mere 24.9 per cent, and it was expected to drop to 12.2 per cent by 1957. Private industry was substantially replaced by joint state ownership, and even individual craftsmen were systematically absorbed in cooperatives. Meanwhile modern industry's share of total industrial and agricultural output rose from 17 per cent in 1949 to 33 per cent in 1954. Producers' goods in this same period jumped from 28.8 per cent of total industrial output to 42.3 per cent.

During the decade 1952–1962, the Chinese hope to raise the annual growth of the economy from 2 per cent at the start to 5 per cent at the end of this period. Meiji Japan, during its period of modernization (1880–1900) averaged from 4 to 5 per cent annually without any natural economic advantages; Communist China, with its totalitarian apparatus, may therefore be able to reach an annual average of from 3 to 4 per cent in 1952–1962. The government already channels from 20 to 30 per cent of the nation's expenses through the budget, and has a firm hold over the direction of the economy. However, Japan achieved rapid industrialization by first stressing improvements in agricultural production—especially through artificial fertilizer—and its textile industry, much of which was cottage production. This pattern is roughly being followed by India today, whose democratic five-year plan is adjusted in emphasis and rate of development to popular desires. India is stressing cottage industries as well as peasant ownership of land, all in sharp contrast to Communist doctrine.

China's production targets were set in 1952 with terminal dates varying from 1957 (the end of the first five-year plan) to 1959 (the end of the Russian aid program begun in 1953). It is difficult to estimate actual production and future expectation because of Communist secrecy, manipulation of figures for propaganda purposes, the inevitable changes made during the first plan, and the changing level of Russian aid. Thus the Russians promised aid for 141 industrial enterprises in 1953; the next year they offered more money for these projects and offered to finance 15 additional enterprises. This program enabled the Chinese to scale the goals upward, since the core of their plan is to build or improve some 600 important industrial plants. The regime estimates that the over-all industrialization program will take almost two generations.

Item	Unit	Pre-1949 Peak	1952	1954	1955 (Estimate)	1957 (Original Target)
INDUSTRY						
Coal	(million metric tons)	62.0	63.53	80.0	92.7	113.0
Pig iron	(million metric tons)	1.9	1.9	2.95	3.7	5.0
Steel	(million metric tons)	0.92	1.35	2.22	2.7	4.12
Cement	(million metric tons)	2.29	2.86	4.60		6.0
Cotton lint	(million metric tons)	0.84	1.30	1.07	1.31	1.63
Cotton yarn	(million bales)	2.4	3.6	4.5		5.0
Electric power	(billion kw-h.)	6.0	7.26	10.9	12.5	15.92
FOOD CROPS (In Million Metric Tons)						
All crops		150	163.9	169.5	177.9	192.8
Rice		53	68.4	70.5	78.5	81.7
Wheat		24	8.1	23.2		23.7
Soy beans		10	9.5	9.2		11.2
FREIGHT TRANSPORTATION (In Billion Ton-Kilometers)						
Railroads			60.2	93.1		120.9
Inland waterways			3.6			15.3
Coastal shipping (billion ton nautical miles)			2.0			5.8
Trucking			0.7	1.9		3.2

Indicative of the rise in expectations were the following revised targets (million metric tons) announced by Liu Shao-ch'i at the Eighth Communist Party Congress in September, 1956:

Coal: 1957—120; 1962—190 to 210.
Steel: 1957—5.5; 1962—10.5 to 12.
Electric power (billion kw-h.): 1957—18; 1962—40 to 43.
The all-crops target for 1962 was set at 250 million tons.

The three tables above show the production achievements and objectives reported by the State Planning Commission (July, 1955) and the State Statistical Bureau (September, 1954).[1] In 1956 the government announced that it

---

[1] Theodore Shabad, "Communist China's Five Year Plan," *Far Eastern Survey*, XXIV, No. 12 (December, 1955), 189–191.

would double industrial production by 1962, with China supplying over two thirds of its own machinery requirements. In addition, 5000 new miles of railway were planned, partly to help industry develop in the interior and reduce its concentration (75 per cent) in Manchuria and the coastal regions.

China's per capita income in 1962 would still be at an underdeveloped level of $62 in United States money, but the share of industry in the gross national product would rise from 7 per cent in 1952 to about 16 per cent in 1962. The workers, who benefited little at first, were promised a 35 per cent rise in real income, with the national income rising 50 per cent by 1960. An addition of six million workers to the labor force will be required during this period. These achievements would be remarkable by Asian standards, especially in the light of the difficult economic situation inherited by the Communists. Moreover, the psychological impact would be magnified considerably by propaganda claims. Chinese military power and communist subversion may be important threats to Southeast Asia, but the long-term economic development of Communist China may have even greater significance. It is up to the West to show how other methods can, as in Meiji Japan, bring progress without the economic deprivation or police-state methods of communism. Specifically, it is essential that India, which is following a more democratic method, attain a comparative degree of success in its program of modernization and improvement of living conditions. Economic development may prove to be the most significant and dramatic form of the struggle to contain communism in Asia. For, even if there is peace, the communists always seek to expand their realm and will not hesitate to use the magnetic attraction of a modernized and powerful China.

Of course it is true that the Chinese are not certain to achieve their goals. A huge population, a low level of productivity, a small industrial base, and restricted sources of foreign aid are bound to mean hardship and bitter reaction from an overburdened people. China sorely lacks adequate technicians, and even with Soviet assistance this deficit will persist. More serious are restrictions on its foreign trade, to some extent self-imposed by political prejudice and economic needs. But some restrictions are due to the embargo imposed by the United Nations during the Korean War and still applicable to strategic materials. Since any trade bringing valuable foreign currency can serve the industrialization program, commerce even in nonessential items benefits Peking. Foreign trade was estimated at only 3 per cent of the gross national product in 1952, but it contributed almost 20 per cent of the capital formation required for investment. The big rise in industrial production in 1955 was attributed by government officials to a bumper crop (184 million tons) which was used in both foreign trade and domestic capital accumulation. The government must concentrate on gathering a surplus of internal production—essentially agricultural—and converting it through foreign trade into capital-goods imports. The strain of accumulating such a surplus is a key problem in China's plans for industrialization.

The Agrarian Problem

Even with increased Russian assistance, China's problem of accumulating sufficient food remains acute. Despite improved farming methods and an increase of 6 per cent in cultivated land, the Chinese face continued deficits in production. Only intensive investments in artificial fertilizer can raise production per acre substantially, but this policy is rejected by the Communists because it would take funds away from industrial efforts. Production per acre is above that of Meiji Japan but below modern Japanese levels. To supply exports, feed the urban regions, and take care of a growing population, China must increase agricultural production by 25 per cent in the decade 1952–1962. The government's target is 35 per cent, in contrast to Western estimates of a 20 per cent rise during that period.

China is still at the mercy of the elements, which can play havoc with all production estimates. Thus, in 1954, the Communist government acknowledged unprecedented floods in the Yangtze and Hwai valleys, and about 10 per cent of the nation's 250-odd million acres was flooded. Production targets were not fulfilled in 1953 or 1954. The 1953 target for food was 170 to 175 million tons as against 165 million produced; cotton fell 10 per cent below its 1952 level, with 1.17 million tons, a good 300,000 tons below the 1953 goal. However, it rose to 1.5 million tons in 1955, and the target for 1962 was set at 2.4 million.

A further problem, common to all communist regimes, goes beyond these investment needs and natural difficulties: the government feels compelled to "socialize" agrarian production in order to increase efficiency, guarantee state control of the produce, and adhere to the doctrine of state ownership of all means of production. The "socialist transformation of agriculture" is a fixed aim of government; if the Russian and East European examples apply, this will antagonize the peasantry and may cause production to stagnate. In their rise to power, the Communists promised and gave land to the individual peasant. This hasty reversal of policy is a measure of the economic and ideological problems confronting the government.

Despite claims to originality, the Chinese Communist approach is depressingly similar to that of the East European satellites. The only novel feature in China's plan is the use of a "mutual-aid" period to precede the two later stages of "producers' cooperatives" and collectivization itself. The mutual-aid team, which introduces the peasant to joint farming operations, is featured by a temporary pooling of labor, with the peasant theoretically in control of his production, consumption, and sales. However, a Communist agent tries to foster a high degree of cooperation and prepare the way for the later stages. The government also uses economic incentives to encourage the formation of producers' cooperatives. These are barely distinguishable from collective farms, since both tools and labor are pooled, with joint cultivation and planning of production; returns are distributed primarily in accordance with labor invested but also, to a lesser degree, with land cultivated. In the collective stage, this last aspect disappears as the peasant loses his right to ownership and the theoretical privilege of withdrawing at will. Russian collectivization was linked with the use of tractors, and the mechanization of agriculture, as levers of political control and substitutes for manpower. In China, collectivization need not be accompanied by these innovations.

In 1954 the government claimed that more than half the nation's approximately 115 million peasant families were organized into mutual-aid teams. At that time it was planned to bring about half the households into 800,000 producers' cooperative units by 1957. Since then, however, the government has claimed phenomenal results. At the end of 1955 Mao Tse-tung announced that 60 per cent of the peasantry was organized in cooperatives, declaring that over 50 million families had been brought in within a few months. Then in September, 1956, 110 million families, or 90 per cent of the total, were reported to be in cooperatives or collective farms. When the government withdrew the dividends paid by cooperatives, the theoretical difference between this form and collectivization disappeared. The government boasted that 67 per cent of the farmers were fully collectivized in the fall of 1956. However, the level of consolidation is far below Russia's, for there are about one million farms in Chinese collectives as compared to 90,000 in the Soviet Union.

To the peasantry, all this has come as a bitter disappointment: exhortations to work, unabashed plans to collectivize recently acquired private property, deliveries at set prices in addition to tax levies on grain, economic assistance—in implements, technical aid, credits—below the level promised, forced savings, and little choice of consumer goods. Peasant unrest remains a latent problem for the government.

Transportation

The reconstruction and development of China's rail network have been given a high priority. Extensive railway plans for the sparsely populated western regions reflect the importance attached to overland trade with Russia. The government is also determined to exploit and eventually settle this vast western hinterland. A modern rail network is essential to China's political-military strength as well as its economy, for it will mean greater unity and more mobility in the transportation of troops and matériel. Eventually China's southwest and far west will be opened, three lines to Russia will be completed, and rail transportation will be possible from Siberia across all of China to the Gulf of Tonkin in Indochina. Even with an extensive labor supply, this program bites into the resources available for industrial expansion, but perhaps the strategic and political factors, plus the long-range economic advantages, outweigh this consideration.

A line through Outer and Inner Mongolia connects the important Soviet industrial complex in the Lake Baikal region with Peking, Tientsin, and the ice-free port of Taku. This link, through which much of China's industrial sup-

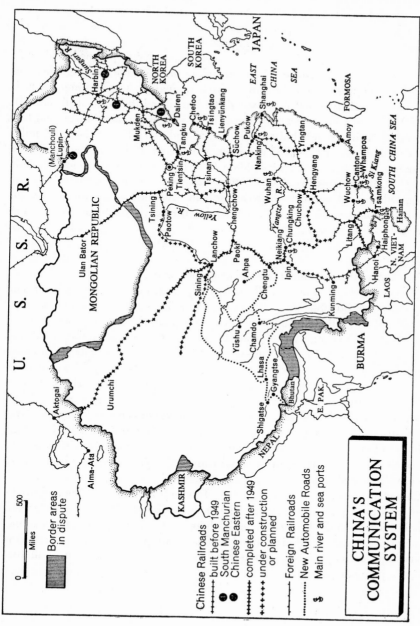

CHINA'S
COMMUNICATION
SYSTEM

Chinese Railroads
━━━ built before 1949
● ● South Manchurian
    Chinese Eastern
┿┿┿┿┿ completed after 1949
+++++ under construction
    or planned
──── Foreign Railroads
········ New Automobile Roads
ᶘ Main river and sea ports

Border areas
in dispute

0   500
Miles

U. S. S. R.

MONGOLIAN REPUBLIC

Ulan Bator

(Manchouli)
Lupin

Harbin

Sungari R.

NORTH
KOREA

SOUTH
KOREA

JAPAN

EAST
CHINA
SEA

FORMOSA

Mukden

Dairen

Chefoo

Tsingtao

Lienyünkang

Shanghai

Tsinan

Sichow

Pukow

Nanking

Yingtan

Tientsin

Tangku

Peking

Tsining

Paotow

Chengchow

Wuhan

Hengyang

Hengyang

Chungking

Chuchow

Lanchow

Sining

Paok'i

Ahpa

Neikiang

Ipin

Chengtu

Kunming

Wuchow

Canton
Whampoa
Tsamkong
Hainan

Amoy

Si Kiang

SOUTH CHINA SEA

Litang

Haiphong

Hanoi

LAOS

N. VIET-
NAM

BURMA

Yüshu

Chamdo

Lhasa

Shigatse

Gyangtse

Bhutan

NEPAL

E. PAK.

KASHMIR

Aktogai

Urumchi

Alma-Ata

Yellow R.

Yangtze R.

Adapted from Theodore Shabad, *China's Changing Map* (New York: Frederick A. Praeger, Inc., 1956). © 1956.

167

plies is expected to come, was completed by 1956. A second railway line will go through 2,000 miles of difficult terrain in Sinkiang, linking Lanchow with Alma Alta in Central Asia; this has grown at the steady, deliberate pace of 100 miles a year since 1952. These lines, plus the existing Manchurian link, will give China three major railways to Russia.

A series of links to China's trunk routes is also being planned. This will include a line from Paochi to Chengtu, linking up with the existing Chengtu-Chungking line; another route will go from Chungking to Kunming, where it will meet the rail line that now extends to Hanoi and the Gulf of Tonkin. In all, 600 miles of railroad were planned for 1955. Peking has claimed that 870 miles of new railway were built in 1949–1953 and that 1,675 of the 2,536 miles projected under the 1953–1957 plan were completed by 1956. In addition, the Chinese planned to cement their hold on Tibet by constructing two motor roads from Central and Northwest China that will converge on the capital city of Lhasa. Other road networks of strategic and economic value are on Hainan Island, off southern China, and in Fukien Province opposite the Nationalist stronghold of Formosa.

The Army

The Communist government moved cautiously in dismantling the large volunteer force with which it had fought its way to power. Its first conscription order went into effect in September, 1954, with 450,000 men called up in a trial run. In terms of eligibility, an average class of potential conscripts would total 3½ million each year; after allowing for various exemptions, there would still be more than 2 million a year. The conscription law of 1955 was first cautiously circulated around the country to test public reaction. It calls for three years of service in the army, four in the air force, and five in the navy. However, this potentially monster force will grow slowly because of high costs and the shortage of a disciplined cadre. Meanwhile the volunteer army, somewhat reduced in size but replenished by new recruits, will remain the backbone of China's military power. However, a professional officer corps is being planned, with candidates going through a regular training program and officers receiving the privileges and rights of rank.

China has only a small air force, dependent on Russia for training and equipment, and hardly any navy as yet. The army embodies its military power and it is the most formidable one in Asia. With its military prowess, economic plans, ideological initiative, and disciplined regime, resurgent China has had an enormous impact on East Asia and is now the most important element in that region's political pattern.

Foreign Relations

China has undergone a striking transformation in its foreign relations. It remains the storm center of Asian affairs, but its relative strength and expansionist tendencies have replaced the old power vacuum that drew foreign conquerors and exploiters to its shores. In this complete about-face, China is extending its influence and political suzerainty over neighboring regions, as in Manchu times. There is also the new ideology with its expansionist bias, seeking to convert the rest of eastern Asia to communism.

The Communists seized the initiative immediately after assuming power. In 1950–1951 China sent over a million men into the Korean War, thereby tying up enormous resources essential for economic development; but it fought the American-led United Nations forces to a standstill. Simultaneously, it invaded and asserted Chinese sovereignty over Tibet and eliminated Indian influence from this mountain region. Through patient negotiation with its Russian ally, China regained full control over Manchuria and Sinkiang, recognizing, in return, the independence of Outer Mongolia. It supported the Vietminh (Communist) rebellion across its southern border and, after the Korean truce of 1953, gave sufficient help to tip the balance against the French. China then participated in the 1954 conference at Geneva that affirmed communist control over at least North Vietnam.

The Peking government is fostering pan-Thai movements on its southern border in order to have an ethnic foothold for subversion against Thailand, the small kingdom of Laos, and perhaps the Shan region of Upper Burma. In 1949, it established what many call an "Asian Communist International" at Peking, in order to subvert Southeast Asia through local Communist parties and labor organizations. It is giving these groups training, inspiration, and direction, and is flooding the area with communist propaganda. Communist China has waged an unceasing propaganda war against the Nationalists on Formosa, and probably only American aid has kept that battered regime from succumbing either to military or psychological pressure. Finally, China's diplomatic leadership in Asia is personified in its Premier and Foreign Minister Chou En-lai, today considered the area's leading diplomat. His most outstanding achievements have been the friendship pacts with India and Burma in 1954, the fine showing he made at the Asian-African Conference held at Bandung, Indonesia, in 1955, and his efforts to bring stability to the European communist camp after the uprising in Hungary and the unrest in Poland late in 1956.

Hostility to the United States

An anchor point in China's foreign policy is implacable hostility to the West, with the United States singled out as the major force of evil. Even that document of temporary moderation—*The New Democracy*—stressed the inevitability of conflict with the West. China did not even acknowledge Britain's recognition of its government in 1950; formal contact with the British chargé d'affaires was first made in 1954, following the Geneva conference. By contrast, ambassadors were quickly exchanged with Asian states that recognized the Communist regime.

Clearly, China is responding with nationalist fervor to its years of helpless degradation. Moreover, a case can be made for an anti-American attitude in the light of American favoritism to the Nationalists in the civil war, lack of recognition after 1949, and support of the Kuomintang on Formosa. Yet the hostility was so intense from the first that China seems to have sought and even encouraged American acts of enmity. Even before 1949 the Communists likened the Americans to their former fascist enemies and held that the United States had replaced Japan as China's leading exploiter. All past history was distorted to show the United States as a subtle imperial power, responsible for every degradation China had suffered in the past, such as the Opium Wars and the Boxer Incident. The Communists denounced an American-Chinese economic treaty of 1946 as the last of the unequal treaties. In 1950, China opened a vigorous hate-America campaign with the United States described as a rotten, strife-ridden, imperialist nation, and a "paper tiger." The Chinese also arrested American nationals, including consular officials, and seized American property. Yet Peking professed to be incensed when it did not gain recognition or China's seat in the United Nations.

The Korean War of June, 1950, and China's entry into the struggle that fall hardened American-Chinese animosity. China aided North Korea at an early stage of the fighting but did not fully engage American troops until United Nations forces crossed latitude 38° into North Korea. The first major encounter took place near the Yalu River frontier of Manchuria; the Chinese argued that they were fighting a just cause in self-defense against an American aggressor who was following in Imperial Japan's footsteps. Flushed with the victory in their own civil war, the Communists sought to sweep the "paper tiger" off the Korean peninsula entirely and ignored early United Nations' appeals for peace. Under American pressure, the United Nations declared China an aggressor in February, 1951, and that May placed an embargo on trade with China in strategic materials. During the two-year stalemate that followed, Chinese propaganda blamed America for starting the war and accused the United States of germ warfare. When a truce was arranged in July, 1953, China treated this as a major victory, just as it had considered all peace overtures as signs of Western weakness.

Since the Nationalists on Formosa posed the only threat to the Communist regime, the fate of that island remained a major issue between the United States and China. The Nationalists were at first uncertain of American support but, when the Korean War began in 1950, the United States neutralized and protected Formosa. The Peking government considered this proof of American aggression and was further angered when the Eisenhower administration in 1953 removed the restriction on Nationalist offensive action. Since then, the United States has signed a defense treaty with the Nationalists but on grounds that preclude Kuomintang assaults on the mainland. The Communists feel that they can easily conquer Formosa, if unmolested, and insist that this is a purely internal Chinese problem. Peking has mixed threats with offers to negotiate only on its own terms.

Friendship with Russia

The Soviet Union, which by definition could not be imperialist or aggressive, was hailed as the leader of the anti-American "peace front." It was considered the source of China's intellectual inspiration and the power that would protect and enhance the communist world revolution. No public hostility resulted from bad advice in the past, earlier Russian support of the Kuomintang, Soviet looting of Manchuria, the detachment of Outer Mongolia, or continued economic privileges enjoyed by Russia in Manchuria and Sinkiang until 1954. The Soviet and Chinese governments seem to have harmonized their foreign policies to a remarkable extent, and to have worked out their mutual relations in a cooperative spirit. The Russians began their long-range programs of extensive aid to China in 1953 and the following year yielded their rights on Chinese territory.[2]

The dominant part of China's foreign trade is with the Soviet bloc, with Russia itself accounting for three quarters of the total. This completely reverses the pre-1949 pattern, when most trade was with the West. China still exports its standard commodities of soybeans, tea, silk, wool, agricultural products, and metals. Instead of consumer goods, however, China now imports primarily industrial raw materials, machinery, and communications equipment.

Chinese-Russian relations are still beset by such traditional handicaps as China's suspicion of foreigners, Russia's long record of encroachment under the czars, and Russia's control—through trade and assistance programs—over China's rate of economic development. Officially, China's faith in the U.S.S.R. remains unshakable, though communist frictions are never exposed to the world short of the rupture point. The Peking government is making every effort to popularize the Russians among its people. Soviet virtues and friendship are extolled in a barrage of literary, radio, and film propaganda, and through such devices as student exchanges. A Sino-Soviet Friendship Association was formed for this purpose, and in 1951 it already had 1,300 branches working to eliminate "vestiges of anti-Soviet thought."

Policy toward Its Neighbors

China seeks to advance the cause of communism in eastern Asia, and will adopt any tactics, however contradictory they may appear, that will serve this purpose. The Chinese count on the attraction of their ideology, the glamour and menace of their power, the alleged results of industrialization, and support of subversive groups abroad. Yet they constantly repeat assurances of peaceful intention and respect for the integrity of other national, anti-imperialist states. The Peking government condemned the Japanese Peace Treaty, calling it illegal, a threat to peace, and a device to keep Japan subjugated, primarily because it was linked to an agreement permitting the United States to retain bases and troops there. By contrast, similar Soviet rights in Manchuria were hailed as guarantees of peace and security.

[2] See Chapter 17, "Russia in the Far East," pages 508–509.

China's ideological interpretation of the situation in South Asia reveals its revolutionary attitude. Peking is willing to support native nationalist movements that are properly led and imbued with "proletarian patriotism" against foreign imperialism. Middle-class nationalists who fight colonial or semi-colonial rule can be used as temporary allies in achieving the proletarian revolution. However, existing middle-class governments that came into power after 1945 were severely criticized for sabotaging the social revolution and were described as mere semicolonial fronts for the departed imperial powers. Presumably, Burma, India, and Indonesia, with whom Peking is cultivating friendly relations, as well as the Philippines, are in this category. Western imperialism remains the main enemy, and China describes itself as the leader of Asia's effort to fight this sinister cause of misery.

A first step was to dominate areas considered part of the national realm. Thus Tibet was freed from itself by an invasion of Chinese troops, and since 1951 has been "protected against foreign imperialists." But Western influence had already ended when Britain turned over its interest in Tibet to India in 1947; in fact, the region had enjoyed political autonomy for more than a century. An Indian offer to hasten a settlement was bluntly rejected on the grounds of interference in China's internal affairs. India was torn by concern for its own security and a strong desire to believe in Chinese good-will. Peking and New Delhi finally reached a settlement in April, 1954. Chinese sovereignty was recognized, Indian military garrisons were withdrawn, and India retained trading rights in certain Tibetan cities. That October there followed a commercial agreement that enabled China to use Indian ports and railways to trade with Tibet.

In North Korea, a Chinese army has remained since the truce, to guarantee Peking's interests and the security of the local communist regime. China and North Korea signed a ten-year treaty of friendship, mutual assistance, reciprocity, and equality in 1953. with the objective of strengthening cultural and economic relations. China, like Russia, offered aid to the battered Korean regime, writing off all wartime expenditures and promising over $300 million for reconstruction by 1957. Chinese influence in Korea has risen markedly as a result of the peninsular war and its aftermath, and North Korea appears to be assuming its historical role of a Chinese satellite.

Just south of the border, Chinese aid to the hard-fighting Vietminh Communist forces in Northern Indochina finally undermined the French military position in the Red River area. With Indian diplomacy playing a contributing role, the Chinese Communists and the Russians induced the Vietminh not to press the war further but allow the French to evacuate the north and accept a temporary partition of Vietnam. During a recess in the Geneva Conference of June, 1954, at which this agreement was reached, Chou En-lai visited Prime Minister Nehru of India, and the two leaders issued a joint statement of principles to which they adhered. These Five Principles, criticized in the West for vagueness, were mutual respect for each other's sovereignty and territorial integrity; nonaggression; noninterference in each other's internal affairs; equality and mutual benefit; and peaceful coexistence. A similar accord was reached with the Burmese, who do not trust China's good faith but are following the policy of a small, neutralist power confronted with a powerful and potentially aggressive neighbor.

Trade-unions and Communist parties in Asian lands have continued to serve as communist weapons. In December, 1949, a conference of Asian and Australasian trade-unions was convened at Peking. It formed an Asian-Australasian Liaison Bureau of the communist-dominated World Federation of Trade Unions (from which democratic trade-unions had long departed). This Bureau and a Peace Liaison Committee established in 1952 at a so-called Asian Pacific Peace Conference may well form a central headquarters for East Asian communist activity. All of Southeast Asia lies exposed to Chinese Communist pressure. Chinese residents there, the weak administration of these states, and the Communist parties offer levers to power. Possessing the most powerful and dynamic force in the Far East, the Chinese government may feel that time is on its side and that Southeast Asia will fall into communist hands eventually, without a major struggle.

The Nationalists on Formosa

When the military situation on the mainland collapsed in 1948–1949, Chiang Kai-shek organized a retreat to Formosa (Taiwan), seeing in it the only haven of refuge that could give his cause some security and so allow him to await his opportunity to return to the mainland. Since Kuomintang power had fallen to such a low state that the Nationalists could no longer account for their own military security, let alone precipitate a counteroffensive, these military-diplomatic questions became primarily issues for American foreign policy and are discussed in that context.[3] It is sufficient to note here that before June, 1950, the island appeared highly vulnerable to a Communist assault because the United States was not committed to its defense. The attack on South Korea completely changed American policy to one of guaranteeing Formosa protection against any assault from the mainland. In addition, with the help of American military aid, in training and matériel, the Nationalists reorganized their forces and have welded their army of 600,000 into a well-equipped disciplined fighting force.

These developments have given both the Nationalists on the island and the native population some sense of security and an expectation that their position there will not be easily overturned despite repeated Communist promises to "liberate" Formosa. On the other hand, the Nationalist exhortation "return to the mainland" becomes more hollow with each passing year, though this remains the party's official aspiration. In any event, Kuomintang officials have concen-

[3] See Chapter 18, pages 537, 540–542.

trated on improving and developing Formosa itself, in order to strengthen their political position and establish a basis for favorable comparison of their work with that of their Communist rivals on the mainland.

The island had suffered serious economic losses in 1944–1945, when American bombings and the effects of United States naval power reduced its productive capacity markedly. The Japanese had built a sizable economic plant in their half century of rule (1895–1945), including a railway network, coal mines, sugar and oil refineries, as well as cement, paper, and metallurgical and aluminum plants. Such crops as rice, sugar, pineapples, tea, and camphor were important exports and made the colony a valuable asset to Tokyo. The effects of the war can be seen in the following statistics: rice production, which stood at 1.4 million tons in 1938, fell to 0.64 million tons by 1945; the use of fertilizer on rice fields had fallen from 389,300 tons to a mere 1,960 tons during these years.

The Nationalists inherited a difficult situation in 1945 when they assumed political rule over Formosa. It was made even worse by the activities of the first Chinese governor, Chen Yi, a former warlord who used this assignment as an opportunity to enrich himself. He was guilty of such oppressive and corrupt practices that the islanders revolted against his rule in 1947. Only after this incident, which was suppressed with considerable violence, did the Kuomintang replace Chen Yi. It was unfortunate that while in power on the mainland the Nationalists permitted the same pattern of misrule that existed in China to occur on Formosa. Only after the disaster of 1948–1949, when confronted with the prospect of utter annihilation, did the Kuomintang institute vigorous reforms on Formosa.

Early in 1949, Chiang Kai-shek placed General Ch'en Ch'eng in authority in order to strengthen the island's internal security and assure Kuomintang control. General Ch'en invoked martial law, arresting and executing many people suspected of communist sympathies. His rule alienated the people of the island further, and matters were made worse because economic conditions did not improve. Later that year the Nationalist government itself moved to the island and General Ch'en was placed in charge of its Executive Yuan. Direction of the provincial government was given to a capable administrator, K. C. Wu. All operations were carried on under the direct supervision of Chiang Kai-shek himself.

Since 1950 the combination of orderly administration, a reform program, and American economic help (about $500 million during 1950–1956) has led to remarkable progress. A major achievement has been land reform, which was begun by reducing the tenant's annual rent from 50 per cent to 37.5 per cent of the crop. The law, unlike earlier Kuomintang edicts on the mainland, was effectively enforced. It led to a rise in peasant income and a drop in land values, with the result that peasants could more easily buy land. A land redistribution program was introduced, some public lands were sold to the peasantry, and many tenants simply purchased the land they worked. As a result, the proportion of owner-cultivated land rose from 50 to 75 per cent. This revolution in land tenure has been acompanied by a 50 per cent increase in agricultural production. Sugar production has been restricted to an annual level of 700,000 tons a year under an international agreement, but rice has reached 1.7 million tons, and the number of hogs is now 3 million, or twice its 1949 total. The government has carried out extensive programs in timber conservation, irrigation, and rural public health. It has received invaluable help in these projects by the American-sponsored Joint Commission for Rural Reconstruction, which has been active on Formosa since 1948.

The Nationalists are also seeking to industrialize Formosa's economy, because the heavy military burden, the limited amount of arable land, and the island's growing population all point to a rising inflationary pressure. The population of 10 million, which includes 2 million mainlanders, is increasing at an annual rate of 3 per cent. Therefore many business leaders feel that industrial products should provide a larger share of Formosa's exports, which now depend heavily on the sale of sugar and rice to Japan. Industrial output doubled between 1950 and 1956, with electric power, for example, rising from a capacity of 150,000–170,000 kilowatts under Japanese rule to about 350,000 in 1956. Many former landowners have been converted into investors in industrial enterprises by the land reform program of expropriation-with-compensation, and industry as a whole is undergoing both expansion and diversification. A major objective is to sell industrial products, such as light electrical equipment, to Southeast Asia, thereby strengthening Formosa's balance-of-trade position and improving relations with the Overseas Chinese.

In the field of education, a fairly high literacy rate had been achieved under Japanese rule, and this was raised to 82.5 per cent in the 1950's. There has been a marked increase in the number of students at all age levels; in 1955 there were more than 1,200,000 children (90 per cent of the total) in grade school. At the higher levels, the government is stressing vocational education, for there is a shortage of skilled workers.

Efforts have been made to gain the support of the Formosan people by allowing them a greater participation in the direction of the island's political affairs. Formosa is administered as a province of the Nationalist Republic of China. It has its own 55-man legislative assembly and is subdivided into five municipalities and sixteen counties, each with a legislative council. There have been three general elections at local levels since 1948, and 96 per cent of the 433 municipal and country councilors elected in 1954–1955 were Formosans. The percentage of natives in the Formosan legislative assembly is only 57 per cent, but more than 70 per cent of the province's administrative officials are islanders.

When K. C. Wu resigned as governor in 1953 he was succeeded by O. K. Yui, who in turn became premier of the central government in 1954. At this time C. K. Yen became governor. The second election of a president and vice-president of the Republic of China occurred in 1954, and the National Assembly's 1,577 delegates chose Chiang Kai-shek and General Ch'en Ch'eng, respectively, to fill these positions. Hence the forms of government adopted on the mainland in 1947–1948 are retained as the Nationalists continue to cherish the hope of regaining control of China. But, as the Communist regime makes rapid strides toward becoming a major industrial and military power, the Nationalist cause, centered on its island stronghold 100 miles off the South China coast, faces a grim future.

Bibliography

CHINA

General

LATOURETTE, K. S., *The Chinese: Their History and Culture.* 2 vols., 3rd ed.; New York: Macmillan, 1946.

CRESSEY, G. B., *China's Geographic Foundations.* New York: McGraw-Hill, 1934.

CRESSEY, G. B., *Land of the 500 Million: A Geography of China.* New York: McGraw-Hill, 1955.

HERRMANN, A. A. L., *Historical and Commercial Atlas of China.* Cambridge: Harvard Univ. Press, 1936.

GOODRICH, L. C., *A Short History of the Chinese People.* New York: Harper, 1953.

MACNAIR, H. F. (ed.), *China.* Berkeley: Univ. of California Press, 1946.

EBERHARD, W., *A History of China.* Berkeley: Univ. of California Press, 1946.

FAIRBANK, J. K., *The United States and China.* Cambridge: Harvard Univ. Press, 1949.

NEEDHAM, J., *Science and Civilization in China.* London: Cambridge Univ. Press, 1954, Vol. I.

CREEL, H. G., *Chinese Thought from Confucius to Mao Tse-tung.* Chicago: Univ. of Chicago Press, 1953.

SHER, T. H., *Agriculture Resources of China.* Ithaca: Cornell Univ. Press, 1951.

WINFIELD, G., *China: The Land and the People.* New York: Sloane, 1948.

KIRBY, E. S., *Introduction to the Economic History of China.* New York: Macmillan, 1954.

Ancient China

CREEL, H. G., *The Birth of China.* New York: Harcourt, Brace, 1937.

CREEL, H. G., *Studies in Early Chinese Culture.* Baltimore: Waverly Press, 1937.

BISHOP, C. W., *Origin of the Far Eastern Civilization.* Washington: Smithsonian Institute, 1942.

WALEY, A., *The Way and Its Power.* Boston: Houghton Mifflin, 1942.

LIU WU-CHI, *A Short History of Confucian Philosophy.* London: Penguin, 1955.

WALEY, A. (ed.), *The Analects of Confucius.* New York: Macmillan, 1939.

WALEY, A., *Three Ways of Thought in Ancient China.* London: Allen & Unwin, 1939.

CREEL, H. G., *Confucius: The Man and the Myth.* New York: John Day, 1949.

SWANN, N. L., *Food and Money in Ancient China.* Princeton: Princeton Univ. Press, 1950.

EBERHARD, W., *Conquerors and Rulers: Social Forms in Medieval China.* Leiden: Brill, 1952.

LEGGE, J., *The Chinese Classics.* 7 vols., 2nd ed.; Oxford: Clarendon Press, 1893-1895.

BODDE, D., *China's First Unifier: A Study of the Ch'in Dynasty as Seen in the Life of Li Ssu.* Leiden: Brill, 1938.

BODDE, D., *Statesman, Patriot and General in Ancient China: Three Shih Chi Biographies of the Ch'in Dynasty (255–206 B.C.).* New Haven: American Oriental Society, 1940.

DUBS, H. (trans.), *The History of the Former Han Dynasty by Pan Ku.* Baltimore: Waverly Press, Vol. 1, 1938; Vol. 2, 1944.

WILBUR, C. M., *Slavery in China during the Former Han Dynasty: 206 B.C.-A.D. 253.* Chicago: Field Museum of National History, 1943.

BINGHAM, W., *The Founding of the T'ang Dynasty.* Baltimore: Waverly Press, 1944.

REISCHAUER, E. (trans.), *Ennin's Diary: The Records of a Pilgrimage to China.* New York: Ronald, 1955.

REISCHAUER, E., *Ennin's Travels in T'ang China.* New York: Ronald, 1955.

WITTFOGEL, K. A., and C. S. FENG, *History of Chinese Society, Liao: 907–1125.* New York: Macmillan, 1949.

FITZGERALD, C. P., *Son of Heaven: A Biography of Li Shih-min, Founder of the T'ang Dynasty.* New York: Macmillan, 1934.

WILLIAMSTON, H. R., *Wang An Shih.* London: Probsthain, 1935, 1937.

RICCI, A., *The Travels of Marco Polo.* London: Routledge & Kegan Paul, 1931.

RICCI, M., *Journals: China in the Sixteenth Century.* New York: Random House, 1953.

MICHAEL, F., *The Origin of Manchu Rule in China.* Baltimore: Johns Hopkins Press, 1942.

WILLIAMS, S. W., *The Middle Kingdom.* Rev. ed.; New York: Wiley, 1883.

HUMMEL, A. W. (ed.), *Eminent Chinese of the Ch'ing Period,* 2 vols.; Washington: Government Printing Office, 1943, 1944.

The Fringe Regions

LATTIMORE, O., *Inner Frontiers of China.* New York: American Geographic Society, 1940.

LATTIMORE, O., *Manchuria, Cradle of Conflict.* New York: Macmillan, 1932.

McGOVERN, W. M., *The Early Empires of Central Asia.* Chapel Hill: Univ. of N. C. Press, 1939.

PARKER, E. M., *A Thousand Years of the Tartars.* 2nd ed.; New York: Knopf, 1924.

LATTIMORE, O., and associates, *Pivot of Asia.* Boston: Little, Brown, 1950.

FRITERS, G., *Outer Mongolia and Its International Position.* Baltimore: Johns Hopkins Press, 1949.

PROWDIN, M., *The Mongol Empire: Its Rise and Legacy.* London: Allen & Unwin, 1952.

HOWARTH, H. H., *History of the Mongols from the Ninth to the Nineteenth Century.* London: Longmans, Green, 1876-1888.

LATTIMORE, O., *Nationalism and Revolution in Mongolia.* New York: Oxford, 1955.

RIENCOURT, A. DE, *Roof of the World.* New York: Rinehart, 1951.

LI TIEH-TSENG, *The Historical Status of Tibet.* New York: King's Crown Press, 1955.

SHEN TSUNG-LIEN and LIU SHEN-CHI, *Tibet and the Tibetans.* Stanford: Stanford Univ. Press, 1953.

BELL, C., *Tibet: Past and Present.* Oxford: Clarendon Press, 1925.

BELL, C., *The People of Tibet.* Oxford: Clarendon Press, 1928.

Contacts with the West

HUDSON, G. F., *Europe and China: A Survey of the Relations from Earliest Times to 1800.* London: E. Arnold, 1931.

MORSE, H. B., *The International Relations of the Chinese Empire.* 3 vols.; New York: Longmans, Green, 1910–1918.

REICHWEIN, A., *China and Europe: Intellectual and Artistic Contacts in the Eighteenth Century.* New York: Knopf, 1925.

GILBERT, R., *The Unequal Treaties.* London: Murray, 1929.

KEETON, G. W., *The Development of Extraterritoriality in China.* 2 vols.; London: Longmans, Green, 1928.

HUGHES, E. R., *The Invasion of China by the Western World.* New York: Macmillan, 1938.

ROWBOTHAM, A. H., *Missionary and Mandarin: The Jesuits at the Court of China.* Berkeley: Univ. of California Press, 1942.

LATOURETTE, K. S., *A History of Christian Missionaries in China.* New York: Macmillan, 1928.

TENG SSU-YU, and J. K. FAIRBANK, *China's Response to the West: A Documentary Survey, 1839–1923.* Cambridge: Harvard Univ. Press, 1954.

SUN E-TU ZEN, *Chinese Railways and British Interests.* New York: King's Crown Press, 1954.

CHIANG, M., *Tides from the West.* New Haven: Yale Univ. Press, 1947.

CHANG, K. N., *China's Struggle for Railway Development.* New York: John Day, 1943.

WRIGHT, S. F., *China's Struggle for Tariff Autonomy; 1843–1938.* Shanghai: Kelley and Walsh, 1938.

TAMAGNE, F. M., *Banking and Finance in China.* New York: Inst. of Pacific Relations, 1932.

LEVI, W., *Modern China's Foreign Policy.* Minneapolis: Univ. of Minnesota Press, 1953.

FISHEL, W. R., *The End of Extraterritoriality in China.* Berkeley: Univ. of California Press, 1952.

The End of Manchu Rule

HAIL, W. J., *Tseng Kuo-fang and the Taiping Rebellion.* New Haven: Yale Univ. Press, 1927.

SMITH, A. H., *China in Convulsion.* 2 vols.; London: Oliphant, 1903.

TAN, C., *The Boxer Catastrophe.* New York: Columbia Univ. Press, 1955.

REID, J. G., *The Manchu Abdication and the Powers: 1908–1912.* Berkeley: Univ. of California Press, 1935.

POWELL, R. L., *The Rise of Chinese Military Power: 1885–1912.* Princeton: Princeton Univ. Press, 1955.

CAMERON, M. E., *The Reform Movement in China: 1898–1912.* Stanford: Stanford Univ. Press, 1931.

The Nationalist Revolution

HOLCOMB, A. N., *The Chinese Revolution.* Cambridge: Harvard Univ. Press, 1930.

MacNAIR, H. F., *China in Revolution.* Chicago: Univ. of Chicago Press, 1931.

SHARMAN, L., *Sun Yat-sen,* New York: John Day, 1934.

CHEN, S., and R. PAYNE, *Sun Yat-sen: A Portrait.* New York: John Day, 1946.

LEVENSON, J., *Liang Ch'i-ch'ao and the Mind of Modern China.* Cambridge: Harvard Univ. Press, 1953.

CH'IEN TUAN-SHENG, *The Government and Politics of China.* Cambridge: Harvard Univ. Press, 1950.

LINEBARGER, P. M. A., *The Political Doctrines of Sun Yat-sen.* Baltimore: Johns Hopkins Press, 1937.

HU SHIH, *The Chinese Renaissance.* Chicago: Univ. of Chicago Press, 1934.

CHIANG KAI-SHEK, *China's Destiny.* New York: Macmillan, 1947.

WOO, T. C., *The Kuomintang and the Future of the Chinese Revolution.* London: Allen & Unwin, 1928.

POLLARD, R. T., *China's Foreign Relations: 1917–1931.* New York: Macmillan, 1933.

LINEBARGER, P. M. A., *The China of Chiang Kai-shek.* Boston: World Peace Foundation, 1941.

FITZGERALD, C. P., *Revolution in China.* New York: Praeger, 1952.

ISAACS, H., *The Tragedy of the Chinese Revolution.* Rev. ed.; Stanford: Stanford Univ. Press, 1951.

The Japanese War and After

BARNETT, R. W., *Economic Shanghai: Hostage to Politics: 1937–1941.* New York: Inst. of Pacific Relations, 1941.

BISSON, T. A., *Japan in China.* New York: Macmillan, 1938.

QUIGLEY, H. J., *Far Eastern War: 1937–1941.* Boston: World Peace Foundation, 1942.

LEAGUE OF NATIONS, *Report of the Commission of Inquiry* and *Supplementary Documents.* Geneva, 1932.

KOO, V. K. W., *Memoranda Presented to the Lytton Commission.* 3 vols.; New York, The Chinese Cultural Society, 1932–1933.

YOUNG, C. W., *The International Relations of Manchuria.* Chicago: Univ. of Chicago Press, 1929.

JONES, F. C., *Manchuria since 1931.* London: Royal Inst. of Int. Affairs, 1949.

CHIANG KAI-SHEK, *The Collected Wartime Messages of Generalissimo Chiang Kai-shek, 1937–1945.* New York: John Day, 1946.

FRIEDMAN, I. S., *British Relations with China: 1931–1939.* New York: Inst. of Pacific Relations, 1940.

Chinese Yearbook. Shanghai: Commercial Press, 1936 ff.

China Handbook, 1937–1943. Rev. ed.; New York: Macmillan, 1933, 1947.

ROWE, D. N., *China among the Powers.* New York: Harcourt, Brace, 1945.

MURPHY, R., *Shanghai; Key to Modern China.* Cambridge: Harvard Univ. Press, 1955.

LIANG YEN, *Daughter of the Khans.* New York: Norton, 1955.

WHITE, T., and A. JACOBY, *Thunder out of China.* New York: Sloan, 1946.

BELDEN, J., *China Shakes the World.* New York: Harper, 1949.

MOORAD, G., *Lost Peace in China.* New York: Dutton, 1949.

The Rise of Communism

BRANDT, C., and others, *A Documentary History of Chinese Communism.* Cambridge: Harvard Univ. Press, 1952.

SCHWARTZ, B., *Chinese Communism and the Rise of Mao.* Cambridge: Harvard Univ. Press, 1951.

NORTH, R., *Moscow and Chinese Communists.* Stanford: Stanford Univ. Press, 1953.

COMPTON, B., *Mao's China: Party Reform Documents: 1942–1944.* Seattle: Univ. of Washington Press, 1952.

MAO TSE-TUNG, *Collected Works.* 5 vols.; New York: Int. Pubs., 1954———.

BOND, C., and W. BOND, *Two Years with the Chinese Communists.* New Haven: Yale Univ. Press, 1948.

WALES, N., *Red Dust: Autobiographies of Chinese Communists.* Stanford: Stanford Univ. Press, 1952.

SNOW, E., *Red Star over China.* New York: Random House, 1938.

STEIN, G., *The Challenge of Red China.* New York: McGraw-Hill, 1944.

EPSTEIN, I., *The Unfinished Revolution in China.* Boston: Little, Brown, 1947.

PAYNE, R., *China Awake.* New York: Dodd, Mead, 1947.

NORTH, R., *Kuomintang and Communist Elites.* Stanford: Stanford Univ. Press, 1952.

PECK, G., *Two Kinds of Time.* Boston: Houghton Mifflin, 1950.

BODDE, D., *Peking Diary.* New York: Abelard-Shuman, 1950.

U. S. WAR DEPT., *The Chinese Communist Movement,* in U.S. Senate Committee on the Judiciary, Hearings before the Subcommittee to Investigate the Administration of the Internal Security Act and Other Security Laws, Part 7a, Appendix II. Washington: Government Printing Office, 1952.

Social and Economic Conditions in Modern China

BUCK, J. L., *Land Utilization in China.* 2 vols.; Chicago: Univ. of Chicago Press, 1937.

TAWNEY, R. H., *Land and Labor in China.* New York: Harcourt, Brace, 1932.

SMITH, A. H., *Village Life in China.* New York: Revell, 1899.

FEI HSIAO-T'UNG, Peasant Life in China. New York: Dutton, 1939.

FRIED, M., *Fabric of Chinese Society.* New York: Praeger, 1953.

HSU, F., *Under the Ancestor's Shadow.* New York: Columbia Univ. Press, 1948.

KIANG WEN-HAU, *The Chinese Student Movement.* New York: King's Crown Press, 1948.

LANG, O., *Chinese Family and Society.* New Haven: Yale Univ. Press, 1946.

LEVY, M., *The Family Revolution in Modern China.* Cambridge: Harvard Univ. Press, 1947.

YANG, M., *A Chinese Village.* New York: Columbia Univ. Press, 1946.

WALES, N., *The Chinese Labor Movement,* New York: John Day, 1945.

Communist Rule

WALKER, R. L., *China under Communism: The First Five Years.* New Haven: Yale Univ. Press, 1955.

SHABAD, T., *China's Changing Map.* New York: Praeger, 1955.

THOMAS, S. B., *Government and Administration in Communist China*. New York: Wiley, 1954.

PANIKKAR, K. M., *In Two Chinas: Memoirs of a Diplomat*. London: Allen & Unwin, 1955.

CAMERON, J., *Mandarin Red*. New York: Rinehart, 1955.

RIGG, R., *Red China's Fighting Hordes*. Harrisburg: Military Service Pub. Co., 1951.

LINDSAY, M., *China and the Cold War*. New York: Cambridge Univ. Press, 1955.

HUTHEESING, R., *The Great Peace*. New York: Harper, 1953.

MORAES, F., *Report on Mao's China*. New York: Macmillan, 1953.

TENNIEN, M., *No Secret Is Safe behind the Bamboo Curtain*. New York: Farrar, Straus & Cudahy, 1952.

YEN, M., *The Umbrella Garden*. New York: Macmillan, 1954.

DUNLAP, A. M., *Behind the Bamboo Curtain*. Washington: Public Affairs Press, 1956.

WU YUAN-LI, *An Economic Survey of Communist China*. New York: Bookman Associates, 1956.

U.S. CONSULATE GENERAL, Hong Kong publications, *Current Background* and *Survey of the China Mainland Press*.

EXILE GROUPS: China News Analysis, Freedom Front, Hong Kong Union Research Institute. See the latter's "Communist China Problem Research Series," especially review article by R. W. Hatch in *World Politics*, Vol. VII, No. 1 (October, 1955).

Nationalists on Formosa

GRAJDANZEV, A. J., *Formosa Today*. New York: Inst. of Pacific Relations, 1942.

HAHN, E., *Chiang Kai-shek: An Unauthorized Biography*. Garden City: Doubleday, 1955.

BATE, H., *Report from Formosa*. New York: Dutton, 1952.

RIGGS, F., *Formosa under China's Nationalist Rule*. New York: Macmillan, 1952.

BALLANTINE, J. W., *Formosa*. Washington: Brookings Institution, 1952.

BARCLAY, G. W., *Colonial Development and Population in Taiwan*. Princeton: Princeton Univ. Press, 1954.

China Handbook, 1953–1954. Taipei: China Publishing Co., 1953, and New York: Pierce, 1954.

TANG HUI-SUN, *Land Reform in Free China*. Taipei: Chinese-American Joint Commission on Rural Construction, 1954.

RAND, C., *Hongkong: The Island in Between*. New York: Knopf, 1952.

INGRAM, W. H., *Hong Kong*. London: His Majesty's Stationery Office, 1952.

PART THREE **Japan**

7 The Japanese Political Tradition

During the last third of the nineteenth century, Japan embarked on a program of industrialization of breathtaking scope. Until the end of the Second World War it met with astonishing success as the country assumed a lead over the rest of the Far East in both national cohesion and material development. This relatively small group of islands was the prime force behind most major events in East Asia and, almost unwittingly, served as a spark that set off a series of crises in that region, which have not yet shown signs of abating.

Under any analysis, the Japanese achievement must be deemed remarkable, since the country had no special attributes—in size of population, availability of technical skill, or abundance of natural resources. Credit must be given to determined leadership, which channeled the entire energy of the nation into revamping the economic and social structure of the Japanese community. A cursory examination reveals great success in emulating both the West's physical attributes and its formal political institutions. Industrial plants grew rapidly— first, light industries like textiles and, later, heavier goods—and the cities developed into modern urban centers like Tokyo, Nagoya, Osaka, and Kobe. Road and rail lines were built, telegraphic communication and electric power spread, and, as befits an island power, the Japanese merchant marine became one of the finest in the world. The development of financial and commercial facilities added further proof that Japan had become an efficient modern power, achieving in two or three generations what had been first accomplished in Britain over several centuries.

The assimilation of Western political techniques, however, was more apparent than real. The form of government adopted was the then fashionable constitutional monarchy, with little power held directly by the emperor. A parliament, or Diet, was created and a beautiful building constructed to house it. The government was directed by a cabinet, and there was even a written constitution in 1890, that accepted guarantee of political stability. Many Western observers were awed into concluding that here was a miracle of thorough modernization, an industrial state with some form of democracy based on a humane standard of life.

With the wisdom of hindsight, we know that this picture of a politically balanced, stable member of the world community was entirely erroneous. The Japanese once again demonstrated their ability to absorb only that part of an alien culture in which they were vitally interested, a technique they developed with regard to Chinese culture during the first millenium A.D.

Basically, modern Japan retained the political and social heritage that it possessed when coming into contact with Western influence. Therefore an understanding of the major political characteristics of the new Japan, and especially its aggressive expansionism, must be based on observations of the traits and attitudes with which Japan started on its violent modern life. It must also be borne in mind that the pressure of modernization posed a severe challenge to the old customs, and that political stability remains an objective still unrealized.

Early Japan

Political Features

Unlike the great political cultures of China and India, Japan had not fostered a mature civilization by the beginning of the Christian era. Instead, at that time the ancestors of the present Japanese people were still settling the southern parts of the islands of Kyushu and Shikoku and the nearby western sections of the main island of Honshu. Though capable of driving the Ainu aborigines —an early Caucasoid type—northward on Honshu and eventually to Hokkaido, the Japanese lacked the culture and political cohesion already flourishing on the Asian mainland. Its relatively late start induced Japan to become acutely conscious of more advanced neighbors and to make rapid progress by extensive cultural borrowing. These borrowings occurred on two great occasions—from China in the sixth to ninth centuries and from the West after 1850.

It is erroneous to conclude that the Japanese were "mere imitators" without originality of their own. Actually, their sensitivity to foreign achievements is in itself a significant accomplishment. Moreover, as we shall see, they borrowed selectively and molded what they learned into a pattern of their own making. Japan entered the modern era as a distinctive political society that mustered the discipline and vigor required to adapt to a new environment. Its very success and tragedy are explicable in terms of its own historical development.

The Japanese who settled in their new island home probably arrived from Korea and from the coastal regions of South China. They had a loose political organization in which the various clans and their leaders enjoyed a large degree of autonomous power. This characteristic was further strengthened by the dislocating impact of migration and the relative isolation and difficulty of communication caused by Japan's mountainous terrain. Gradually, a central imperial power was established on the Yamato Plain, near the modern city of Nagoya on Honshu, at the start of the Christian era.[1] It was asserted that the

---

[1] The traditional Japanese date of February 11, 660 B.C., for the founding of the empire is not given much credence even among conservative Japanese scholars.

emperor was a supreme ruler and a descendant of the Sun Goddess, but his control over the clans was not effective. Eventually his position became based more on prestige and inviolability than on actual power, because the great clans could not be taxed or compelled to act against their own interests.

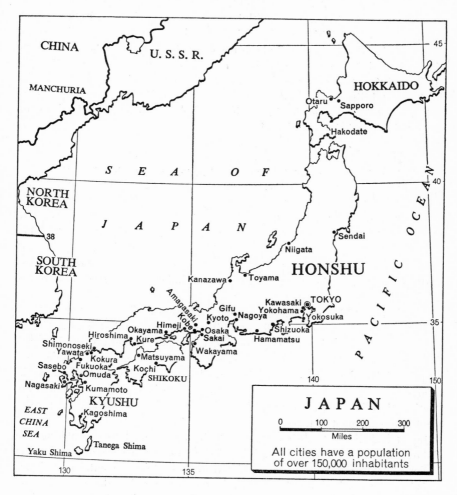

These powerful clans were, however, envious of one another, and an uneasy political balance developed with its focal point in the emperor. The imperial family remained the sacred, legal repository of sovereignty through the centuries, enjoying a continuity of rule without power, while the great clans fought bitterly to gain actual control of the government. This was a dual system of government; sovereignty remained vested in the emperor, but real authority lay elsewhere. There developed a political pattern that prevailed until modern times: a struggle among the clans, the ascendancy of the victor, rule through

185

the sacrosanct imperial family, its attempt to subjugate rivals and consolidate power, and its eventual fall. Thus Japan developed quite early the distinctive feature of a dual system of government, with a theoretically all-powerful emperor who served primarily to attract popular loyalty to the regime in power.

Contests for power at the center had their counterpart in the center's struggle to assert its authority over the outlying regions. Japan's ruling class, which engaged in these activities, was an aristocracy based on birth. In this respect, it resembled a Western society and was markedly different from the "aristocracy of learning" that, in theory at least, characterized China's official class. In fact, rule by aristocratic *family* predominated, and it was family or clan solidarity that gave stability to the Japanese political system. Reliance on these bodies and other collective agencies in making vital decisions has remained an important characteristic in modern Japan.

The Chinese Impact

Japan's rudimentary social and political order came under the influence of China's great civilization in the sixth century, during the dazzling T'ang dynasty. Buddhism as a religious force and as a vehicle for the transmission of advanced culture so impressed the Japanese that they adopted the belief. This Chinese-Buddhist orientation began about 550 A.D., and its advocates triumphed over opposition elements in 587. A conscious effort was undertaken to absorb Chinese ways under the direction of Prince Shotoku, who sent a large embassy to China in 607. During the next 200 years, scholars and specialists were systematically dispatched to China for this purpose. In 645, students who had returned from China engineered a successful coup at the Yamato court and sought to reproduce the magnificent Chinese governmental structure. Capital cities were constructed on the Chinese model, first near modern Nara (710) and then at Kyoto (794). The central government under the emperor was declared all-powerful, and a vast bureaucratic network was created, with even provincial affairs under its control. As in China, land was to be equally distributed and "nationalized" so that no one could stand between the peasant and the government in the payment of taxes.

Japan lacked the tradition and the trained personnel to execute such an elaborate political reform. The nation-wide bureaucracy never really took effect, because local aristocrats were appointed to these "governmental posts." The civil bureaucracy in the capital lacked the power to regulate the possession and distribution of land, taxation, or the apportionment of agricultural produce. The government could not control provincial affairs, even though it operated in the name of the imperial court, had the power to make laws, and bestowed highly valued court honors. Gradually the so-called national domain disappeared as tax-free estates were formed through the collusion of court aristocrats and local gentry. By the tenth century the emperor's domain became simply lands that were his private estates.

In copying the Chinese techniques of administration, the Japanese permitted only their aristocracy to take "competitive" examinations and so perpetuated this rule. Yet, despite these distortions and failure to overcome political decentralization, the Japanese did retain much of the Chinese example. In the fields of fine arts, writing—where they adopted the cumbersome Chinese system of ideographs—literature, and religion, what they learned from China gave the Japanese a substantial foundation on which to develop an advanced culture of their own. China's influence was at its peak from the sixth to the ninth century. In the centuries that followed, Japan developed a native art and literature and embarked on its own modifications of Buddhism.

The Feudal Era

The Rise of Military Feudalism

The failure of the Chinese system of centralized rule to take hold in Japan seriously weakened the political power of the imperial family. In the countryside the noble families and Buddhist monasteries became decentralized centers of authority, much like the manorial lords of feudal Europe. The dual system of government evolved when a wealthy and large courtier family, the Fujiwara, asserted its dominance over imperial affairs. It cemented its direct control over the throne, by the ninth century, through intermarriage with the imperial family. Fujiwara leaders became the regents when minors were on the throne, and civil dictators at other times. The pattern they established at the court became inviolable; in fact, the Fujiwara family retained its control over the major court positions for about one thousand years.

However, with the decline in the court's authority, the Fujiwara's position became devoid of political importance. By the eleventh century, real power passed to a rising military aristocracy, which managed and defended the independent country estates. The knights of the military clans fought among themselves and gained prestige in campaigns against the Ainu aborigines. When the court aristocracy itself called on these forces to settle disputes, or defend the court against nearby clans or monasteries, the age of military feudalism had dawned. Two competing military clans, Taira and Minamoto, arose in the twelfth century. At the end of a victorious war in 1160, the Taira leaders moved into Kyoto and took control of the court, but the Minamoto forces slowly marshaled their strength in eastern Japan and completely destroyed the Taira leaders in the war of 1180–1185. Henceforth all the struggles for supreme power were dominated by the military clans.

Minamoto Yoritomo, leader of the victorious faction, believed that the Taira clan had fatally weakened itself by settling at the effete and decadent court at Kyoto. He therefore established his headquarters at Kamakura, created the post of shogun or generalissimo, and ruled from this vantage point. Hereafter, the head of a victorious clan assumed control of the shogunate and continued the practice of dual government by directing the affairs of state from this position.

187

The emperor remained firmly excluded from a position of actual power; yet the shogun always acknowledged his prestige, so great was the tradition of reverence for the imperial family. Even these military dictators could not assert full control over all Japan. Each ruling clan had to depend on feudal retainers, for it was always apprehensive that these supporters or rival clans would challenge its rule.

The military rulers at Kamakura dispatched loyal estate managers and knights to control individual estates and maintain security throughout the land. This system of rule, which lasted over 150 years, was weakened by the pull of regional loyalties as the original binding ties to Kamakura lost their immediacy. In its late stage the Kamakura system still had the strength to rally a defense force against an invasion by the Mongol hordes of Kublai Khan, conqueror and ruler of China. In 1281 a "divine wind" destroyed much of the invading fleet off Kyushu, and the defenders defeated those of the 150,000 invaders who managed to land. Fifty years later, in 1331, the Minamoto shogunate was destroyed in a revolt by an ex-emperor who aspired to reassert authority. Instead, another military clan, the Ashikaga, assumed power and maintained the shogunate system.

Effective Ashikaga rule barely lasted to the end of the century, and with its decline Japan entered two centuries of civil wars and indecisive struggles for power. The Japanese society, its military clans included, had grown so rapidly that a more complex system than personal loyalty to the center was required for political order. In effect, a true feudal structure developed, as various estates became consolidated into fewer and larger domains under the control of a lord, or *daimyo*. The consequence was that the knights, immediately below the lords in the social order, lost their economic independence and, as peasant armies were developed, some of their military significance as well.

The mounting strength of the individual daimyos, actual rulers over their own domains, pointed toward an eventual struggle for absolute power. Finally, in the latter half of the sixteenth century, national unity was achieved through the efforts of three remarkable leaders. These were the daimyo Oda Nobunaga, his ablest general Hideyoshi, who gained power on Nobunaga's death; and Tokugawa Ieyasu, who destroyed Hideyoshi's family after the latter's death in 1597. Shortly after 1600, the Tokugawa Ieyasu shogunate was established, which lasted for over 250 years. Its founder carefully planned to keep his family in power, obsessed as he was by the failure of both Nobunaga and Hideyoshi to achieve this end. The consequences for Japan, as we shall see, were far-reaching.

The Development of a Japanese Culture

Although the period before 1600 was characterized by political chaos, Japan made significant progress in the fields of cultural and economic development. The growth of a military tradition of chivalry became a major theme in Japanese life. The soldier's virtues of self-discipline and combat readiness were further glorified by his ability to remain indifferent to suffering and steadfast in his personal and family loyalties. Military themes, based on the Taira-Minamoto clash and succeeding struggles, illustrated this outlook and became an important part of Japanese literature. Japanese civilization became permeated with the virtues of physical endurance and unswerving loyalty that, in the feudal system, evolved into an ethic of devotion by the vassal to his lord. In addition to these binding obligations, there were material benefits to both lord and vassal derived from the feudal system of land tenure. This pattern of relations was strengthened by the Confucian doctrine of obedience to superiors, which in China fostered respect for the state and the bureaucratic order of civilian officials; in Japan it was applied to the soldier-vassal (*samurai*) and his lord.

In the twelfth and thirteenth centuries the growing national culture of Japan expressed itself in extensive modifications of Buddhism. This religion had already undergone considerable change during its long journey from India. At its source of origin Buddhism was a somewhat austere and ascetic religion whose essentially passive and pessimistic outlook on life was reflected in its major purpose of "breaking the life cycle," with its hardship and pain, and entering the void of nirvana. The military influence in Japanese culture was reflected in the rise of the Zen Sect of Buddhism, which stressed the virtues of insight, mental concentration, and physical self-discipline. It gained a wide following in military circles that continued into the modern era. There also developed the Pure Land Sect and its offshoot, the True Pure Land Sect. These groups popularized Buddhism by turning nirvana into a paradise. The sects also preached that salvation was easily attainable by the faithful, through the intervention of lesser gods existing in this Buddhist system. Another offshoot, the Nichiren Sect, displayed still another contrast to traditional Buddhism by its intolerance of other sects and religions, extreme nationalism, and a bellicose, violent nature.

The Kamakura period was an era of broad cultural development. The higher culture recently borrowed from China was diffused from its narrow base in the Kyoto region to the outlying provincial centers. This expansion established a foundation for the later rise of a class of leaders, numerous and competent enough to operate a central government.

The era of the Ashikaga shogunate was noted for its architecture, painting and literature, and the development of the no dance with its accompanying poetic recitations. At this time such characteristic practices as landscape gardening, the tea ceremony, and flower arrangements were introduced. The Zen Sect was influential in developing and propagating these activities, together with their distinguishing traits of simplicity, calmness, and self-discipline.

Nevertheless, this was not an era of the strict self-discipline and reticence that were to mark Japan at a later age. The thriving Japanese economy underwent considerable urbanization, and the great commercial center of Osaka developed free of daimyo control, though dominated by a powerful monastery of the True Pure Land Sect. Japan at this time, especially after the collapse of the Ashikaga, engaged in international trade, which assumed great importance in the nation's economy, and Japanese communities were established in the Philippines and Southeast Asia. By the sixteenth century, Japanese pirates were ravaging the coast of Ming China. The Japanese also came in contact with the Europeans, newly arrived in the Pacific. Christian missionaries practiced in Japan and achieved a notable record of conversions, especially in the outlying regions of Kyushu. What the country lacked in political unity it possessed in an aggressive outlook on the world, expanding economic interests, and a lively cultural development that stemmed from a sense of national confidence. Its people behaved in a manner similar to that of contemporary and modern Korea —vigorous, self-expressive, quite volatile, and with an "uninhibited personality." In many of these respects Japan was more modern in 1600 than it was two centuries later. By 1850 the country had undergone 250 years of Tokugawa rule, which had tried, with considerable success, to prevent changes in the political and social order. It saw in this policy the only way to maintain internal peace and stability and sustain its own power.

The Tokugawa Shogunate (1615–1868)

The Tokugawa shogunate introduced an era of isolation and rigid internal stability, when many traits in Japan's political culture became crystallized or recast to serve political ends. The regime claimed that it was merely preserving the traditional social order. In fact, it used and embellished traditional political concepts and developed or borrowed new ones that contributed to political stability. The Japanese system had never been fixed or stable, and now, at its point of most rapid change, it was frozen by political fiat. The mold of thought and behavior created by the Tokugawa actually changed the nature of Japanese society and the direction of its development, so deep was its impression on the people.

The Tokugawa regime established itself at Edo (Tokyo), protected by an elaborate system of security checks, including traffic controls and a network of espionage. Preferences in land, taxes, and power were bestowed on clans who supported the Tokugawa in their rise to power. All potentially rival clans had to leave hostages with the shogunate. An attempt was made to fix the social order permanently through legislation that forbade any man to leave his hereditary station in life. A sharp separation between warrior and peasant, inaugurated by Hideyoshi, was reinforced and extended by the Tokugawa. Adapting the Confucian hierarchy of classes, the shogunate ranked the warrior, or samurai, first, then the peasant, the artisan, and finally the merchant. Symbolically, the peasant was disarmed, and sword bearing was made a badge of warrior rank.

This stratification was artificial in that it failed to reflect the material and cultural importance of the commercial class in Japan. The attempt to retain the old order by glorifying the samurai class occurred just as the re-establishment of peace had made this group superfluous. The samurai were still classed as warriors who owed allegiance to their feudal lords, but they did no labor and now subsisted on a rice stipend. A petrifying desire to avoid change led the government to exhort the samurai to accept the new situation and live with the flourish of olden times, but inactively and obediently. The warrior code was developed into an impersonal national ethic of loyalty, called *Bushido*, or the Way of the Warrior, in an effort to retain a useless warrior class without endangering the social fabric.

In international affairs, the government attempted to insulate Japan completely against all foreign contacts, especially intercourse with the West. Foreign trade in Japanese ports was eliminated, save for a restricted Dutch post; travel abroad by Japanese nationals was forbidden; and those residing overseas were forbidden to return. There were some clandestine trade and contact with the outside, but generally the policy of exclusion (*ca.* 1630–1854) was successful. Christianity and other Western influences were ruthlessly eliminated, primarily because they threatened the stability of the social order. These new forces also endangered the political balance, since hostile western and southern clans were gaining strength through their economic contacts with foreigners. An important effect of the exclusion policy was the prevention of early Japanese participation, however tenuous, in the industrial revolution and the new currents of intellectual and scientific thought then developing in Europe.

The Tokugawa naturally leaned heavily on the authoritarian tradition they had inherited. They also made full use of the Japanese concept of society as an integrated structure. All elements in society and their functions as well were considered to have meaning only as parts of a unified order. Although extremely class-conscious, the Japanese viewed each social stratum as part of the total group. Within the protection of this enveloping sense of unity, they graded all community activities and then established detailed hierarchies of competence within each field, be it carpentry or wrestling. The pyramid of political power and influence was of primary importance because obligations to the state took precedence over all other commitments, including family duties.

Also vital to the Tokugawa system were the Japanese concepts of law and the religious structure. In addition, an elaborate system of social etiquette and sanctions was developed to strengthen the government's control over society.

The inequality of man was a basic philosophical belief supported by the Confucian pattern of superior-inferior relations. The Chinese view that government should be in the hands of the superior—in wisdom and virtue—was simply used to justify aristocratic rule. From this belief it followed that government by man was superior to government by law and that the lawmaker and administrator were above the law. Moral government and ethical administration of the law were dependent on the personal integrity of the morally superior rulers, because in resolving an issue their consciences were considered better guides than an inflexible law. Officials could therefore interpret law to the extent of deciding when punishment should be meted out. Actually, Japanese law was a more precise tool than the Chinese version, especially with regard to the legal relationships established under feudalism. Still, it was conceived as a temporary expression of the opinion of the ruling class.

Since the individual was simply part of the community, he could not depend on the law as a breakwater to protect himself against other individuals or the government. Law was to bind the society together and stressed the duties, rather than the rights, of the emperor's subjects. On one occasion, as an extreme example of this type of rule, the people were not even told what the law was, out of suspicion that they would evade it. Ignorance, presumably, would contribute further to righteous living, under the guidance of a superior ruling class.

The native religion of Shintoism also supported the dominant ideology. It developed early in Japanese history and was a primitive belief based on an appreciation and awe of nature. The Shinto theory that a blood tie existed between the imperial dynasty and all other families strengthened the concept of a unified Japanese society. The highest religious sanction for the inequality of people was derived from the Shinto myth that the emperor descended from the Sun Goddess. One's level in society was therefore determined by the closeness of his blood relationship with the throne, another justification for the right of a small aristocracy to retain political power.

Shintoism was not a major force during the Tokugawa period; in fact, it had long held a secondary position to Buddhism, the official religion of Japan. Only in the modern era, after the fall of the shogunate, was Shintoism brought to the fore as a state creed. The new rulers, seeking to build up the authority of the central government after 1868, developed a state Shintoism: an intensely patriotic devotion to things Japanese and a symbol of service to the nation. This political edifice was capped by worship of the emperor as the national symbol of unity.

It was in the realm of social relationships that the Tokugawa rulers, relying heavily on Confucianism, made their greatest imprint. A considerable degree of social tension was generated in the stifling atmosphere of exclusion and isolation created by an oppressive regime, especially as the population increased during 250 years of peace. Before 1600, formalistic Confucian tenets had made little headway in a Japan characterized by independent and disobedient behavior. For the Tokugawa regime, Confucianism presented an ideal rule book for social comportment, and its stress on etiquette and ceremony was of particular value in curbing asocial activities. Formal routines of conduct and proper ways of behavior were devised for all occasions and with regard to all types of persons. Reliance on rules of etiquette came to characterize social encounters, and these regulations eased the operation of the tightly constructed social system of Tokugawa Japan.[2]

The Western concepts of sin or religious sanctions were nowhere evident as means for enforcing and perpetuating this type of social relationship. Rather, the threat of shame was used as a sanction to prevent irregular behavior; guilt, then, stemmed from improper or erroneous conduct, which therefore had to be

---

[2] The cult of cleanliness and the love of small and simple objects and designs antedated the Tokugawa era but, under the impact of close living, were heavily stressed at that time.

192

avoided at all costs. Self-respect is a most taxing master. The best way to save face was to follow the rule book and live up to all duties and obligations owed to the state, the family, and other groups. Hence, completing the circle, etiquette and ceremony were utilized to save face, as this latter necessity became a basic aspect of Japanese ethics. Sincerity in this context was not equated with frankness but with knowing and following the rules required to maintain the self-respect of all concerned. To win social approval by avoidance of *faux pas* was more important than cultivating virtue in the Western sense of that term.

If a person acted so that he was shamed before society, he could find no protection anywhere against this loss of face, for not even his family could or would serve as a shelter. This ethic placed extreme dependence on the judgment of society as a whole and clearly implied the existence of fixed, unavoidable obligations that were publicly known. The Japanese tended to avoid the burden of individual responsibility and decision making, since the satisfaction of individual desires was not the purpose of social behavior and the individual was not the basic unit of society. Life, however, remained extremely competitive, and failure in the social context was bound to be very bitter. Yet outwardly the individual was compelled to avoid any dramatization or emotional demonstration of his feelings.

Despite some failures, the Japanese system of stylized behavior was maintained as long as the environment remained familiar and the rules clearly applicable. This pattern of social relationships became an integral part of the Japanese scene by the end of the Tokugawa era and remained an outstanding characteristic of modern Japan after the shogunate system had collapsed.

Opposition to the Tokugawa

In the long run, the Tokugawa was menaced by its own thoroughness and success. Dislocations arising from the inevitable changes in living conditions could not be repaired gradually, and eventually led to quick and violent reforms.

As the nation developed a more complex economy, including a money exchange, the old system began to falter. Vast fluctuations in the price of the major crop, rice, typified the great havoc caused by new, ill-understood forces. These new conditions, stimulated by internal tranquility, strengthened the wealthy business and commercial class—the chonin. The daimyo and samurai often found themselves deeply in debt to these socially inferior financial leaders.

The feudal elite, however, retained its ascendancy, and the new class, for all its wealth, remained politically subservient. The chonin in turn developed a narrow view toward economic operations. They were less interested in investment or production than in maximizing profits on the basis of purely commercial and speculative activities. As a result, they could neither envisage nor increase their power through an industrial revolution. They even lacked the ability to grasp the initiative when Japan was opened to the West.

Unlike the middle-class leadership of Western Europe, the chonin played a secondary role to the more vigorous feudal leaders in modernizing Japan. In feudal times their contributions took the form of developing a system of communications and commerce that eventually ruined the feudal economy. More directly, they supported with vast funds any movement that promised to eliminate the hateful shogunate and give businessmen more leeway.

The major force working for a change, ironically, was the samurai class, the one so assiduously cultivated by the Tokugawa. Samurai hatred of the government was climaxed when their lords reduced rice stipends in an economy move. This retrenchment created an untenable situation for a class that had lost its social purpose when it was removed from the land and denied the right to fight. Many samurai severed their allegiances as vassals to their lords and studied Western ways of life. Others, duplicating the shogun-emperor relationship on a smaller scale, actually governed their clans, with the daimyo serving as figure-heads. Abetted by the merchants, these elements of the samurai class formed the backbone of the antigovernment movement.

However, the spearhead of an attack on the shogunate had to have well-organized, respectable leadership, with a secure geographic base. This was found in the four powerful clans of southern and western Japan, far enough from Tokugawa centers of rule to be nearly autonomous rivals of the government. The major rival clan was the Satsuma, on Kyushu. They were proud, fierce fighters, who had good sources of revenue bolstered by an illegal China trade. The Satsuma were supported by three neighboring clans—Choshu and, of lesser significance, Hizen and Tosa.

Political opposition gradually became organized in the nineteenth century, as the more daring nobles (kuge) of the emperor's court joined forces with the four dissident clans. It is clear that the Japanese government was teetering on the edge of collapse and might have been overthrown from within, as it had been on so many previous occasions. This time it was the intervention of the Western powers that precipitated the final blow against the shogunate and the policy of national seclusion. The Japanese forces behind the thrust were motivated by domestic drives—disgruntled samurai and merchants, plus daimyo of rival clans who simply wanted to supplant the Tokugawa and assume control of the shogunate.

The Meiji Restoration (1867–1868)

Events moved Japan into the currents of world affairs after 1850, although it had already granted maritime coaling rights to foreign ships under European pressure earlier in the century. This end to isolation placed the shogunate in an embarrassing position because it had encouraged antiforeign (antibarbarian) sentiment, already a dominant feeling in Japan. The government's vulnerability was increased when the naval mission of United States Commodore Perry forced Japan in 1853–1854 to establish relations with the outside world. Commercial and diplomatic agreements made under the Japanese-American Treaty of 1858 served as a model for similar pacts with European powers. Unfortunately, the treaty fixed the tariff that Japan could levy on imports and exports and so deprived the government of the right to raise revenue rates during the trying years of modernization. A severe blow to Japan's prestige was the inclusion of the right of extraterritoriality—allowing alien residents in Japan to be tried in courts of their own consuls under their own laws.

The feudal economy suffered severely from the rapid increase of trade with the West and the loss of gold, which followed from an unrestricted exchange of coin. Restricted revenue from taxes, debased coinage, and monetary speculation all pointed to a steep inflationary rise in prices. The peasants, who had been treated harshly by the Tokugawa, and the samurai came to resent the government even more.

The Satsuma and Choshu opposition used the rallying cry "Expel the Barbarians" to undermine Tokugawa prestige. These warrior clans, however, underwent Western naval bombardments at Kagoshimo (Satsuma) and Shimonoseki (Choshu) in 1862–1863, in retaliation for assaults on Western nationals. They came to respect this power and decided to learn from the West how to increase Japan's might. Their antiforeign line had been simply a means to domestic rule; once in office in 1868, the new regime promptly punished those who continued to attack foreigners.

Another effective slogan was "Revere the Emperor," a shrewd maneuver to turn the shogunate's own stress on loyalty against the Tokugawa. Study of Shinto religion and theory was revived, and effective propagandistic use was made of its stress on the emperor's supremacy. Since reverence for the emperor had never died out, the portrayal of the shogun as a usurper of his power had tremendous effect.

A memorial sent to the new shogun in 1867, with the backing of the four western clans, asked that actual power be transferred to the new emperor, Mutsuhito. The shogun resigned, expecting all clans to receive equal treatment from the throne. When the Choshu and Satsuma leaders promptly monopolized governmental power, the Tokugawa clan fought back, but was suppressed in 1868–1869. This was the "Meiji Restoration," named after the title of Mutsuhito's reign. The Hizen and Tosa clans also derived some advantages but were held to secondary positions.

The New Order Consolidated

The task before Japan was so great that its astute new leaders knew that it could never be achieved within the framework of the old feudal order. Primarily, Japan's vulnerability to foreign domination and rule had to be eliminated in favor of a strong, secure position in world affairs. The country was given a breathing space by the tense diplomatic situation in Europe between the Crimean and the Franco-Prussian wars, and by the greater attraction China held to European expansionists. To attain its objective of security, Japan had to organize a modern central administration, create an up-to-date army and navy, develop a strategic industrial base, and instill a concept of national solidarity in the population.

The success of such an enterprise is astonishing when note is taken of the country's weakened condition, shackled as it was by feudal restrictions, and torn by dissent and civil strife. Such a change had to be administered from above by a powerful government that could move rapidly and pull a half-aware nation along after it.

An ominous portent of what the new rulers had in mind after Japan's security was assured can be gleaned from a curious debate over government policy in 1871–1873. One faction wanted to use some incidents of friction with Korea as an excuse to launch an expedition against that country. In this way it was hoped to relieve pressures and tensions at home caused by the political changes, especially with regard to the uncertain status of the samurai class. Wiser heads prevailed when it was pointed out that the government had to build the country's industrial, military, and political strength before undertaking foreign expansion.

A further disquieting feature was the use of terror and the weapon of political assassination against government officials during the last days of the shogunate and at the start of the new regime. Under feudal rule recourse to such methods was one of the few ways to redress grievances. In the twentieth century, "patriotic" fanatics frequently committed political murder against those who advocated liberal or moderate policies at home and abroad.

The New Rulers

The new governing class reflected a shift of power from the upper nobility to the lower members of the samurai class. These lesser samurai had acquired valuable experience in directing their clans' activities. They had reorganized the administration of their clans, making them economically viable, with expanding commercial and manufacturing facilities. The attitude of these samurai was that of the paternalistic bureaucrat, imbued with a disciplined spirit and a devotion to duty that were later transferred to the Imperial government. The ability of these determined young civilian and military bureaucrats, plus the magnetic centralizing effect of the throne, made the Meiji Restoration a success.

This autocratic bureaucracy could not rely on the lower classes for support. Because capital accumulation had been retarded by feudal restrictions, the new government was forced to rely mainly on a land tax to finance its way. At times the peasant was compelled to yield 60 to 75 per cent of his produce, and until 1890 the land tax averaged about 70 per cent of the government's annual income. In addition, the peasant became confused by the radical changes in the form of government.

In this predicament, the government received assistance from the merchant, or chonin, class. As noted earlier, the wealthy chonin were so uncertain of their ability as industrial innovators or political leaders that they were perfectly willing to follow and support the new samurai-dominated regime. They even depended on government initiative to develop modern industry. Help from the chonin, especially in Osaka, where 70 per cent of Japan's nonagrarian wealth was concentrated, enabled the new regime to avoid immediate bankruptcy. The government was able to organize internal security forces, undertake reconstruction activity, and establish heavy industries.

This coalition of lower samurai and merchants was the culmination of developments that had been going on under Tokugawa rule. At that time the impoverished nobility often sold samurai rights to wealthy chonin or adopted them, in order to avoid economic collapse. This permitted many merchants and even some wealthy peasants to infiltrate into the ranks of the lower samurai. Now with social and class restrictions gone, the chonin and samurai leaders could work unimpeded, along the lines of economic development begun during feudal days.

The potentially dangerous feudal lords were won over by a policy of appeasement. Although the feudal structure was dismantled, the lords retained their high standing in the social system. In 1871 clans were formally abolished and their registers of land and people were relinquished to the central government. The latter established administrative subdivisions all over Japan, called prefectures, each under a centrally appointed governor. Feudal dress and class inequality were abolished, Buddhism was disestablished as the state religion, and people gained the right to alienate land and choose an occupation.

As the new national army gained strength, the feudal lords lost the physical power as well as the public support required to maintain their strongholds. Their capitulation was softened by a generous grant of government bonds in exchange for all feudal revenues. Thus the old territorial magnates retained economic power in the form of finance capital. By purchasing large tracts of land and investing heavily in the new national banks, they joined the military and civilian bureaucrats and the merchants as the pillars of the new order.

A new peerage, based on the German model, was created for the court and feudal nobility in 1884; the reorganized nobility was given considerable political power in 1889 when the House of Peers was formed.[3] The same groups that had dominated feudal society continued their joint mastery, although their mutual relations had altered somewhat.

Even though most of the new official and administrative positions were filled with samurai, only a relatively small number of this class could be so employed. Samurai made up 5 per cent of a population of 34 million in 1870. The bulk of this class felt more wretched and uprooted than ever, for it had lost prestige and lacked a place in the new society. Then a government act in 1876 reduced the pension samurai were to receive in lieu of the rice stipend. Led by some of the Satsuma who were disgruntled with the turn of events and the failure of

---

[3] The ranks of nobility, in descending order, were prince, marquis, count, viscount, and baron.

their clan to replace the Tokugawa within the old framework, the samurai undertook a bloody uprising in 1877. The new army of conscripts finally defeated them and ended the last serious attempt to upset the new order.

The Struggle for a Constitution

The governmental institutions developed during the early days of the Meiji era established a pattern of politics that lasted until upset by military extremism in the 1930's. In view of what has been described, it is not surprising that the "restorers" of the emperor, victors of a bitter ten-year struggle (1867–1877), should perpetuate their own power. The futile struggle of the liberal element for a democratic constitution only emphasized how deeply the conservative rulers were entrenched.

Some specious concessions were made to liberal demands in the era between the Restoration of 1868 and the promulgation of the Constitution of 1889. An Imperial Oath of 1868 recognized the right to public debate and discussion and asked for the pursuit of all knowledge to strengthen the nation. Also in 1868 a Deliberative Assembly was formed, consisting, however, only of nobles. To head off mounting demands for representative institutions, the government created prefectural assemblies in 1878 that had a restricted electorate and no power over the centrally controlled prefectural bureaucracy. Another inadequate concession was an Assembly of Prefectural Governors, all agents of the central government. The clamor for reform finally led to a promise in 1881 that Japan would have a constitution and national assembly by 1889.

Early Political Parties

This retreat from tight autocratic control was hastened by the formation of political parties in 1881. The Jiyuto, or Liberal party, was a major center of opposition, and its composition was a revealing commentary on the Japanese scene. It was formed by an amalgam of local political associations in 1881 under Itagaki of Tosa. The leaders of this clan had been shunted aside by the Choshu and Satsuma forces and so turned to the democratic opposition as a means of striking back. The party's main base of support was the disgruntled peasantry. In addition to burdensome taxes, these farmers suffered a loss of land, as tenancy jumped from 10 to 45 per cent of all landholders in the generation after 1868. The movement was given important backing by landlords as well, for they too opposed the high land tax. In addition, there were small manufacturing interests whose traditional operations were endangered by the program of modernization, especially in view of the favoritism, subsidies, and protection lavished on government-sponsored enterprises. Some disaffected samurai joined, willing to support even a liberal opposition. A coalition of such divergent interests could not last long, especially since many grievances were of a short-range nature.

The Jiyuto program favored broader personal liberties, a sound constitutional system, and a vigorous foreign policy. A more moderate opposition group, the Kaishinto, or Progressives, appeared in 1882 under Okuma of Hizen, the last of the four western clans. Whatever policy differences existed between the two factions were not important enough to warrant this split in the opposition camp during these critical formative years. A progovernment Imperial party was also formed in 1882, but it did not gain a widespread following. On the question of where ultimate sovereignty lay, the Imperialists placed it in the person of the emperor, the Liberals associated it with the people, and the Progressives stated that it was shared by the emperor and the people's assembly.

The government assiduously played the two opposition groups off against each other and won some support by means of bribery and favors to the two clans. With the parties weakened and confused, the central authorities enforced severe regulations restricting meetings and associations. Under such pressure, rather than continue with illegal activity, the two opposition parties dissolved themselves in 1884 and did not re-form until 1890, when the constitution was put into operation.

The Constitutional Order

The Constitution of 1889

The leading architect of Japan's first modern constitution was Ito Hirobumi of Choshu, a civilian aristocrat. He worked cautiously and in secrecy while the government expanded its military and civilian bureaucracies. Ito studied European constitutional systems abroad and chose the Prussian model as the one best suited for Japan. He even established certain vital agencies, particularly the cabinet and the Privy Council, before the constitution was completed. The Privy Council was formed in 1888, with Ito as its head, to pass "critical judgment" on the new basic law.

As the date for its presentation drew near, the government intensified its internal security system. A press control law of 1875 was strictly enforced, and, when the constitution was promulgated in 1889, the radical press was banned and all other newspapers were forbidden to offer immediate comment. In addition, a Peace Preservation Law of 1887 was passed to strengthen the government's police powers still further. In order to insure maximum secrecy, Ito created a special bureau to work on the constitution and placed it under the Imperial Household Department. There it could work in full freedom, shielded by imperial prestige from all public scrutiny. The conservatives also won a significant symbolic victory—the document was presented as the gift of a merciful and bountiful ruler.

The Constitution of 1889 provided for a theocratic monarchy under an emperor of heavenly ancestry, but actual power was held by an authoritarian ruling class. Another important aspect of administration, in line with historical tradition, was the separation of the civilian and military functions of this leadership. The conservative civilian aristocrats and bureaucrats failed to perceive how easily their military confreres could make a bid for domination once Japan seriously embarked on an expansionist foreign policy. So eager was the dominant aristocracy to check the liberal democratic opposition which soon arose that it prevented the formation of an effective united front against the militarists. Even when the danger of uncontrolled military leadership became apparent, very few civilian aristocrats would join forces with democratic elements, and then only in a half-hearted manner of distasteful expediency.

The constitution faithfully reflected the new order in Japan and marked out the political landmarks around which much of the struggle for power later occurred. The new legal framework can best be grouped around the role of the emperor, the undemocratic civilian organs, the concessions to democracy, and the substantial powers allotted to the military.

THE EMPEROR

In theory the emperor held broad powers over all phases of government. He alone could initiate constitutional amendments, a power never utilized, for the legislature (Diet) to approve. Imperial Ordinances, unlimited in scope, were allowed during emergencies when the Diet was not in session, but required prior confirmation of the Privy Council. To remain in effect these ordinances needed later support of the Diet. As in all the emperor's important powers, ordinances had to be countersigned by a responsible cabinet officer, for the ruler could never act except on the advice of others.

Nonetheless, the emperor's prerogatives and attributes of sovereignty were staggering at first glance. He was empowered to convoke, open, close, and prorogue the Diet, as well as dissolve the lower house; determine the organization of the administrative apparatus, and the salaries and appointments of all officials not provided for in the constitution; declare war and make peace; conclude treaties, with the concurrence of the Privy Council but without having to consult the Diet; proclaim martial law; and confer honors and titles. He was also commander in chief of the army and navy in the field and in administrative affairs.

But in all these matters the emperor was not supposed to demonstrate a will of his own, or act against the wishes of his advisers. He could only endeavor to induce his advisers to change or modify their recommendations. This held true even with regard to his own family affairs, which were the responsibility of the Minister of the Imperial Household. The imperial family, with the emperor as its patriarch, was one of the richest in Japan. It received an annual allotment of $1,500,000 and owned large tracts of land and substantial shares of industrial and financial enterprises.

The real rulers of Imperial Japan were those who operated through the emperor. The vital struggle for power was to control the machinery of state and so be able to "advise" the emperor what to do. Thus we see a picture of many forces struggling, sometimes quietly, sometimes violently, never altogether

CONSTITUTIONAL STRUCTURE AFTER 1889

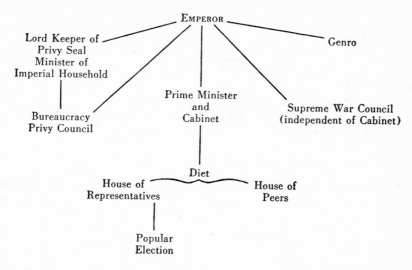

For a democratic, responsible government to evolve out of the Constitution of 1889, the following would have had to occur:

1. Cabinet responsibility to the Diet, presumably through a party system; and House of Representatives domination of the Diet, by making the Peers subservient to its wishes.
2. Cabinet control over the Privy Council, eliminating its restrictive influence.
3. Cabinet control over the bureaucracy.
4. Cabinet control of the Supreme War Council and military leadership in general.

openly, to control the sources of political power. The leading contestants were the aristocratic bureaucrats, the militarists, and the democratic politicians.

THE GENRO

It is significant that the first center of power in post-1889 Japan was a body not even mentioned in the constitution and one that had no official sanction. This was a small group of elder statesmen—genro[4]—who had led the Meiji Restoration and continued to determine high policy until the end of the World War. All important domestic legislation, treaties, foreign-policy decisions, and appointments of prime ministers required their approval. All but one were either Choshu or Satsuma, and, again with one exception, only they or their loyal followers were prime ministers until 1918. They also dominated the presidency of the Privy Council. On the whole, the genro conducted government-by-aristocracy, though on a very competent level.

This group was actually a corporate and operating embodiment of the "em-

[4] The genro were Ito, Yamagata Aritomo, Inoue Kaoru, and Katsura Taro of Choshu; Oyama Iwao and Matsukata Masayoshi of Satsuma; and Saionji Kimmochi, a court noble and protégé of Ito.

peror's will." Yet the genro did not always agree among themselves, and a split developed between the civilian and military members. These two wings were led, respectively, by Ito and his fellow clansman General Yamagata Aritomo.[5] Neither tried to smash the other's power as they sparred for position within the new political framework. However, the redoubtable Yamagata gradually gained his point and laid the groundwork for the later disintegration of civilian rule. In this he was aided by the privileged constitutional position Ito himself created for the militarists. Yamagata also learned quickly how to play along with the Diet, corrupt it, and steal his opponent's thunder in dealing with the democratic politicians.

UNDEMOCRATIC GOVERNMENTAL INSTITUTIONS

A glance at the institutions of government is sufficient to reveal how carefully the framers of the constitution hemmed in the democratic elements. These democratic groups were placed under a severe handicap even in competing for control of the branch of the government dealing with civilian affairs, for they faced a formidable array of opposition in the House of Peers, the bureaucracy itself, and the Privy Council.

The peers formed the Upper House of the Diet, and contained all royal princes and many other nobles, some imperial life appointees, and indirectly elected high tax payers. This ultraconservative body had equal legislative power with the House of Representatives, and its members served as prime ministers and cabinet officers. No reforms of the House of Peers could be undertaken without its consent, and the liberals could never curtail its power, as was done to the British House of Lords in 1911 and 1950.

An important prop bolstering the ruling class was a loyal bureaucracy whose civil servants eventually numbered 450,000. Its leading figures were the Lord Keeper of the Privy Seal and the Minister of the Imperial Household. The former was very influential because he held the seals required to make any law or ordinance official, and the latter wielded power because of his closeness to the ruler. As the channels through which all imperial audiences were granted, these two men were able to deny access to the throne to political opponents or persons whose views were considered unsound. They were appointed and dismissed by the emperor on the advice of the prime minister but actually were able to hold their posts as long as they chose. The bureaucracy was made more efficient, loyal, and "nonpolitical" by the institution of a civil service examination system and the use of Tokyo Imperial University as a training center for government careerists.

The third citadel of civil aristocratic rule was the Privy Council, whose members were life appointees chosen by the emperor on nomination by the prime minister, and with the consent of the Privy Council, especially its president. Its

---

[5] The civilians were Ito, Inoue, and Saionji. The militarists were Yamagata, Oyama, Katsura of the army, and the naval leader Matsukata.

extensive powers included consultation on all important matters concerning the imperial family, approval of supplements and amendments to the constitution, settlement of constitutional disputes among government organs, approval of treaties and emergency ordinances, and, in fact, approval of any important decision on national policy. Since it was a seat of privilege and shared many powers with the cabinet, the House of Representatives constantly sought to reduce its influence. Theoretically, a prime minister, supported by the lower house, could pack the Council with his allies or have the emperor refuse to lay important matters before it, but it was extremely difficult to muster the political power and courage for such attempts.

THE HOUSE OF REPRESENTATIVES AND THE CABINET

The one concession to Western liberal institutions was the House of Representatives, from which sustained assaults were launched to "Anglo-Saxonize" Japan. The rather meager weapon at hand were the powers of this lower house, eventually of 466 members, popularly elected every four years. The Diet, composed of the House of Peers and the House of Representatives, was convoked annually by the emperor. It met for only three months, from December to March, though it could be reconvened in case of emergency. The emperor could prorogue the Diet for no more than fifteen days and he could dissolve the lower house. In this latter case, elections for a new House of Representatives had to take place after a lapse of not more than five months. The weapon of dissolution was abused repeatedly by prime ministers who lacked the confidence of the lower house.

All statutes required a majority vote in each house; thus the Peers were equal to the Representatives, save that financial legislation had to be introduced in the lower house. The emperor had an absolute veto power over all laws. Following the European pattern, bills were generally presented by the cabinet and rarely originated on the floor of parliament.

So weak was the House of Representatives that even the power of the purse, the pride and strength of democratic assemblies, was severely restricted. It had no control over budgetary items listed as "fixed expenditures." These included salaries of officials, Imperial Household expenses, ordinary expenditures of the army and navy and other branches of administration, expenses arising from treaties, and expenditures due to laws or legal obligations of the government. Nor could it control administrative revenues from postal services, government railways, and passports. Unlike Western democracies, if the Diet refused to pass a new budget on the items it could legally control, the government could continue to operate under the old law. Nevertheless, the Diet's approval was required on many appropriations where increases were desired. It could and did use this power, especially when increases in military strength were involved, to assert its will.

The primary goal of the House of Representatives was to "capture" the cabinet by making it responsible solely to the Diet. Cabinet responsibility was primarily to the emperor and then to the Diet and other organs of government. After the death of all the genro but Saionji in 1924, the emperor chose his prime minister on the advice of the Lord Keeper of the Privy Seal and the Minister of the Imperial Household. The cabinet as a whole came under the prime minister's control, with the exception of the war and navy ministers, whose special position is discussed below.

Though often in conflict with the Diet, the cabinet was not a conservative stronghold. It was rather a political no-man's land vulnerable to attack from several directions. Its composition reflected the pull of political forces in the nation and mirrored the balance of power among the competing nobles, bureaucrats, militarists, and politicians.

All groups sought to control the cabinet because it was from this operating executive organ that a program could be carried out over the nation as a whole. Though the cabinet could be overturned by a vote of no confidence in the lower house, usually it would take the preventive step of dissolving the House of Representatives and calling new elections. Also, cabinets could not withstand the hostility of aristocrats (House of Peers), bureaucrats (Privy Council), or militarists. Public criticism in the form of riots or mob violence, and successful or even attempted assassination also ended cabinets in later years.

Although the lower house was not the sole source of danger to a cabinet, good relations between the two were essential to the smooth operation of government. Thus the cabinet was exposed to popular attack channeled through the Diet. Because the cabinet was in a vulnerable position and liable to capture by democratic forces, the organizers of modern Japan took great care not to make it the powerful institution that it was in Europe. This is the chief reason why the cabinet was surrounded by authoritarian bodies like the Privy Council, which severely limited its power.

The Party System

The lower-house effort at self-assertion was expressed through political parties that continued to gain in cohesion and strength after being re-established under the constitutional system. During the ensuing half century the parties made considerable penetrations into the strongholds of the civilian bureaucracy before being crushed by the military extremists. Despite this progress in the face of formidable antidemocratic forces, the party system proved incapable of providing Japan with purposeful policy direction or strong political leadership. The weaknesses revealed from 1881–1884 became even more apparent after 1890.

Such defects are inevitable when so subtle and exotic a mechanism of government is transplanted to a foreign political culture. Neither the routine of daily operations nor the abstract principles and techniques of democracy can be grasped, even by their advocates, without considerable difficulty. In Japan both the political tradition and the governmental structure were hostile to successful party rule. The party system has often proved inadequate even in traditional democracies where popular loyalty, experience, and understanding can be depended on. Japan's painful experience in developing the competence and public support required for effective party government should be a sobering example in analyzing the present attempts at democratic self-rule in Korea and elsewhere in East Asia.

The parties were unable to formulate cohesive programs with firm social and economic bases that would attract wide followings. Groups constantly crossed party lines, and the parties themselves led mercurial and erratic existences. Clan differences, the importance of personality conflicts, and the readiness to form factions on the basis of individual leadership revealed an immaturity that persistently weakened Japan's party structure. The lack of party loyalty and the stress on personal allegiances made for fragmentation and factionalism even within parties.

Another important reason for the weakness of democratic party forces was the absence of middle-class sponsorship or support. This element was the fountainhead of Western liberalism, but in Japan the commercial class worked closely with the ruling aristocracy and was little concerned with the democratic movement. In fact, Japan's rapid economic progress was founded on a narrow industrial and financial base. Its heavy reliance on government supervision and direction led to an economic structure and theory far removed from middle-class individualism and laissez faire.

A monopolistic system in trade, industry, and finance culminated in a series of huge interlocking directorates run by the great moneyed families (zaibatsu).[5] These groups did not challenge the ruling class of aristocrats and ex-samurai and, though their trusts controlled a large part of the economy, they were content to play a subservient role in government until the First World War. The failure of the urban industrial society and its economic leaders to insist on popular control of the government not only made party government more difficult to attain but also facilitated the eventual triumph of extreme militarism.

The Position of the Militarists

In the formative years after 1868 the militarists created a political base for later efforts to capture control and direction of governmental affairs. The army became the most important element in the development of Japan's foreign policy, as the chief architect and executor of the program of expansion. Its secure position, achieved before 1918, enabled it to weather the temporary eclipse of the 1920's, and it made a successful bid for domination after 1930. Yet, even in its period of "glory" (1931–1945), it was compelled to wage a long struggle for leadership. It never did attain the total power required to crush all opposition and to rule undisturbed on the Japanese scene.

The political strength of the military was actually greater than depicted in the constitution, for in 1898–1899 Prime Minister General Yamagata put through an Imperial Ordinance that listed persons eligible to be ministers of war and navy. Only active generals, lieutenant-generals, admirals, and vice-

---

[5] The leading families were Mitsui, Mitsubishi, Yasuda, and Suitomo.

admirals were named, and they could assume or remain at their cabinet posts only with permission from the military leaders. Since even a party cabinet would collapse without an armed-service minister, the military bureaucracy thus acquired a virtual stranglehold over the government. Of course, in a national crisis political will power and prestige were as important as ordinance regulations, but the insecure nature of the civilian opposition and the arrogant self-confidence of the militarists, as reflected in the ordinance itself, offered little hope that the army could be forced to retreat from its legally won position.

This negative power was merely of supplementary importance, compared with the militarists' ability to affect the course of events directly. Their authority was derived from the emperor's supreme command and absolute control of the armed forces. Superficially this resembled Western constitutional arrangements, but in Japan there was no direct or ultimate civilian control over the movement and use of the nation's armed might.

It was a typical Restoration maneuver to center personal command of the armed forces in the emperor, for it added to the power of the Satsuma-Choshu rulers. Ito himself claimed this absolute right for the ruler, on the completely inaccurate grounds that emperors always had led their armies in the field. Actually, the shogunate rarely permitted them to leave the old capital of Kyoto. Ito observed also that independent control of the armed forces was essential to the successful prosecution of a war. Since control by the Diet or cabinet would hamper military efficiency, no one was allowed to interfere with the "military will of the emperor."

Such control meant dual government, with the military command separate from the organs that dealt with all other governmental questions. Cabinet ministers and the Privy Council could advise the emperor on civilian affairs, but only military advisers gave counsel on matters affecting the armed forces. Only the emperor's person united the civilian government with his "military camp." Thus the military leaders could pursue their own policy without civilian obstruction, and use their control of the armed-service ministries to block, influence, and guide the civilian affairs of state. This power is almost a complete reversal of that vested in civilian and military officials in democratic states.

The army successfully maintained that it alone could determine the size, recruiting system, and equipment of the military establishment. It maintained that the legal term "responsible ministers" in these matters referred only to the armed-service ministers and not the cabinet as a whole. The war and navy ministers could always resign if the cabinet or Diet tried to strike back through budgetary slashes. Clearly, Yamagata's coup guaranteed the independence of the armed forces from the rest of the government. All military administration and the entire conduct of troop movements, including the size of the force involved, were removed from the jurisdiction of the cabinet.

The military advisers to the emperor were formally organized in the powerful Supreme War Council, a body of about a dozen men, including all Fleet Admirals and Field Marshals (usually of imperial lineage during peacetime and therefore not very important), the armed-service ministers from the cabinet, the chiefs of staff, and other important officers appointed by the emperor. This group decided on all military programs and regulated the military administration. Its advice was always followed by the emperor. By Imperial Ordinance, the Chiefs of Staff were directly responsible to the emperor and not to the war and navy ministers. Usually, the general staffs alone controlled plans for national defense and the disposition of troops, and merely informed their respective ministers of decisions taken.[7] After the death of Field Marshal Prince Yamagata Aritomo in 1922, there was no recognized head of the army, and its various factions often fought strenuously for the control of this powerful machine.

In the early years, the closely-knit unity of the Choshu clan may explain why the army, which it controlled, played such a decisive political role in the island kingdom. At first Satsuma and Choshu influences were about equal in the army, but when the great Satsuma militarist, Saigo Takamori, left the government and led the samurai revolt of 1877, his clan lost the one man who could rival Yamagata. In turn, the Satsuma leaders found their field of influence with the creation of a modern navy.

In 1870, Yamagata studied foreign military organizations in Europe. He returned to organize a system of conscription in 1873, under which all men had to serve three years on active duty and four years in the reserve. Until this new force was organized, the army, which consisted mainly of garrisons scattered in the capital and other large cities, was composed of anti-Tokugawa samurai. The new conscript force proved, during the revolt of 1877, that peasants and workers could fight as well as hereditary warriors.

The army's program of military education continued the public-school emphasis on loyalty to the emperor, mixed with military obedience and discipline. Later, the army tried to retain control over the minds of ex-soldiers by organizing militaristic veteran and patriotic groups. Among these were the Imperial Ex-Servicemen's Association, which later reached a membership of 3 million, and the infamous Black Dragon Society. These organizations were generally imperialist, stressing loyalty to the emperor and the glory of war.

With internal security assured after 1880, the army revised and expanded its structure in preparation for foreign war. The immediate increase was from sixteen to twenty-eight infantry regiments and a proportionate rise in all other service arms. The navy program of 1882 for forty-eight ships in eight years was raised in 1886 to fifty-four vessels. These forces were soon put to use as Japan turned its attention beyond its horizons.

---

[7] As in other aspects of government, the formal head of the general staff was often not its actual leader. When a royal prince, for example, was chief of staff, the real leader might have been the war minister, the inspector-general of military education, an influential military leader who held no major post, or a group of officers.

8 Japan under the Constitution (1890−1931)

The Japanese political structure absorbed its new constitutional rules without serious strain, despite sharp struggles among various organs of government. These institutions were feeling their way toward the limits of power attainable by the social and economic forces they represented. Yet, as the country came to assume an important position in Asia, it could not be said that Japan was definitely charting a course toward totalitarian excessiveness, for there were several indications of the growing strength of democratic and moderate elements. The issue remained in doubt all during the period of constitutional government and was kept alive even after the crucial Manchurian affair of 1931–1932.

The strength of militarism at home was intimately dependent on the success of an aggressively expansionist foreign policy. This was immensely successful, involving a war every ten years (China, 1894; Russia, 1904; Germany, 1914). In fact, foreign affairs had so great an impact on domestic politics that the early development of constitutional government must be examined in the light of Japan's international position.

The Era of the Genro

The era of genro rule extended from 1890 until the end of the First World War. All premiers except Okuma were genro or loyal followers of this group. The genro also dominated the presidency of the Privy Council. Though expansionist, these elder statesmen followed a policy of limited conquest and did not undertake commitments that imperiled Japan's security. They remained antidemocratic and paternalistic in domestic politics but generally worked within the letter, if not the spirit, of the new constitution.

The First Diet Sessions

The first Diet, which met in 1890, was chosen by an electorate that was limited because of the property qualifications for voters. The two major parties in the

LEADERS OF JAPAN'S TWO MAJOR PARTIES
1890–1932

Seiyukai (1900–1940)	Kenseikai (1915–1927) Minseito (1927–1940)
1890 Itagaki Taisuke (Tosa)	Okuma Shigenobu (Hizen)
1900 Ito Hirobumi (Choshu)	
1903 Saionji Kimmochi (Kuge)	
1914 Hara Kei (Takashi) (1921*)	
1916	Kato Takaakira
1921 Takahashi Korekiyo	
1924 Tanbaka Gi-ichi	
1926	Wakatsuki Reijiro
1927	Hamaguchi Yuko (Osachi) (1931*)
1931 Inukai Ki (Tsuyoshi) (1932*)	
1932 end of party rule	

* Assassinated.

lower house, led by Itagaki and Okuma, won 170 of the 300 seats. Their power was hampered by the autocratic constitution and their own peculiar ability to stand for the same things while remaining hostile foes over questions of personality and leadership. Although they remained ineffectual against the Satsuma-Choshu governments, which had no party support, they constantly attacked these cabinets in a vituperative and bitter manner. The various prime ministers casually bought off the Diets with "compromises," more often with bribes (a precedent cynically begun in the first Yamagata cabinet of 1890), or a worthless promise to work together with one of the parties. If these efforts failed, the prime minister would dissolve the lower house and make a deal to support the minority element in the next election.

In 1891–1894 the parliamentary groups sought to checkmate the government because it constantly refused to form cabinets responsible to the Diet. In the 1891–1892 session, the lower house blocked the government at every point; unable to force its own program through, it brought the administration of affairs to a standstill and was dissolved. Prime Minister Matsukata's flagrant efforts to force a victory for his candidates failed in the election in February, 1892, and he had to resign. When Ito assumed the premiership, the Diet promptly cut the regular budget and reduced the annual extraordinary fund for the naval construction program. Ito triumphed in a very significant and characteristic manner—by an imperial rescript from the throne, which ordered all officials (including Diet members) to contribute 10 per cent of their salary to the navy fund. Before an attack from so august a body as the emperor, the Diet yielded on this budgetary question. Nevertheless, as it continued to be obstructive, two dissolutions were required in 1893–1894.

Hizen and Tosa desires for a share of wealth and power may have been behind the Diet's struggle for responsible government. The fact remains that by 1894 the government was fought to a near deadlock. Every session of the

JAPANESE PREMIERS

1890–1918 (Clan Domination)

Ito Hirobumi (C, G) 1885–1888; 1892–1896; 1898; 1900–1901
Kuroda Kiyotaka (S) 1888–1889
Yamagata Aritomo (C, G) 1889–1891; 1898–1900
Matsukata Masayoshi (S, G) 1891–1892; 1896–1898
Okuma Shigenobu (H) 1898; 1914–1916
Katsura Taro (C, G) 1901–1906; 1908–1911; 1912–1913
Saionji Kimmochi (K, G) 1906–1908; 1911–1912
Yamamoto Gombei (S) 1913–1914
Terauchi Seiki (C) 1916–1918

    (C—Choshu; S—Satsuma; H—Hizen; K—Kuge, or Court Noble; G—Genro)

1918–1932 (Party Government)

Hara Kei (Takashi) 1918–1921
Takahashi Korekiyo 1921–1922
Kato Tomosaburo (Admiral) 1922–1923
Yamamoto Gombei (Admiral) 1923–1924
Kiyoura Keiga (Privy Council) 1924
Kato Takaakira 1924–1925
Wakatsuki Reijiro 1926–1927; 1931
Tanaka Giichi 1927–1929
Hamaguchi Yuko (Osachi) 1929–1931
Inukai Ki (Tsuyoshi) 1931–1932

1932–1945 (Military Leadership)

Saito Makoto (Admiral) 1932–1934
Okada Keisuke (Admiral) 1934–1936
Hirota Koki 1936–1937
Hayashi Senjuro (General) 1937
Konoye Fumimaro (Prince) 1937–1939; 1940–1941
Hiranuma Kiichiro 1939
Abe Nobuyuki (General) 1939–1940
Yonai Mitsumasa (Admiral) 1940
Tojo Hideki (General) 1941–1944
Koiso Kuniaki (General) 1944–1945
Suzuki Kantaro (Admiral) 1945
Higashikuni Naruhiko (Royal Prince) 1945

Diet was a hectic one, involving a budgetary crisis. Partly to relieve this tension and partly because it appeared to be a sound move from the viewpoint of national policy, Prime Minister Ito decided to support those demanding a war with China. This move won patriotic support from the Diet, which fell in line and passed huge emergency budgets. The war cost Ito dearly, however, as victories in the field raised the prestige of Generals Yamagata and Oyama, whereas he suffered a diplomatic defeat at the close of the conflict.

A Foreign Policy of Expansion

Much has been said about the motivations behind Japan's outward thrust so soon after it had put its own house in order. The answer can be traced to a combination of causes: the intense ambition of its rulers, the devoted nationalism and obedience of the people, the struggle to retain security and independence in the modern world, and the desire for foreign markets of investment.

The Japanese had a strong sense of national sentiment well before Western intervention occurred, and were accustomed to military leadership. Support for expansionist undertakings after 1890 was not confined to professional fire-brands and militarists but had a wide popular base. The Chinese and Russian wars were fully supported in the Diet, for the liberals and party politicians then were as glory-minded as any other group. Memorials for expansion in Asia, especially in Korea, were constantly presented to the emperor by the new intellectual class in the decade after 1890. Military and diplomatic victories in turn fanned the flames of the new, modern nationalism. A keen sense of national honor was heightened by the unequal treaties, which were slow to disappear.[1]

Japan sought to become a great power and, observing the frenzied imperialist activities of the Western states in Asia and Africa, it could see no ethical or moral reason to refrain from joining the scramble for empire. In such an international setting, the Japanese could argue that one became either a colonizer or a colony. In fact, the Russian thrust at Manchuria and Korea made Japan's vigorous counteraction on the continent partially understandable in the name of self-defense.

Japan's rulers realized the need for military and industrial strength before embarking on a war with China, let alone challenging the dominant world powers. They also knew that European influence in Asia could be undermined only when these Western powers were at one another's throat. Then Japan could attack the one most vulnerable in Asia—as it turned out, first Russia, then Germany, and finally the democratic states. It could then become the dominant power in the Orient.

Economic developments further bolstered this ambition. Rapid industrialization on a narrow base meant that capitalization had been emphasized at the expense of consumer-goods production. This unbalance weakened domestic markets and purchasing power, thereby encouraging investment abroad. The first areas of Japanese economic penetration were Korea and adjacent Chinese territory. Moreover, the scarcity of raw materials and, later, food in the home islands meant the need for a navy to protect the sea lanes. It also served as an excuse, long used by the Europeans, to control foreign domains that produced the required products.

The Sino-Japanese War of 1894–1895 and Its Aftermath

The focal point of friction on the continent was Korea, long a bone of contention between China and Japan, and now a target of Czarist Russian expan-

---

[1] These were the treaties signed in the last years of the shogunate. The judicial structure was modernized with the help of French and German legal advisers. Extraterritoriality was ended in 1899; tariff autonomy was gained in 1910.

sion. In 1592 a Japanese force of 200,000 under Hideyoshi had all but con-
qured Korea, as a prelude to an attack on China. However, it had withdrawn
in the face of a large Chinese force, only to return in 1597 to engage in fierce
indecisive combat with Chinese and Korean troops. The war-weary Japanese
had withdrawn again when Hideyoshi died, leaving the countryside devastated.
Thus there had been instilled in the Koreans a fear and hatred of the Japanese.

Korea remained in isolation, under China's nominal rule, until modern
times. To Japan, control of the peninsula was important both to keep the Russians at bay and to serve as a springboard for further expansion. The very
idea that a small island power could conquer portions of a continent ruled by
Russia and China seemed as inconceivable in 1890 as it was to appear after
1950.

Japan, which had already established its control over the Ryukyu Islands,
including Okinawa, incorporated them as a prefecture in 1879. In spite of
treaties that gave Japan certain rights in Korea, the Chinese tried to establish
a full protectorate there. The Koreans did not offer strenuous objections and
the foreign powers registered only passive opposition. Only Japan would fight
to "preserve Korea's independence." An abortive revolt in Korea led both
China and Japan to send troops there and in 1894 the rivals confronted each
other near the capital city of Seoul. The original decision to send troops to
Korea and so precipitate a war was taken at a cabinet meeting attended by
Yamagata, then army chief of staff and president of the Privy Council. The
first modern Sino-Japanese war began when China would not recognize the
peninsula's freedom.

China, which could get no foreign aid, was quickly beaten by Japan's land
and naval forces, which thereby gained considerable military prestige. China
was compelled to yield to the victor's demands in the Treaty of Shimonoseki
in 1895. Korea was made free and independent; China had to pay Japan an
indemnity of 3,000 million taels and give Japan most-favored-nation trade
privileges, plus the right to trade in many Chinese ports. The Japanese even
obtained extraterritoriality in China before they had got rid of this burden
in their own country. China was forced to cede Formosa and the nearby Pescadores Islands to Japan. Finally, the indemnity enabled Japan to adopt the gold
standard. Its rulers were convinced that carefully planned expansion clearly
brought handsome rewards.

The settlement, however, brought a diplomatic defeat that underscored
Japan's isolated position. China had yielded to Japan control of the Liaotung
Peninsula (including Port Arthur) in Southern Manchuria. The European
powers intervened as Russia, supported by its French ally and an ambitious
Germany, sponsored the Triple Intervention of April 23, 1895, "advising"
Japan to drop this claim. Ito had foreseen this eventuality but had been unable
to resist militarist efforts to demand Liaotung. The German Ambassador pro-
voked Japanese resentment against his government by crudely threatening war.

Japan yielded to this solid front in return for a slightly larger indemnity. Ito thus appeared to suffer a diplomatic defeat, but the military victory raised the prestige of Generals Yamagata and Oyama.

Aware of this shift in power, Ito sought to redress the balance by having political parties assume office. Because of his efforts, then, Okuma and Itagaki were suddenly ordered by the throne to form a cabinet in 1898. With control of two thirds of the lower house, the parties' position seemed secure; then Ito left on a trip to China. The experiment proved an utter fiasco, for Prime Minister Okuma and Foreign Minister Itagaki were barely in office when a quarrel over the spoils of patronage caused Itagaki to resign. The cabinet soon fell, and Yamagata took over. By bribing Itagaki's faction, the great militarist pushed through his ominous Imperial Ordinance of 1898, which gave the military command virtual control over the armed-service ministries.

The angered Ito, on his return, joined forces with the duped Itagaki faction and formed a new party in 1900, the Seiyukai. This former liberal body was now a conservative party of landowners and businessmen who sought responsible government. Ito was party leader for only three years. The Peers were angered by his association with a democratic political group, and his party became restive when he supported a high tax program necessitated by the impending war with Russia. He finally yielded Seiyukai leadership to his protégé Saionji, a firm believer in party government.[2]

Before considering the war with Russia, it may be noted parenthetically, Saionji fared no better than his mentor in dealing with Yamagata. The Saionji cabinet in 1912 had persistently refused to grant the army's request for two new divisions in the Korean sector. War Minister General Uehara resigned, and the cabinet fell when the army would not appoint a replacement. Saionji then became a genro, the last so designated, and continued his struggle against the militarists from that vantage point. Hara Kei, a commoner, then became the Seiyukai leader.

The British Alliance and War with Russia

The recurrent nature of some Far Eastern problems was reflected in the decade between Japan's wars with China and Russia. The Chinese indemnity of 1895 was financed by Russia in return for a military defensive alliance against Japan in 1896, which bears more than a passing resemblance to the Sino-Russian Treaty of 1950. China also permitted Russia to build a short cut for its Trans-Siberian Railroad across Manchuria. This vital east-west line, called the Chinese Eastern Railway, was completed in 1904. Also in 1896, Yamagata went to Russia to seek a compromise. His proposal that Korea be divided into

[2] Ito's last antimilitarist effort was his opposition to the annexation of Korea. He used his great prestige and position as resident-general of Korea after 1905 to this purpose. Ironically, he was assassinated by a Korean in 1909, and, in the wave of popular indignation that followed, the expansionists annexed Korea in 1910.

spheres of influence at latitude 38° was rejected by the ambitious Czarist government. Instead, a vague agreement was reached to keep law and order in Korea, making it practically a joint protectorate.

This delicate balance in the Far East was upset in 1898 when Germany obtained the Kiaochow leasehold, a region in China aspired to by Russia. The Russians immediately gained control over Port Arthur and the Kwantung Peninsula (southern tip of the Liaotung Peninsula), thereby moving into the very spot Japan wanted in 1895. Russia was also allowed to build a north-south rail line in Manchuria to link its new leasehold with the Chinese Eastern Railway. Finally, it did not escape Japanese attention that the Russians used the Boxer Rebellion as a pretext for occupying all Manchuria in 1900. The benefits won in 1894–1895 seemed to be passing bloodlessly into Russian hands.

It was at this juncture that Britain and Japan, brought together by fear of Russia, signed their famous Alliance of 1902 and ended the uncomfortable diplomatic isolation that each had suffered. This treaty blocked a Russo-Japanese agreement that could have threatened British interests in the Orient. Ito had sought a settlement with Russia in order to avoid a war, but the cabinet and the rest of the genro favored a British alliance instead.

The alliance stated its support of the status quo and peace of Asia. It recognized the special interests of each power in China, and the special interests of Japan in Korea. Each promised to remain neutral if the other was at war but to come to its aid if attacked by more than one power. The Diet gave its unanimous support and the alliance became the cornerstone of Japan's foreign policy for twenty years.

Japan could now turn to meet the menace of the insatiable and irresponsible program of expansion devised by the Czar's ambitious agents in the Far East. Most disturbing was Russia's refusal to recognize Japan's supremacy in Korea or to make good on a promise to China in 1902 to evacuate Manchuria. Tokyo's attempt to recognize Russia's right in Manchuria in return for a reciprocal acceptance of its own position in Korea was rejected in 1903. General Oyama, genro and chief of the general staff, then persuaded his government to go to war while Japan still held a military advantage.

During these years, negotiations were shrouded in diplomatic secrecy, but it must be emphasized that Japan's rulers were willing to negotiate a moderate settlement. The public at large and the Diet, bitter over the failure to check Russia, clamored for war. Educators and newspaper men were particularly insistent, and in 1903 the advocates of a "speedy solution" banded together to press their case. Finally, on February 4, 1904, the Japanese launched a naval attack on Port Arthur and declared war two days later.

With an army totaling only 850,000 men, the better-prepared Japanese quickly forced their way from Korea into Manchuria. At the start of 1905 they won two important victories, the capture of Port Arthur and the battle of Mukden. In May, 1905, the Russian Baltic Fleet, after traveling around Eurasia, was wiped out by Admiral Togo's forces in the Sea of Japan. However, the Japanese had run low on money and manpower, and the army command in Manchuria secretly demanded an end to the fighting. At Japan's request, President Theodore Roosevelt arranged a peace conference at Portsmouth, New Hampshire, in June, 1905, a move resentfully branded as "intervention" by the Japanese public.

The Japanese won their minimum demands: recognition of Japan's dominance in Korea, Russian evacuation of Manchuria, Japanese acquisition of the Kwantung leasehold, and control of the railway zone between Port Arthur and Changchun. Negotiations became snarled when the Russians refused to pay an indemnity, but, when the army insisted that peace was absolutely essential,

215

Japan dropped this demand in return for the southern half of Sakhalin Island. Both sides agreed to leave Manchuria, except for railway guards, and restore the administrative rule of that region to China.

The Closed Door: Korea and Manchuria

The public was so aroused at the failure to obtain an indemnity and greater territorial concessions (e.g., Russia's Maritime Province) that martial law was declared in Tokyo. Foreign Minister Baron Kuroda, who negotiated the final agreement against his will, had to be protected by an armed escort on his arrival home. Not even publication of the revised Anglo-Japanese Treaty, in September, 1905, could appease the people, though each signatory now promised to aid the other should there be an unprovoked attack by a third party. In return for a free hand in Tibet, Britain recognized Japan's similar right in Korea. Japan also won American recognition of its special rights in Korea in 1905. The peninsula was annexed in 1910, under the guidance of War Minister General Terauchi, who was also Korea's resident-general.

Meanwhile, the former antagonists were sharing Manchuria, the northern portion going to Russia and the southern to Japan. The two powers jealously guarded the exclusiveness of these economic preserves against foreign encroachment. Those Americans who thought that Japan had fought to maintain equality of economic opportunity (the Open Door) were quickly undeceived. Manchuria, with two powers in it, was as closed a pasture as before 1904. The Russians and Japanese signed secret treaties in 1907, 1910, and 1917 that divided Manchuria into spheres of influence, especially regarding rail and telegraph lines. The published treaties repeated the standard hypocrisies about the status quo, respect for China's integrity, acceptance of the Open Door, and equal economic opportunity for all.

Japan's policy at this time was to strengthen its economic position in South Manchuria and so lay the groundwork for future political absorption. In negotiation with China, notably the Treaty of Peking in 1905, Japan acquired lumbering rights on the Yalu River and mining rights in the fields formerly controlled by Russia, as well as cable and telegraph privileges.

Most important was the stranglehold Japan gained by treaty and pressure over railway construction and management. No other foreign concerns were able to construct routes there, and China itself had to agree not to build a competing line in the neighborhood of the South Manchurian Railway (the new name of the north-south line connecting Changchun with Port Arthur). The Chinese were, in effect, compelled to obtain Japan's permission and financial assistance to build railroads in South Manchuria. Thus, economic penetration, spearheaded by railway control, foreshadowed later Japanese efforts at political domination. In the Kwantung leasehold, Japan established direct rule, with a governor-general responsible to the cabinet in Tokyo.

The First World War—A Divine Wind

The First World War came as a blessing, for it gave Japan practically a free hand in the Orient. Japan joined the Allied side and took advantage of Germany's vulnerability to capture its territories and concessions in the Pacific. It then sought to take advantage of the withdrawal of European power from the Far East to dominate a China torn by the confusion following the fall of the Manchu Dynasty.

Assuring its uneasy British ally that it wished only to eliminate German influence in China, Japan captured the German leasehold at Kiaochow and the new port of Tsingtao on the Shantung Peninsula. A Chinese declaration of neutrality and a later proclamation limiting the war zone to Kiaochow were ignored. By the end of 1914, Japan took over German rights in Shantung. Germany had held a ninety-nine year lease on Kiaochow Bay and its adjoining territory, rights to railroad construction (the Tsingtao-Tsinan Railroad resulted), coal mining along the railway, and a priority in supplying capital for any undertakings in Shantung. In the Pacific, Japan occupied all German colonies north of the equator, extending more than halfway to Pearl Harbor. By the end of 1915, its war effort was essentially concluded.

The veteran politician, Okuma of Hizen, was prime minister (1914–1916) during this period, but his position did not signify responsible party rule, for the Seiyukai opposition held a majority in the lower house. Okuma's tenure of office was highlighted by an aggressive China policy that proved as expansionist as bureaucratic rule had ever been. The House of Representatives could not get Okuma or Foreign Minister Kato to divulge the nature of the government's negotiations with Britain or Germany. Nor could it force a vote, in December, 1914, to restrict the war or return the Kiaochow leasehold to China. When the Diet would not provide funds for the establishment of two new army divisions, Okuma called for and won an election in March, 1915.

This nongenro government also undertook a major effort to subjugate China. Foreign Minister Kato Takaakira, who had reorganized his staff in order to pursue a more vigorous foreign policy, demanded extensive rights in Manchuria and Mongolia.[3] The public as a whole favored a "strong" China policy, and it was aroused when the Chinese government declared the Kiaochow war zone abolished on January 7, 1915. Kato had been awaiting such an opportunity, and the next day China was presented with Japan's infamous Twenty-one Demands. They were divided into five groups, with the last and most onerous labeled as "requests." Their acceptance would have made China a Japanese puppet state.

---

[3] At this time Japan's interests included the Shantung and Kwantung peninsulas, the South Manchurian Railway zone, and another rail line in Manchuria running from Mukden to Antung.

217

Twenty-one Demands

Group I concerned Shantung. The Germans were to be kept out, with Japan acquiring all their rights, plus the ability to extend railroad construction; and the future peace conference was not to hinder this arrangement. The Japanese were most persistent regarding Shantung; they reasoned that the cost of defeating the Germans had to be met and that China, which "benefited" from this campaign, should make concessions.

Group II, based on long and continuous negotiation, dealt with Manchuria and Eastern Inner Mongolia. Japan demanded a ninety-nine—(instead of twenty-five) year lease for Kwantung, the existing railways (South Manchurian and Mukden-Antung), plus a new railroad to run from Kirin to Changchun. Japan also demanded the right for its citizens to enter South Manchuria at will, own land, and operate mines there. Foreign capital for railway or industrial purposes was to be controlled by Japan. Regarding Inner Mongolia, Japan sought the same control that Russia was in the process of establishing over Outer Mongolia.

Group III was to give Japan control over iron resources by making the Chinese Hanyehping Company, which controlled rich iron and coal properties in Central China, a joint Chinese-Japanese concern with a mining monopoly in the Yangtze Valley region. This measure was an answer to Chinese nationalization of the company; because the company had become heavily in debt to the Japanese, they had gained control over its ore produce.

Group IV called on China not to cede or lease any coastal harbor, bay, or island to a foreign power.

Group V—the requests—included the desire that Fukien, near Formosa, be made a Japanese sphere. This was the only point in Group V that was mentioned in the final settlement of May, 1915. For the rest, Japan wanted China to hire Japanese as political, military, and financial advisers; allow Japanese to own hospitals, temples, and schools in China; place the Chinese police under joint Chinese-Japanese control in areas where disputes might arise; receive arms from Japan or establish a joint arsenal; give Japan rights to construct railroads in South China; and allow Japanese to preach in China.

The Demands were so obnoxious that China rejected them, and world public opinion was aroused against Japan. After considerable negotiation (January-May, 1915) Kato dropped the fifth group and presented the rest as an ultimatum. Preparations were made for general mobilization, but China capitulated on May 9, 1915.

Even though this was a great victory for Kato, the genro and particularly Yamagata became his bitter opponents, primarily because of the Foreign Minister's insistence that the Foreign Office be independent of all outside influence. He did not present major questions to the genro or show them all the important documents of state. Kato followed his own course, not yielding to advice of caution and moderation by Yamagata or to extremist proposals for a show of force by Minister of War General Oka.

The Seiyukai minority proposed a vote of censure, on the curiously mixed grounds that the ruthless Twenty-one Demands aroused widespread antagonism in China, and that the government's promise of "eventual" restoration of Kiao-chow to China was detrimental to Japan's interest and prestige. This confused and futile political gesture was nevertheless the first occasion on which a government was accused by the organized political opposition of being too expansionist.

Further negotiation led to a final agreement of May 25, 1915, providing for the return of the Shantung leasehold to China after the war, with the area recognized as a Japanese sphere of influence. The Kwantung leasehold was extended to ninety-nine years, and Japan gained railway and other privileges in South Manchuria. In sum, Japan's Manchurian and Kwantung interests were safeguarded, but this could have been achieved in a quieter manner. The other vague gains could not have compensated for the hostility aroused in China and elsewhere.

The Siberian Venture

When Okuma retired, he refused an offer to join the genro, for the "Tribune of the People" had always been disdainful of that august body. The new prime minister was the militarist bureaucrat General Terauchi, a protégé of the aging Yamagata. His government was seriously troubled by the wartime inflation, which reached dangerous proportions in 1917–1918. The high cost of living led to "rice riots" and resulted in a change of government in 1918.[4]

Before leaving office, however, General Terauchi succeeded in launching Japan on its last wartime adventure—in Siberia, where a power vacuum was created by the Russian Revolution. The United States reluctantly proposed a joint intervention in Siberia in order to aid some Czech troops moving eastward across Russia and to protect supply centers on the Russian Pacific coast. Britain, France, and Japan were also determined to work against the Bolsheviks.

In addition, Prime Minister Terauchi saw a favorable occasion for expansion, and contemplated sending an "independent expedition" in July, 1918. At that time in Japan there was a short-lived body called the Advisory Council on Foreign Relations, whose consent for this scheme was required. Hara Kei, who as the Seiyukai leader was a member, vigorously opposed such a vague and costly project. Terauchi yielded but reserved the freedom to dispatch additional troops if the Czechs were in distress. He had to promise to withdraw the troops when the purpose of the expedition was accomplished. The whole con-

---

[4] Earlier riots were politically motivated. Rioting and bloodshed had featured the first Diet elections after 1889. Threats, exhortations to assassination, and riots followed the peace treaty that ended the Russian war in 1905.

cept of a Siberian adventure was evidently engineered by Yamagata, who pressed vigorously for an independent expedition.

The United States, which proposed that each party dispatch 7,000 men, eventually sent 9,000 troops under General Graves. The Japanese, reserving freedom of action and professing no territorial or political designs on Siberian territory, sent more than 72,000 men.

When the Terauchi cabinet fell, it was replaced by the Seiyukai under Hara Kei, a professional politician and the first commoner ever to become prime minister. Many felt that this innovation symbolized the culmination of an evolution toward party government. An understanding of the power still held by the militarists and bureaucrats, plus an appreciation of the limited importance of the cabinet, leads to a more modest interpretation. Even if party control of the cabinet could be claimed in 1918, the advocates of representative government had merely reached a position from which they could carry the fight to its critical stage.

Hara inherited not only the domestic issue of responsible government but a wide variety of problems in foreign relations as well. These concerned the extent of Japanese control and influence on the Asiatic mainland, naval relations with the Western powers, and the growing tension with Britain and the United States. Japan had definitely come of age in 1918. The question now was, which way would it turn?

The "Period of Normal Government"

A sustained effort to attain democratic rule in Japan occurred during 1918–1931, as the cabinet became responsible to the lower house. Save for an interlude in 1922–1924, prime ministers were chosen with consideration given to their party support in the House of Representatives. A cabinet resigned following its party's defeat in an election or the collapse of party discipline in parliament. However, a prime minister could still dissolve a recalcitrant lower house and the government was able to influence the ensuing election through the Home Ministry's manipulation of prefectural administrative machinery.

With the passing of the genro the political situation became more fluid; governmental activities during the 1920's reflected both a relative strengthening of the democratic system and the persistent influence of nondemocratic and militarist elements. Both aspects can be discerned from a study of the more important cabinets that held office at this time. A similar balancing of these forces is reflected in other developments on the Japanese scene: the changed role and prestige of the army, the development of the economy, and the quality of party politics in this crucial hour of leadership.

Decline of Militarist Prestige

One of the most striking changes in the political atmosphere after 1918 was the army's sudden decline in prestige, due in good part to a change in popular attitudes toward aggressive diplomacy. Antagonism to expansionist policies, already apparent with regard to China, became greatly intensified during the long and costly Siberian adventure. The failure of the Terauchi cabinet to maintain political and economic order at home also affected the army's prestige. Moreover, the Japanese were impressed by the victory of the Western democracies over the German military oligarchy, which had served as a model for many of Japan's modern political institutions.

The army shortsightedly persisted in occupying Siberia, and the Hara cabinet could take office only by making General Tanaka Giichi—another Yamagata protégé from Choshu—minister of war with administrative control of the affair. In fact, the Seiyukai government (1918–1922) proved unable to recall the Siberian expeditionary force, a fact reflecting again the limitations of cabinet authority. Public and parliamentary opposition to the project became increasingly vehement even in the face of sponsorship by the Choshu clique (Yamagata, Terauchi, and Tanaka), genro support, and repeated appeals to patriotism, but opposition was checked by ruthless suppression of speech and the press.

The government's right to dispatch troops without parliamentary approval was challenged in the lower house; even the Peers were disturbed by the clash of opinion within the cabinet. The Diet demanded that no more troops be sent to Siberia. When 700 Japanese were massacred at Nikolaevsk in 1920, the public displayed no interest in revenge but called for the withdrawal of the occupation forces. The Kenseikei opposition party—formed by Okuma in 1915 and now led by former Foreign Minister Viscount Kato and Hamaguchi Yuko —demanded immediate evacuation and accused the militarists of governing from behind the scenes. The liberal element tried to curb the army's power to make independent decisions committing the nation so deeply.

Matters were further complicated by the discovery that War Minister Tanaka was making unauthorized use of the funds allocated for the Siberian forces to aid the White Russians. This interference in the civil war was contrary to the Foreign Ministry's policy of neutrality. Such a flagrant example of dual government aroused the public even more against the army. The Siberian venture was finally ended by the nonparty government of Admiral Kato in October, 1922. In a sense this accomplishment exemplified the more moderate attitude of the navy and indicated that the armed services were not always in total accord. However, it also revealed the inability of political parties to achieve their objectives without this kind of support.

As the decade wore on, the "army steamroller" lost much of its effectiveness. As General Tanaka learned when prime minister in 1927–1929, one could no longer be certain of rallying popular support for chauvinistic enterprises. After Yamagata died in 1922, the army temporarily refrained from undertaking heavy-handed ventures in the field of foreign relations. The partial eclipse of the army's political power was matched by its reduced attraction as a career for ambitious young men. Inflation and restrictive budgets meant low real wages for young officers. Moreover, the road to political influence now appeared open to politicians and economic leaders, and a career in Japan's expanding economy offered high social status as well as a good income.

Economic Development

As the Japanese economy matured under relatively prosperous world economic conditions, the zaibatsu and other business interests discarded their earlier role as mere agents of the state. Their efforts to direct government policy were made through the middle-class parties and democratic institutions, which benefited at first from such support. The nature and rate of Japan's economic growth after 1918 thus had important political consequences.

With the development of industry, the national income almost doubled between 1914 and 1930, while the population increased by 25 per cent, from 51 million to 64 million. Real income of workers rose about 50 per cent, but the peasantry, though benefiting somewhat, did not enjoy as large a gain.

Even so, the industrial revolution was not yet in high gear by 1930, and only one fifth of the population was connected with manufacturing, compared to nearly one half in agriculture. Of course, compared to the rest of the Orient, Japan's progress was remarkable. In the vital iron and steel industries Japan made moderate progress after the state-owned Yawata Iron Works opened in 1901. By 1913, Japan was producing 253,000 tons of pig iron and 255,000 tons of finished steel, or about one half and one third, respectively, of home consumption. Most of this was made at Yawata, and no firms, private or public, were as yet profitable. The production of steel rose to 533,000 tons in 1920 and over 2 million tons by 1929, supplying 70 per cent of Japan's needs. Pig-iron production in 1920 was twice its 1913 level, and this was doubled again by 1929. Many private plants had been constructed by 1930, but Yawata still overshadowed them all. As Japan's experience clearly demonstrated, the development of heavy industry is a difficult and time-consuming process.

Greatest progress was recorded in the textile industries, especially silk and cotton. So well developed were these two light industries that in 1913 they accounted for more than half of Japan's exports, with raw silk alone accounting for about one third of the total. With the United States as the major market, raw-silk production tripled between 1913 and 1929. This expansion brought 40 per cent of all farming families into the silk-raising industry and led peasants' daughters to work at reeling mills built near the sources of supply. Silk thus became an important source of cash income and was responsible for the improvements that did occur in peasant living conditions. This intimate tie of Japan's farming population to the American silk market had disastrous economic and political repercussions when the market collapsed after 1929.

In cotton production, the number of spindles rose from 2½ to 6½ million between 1913 and 1929. Generally, the textile industry, having gotten off to a fast start after the Restoration of 1868, was quite thoroughly modernized by

1929, and employed one quarter of all Japan's industrial labor. Its importance was again reflected in foreign trade: cotton and silk totaled 53 per cent of the exports in 1914, and 65 per cent in 1929.

Shipping, like iron and steel, showed some progress but could not compare with textiles. It was only just prior to the First World War that Japanese yards undertook the construction of ocean-going vessels and warships. Between 1909 and 1913 Japan produced annually about 50,000 tons of steamships, and by 1914 had six yards able to build ships of 1,000 tons or more. The war was a tremendous boon to shipping, and 650,000 tons were launched in 1919 as compared with 85,000 tons in 1914. However, as cutbacks were soon necessitated by high costs and foreign competition, in the 1920's a yearly production of 150,000 tons was considered good.

As industrialization progressed, the role of government in economic affairs changed. By the end of the Meiji era, the industries directly administered by the government were declining in relative importance. Some monopolies, like salt, tobacco, and camphor, were retained for revenue purposes, and the government also managed railways, dockyards, and munition plants. But iron and steel production was the only major field in which the state predominated; the Yawata works in 1931 still produced three quarters of the pig iron and one half of the ingot steel made in Japan. Some other strategically important concerns, however, were helped by such financial devices as direct subsidies through the Industrial Bank of Japan. The major colonial enterprise thus aided was the South Manchurian Railway Company, which controlled the railroad and most large-scale enterprises in the railway zone.

Otherwise, government control over industrial life was fairly restricted, because the classical economic theory of liberalism prevailed in the 1920's. What enabled the government to retain intimate contact with economic developments was its tie with the vastly influential zaibatsu and some lesser families. These relatively few groups gave the economy central direction and control, since each family was a huge vertical trust holding interests in all facets of the Japanese economy. Zaibatsu associations with political parties were common: the Mitsui family backed the conservative Seiyukai, whereas Mitsubishi supported the more liberal Kenseikai and its successor, the Minseito.

Unlike other nations, Japan did not undergo an immediate deflation after 1918, partly because the government feared the political effect of widespread unemployment and partly because the zaibatsu would not sacrifice unprofitable industrial enterprises to financial considerations. However, during the next ten years the zaibatsu loomed larger than ever in the Japanese economy, as many lesser rivals were eliminated. Japan finally became adapted to peacetime conditions of production and trade. Unfortunately, the great American collapse of 1929 administered a severe shock to this vulnerable economic structure.

Two major problems, then, were Japan's heavy dependence on favorable world economic conditions and the concentration of so much power in the zaibatsu. This dominance meant that the business community failed to develop a wide base of political support for middle-of-the-road policies. When the militarists attempted to regain power after the depression of 1930, the middle class was unable to offer effective resistance.

Weaknesses of Party Government

The numerous difficulties confronting the effort to establish responsible party rule were generally underestimated. Some support was given by Prince Saionji, abetted by the liberal Lord Keeper of the Privy Seal Makino and Minister of the Imperial Household Ikki. However, the aristocracy as a whole had no intention of capitulating simply because the despised Diet had captured the cabinet. The army and the bureaucracy, though in a defensive posture, remained very powerful and could be curbed only by an intelligent and concerted campaign. Yet the forces required for this campaign were too diversified, ranging from conservative business leaders to peasant farmers and radical labor groups. Such elements actually encompass the major forces that compete vigorously for political power in a democratic community. It would have required statecraft of the highest order for these conflicting groups to combine against their wily, entrenched foes. That such brilliance was not forthcoming was an unfortunate but not surprising development.

The two leading parties—Seiyukai and Kenseikai (later Minseito)—were unable to assert competent leadership even after they had become middle-class strongholds. Their continued competition for power, even in the face of a common danger, and their inability to generate the political discipline needed for survival revealed the persistence of the faults that first characterized the Japanese party system. Perhaps two generations proved too short a time for the growth of a resilient democratic tradition.

The parties remained somewhat amorphous because they did not grasp the importance of formulating and standing by certain principles. There was a bewildering profusion of splinter groups, constantly shifting their political allegiances. Personal leadership remained the most significant factor in determining a party's policy and strength, and even its existence. When violent death removed Hara, Hamaguchi, and the few other capable politicians who did appear, the fragile structure of party rule and responsible government was irrevocably damaged.[5]

The continued presence of corrupt practices was especially damaging. Other elements in the government were also guilty, but the parties could not fall back on a protective reserve of prestige or respect, and depended directly on public support in their fight for political power. Since parties now held responsible positions, their conduct attracted greater attention than before 1914, when they were primarily obstructionist.

---

[5] Too much has been made of premierships held by commoner-politicians. Although four commoners (including Hara and Hamaguchi) held this office, it was also occupied by two admirals, one bureaucrat, one nobleman-politician, and one general during this period.

The pattern of party policy in the Diet demonstrated a naive and dangerous type of opportunism within the democratic camp. In 1922, the liberal Kenseikai opposition supported "big navy" attempts to defeat the conservative Seiyukai cabinet policy of retrenchment. Later, in 1928, the liberal Minseito party sided with the extreme chauvinists, who accused a Seiyukai administration of infringing on the constitutional sovereignty of the throne when it signed the Kellogg-Briand Treaty "on behalf of the people." The Minseito was partly to blame for the antidemocratic sentiment aroused by this incident.

Similarly, the Seiyukai behaved myopically when out of power in 1930. It sided with the naval opponents of a Minseito cabinet that had accepted a modest ratio of naval power in a treaty with the Anglo-American powers. Finally, even in the great Manchurian crises of 1931–1932, the two parties failed to form a coalition or operate together; partisan advantage seemed so attractive that it was pursued even at the cost of representative government.

The Cabinets of 1919–1932

The Hara Cabinet and After (1918–1924)

Each party cabinet during this period revealed in turn the complex issues besetting popular government. The rapid chain of events occurring during the years 1918–1924 graphically illustrated the instability of Japan's representative institutions. The brave experiment in party rule begun under Hara and the Seiyukai terminated in chaos, terror, and "transcendental" nonpartisan government.

Hara was a conservative politician without reformist ideals who ran the Seiyukai with a heavy hand. His party had gained a plurality in the 1917 election. When the Kenseikai demanded a universal manhood suffrage law, he bluntly dissolved the lower house and won a majority in the election of January, 1920.

The major Seiyukai achievement lay in implementing a moderate foreign policy. In 1919, Japan attended the Paris Peace Conference and ratified the Treaty of Versailles. Japanese interest was centered in three issues—Shantung, the German island conquests, and racial equality. Japan sought outright annexation of the former German islands and could cite similar colonial ambitions among its allies. American opposition, although not strong enough to block Japanese rule, succeeded in bringing these islands under the League mandate system. Japan received a Class C mandate, tantamount to annexation, but the Japanese accepted this compromise grudgingly.

Japan insisted in vain that a declaration of racial equality among states be a basic principle of the League of Nations. Britain feared that this would embarrass its Middle Eastern position, and Australia opposed it as a threat to its immigration policy. This failure made the Japanese adamant regarding Shantung. Treaties with China in 1915 and 1918 had transferred German economic privileges to Japan, with the leasehold restored to Chinese sovereignty. Japan won Western acceptance of this provision, but the Chinese refused to sign the Versailles Treaty.

Japanese-American relations were at a low ebb because of differences over Japan's policy of expansion in the Pacific and on the Asian mainland. Tension was sharpened by the danger of a naval arms race. Although the United States was unwilling to use force to preserve China's integrity, the war left it with a large naval establishment at sea and under construction. Though domestic American politics might have curtailed the building program, Japan was impelled to seek an international-control agreement. Of a budget of about 1½ billion yen, 48 per cent was already going to the army and navy. In a naval race with the United States, Japan would have been forced to spend even more money in a contest it could not win.

Under the terms of the Anglo-Japanese Alliance, Britain might have been obliged to side against America in a major Asian war. The naval and diplomatic issues came to a head when the alliance came up for renewal and the British sought to replace it with a broader pact.

Japan agreed to attend a Pacific Affairs Conference held at Washington in 1921–1922. Hara sent a delegation that included Navy Minister Admiral Kato, architect of Japan's modern navy. It was authorized to accept reductions in naval power and military bases provided they did not impair Japan's security.

The expendable Anglo-Japanese Alliance was replaced by a general political arrangement. This was the Four Power Treaty (United States, Britain, Japan, and France), which provided for a pledge of consultation among the signatories. In addition to recognizing no special interests—at American insistence —the signatories agreed to respect one another's territory in the Pacific, confer jointly in case of controversy, and communicate with one another in case of aggressive action by another power.

The best-known achievement of the Conference was the Five Power Naval Treaty. The United States proposed to limit all naval vessels, but Britain and Japan restricted the agreement to capital ships. A ten-year holiday in construction of this class was agreed on, certain vessels were scrapped, and battleships and aircraft carriers were limited as to tonnage and size of guns. The ratio of capital ships was set at 5:5:3:1.75:1.75 for America, Britain, Japan, France, and Italy. However, the political and naval agreements made sense to Admiral Kato only if Japan was assured of supremacy in the western Pacific, which he regarded as "home waters." The other powers satisfied Japan's security requirements by agreeing not to add new fortifications and bases in this area and to make no changes in existing establishments.[6]

This agreement assured Japan military supremacy as well as security in the

---

[6] New construction was forbidden at the following sites: the United States—Aleutians, Guam, Pago Pago, Philippines; Britain—Hong Kong and the Pacific Islands east of 110 east longitude except those near dominion waters; Japan—Kuriles, Bonins, Amami-Oshima, Ryukyus, Formosa, and the Pescadores. Mandated islands were already forbidden to have fortifications.

western Pacific. As a mild diplomatic counterweight, a Nine-Power Treaty, which institutionalized the principle of the Open Door in China, was also concluded, at the desire of the United States. The burden of respecting this principle was now shared by the five signatories of the naval agreement, plus Belgium, Holland, and Portugal. The treaty powers agreed to respect China's independence and integrity, establish equal economic opportunity for all, enable China to develop a stable government, and respect its neutrality. No previously acquired rights were surrended, and the only weapon of enforcement remained the good faith of the signatories. Since China's rights had already been solemnly recognized in many previous treaties, all to no avail, there seems in retrospect to have been little reason to hope that Japan would keep its pledge once the balance of military power again shifted in its favor.

The Shantung question was also resolved at Washington under Anglo-American pressure. The Sino-Japanese Treaty of 1922 was a compromise that returned Shangtung to China but gave Japan control of the Tsinan-Tsingtao Railway for fifteen years, the life of a loan that enabled China to buy back the road.

Admiral Kato had the prestige and power required to keep the "big navy" advocates under control and speed the agreements through the Privy Council. Public opinion in general favored the treaties, since they assured security, relieved the tension in the Pacific, and simultaneously reduced the tax burden. Although the extremists were upset, Japan in effect obtained a sound naval position in the Orient, an excellent resting point from which an aggressive program could later be launched.

The Hara government was less fortunate in domestic affairs, where internal party dissension acutely weakened its freedom of action. In addition, economic conditions remained unstable after the end of the war. Inflationary pressures at first continued to distort Japan's cost-price structure and keep food prices high. Then a sudden though temporary reversal in April, 1920, sent prices into a spin. The wholesale price index, which stood at 100 in 1913 and was 322 at the start of 1920, fell to 190 in 1921. Economic pressure was somewhat reduced, however, by wage increases and the competent management of Finance Minister Takahashi Korekiyo.

The uncertainty of the times and blatant corruption in the government led a young railway employee to murder Hara on November 24, 1921. Takahashi became premier, but as he lacked the ability to keep his party in line he had to resign in 1922. Not only was he unable to control the Seiyukai, but during his premiership Diet members became so unruly and irresponsible as to resort to violence on the floor of the House of Representatives. A marked swing to the left had arisen in many centers of popular thought, and this condition also was reflected in the Diet. Simultaneously, the nascent labor movement grew to 300 unions of more than 100,000 members by 1921. Takahashi's resignation put a temporary halt to party government for two years.

The Kenseikai leader was Viscount Kato, successor to former Premier Okuma, who, as foreign minister in 1915 had antagonized the genro. He was bypassed in the search for a new premier until his genro antagonists passed away in 1924. In the light of mounting economic and social unrest, three "transcendental" nonparty governments were formed during 1922–1924. The first two were led by Admirals Kato and Yamamoto; during Yamamoto's regime, physical attacks on labor and liberal organizations became frequent. Hara's death had touched off a series of assassinations, and hired groups were used to smash labor-union centers and the more liberal press. The climax occurred during the great earthquake of September, 1923, which almost destroyed Tokyo. The police used the occasion to arrest thousands of citizens, mainly Socialists. One police captain went so far as to arrest and strangle a prominent labor leader and his family.

A caretaker cabinet of peers under Viscount Kiyoura then held office, until the election of 1924 brought the return of party government. The extremist threat subsided, but five years had passed in which democratic self-rule had made little progress. In spite of this ominous warning, the middle class did not close its own ranks, let alone enlist the support of the rising labor elements.

The Kenseikai in Power (1924–1927)

The second opportunity at responsible cabinet rule was more promising than that in 1918. The party in power was more liberal than the Seiyukai, and Prime Minister Viscount Kato, while not a commoner, was an able politician who had studied and understood the British system of parliamentary rule. Economic affairs were more stable than in 1920–1921, and the Mitsubishi group, which backed the government, was much more liberal than its rival Mitsui.

This Kenseikai regime was a representative sample of Japanese liberalism, reflecting its strong points and its grave defects. On the credit side was the passage of a universal manhood suffrage act in March, 1925, by a coalition Kenseikai-Saiyukai cabinet.[7] Both parties could thus take credit for its passage. This statute marked considerable progress in electoral reform since the first election of 1890. Then 460,000 were eligible to vote under a law that qualified only those who paid a direct national tax of fifteen yen a year. This tax was first lowered in 1899 to five yen and then set at ten yen in 1900, allowing 1,250,000 to vote. Yamagata supported the reform in order to reduce the influence of the landed interests in the Diet, for they had blocked an increase in the land tax required for a military expansion program. Labor and socialist leaders then pressed unsuccessfully for further reform, an issue serious enough to cause riots in 1912 and 1913. Hara lowered the qualifying tax from ten to three yen in 1920, creating a total of more than 3,000,000 voters. The first election under the new universal manhood suffrage law of 1925 took place in 1928, with more than 12,500,000 eligible voters.

Kato had authored the Twenty-one Demands in 1915, but was no longer an

---

[7] The coalition lasted until 1925, when it split because of tax and foreign-policy issues. Kato then formed a Kenseikai government, which lasted after his death in December, 1925, until April, 1927.

advocate of a "strong" China policy. The appointment of the conciliatory Baron Shidehara to the Foreign Ministry confirmed the policy of moderation. The Kato government also carried on a program of retrenchment under Finance Minister Hamaguchi, to the dismay of the bureaucrats and the militarists. Under this policy the army was reduced from twenty-one to seventeen divisions in March, 1925, a move hailed as a victory for liberalism and proof of Japan's westernization. The army opposed the cut vigorously, but an economy-minded public supported the government. Actually, this retrenchment was a blessing in disguise for the army. The number of troops was still ample for peacetime needs; officers freed from routine divisional duties were not retired but were assigned to organize military training in civilian schools. The money saved remained under army control and was invested in tanks, planes, and other equipment then lacking. Thus the army, though smaller, was better trained and equipped, and the number of Japanese subjects given military training and indoctrination actually increased.

The infamous Peace Preservation Law of April, 1925, indicated even more clearly the limitations of Japanese liberalism. It provided for up to ten years' imprisonment for those who formed or joined societies that sought to alter the national constitution or form of government, or repudiated the system of private ownership of property. Clearly aimed at left-wing reformers, this act was supported by the same liberals who voted for universal suffrage. It was strongly defended by Home Minister Wakatsuki Reijiro, who succeeded Kato in December, 1925, as party leader and premier. The law led to political arrests on a large scale, a feature which was to become quite common to the Japanese political scene.

The Seiyukai, seeking to mend its political fences, turned to a former war minister, the Choshu militarist, General Tanaka, for leadership. As a protégé of Prince Saionji, Tanaka seemed a likely candidate for the premiership. To bolster its other flank, the party won over Inukai Ki, a popular politician who could give the party a mass appeal under the new election law. The Kenseikai government under Wakatsuki displayed confusion and hesitation, and wavered under the Seiyukai criticism of its "timorous" China policy, lack of discipline, and corruption. Though vulnerable to such reactionary attacks, the Kenseikai failed to reach a compromise with the radicals, as the Peace Preservation Law attests. For example, in 1925, it permitted a Farmer-Labor party of 140,000 members to organize and then ordered it disbanded the same day.

Beset from left and right, the government adopted the negative policy of attacking the moral stature of the Seiyukai, centering its charges of gross corruption on Tanaka himself. When the Privy Council opposed a cabinet financial policy in April, 1927, Wakatsuki resigned. The more dynamic Hamaguchi then assumed Kenseikai leadership and reorganized the Kenseikai as the Minseito, or Democratic party. In spite of a Minseito plurality, Saionji held that the public wanted a change and recommended Tanaka for premier. It was hoped that the nationalistic Seiyukai would satisfy the conservatives and militarists while assuring the continuation of party government.

The Second Seiyukai Regime: General Tanaka

The decline in prestige of parliamentary rule after the death of Viscount Kato in 1925 was accelerated under the Seiyukai cabinet. In contrast to his predecessor, Tanaka displayed too much resolution. He became foreign minister and premier, and was therefore a target for opposition attacks in both domestic and foreign relations. The Minseito used its greater parliamentary strength to harass the government and continually harped on Tanaka's alleged misuse of funds in Siberia while war minister. The Diet was prevented from declaring no confidence in the government only by dissolution at the start of the 1927–1928 session. Although the Seiyukai controlled the administrative apparatus and spent a great deal of money on the 1928 campaign, it became the second government since 1890 to lose an election. When Tanaka would not resign, the Diet continued to challenge his position; the special session of 1928 was suspended twice to prevent the passage of resolutions of no confidence. After weathering the regular 1928–1929 session, the government was so battered that it resigned shortly after the Diet adjourned.

The Tanaka cabinet made little headway on internal matters but adopted a "positive policy" toward China, which involved it in serious complications. At an important state conference in the summer of 1927, a distinction was made between China Proper on the one hand and Manchuria and Eastern Mongolia on the other. The latter were considered areas of special interest, in which Japan was obliged to keep the peace.[8] An opportunity to implement Tanaka's somewhat vague ambitions arose in the spring of 1928. Chiang Kai-shek's Chinese Nationalist armies were moving northward toward Manchuria and posed a threat to its warlord ruler, Chang Tso-lin, considered friendly to Japan. That May, Japan's Kwantung army forces were dispatched to Tsinan in Shantung, ostensibly to protect Japanese property and economic privileges. The military command worked with Tanaka but paid little heed to the civilian authorities or even the War Ministry.

As the Tsinan affair grew tenser, Chang Tso-lin was assassinated in Manchuria, under suspicious circumstance implicating the Japanese. Tanaka then decided to withdraw Japanese troops from China Proper because of considerable public opposition. When the House of Peers joined in voicing concern over his policies, Tanaka stalled negotiations with China until the Diet adjourned in 1929. Even then, he concluded an executive agreement rather than a treaty, in order to keep the Privy Council from scrutinizing it. That body then joined the ranks of his opponents.

This retreat was in marked contrast to events that were to take place only two years later, but it was significant that even a half-hearted expansionist effort

---

[8] The Chinese later produced a "Tanaka Memorial" that, they claimed, incorporated findings of this conference. The document purported to show that Japan had extremely aggressive designs in Asia. Its authenticity is doubtful, but as a predictive description of Japan's later actions it was remarkably accurate.

could be made during a period of "normal government." The lacklustre performance of the parties was all the more damaging because this "dry-run" Tsinan affair demonstrated the army's aggressive intentions and its eagerness to be rid of cabinet control.

The failure of his China policy and the accusations leveled at his cabinet's adherence to the Kellogg-Briand Pact were personal disasters for Tanaka. It was ironic for a Choshu militarist to be accused of lacking sufficient nationalist ardor. He resigned in July, 1929 and died, a broken man, at the end of the year.

The Efforts of Hamaguchi

The Seiyukai failure presented the Minseito with what proved to be the final opportunity to secure party government. Some progress was made before its capable leader, "Lion" Hamaguchi, was cut down by an assassin. Thereafter, with Wakatsuki again prime minister, the government lost control over the situation.

When Hamaguchi became prime minister, Baron Shidehara returned to the Foreign Ministry, and he promptly staffed it with moderates who carried on his policy of conciliation. Relations with China improved, and the public welcomed a change from the crude Tanaka approach that had aroused Chinese hatred. Except for Home Minister Adachi, the cabinet was very liberal; it quickly won a decisive election victory over the discredited Seiyukai, gaining 273 seats to 174.

Perhaps Hamaguchi's greatest achievement was the ratification of the London Naval Limitation Treaty of 1930. His success in standing up to the military command and the Privy Council might well have set the pattern for the future political development of Japan. Instead, it became the isolated highwater mark of responsible government. The basic issues developed over the navy's demand for a 7:10 ratio with the United States in large cruisers and all auxiliary craft. The navy argued that the proposed lower ratio of 6:9 would endanger Japanese security. The government, however, accepted this latter ratio, and extended the earlier capital-ship limitation from 1931 to 1936.

In this struggle, Hamaguchi presented an important constitutional argument developed by the liberal theoretician, Dr. Minobe Tatsukichi. He contended that the cabinet could be advised by the military "technicians" but was under no obligation to obey them, for the cabinet had to make the crucial tax and policy decisions of the government. With important support in the Imperial Court, Hamaguchi relieved the vice-chief of naval staff and the vice-minister of the navy of their posts. He went further and declared that an unfavorable report by the Supreme War Council had no legally binding effect.

In the course of seeking the Privy Council ratification required for the treaty to become law, Hamaguchi divulged no confidential information. It was even hinted that this august body would be packed if it proved recalcitrant. A favorable recommendation was returned, and the treaty was ratified in October, 1930.

This incident did not actually clarify the role of the military command in government. Nor was the constitutional struggle between the cabinet and the Privy Council settled. Nevertheless, the passage of this relatively minor treaty was a notable victory for the progressives. Credit was due to strong support in the Imperial Court, favorable public reaction to the treaty, and the firm determination of Hamaguchi, solidly backed by his majority in the House of Representatives.

The Minseito government handled economic affairs in the classical liberal manner. In 1929 it sought to balance the budget, avoid foreign loans, and bring an end to an embargo on gold. This program depended on continued American prosperity and high demand for silk, Indian purchases of cotton, and a high level of world trade. Matters went well in 1929, the first year in a decade in which Japan's exports exceeded imports, but when the depression struck in 1930 the government resorted to the traditional liberal devices of deflation and retrenchment. Administrative reforms to curtail expenses included a reorganization of the army. This act incurred the wrath of the newly crystallized young officer clique, already hostile to the cabinet's moderate foreign policy. All non-democratic elements were antagonistic to Hamaguchi because they felt that their favored position in government was seriously menaced.

The impact of the depression on this tense political situation was disastrous. The new liberal trade policies exposed Japan to the full brunt of economic shocks from abroad. The economy underwent a severe deflation, and Japan's price level fell 35 per cent, as compared to a decline of 27 per cent in the United States. Japan's export trade as a whole decreased by 27 per cent, with the silk industry particularly damaged. The price of raw silk fell by 50 per cent in 1930; silk exports weighed 82 per cent of the 1929 total but had a value of only 53 per cent.

The peasants, always vulnerable, were hit hard by the fall in value of their silk cash crop, and the failure of their daughters to gain supplementary employment at cotton and silk mills. In 1931, an Indian tariff and a Chinese boycott depressed prices further. To make matters worse, a series of good harvests lowered the price of rice, which fell from twenty-nine yen per koku to seventeen in 1930. Finance Minister Inoue persisted in a classical liberal program of deflation, seeking still lower military expenditures. A large part of the army and its officer corps now stemmed from an agrarian background, and peasant unrest was quickly sensed in these circles. The militarists found in this situation further encouragement for their plans to regain a position of political dominance.

The End of Party Government

The extremists were given their golden opportunity when a young fanatic shot Hamaguchi in November, 1930, the month after the London Naval Treaty was ratified. Although Hamaguchi did not die until the next year, Shidehara was compelled to assume the premiership. Neither he nor Wakatsuki, who became prime minister when Hamaguchi died, had the prestige to maintain discipline in the Minseito. The loss of a man who was both a capable politician and a fearless democrat was too stunning a blow to be absorbed.

The army met Wakatsuki's effort at retrenchment with demands for a bigger force on the continent and a larger air force. A debate also went on during the summer of 1931 between the army and Shidehara's Foreign Ministry over the method to be used in liquidating certain issues between China and Japan. The army abruptly undertook an invasion of Manchuria in September, 1931, in defiance of the civilian government. Following this success, the military extremists continued to act independently. The Foreign Ministry was reduced to accepting one *fait accompli* after another, and justifying them to the outside world.

These developments were too much for the Minseito, even though it soundly defeated the Seiyukai in the prefectural elections of October, 1931. The Seiyukai argued that the administration's policy was weak and so detrimental to Japan's prestige that it provoked military action in Manchuria. Irresponsibility spread to the cabinet itself, when Home Minister Adachi refused to attend meetings because the Minseito would not agree to a coalition government, presumably under his leadership. Since he was too powerful to be ousted, the cabinet had to resign in December, 1931, despite its large legislative majority.

The Seiyukai then took office for its third and final attempt at party rule. The cabinet was headed by the old politician Inukai, who had succeeded Tanaka as party head in 1929. He opposed a coalition government of the type then adopted in Britain. He reasoned that British parties were based on policies and so could alter their positions in harmony with changed circumstances, whereas Japanese parties were mere associations of politicians who were seeking office. Even the imminent threat to the survival of party government could not shake Japan's political leaders out of their old habits.

Desirous of capitalizing on the war crisis, Inukai dissolved the House of Representatives in January, 1932, and won a thumping victory over the Minseito, 304 to 147, the following month. The Seiyukai then tried to run affairs on the basis of a vigorous China policy. However, the army had tasted power when the civilian government failed to check it in 1931, and it now sought further domination of affairs. When a bomb was thrown at an Imperial Procession in January, 1932, the cabinet offered to resign, but this offer was rejected. The next month former Finance Minister Inoue was killed, and in March, Baron Dan, manager of the Mitsui interests, was murdered.

The final crisis came on May 15, 1932, when young officers terrorized Tokyo, attacking banks, police headquarters, and the Seiyukai party headquarters. Inukai was assassinated. The veteran Finance Minister Takahashi, who had served under Hara, became premier, but the era of civil authority and party rule was at an end. Crippled by conservative and military elements in the government, responsible rule was destroyed under the pressure of personal attacks and uncontrolled military action on the Asiatic mainland.

9 *Japan's Road to War*

The violent years 1931–1945 were highlighted in Asia by Imperial Japan's great bid for world power. The disaster that climaxed this effort was in true proportions to the epic nature of the gamble. The conquest of Manchuria in 1931–1932 started this adventurous policy, and its unqualified success undoubtedly encouraged the aggressive dictators of Italy and Germany to embark on their military conquests. Since this episode abruptly closed the period of democratic rule in Japan, it can justly be described as a disastrous turning point in world politics. Yet it would be too sweeping to claim that the course charted by the army in 1931 led inevitably and directly to the military dictatorship and world war that Japan spawned a decade later. Japanese politics was too uncertain, with too many divergent groups competing with one another, for foreign policy to develop as a coolly elaborated master plan of expansion.

A militarist foreign policy required a military dictatorship at home, but the army did not win such sweeping control as a result of the Manchurian episode. Domestic politics during the 1930's was shaped by the differences and compromises between the increasingly powerful expansionist elements and their influential moderate opponents, with the focus of power often shifting unexpectedly. Japan's pattern of internal political power, its diplomatic alignments, and its military plans were closely interdependent. Foreign events had a major influence over their development; in fact, it was the amazing rise of Hitler's Germany that ultimately placed political control in the hands of the extremists.

In 1936, the empire's last year of peace, the cumbersome Japanese political machine was still not committed to a major war. Nevertheless, the events of the five previous years had clearly strengthened the position of the militarists and enabled them to seize the opportunities that then arose to force Japan into its most desperate venture.

Expansion in China

Sino-Japanese Dispute in Manchuria

The most direct cause for Japan's conquest of Manchuria lay in the real danger its leaders saw to Nippon's privileged economic and political position. China was still lacking in unity and real military power, but its political resurgence during the 1920's under Kuomintang leadership portended future trouble. Its strident nationalism and anti-Japanese propaganda in Manchuria at the end of that decade pointed up this menace. Japan considered Manchuria a hard-won security buffer zone, a suitable region for industrial and commercial expansion, and a source of vital raw materials. It was, in short, an area that would guarantee Japan the degree of self-sufficiency required by a great power.

To the Chinese, Manchuria was an important granary, an outlet for its over-populated northern provinces, and national domain over which sovereignty had to be reasserted. In this context, the continuation of Japanese privileges regarding taxation, education, and police protection, established under existing treaties, was bound to be disputed.[1]

Railroad policies were another cause of grave differences. Though China had promised not to build railroads rivaling the South Manchurian Railway system, it constructed parallel lines that drew traffic from Dairen to the Chinese ports of Yingkow and Hulutao. The Chinese also refused to repay Japanese loans, valued at Y150 million in 1931, extended to finance new railways and pay Japanese technicians. They claimed that Japan was spending this money to strengthen its political hold and protect its railway monopoly. Not even the Minseito's conciliatory Foreign Minister Shidehara could resolve these disputes, and his attempt to negotiate a settlement early in 1931 was a failure. No respectable political leader could yield Japan's "special position" or accept full Chinese sovereignty over Manchuria.

The Conquest of Manchuria

Meanwhile, in Japan itself, the army's privileged status was being seriously challenged. The Hamaguchi cabinet attempted to follow its success in cutting the naval arms program with a reduction in the size of the army, which in 1930 had seventeen divisions and four independent brigades. The cabinet had also demonstrated its intention to reduce the military command to an advisory body whose findings did not bind the government. It admitted that the emperor was commander in chief of the army but held that constitutionally this role was subordinate to his position as chief of state. This interpretation clearly implied the supremacy of the civilian government. The army's spirited defense of its position was poorly received, and its stress on the importance of the Manchurian impasse was criticized as an attempt to divert public opinion from the need for budgetary cuts.

The military command decided to strike on its own, to protect what it considered to be Japan's and the army's vital interests. Its freedom to act stemmed from the military's traditional autonomy from civil control, the weakness of civilian rule after the shooting of Hamaguchi, and the instability caused by the great depression of 1930–1931. On September 18, 1931, three days after a gen-

[1] The Chinese claimed that Japan's insistence on police rights to protect Korean minorities was a cloak for expansion. The population of Manchuria in 1930 included 28 million Chinese as against 800,000 Koreans, 230,000 Japanese, and 150,000 Russians.

eral staff conference in Tokyo, the Kwantung army presented a trumped-up charge that Chinese agents attempted to blow up a railway line; its troops occupied Mukden, and the conquest of Manchuria was begun. The cabinet tried to follow a "policy of nonaggravation" while the army, unmolested by its own government and encountering little armed resistance, occupied the entire region. The military command refused to discuss its plans with the government and actually sent reinforcements from Korea as an "order of the field commander" over cabinet protest. This action was in sharp and tragic contrast to the military-civilian clash of wills during the naval crisis of 1930.

The occupation of Manchuria led to a Chinese boycott of Japanese goods; the army responded by attacking Shanghai in January, 1932. Here the Chinese resisted valiantly and the invader withdrew in May. Meanwhile, in February, the army had created a new state, Manchukuo, of its conquest and made Henry P'u-yi, China's last emperor, its regent and then its ruler. The international reaction to this adventure was hostile indeed, with the American government, through Secretary of State Stimson, declining to recognize the validity or legality of any Japanese conquest. In 1932, easy military victory and foreign opposition enabled the military leaders to rally popular sentiment in support of their cause. With its position secure at home and in Manchuria, the army permitted the League of Nations to undertake an investigation of the incident.

The Lytton Commission of Inquiry submitted an unfavorable report to the League. It recommended a denial of diplomatic recognition to Manchukuo, a government for Manchuria compatible with Chinese sovereignty, and an invitation to China and Japan to negotiate under the League's good offices. Japan, which had already invaded neighboring Jehol Province, responded to this Report by withdrawing from the League in March, 1933. With its armies below the Great Wall of China, Japan signed a truce with the Nanking government at Tangku in May, 1933. This agreement established a wide demilitarized zone at the military frontier, from which Chinese forces were excluded. It favored Japan in many other details, for Chiang Kai-shek at this time was anxious to avoid a full-scale war and was willing to guarantee a cooperative Chinese policy in the north.

However, the militarists now extended their area of interest and spoke of an "economic bloc" comprised of Japan, Manchukuo, and North China. The Manchurian adventure succeeded because the army command in Tokyo had kept the civilian government from interfering with the operations of allegedly independent field commanders. Continued expansion now depended on the army's ability to retain the initiative and institutionalize its independence of action. The impetus for action came from the Japanese North China garrison army, which was jealous of the success enjoyed by the Kwantung army in Manchuria and sought to emulate its rival with new conquests. The Tokyo command did not try to curb these ambitions because further military adventures would improve its position within the government. The Japanese military machine therefore tried, in a somewhat erratic fashion, to detach North China and create an autonomous region including Shantung, Chahar, Suiyuan, Shansi, and Hopei Provinces. It was this threat to the integrity of China Proper that aroused Chinese nationalist sentiment and finally compelled Chiang Kai-shek to make peace with his Communist rivals and confront the Japanese menace.

Internal Political Developments (1932–1936)

The uneasy years of peace between the Manchurian affair and the 1937 invasion of China witnessed an indecisive struggle for power within the Japanese government. Although party government was dead after 1932, the army could not eliminate the influence of the parties or the other elements of power—the bureaucracy, the zaibatsu, and the imperial advisers. On the other hand, although the two cabinets of 1932–1936 were headed by moderate dignitaries, Admirals Saito and Okada, the opponents of army rule could not regroup their forces under these National cabinets. The Saito regime, for example, was seriously weakened by scandal and corruption. During this time, the Seiyukai split over the issue of supporting a nonparty administration, and did itself a grave disservice by adopting a military expansionist platform under the guidance of its president Dr. Suzuki.

The extremists were a growing voice in public opinion, and ultrapatriotic groups challenged all concepts deemed insufficiently loyal to the emperor or to the mystical Imperial Way. The issue of "national polity," which caused a furore in 1935, typified this political trend. Dr. Minobe, the liberal constitutional theorist, had once argued that the emperor was only an organ of the state and not its actual embodiment. This concept was now denounced as treasonous, and its author was forced to resign from the House of Peers. The cabinet was compelled to proclaim that sovereignty did reside in the emperor and not in the state.

As the army threaded its way toward greater power, it was confronted with a factional conflict within its own ranks, which burst into the open in 1935–1936. The rise in military prestige and the determination of the army leaders to attain political domination led the militarists to ignore completely the constitutional injunction to stay out of political affairs. But, though the army as a whole agreed that it alone could save Japan from the vices and decay of modern life through a "national reconstruction," there were differences of opinion over procedure. The Kodoha (Imperial Way Group), composed of young officers, sought power by extremist methods of violence. It advocated radical economic and political reform that would destroy capitalism and protect the peasantry; paradoxically, its foreign policy was comparatively moderate and not expansionist. The Kodoha worked actively with civilian terrorist societies but lacked the central organization and direction required for ultimate success. It was represented, though not actually led, by Generals Araki and Mazaki in the higher echelons.

Its more successful rival was the Toseiha (Control Group), which sought power by less flamboyant methods. It favored a grandiose policy of expansion and included among its leaders Generals Tojo and Nagata.[2] This was the group that controlled Manchuria and made plans to build a buffer in North China and penetrate Inner Mongolia. General Tojo and some of his colleagues called for an early war to strike down the Nanking regime while it was still weak. It was his group that eventually led Japan into the Second World War. Unlike the Kodoha, which sought to eliminate "Western influences" and shift the tax burden from the peasant to the capitalists as a prelude to more drastic reforms, the Toseiha wished to preserve the existing structure and compel the bureaucracy and the zaibatsu to work under military direction.

The two factions managed to work together until 1935, though the young officers plotted coups and assassinations annually after 1930. General Araki obtained large military appropriations while war minister (1931–1934) by stressing the "crisis of 1935–1936"—when American-Japanese antagonism was supposed to reach a climax. The public, however, knew little of the army's internal split, for the military command defended all its personnel when plots against the government were uncovered in 1931 and 1934. The Toseiha was slow to take action against the terrorists because army prestige was at stake. Also, Kodoha extremist action did paralyze the forces of moderation and improve the army's political position. For similar reasons, it encouraged the growth of patriotic societies; over half of the 235 patriotic organizations existing in 1936 were founded after 1930.[3]

In 1935, however, the extremists struck at the army itself. The crisis was precipitated by the decision of General Nagata, the brain behind the Toseiha, to rid the army of its radical element by reshuffling military commands and assignments. Among the 3,500 changes was the removal of General Mazaki from the key post of inspector general of military education. That August, an officer being transferred to Formosa murdered General Nagata at his office in broad daylight. The fanaticism of the extremists was now clearly revealed, and the public realized that something was drastically amiss with the army's vaunted discipline.

The Last Years of Peace (1936–1937)

The struggle within the army and the political situation in the nation as a whole reached a turning point in 1936. The results of the national election at the start of the year, featured by a large turnout of 11 million voters, sharply rebuffed the superpatriots and supported a moderate policy. The Minseito, running with a slogan "Which shall it be—parliamentary government or fascism?" won a large majority of the seats. But the democratic system was no longer operative, and these results did not unseat the army or bring the Minseito back to power. In fact, this popular support of moderation was followed by a fanatical extremist response. On February 26, 1936, four days after election

[2] Others were Generals Matsui, Minami, Itagaki, Tatakawa, and Watanabe.
[3] The leading societies were the Imperial Ex-Servicemen's Association, the Imperial Way Society, and the Imperial League of Young Officers.

returns were in, twenty junior officers led a regimental revolt in Tokyo aimed at overthrowing the government. Many important military and bureaucratic leaders were assassinated. Prime Minister Okada escaped death only through a case of mistaken identity, and for four days Tokyo was in a state of siege and terror. Finally the 1,900 rebellious troops yielded to an imperial order to surrender. The Toseiha realized the damage caused to the army's prestige by this mutiny; the culprits were quickly punished and the Kodoha was effectively smashed as a rival force within the army.

Despite the immediate loss of prestige, the army ultimately benefited from this terrorism, for the behavior of the moderates over the next nine years was seriously inhibited by fear of militarist uprisings and even revolution. The army even made further political inroads when it won restoration of the requirement that war and navy ministers had to be general officers on *active* duty.[4] From 1937 on, the war minister became a more powerful figure than the chief of the general staff or the inspector-general of military education. The new edict was invoked to prevent the retired General Ugaki from forming a moderate cabinet in 1937. On the other hand, parliamentary opposition to the militarist cabinet of General Hayashi in 1937 compelled the government to hold an election. The two major parties were in opposition to the administration and, in a light turnout, again decisively defeated the extremist candidates.[5] Efforts were now made to find a premier who was acceptable to both the parties and the militarists. In June, Prince Konoye, a court noble and protégé of Prince Saionji, was selected. This move was publicly hailed in the hope that Konoye could block the drift toward military rule.

Japan's last year of peace also witnessed the adoption of the army's program for "national renovation." Its main features were a determined effort at economic modernization and development, and a five-year rearmament and a six-year military renovation program. In view of world conditions and the state of Japan's economy, these efforts could be treated as legitimate security measures. A policy of prudence would also have called for a rapid economic build-up of Manchuria and a cautious neutrality in world politics. At this time, Japan was not committed to war by any diplomatic obligations.

The Japanese keenly felt the political isolation resulting from their conquests of Manchuria and further encroachments in northern China. Yet in 1936 they terminated the naval treaties with the Anglo-American powers when their demands for equality were rejected. Nor were their delicate relations with the Soviet Union improving. The Russian refusal to renew Japan's long-term fishing rights in Soviet waters and Moscow's defensive military agreement with Outer Mongolia were signs of a growing tension. Army pressure and the desire for a political ally thus led Japan to sign the 1936 Anti-Comintern Pact with

[4] During the period of the army's political eclipse, retired general officers were eligible for these posts.

[5] The Minseito won 179 seats and the Seiyukai 175 seats; even the new Social Mass party showed strength with 37 seats.

Nazi Germany, an agreement that expressed antagonism to international communism. Its major provision was a secret promise by each party not to aid the
Soviet Union if the other was at war with Russia. This treaty was, therefore,
merely a guarantee of neutrality, but it was the first step in the formation of
the Axis Alliance (Germany, Japan, Italy) of the Second World War.

The Chinese "Incident"

Even though Japan favored a policy of expansion over neutrality, it could
have exploited the European crisis more advantageously had it kept free of a
Chinese war. Despite the worried cries in Tokyo for a preventive war, the Chinese Nationalist regime was too weak and Russia too busy in Europe for either
to present a real threat to Japan's security. However, the army went to war in
1937, and Japan became mired in a Chinese conflict that it could not end with
a political or military victory. This meant austerity at home and some curtailment of Manchuria's development, partly because of the loss of potential foreign
capital. The war was a constant irritant, and one cause for the rash series of
diplomatic maneuvers that placed Japan in an untenable position by 1941.
There was tragic irony in a war that proved fatal to both contestants and did
more to advance the cause of communism in Asia—the avowed foe of the Japanese warlords and the Nationalist Chinese—than any other event.

The militarist attempts to infiltrate North China and establish autonomous
puppet councils there proved a dismal failure, as did General Tojo's effort to
use Mongolian forces to subjugate Eastern Inner Mongolia in 1935–1936. The
army still coveted these areas as strategic buffers and economic adjuncts to the
grand prize of Manchuria. Between 1931 and 1938, Japanese investments in
Manchuria rose from Y1.6 billion to Y3.4 billion, and by still another billion
yen in 1939. With this increase in industry and electric power in Manchuria,
North China took on greater significance as a source of coal, iron, and cotton
and as a market for manufactured exports.

By 1937 an open assault was the only way the determined militarists in North
China could gain control over that region, but it was now easier for the field
commanders to precipitate an act of aggression than in 1931. The assault began
with an incident at the Marco Polo Bridge at Peking in July. The Konoye government, barely in office, was swept along with the tide, improvising policy in
the wake of the army's campaign. Still, it was able to make a reasonable peace
offer in November, 1937, through German diplomatic channels, which promised
to leave China Proper intact.[6] The Nationalist government still had strong
forces in the field and had false expectations of appreciable foreign aid. It
refused the offer at that time. The following month, with his field armies
beaten, Shanghai lost, and the fall of Nanking imminent, Chiang Kai-shek was

---

[6] The main provisions of this offer were for (1) the autonomy of Inner Mongolia, (2) a demilitarized zone in North China extending below the Peking-Tientsin line but *leaving the
administration of all North China to the Chinese,* (3) an extended demilitarized zone in
Shanghai, and (4) an end to anti-Japanese policies.

willing to agree. Now, however, the Japanese militarists were flushed with success and expected to knock out the Kuomintang regime and so attain a decisive victory. The prophetic advice of the German ambassador in Tokyo went unheeded: that a continued war would ruin Anglo-Japanese relations, open China to communism, and weaken Japan with regard to Soviet Russia. When Nanking fell, the Japanese commanders gave vent to their rage over Chinese resistance by permitting their highly disciplined troops to ravage the city, in an incident known as "the rape of Nanking."

The sincere desire of the Konoye regime for peace was a measure of the premier's ineffectiveness. He could not check the army, but the promised victory did not materialize despite the occupation of all major coastal cities and of other urban centers in North and Central China. The Japanese forces remained uncoordinated as the war progressed and lacked a commander in chief. The major army groups displayed localist attitudes in conducting their campaigns and in establishing rival puppet regimes in Peking and Nanking in 1938. By 1939 the China campaign had degenerated into a wearisome colonial war; diplomatic efforts to isolate the Nationalists failed, as aid from Russia and then from the West continued to trickle in. This assistance was comparatively meager, but it had great psychological value in bolstering the morale of the badly shattered Kuomintang regime.

Japanese Plans in China

Presumably the Japanese could have captured the great province of Szechuan and the wartime capital of Chungking. This decision would have forced the army into an even costlier campaign, especially if Chiang continued to resist from his deep interior bases. As it now stood, the China campaign was not as great a strain on Japanese resources as was supposed abroad; it actually served as a training ground for new troops. With a southern army based on Canton, the lower Yangtze secure after the capture of Hankow, and communications between North and Central China assured by two rail lines, the Japanese decided to revert to a defensive posture. They hoped to use less direct methods to bring about the fall of the Kuomintang: terrorize Chungking with air raids, crush all Chinese counteroffensives, and establish a new regime at Nanking.

The militarists won a victory at home when a China Affairs Board, which they dominated, was created in December, 1938. This agency was given wide powers to control almost all aspects of Chinese affairs; only diplomatic problems, narrowly defined, were left under the jurisdiction of the Foreign Ministry. An economic bloc was envisaged in which Japan would specialize in advanced precision industries, while Manchuria became a center of heavy industry and electrochemistry, and North China developed light industry. The political basis of this scheme was rooted in the hope that Japanese control would bring stability and order to this rich, populated area. Toward this objective, the rival regional armies joined under a single command and agreed to establish a central Chinese government under Wang Ching-wei, former Kuomintang leader, rival of Chiang, and advocate of appeasement. This government was installed in March, 1940, but it had little political value, because supplementary agreements showed the Japanese to be harsh masters who retained extensive power. Thus any claim Wang could make to sovereignty and independence was a mockery.

Nor could diplomacy resolve the stalemate, since Chiang would not accept the Japanese army's terms for peace. These included close economic collaboration, an anticommunist pact, recognition of Manchukuo, the establishment of Inner Mongolia as a special buffer zone, and the right of Japan to keep troops in China—especially in the north—in order to protect its hard-won privileges. By the time the Second World War began, in September, 1939, the China struggle had become a major annoyance because it hampered concentrated preparations for a large-scale war against a major enemy—assumed to be Soviet Russia before 1940. This problem became even more troublesome after the Nazi triumphs of 1939–1940 presented Japan with a great opportunity to expand southward into the colonial possessions of the battered West European democracies.

Toward Dictatorship and War

Diplomatic Relations with Germany and Russia (1939–1941)

The central point of Japan's foreign policy was its relationship with Nazi Germany. The army remained the main advocate of closer ties to Germany, for Hitler's successes meant a great opportunity to extend Nippon's rule in Asia. Yet Japan's ties to the erratic and secretive Hitler regime proved ill-starred, and from the beginning of the Axis alignment, the two partners worked independently and at cross-purposes.

Before the outbreak of war in Europe, Japan initiated bitter undeclared border conflicts with the Soviet Union, notably at Changkufeng in Manchuria in 1938, and Nomohan on the Manchurian-Outer Mongolian frontier during May-August, 1939. The Kwantung army fared poorly in these clashes, and the stiff Russian resistance may have induced the army to seek more fruitful grounds for expansion. During this period of negotiations (1938–1939) with Germany, the peace party in Tokyo was strong enough to block a military alliance; Germany wanted a Japanese commitment to join in a fight against the West as well as Russia. Then came a bombshell—the Russo-German Non-Aggression Pact of August, 1939; this violated the spirit of the Anti-Comintern Pact of 1936 and even the letter of its secret protocols. The Japanese, from this point on, veered sharply away from thought of war with Russia and sought to make Soviet-Japanese-German collaboration the cornerstone of their diplomacy. With the army's diplomatic gambit temporarily discredited, the advocates of caution prevented any binding commitment to Germany.

Then the great German victories of 1940, like a new spin in the wheel of fortune, opened the way for expansion into Southeast Asia. They reduced still further the chances of a diplomatic settlement in China. The Nazis urged an immediate assault on possessions of the defeated French and Dutch, coupled with an attack on the great British base at Singapore. Japan, however, was still not prepared for such a decisive move, even though Britain stood alone in Europe in July, 1940. That summer, Prince Konoye formed his second cabinet, after an absence from office of a year and a half. His foreign minister was the unpredictable Matsuoka Yosuke, who had totalitarian and expansionist ambitions. His immediate objective was to use the European Axis alignment to further Japanese ambitions in Southeast Asia but not to commit Japan fully to a German alliance. The result was the Tripartite Pact of October, 1940, in which Germany, Japan, and Italy agreed to aid one another if attacked by a power not involved in the European or Chinese conflicts. This pointed reference to the United States was emphasized by the definite exclusion of Soviet Russia as a target of the alliance. For Japan, this treaty had two purposes: to paralyze the United States with fear of a two-front war and so keep it from acting in Europe or Asia, and to get Russia to stop helping China and so induce Chiang to sue for peace.

Both calculations misfired. The United States became increasingly antagonistic, and Chinese resistance, with Russian and Western help, persisted. Matsuoka then sought to retrieve his position with a Soviet nonaggression pact. While in Berlin early in 1941, he explained that Japan decided to move southward and that he would seek an accommodation with Russia in order to protect the northern flank. The Germans dropped some veiled hints, but Hitler did not confide his plans for an invasion of Russia; in April, 1941, Japan signed a neutrality pact with the Soviet Union on the latter's terms—a promise to yield economic concessions enjoyed in Russian-owned Northern Sakhalin. When Germany attacked Russia two months later, Japan was again taken by surprise.

The Germans now urged military cooperation against Russia, and Matsuoka advocated renunciation of his own Soviet neutrality pact, but the Japanese government refused to act. Germany was now fully engaged in a two-front war, but Japan remained uncommitted. It had turned away from a Russian war almost simultaneously with the Nazi decision to fight there, and without launching an invasion to the south. When the cumbersome Japanese governmental machine finally decided to move against the Western powers, it meant a war fought in isolation. The lack of coordination displayed in Axis diplomacy was to continue in the field of military strategy, for Germany and Japan never developed a unified global strategy or a real coalition effort.

Japan and the West (1939–1941)

The Japanese militarists had already made threatening gestures toward the south in 1939, the one direction that could involve them in war with the Western powers. At that time they occupied Hainan and the Spratly Islands off the South China coast in an effort to halt Anglo-American support of Chiang Kai-shek. The West, however, maintained and even increased currency and credit support of China. In July, 1939, the United States gave Japan a six-month notice that it was ending its Commercial Treaty of 1911, though the full consequences with regard to trade policy were left ambiguous. This climaxed a series of unpleasant developments that had started in 1937, when an American gunboat, the "Panay," was sunk in Chinese waters and British subjects were made to suffer personal indignities in China.

The American reaction to the "Panay" incident was to avoid further provocations; the Japanese people were profoundly dismayed, and their government extended a sincere apology. However, as the war progressed, Japanese atrocities and the terror bombing of Chungking and other Chinese cities aroused American indignation. A moral embargo in 1938 was invoked against the shipment of aviation equipment and high octane gasoline to Japan. In addition, the end of commercial relations in 1939 eliminated legal obstacles to an embargo on all war materials, the greatest pressure short of war that the United States could place against the vulnerable Japanese economy. The tortuous diplomacy that led to Pearl Harbor was played against a background of Japanese thrusts to the south followed by United States economic retaliation, which in turn made the rich colonial lands all the more attractive to the expansionists of Nippon.

With Russian relations stabilized in 1940, the Japanese resolved to make their major expansionist effort southward, hoping to use the German victories in Europe to achieve easy conquests. Japanese propaganda made much of a regional bloc that now included the countries of East *and* Southeast Asia. Peace was declared possible only if there was stability in each important region of the world. As Foreign Minister Arita put it, under compulsion from the army in June, 1940, only a "stabilizing force" could bring security and progress to each region. The task in the Far East fell to Japan, which was to achieve a new order in the Orient through the formation of a Greater East Asia Co-Prosperity Sphere.

Japan, however, moved cautiously in 1940, and was satisfied with Britain's agreement in July to close the Burma Road to China for three months. This concession, made when Britain was fighting for survival, occurred during the rainy season when shipment of supplies was sharply reduced by the weather. The other Japanese move was the occupation of northern French Indochina. This too could be interpreted as part of the China campaign, inasmuch as control of this region gave Japan tighter control over the communication network of southern China. The southern portion of the French colony, however, was considered the vital jumping-off point for a major assault on British and Dutch possessions. Japan exerted economic and political pressure on the Dutch East Indies in the hope of gaining control over this rich colony without a struggle, but was sharply rebuffed by Dutch officials.

When the Nazis invaded Russia in June, 1941, the Japanese militarists made their momentous decision not to invade Siberia until a German victory was certain. Instead, they pushed southward even at the risk of war with the Anglo-American powers. The final act in this drama opened with the Japanese occupation of southern Indochina, an ominous threat to British security in the Pacific. This occupation threatened to undermine Britain in its struggle against Germany, then the central concern of American foreign policy. The United States government was compelled to react vigorously, even if to do so meant war with Japan at a time when the European theater was of primary strategic importance. It therefore froze all Japanese funds and assets in the United States on July 26, 1941, and followed this on August 1 with an order banning the export to Japan of certain materials and gasoline. The Japanese were surprised at the forcefulness of this response, but it was still far short of a total embargo and allowed for moderation in return for a Japanese withdrawal from Indochina.

The militarists continued their preparations but still lacked the strength to sweep the country into a major war. The advocates of a peaceful settlement with the Western powers were still strong enough to insist on diplomatic negotiations with the United States. These were intensified during the latter half of 1941, but the vital issues under consideration went well beyond the question of Indochina. The discussions assumed a logic of their own, and, once the entire situation in the Far East came under review, China became the great immediate obstacle to a settlement.

Drift to Dictatorship (1937–1941)

Political developments within Japan, during this twilight era between peace and war, weakened the chances for a compromise settlement. The army had steadily improved its position and was adamantly opposed to delaying an assault in Southeast Asia until the fate of the Nazi adventure in Europe was decided. Though still unable to force the government into a major war, it could block any major concessions in China. It had not suffered a military setback there and would not yield the fruits of its labor; on this point it was assured of popular support.

In any event, the army's domestic political position was almost impregnable. The Diet was virtually paralyzed after 1936, as the party system had disintegrated and the zaibatsu had made peace with the new order. It had been under sharp attack by the army radicals and was glad to come to terms with the Toseika in 1936. The army, on its side, was anxious to win the support or passive acceptance of the capitalists and bureaucrats in order to carry out its program of national renovation. The zaibatsu, in fact, had never formed a homogeneous group; Mitsui constantly favored a more positive foreign policy than did Mitsubishi and Suitomo. In addition, the army sponsored new capitalist concerns in Manchuria and elsewhere; these elements were committed to the army and the expansionist program that enabled them to break the old zaibatsu monopoly.

Political freedom and civil liberties, never deeply rooted in the Japanese scene, withered rapidly and disappeared in a hostile environment. The sweeping legislation of 1936, which established the basis for expanded production, also created a new press law with stringent controls over freedom of expression. At the end of the year, the Diet met in its sumptuous new building in the heart of Tokyo, but it was powerless to oppose the militarist and ultranationalist extremists. At that time the army did not want to eradicate parliament as an institution, since this was a gift of the Meiji emperor, but it did seek to eliminate parties, turn the Diet into a rubber stamp, and limit suffrage to a properly indoctrinated electorate. Many bureaucrats and court nobles remained opposed to the military extremists and their dangerous ventures; they believed that the army would even overthrow the imperial order to attain these objectives. In the end, the moderates were thwarted by the oppressive power of the army and their own inability to cooperate with the despised democratic elements.

The cabinets of 1937–1940 reflected this precarious state of affairs. The premiers during this period were moderate bureaucrats or officers unable to counterbalance mounting extremist pressure. Thus the army forced into law plans for rapid economic change through strict central controls. A Planning Board was established in 1937 under army direction, as a general headquarters to direct the national economy. Another step toward totalitarian rule was the National General Mobilization Law, passed over vigorous Diet opposition by threat of dissolution and a promise, immediately broken, to delay its implementation. The law gave the cabinet almost full powers to govern by ordinance, thereby making the legislature superfluous. The army was also able to thwart Premier Yonai's efforts at a *rapprochement* with the West in 1940. When Foreign Minister Arita unsuccessfully sought to undertake a foreign policy of conciliation, the army informed him that his ministry and the administration as a whole had no foreign policy! Finally the militarists ordered War Minister General Hata to resign, refused to nominate a successor, and so caused the Yonai cabinet to fall.

When Prince Konoye formed his second cabinet in July, 1940, he represented the moderates' last hope of controlling the army. An arch-conservative who did not believe in the party system, he was willing to go along with the militarist idea of a single party. However, he sought to base his own political strength on this body, support the army's policy up to a point, but gradually confine the limits of its ambitions. To cooperate with the extremists he included two firebrands in his cabinet—General Tojo as war minister, from the Kwantung army, and Matsuoka, who had served with the South Manchurian Railway, as foreign minister. The government also tried to overcome popular apathy with a propaganda campaign for "spiritual mobilization," stressing the goal of a new order in East Asia and eventual world peace. A renewed effort at industrial expansion placed emphasis on chemicals and machine tools. National health standards were improved in response to the army's growing need for manpower, education was reorganized along ultrapatriotic lines, and a program was inaugurated to foster population growth in a land whose imperialists justified aggression on the grounds of overpopulation.

By 1940, the parties had become so helpless that the Diet was forced to expel a Minseito member who had challenged the government's harsh terms for peace in China. Prince Konoye decided to create a "unified national structure" and, in a move reminiscent of the 1880's, the parties were obliged to dissolve them selves in the summer of 1940. After considerable preparatory negotiations among bureaucrats and militarists, an Imperial Rule Assistance Association (IRAA) was formed in October, 1940. Konoye insisted that it was not a political party or a totalitarian device. Yet it was clearly a governmental agency, with a central office in Tokyo and branches in all other important cities. Its purpose was to harmonize the nation's political interests with state policies. The association's president had the power to direct and alter the organization— a right later utilized by Tojo when he succeeded Konoye. Despite Konoye's protestations, the staff of the IRAA conducted its affairs along totalitarian lines, in accordance with army wishes. The new apparatus, therefore, proved inadequate to check the army and was later used by the militarists to prepare and conduct a full-scale war effort.

The Failure of Diplomacy

In the summer of 1941, Japan was at the crossroads in its diplomacy, internal politics, and military plans. The army still held the initiative, but Prince Konoye claimed to be a man of peace, and he made a vigorous and dramatic effort to reach a settlement. But the Anglo-American powers, as well as Japan, had very little room for diplomatic maneuver. American-Japanese negotiations, difficult enough early in 1941, were temporarily suspended when Japan occupied southern Indochina in July, 1941. The adoption of economic sanctions by the West brought an end to Japan's attitude of procrastination and aroused its interest in a speedy settlement, for fear that its stockpile of essential materials would fall below the critical limit.

Not all army leaders were eager for war, but the desire for caution was felt more deeply in the navy. It reacted unfavorably to the army-inspired diplomacy that produced the 1940 treaty with Germany. Admiral Yamamoto Isoroku, commander in chief of the combined fleet, was worried about the expansionist mood that led to this pact and the threat of war with the United States, which it implied. His fears were twofold. One concerned the fact that Soviet Russia would remain a nearby menace while Japan exhausted itself in a war far across the Pacific. Even a nonaggression pact with Russia lacked value unless Japan had the power to compel Soviet neutrality. Secondly, Japanese Naval Staff College exercises pointed to a defeat in a war with the United States, a finding which troubled the emperor considerably. However, this pessimistic current of thought remained a minor theme in Japanese policy making, despite its strategic soundness and support in high bureaucratic and naval circles.

The peace party's hopes centered in a proposed meeting between Prince Konoye and President Franklin Roosevelt to reach a compromise settlement. Konoye then hoped to confront the extremists with an accomplished fact and rally enough popular support to thwart a rash militarist response. However, he evidently had little leeway to negotiate, for the army agreed to the meeting

247

with the provision that it acknowledge Japan's minimum demands in Asia. The American government was suspicious of Konoye's motives and doubted his ability to force a real compromise arrangement on the Japanese army. Secretary of State Cordell Hull insisted on a carefully prepared agenda, and preliminary discussions during the summer of 1941 focused on three main problems. The first was the American desire to have the Tripartite Pact of 1940 nullified as a guide to Japanese policy. The second concerned the evacuation of Indochina and the end to American economic sanctions. On these two points, apparently, agreement was possible, if the China issue could be settled. Japan could back down on Indochina if America accepted some of its claims in China.

Premier Konoye hoped to avoid a war, keep the Japanese fleet intact, and be guided by later developments elsewhere. But General Tojo and his colleagues would not allow the premier to follow his own inclination and withdraw all troops from China as part of a general agreement. The militarists wanted to annex part of China, though they were willing to reach a settlement if Japan could keep Manchuria, establish a political link with China through an anti-communist pact, retain troops in North China and Inner Mongolia, and preserve control over economic concerns established in these regions. Konoye's diplomatic approach along these lines was unacceptable to the United States, and, given British coolness and bitter Chinese hostility toward any meeting, the high-level conference never took place.

The Japanese government became committed, at an Imperial Conference of September 6, 1941, to a policy of military action should diplomacy fail. It is therefore arguable that the Western powers could have aided the peace party by agreeing to a limited conference to deal with the immediate crisis over Indochina. Without even a partial settlement, Konoye had to resign. Still Tojo had to wait for his war. He was made premier in October, 1941, with the obligation to try once more for an American settlement. Had the discussions that he dutifully continued lasted long enough for Germany's difficulties in Russia to become apparent, Japan might have taken a more conciliatory position. As it was, the negotiations quickly reached the familiar impasse over the fate of China. At the Imperial Conference of November 5, Japan committed itself to go to war if the diplomatic talks had not succeeded by November 25. Even at that date, Tojo's opponents sought further delays, but the premier, his obligations fully discharged, eagerly and successfully held them to their agreement. Japan's cumbersome machinery for group decision making finally produced a definite, if tragic, policy.

The most serious error of the Anglo-American powers was their failure to realize that Japan would fight rather than yield, despite persistent warnings by Ambassadors Grew and Craigie to their superiors in Washington and London. The Western powers, with their greater war potential, did not realize what Japan could accomplish before they could marshal their forces. But Japan also underrated the West, its determination to persist in a long war, and its ability to unleash great destructive offensives against the home islands. The army's final haven was the delusion that, no matter what followed, Japan's higher moral spirit and discipline would prevail over the materialist might of a decadent opponent.

Japan's War Moves

Japan conceived of war in limited terms for specific purposes, and not as an assault on the very survival of its foes. Strategic and tactical plans were developed with this principle in mind. The main Japanese objective was to secure control of a wide area around the home islands and carve out a regional empire in Southeast Asia. An attack had to be made before the end of 1941, for delay would bring on bad weather and force a postponement until the following spring. Oil stockpiles were too low for the navy to risk such a long wait. Even at this late date, the navy agreed only grudgingly to fight, as "an action in self-defense" to preserve Japan from the squeeze of economic sanctions and intimidation. Some naval leaders still held that they were fatalistically following the army's lead.

The attack against Pearl Harbor had the defensive-offensive purpose of defeating the American navy in order to attain these nearby objectives. At no time was a long-range attack on the United States contemplated, and, when military victory exceeded all expectations in 1942, Japan did not sweep on against India with any sustained effort. In fact, its island conquests were to prove an overcommitment of Japan's armed might. Strategy dictated the capture and consolidation of this new empire, thus causing the enemy to make peace rather than undertake the enormous effort of crossing the Pacific and assaulting these bastions. The war, then, was to last long enough for Japan to gain its empire and reveal its determination and ability to hold it. Admiral Yamamoto had warned, with remarkable accuracy, that the navy could win early victories but that Japan would have to disengage itself within eighteen months, because then the tide would turn rapidly in favor of the United States.

The Japanese navy followed its success at Pearl Harbor with a brilliant strike against the more exposed British naval contingent at Singapore, sinking its two capital ships, the "Repulse" and "Prince of Wales." With control of the seas and a highly trained jungle force, the invaders made excellent use of amphibious operations to sweep through all of Southeast Asia. The Malayan Peninsula was conquered rapidly, before British reserves could be rushed to stem the attack; Singapore was taken from the rear, while its great defense works pointed uselessly toward the sea. The Philippines fell after a bitter defense by American and Filipino forces on Bataan Peninsula, Luzon Island, in the spring of 1942. The Dutch East Indies were quickly occupied after a sharp naval engagement in the Java Sea resulted in the destruction of a light Allied force under Dutch command. Back on the mainland, Burma was quickly overrun, with British forces hurled back to India. The extremes of the westward thrust

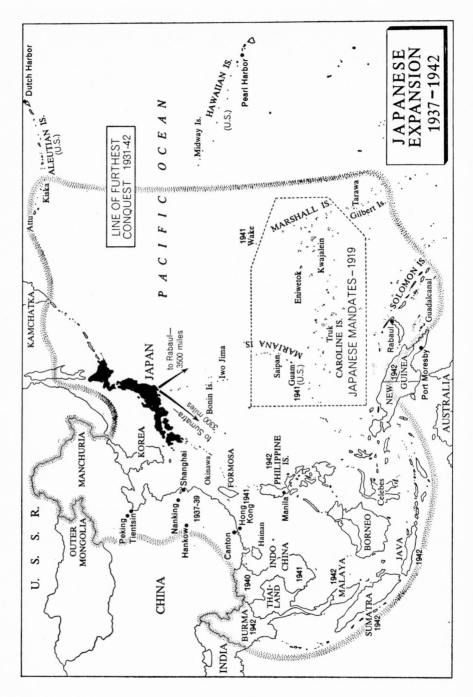

JAPANESE
EXPANSION
1937–1942

LINE OF FURTHEST
CONQUEST 1931-42

PACIFIC OCEAN

Dutch Harbor

ALEUTIAN IS.
(U.S.)

Kiska

Attu

Midway Is.

HAWAIIAN IS.
(U.S.)

Pearl Harbor

MARSHALL IS.

1941
Wake

Gilbert Is.

Tarawa

Eniwetok

Kwajalein

CAROLINE IS.

Truk

JAPANESE MANDATES – 1919

MARIANA IS.

Saipan

Guam
(U.S.)
1941

SOLOMON IS.

Rabaul

1942

Guadalcanal

NEW GUINEA

Port Moresby

AUSTRALIA

KAMCHATKA

JAPAN

to Rabaul—
3500 miles

to Sumatra—
3300 miles

Bonin Is.

Iwo Jima

KOREA

Okinawa

FORMOSA

Shanghai

Nanking

1937-39

Hankow

Hong
Kong

1941

Hainan

PHILIPPINE
IS.

1942

Manila

Celebes

BORNEO

JAVA

1942

MALAYA
1942

SUMATRA
1942

INDO
CHINA

1941

THAI-
LAND

Canton

1940

BURMA
1942

INDIA

CHINA

Peking

Tientsin

MANCHURIA

OUTER
MONGOLIA

U. S. S. R.

250

brought the Japanese navy into the Indian Ocean, where it damaged British merchant shipping, and was able to capture the Andaman Islands. To the south, the invaders advanced through the northeastern part of New Guinea toward the final objective—Australia. The military leaders were proved most accurate in their prediction that Southeast Asia could be conquered in a five-month campaign.

But in the jungles of New Guinea and its Owen Stanley Mountains the land assault came to a halt. A simultaneous failure occurred in the Coral Sea during the spring of 1942; in a battle dominated by naval air power, the Japanese force was driven back. A small but spectacular American naval air raid on Tokyo occurred at this time and emphasized the exposed position of the home islands. The naval command determined to seek out and destroy the American fleet and capture bases in the Central Pacific, in order to protect Japan itself and create a military situation in which a favorable peace could be won. This decision led to the great battle of Midway in mid-1942, in which the bulk of the Japanese fleet was defeated in its attempt to gain dominance over the Hawaii-Midway area. From this point forward, beginning with the amphibious American counterattack on Guadalcanal in the Solomon Islands in the extreme southeastern corner of Japan's new empire, the initiative passed to the Allied forces. Despite vigorous resistance and an occasional offensive threat, such as the Burma-based assault on the Indian frontier city of Imphal in 1944, the area of Japanese dominion shrank under the pressure of Allied amphibious operations.

This turn of events wrecked the sequence envisaged in the Japanese war plan, that is, rapid conquest, then military stalemate, followed by a peace settlement recognizing these gains. American determination and the sudden rise of its naval power were the major causes of this disaster. However, it was significant and perhaps equally decisive that Japan fought the war in almost complete isolation from its Axis ally, in sharp contrast to the Anglo-American integration of effort. Even the democracies' ties with Russia were close in comparison with Japanese-German relations. It is true that Hitler declared war on the United States in December, 1941, in the belief that otherwise America would first dispose of Japan and then be able to turn its undivided attention to Europe. But his decision was not followed by any combined military policy or an effort to establish liaison agencies.

The major Japanese mission by the spring of 1942 was defensive, and further thrusts beyond the conquered regions were not adequately planned. However, there was an attempt to cut America's communications with Australia, thwarted in the Battle of the Coral Sea; and one powerful naval air assault was launched against the British base in Ceylon. It is most significant that Japan's major thrust in 1942, the last year of Axis military superiority, was eastward across the Pacific toward Midway and Hawaii in a desperate lunge against the United States. There were cogent reasons for such an offensive, if viewed in the narrow terms of a Japanese-American struggle. Yet the only Axis chance of victory was probably a coordinated assault on the Middle East and a linking of forces. Instead of careful, long-range planning in terms of joint needs, each Axis partner struck in blind isolation against his major foe at the defender's strongest point.

Japan at War

In 1942 it became clear that Japan was involved in a long war for which it was unprepared. The country had to improvise domestic political controls, economic mobilization, and even grand strategy.

The Political Scene

The army tried to meet this situation by developing an efficient, totalitarian structure of rule, but it failed to subjugate the other groups. It could not overcome the strong Japanese tradition of preserving group interests and arriving at decisions through intergroup compromises. The career of General Tojo Hideki reflected these limitations. In October, 1941, he was war and home minister as well as premier, a post that had grown steadily in importance after 1930. However, he had been accepted only because the war policy of the army extremists carried the day, and he was their leading representative. Tojo's leadership, always conditional, was completely undermined by the military defeats of 1943–1944, and he was forced from office in July, 1944, when the key defensive island of Saipan fell. General Koiso, an extremist who did not, however, have the army's confidence, then formed a cabinet still committed to a full war effort. But in April, 1945, the army's supremacy was ended when the moderate Admiral Suzuki Kantaro became premier and the peace effort gained momentum.

An important consequence of the pattern of compromise and group responsibility was the development of many high-level policy agencies with overlapping powers. In addition to the Privy Council and the cabinet, an inner cabinet composed of key ministries was formed in 1940, but it never gained control over political affairs. Even in time of national crisis, rival groups gave due consideration to the balance of power among themselves. For example, marked hostility existed within the armed forces. During the critical campaigns of 1942, the navy observed that the army "was taking a walk on the Asian mainland"; and only because it controlled the tankers could the navy be certain of a fair share of army-controlled oil production.

Another coordinating device was the full-dress Imperial Conference, attended by all important officials, which formally announced state policy after a decision was reached by influential smaller bodies. Even these official policies could be reversed: the September, 1941, decision to fight was temporarily suspended and the army-inspired commitment against surrender in June, 1945, was soon reversed. Symbolic of the importance of nonofficial, informed centers of influence was the *jushin*, an advisory council of ex-premiers.[7] A pale reflection of the genro, this group had no legal powers, but it became a rallying point for the peace party as Japan's war fortunes declined. Such moderates as Prince Konoye and Admiral Yonai were joined in their efforts by Lord Privy Seal Marquis Kido Koichi, the emperor's personal representative in government. The jushin was able to precipitate the fall of the Tojo cabinet and influenced the choice of personnel in its successor. From this point forward it was a major factor in blunting the extremists' power.

A similar shift of power can be traced through the liaison between the army and the government. At first such liaison conferences were guided and directed by a military secretariat controlled by the extremists. A new high agency was established by Premier Koiso in 1944, a Supreme War Council composed of the premier, the foreign minister, the war and navy ministers, and the army and navy chiefs of staff. Ignored at first by the overconfident army, this agency grew in importance, formed its own loyal staff, which bypassed the military secretariat, and conducted its meetings in a secrecy respected by its uniformed members.

While premier, General Tojo tried to cut through this maze of high-level councils and consolidate his position with a totalitarian party system. In 1942 he sought to control the Diet by having the people elect a slate of hand-picked candidates. The government also sought to breathe new life into the IRAA, and organized the Imperial Rule Assistance Political Society and an IRA Youth Corps to strengthen its control over political affairs. Coercion was used against opposition candidates, but even the election of a government-endorsed slate still left the Diet a center of opposition to totalitarian army rule. An effort was also made during this election to mobilize popular support for the war effort, as had been attempted in the National Spiritual Mobilization movement of 1940. The people remained loyal and willing to endure numerous sacrifices, but, except during the victory campaigns of early 1942, they did not display excitement or enthusiasm.

Economic Mobilization and Production

The Japanese were slow to undertake a total war effort in 1942, for they were bemused by victory and expected an early peace. Administrative agencies sprouted like jungle growths, but they suffered from inexperience and army domination. Even with a Planning Board, a National Mobilization Council (1938), and a Price Policy Council (1940), most economic activity as late as 1940 remained free from state controls. The army's dominance of the Technical Board (1942) led to suspicion and hostility among other elements, and prevented it from achieving adequate scientific mobilization.

The zaibatsu welcomed efforts to create central controls but only if its own

---

[7] These included Baron Wakatsuki Reijiro, Admiral Okada Keisuke, the diplomat Hirota Koki, General Hayashi Senjuro, Prince Konoye Fumimaro, Baron Hiranuma Kiichiro, General Abe Nobuyuki, Admiral Yonai Mitsumasa, and, later, Generals Tojo and Koiso.

members could direct affairs. It resented the imposition of retired generals and the Kwantung clique in key positions and held out for civilian management, for the sake of efficiency and self-preservation. The militarists yielded in 1943, and a new Munitions Ministry was created to direct industrial mobilization. This and other new agencies were dominated by the business community, adopted its control programs and policies, and expanded production considerably. After Tojo fell, a member of the zaibatsu became munitions minister, thereby consolidating its position.

Japan's peak production year was 1944, when it turned out 28,180 planes and 4,652,000 tons of finished steel products. The Supreme Council had called for 40,000 planes, 5 million tons of steel and 1,800,000 tons of merchant shipping. Despite heroic efforts, which produced 1,590,000 tons of shipping in the last year of the war, losses were so severe that total available shipping fell from 6,000,000 to 2,000,000 tons by the end of the war. Nor could steel and airplane production be sustained in 1945 in the face of such losses and the heavy bombing of cities.[8] Food consumption also fell from 2,000 calories per day in 1940 to 1,900 in 1944, and to a bare 1,680 in 1945. The military drain on farm workers and the lack of fertilizer, the key to Japan's high productivity, contributed to this decline. As a result, a black market and a runaway inflation developed as currency doubled in volume, and consumer goods became scarce. Finally, the B-29 assaults, beginning in November, 1944, and reaching a crescendo in the four great fire raids of March, 1945, destroyed almost half the houses of Tokyo and Yokohama and about one third of those in Osaka, Kobe, and Nagoya.

Yet it must be remembered that Japan was able to wage a major war for almost four years. Its industrial machine worked vigorously and produced many fine planes and ships. Its army, outgunned and undermanned, fought with legendary tenacity and fanatical devotion. Even in the light of the final disaster, its effort remains a startling achievement, which altered the future of the areas it temporarily conquered.

The Greater East Asia Co-Prosperity Sphere

Japan's policy for its occupied territories was set before the Pacific War began. Its first stage was to be a military rule that used native administrations and respected local customs. Sincerely committed to Asian self-rule, the Japanese also planned to give the nations of Southeast Asia freedom by degrees, depending on their level of cultural development, and provided that they were militarily secure. Since Burma and the Philippines were the most advanced, nationalist regimes were established there, and in Indonesia as well. However, the Japanese, who followed the pattern of their 1940 treaty with the puppet regime in China, made very few political concessions at first. Malaya and Hong Kong were to be kept as colonies. Indochina held an intermediate position,

[8] Average monthly plane production: 1941—424; 1942—738; 1943—1,391; 1944—2,348; 1945 (to August)—1,475.

complicated by the embarrassing continuation of the Vichy French administration under Japanese control; this policy enabled the Japanese to enjoy security there and use their own skilled personnel elsewhere.

The entire region of Southeast Asia was placed under the jurisdiction of the army, which subjected it to economic exploitation. The army asserted its authority through a new Greater East Asia Ministry, created in 1942. Military officials concerned with grand strategy appreciated the political complexities of the area, but their colleagues saw only an opportunity to harness the strength of the area to Japan's war effort. Raw materials and food resources—rice, cash crops, and minerals—were vigorously exploited under an elaborate regional plan in which Japan promised to send consumer and capital goods in return. However, Japan could not deliver these goods during the war because of its own military effort and Allied control of the seas; the economic systems in Southeast Asia created under Western rule virtually disintegrated. Even Thailand, Japan's ally since 1941 and not directly hit by the war, found its economy badly dislocated. However, it had increased its territory at the expense of Burma, Malaya, and Indochina. When the Western powers returned to Burma and the Philippines, bitter Japanese resistance caused enormous destruction. Another act of harshness was the construction of the infamous Burma-Siam railroad, through very difficult terrain, which proved a graveyard for many thousands of Burmese and other conscript workers. Japan could only apologize and explain how vital this link was for the entire region. Postwar reparation claims by the nations of Southeast Asia were based on these Japanese actions.

Japan's political program for the region was even less successful, because the theoretical concepts on which it was based proved unrealistic. Up to a point, it struck a responsive chord with such slogans as "Asia for the Asians" and an "Asian Monroe Doctrine." The victory of 1942 destroyed all illusions of Western invulnerability and gave decisive help to local nationalists. But Japan was supported only as long as it cleared the road to freedom; it could never gain adherence to its own vision of a Nippon-led political community. Japan considered itself the new "Light of Asia" that would carry on the functions performed in antiquity by China. Its leaders believed that their culture was ethically and intellectually superior to that of their "younger brothers" and represented a way of life well worth copying. These beliefs were completely unacceptable to the new nations of Southeast Asia, especially since they implied further foreign domination. The overbearing manner of Japan's soldiers and the erratic behavior of the occupation officials, who mixed harsh and brutal actions with stiff correctness and grand promises, antagonized the Southeast Asians further. The Indonesians were especially upset by the forceful propagation of the Japanese language and the Shinto religion with its emperor worship.

The Effect of Political Concessions

Foreign Minister Shigemitsu Mamoro induced the army to agree to a policy of political concessions in 1943. However, the colonial revolutionaries realized that Japan was bargaining from weakness. Tokyo had hoped that this move would give the Asians a stake in the Japanese order and encourage them to side with Japan against Western counterinvasions. But the colonials simply accepted political rights without committing themselves to Japan. They remained devoted to the single purpose of independence, and Japan was the leader of Asia only in hastening this development.

Shigemitsu's first move was to make a liberal settlement with the Nanking puppet regime in order to show Japan's good faith. Japan renounced its concessions in Chinese cities and yielded its Boxer indemnities. It made a new pact with Nanking in 1943 calling for mutual cooperation and respect for each other's territorial integrity. This was also an indirect offer to Nationalist China to collaborate as equals; Chiang refused to compromise, believing that Japan was on the road to defeat.

Burma was given its independence in return for a declaration of war against the West. The Philippines under President Laurel gained the same right but did not declare war until the American invasion of Leyte led Japan to insist upon this. Even though real self-government was still not granted, Japan's policy was a challenge to the Western imperial powers. Finally, at the very end of the war, Japan made far-reaching changes in Indonesia. Its leaders had been pressing for a grant of independence and were suddenly granted their wish in the confused final days of the war. In Indochina, Japan uncovered a French plan for a coup early in 1945, disarmed and interned the French, and recognized the independence of Annam, one of the Indochinese states. By midsummer, the independence movement had come under the control of the local Communist leader Ho Chi Minh.

Even in defeat, Japan's militarists believed that this was merely one phase of a hundred-year war in which the struggle between the imperial powers and their colonies would give Japan another chance to dominate the region. They did not realize that colonialism was dead and that their own actions had helped destroy it. The nationalists of Southeast Asia, moreover, were convinced that the West would yield political freedom at war's end and so helped destroy Japanese power in 1944–1945. In the Philippines, where anti-Japanese sentiment was strongest, guerilla activity never ceased, and Filipino troops participated in the Leyte and Luzon campaigns. Many Burmese leaders went underground and gave Britain the widespread military support in 1945 that was so markedly absent in 1942. Even in Thailand, the pro-Japanese regime fell when Tojo lost power. It was replaced by a pro-Western faction that allowed an Allied intelligence network to operate in Bangkok itself. The Japanese, taxed to the limit by their military obligations and committed to the area's political freedom, found themselves unable to check the military or political turn of the tide.

Military Defeat

In 1944, Japan's military position deteriorated on all fronts except China. It opened an offensive into southern China against the still-isolated Kuomintang army in order to destroy a group of newly completed B-29 bases. Despite marked success by the end of the year, defeats elsewhere forced the Japanese to pull back toward the coast. The Burma front was endangered by a joint Anglo-American-Chinese operation which had already cleared the mountainous northern frontier region. In the Southwest Pacific, the Solomons, New Guinea, and the southern Philippines were cleared, with new assaults prepared against the Dutch Indies and the northern Philippines. Defeats in the central Pacific, especially the fall of the Mariannas, tore apart the core of Japan's inner defenses and opened the country to strategic bombing attacks.

Early in 1945, nearby Iwo Jima fell, and, that spring, Okinawa was lost after a fanatical defense featured by the very effective use of suicidal air assaults (kamikaze) on American ships. The Imperial Japanese Navy was now virtually destroyed, but the extremists argued that the Okinawa campaign proved that Japan could be successfully defended against invasion. In 1942 they had argued that the conquered empire could be held and a negotiated peace won; in 1943 the argument had been that the inner defense core of the empire was invulnerable. Now, with control of the air and sea lost, the army maintained that invasion of the home islands would be so costly to the United States that Japan could still emerge victorious. The militarists continued to terrorize their opponents with the menace of violence and assassination, and the additional threat of a revolutionary coup.

Efforts to End the War

The peace party won its first victory in 1943 when Shigemitsu became foreign minister, though he failed to mediate a Russo-German truce as a prelude to a Far Eastern settlement. In 1944, the jushin was able to get the moderate Admiral Yonai into the stopgap Koiso Cabinet, as extremists and moderates sparred for position. The Allied demand for unconditional surrender in 1943 strengthened the case for resistance because it threw doubt on the future of the institution of the throne, the one point on which the Japanese would not yield. At Cairo, in November, 1943, the Allies decided to strip Japan of all colonies gained since 1895. Yet the defeats of 1945 brought Admiral Suzuki to power; the eighty-year old premier became a wavering advocate of peace after he was briefed on the deplorable military situation. That spring the Supreme War Council was evenly divided: Suzuki, Foreign Minister Togo and Navy Minister Yonai for peace, as against War Minister General Anami and the two chiefs of staff, General Umezu and Admiral Toyoda.

It was to take a powerful combination of military blows plus a less rigid Allied stand to end the war. The defeat of Germany that spring exposed Japan to a Russian attack. The Soviet government denounced the Neutrality Pact of 1941 in April, and Russian troop movements forced Japan to reverse its policy of stripping down the Kwantung army. After it had been dropped from 700,000 in 1942 to 400,000 in 1944, this force was raised to 650,000 men. But with reduced combat efficiency it was expected to wage only a defensive struggle, falling back from Manchuria to a main line of resistance in northern Korea.

As late as July, 1945, Japan was still trying to have Russia mediate a settlement in the Pacific. Instead, the Potsdam Declaration of July 26, to which the Soviet Union adhered, presented terms for surrender. The conditions were harsh— total disarmament, extensive economic reparations, and loss of empire—but they left room for negotiation concerning the throne. The advocates of sur- render now faced a difficult problem: challenge the army and perhaps force a coup, or fight on while the old order crumbled and communism emerged from the chaos.

Though his government gave serious consideration to the Potsdam terms, the impression was created that Premier Suzuki intended to ignore them, thereby making Japan seem more intransigent than it really was. There followed the multiple catastrophes of the atom bombing of Hiroshima on August 6, a Soviet declaration of war two days later, and the second atomic assault, on Nagasaki, the following day. The question of surrender became one of national survival.

The Surrender

All factions agreed that Japan had to keep the imperial dynasty. But the army still insisted that Japan demobilize itself, try its own war criminals, and not be occupied. On August 9, the Supreme War Council was deadlocked 3–3 on the issue of accepting Allied terms, and the extremists were outvoted 12–3 in the cabinet. That night the Supreme War Council met again and Premier Suzuki dramatically called on Emperor Hirohito to decide. Such a policy move had not been made since the days of the Meiji emperor. Hirohito advised surrender, provided that the imperial institution was preserved. The cabinet quickly approved, and four harrowing days of negotiations with the United States followed.

The American position regarding the throne was vague enough to enable the militarists to cause a new deadlock in the Supreme War Council. Young officers plotted coups while the emperor met with all leading officials in order to get the issue settled. It took an Imperial Conference on August 14, summoned secretly and unexpectedly, to end the suspense. After all parties spoke, the emperor had the final word and formally decided on surrender. Since he was supported by all princes of the blood, the extremists were without a suitable replacement even if they did try a coup. An attempt to destroy the emperor's recorded statement of surrender was thwarted, other acts of violence were sup- pressed, and the announcement was made public on August 15. Imperial princes were dispatched to all field headquarters to ensure army compliance with this order. War Minister Anami committed suicide, as did many other officers; General Umezu stayed at his post and became Japan's military repre- sentative at the formal surrender ceremonies aboard the U.S.S. "Missouri" in Tokyo Bay on September 2.

The Japanese public was utterly astonished by the emperor's announcement. The fate of the entire country had actually come under the control of a handful of men who struggled bitterly for power while Japan suffered unimagined horrors. A milder American policy probably would not have ended the war so early, and it is difficult, even with the advantage of hindsight, to argue that Far Eastern affairs would have then developed more favorably for the United States.

The harsh terms of peace, however, weakened the Western position in the Orient, for the disintegration of Japanese power and the reduction of the imperial domain to the four home islands created a power vacuum that the West found difficult to fill. Had the original plan to reduce Japan's economic plant through reparations been carried out, the consequences might have been disastrous. On the other hand, a less sweeping policy of occupation and disarmament might never have shattered the old order of militarist domination.

In the end, Japan emerged battered but intact. Its economy suffered from intensive use, distortion, and destruction, and the nation was confronted with the unknown dangers of a foreign occupation. But the throne was preserved as a rallying point that enabled the nation to retain its sense of national identity. Japan remained the most modern, industrialized state in Asia, its home territory was not partitioned, and its administrative apparatus, the backbone of its government, was still intact. Despite the catastrophe and humiliation of 1945, Japan still had the opportunity to regain a position of prominence in world affairs through a determined effort at reconstruction.

10 *Japan after Defeat:*

Occupation and

Independence

Peace in 1945 meant more to Japan than the humiliation of defeat, loss of empire, and economic privation. It also brought a foreign occupation that sought to remold the country in the victor's image of the good society. But the bitter turn of world politics from the expectations of Allied cooperation in 1945 to the Cold War just a few years later compelled the Americans to modify their original plans. As the situation in Asia disintegrated and warfare occurred in the former Japanese empire—China, Korea, and Indochina—Japan itself became a major prize. Its quest for sovereignty and security in international politics now rivaled its concern with internal affairs.

Nevertheless, the major political development in Japan was the reintroduction of liberal democracy. Although the optimistic claims of complete democratization that were made by occupation leaders must be discounted, many achievements were recorded. Much will depend on the strength of Japan's revived democratic traditions and the country's ability to attain economic stability under difficult circumstances.

Defeat and Occupation

The Consequences of Defeat

Japan did not surrender unconditionally, since it was given the opportunity for economic revival along democratic lines. However, the terms of peace in reparations and territory were severe. Had the reparations policy been carried out, economic duress and political instability would have resulted. Steel, chemical, and machine-tool equipment were to be removed and the economy reduced to its level of the 1930's. Colonial losses meanwhile ended Japan's exploitation of Korean rice, Formosan rice and sugar, and Manchurian industrial raw materials. Profitable trade elsewhere in Asia and the merchant marine were virtually destroyed in the war. The influx of Japanese people from overseas gave the impoverished homeland more than 80 million inhabitants in 1945. A total of over 100 million was expected in the 1960's.

The United States modified its stand on reparations after 1947, for its own taxpayers would have had to support a dismantled Japanese economy. Futhermore, a prosperous environment was considered essential if democracy was to check a resurgence of militarism. When the Cold War arrived and Japan became essential to American security plans for Asia, the reparation policy was doomed. Only military installations were removed, and even this action was halted in 1949. The amount of industrial equipment taken from Japan was valued at less than $50 million. Reparations remained a major issue between Japan and the nations of Southeast Asia, to be negotiated diplomatically after the occupation ended in 1952.

Japan was less fortunate in territorial settlements. It lost not only the conquests made after 1931 but all possessions gained after the Meiji Restoration, even though these had previously received legal recognition. The Kurile Islands and Southern Sakhalin went to Russia, the Bonin Islands, below Honshu, and the Ryukyus (including Okinawa) came under American control, but their obvious Japanese composition was a deciding factor leading to their partial return a decade later. However, the United States retained a trusteeship over the Pacific Islands that Japan had won from Germany at Versailles. Manchuria and China Proper were evacuated, and Formosa and the Pescadores were returned to China. Finally, Korea was given its independence. Many of these former possessions quickly became storm centers of the Cold War. Had the Japanese Empire not gone to war in 1941, it might well have survived almost intact, as a powerful independent makeweight between East and West.

What was left of the imperial war machine was completely dismantled. Though the navy had been all but destroyed during the war the army and a sizable air arm were intact in 1945. Six million soldiers and civilians overseas were returned except in Soviet-controlled areas, and all military units were disbanded. War industries were closed and the powerful service ministries abolished. Professional officers were put on purge lists and barred from holding public office. These negative reforms of demobilization and demilitarization were most essential in ending the army's stranglehold over the government. However, in the light of the army's traditional position in political affairs, it remains to be seen whether a civilian administration can control a new military arm, even one with a limited scope for operation.

The shock of defeat, hope for an orderly world community, American idealism, and fervent Japanese pacifism combined to make an astonishing contribution to the new Japanese constitution. Article 9 stated that, "land, sea, and air forces, as well as other war potential, will never be maintained," in support of the claim that "the Japanese people forever renounce war as a sovereign right of the nation." The qualifying right of self-defense was retained, and a two-thirds majority in the legislature can amend the constitution, but this clause has now become a rallying point for those who fear the militarists or oppose siding with the United States in foreign affairs. The occupation authorities soon argued that Japan required self-defense forces in order to avoid utter dependence on American protection. A National Police Reserve of 75,000 men was created in 1950 and almost doubled in size in 1954. Trained in light infantry weapons, this force could be the nucleus of an army; but it is not obligated to serve overseas, and Japan still lacks a full military organization and heavy equipment. Rearmament became a major political issue, involving serious consideration of economic costs, direction of foreign policy, and the future of the constitutional order.

The American Occupation

Unlike its less fortunate German ally, Japan suffered neither from partition nor joint Allied rule. The Russians tried unsuccessfully to gain an occupation zone in Hokkaido, but neither they nor the British could effectively interfere with American rule. The dominant American position was partly due to the fact that it was able to establish immediate control under General Douglas MacArthur when Japan suddenly collapsed. As Supreme Commander for the Allied Powers (SCAP), MacArthur operated only under the broad directives of his government, and his own prestige with right-wing Republican critics of the Democratic Truman administration served to keep Japanese questions out of domestic American politics. It is true that the United States agreed to an eleven-nation Far Eastern Commission that could define policy toward Japan by a majority vote, including American, Russian, British, and Chinese approval, but any Commission proposal was subject to an American veto. In addition, the United States could issue interim directives to SCAP headquarters in Tokyo. Even the Allied Council for Japan, established in Tokyo, had only advisory powers and was treated coolly by General MacArthur.

Of equal importance was the American decision to rule through the existing Japanese government. Thus there was a continuity of authority, although at first the abdication of the emperor was seriously considered. With Hirohito retained, the country enjoyed a stability of rule that extended through the entire bureaucratic system. SCAP had only 2,000 people in its own headquarters to issue orders and suggestions but not to operate the government. An equal number served in military government units in the prefectural capitals, again to advise and admonish. The occupation did not bear directly on the people and General MacArthur quickly estimated that it could be effective for only three or four years. Clearly the Japanese themselves had an important role to play in making the proposed reforms work.

Problems Confronting Reform

The old-line political leaders and bureaucrats, even those opponents of militarism who now inherited the mantle of leadership, were unsympathetic to these American-inspired ideals. All they could do was offer covert resistance, go along with the tide, and await the end of the occupation. Although the bureaucracy, like the rest of the country, was jolted by defeat, it was able to reassert its prestige and privilege. Its sense of superiority and arrogance toward the Japanese people, far different from the Western concept of a civil service, could not be dispelled as long as the bureaucracy remained the backbone of the state.

Another dilemma lay in Japan's readiness to submit to foreign rule. This aided the occupation in fostering reform but it also reinforced the country's long tradition of obedience to recognized authority. Moreover, the authoritarian, military nature of the occupation was not offset by attempts to have the Japanese take the initiative. SCAP directives overrode the wishes of Japan's representative government because this was often the only way in which essential reforms could be achieved. The distant manner of the Supreme Commander may have further strengthened obedience to authority; yet he was deeply committed to the task of democratization and pursued it with a zealous devotion. His headquarters often erred in claiming rapid, sweeping success, but its more modest accomplishments must not be overlooked.

The Japanese, adept at borrowing from alien cultures, were most anxious to become acquainted with foreign ideas because they had been cut off from these trends for some years. Nevertheless, the country could not be certain that reform would occur without great effort. Though overthrown by force in 1931–1932, democracy had displayed serious weaknesses that were not necessarily cured by fifteen years of suppression. Equally important is the selective nature of Japan's cultural borrowing, always molding alien contributions into a native pattern. In early times, a feudal order survived the period of T'ang culture and later the Meiji Restoration modernized the state but kept the basic social-political pattern of Tokugawa Japan. It is true that a modern setting and the shock of defeat in 1945 were bound to have modifying effects. But the occupation covered a brief period of seven years, and the complex bases of society are slow to change. The occupation may be viewed as a dynamic event, occurring at a key moment in Japan's long-term evolution, but it will have succeeded only if democracy is adapted to a Japanese pattern that is workable and respected.

Preliminary Reforms

The occupation authorities were most systematic in their negative task of clearing away much of the old order. The apparatus of state control was removed, together with restrictions on individual freedom. The Home Ministry and the dreaded thought police were abolished. The regular national police system was decentralized, even though law and order suffered as a consequence. Ordinances restricting individual and group action were removed and political prisoners, including Communists, were released. The formidable array of militarist, terrorist, and ultrapatriotic associations was declared illegal.

The position of the emperor was modified so that imperial prestige would no longer serve to bolster authoritarianism. People were now permitted to discuss the emperor and the throne without fear of reprisal, thereby opening the topic to vigorous debate. The occupation authorities sought to have the emperor treated as a ruler and not a personage of divinity. His advisers opposed this for fear that the throne would fall in repute, but Hirohito agreed and had a rescript issued in 1946 denying both the emperor's divinity and Japan's superior mission to rule.

State Shintoism was disestablished as the official religion because it had been used by the militarists to spread their doctrine of a divine mission of conquest. The teaching of Shintoism and militarism in schools was forbidden, and the emperor's picture, the most valued and sacred item in a school, was ordered removed. The injunctions to teach a new ethic fostering democracy and to remove ultranationalistic teachers were important but difficult to enforce.

An attempt was made to purge leaders responsible for Japan's ill-fated aggression. Twenty-eight were tried as war criminals and found guilty in 1948, with sentences ranging from prison terms to death for former Premier Tojo and others. All those who held positions of authority during the imperialist venture were prohibited from holding office or engaging in public affairs. This group included military leaders, members of patriotic societies, secret police, high officials in public corporations or overseas territories, and parliamentarians approved by the Tojo cabinet. The press, labor, business organizations, and similar vocations were also included, so that more than 200,000 persons were affected by 1948. Such a rapid and sweeping reform was bound to punish moderates and extremists alike, and, since the Japanese administered the purge, personal and political considerations played an important role. Often the chief official of an agency would be purged and his subordinate, who differed only in being younger, would succeed him.

However, following honored custom, the formal leaders consulted with former officials or family relations who had been purged. As the Japanese regained control of their affairs, the purge was brought to an end by 1949. A screening board considered appeals and was lenient where association rather than individual action caused the purge. When the occupation ended, the purge was lifted, with full rights restored to the depurged. Japan since 1952 has attempted to induce the United States to release former leaders still jailed for war crimes.

Constitutional and Political Reform

American animosity toward Japan was intense during the war, and the belief grew that only total reform would save this defeated enemy. But it is extremely rash for one nation to attempt to redirect the basic political outlook of another advanced culture. The Americans, who considered the field of government and political action restricted in scope, limited their reform program accordingly.

Other reforms in social and economic affairs were undertaken, but primarily to remove obstacles to political democracy. There was no attempt to reorder Japanese society with the thoroughness of purpose and action we have come to associate with a Soviet totalitarian occupation.

The reformers hoped that a new constitutional structure would be the core around which a truly open society would crystallize. A new Constitution of 1947 replacing the Meiji statute embodied two fundamental changes in the political order. The source of sovereignty was transferred from the emperor to the people. The Meiji Constitution had been a gracious gift handed down by the monarch, but the new document's preamble contained the novel assertion: "We the Japanese people . . . do proclaim that sovereign power resides with the people and do firmly establish this Constitution." A second major step was the creation of a constitutional monarchy and parliamentary government, with the legislature as the supreme ruling organ. A cabinet, responsible to the Diet, was given authority in executive affairs.

SCAP had issued a directive to the Japanese to institute these sweeping reforms, but the change was attained in a startling manner. The conservative leaders of Japan in 1945–1946 had continued to represent the traditional order. Baron Shidehara, famous for his moderate China policy in the 1920's, headed a government that wished to modify the Meiji order only where absolutely necessary, by redrafting sections of the old constitution. A cabinet committee and private study groups agreed to retain the "emperor system" and the "national polity" but presented unsatisfactory constitutional drafts. SCAP then had its own Government Section secretly formulate a draft constitution in February, 1946, to avoid riding roughshod over the government in public. Most conservatives, including Foreign Minister Yoshida Shigeru, were bitterly opposed, but the premier and others felt obliged to accept this constitution. Again Emperor Hirohito exercised decisive influence, siding with the premier. After public scrutiny and general support by the parties and the press, it was approved by the old legislature and accepted by the Privy Council. Promulgated on November 3, 1946, it became Japan's basic law six months later.

The Emperor

The position of the monarch was reduced to "a symbol of the state and of the unity of the people," with none of the shadowy broad powers enjoyed under the Meiji system. He was to perform only formal and ceremonial functions, and all his actions required the advice of the cabinet. The imperial family's immediate affairs and economic interests were now controlled by responsible public agencies. The Diet appropriated imperial income and the state registered its property. The Imperial Household was reduced to a department dealing with ceremonial court functions, and the Imperial Family Council was replaced by a council dominated by the Diet and cabinet. The number of imperial princes was sharply reduced.

The emperor, save for the crisis of 1945–1946, had not made policy decisions, but as the embodiment of the state he remained enveloped by an atmosphere of power and prestige. It is most difficult to transfer this dignity and supremacy to a Diet and cabinet, whose past record was uninspiring and whose daily purpose is partisan conflict. The imperial family has endeavored to live simply and has had Crown Prince Akihito trained by an American Quaker governess. Hirohito has scrupulously adhered to his constitutional role. Yet the symbol of the emperor persists as a vital social, religious, and psychological force in the Japanese order. He is still at the center of an intricate web of duty and status that mark Japanese society and will so remain as long as this order pervades the country at large.

Undoubtedly the imperial system continues to signify loyalty to the state and religious devotion to the throne. However, militarism and authoritarian rule are not inevitably part of this institution, and the throne need not be an obstacle to democracy. The destruction of the old order in Central and Eastern Europe in 1917–1918 helped open the way to violent totalitarianism instead of moderate self-government. The imperial system may be a stabilizing force in an era of disquieting changes and so aid the chances of democracy to survive. On the other hand, authoritarian opponents of the new order may try to destroy it by calling for a "restoration of imperial power"; they can always denounce the present constitution as a betrayal of native traditions, imposed by foreign pressure. In any event, this menace can be thwarted only if democracy proves itself by positive results; under these circumstances, the maintenance of the imperial system appears the wiser choice.

Parliamentary Government

All old antidemocratic institutions were swept away: the military, the Privy Council, the Lord Privy Seal, the Minister of the Imperial Household, as well as the jushin, and various other autonomous agencies. The bureaucracy remains, but executive authority is now vested in the cabinet. Unlike the old order, the cabinet is directly responsible to the Diet, which is "the highest organ of state power, and . . . the sole law-making organ of State." The premier and a majority of the cabinet have to be members of the Diet, following the British theory of the cabinet as the legislature's "executive committee." A vote of no confidence in the House of Representatives can overturn a cabinet, but the latter can respond by dissolving the House and holding a general election.

The Diet has extensive powers, with full control over national finances. It approves all taxes and expenditures, including the budget drawn up by the cabinet. Its composition remains bicameral, but the lower house is superior to the House of Councilors, which replaced the House of Peers when the aristocracy was abolished under the occupation. In case of disagreement, the lower house can override the Councilors by a two-thirds majority, and in treaties and the budget not even this is required. Failure of the Councilors to act within sixty days on measures approved by the lower house is treated as a rejection that can then be overridden. However, half the 250 members of the upper house are chosen every three years, and the chamber is not dissolved when the lower house is undergoing an election. It is closed on these occasions except when the cabinet requires emergency measures, which must later gain retroactive approval of the Representatives. This heavy reliance on law and regulation to protect the power of the legislature is a result of anxiety based on past experience. Although such elaborate constitutional safeguards are of value, security rests ultimately only in the adequate direction of public affairs.

A Diet Law of 1947, based on the American model, was passed to improve legislative efficiency. It provided for five-month sessions, to be extended by Diet decision; twenty standing committees with their own staffs to give the legislature expert help, continuity, and prestige in dealing with the executive; public committee hearings, important levers of power and influence; and salaries and allowances at respectable levels; moreover, the cabinet was forbidden to interfere with the Diet's ability to function as it saw fit. This assertion that the legislature is an independent counterweight to the executive is in marked contrast to British parliamentary democracy.

There are 466 members of the lower house, elected for four years. Under the suffrage law of 1945 the voting age was reduced to twenty, and women gained the right to vote. The electoral districts are small, but several representatives are chosen from each district. This is in effect a type of proportional representation in which each major party often wins one seat in a district. Thus it is difficult in a multiparty system for one party to win a legislative majority, a situation that adds to the obstacles of responsible executive leadership.

Democratic rule is confronted with an institutional dilemma. Parliamentary supremacy seems to be its chief safeguard, but legislatures cannot actually direct the affairs of state. In the modern era, efficient parliamentary rule has depended on the competence and decisiveness of the cabinet, exercising responsible leadership on the basis of its legislative majority. The lower house in this system has the vital task of reflecting the popular will and transmitting this authority, through disciplined parties, to the executive. The alternative appears to be cabinet instability and impotence in the face of undisciplined parties and legislative supremacy. As the Japanese system has developed since 1947, the cabinet has exercised its authority in a manner approaching the British system but without a similar public or legislative acceptance. In both the Diet and the press, the rise of cabinet power is decried as an usurpation and a step toward dictatorship.

The premier is chosen by the Diet, but he in turn selects and removes members of his cabinet. When Yoshida Shigeru was premier for six years, he became the cabinet's primary figure and made crucial policy decisions, especially with regard to dissolving the lower house. The staff and size of the premier's office have also expanded considerably since 1947. The cabinet as a whole has the constitutional power to formulate, execute, and administer national policy. It prepares the budget and drafts legislation for the Diet to consider, but must be prepared to defend its position in parliament by speeches and responses to questioning. It must account for all expenditures, including a reserve fund granted to meet emergencies. Unlike pre-1945 governments, the new executive can issue ordinances only to execute laws passed by the Diet.

Difficulties Confronting the Diet

Ultimate control rests in the Diet, yet the cabinet can initiate and direct policy and demand disciplined party support in the legislature—a situation that is normal in Britain but has confused and irritated the Japanese political scene. The difficulty goes beyond parliamentary irresponsibility and poor party discipline, which marked Japan's earlier democratic period. Britain's parliamentary tradition, for example, enabled the people to divide its loyalty faithfully between the crown and parliament, even after "parliamentary supremacy" had been modified by a cabinet-party rule. But how will this system fare in an alien Japanese culture? Can the Diet truly act as the symbolic and political repository of Japanese sovereignty called for in the constitution? It is difficult to see the average Japanese treating the emperor and the Diet with equal reverence and respect and, in light of cabinet-Diet relations, accepting it as the highest political authority.

In its early years, the new Diet lost an opportunity to gain popular support by failing to act with the competence and dignity expected of it. Mounting popular criticism and lack of interest in parliamentary debates indicated a decline in prestige. Parliamentary debates had little public appeal because much of the free discussion required by law is directed through party channels, so that all major groups can be heard, and much of the important work is done in committee. The negative acts—criticism, obstruction, filibustering—caught the public eye, and the Diet gained a reputation of being unproductive. These complaints, however, occur in all democracies, and a more modest evaluation of the Diet may produce a more realistic appreciation of its functions.

Unfortunately, the difficulty does not revolve simply about an understanding of parliamentary government. The Diet engaged in such practices as rowdyism, displayed a vulnerability to crude lobbying, and experienced an extraordinary degree of corruption. The decorum and politeness associated with British parliamentary procedure were absent; and there were outbursts of violence in heated parliamentary debates. In 1956, for example, the Socialist opposition resorted to sit-down strikes, and the blocking of corridors to stop the passage of laws. Strained relations with the Yoshida cabinets, inspired in part by the premier's contempt for parliamentary and party pressures, did not enhance either side's prestige. The reversion to the fine arts of bribery and corruption in a manner reminiscent of the 1920's has even led to a systematic classification of these types of influence!

The Diet has much to do if it is to hold its own in competition with the cabinet and the bureaucracy. One approach is through its standing committees, which can develop their own spheres of competence, produce adequate bureaucratic staffs, and confront the executive on equal terms. From a more general view, the Diet has the advantage of the status quo, which only a major upheaval can destroy. The parliamentary system of the 1920's, established by Japan itself, was accepted by the people and endorsed in elections as late as 1936, despite a record of weak cabinets, party instability, corruption, and mismanagement. There is thus a high level of tolerance for this system, but it is of a passive nature and in itself may not be enough to sustain democracy if its enemies regain their former strength. The present order must win some enthusiastic and positive support during the years in which it can operate unmolested. Much will depend on the success of the government in confronting the issues that trouble Japan today, and here the party structure and its leadership play a vital role.

Political Parties and Leadership

A striking feature of Japanese politics has been the continuity of party traditions and voting patterns from the premilitarist period. The major change has been the rise of socialist strength, due to the more liberal atmosphere of the occupation and the development of Japan's urban services and industrial enterprises since 1936. The majority of the country still favors the conservatives— now united in the Democratic-Liberal party—who continue to win support from business leaders, landowners, and the peasantry. The rural regions remained conservative strongholds during the period of sweeping land reform, because the peasant continued to follow his local political leader and former landlord.

The electoral base of the right wing has been reduced by the rise of a politically conscious white-collar element and the development of trade-unions after 1945. The left wing is now a major competitor for power, with most of its strength centered in the Socialist party. The first substantial effort at leftist party organization occurred in 1925, when universal suffrage was attained.

THE MAJOR PARTIES SINCE 1945

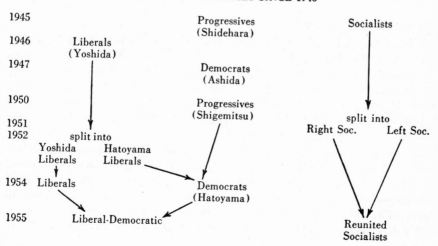

269

CABINETS SINCE 1945

		Time in Office
August, 1945	Higashikuni Naruhiko	2 months
October, 1945	Shidehara Kijuro (Progressive)	5 months
May, 1946	Yoshida Shigeru (Liberal)	1 year
June, 1947	Katayama Tetsu (Socialist)	8 months
March, 1948	Ashida Hitoshi (Democrat)	7 months
October, 1948	Yoshida Shigeru (Liberal)	6 years, 2 months (four consecutive cabinets)
December, 1954	Hatoyama Ichiro (Democrat; Liberal-Dem.)	2 years
December, 1956	Ishibashi Tanzan (Liberal-Dem.)	2 months
February, 1957	Kishi Nobusuke (Liberal-Dem.)	

There were four rival groups, which won almost 500,000 votes in 1928 and 300,000 in 1932. A consolidation of effort under the Social Mass party made them a factor in the 1936 election, but this movement was suppressed by the rise of authoritarian rule. In the postwar period trade-unions, along with some white-collar workers, students, and intellectuals, have supported the Socialists. Japanese labor unions have concentrated heavily on politics, in sharp contrast to American practices. The Communist party and the extremists on the right have thus far failed to attract votes; postwar Japan could boast that its major parties tolerated each other and accepted the democratic system.

This pattern of attitudes, the development of meaningful party alternatives within a constitutional framework, and the continuity of electoral allegiances from an earlier generation are signs of political maturation. The voter has become more concerned with platforms and issues, and party discipline and public responsibility have improved since the 1920's. Compared to its own past record and the contemporary situation elsewhere in Asia, Japanese democracy is relatively advanced. However, the party structure still leaves much to be desired and is open to searching criticisms.

Persistent Difficulties

Among the major difficulties confronting the parties have been instability and lack of cohesion, an absence of national party structures, and the problem of corruption. Despite better discipline over individual parliamentarians, party leaders were still plagued by bolting splinter groups, which often joined the rival side. Cliques and the tendency to peg party allegiances on personalities remained common political features. Thus, in the decade after 1945, the right wing was split into two factions, the Liberals and the Progressives (or Democrats), with a remarkably frequent shift of membership, and even leadership, between the two camps. Their major opponents, the Socialists, remained united until 1951, then split into rival parties for four years. Only at the end of 1955 did the Socialists reunite and thus compel the quarreling right-wing faction to patch up its differences and establish the Democratic-Liberal party.

Another serious problem has been the close relationship between party machines and illegal organizations. Parties have central offices in Tokyo that perform many essential tasks and exercise discipline in parliament. But they lack effective vote-producing, nationwide organizations, and do not enjoy adequate financial support. In their search for votes and money in the cities, parties have depended on the illegal *oyabun-kobun* system, in which underground leaders (*oyabun*) exercise a feudallike control over their followers. These elements control day-labor activities, street stalls, and other legal enterprises, as well as gambling, and a variety of illegal pursuits. In rural regions, the influence of former landlords and local leaders remains the major channel for vote-getting. The old official organizations—neighborhood associations in the cities and similar groupings in the countryside—were outlawed under SCAP as feudal and fascist remnants that stifled individual self-expression. Yet these have persisted and, in modified form, can serve as building blocks in the con-struction of efficient party machines.

The problem of corruption involves financial aid from business interests, labor unions, and other elements seeking benefits in return. The black market, which began late in the war, the decay of the militarist structure, and the diffi-culties of adjusting to the postwar situation lowered the moral tone and fostered a disrespect of the law. After 1945 the Foreign Ministry replaced the Home Ministry as the source of patronage and support, since it was the channel through which American aid was disbursed. In internal affairs *oyabun* handled vast construction assignments, black marketeers dealt in military surplus, and business leaders entered the picture as the economy recovered. There were many instances of bribery in the parties and the bureaucracy; a major scandal in-volved the Showa Denko (Electric) Company in 1948 and overturned a cabinet.

The continued dependence of the parties on popular support has served as a check against continued excesses. A long period of honest and free elections may eventually be a determining factor in bringing about political order, firmer party lines, and cleaner government. Because parties have become the instru-ment through which real political power can be attained, the political order possesses a significance and vitality it lacked in the past.

Early Postwar Politics

In 1945 party politicians sought out respectable bureaucrats to assume politi-cal leadership, and foreign-affairs officials like Baron Shidehara, Yoshida Shigeru, and Ashida Hitoshi became party leaders. Experienced parliamentari-ans were scarce because many who were removed by the purges did not regain their former positions until after the occupation. A most spectacular example was Liberal party leader Hatoyama Ichiro, a veteran legislator who had bolted the Seiyukai in 1939 because it was promilitarist. Yet he was suddenly purged in 1946 for having defended Japan's policy of expansion during the war. He was ousted shortly after forming the Liberal party in an effort to unite all anti-militarist conservatives. Hatoyama then entrusted the party leadership to Yo-shida Shigeru until his return. By that time (1951–1952) the latter had proved

ELECTIONS SINCE 1946

PERCENTAGE OF VOTES

	April 1946	April 1947	January 1949	October 1952	April 1953	February 1955 (approx.)
Liberals	24.4	26.5	43.8	48		
Yoshida					38.94	27
Hatoyama					8.93 ⎤	37
Progressive-Democrat	18.7	25.9	15.8	18.2	17.78 ⎦	
Socialist	17.8	26.2	13.5	(21.1)*	(26.59)	(29)
Right				11.4	13.36	14
Left				9.9	13.23	15
Cooperative	3.2	7.1	3.4			
Labor-Farmer (from 1952)				0.7	1.04	1
Communist	3.8	3.6	9.6	2.5	1.89	2
Other parties	11.7	5.7	7.3	2.8	.42 ⎤	5
Independents	20.4	5.0	6.6	6.5	4.41 ⎦	

SEATS IN THE HOUSE OF REPRESENTATIVES

	April 1946	April 1947	January 1949	October 1952	April 1953	February 1955 (approx.)
Liberals	141	132	264	240		
Yoshida					202	112
Hatoyama					35 ⎤	185
Progressive-Democrat	93	126	68	85	77 ⎦	
Socialist	92	143	49	(111)*	(138)	(156)
Right				57	66	67
Left				54	72	89
Cooperative	14	31	14			
Labor-Farmer (from 1952)				4	5	4
Communist	5	4	35	0	1	2
Other parties	39	18	24	7	1 ⎤	8
Independents	80	12	12	19	11 ⎦	

* The Socialist party was split in the 1952–1955 elections, the two wings running as competitors.

his competence as party leader and premier and refused to yield to Hatoyama. Hatoyama promptly split the Liberals by forming his own faction and then bolting the party.

The Liberals inherited the old Seiyukai structure, its party discipline, and many of its old zones of influence. However, in personality and policy, a distinct break was made with the past. Similarly, the rival conservative party (alternately the Progressives or Democrats) depended on the old Minseito organization and its urban strongholds. Since it included many former officials at first, it suffered heavily from the purge. It was then given a more liberal orientation under the leadership of Baron Shidehara and especially by Ashida Hitoshi in 1947–1948, after he bolted the Liberals.

Meanwhile, the trend of government in the early postwar years was to the left. The last wartime cabinet under Prince Higashikuni gave way to Shide-hara's cabinet of bureaucrats in 1945. The election of 1946 was a conservative triumph, but the Liberal Yoshida government that followed failed to act in the face of an economic crisis. When the Socialists refused to join the cabinet, a second election was held in 1947. The Socialists emerged the largest party and formed their first administration, with the support of Ashida's Democrats. However, since it lacked an absolute majority, the Socialist party could not pursue a policy of nationalization or extensive economic controls. Low coal production, inflation, and inadequate food supplies created difficulties that the inexperienced and cautious cabinet could not overcome. The Americans had now decided to rehabilitate Japan, but their aid arrived too late to benefit the Socialists. In 1948 this leftist coalition was re-formed, and the Democrats ruled with Socialist support. But both parties suffered from internal conflicts, and, when a scandal broke involving leading Democrats, including Premier Ashida, the coalition fell and the country entered a six-year period of Liberal rule.

The Yoshida Regime (1948–1954) and Its Opponents

The Liberals won a clear majority in the January, 1949, election and held it for four years. As this margin declined, Premier Yoshida reshuffled his cabinets, held elections in 1952 and 1953, and set a record as premier of five cabinets before retiring in 1954. His vigorous competence in controlling his party and getting legislation through the Diet won popular approval in a nation unaccustomed to incisive democratic leadership. Yoshida was assailed as both a dictator of Japan and a puppet of SCAP. He did follow a pro-Western foreign policy, but his determined effort to modify the reform program of the occupation proved his independence and conservatism. Yoshida also succeeded in getting the occupation ended and Japanese sovereignty restored in 1952.

However, with independence came a treaty giving the United States the right to keep troops in Japan in order to defend it. This policy required considerable political skill and courage and was carried through during Yoshida's third cabinet (1949–1952), when the Liberals enjoyed a comfortable parliamentary majority.

Yoshida also sided with the West on the question of foreign trade and its relation to the Japanese economy. Japan sought economic aid under the American Mutual Security Program, membership in the Colombo Plan (achieved in 1954), and extensive contacts with Southeast Asia, an area hungry for capital and industrial equipment. The premier was willing to trade with Communist China but did not press for extensive markets. He followed the American-United Nations lead after 1950, when an embargo was placed on trade with Peking in strategic materials. Yoshida was extremely cautious with regard to rearmament. He refused to seek an amendment to the constitution permitting Japan to rearm, but created the National Police Reserve in line with the MacArthur interpretation that the constitution permitted Japan to defend itself against invasion or subversion.

His opponents during this time were busy rebuilding their strength after the defeat of 1949. The Democrats won only sixty-seven seats that year; reorganized as the Progressives under a depurged former foreign minister, Shigemitsu Mamoru, the party adopted a more conservative view. In the 1952 and 1953 elections it won eighty-five and then seventy-seven seats. Right-wing opposition was strengthened when the Hatoyama faction of the Liberal party sought to undermine Yoshida's position. It organized a Democratization League of Diet Liberals, sought cabinet posts, and demanded positions in the party executive. The Liberal majority in 1952 fell to 240, compared to 264 in 1949. When the Hatoyama group defected and cost the government a vote of confidence, Yoshida dissolved the lower house and held a new election in 1953. The Hatoyama Liberals won only thirty-five seats, but the Yoshida Liberals were reduced to 199 in the premier's last cabinet (1953–1954). The opposition was now strong enough to control the key posts in the Diet and harassed Yoshida from this stronghold. The Hatoyama Liberals and Shigemitsu Progressives merged as a new Democratic party in 1954 under Hatoyama, determined to wrest the majority conservative vote from the Liberals.

The Socialists suffered a staggering defeat in 1949 when their 1947 high of 143 seats was reduced to forty-nine; by contrast, the Communists jumped from four to thirty-five seats. Adversity caused a split between the Right and Left Socialists, who formed separate parties as a result of a dispute over the Japanese-American peace treaty. The Left Socialists retained control of the party machine and the General Confederation of Japanese Trade Unions (*Sohyo*). In foreign policy they were neutralist, opposed to a peace treaty not signed by Russia, and completely against rearmament. The Right Socialists supported the peace treaty and recognized the need for some defensive forces. This group resembled the moderate British Labor party in ideology, and maintained its strength by sponsoring a Council for a Democratic Labor Movement (*Zenryo*). Both factions still agreed to oppose a laissez-faire capitalist economy and sought state control over coal, iron, steel, and fertilizer production. They were also united in demanding more trade with China, on both ideological and economic grounds, and bitterly resented the strategic restrictions imposed by the United States.

Even with the split, the Socialists vote mounted, with a combined total of 111 in 1952 and 138 in 1953. They joined with the new Democratic party, which had 112 seats, to control the 1953 Diet and challenge the government. This opposition capitalized on the government's reduced popularity and the critical attitude toward Yoshida displayed in the press. It challenged the premier's moderate foreign policy and adopted a strident nationalist tone.

The Japanese people, anxious to attain complete sovereignty, criticized the defense treaty, the presence of American ground troops, and the military bases. Like the Socialists, the business community sought more trade with China, recalling the profitable ties that existed until 1945. Any radical change, however, would have endangered essential economic relations with the United States.

In other matters, however, the Democrats and their supporters were far to the right of the Socialists. They wanted a more independent foreign policy and sought modifications in the treaties with the United States. But they sought a constitutional amendment to permit a more extensive program of rearmament. Beyond this, Hatoyama, Shigemitsu, and other depurged leaders wished to revise the constitution, re-establish the theory of imperial rule, and thus effect a partial return to the old order.

A Two-Party System

Despite these differences, the opposition finally achieved the resignation of Yoshida at the end of 1954 and brought Hatoyama to power. In this it was aided by the growing unrest within the Liberal camp and a shipping scandal that involved Liberal ministers and parliamentarians. The elections of February, 1955, confirmed the new balance: the Democrats won enough seats to form a government but lacked a majority without Liberal or Socialist support. As a result, the Hatoyama regime continued to preach an independent nationalist line but did not actually depart from the more moderate Liberal position.

In October, 1955, the two Socialist factions finally reunited, though important elements of each camp resented the concessions made in the compromise settlement. The left wing dropped its "no arms" pledge and accepted the right's program for a small defensive force, which would be admittedly too small to be useful. The right in turn dropped its argument that Japan had been in the free world's camp ever since it signed the peace treaty. The party now held that Japan, though nominally independent, was not really free because of American military and economic pressure. The left agreed to yield its demand that the treaty be abrogated, but the right accepted the other's view that Japan should seek closer ties with other Asian states and avoid entering the American or Russian camp. Like this new platform, the number of high party officers was expanded to accommodate the leaders of both camps. Leftist Suzuki Mosaburo became Chairman of the Executive Committee, and rightist Kawakami Jotaro became "supreme adviser."

This maneuver spurred the two conservative groups to unite the very next month as the Liberal-Democrats with Hatoyama still premier. This new party was lacking in internal stability, for the aged and infirm Premier Hatoyama could not exercise the strong leadership which Japan had experienced under Yoshida Shigeru. In 1956 nine competing groups could be found within the Liberal-Democratic camp. However, the long-sought merger gave the new party 298 of the Diet's 467 seats. With Liberal influence again strong in the government, the new right-wing party based its foreign policy on close cooperation with the United States, as against the neutralist views of the Socialists. However, there are extreme rightists who still favor a more independent policy, while the extreme left leans more definitely to the Communist bloc. In domestic affairs the two parties offer a clear-cut choice between private enterprise protected by government and a state-controlled economy stressing nationalization. In light of the personality and organizational clashes and the divergent policies still sponsored within each party, it is not yet clear whether the new two-party system will prove durable.

The Political Extremes

American economic assistance and unexpected purchases resulting from the Korean War contributed to political stability and reduced the appeal of extremism. However, Japan has suffered severe economic and political dislocations in recent decades and is far from secure against an authoritarian revival. Elsewhere this menace has come from the communist left and the totalitarian right simultaneously, for these natural enemies remain bitter foes of democracy. In Japan, the first organized challenge has come from the Communists instead of the traditionally powerful right. This is partly due to the early occupation policy of allowing the Communists wide latitude while jailing the right extremists. Consequently, the Communists made rapid gains and reached an ominous peak in 1949 before undergoing a decline. Though weakened as a political party, communism remains a potent force, with many sympathizers in intellectual circles.

Before the war the Communist party was a weak, detested agent of a hostile power, hunted by the police. Irreverent criticism of the emperor and appeals to violence also reduced its influence. Early in 1946, Nozaka Sanzo, the party's most popular leader, returned from a long stay with the Chinese Communists. Under his direction, the party embarked on a policy of moderation and sought to gain mass electoral support. Its effort to be "lovable" was linked to the assertion that the party was independent of all foreign influence. Skillful propaganda, exploitation of economic difficulties, and appeal to intellectuals and students all had their effects. By 1949, party membership rose to 100,000, with supporters estimated at 3 million, and its numerous publications enjoyed wide circulation. It made serious inroads into organized labor, especially the railway and electrical unions, and won 10 per cent of the popular vote in that year's election.

However, the party's professed moderation was disproved by its persistent efforts to hamstring economic recovery and foster strikes and riots. More important, the international communist movement had embarked on a program of violence after 1948, and in 1950 the Cominform denounced Nozaka's cautious attitude and, though he publicly recanted, placed the "internationalists" in control of the party. This revelation of Russian domination and recourse to violence again cost the party dearly. Meanwhile SCAP curtailed strikes and demonstrations, restricted labor's privileges, and allowed the Japanese government to control the Communist party. When the Korean War began, SCAP barred the Communist Central Committee from party office and banned the party's newspaper. It suggested that the party be outlawed, but the Yoshida government would not take this dangerous political step. The Communist party won no seats in the 1952 election, its membership was halved, and it lost much of its control over labor unions to the resurgent Socialists.

Suffering from internal dissent and without an attractive platform, the Communists embarked on a vitriolic anti-American campaign, parading neutralism and nationalism as interdependent policies. They denounced the government as an American puppet and the treaty arrangements with the United States as evidence of colonial rule that justified acts of violence. This brought such a sharp public reaction that in 1953 party leaders again reversed their tactics and promised to operate legally. Recently the Communists have infiltrated the left-wing socialist and labor organizations with some success. The party continues to develop its secret revolutionary apparatus, together with small, illegal, military units, while using the regular party structure to campaign against the government and pro-Western policies.

The extreme right has not presented such an active threat, but its latent strength may be much greater. Its revival after 1950 has not produced a distinctive national party. It too has infiltrated the parliamentary system from the other extreme and seeks to capitalize on any antigovernmental revolutionary sentiment that may arise. Militarism has suffered because of its ineptness and defeat, and General Tojo and his colleagues were condemned by the public on these grounds rather than for any moral crimes. The deep imprint of the military tradition and extremist nationalism cannot be uprooted in a few years. Many ultranationalist societies composed of ex-soldiers have been formed. One example is the Revolutionary Chrysanthemum Flag Association in the old feudal stronghold of Kyushu; its very title contains the symbols of imperial tradition. Its platform of mass democracy, socialism, and nationalism is reminiscent of the post-1918 German Nazi (National Socialists) appeal. The electoral strength of these groups has been negligible thus far. Still, much of the antagonism to rearmament is rooted in the fear that a new army will try to reassert its political authority, especially if the economic or international situation takes an unfortunate turn.

Administrative Legal and Social Reforms

The Bureaucracy

SCAP reforms did not prove as durable in the field of administration as in the constitutional order. The importance of consent, implied in a brief period of occupation, was revealed by the speed with which the old Japanese pattern of administration reasserted itself.

SCAP sought to maintain the efficiency of Japan's administrative system while placing it under effective democratic control. The powerful civilian bureaucracy, with a tradition of prestige and leadership, benefited from the removal of military rivals. Its long-standing contempt for parliamentary rule served as a warning that a simple constitutional declaration of Diet supremacy would not make the Japanese bureaucracy a Western-style "servant of the people." The dependence of the relatively inexperienced parliament on the bureaucrats for the drafting of legislation, a practice common enough in the West, has more significant overtones in Japan. Only effective party government, competent cabinet administration, and the development of a reliable legislative staff can make democratic control over the bureaucracy a reality.

Efforts at legislating reform have not been too successful. A Japanese law in 1946 merely simplified the unwieldy structure that had evolved during the militarist era. The Americans prodded the government to create a merit system under democratic control, but even the Socialist cabinet, under Katayama Tetsu, could not effect a sweeping reform, since it was only nominally supported by its allies. A National Public Service Law of 1948 improved standards of pay, classification, and examination but failed to end the power of the old bureaucratic clique. It did create a National Personnel Authority that could serve as an agency of control and reform, but this body's effectiveness is still unproved. Meanwhile, the number of government employees continued to rise; now, despite a temporary cut in 1949, Japan's bureaucracy is among the largest in the world.

Decentralization of Authority

Another type of reform was to curtail the power of the center in civil and police affairs, and give prefectural and local authorities real power and responsibility. SCAP hoped to increase grass-roots participation in political affairs, create scattered centers of political power, and so strengthen democracy in Japan. Since the country was a unitary state, the American federal system could not be applied, but it apparently was used as a model for reform. Under the Local Autonomy Law of 1947, all officials—from village and ward chiefs to prefectural governors—were elected, to represent local interests instead of serving as appointed agents of the center. Elected provincial assemblies were created with broad powers, especially in budgetary and appointive affairs, as checks on the governors. All elections, local and national, were to be supervised by local committees instead of personnel from Tokyo.

This sweeping reform proved too great a change. The multiplication of executive and legislative officers led to inefficiency, overlapping of authority, burdensome costs, and corruption. Popular participation in local contests was below that of national elections, and there was often only one candidate for a local office. Traditional leaders continued to dominate provincial and local politics.

A Police Reform Law of 1947 ended the national police system and made municipalities of 5,000 or more responsible for their own law and order. This law gave Japan 10,000 police units, each under a civilian public safety commission appointed by a local assembly. The remaining one quarter of the police was organized as the National Rural Police under civilian control in Tokyo. The local units lacked the funds or competence to develop adequate police systems, and the incidence of crime increased rapidly. Control of education was also decentralized under the School Education Law of 1947, which transferred control over curriculum, personnel, and administration to local authorities. The

Ministry of Education retained jurisdiction over the universities and continued to control research and guidance in planning educational standards.

Additional transfers of authority over roads, buildings, and other services meant a great increase in the cost of prefectural and local government. However, the old tax structure, which allowed local agencies few independent sources of income, was barely changed: local officials collected taxes, turned the revenue over to the center, and received funds to cover 80 per cent of their normal expenses. The poorer prefectures were especially hurt by this, and the rich ones resisted a tax to equalize the burden. On the whole Tokyo proved reluctant to cover the new expenses, even for police work, since it could not control the local distribution of funds or performance of services. Moreover, the Diet, after authorizing new local taxes, reduced them by half in a pre-election maneuver in 1951. Local authorities were therefore at the mercy of a central regime acting in its own interests, and grave budgetary deficits accumulated during 1952.

As the occupation ended, many local units surrendered their powers and expenses to the central government. Cities placed themselves under Tokyo's financial control by various subterfuges, by becoming centers of reconstruction or special cities for tourism and culture. The constitutional requirement for a referendum before power could be transferred was met with overwhelming majorities. The lesser villages and town units, numbering over 10,000, sought to merge their administrative functions, and a Town Amalgamation Promotion Law of 1954 reduced the number of self-governing units to one third of their original total.

The need to maintain order in the face of crime and communist violence forced Japan to raise its police force to 125,000 in 1952, compared to 84,000 a decade earlier. This great expense compelled a recentralization of authority. In 1951 the Diet allowed local police units to merge with one another or the National Rural Police, which then numbered 30,000. By 1953 most towns voted to join the National Rural Police, with only 200 units remaining independent. That year, the Yoshida government planned a return to the prewar system, promising that it would not serve as an instrument of political oppression. It proposed a National Security Board, under a cabinet official, to unify the police and fire services; except for the six largest cities, prefectural forces would replace the local police and be responsible to the Board. Fears of a police state led the Socialists to challenge the constitutionality of this plan, but the government went ahead with it nonetheless.

The Courts

In its effort to make the law a weapon of individual freedom instead of suppression, SCAP sponsored an independent judicial system and a new group of constitutionally guaranteed legal and political rights. The Constitution of 1947, the supreme law of the land, ended the bureaucratic control over the courts exercised through the Ministry of Justice. Administrative authority was vested in the hands of the judiciary itself. This consisted of a Supreme Court and a new network of lower courts established by a Diet law of 1947. The Supreme Court has the multiple duties of administering the legal system, deciding final appeals on the basis of the legal issues involved, and exercising the unprecedented function of judicial review or determining the constitutionality of law. Special administrative courts have been abolished, and the regular courts pass on complaints against administrative officials. This more elaborate Anglo-American legal system may be necessary in the light of Japan's recent history, but it has yet to gain the prestige and influence it has earned in the West over the centuries.

Even prosecutors and other attorneys come under the court's rule-making procedures since the abolition of the Ministry of Justice. A new office under the attorney-general handles all cases involving the government, gives legal advice to the executive, and reviews cabinet bills from a legal standpoint. The President of the Supreme Court is designated by the cabinet and officially appointed by the emperor, while his colleagues are chosen directly by the cabinet. Ten of the court's fifteen judges are chosen for their professional skill; the rest may represent other interests. Appointments are for ten years, after which they are subject to popular electoral review.

Legal and Political Rights

In revising their legal statutes, Japanese lawyers retained the Civil and Commercial Codes originally adopted from the West. However, they substituted the individual for the family as the responsible unit in legal contracts. The entire Criminal Code was overhauled and the safeguards granted under Anglo-Saxon law—method of arrest, habeas corpus, treatment in jail, procedural due process under law—were all adopted. The competence of the judges and lawyers will greatly determine the extent to which police habits are altered in practice.

A Bill of Rights in the constitution is more elaborate than its American model. The abolition of rank, with stress instead on equality below the imperial family, is another radical change in Japanese society whose effectiveness is yet to be judged. Traditional political freedoms are now granted without the crippling qualifications found in the 1889 constitution. Additional economic guarantees include right of property, collective bargaining, and free choice of residence and occupation. Social welfare, health, and education benefits are also stressed. Given Japan's present economic condition, the level of well-being implied here represents an ideal aspiration rather than an immediate possibility.

The traditional atmosphere of the police state weighed heavily on the press, which had been under censorship since the Restoration. In 1945 newspapers were given freedom to report on all matters and were admonished to give an accurate account of the past, especially the war years. The number of publications grew at a phenomenal rate, with the result that by 1950 newspapers alone had a daily circulation of more than 50 million. The press adopted a code of ethical reporting and guarded its new freedom zealously. Despite early occupation controls and later anticommunist restrictions, freedom of the press became a reality, as evidenced by the constant criticism of the Yoshida administration and American policy.

Social Reforms

The occupation authorities hoped that democracy would be strengthened over the long haul by an educational system that would inculcate these beliefs in lieu of militant nationalism. The Educational Law of 1947 opened schooling to all on a basis of equality and liberalized chances for advancement to higher education. The minimum period of education was raised from six to nine years. Even more ambitious was the attempt to give a democratic orientation to the entire school system. Adult education and other ways of spreading the new political creed to the family circle and other social units were also encouraged. Decentralization was achieved at first by having each school board elected locally. However, in 1956, partly to reduce the power of the left-oriented Japan Teachers Union, the Diet made these posts appointive, under central authority.

The role of the family involved the question of women's rights, which had reached a low point during the Tokugawa era. The impact of modernization brought about female education, work in factories—under strictly regulated conditions—and the rise of feminist societies. This new trend facilitated SCAP's effort to replace female subordination with an equality guaranteed in the constitution. The right to vote and hold office brought thirty-nine women to the Diet in 1946; since then the novelty has worn off and fewer women vote or seek office. However, this is but one aspect of the reform movement. The Civil Code gave women full rights, the educational law provided for coeducation in the higher schools, and labor standards were to guarantee equal pay for equal work. Women's organizations grew rapidly until there were 10,000 groups claiming 6 million members in all. Feminist leaders are conducting training programs in civic and political affairs to help others overcome their lack of knowledge in these fields.

If successful, reform in this field can make fundamental alterations in the Japanese social fabric, changing the family structure from a feudallike hierarchy to one approximating equality. These advances in turn may help relax the taut formalism that has characterized Japanese modern society. Progress has been greatest in the cities, where agitation for reform developed, but in the countryside the old hierarchy of status persists. With the occupation ended, such groups as the Japanese League of Women Voters and the League of Democratic Women will have to make sustained efforts if they are to maintain and extend their rights. A return of authoritarian rule would mean a sharp reversal of this program, though, ironically, it was the military requirements of the war that brought women more fully into economic and social work, gave them greater economic freedom, and so prepared them for the postwar reforms.

Labor Reforms

The Japanese labor unions had only 100,000 members at their prewar peak, and even this gain was wiped out by the militarist regime. SCAP attempted to create a strong labor force to serve as a democratic counterweight to vested economic interests and to protect labor's rights and enhance its welfare. Old restrictions were eliminated, and the Diet passed a Trade-Union Law in December 1945 modeled on the American pattern. It allowed unionization, collective bargaining, and the right to strike. Working standards, insurance, and the settlement of disputes were brought under public regulation, and a Ministry of Labor was created in 1947. Unions developed rapidly and claimed more than 6 million members in 1949 in 36,000 locals—or 40 per cent of the nonfarming labor force.

This development, however, posed many serious problems. One was communist infiltration, which the democratic unions tried to meet by forming democratization leagues and a National Federation of Industrial Unions. An additional difficulty was the large number of unionized government employees. After a strike was prevented by SCAP in 1948, the National Public Service Law was revised to prohibit strikes by public service workers. In addition, in order to bolster Japan's shaky economic position, workers in private industry were urged not to strike. Because of these and other restrictions, the unions were reduced to 30,000 locals and some 5,000,000 members.

The unions have become deeply involved in politics, especially the Socialist party split, an indication that labor still enjoys considerable freedom. The future of labor will undoubtedly be closely linked to the fate of the democratic left.

Social welfare in the past had remained under the care of one's family or employer, but social services, like wages, had been kept at a minimum so that capitalization and economic expansion could be pursued. Labor, now demanding a change, was aided by SCAP in obtaining health services and a social security program. Wages rose above their depressed prewar levels, standards were enforced with regard to accident prevention and compensation, and unemployment relief was extended. However, labor's well-being still depends on the fate of the Japanese economy as a whole.

Economic Reforms and Prospects

SCAP attempted two major economic reforms—a redistribution of land and the elimination of the zaibatsu. In both activities the Americans sought to end excessive concentration of wealth and bring about a wide diffusion of property. In this way, it was hoped, they would enlarge the middle class and make it a self-reliant defender of the new democratic order. But again they were confronted with the fact that political relationships and attitudes change slowly.

Japanese farming is noted for its efficiency and high-acreage yields, and its industry benefited considerably from its high degree of concentration. Even if carried out with a minimum of friction, the reform program could not guarantee further improvements in production. On the whole, land reform was successful, since the new owners proved able to manage their property and appeared determined to preserve their gains. To diffuse industrial and commercial ownership and to maintain economic efficiency, however, were proved much more difficult. The arrival of the Cold War induced SCAP to curtail its policy in these fields, and the postoccupation government undertook further retrenchments.

Land Reform

Although Japan was far more industrialized than any other Asian state, before 1940 more than 34 million people still depended on farming for a livelihood. Tenancy, which had been mounting since the restoration, encompassed over 70 per cent of the 5 million families engaged in agriculture. A few landlords owned large tracts, but there were many small owners who rented property; led by its wealthier element, the class dominated the countryside, economically and socially. Rent and debt kept peasant income low and curtailed Japan's domestic market for manufactured products. Land reform therefore had the multiple objective of, on the one hand, creating sturdy independent farmers with a stake in democracy, bringing economic relief to the peasants, and removing grievances that the communists skillfully exploited elsewhere in Asia, and, on the other hand, giving Japan the economic impetus to expand production without relying so heavily on foreign markets.

The Japanese government in 1945 did not volunteer to institute reform, and its leaders fruitlessly opposed such a program in later years. In November, 1945, SCAP issued its basic directive on land reform, which resulted in a cabinet bill to take all land over 3 *cho* (7.5 acres) from its owners and distribute it to the peasants over a five-year period. This reform would have meant the sale of 1.5 million of the 2.6 million cho then rented. The Diet raised the minimum owner level to 5 cho, which would have affected less than 1 million cho, leaving unmolested the 940,000 owners of 1-3 cho and the 220,000 owners of 3-5 cho. Only the 106,000 peasants who held 5-10 cho and the 45,000 who had more than 10 cho would have lost property.

SCAP rejected these proposals, and in October, 1946, got an acceptable law that gave land ownership to 3,000,000 of Japan's 3,800,000 tenant families. Under its provisions, absentee owners had to sell their land, and resident owners could keep only the land they worked, plus 1 cho of tenant-operated land, a concession to protect the small owner. This meant a redistribution of 2,000,000 cho of rented land, to be sold to tenants at fixed prices. The remaining 600,000 cho of tenanted land was carefully regulated, with rents set at money values equal to 25 per cent of the rice crop and 15 per cent of dry crops.

The program was carried out during the occupation period. A continuing inflation insured high prices for crops and enabled the new owners to pay their fixed costs of purchase very rapidly. The dispossessed owners complained bitterly over such loss of property without adequate return, but to no avail. Several questions still remained: would the peasant prove a competent owner, would a postoccupation administration try to undo the program, and would the peasant become an active factor in national politics? Because peasants had never been exploited as harshly as in other Asian lands, reform of tenure was no guarantee of better living conditions. Many of them encountered grave difficulties in operating their farms and secretly tried to alienate their land to their former owners in violation of the law. Moreover, they did not demonstrate new political skills. The old parties have not yet felt the need to reorganize and cultivate an independent peasant vote. They work effectively through traditional local leaders, and no new party has arisen to serve the interests of the peasants as the Socialists served the interests of the urban workers.

However, the reform is still a recent achievement; as the peasantry grows accustomed to its new position, it is almost certain to gain political influence. Moreover, the conservative leaders may be compelled to revise their policies, if only to retain the mass rural vote, which is the basis of their majorities. Inasmuch as the dislocating effects of reform have been comparatively mild, the farmers can retain their economic independence if there is adequate government assistance in such fields as rural credit and marketing. All in all, the land reform is the greatest achievement of the occupation and can serve to contrast the American attitude toward the Asian peasantry with the policy of enforced collectivism adopted in the 1950's by Communist China.

Zaibatsu Dissolution

The attempt to dissolve the zaibatsu and establish broader ownership of commercial and industrial property conflicted with established cultural patterns. Industrialization has not yet exerted revolutionary pressure on the Japanese social order, for it did not develop in accordance with the liberal doctrines of Western capitalism. The zaibatsu adhered to the social code of the leaders of the Meiji Restoration: rule by a privileged oligarchy operating through group action and a quasifeudal structure of relationships. Their organizations were governed by absolutism, status, and a hierarchical structure—from the ruling family through the upper administrative levels down to the lowest workers. The Mitsui family, for example, had its own household code of law; it was governed in personal as well as financial matters by a family council, under the direction of the head of the main family (there were eleven branches). At the next level, managers, technicians, and directors owed allegiance to their superiors; the resulting cohesiveness was invaluable in integrating the family's vast enterprises. To join a rival combine was a violation of a most solemn moral code; the Mitsui family in turn was obliged to discover, train, and advance the competent young men in its employ. Salaries were low and the interests of the firm were paramount. The laboring class was included in this great paternalistic order, which often mitigated the harsh operations of the market through bonuses, retirement pay, uneconomical employment in a depression, and sickness benefits.

By 1945, Mitsui employed 2 million and Mitsubishi 1 million in Japan alone. The fourteen combines that dominated commerce and industry avoided friction by cartel arrangements or, more frequently, through informal understandings. Less profitable enterprises were still conducted by home industries and small factories, each producing 27 per cent of all factory-value goods in 1930, but only 18 and 20 per cent, respectively, in 1939. Their decline continued under the pressure of wartime concentration.

A further justification for dissolving the zaibatsu was the belief that they were partly responsible for the rise of militarism and the subsequent policy of expansion. It was hoped that reform would bolster the new party system and enhance individual freedom and self-respect in an environment of open economic competition. Labor and agriculture were also expected to gain in strength from the reduction of zaibatsu power. Defenders of the old order pointed to its record of efficiency and high levels of investment, which gave Japan the highest living standard in the Orient. The reformers countered that wages were kept at excessively low levels and that the fruit of labor's effort was dissipated in a military venture. The Americans therefore proceeded with zaibatsu dissolution and purged all its leaders from their economic posts. Antitrust legislation along American lines was added to reinforce this program.

Each zaibatsu combine had been organized with one holding company directing its vast enterprises. These companies were dissolved in the first and most enduring reform. A Holding Company Liquidation Commission was formed in 1946 to review the securities and properties of the fourteen leading zaibatsu holding companies; in addition, fifty-six persons in ten combines had to yield their securities, which were to be sold to as many different buyers as possible, with the dispossessed being compensated with securities that were nonnegotiable for ten years. Zaibatsu leaders and their executives were forbidden to hold office in sixty-seven holding companies and 4,500 subsidiaries. New business leaders arose, especially when the purge went beyond this Zaibatsu Appointees Law of 1946 and, in 1948–1949, included lesser officials. By 1948, 325 companies were designated as having excessive economic power, and plans were made for their dissolution. A sternly worded Antimonopoly Law of 1947 had already prohibited unreasonable restraint of trade, unfair methods of competition, and interlocking directorates. A Fair Trade Commission was now created to enforce this act and the Trade Associations Law of 1948, which forbade private control of prices and restraint of trade.

Even with the removal of top zaibatsu leaders, their subordinates continued to operate in the traditional manner. A complete purge would have taken over a decade of strict economic controls. A further difficulty was the lack of independent sources of capital to buy the accumulated zaibatsu properties. In 1950–1951 only limited controls were placed on new flotations of stock, and two thirds of the shares issued fell to 10 per cent of the shareholders. On the whole, deconcentration was most substantial in the commercial sphere, less so in industry, and practically without effect in banking because financial institutions were exempted in 1948 from the deconcentration law.

The business community opposed the entire program as unjust and condemned it as imposing wasteful methods of competition on a poor country. It therefore sought state assistance in regaining its privileged status and protection. In 1949 the need to bolster the Japanese economy induced the United States to

285

halt its program of deconcentration after only eleven companies had been broken up and eight more modified. That year the Japanese relaxed the restrictions against collusion in the Antimonopoly Law. In 1953 they permitted trade combinations in time of depression and when deemed essential for greater mechanization of industry. Meanwhile the old leadership, depurged in 1950–1951, returned to posts held by subordinate officials. The government also removed 250 of the 325 companies scheduled for deconcentration and then abandoned the project altogether.

Old zaibatsu trademarks and names, forbidden under the occupation, returned with independence in 1952, and a considerable degree of concentration and merging occurred. Though the old holding companies are gone, personal and traditional ties have proved to be adequate substitutes for cohesion.

Economic Conditions

The devastating effects of the war left Japan with its industry in poor condition, unable to compete effectively in world markets. As in the period after 1918, Japan was slow to rationalize its economic plant; therefore, in 1948–1949, an American mission was brought in to devise a rehabilitation program. It recommended a policy to check inflation, increase production, stabilize wages and prices, and expand exports. Austerity and deflation were the prescribed remedies, and, though the adjustment caused some unemployment, exports rose from an alarming 38 per cent of imports to 60 per cent. Over the following six years, the government sought to improve its domestic and international financial position by reducing the money supply, restricting credit, curtailing public expenses, and restricting imports. It brought moderate pressure on the economy to reduce prices, curtail nonessential consumption, modernize its industrial plant, and cut production costs.

Production in industry began to rise; by the end of the occupation it was above its prewar peak.

	1934–36	1952	1953	1954
Industrial over-all production	100	126.4	155.1	165.2
Mining	100	114.2	122.6	116.6
Durable manufactures	100	171.8	209.9	213.0
Nondurable manufactures	100	104.5	131.8	147.7

SOURCES: Ministry of Finance, *General Survey of the Japanese Economy, 1954* (Tokyo, 1954), p. 100; and Economic Council Board, *Economic Survey of Japan, 1953–1954*, p. 178.

The trend toward modernization and the development of public and private service industries was interrupted by the war, but this too showed a resumption of its earlier pattern by the end of the occupation. The development of Japan's industrial structure is reflected in the following breakdown of its working population according to primary (agriculture, lumber, fishery), secondary (mining, manufacturing, construction), and tertiary (banking, commerce, insurance, transport, public services, etc.) industries.

WORKING POPULATION

(In Thousands)

	Primary	Secondary	Tertiary
1920	14,442	5,576	6,434
1940	14,192	8,419	9,403
1953	17,780	8,950	12,530

Source: *Economic Survey of Japan, 1953–1954*, p. 124.

In 1953 the national income was derived in the following proportions: primary industry, 22.5 per cent; secondary, 31.5 per cent; and tertiary, 46.7 per cent. Unfortunately, underemployment has so characterized the tertiary industries that Japan has never actually experienced a condition of full employment.

Japanese exports expanded considerably by 1954 and, with imports restricted, the unfavorable imbalance fell from $1.1 billion in 1953 to $770 million in 1954. This difference was due to the general expansion of trade among the non-Communist nations, and a partial relaxation of import restrictions in Britain and the rest of the sterling area. However, Japan also employed a "link system" by which raw-material imports were linked to manufactured exports; another "link" was a hidden subsidy to exporters of unprofitable items, by giving them lucrative import licenses. These unfair trade practices have been resented by Britain, which opposed Japan's entry into G.A.T.T., the formal international trade organization of the free world. Textiles still dominate the nation's export commodities, accounting for 40 per cent of total export values in 1953–1954; other leading products were metals, 15 per cent; machinery and transport equipment, 12 per cent; food, 8 per cent; and chemicals and nonmetals, 4 per cent each.

Japan hopes to become the workshop of Asia and supply the new states of South and Southeast Asia with industrial equipment. However, after a good start, Japanese exports declined after 1951, partly because these countries experienced a decline in their own export sales and could not pay for imports. Thus, in 1951, Southeast Asia absorbed $554 million or 41 per cent of Japan's total exports; in 1953 this figure fell to $384 million, or 30 per cent of the total. This area has engaged heavily in foreign trade during modern times and remains a potentially lucrative market.

Yet, even before trouble arose here, Japanese business interests sought to revive and expand trade with China. The Peking government presented a glowing picture of commercial possibilities but insisted on trading in strategic items placed under an embargo by the United Nations. China, the United States, and Britain were the main trading partners of prewar Japan, but in 1935–1936 China took only 17 per cent of Japan's exports—much more than the 0.4 per cent registered in 1953 but nothing like the 40 to 50 per cent attained in 1940. Much of this wartime trade yielded profits because of favorable terms of trade, blocked currencies, and other devices dependent on military superiority. Today, Communist China does not want consumer goods but seeks imports that will strengthen its own industrial base. Moreover, the communists use trade as a political weapon and can turn it on and off at will; their record in this field is not one of steadiness and reliability.

In summary, Japan suffered permanent economic reverses when it lost its colonies and position of dominance in East Asia. It will be compelled to travel further and pay more for imports such as rice from Southeast Asia, and coal and metals from the United States. Nor has trade reached its prewar volume, with exports barely at 50 per cent and imports at 75 per cent of the level reached in the 1930's. However, though this condition is unsatisfactory, Japan has progressed in the field of metal and machinery exports and continues to lead its competitors in products requiring considerable skill and labor. The boom created by the Korean War enabled Japan to accumulate capital, invest in new machinery, and raise its living standards. Industrial production more than doubled, and the value of exports increased by more than 40 per cent between 1950 and 1954; per capita consumption rose by one third in the cities and one half in the countryside. The national income in 1954 was one third higher than before the war so that per capita consumption, even with a population of 88 million, was greater. However, these gains came largely from American aid— $2 billion before 1950 and $3 billion since then through special procurements. Japan is confronted with the tasks of continuing its economic growth after this aid tapers off, averting a major inflation, and reducing the wide gap in its foreign-trade balance.

Foreign Relations

The shock of defeat, disarmament, and a protective foreign occupation all combined to create an air of unreality in the field of foreign policy. Relations with the United States have been most complex because of the intimate tie between the two states and the dependence of one on the other. As a result, American policy has been subject to constant criticism by the Japanese press, pressure groups, and even government officials. This situation is most apparent with regard to treaty relations and the question of rearmament.

Japanese-American Difficulties

Japanese attitudes have often been contradictory. The nation seeks full sovereignty and has chafed under American tutelage and protection. Yet the Japanese were unwilling to prepare their own self-defense or develop a consistent diplomatic position in the Cold War. A policy statement by an American official that the United States considered its position in Japan an overextension of strength created a sensation in Tokyo in 1948. Japanese still fear that the United States has not made a "hard commitment" to defend their country in any emergency. They are also afraid of being quickly conquered by an aggressor at the start of a war. They value both a defense treaty and neutrality and want a defensive army of their own but refuse to shoulder the cost.

Some progress was made by Premier Yoshida in clarifying these issues, but matters have been at a standstill since 1951. During that year, after careful negotiation, a peace treaty was signed, restoring Japanese sovereignty and freeing Japan from any obligation to maintain statutes passed under the occupation. Japan committed itself to the principles of the United Nations charter and accepted the territorial losses outlined in 1945. Japan was also obliged to reach reparation settlements with former enemies and refrain from using force in international relations. However, it was not permitted to provide its own defense. Though occupation forces were to leave ninety days after the treaty took effect, foreign troops could remain in Japan through defense-treaty arrangements. A Security Pact with the United States was in fact signed on the same day as the peace treaty, permitting the Americans to remain in Japan to fight against foreign invasion and aid in subduing major internal disturbances. Japan also agreed not to grant similar rights to a third power.

The American government has since sought to have Japan provide a greater share of its own defense, in order to restore a sense of self-reliance and confidence to Japan and relieve the United States of a thankless burden that only bred antagonism. The Japanese also have sought "full sovereignty," which they interpret to be greater diplomatic freedom and the removal of American military controls, but not extensive rearmament. Premier Yoshida, mindful of constitutional restrictions and the political explosiveness of this issue, moved cautiously in converting the National Police Reserve into a Self-Defense Force. The army received some heavy equipment, the navy acquired old American vessels, and an embryo air force was created. In 1956, the army had 160,000 men organized in six divisions, the navy 19,000 and the air force just over 11,500.

By this time the Americans wisely relaxed their pressure on Japan to rearm, for pressure only strengthened the political opponents of the program. Not even the nationalistic Democratic government was willing to institute a radical change in policy. By 1955, the conservatives held only 65 per cent of the Diet, falling below the two-thirds vote needed to effect a constitutional amendment permitting rearmament. The Hatoyama administration agreed to a modest increase in military strength only after the United States made important concessions to finance the program. The United States reduced Japan's contribution to the cost of keeping American defense forces in Japan from $150 million a year to $105 million. Japan's plans for 1960 included an army of only 180,000 men, an air force of 1,300 planes and a navy of 1,250,000 tons. While visiting Washington in 1955, Foreign Minister Shigemitsu proposed that American troops be evacuated when the army's target was attained. The Americans refused to fix a date for departure, even though they had only about 30,000 ground troops there, for they placed Japan's minimum needs at 350,000 soldiers.

During the following two years, Japan sought to have the 1951 security treaty replaced by a defense arrangement that was not as one-sided in favor of the United States. However, despite its plea for an alliance of "equal partners," Tokyo refused to carry out an agreement to raise its budget on military expenditures. As a result, the planned annual increase of 10,000 men was not provided for in 1957 even though it was the major element in a six-year program to make Japan militarily self-sufficient.

The constitutional fiat against war and armies, the appeal of neutralism, and the division of opinion within conservative ranks have kept Japan from proceeding any further, though a Constitution Research Council was formed in 1956 and authorized to recommend changes in Article 9. Although China declared in 1955 that a minimum of 24 per cent of its national budget had to go for defense, the Japanese finance minister averred that his country could not spend more than 3 per cent of its budget on security. Meanwhile, popular antagonism mounted against the pressure of American troops, demonstrations and petitions greeted atomic artillery in Japan and compelled its withdrawal, villages opposed the extension of American airfields and use of artillery ranges, and American aid as a whole was derided by the Socialist opposition. On the important American base at Okinawa, popular protests were raised in 1956 against the presence of atomic munitions. This was accompanied by calls for the return of administrative rule over the Bonin and Ryukyu Islands to Tokyo. However, the United States continued to recognize Japanese sovereignty over these islands but retained practical control in its own hands. In all, impatience and restiveness continued to characterize Japan's attitude toward the United States.

Negotiations with Soviet Russia

An important factor in Tokyo's negotiations with the United States is Japan's new-found belief in its own strategic value. That the country has strategic value is true to a certain extent, but the Japanese tend to exaggerate its significance. This fact may help to explain why Tokyo has bargained so stiffly with the United States and why it took an extreme position in negotiations with Soviet Russia, during 1955. The Soviet government, having refused to sign the 1951 treaty, sought to normalize relations with Japan at the end of 1954. Premier Hatoyama made great capital of these forthcoming negotiations during the election campaign of February, 1955. The Japanese began to hope for a series of concessions in return for agreeing to re-establish normal relations.

Hence Japan asked for the return of all prisoners still held by Russia; the return of Habomai and Shikotan Islands just off Hokkaido, and the Kuriles and Southern Sakhalin as well; a comprehensive fishing agreement allowing Japan to operate in waters now closed by the Russians; a trade agreement; diplomatic recognition; and support of Japan's entry into the United Nations. The Russians at first refused to discuss anything until diplomatic relations were established. In December, 1955, they even vetoed Tokyo's admittance to the United Nations, causing great popular antagonism to spread throughout Japan. Negotiations continued until October, 1956, when a compromise agreement enabled Premier Hatoyama to fulfill his promise to end the state of war with Russia.

The "peace declaration" then signed differed from a formal peace treaty only in its omission of a territorial settlement. Moscow recognized Japan's future claims to the Habomai and Shikotan islands just off Hokkaido, but would not recognize the additional claims of Kunashiri and Etorofu Islands in the southern Kuriles. Both parties agreed on this basis to continue territorial negotiations in quest of a formal peace treaty. Other provisions of the settlement were an end to the state of war, the re-establishment of diplomatic relations, regard for the principles of the United Nations Charter, Russian support of Japan's entry into the United Nations (achieved in December, 1956), the repatriation of all Japanese citizens still held in the Soviet Union, the enactment of a fishing agreement reached in March, 1956, and a joint promise to strengthen trade relations.

Premier Hatoyama held that this treaty would prove Japan's freedom of action and so reduce its apparent dependence on the United States. This he hoped would reduce friction and irritations in American-Japanese relations. He also added that Japan would not immediately seek normal relations with Peking. With Socialist support, the settlement was handily approved and the aged premier could retire at the end of 1956. His successor, Ishibashi Tanzan, was the first premier chosen in an open party vote. He followed in Hatoyama's footsteps by moderating his critical views of the United States and toning down proposals to trade with Communist China. The pressure of maintaining a balance among the various factions in the conservative camp seemed to preclude any rash departures from this policy.

Conclusion

Japan found itself in a precarious international position because of the sudden rise of Chinese power, its own military weakness, and the scars resulting from its imperial conquests. South Korea bitterly refused all Japanese aid in 1950 and has forbidden Japanese ships to fish within its "Rhee line"—its continental shelf, well out to sea. The nations of Southeast Asia, while less vehement, are also wary of the Japanese, and see in offers of friendship and economic aid a possible means of dangerous infiltration. Commercial rivalry with Britain, the ambivalent relationship of dependence-antagonism with the United States that Japanese policy seems to intensify, and the long tradition of hostility to the Soviet Union combine to present a formidable challenge to Japanese statecraft. The Socialist slogan of neutrality, disarmament, and the elimination of foreign bases is considered too unrealistic to gain majority support, but the governing conservative parties have been unable to develop a concise and forceful alternative course. Behind this lies the question of whether rearmament would bring about a revival of militarism and so destroy democracy from within. National security and the survival of democratic reforms both hang in the balance. A satisfactory resolution of these problems requires statesmanship and patience on the part of Japan and the United States.

Bibliography

JAPAN

The Japanese Setting

GROOT, G. J., *The Prehistory of Japan.* New York: Columbia Univ. Press, 1951.

REISCHAUER, R. K., and J. REISCHAUER, *Early Japanese History.* Princeton: Princeton Univ. Press, 1937.

SANSOM, G. B., *A Short Cultural History of Japan.* New York: Appleton-Century-Crofts, 1943.

ASAKAWA, K., *The Early Institutional Life of Japan: A Study of the Reform of 645 A.D.* London: Probsthain, 1909.

HONJO, E., *The Social and Economic History of Japan.* London: Luzac, 1935.

DENING, W., *Japan in the Days of Yore.* London: Routledge & Kegan Paul, 1906.

SADLER, A. L., *The Maker of Modern Japan: The Life of Tokugawa Ieyasu.* London: Allen & Unwin, 1932.

ANESAKI, M., *Nichiren: The Buddhist Prophet.* Cambridge: Harvard Univ. Press, 1916.

ANESAKI, M., *History of Japanese Religion.* London: Routledge & Kegan Paul, 1930.

CHAMBERLAIN, B. H., *Things Japanese.* 6th ed.; Kobe: Thompson, 1909.

GULICK, S. L., *The Evolution of the Japanese.* Westwood, N. J.: Revell, 1903.

HEARN, L., *Japan: An Attempt at Interpretation.* New York: Macmillan, 1905.

KATO, G., *A Study of Shinto.* Tokyo: Meiji Japan Society, 1926.

NITOBE, I., *Bushido: The Soul of Japan.* New York: Putnam's, 1905.

ELIOT, C., *Japanese Buddhism.* London: Arnold, 1935.

REISCHAUER, A. K., *Studies in Japanese Buddhism.* New York: Macmillan, 1935.

TREWARTHA, G. T., *Japan: A Physical, Cultural and Regional Geography.* Madison: Univ. of Wisconsin Press, 1945.

REISCHAUER, E. O., *The United States and Japan.* Cambridge: Harvard Univ. Press, 1950.

ACKERMAN, E. A., *Japan's Natural Resources and Their Relation to Japan's Economic Future.* Chicago: Univ. of Chicago Press, 1953.

Modernization of Japan

BORTON, H., *Japan's Modern Century.* New York: Ronald, 1955.

QUIGLEY, H. S., *Japanese Government and Politics.* New York: Century, 1930.

YANAGA, C., *Japan since Perry.* New York: McGraw-Hill, 1949.

WALWORTH, A., *Black Ships off Tokyo.* New York: Knopf, 1946.

SANSOM, G. B., *The Western World and Japan,* New York: Knopf, 1950.

HOLTOM, D. C., *Modern Japan and Shinto Nationalism.* 2d ed.; Chicago: Univ. of Chicago Press, 1947.

NORMAN, E. H., *Japan's Emergence as a Modern State.* New York: Inst. of Pacific Relations, 1940.

GUBBINS, J. H., *The Making of Modern Japan.* Philadelphia: Lippincott, 1922.

McLAREN, W. W., *A Political History of Japan during the Meiji Era: 1867–1912.* New York: Scribner's, 1916.

OKUMA, S., *Fifty Years of New Japan.* 2 vols.; London: Smith, Elder, 1910.

IKE, N., *The Beginning of Political Democracy in Japan.* Baltimore: Johns Hopkins Press, 1950.

SCALAPINO, R., *Democracy and the Party Movement in Prewar Japan*. Berkeley: Univ. of California Press, 1950.

NITOBE, I. O., *Japan*. New York: Scribner's, 1931.

LOCKWOOD, W. W., *The Economic Development of Japan*. Princeton: Princeton Univ. Press, 1954.

ALLEN, G. C., *A Short Economic History of Japan: 1867–1937*. London: Allen & Unwin, 1946.

ALLEN, G. C., *Modern Japan and Its Problems*. London: Allen & Unwin, 1928.

KENNEDY, M. D., *The Changing Fabric of Japan*. London: Constable, 1920.

YOUNG, A. M., *Japan in Recent Times*. New York: Morrow, 1929.

OMURA, B., *The Last Genro*. Philadelphia: Lippincott, 1938.

ISHIHASHI, Y., *The Washington Conference and After*. Stanford: Stanford Univ. Press, 1928.

ISHII, K. (ed. and trans. by W. R. LANGDON), *Diplomatic Commentaries*. Baltimore: Johns Hopkins Press, 1936.

DENNIS, A. L. P., *The Anglo-Japanese Alliance*. Berkeley: Univ. of California Press, 1933.

OGAWA, G., *Conscription System in Japan*. New York: Oxford Univ. Press, 1921.

Expansionist Japan

BALLARD, G. S., *The Influence of the Sea on the Political History of Japan*. New York: Dutton, 1921.

FALK, E.. *Togo and the Rise of Japanese Sea Power*. New York: Longmans, 1936.

JAMES, D. H., *The Rise and Fall of the Japanese Empire*. New York: Macmillan, 1951.

TAKEUCHI, T., *War and Diplomacy in the Japanese Empire*. Garden City: Doubleday, 1935.

JANSEN, M., *The Japanese and Sun Yat-sen*. Cambridge: Harvard Univ. Press, 1954.

JONES, F. C., *Japan's New Order in East Asia*. New York: Oxford Univ. Press. 1954.

REISCHAUER, R. K., *Japan: Government-Politics*. New York: Nelson, 1939.

MAKI, J., *Japanese Militarism: Its Cause and Cure*. New York: Knopf, 1945

COLGROVE, K., *Militarism in Japan*. Boston: World Peace Foundation, 1936.

ALLEN, G. C., *Japan: The Hungry Guest*. New York: Dutton, 1938.

ROYAMA, M., *Foreign Policy of Japan: 1914–1939*. Tokyo: Inst. of Pacific Relations, 1941.

LORY, H., *Japan's Military Masters*. New York: Viking, 1943.

TOLISCHUS, O., *Tokyo Record*. New York: Harcourt, Brace, 1943.

BORTON, H., *Japan since 1931: Its Social and Political Development*. New York: Inst. of Pacific Relations, 1940.

BYAS, H., *Government by Assassination*. New York: Knopf, 1942.

DEPARTMENT OF EDUCATION, JAPAN (ed. by R. K. HALL, trans. by J. O. GAUNTLETT), *Kokutai no Hongi*. Cambridge: Harvard Univ. Press, 1949.

HALL, R. K., *Shushin: The Ethics of a Defeated Nation*. New York: Teachers College, 1949.

EMBREE, J., *Suyemura: A Japanese Village*. Chicago: Univ. of Chicago Press, 1939.

YOUNG, A. M., *Imperial Japan*. New York: Morrow, 1938.

YOUNG, A. M., *The Rise of a Pagan State: Japan's Religious Background*. New York: Morrow, 1934.

SCHUMPETER, E. B., and others, *The Industrialization of Japan and Manchuria, 1930–1940*. New York: Macmillan, 1940.

COHEN, J. B., *Japan's Economy in War and Reconstruction*. Minneapolis: Univ. of Minnesota, 1949.

KASE, T., *Journey to the Missouri*. New Haven: Yale Univ. Press, 1950.

KATO, M., *The Lost War*. New York: Knopf, 1946.

AZIZ, M. A., *Japan's Colonization and Indonesia*. The Hague: Nijhoff, 1955.

ELSBREE, W. J., *Japan's Role in Southeast Asian Nationalist Movements: 1940–1945*. Cambridge: Harvard Univ. Press, 1946.

BUTOW, R., *Japan's Decision to Surrender*. Stanford: Stanford Univ. Press, 1954.

REEL, A., *The Case of General Yamashita*. Chicago: Univ. of Chicago Press, 1949.

FUCHIDA, M., and M. OKUJIMA, *Midway*. Annapolis: Naval Institute, 1955.

SAKAMAKI, K., *I Attacked Pearl Harbor*. New York: Associated Press, 1949.

HACHIYA, M., *Hiroshima Diary*. Chapel Hill: Univ. of N. C. Press, 1955.

HERSEY, J., *Hiroshima*. New York: Knopf, 1946.

UNITED STATES ARMY AIR FORCE, *Mission Accomplished: Interrogation of Japanese Industrial, Military and Civil Leaders of World War II*. Washington: Government Printing Office, 1946.

See also Hearings before the Joint Committee on the Investigation of the Pearl Harbor Attack, 79th Cong. 1st Sess. (Washington: Government Printing Office, 1945), and the *Report* of the Joint Committee (1946); and

The International Military Tribunal for the Far East for translations of Japanese documents, memoirs, and affidavits.

The Occupation and After

QUIGLEY, H. S., and J. E. TURNER, *The New Japan*. Minneapolis: Univ. of Minnesota Press, 1956.

MARTIN, E. M., *The Allied Occupation of Japan*. Stanford: Stanford Univ. Press, 1948.

FEARY, R., *The Occupation of Japan: Second Phase*. New York: Macmillan, 1950.

G.H.Q., SCAP, CIES, *Education in the New Japan*. 2 vols.; Tokyo, 1948.

HALL, R., *Education for a New Japan*. New Haven: Yale Univ. Press, 1949.

BALL, W. M., *Japan, Enemy or Ally?* New York: John Day, 1948.

WAKEFIELD, H., *New Paths for Japan*. New York: Oxford Univ. Press, 1948.

LEWE VAN ADUARD, E. J., *Japan from Surrender to Peace*. The Hague: Nijhoff, 1953.

U.S. DEPARTMENT OF STATE, *The Far Eastern Commission: A Study in International Cooperation, 1945–1952*. Far Eastern Series 60; Washington: Government Printing Office, 1953.

GAYN, M., *Japan Diary*. New York: Sloan, 1948.

TEXTOR, R., *Failure in Japan*. New York: John Day, 1951.

WILDES, H., *Typhoon in Tokyo*. New York: Macmillan, 1954.

TRACY, H., *Kakemono*. New York: Coward-McCann, 1951.

GIBNEY, F., *Five Gentlemen of Japan*. New York: Farrar, Straus & Cudahy, 1953.

CLIFTON, A. S., *Time of the Fallen Blossoms*. New York: Knopf, 1951.

HARING, D. G. (ed.), *Japan's Prospects*. Cambridge: Harvard Univ. Press, 1946.

MINISTRY OF FOREIGN AFFAIRS, TOKYO, *Provisional Verbatim Minutes of the Conference for the Conclusion and Signature of the Treaty of Peace with Japan*. Tokyo, 1951.

STOETZEL, J., *Without the Chrysanthemum and the Sword*. New York: Columbia Univ. Press, 1955.

BROWN, D., *Nationalism in Japan*. Berkeley: Univ. of California Press, 1955.

PRICE, W., *Journey by Junk*. New York: John Day, 1953.

MISHIMA, S., *The Broader Way: A Woman's Life in the New Japan*. New York: John Day, 1953.

CRESSY, E., *Daughters of Changing Japan*. New York: Farrar, Straus & Cudahy, 1955.

MATSUOKA, Y., *Daughter of the Pacific*. New York: Harper, 1952.

HEWES, L., *Japan: Land and Men*. Ames: Iowa State College Press, 1955.

GRAD, A., *Land and Peasant in Japan*. New York: Inst. of Pacific Relations, 1952.

BISSON, T., *Zaibatsu Dissolution in Japan*. Berkeley: Univ. of California Press, 1954.

COLBERT, E., *The Left Wing in Japanese Politics*. New York: Inst. of Pacific Relations, 1952.

FARLEY, M., *Aspects of Japan's Labor Problems*. New York: Inst. of Pacific Relations, 1950.

SWEARINGER, R., and P. LANGER, *Red Flag in Japan*. Cambridge: Harvard Univ. Press, 1952.

SMITH, T. C., *Political Change and Industrial Development in Japan*. Stanford: Stanford Univ. Press, 1955.

ECONOMIC PLANNING BOARD, *Economic Survey of Japan*. Tokyo, annual.

PART FOUR **India and**
Pakistan

11 *Hindu India*

The sudden emergence of India as an independent and powerful state was a most unexpected occurrence in world affairs after 1945. This development would appear perfectly natural for such a large and strategically located state were it not for the contrast with its passive international status during the long period of British rule. Because India must now play a pivotal role in the critical ideological and power struggles going on in Asia, it is essential that we understand the country's history and the political forces at work today in this subcontinent.[1]

That independence in 1947 was accompanied by a violent act of partition immediately raised doubts concerning the political stability and security of the new states of India and Pakistan. Clearly, the complex nature of modern Indian politics can be analyzed only in terms of certain fundamental considerations. What is the strength of this civilization that enabled it to rise to prominence immediately after two centuries of European rule? What other points of tension and disunity exist besides the Moslem-Hindu clash? How do the unifying forces compare in power with these disruptive tendencies and to what degree have they fostered social cohesion? Only with these considerations in mind can questions regarding Indian political stability, contemporary foreign policy, and ideological orientation be adequately answered.

One of India's outstanding characteristics is the bewildering and complex array of peoples and cultures that seem to have made the subcontinent a vast container of hopelessly divergent groups. The land was for centuries fragmented into small, politically independent states, constantly at war with one another. Under these conditions, not only was cultural integration retarded, but racial fusion was so incomplete that even today in India seven distinct physical types can be discerned.

Yet, however difficult it may be to perceive at first glance, India did evolve a great and distinctive civilization with a remarkable degree of continuity. Moreover, this culture, as far as its concepts and principles are concerned, was developed in relative isolation from the outside world. In evaluating the factors that contributed toward making India a "cosmos in itself," major emphasis must be placed on the Hindu religion, both as a philosophy and system of

---

[1] For maps of the Indian subcontinent see pages 327, 368, and 377.

values, and on the social and institutional aspects that embody these beliefs.

India has been occupied by three cultures—the Dravidian, which prevailed until approximately 1500 B.C.; the Aryan, which conquered northern India after that date and held political sway until 1000 A.D.; and the Moslem, whose invasions began at that time and led to Islamic domination of India until the British arrived in the eighteenth century. It was during the era of Aryan rule that modern Indian civilization acquired its unique form. But our attention must first be centered on the initial major clash—between Dravidian and Aryan—and the civilization that evolved from this struggle. The impact of the Moslems and the British will then be examined.

The demarcation proposed is not simply one of chronological convenience, for out of the Aryan invasion there arose a Hindu India with a way of life that later conquerors modified but could not fundamentally alter. The history of the Dravidian peoples who occupied India is as yet unclarified. Archaeological research, however, has uncovered a highly developed "Harappa culture," which existed in pre-Aryan days along the Indus River in western India and is presumed to have been under Dravidian influence, at least in its later stages. It was a politically integrated, urbanized civilization, with a form of writing as yet undeciphered. It contrasted sharply with that of the Aryan invaders, who were a rural people, organized along tribal lines, with little material culture. The Dravidians, defeated in battle, were driven out of the Indus valley about 1200 B.C. During the next five centuries the Aryans advanced eastward to the Ganges-Jumna river valley and eventually drove the Dravidians to the south below the Narbada River.

In the Ganges-Jumna region, where Aryan control was not yet predominant, the two cultures fused and developed into a common Hindu civilization. The area itself is known as historic Hindustan. It is difficult to estimate the exact proportion of the contributions made by the two elements, but it seems clear that the Dravidian share was much larger than had been assumed. It is probable that many of the religious symbols of worship and perhaps India's unique social institutions, like the caste and the joint family, can be traced to the pre-Aryan settlers. Of the great philosophical and theological contributions of Hinduism, it can be said that these developed in India under the stimulus of close contact between Aryan and native elements in the centuries after 1000 B.C.

Factors Causing Diversity

Whatever may be said of India's common culture and its source of origin, the elements that made for diversity are of vital significance and therefore must be carefully considered. One factor was the geography of the subcontinent, which encouraged the development of regional differences. Another factor was the variety of races, for this hospitable terrain continued to receive numerous peoples who came from Central Asia in recurrent waves of folk movements or invasions, bringing their divergent languages and customs with them. Finally, there was the decentralization of government. The Aryan rulers proved unable to develop a strong political and administrative structure and so failed to provide the governing hand needed to check the natural centrifugal tendencies of these divergent groups.

The Geographic Setting

It would be an oversimplification to classify the physical background simply as a contributor to diversity. The very nature of India's location made it literally a geographic expression—a large peninsula whose headlands in contact with the rest of Asia were well protected by natural barriers. To the north lay the protective shield of the great Himalaya Mountains, flanked on each side by lesser ranges. In the west, smaller ranges, backed by desert lands, made that sector difficult to penetrate, although accessible mountain passes existed. The eastern frontier province of Assam was a backward region, almost isolated because of its dense jungle terrain. The sea was an avenue for commerce and Indian colonization efforts, but remained a quiescent military frontier until the Western powers arrived after 1500.

Despite these natural endowments, India was repeatedly invaded by peoples from Central Asia and military adventurers from Persia and Afghanistan who came across the famed northwest mountain passes. Still, this geographic entity seemed to "seal in" the various peoples who entered it, and enabled the Hindu civilization to develop in its own fashion without intimate contact with other cultures. Moreover, the Indian terrain itself offered no insuperable obstacles to the movement of peoples or the flow of ideas within its own frontiers. The Hindu way of life could be spread inexorably over the entire subcontinent, a process which today is in its last stages of penetration into the unattractive jungle and hilly regions of the land.

The geographic pattern was an obstacle to political integration, that aspect of culture which in Indian ingenuity and creativity were at a low ebb. The political center of gravity lay in the great northern plains fed by the Indus River system to the west and the Ganges-Jumna region to the east. Invaders from beyond the mountains always found the first and major task to be the subjugation of the north, for the path to power lay in this achievement.

The region below these great river valleys presents the first physical hindrance to a southward movement within India. This area, where the peninsula proper begins to jut out into the sea, is the Deccan. Its northern reaches contain the Vindhya Hills and the Narbada River, barriers reinforced by hills and jungles cutting across the peninsula in an east-west direction. Conquerors from the north were not stopped here, but the increased effort these obstacles demanded may well have been crucial at various times in Indian history. Since the extreme south is an open region, with a central plateau sloping down to the sea in both the east and west, many northern rulers were tempted to extend their rule over the entire subcontinent. Actual invasion often proved less of a problem than the burden of maintaining a garrison there in order to retain control of the region. Such efforts invariably strained the resources of the home base and led to a collapse of the northern empire itself.

The sharpest cultural differences within India have been those distinguishing north and south. The languages, races, literature, and music of the south were expressed in markedly different forms and content, a development traceable to specific historic circumstances. Yet the persistence of these variations is due in good part to the degree of separation caused by topography and distance.

Within the major geographic divisions lies a multitude of physical subdivisions that can be distinguished as regional entities. These territorial pockets proved to be an admirable environment for the nurturing and propagation of different culture traits in each region. The protective environment served to safeguard the individuality of a people who brought its own peculiar characteristics to India; it also encouraged the development of new traits within one element of a larger common group. Thus almost all the major provinces of India have developed their own distinctive characteristics. The Punjabi, Bengali, Rajputi, Tamilians, and Gujarati—to name some of the outstanding ones—have identifiable traits that stem primarily from the regional nature of their development.

Invasion; Racial Differences

The compartmental, though permeable, nature of India's topography served as a passive, friendly setting for the many different peoples who entered the land. One of the decisive features in the growth of Indian civilization has been the recurrent appearance of invaders, their clash with the native culture, and the very difficult process of resolving the disharmonies thus created. The clearest evidence of the scope of these invasions is found in the bewildering assortment of racial types existing in India today. The three basic races of mankind are represented. Negroid peoples evidently occupied the land when the Caucasoid invaders mingled with them in varying degree; the Mongoloid element has been the most recent arrival, filtering in from the north.

When the Dravidians entered India, they apparently intermarried with Negroid aborigines and, although their more advanced culture prevailed, they acquired some of the physical characteristics of the earlier inhabitants. Though the lighter Aryan invaders despised the Dravidians, for their dark color as well as for their "false gods," some further fusion of peoples and races did take place. The result is sometimes classified as a "Hindu type"—short and slender, dark of skin—yet with "white" facial characteristics, described as a Caucasoid peculiar to India.

The effects of this process are reflected in contemporary efforts to classify the major physical types in India. The Dravadians, short and dark, dominate most of the peninsula in the south. The Aryo-Dravidians are found, as would be expected, in Hindustan—the region east of the Punjab, along the mid-Ganges, the United Provinces, and Bihar. The Mongoloids, including the

Gurkas from Nepal, have settled in the northern mountain regions, and the Mongolo-Dravidians are located to the east of Hindustan, in Bengal and Assam. At the northwestern end is a relatively recent arrival—a Caucasoid type similar to the Europeans; these tall and fair Indo-Aryans are found in the frontier mountain region, Kashmir, and the Punjab.[2]

These "races" retained their distinctive features because they were relatively isolated. Once a group settled in an area, it found little reason to undertake further migration. Poor communications and a subsistence economy offered little incentive to travel, save during famines when sporadic movements occurred. Still, occasional intermarriage blurred the boundary lines between races, and it is likely that there were more numerous racial categories in the past than there are today.

It would have required complete social freedom to achieve a fusion of races. Yet the conscious human direction exercised in this matter pointed toward an opposite goal. Unlike the Chinese, who fostered the equality and homogeneity of peoples willing to accept their classical culture, the Indians based their Hindu civilization on physical separation and group inequality. This was expressed in the caste system, which gave religious sanction to the maintenance of marriage taboos and prohibitions even against ordinary social contacts with other castes. Whatever unifying effect Hinduism had in its other manifestations, its social philosophy was firmly based on the perpetuation of social stratification.

A Diversity of Tongues

The existence of many languages in India reflects the phenomenon of clashing cultures and has actively contributed to the continuance of group antipathy. There are five major language groups, of which only the Dravidian and Aryan are currently important, although over 200 different languages and dialects can be listed as separate entities. One lesser group—the Munda—may have preceded the others, but it has now been pushed into the hilly parts of east-central India, where its speakers have remained in a tribal state with a low level of economic development. The other secondary groups are Khasi, in the Assam jungles, and Tibeto-Chinese in the fringe and mountain lands. These, along with some Dravidian elements, generally occupy the agriculturally less productive land.

Although pushed out of north India by the Aryan invaders, the Dravidian languages, which are quite different from the Aryan, prevailed in the south. These Dravidian languages themselves are closely related, each has a well-developed literature, the two leading tongues being Tamil, in the Madras region, and Telegu, in the nearby Andhra country and parts of the former state of Hyderabad. Overseas commercial and colonizing ventures have stemmed

---

[2] The two other racial groups are Turko-Iranians in the northwest and Scytho-Dravidians in the upper part of the Deccan east of the Indus River.

from these regions. The Dravidian sense of resentment against the Aryan-speaking peoples stems from many historical and social sources. Yet there is little doubt that the sharp language diversity has given each group a strong sense of separate identification and has served as a protective shield behind which other divisive elements could be bred.

Hostility does not simply move along Aryan-Dravidian lines, for there is considerable tension between Tamil and Telegu elements today. The latter were fearful of remaining under the political control of their more powerful Tamil neighbors and after independence successfully demanded the creation of a separate Andhra State out of the contiguous Telegu-speaking areas. The vehemence of this demand can be measured by the government's acquiescence, even though this concession might encourage separatist tendencies in other parts of India.

The Aryan tongues, which became the dominant languages, are of Indo-European derivation. Each tribal group among the Aryan invaders had its own tongue, though all were somewhat closely related. Sanskrit, which was one of these languages, was standardized in the Hindu religious scriptures and so became the common tongue of the Aryan culture. As the chief classical language of Hindu India, it was the one in which intellectual theories and spiritual beliefs came to be expressed. It quickly became the means of communication among the learned, and, as Hinduism spread into Dravidian lands, the educated classes there also used Sanskrit. As a result, it served as a vital means of diffusing a common concept of life throughout India.

As the spoken Aryan tongues continued to evolve, Sanskrit became a dead language, but it still retained its importance in learned circles of orthodox Hinduism. Moreover, the Aryan languages all modeled their own forms on Sanskrit and used it as a reservoir for words. Today they are inter-related in a way similar to the European Romanic languages.

The Indian government at present is committed to adopting Hindi, spoken in the Hindustan region, as the official state language. This effort of a central administration to assert a unifying influence is understandable, but it runs counter to the interest and pride of the other Aryan language groups—Bengali, Punjabi, Gujarati, and Rajputi, among others—as well as the Dravidians. Accommodation on this score will at best be a painful and slow process.

The Political Framework

India's failure to attain political and administrative stability during the 2,500 years between the Aryan and Moslem conquests was a major cause of the persistence of so many regional, linguistic, and racial differences. Such weakness at the center prevented its rulers from fostering the degree of uniformity essential for the further consolidation of their power. The Indian political scene thus presented a continuously changing array of independent princedoms, and the inability to develop a large, stable empire was to plague the land for millennia.

An explanation of this failure in terms of the physical environment—size of the land, low level of technology, and undeveloped administrative techniques—is insufficient in the light of China's experience. It is true that India was an inviting target for invaders who could seriously handicap efforts at political unity, but it was the political weakness itself that made the act of invasion so simple and attractive. The basic causes of the country's instability must also be traced to an absence of originality of thought in the fields of political theory and organization.

India did not develop the concept of a single, "universal" empire such as that evolved by the historically oriented Chinese, who considered cultural and political development as two sides of the same coin. There was no strong belief in the principle of a single rule over mankind, though Indian political thought did accept a universal emperor (Chakravartin, or wheel-turner), and many princes aspired to this position. However, its occupant was not to dominate in any real sense but to be an overlord who received tribute and maintained a vague suzerainty over local rulers. The rulers, in turn, trying to exercise unimpaired control over their lands, used the concepts of divine right or omnipotence of kings to bolster their assertion of complete sovereignty over their own realms.

The evolution of political organization in Aryan-controlled India was a difficult process. The original tribal structure of the conquerors gradually developed into the more advanced forms of kingship, republic, and oligarchy, with the kingship eventually predominating. Although the larger kingdoms absorbed some of the lesser states, there were still sixteen kingdoms and other lesser principalities in North India alone as late as the seventh century A.D. These states warred constantly on one another and so were more easily exposed to attacks from abroad; they were also quite vulnerable to internal social disorders and political rebellions.

There were only two notable exceptions to this dreary chronicle of Indian political history. The Maurya (321–237 B.C.) and Gupta (318/9–500 A.D.) dynasties established effective rule over wide areas and maintained stable administrations for more than one generation. However, they held power for relatively short periods and were so widely separated in time that their cumulative effect on Indian political habits and thought was slight. With a political pattern the reverse of China's—dynastic interludes in a mainstream of political chaos—the structures they created were dissolved by the harsh competition for power and survival among their successors.

The Mauryan empire rose shortly after the abortive conquest of northwest India by Alexander the Great in 327–325 B.C. Greek culture did not make more than a marginal impression on India after the conqueror's voluntary withdrawal, despite the persistence of Hellenistic kingdoms and culture patterns in Central Asia during the following centuries. One effect of Alexander's exotic incursion, however, was the collapse of many small Indian states. Chandragupta Maurya was able to seize this opportunity to bring unity to northern India. The founder gave his empire its distinguishing characteristics, although it reached its territorial zenith under the great Asoka (274–237 B.C.), whose rule was colored by a strong attachment to Buddhism. The regime was heavily centralized and impinged severely on the ordinary routine of life in the towns, in a manner reminiscent of what archaeologists infer was the pattern of rule in the pre-Aryan Harappa culture. A battery of restrictive orders extended from curfew laws and price regulations to the control of female morals. A loyal, highly trained, and well-paid bureaucracy carried on government work and effectively collected land revenue from the peasantry. Such stringent rule required harsh restrictions on personal freedom and a well-developed espionage network to function properly. This may well have been the price required for the establishment of dynamic political rule. Yet the regime collapsed after Asoka's death. Even so, the Maurya dynasty was atypical because it lasted three generations.

The millenium that began around 600 B.C. was the approximate era in which the Hindu culture evolved into its modern form. A political highpoint in its late stages was the Gupta dynasty, founded by another Chandragupta in 318/9 A.D. This regime was less despotic than the Mauryan and controlled affairs with a looser rein. Its official chain of authority extended down to the village headman, though a degree of local autonomy was retained. With the collapse of this dynasty around 500 A.D., India did not experience another empire of note in pre-Moslem times. In fact, it was not until 500 years after the Moslems appeared, in the sixteenth century, 1,000 years after the Guptas, that the Moguls established the third major Indian empire.

Although the Aryans had arrived 2,500 years earlier, North India was as far from unity in 1000 A.D. as it ever had been. Hindu India was to pay a great price for its inability to attain a higher level of organization, or even to unite in the face of the Moslem threat. Mutual suspicion among Hindus was so intense that even after the nature of this new foe had become common knowledge, they still failed to coordinate their defenses. At the famous Battle of Tarain in 1192 A.D., this lack of cooperation doomed Hindu rule and ensured Moslem domination over northern India.

The Administrative Pattern

Government rule in this type of political climate suffered from a backwardness in such public services as irrigation, communications, and famine relief. The administrative apparatus was devoted primarily to revenue collection, though efficient dynasties cut deeply into the autonomy enjoyed by villages in other administrative matters. This eclipse was always temporary. Village authority was eventually restored when the higher political order collapsed.

The original nature of land ownership in India is not clear, but some of the attributes of title, if not possession itself, were vested in the ruler. The king was entitled to a fixed share of the crop, at a minimum of one sixth to one quarter, payable in money or in kind. The state was supposed to guarantee peace and security in return, but to the peasant it was simply a drain that taxed his efforts. The more efficient governments established higher and more regular collections. When other imposts and duties were added, and corrupt officials tried to exact profits for themselves, it was little wonder that the cultivator preferred a weak government that left him alone in return for minimum payments.

The absence of a sense of obligation and the lack of administrative skill account for the meager record of public service. Communication facilities could not support even a moderate level of traffic, and trade in commonly used goods was impossible. On the whole, only the rich and the ascetic traveled, and the only commodities worth shipping were luxury items of small bulk and high value. Each area had to be self-sufficient, for even in time of famine a neighboring province could not be counted on for aid. Such a communications system weakened the hold of a government over its outlying districts and encouraged provincial administrators in their inclination to break away from the center.

Irrigation facilities were most inadequate for a community so overwhelmingly dependent on the land. Even a vigorous ruler's action was impaired by the lack of cooperation among states and the likelihood that his successor would let the work fall into disrepair. Flood control was also characterized by sporadic efforts, although this too bore directly on the problem of famine prevention.

Famine was an ever-present menace, because a crop failure was bound to occur in some region even if an India-wide drought was unlikely. Such local crises meant starvation in this politically fragmented land. If a government had taxed the people oppressively, then even a reserve supply to cushion the blow would be absent. The rulers recognized their obligation to undertake preventive and relief measures, but, even under the great Mogul emperors, these were pitifully inadequate. Assistance was usually confined to the capital city and a few large towns, and even then was often administered only in the presence of the emperor.

The difference between the Chinese and Indian attitude toward the bureaucratic apparatus can be seen in the contrasting position of the Confucian scholar and the Brahmin. Unlike the Chinese scholar to whom the government service was a rewarding career, the Brahmins, who were the priestly class in the Aryan structure, remained outside the government. As Hindu rulers came to assert the divine right of kings, the Brahmins became more resentful and hostile, and this accelerated their separation from political affairs. The Brahmins focused their influence and leadership on the religious and social aspects of Indian life, and eventually became the backbone of the Hindu cultural order. As the civilization matured and came under foreign political control, 'it was in the Brahmin-led fields of social organization and religious-philsophical outlook that India displayed its greatest continuity and strength.

The Development of Indian Religion

The strongest sense of Indian unity and originality is firmly rooted in the Hindu religion, which served as an inspirational source for the powerful sanctions and impulses needed to develop a unique form of society. A common way of life was imprinted through this medium on hundreds of thousands of widely separated and, at times, otherwise totally unrelated villages. Yet it must be recalled that the religion accepted and even regulated and reinforced certain differences that existed among the Indian people. Though the result was a highly stratified society, it proved to be one with a tremendous capacity for resilience and survival.

The central importance of religion was reflected by its presence in almost all aspects of life. The entire social order, the economic structure, and all crises in the life cycle were anchored in religious precepts. Law was so closely related to religion that no clear distinction was made between secular and sacred law. The great legal works—the Shastras—were considered to be divinely inspired, and obedience to legal ordinances became a religious obligation and not merely a social duty. Except in the south, where secular literature enjoyed an independent growth, most written works were devotional. A similar concentration of attention was found in the fields of architecture and sculpture.

The evolution of this all-pervading religion, marked by dramatic fusions of cultures and the development of philosophical concepts, demonstrated the powerful, spongelike absorptive capacity of Hinduism. The early religion of the Aryan conquerors, as revealed in their great religious tracts—the four Vedas—was little more than a personification of the powers of nature. The most important work, the Rig Veda, was formulated around 1200 B.C.; it is thus perhaps the oldest text in the Indo-European language. As this Vedic religion developed, it became highly ritualistic, with many fire sacrifices. However, it was capable of encompassing a vast complex of cults from non-Aryan sources and giving them new form within the context of its own structure. The continuity between the pre-Aryan Harappa and the historic Hindu culture can be judged from the presence in both of such sacred symbols as the bull and the pipal tree, the practice of yoga, and the importance of phallic and mother-goddess worship. It is also quite possible that the caste system and other unique cultural features originated in the extremely rigid Harappa culture that the Aryans overwhelmed. The conquerors, at the eastern fringe of the Indo-European peoples, may have adopted sharp class distinctions in order to bolster their own exposed and isolated position.

The cold, formalistic nature of this religion, as well as its Brahmin priesthood, underwent considerable criticism as Aryan rule became established over north India. It was through the interaction between the old and the new cultures, especially in the east along the Ganges-Jumna where Aryan influence was not yet so overpowering, that the great Hindu beliefs took their modern form. The eastern part of Hindustan, Bihar, witnessed this effort in its most intense form, as the non-Aryan leaders of the local society struggled for a social position commensurate with their wealth and power. Significantly, attention was directed toward the realm of the religious and philosophical concepts.

The orthodox elements continued to recognize the Vedas and the sacrifices as divinely inspired, but rigorously challenged the priesthood's claim to intellectual supremacy by mere fact of birth. More significant was the development of speculative texts—the Upanishads—which marked a considerable advance in religious philosophy. The concept of the unity of the universe was set forth, with the Hindu theories of the soul, immortality, and the immanence of God. These achievements placed Hinduism among the world's most advanced, speculative religions.

The Challenge of Buddhism

However, the powerful religious movement which reached its culmination around 600 B.C. also brought forth Buddhism, a great challenge to Hindu supremacy. Together with other heterodox faiths, it rejected the authority of the Vedas and the caste system, and taught the ethical principle of noninjury to living beings (ahimsa).[3] Its warmer, more humanistic outlook won it widespread support, especially among non-Aryans. During the ensuing centuries, it spread over all India, posing a formidable threat to Hinduism for more than 1,000 years. It had the support of powerful social elements and ruling princes, including the great Maurya emperor Asoka, but it never succeeded in becoming the dominant religion. When the Moslems arrived, Buddhism was already in its last stages of decay as a force in Indian spiritual life; today it has no more than a million adherents in its homeland.

This phenomenon can be explained partly by the more tenacious and adaptable nature of Hinduism, which was able to incorporate the more popular aspects of Buddhism within its own firmer social and religious structure. This task of absorption was facilitated by the basic similarity between the two faiths: both leaned heavily on the doctrine of reincarnation and maintained an essentially pessimistic philosophy of life. The great Buddhist contribution was an endeavor to break the cycle of endless rebirths—so painful because to exist meant to suffer. In Buddhism, life and suffering were inseparable, and desire was the cause of suffering; therefore one could snap the chain of life cycles by eliminating desire. Buddhism presented a way of life geared toward this objective, which would then enable one to reach nirvana—the void in which one was released from the tragic consequence of birth and rebirth.

Hinduism adopted the popular principle of nonviolence, which became so deeply rooted in Indian tradition and played such an important political role in the twentieth-century independence movement. In both its religious and social manifestations, this principle signified a major change in the philosophical outlook of the Aryans from their early warlike attitudes, as reflected in the Rig Veda. Hinduism also incorporated the doctrine of escape from the life cycle, on the grounds that existence was mere illusion. This belief gave it an otherworldly bias, though such an outlook remained but one aspect of the religion.

Hinduism thus modified its belief pattern and structure so that it could vie

---

[3] This doctrine was vigorously propounded in the Jain religion, which still persists in India today, with 1,500,000 followers.

in popularity with rival religions; in this way it diminished the attraction of these new faiths. However, it never yielded on any critical matter to the extent of surrendering its individuality. Its combination of tenacity and flexibility may account for its success in India; it may explain also why Hinduism was localized there. Buddhism evidently had a more universal appeal, for it served as the vehicle through which India made its most profound and lasting impression on other lands of the Far East.

The Basic Concepts of Hinduism

The otherworldly aspect of Hinduism is found in Atman or Brahman—the absolute truth, consisting of pure existence and bliss unbounded by time or space. This highest religious level, attained by a few ascetics, or holy men, is based on the doctrine that life is an illusion (maya), and that man's major task is to break out of this cycle of misery. In actual practice the attainment of Atman is considered far beyond ordinary man, who is more concerned with the questions of material happiness and reverence for his local gods. Hence the religion devotes considerable attention to regulating the practical affairs of life.

Here Hinduism differs sharply from Western beliefs, which hold that life on earth is the vital testing ground of one's eternal fate. To the Hindu, a single existence is far less important because one goes through a series of life cycles. The Hindu holds that conduct during previous lives inexorably determines one's present position in society. This is the doctrine of moral consequences (karma), and it is clearly the moral and religious justification of the caste system. Whatever caste one is in expresses the result of a cumulative past record. A clean slate can never be achieved, and any one existence merely adds its weight to the total picture. The lowly are thus given hope that exemplary behavior will mean a gradual improvement in future lives, and the high-born are warned that improper deportment will also bring its just desserts in the next incarnation.

Just as karma explains why one is in a specific caste, dharma tells what the duties of this position are. One's future is decided on the basis of how well these caste functions, covering a multitude of daily routine activities, are executed. In this way religious sanctions are tightly woven into the pattern of everyday existence. It is also believed that the Creator and all creation are one and that, since God exists in every person, God and the soul of man are identical. In this sense, the individual is of considerable importance, for only by his own worship can man attain his religiously ordained goals.

On a less metaphysical level, inhibitions concerning touch and food, as well as the taking of life, occupy a prominent place in the Hindu scheme of things. Touch is related to the varying levels of purity that each caste must maintain. The higher castes have the strictest rule of association, and those at the bottom of the caste order have literally been untouchables. The proper handling of food and its ceremonial purity are of primary importance, especially among the Brahmins. Beef is one of the foods that may not be eaten. The sight of it is liable to make a Hindu ill, for the cow is venerated as a symbol of fruitfulness. It is also related to the sacredness of life and the basic ethic of noninjury to living creatures, a principle that has great strength in Gandhi's region of origin, Gujarat.

The Appeal of Hinduism

The ability of Hinduism to absorb new peoples within India and its ability at the same time to accommodate itself to new religious precepts and customs were two inseparable aspects of its growth. As it spread over the subcontinent, Hinduism became increasingly complex, acquiring the luxuriance of forms and symbols that characterize it today. Although the southern reaches of India remained racially and culturally Dravidian, the Brahmin priesthood penetrated below the Narbada River and undertook to spread its faith there. It gradually converted all except those in the regions most difficult of access. Even today, the Brahmin element in the south is considerably lighter in color than the rest of the population, and resentment against its position of high privilege is now acute.

The Brahmin accomplishment was remarkable because it brought the new elements into the Hindu fold in the lower ranges of the social order. The newcomers were induced to accept this inferior status on the grounds that it was but a consequence of sins committed in past lives. The Dravidian and less-developed tribal peoples were fitted into the lower echelons of the caste system in positions closely related to their degree of political and economic weakness. However, a powerful new invader could be pacified only by a more rewarding decision. Thus the Rajput invaders were "embalmed" in the Hindu system by being placed in the high warrior-noble caste.

As the Brahmins advanced the cause of Hinduism, they found that the inhabitants insisted on retaining their grosser, more superstitious forms of worship. The Brahmins wisely adapted themselves to a compromise permitting a "popular" Hinduism to develop alongside the more intellectual and abstract religious philosophy. In this manner, local gods and regional ceremonies and symbols were incorporated into the Hindu system. One effect of this colorful diversity was the elaboration of works and ceremonial activities, a tendency that raised the status and importance of the Brahmin priesthood.

Thus not only did Hinduism permit geographic variations, but within each region it was pitched at a variety of intellectual and emotional levels. By allowing local practice and by appealing to a wide range of individual attitudes—from the crudest form of animism to the most abstract monist philosophy—Hinduism became a most attractive religion to the diverse peoples of India. This acceptance of divergence in creed was rooted in the belief that all humans were unequal. Since men varied in their intellectual capacities, according to Hinduism, only a few could comprehend the pure truth; for the rest, whatever they grasped was all that could be expected. For example, images are widely used in Hinduism; the more sophisticated consider them symbols of higher values, while others look on these forms as actual deities.

Hindu Social Customs and Institutions

The belief in the basic inequality of man of course lends support to the caste system. This basic institution, through which the complex Hindu social code has functioned, operated in conjunction with two other major social structures, the joint family and the village community. These units gained prestige and authority in the course of their successful activities, but it must be remembered that their strength depended not merely on performance but also on the persuasive powers of the ideas behind them. It was the flexible combination of concepts and customs that gave Hinduism its great capacity to resist or absorb rival systems. In fact, the grave questions of how well Hinduism can endure the shock of modern times must be examined from the ideological as well as the material standpoint.

Still, the social structure was the agency through which Indian culture maintained its continuity despite countless political upheavals. A salient feature of this system was its fundamentally authoritarian nature. It was not simply that the caste system was undemocratic and, to Westerners, socially repugnant. All these bodies were authoritarian regimes that closely controlled individual action and operated in terms of collective responsibility and conformity to group standards. Although the village, caste, and family had considerable autonomy in their own spheres, their form of self-rule was far from democratic. Indian society, moreover, was regulated by status and was not exposed to the leveling interplay of competition. This practice made for stability, but the high degree of conformity to group needs made progressive development and change exceedingly difficult. The nation as a whole was weakened, since people thought in terms of their immediate group. Nevertheless, these social agencies, by contributing vitally to the creation of a unique and uniform Indian culture, laid the groundwork for the development of modern nationalism.

The Caste System

India's most unique and famous institution, the caste system, is a self-regulating community without territorially defined limits. Its boundaries are social, for a caste can be described as a class into which a person is born and which he cannot leave. A common bond exists among members of the same caste: they have their own standards of life and conduct, and enforce the caste's will in matters coming under its jurisdiction.

A ban on intermarriage underlies the principle of separate castes, and wedlock is indeed the regulator of the Hindu social order. Marriage rules abound for each caste, and restrictions are so severe that they take effect even within subcastes. This complex arrangement is heavily dependent on early, parentally directed marriages; otherwise independent human action could seriously endanger the entire structure. The mild relaxations of controls that have occurred recently are directed toward removing lesser barriers among subcastes, effecting marriages later in a person's life, and consulting the principals involved. These modifications, of course, have appeared only among the few advanced elements in society; for the vast majority, the old tradition prevails.

A man not only took his wife from his own caste but ate only with his caste fellows. These practices posed a serious block to social intercourse with one's coreligionists, let alone with foreigners or even Indians of a different faith. Historically, each caste also stood for a specific, separate occupation, making the specialization of function hereditary. As many subdivisions of caste and occupation evolved, people did not always assume their traditional roles. Today, many castes enjoy a wide selection of jobs, especially in the public service and new types of work. This modern trend is more common in the cities, but even there the hereditary process sets in once new occupational lines have been established.

The process of subdivision within castes developed to such an extent that Indian society is stratified into more than 2,000 of these mutually exclusive bodies. Most of the subgroups have a limited geographic extent so that no more than from fifty to a few hundred of these exist in an average community. The basic structure of the caste system is fairly simple: there are three upper levels —Brahmin (priest), Khsatriya (warrior), and Vaisya (merchant)—and the fourth caste of Sudra (laborer). The last group, because traditionally considered to be of non-Aryan origin, was let into the Hindu structure on less favorable terms. Generalizations about the relative well-being of the various elements today are difficult to make; for example, the position of the Sudras in the south is quite good. Still, a ceremonial difference separates them from the other castes: only boys of the upper three groups undergo an important initiation ceremony into their castes and are considered "twice born." Of later origin is the "fifth" caste, or outcaste, now totaling 50 millions, absorbed into the system under extremely unfavorable terms.

It is clear that conquest and occupation were intimately related to the development of the caste system, but racial and color factors must also be emphasized. In fact, the Sanskrit word for caste is varuna, or color, and social differences based on skin pigmentation were embedded early in the caste system. Even today, when skin pigmentation in itself is not a potent political or social force in India, fairness of color is still highly prized, if only in the aesthetic sense.

Continued political instability and the mounting importance of Hinduism as a unifying force in Indian society helped raise the prestige of the Brahmins above that of the warrior and ruler. Today their various subcastes total about 6.4 per cent of the Hindu population. The Brahmins define social position, officiate at religious ceremonies, have custody over sacred lore, and enjoy a number of great social privileges. Their intellectual-religious leadership played a major role in gaining for Hinduism its remarkably dominant position in India's civilization.

The caste system would have been unable to serve as the backbone of the Hindu social system had it always been absolutely rigid. The amazing growth of groupings—called subcastes by orthodox Hindus—within the four major caste divisions left some room for social maneuver and averted total stratification. Traditionally, each subcaste could better its position within its major caste boundary. Some groups actually succeeded in rising in the social scale by dint of conscientious effort. The degree of social flexibility might have been even greater had Hindu political rule not suffered an eclipse with the advent of the Moslems. Until then, Hindu rulers competed with the Brahmins as regulators of society, raising or lowering the status of various subcastes and so keeping the barriers between them from becoming impenetrable. After the Moslem conquest the Brahmins became the unchallenged leaders of Hinduism, and in an era of Islamic dominance, guided Hinduism into its shell of passive resistance. Caste lines were considerably tightened under Brahmin leadership as the entire Hindu structure developed a greater rigidity of outlook and practice.

A spectacular contemporary issue facing the caste system involves the outcastes or untouchables. Incorporated into the Hindu system about 1,800 to 2,000 years ago, they have been compelled to perform the most degrading types of work and suffer humiliating disabilities. In some areas they could not even use village well water and were often driven to supply themselves from totally unsanitary sources. Another well-known restriction was their inability even to approach certain other castes. These peoples, generally descendants of subdued aborigines, have endured a "slavery of the mind," convinced as they are of their moral and spiritual inferiority under the Hindu system.

They commonly live segregated from the four castes, and are themselves divided into subgroups with a gradation of status and prestige. Their over-all condition varies markedly in different locales, ranging from comparative freedom and vigor in the Punjab to extreme squalor in the south. The new Indian government has legislated the caste system out of existence, but, because a sweeping social change cannot be attained overnight simply by constitutional fiat, the outcasts are only gradually being integrated into the Hindu system on more humane terms. Many feel that Mahatma Gandhi's main achievement may well have been this improvement in the position of the *Harijan*—children of God—as he called them. The outcasts' defenders have argued that the divine being never intended to inflict such pain on living creatures and that it was sinful to burden them with such tremendous disabilities. This grave issue highlights the difficulties besetting the Hindu order in its effort to modify its principles, under the impact of modern economic changes and ideological pressures, and still serve as a dynamic force in Indian society.

The Joint Family

The family unit, firmly related to the caste structure, is the atom of the Hindu social order. It is a joint family, differing in structure and purpose from the traditional Western type, which is regarded by Hindus as selfish and lonely. In India, a group of these single families lives together, the unit consisting of a patriarch, his wife, and all their descendants except females who have married. A sense of common pride and a strong community of feeling prevail in this family unit. On the death of the patriarch, the oldest son may take over, or the sons may separate and lead new family groups of their own.

The joint family is collective, since its property is owned in common by the male descendants of a common ancestor and is worked for the benefit of the family as a whole. Any earnings derived from other sources by the individual members are also pooled and shared in some measure by all. The family also extends financial allowances and aids its unemployed members. However, the individual remains heavily dependent on the family manager of his economic affairs.

There is, moreover, a burdensome absence of privacy. Wives are brought into the family circle subject to the rule of the matriarch, while the children are reared by the family as a whole. This is an admirable environment for the very young, for they receive constant care and companionship and acquire a strong sense of security and participation in all their daily activities. However, this is an extremely taxing situation for the adolescent and young adult, who are severely hampered in their effort to strike out on their own. Obligatory ties to the parental group have a powerful hobbling effect on their ability to display individual initiative and arrive at decisions independently. The strict control exercised by the family leaders within their limited sphere of jurisdiction reinforces the authoritarian tradition already evident in political and religious affairs. An unhealthy docility is a consequence of this reverence for, and dependence on, parental authority.

The strength of family loyalty has persisted even where modern conditions have breached its formal structure, and it has been a root cause of nepotism in public affairs. Even among the more modernized elements in society, the spiritual and social power of the family retains much of its vigor. In studying the dilemma of conflicting loyalties and desires in modern India, the strength of the caste and the family cannot be understood merely by observing their more striking prohibitions and restrictions. Both are touched with religious inspiration—to preserve the family unit and the closely related caste customs, to perform the highly important ceremonies related to these institutions, and to pass on the entire system intact to the next generation. The powerful urge for continuity is reflected in the modification of Hindu precepts that permits a family to adopt a son. This act is couched in religious rather than secular terms, and the new member is expected to perpetuate all ceremonial rites essential to the salvation of his adopter and the latter's ancestors.

Women of all castes have been the citadels of orthodoxy, for this religious culture is domestically oriented and closely tied to the family. The Hindu woman is clearly subordinate to her husband and thus has no social role to play when he dies. Yet within the context of their relationship she holds a distinct and divinely inspired place. Although her position depends on the family's status and the number of children she bears, she is revered in her many capacities as wife, mother, and sister, and in this way she attains an important sense of dignity and purpose.

However, the average woman led a most restricted existence, for she was expected to have no interests beyond immediate family affairs. In this century, some women have entered the fields of political, professional, and economic activity, thereby indicating that some adjustment, however difficult, is taking place.

The Village

Like the caste, the village exercised wide powers of self-government, but as a community with definite territorial limits and a nearly self-sufficient economy. It has continued to predominate in a land so overwhelmingly agricultural, and a large majority of the population resides in the approximately 600,000 Indian villages. Families formed the fundamental unit in the village, which was often under the direction of a headman who bore some resemblance to the family leader in communal matters. In some instances the village resembled the family more closely, with a common ancestry and collective ownership of property. More often, the family held its own property and the village had separate though related areas of activity to regulate.

A major achievement of village organization was its ability to function through a long series of political upheavals. State controls were rather slight, as is evidenced in the minimum of governmental functions and the lack of administrative forces at the village level. Aside from collecting revenue and seeing that the land, the source of income, was properly cultivated, the government's main functions centered around police and military protection. Civil functionaries were located in cities and towns only, and the judicial administration and courts were similarly centralized. Only the local officials who were charged with police patrol and revenue action, with headquarters in towns, served as governmental contacts with the villages.

The village frequently was responsible for communication facilities, water supply, and certain judicial functions. The village watchman was left to check petty crimes, and the headman, with a council of elders (panchayat), handled petty legal cases. They administered swift and cheap justice in civil property cases, in a system which operated without lawyers and by arbitration. Thus the parties could not be compelled to appear, though social and customary pressure enabled this native system to operate adequately. Yet, panchayat justice gave way to the compulsory British legal system in the nineteenth century, even though the Western codes were terrifyingly incomprehensible.

The village leadership also organized self-protecting forces against aggressive neighbors and resisted unjust demands of the government. These government levies never included military service, which was neither offered nor expected, for only military castes and professionals fought. The cultivator was not an active participant in wars and political struggles, for in the premodern era he cared less who ruled than how well he was governed. The nationality, religion, or even civilization of the ruler was a secondary consideration to how well the revenue issue was handled. For example, when the Arabs conquered Sind before 1000 A.D., the peasants remained indifferent or actually took sides with the invaders because the Hindu rulers had been intolerably oppressive.

It should be remembered that throughout India's history a strong central government meant a sharp restriction of village autonomy. As the king's power grew, his right to dismiss village officials became widely recognized. Moreover, revenue collection was a powerful lever of interference in daily affairs. An oppressive tax system combined with venal officials could quickly make economic conditions unbearable. In such times, the peasants were likely to flee from their lands, at great economic cost to themselves, the tax collectors, and the country as a whole.

Ordinarily, the lines of village and state interest and authority did not clash in such a vigorous manner. The economy was geared to the placid routine of self-sufficiency. If an area did not happen to be engaged in the export of luxury goods, it was well insulated economically from the outside world. Any deficiency in village production could be remedied by barter with another village three or four miles away; the real economic unit could therefore be considered a compact group of villages. The noncultivators—from artisans to priests—performed their tasks in return for traditionally allotted shares of the produce. The caste system acted as the regulator assuring an adequate and evenly distributed flow of specialists in the various village activities.

Economic life was essentially static, with little effort made to go outside the well-beaten paths of hereditary occupations or to seek an improved standard of living. Those industries that did exist were quickly stereotyped in operation and training. The large centers of trade geared to foreign or imperial markets were too few to make a significant impression on the standard economic pattern. Moreover, urban society, which was centered about imperial or noble courts, was devoted to satisfying their needs. Thus cities did not perform the intellectual or economic functions that they carried on so spectacularly in the West; nor was there an active, self-reliant urban middle class of any size or importance.

The social and economic center of gravity therefore remained in the village. While deficient in elements fostering originality and change, the village served as a minute vessel, located all over India, which served to unify the distinctive elements in Hindu civilization. Our task now is to examine the profound effects that the Moslem incursions and later Western invasions, culminating respectively in Mogul and British rule, had on this Hindu culture.

315

12 *The Moslems and the British in India*

The Hindu culture, which had crystallized by 1000 A.D., was placed under severe pressure during the succeeding centuries by two sets of invaders. These conquerors, Moslems and British, brought new ethical and philosophic viewpoints in their train and undertook what amounted to a revolutionary assault on the entire Indian way of life. Each arrival made a significant contribution in his own cultural sphere, and the cumulative effect of these complementary pressures was profound. It is a tribute to Hinduism that it remained the major strand in India's social and political fabric.

The Moslem Conquest

The impact of the Moslems reached its climax in modern times when the attainment of Indian independence in 1947 took the unexpected but dramatic form of a partition into two sovereign national states divided along religious lines. The recurrent Islamic invasions began in earnest around 1000 A.D. and continued for about 500 years. They took the form of succeeding waves of invaders, each in turn a recent convert to Islam, sweeping in from the north and west. The net effect was that of a series of assaults by religious zealots—Arabs, Turks, Persians, Afghans, Central Asian tribesmen, and Mongols—who sought to convert others to their true faith.

When invaders with advanced cultures encounter a backward native people, they usually succeed in establishing their own way of life in a newly won land. Conversely, an invader who is advanced only in military prowess may leave his mark on a higher native culture but is eventually absorbed by it. The Hindu-Moslem case fits neither category. These cultures clashed under geographic and political conditions that tended to neutralize their effect on each other. Islam achieved a formidable record of conversion after it exploded out of Arabia in the seventh century—extending westward to the Atlantic coast of north Africa and eastward to Indonesia and the southern Philippines. The more passive Hindu tradition possessed a powerful absorptive capacity within its own land

316

of origin and successfully resisted efforts to destroy its hold over the Indian people. It could not eliminate the influence of Islam but did manage to strengthen its own precepts and social-religious institutions. The Moslems at first won some converts, it is true, but in the long run were forced into a defensive posture as a religious minority element.

It may be an unfair dependence on hindsight to argue that this encounter was bound to have a disintegrating effect on the subcontinent's political stability and unity. Yet Indian unity, achieved in the face of numerous obstacles, had been dependent on a common religious outlook, basic philosophy of life, and intellectual pattern of thought. The introduction of a different religious and philosophical outlook was far more serious than the arrival of a new people, another language, or even new economic techniques or political ideologies. When Islam became the creed of more than one fifth of the Indian people, the basic underpinning of Indian unity—a common concept of civilization—was fatally shattered. With the passage of time, the Moslem community became adjusted to its Indian environment but remained a distinctly separate group. For an adequate understanding of this phenomenon we must examine the Islamic creed.

Principles of Islam

In the basically Western-oriented Moslem religion, the creator was conceived as a positive and permanent being, existing separately from and above mankind. Mohammed was the Prophet but not a god, for the gap between man and the deity was clear and unbridgeable. To the Hindus, this concept of the unity and transcendence of God contrasted sharply with their fundamental belief that God resided everywhere and was unseparable from the human soul. For their part, the Moslems were repelled by the apparent polytheism, portrayals of the divine in human form, and especially the idol worshiping which they found in Hindu India.

Like other Western religions, Islam has definite attributes—a creed, a book, one view of God, one series of revelations, doctrinal uniformity (though divergent sects did develop), and belief in a brotherhood of equality for all Moslems. Life on earth was of tremendous importance, serving as a probationary period for the next world. Hinduism, on the other hand, is so amorphous and doctrinally vague that it has been described as best recognizable by its "atmosphere." Its theory of life cycles and rebirths clearly removed from any "one existence" that dramatic emphasis usually found in Western creeds.

The tone of Moslem worship was stern and puritanic, and its form was simple and austere, with no idols or pictures allowed in a mosque. Its stress on personal equality also meant strong communal discipline, and the leveling effect of worship was expressed in uniform, almost regimented, congregational prayer. Formal duties, such as the outward observance of rules and customs, were heavily stressed. These practices were alien to the Hindu, with his private devotions, divergences of form, and individualistic pattern of ritual.

317

The Moslems, in theory at least, were opposed to the caste system and its emphasis on exclusion and inequality; they were particularly antagonized by Brahmin claims of superiority and privilege. Furthermore, Islam was a proselytizing creed, for if all men are equal, they must have been born Moslem; duty therefore lay in "reconverting" them to this single revealed standard. From this belief derived other traits—all contrary to Hindu beliefs—cultural uniformity, the use of the state as an instrument of conversion both within its frontiers and abroad, and the practice of discrimination against nonbelievers.

This wide gulf in ideas and conceptions was reflected in the practices of everyday life. Socially, the Moslems adhered to their own eating customs, dress, and manner of greeting. They developed their own private law, had their own teachers, and lived apart from Hindus in separate sections of the villages. Learned and religious leaders would hear their legal cases and refer to the Koran for guidance. Clearly, the religious communities, by taking advantage of the high degree of legal and administrative autonomy that the village enjoyed, were able to go their separate ways.

Intermarriage was out of the question, for Hindus would not even marry beyond the narrow limits prescribed by the detailed regulations of their subcastes. Since Moslems married within their own faith, and marriage was a principal regulator of the caste system, the Hindus naturally came to consider the Moslems as a caste in themselves! Differing food customs and other Hindu caste regulations that prevented the development of normal social relations proved to be a serious source of friction. The Moslems would not eat pork and intensely resented Hindu violations of this taboo; on the other hand, Hindu veneration of cows was incomprehensible to them. Music was another cause of trouble, for it was forbidden in a mosque and was not supposed to be heard during Moslem prayers. Yet Hindu festivals and religious processions relied heavily on music, which was heard all too frequently during periods of Moslem religious devotion.

Degree of Accommodation

The formidable barriers to social cohesion created by these opposing views of society became intensified through historical experience and led to political hostility in the modern era. Nevertheless, some interpenetration of thought and custom did occur, and efforts were made to reach common grounds of understanding. A parallel attempt was also made during this century in political affairs when important elements in both communities tried to reconcile their differences and retain a unified state. The failure of these efforts must be appreciated in light of the magnitude of the task. The fusion between Aryans and Dravidians required many centuries, was at best a partial success, and depended heavily on a rigid social order. The relatively recent Hindu-Moslem encounter was exploited by the disruptive forces of modern political nationalism before a firm accommodation could be achieved. The remorseless power of nationalism in splintering sovereign states is after all a world-wide phenomenon. The Moslem-Hindu political clash attained dramatic intensity because the Moslems had developed a strong sense of being Indian and looked on India as their homeland.

In efforts at accommodation, the Moslems exerted greater influence in theology and the Hindus in social affairs. Since the conquerors themselves were a small minority and many followers of Islam were converts from Hinduism, several Hindu customs were adopted by the Moslem community. Some Moslem groups adopted social gradations and marriage restrictions along caste lines, even though such intent was vigorously denied and the caste system itself remained theoretically repugnant. Admittedly, these distinctions were not as rigid as in Hinduism; nor was the practice supported by the driving force of religious sanction. Violations did not exclude one from the brotherhood, but social pressure for conformity was applied, and the effect was to distort the Moslem concept of equality.

On the other hand, some Hindus in parts of north India adopted the Moslem practice of purdah—the physical seclusion of women. This was not divinely sanctioned in the Islamic creed, but its prevalence reflected the depressed condition of Moslem women. On paper, they had advantages not enjoyed by Hindu women: they could hold property and receive specific shares of inheritance. But Islam permitted a subordinate-wife system and treated marriage as a contract rather than a sacrament, thus permitting divorce and remarriage. The position of Moslem women was further undermined by the almost complete absence of female education, a handicap that reduced their capacity to earn an independent livelihood and kept them in ignorance of the few rights they possessed. Finally, Hinduism gave its women a spiritually higher status by touching them with divinity, which in practice more than compensated for the Moslem woman's greater legal rights.

The theological impact of Islam served to encourage Hinduism to move toward monotheism, a direction already followed by many philosophers. It also induced a tendency among Hindus to minimize idolatry. Many Hindus, attracted by the unified concept and moral character of Islam's deity, established groups that sought to bridge the gap between the two religions. The most famous of these were the Sikhs, a religious sect, in the Punjab region, that evolved into a separate people. Their leader, Nanak (1469–1538), believed in one superior being and denounced caste in favor of equality for all. Although he was considered a saint by some Moslems, later persecution and discrimination by Moslem rulers drove the Sikhs into bitter political opposition. A basic antipathy developed between these groups; in the end the Sikhs became political allies of the Hindus, despite sharp differences on religious issues.

The Moslems took firm root in India during the great period of Mogul rule in the sixteenth and seventeenth centuries.[1] There was a marked blend of Hindu

---

[1] Court personnel came from all parts of Moslem Asia during the epoch of Moslem rule, but by the third or fourth generation their descendants were brown of complexion and adopted the more languid manners of their birthland. Ironically, these latter elements were less respected than the constant stream of newcomers.

319

and Moslem approaches in the fine arts and architecture. A notable linguistic development was the evolution of a hybrid tongue, Urdu. This Moslem court and camp language developed from the necessary contacts between the conquerors and their Hindu subjects. Urdu had a Hindu grammatical syntax, onto which were grafted a Persian and Arabian vocabulary and the Persian alphabet. Evolving primarily in the Delhi region, it bore a close resemblance to the local Hindu dialect. Urdu developed a vigorous literary tradition as it spread southward to the Deccan; Hindus made great contributions to this effort and fostered the introduction of Persian influences. Thus Hindi and Urdu bear a striking resemblance to each other in their elementary forms, but the similarity wanes in their more advanced stages. Though Hindi turned to Sanskrit, and Urdu to Persian, for additional words, their relationship was still close enough to bring forth a common oral tongue, Hindustani, which became the medium for everyday speech in the north-central region.

Linguistic relationships, already complex in Hindu India, took on added depth. In modern Pakistan, the decision to make Urdu the official language was greeted with dismay and anger in East Bengal. Similarly, when there was an effort to purge Hindi—the official language of independent India—of Urdu elements, the Moslem citizens of the new republic were upset. On the whole, then, efforts at cultural fusion became tangled in the same obstacles that hindered political unity. In the end, the common sympathies and attitudes essential to national cohesion were not developed.

The Moslem Conquests

First in the long series of Moslem invaders were the Arabs, who came from the West and conquered Sind Province in the ninth century. They were checked by the desert and other geographic obstacles; the major inroads came later, across the northwest mountain passes. These continued bloody assaults from the eleventh to the thirteenth century broke the disunited Hindu power in northern India. However, Moslem rule presented the same chronicle of failure, with petty princes fighting one another, and succeeding Islamic invaders destroying the very states their coreligionists had created.

The strategic city of Delhi became the focal point of Moslem rule after the twelfth century, and its control conferred political prestige as well as military advantage. The ruler who occupied the surrounding region was the leading political figure of northern India, but he remained simply one among several competitors for power. These territorially restricted Delhi kingdoms were often too weak to control even their own outlying provinces, and the bewildering rapidity of dynastic successions further diminished their stability and influence. In theory, however, the concept that the ruler held absolute power became widely accepted, thereby easing the way for the later assertion of supremacy by the successful Mogul conquerors.

The early Moslem invaders were primarily raiding parties whose success gave the conquerors political power, which in turn induced other Moslems to migrate as professionals in the new rulers' service. Though they arrived in numbers large enough to form compact communities, they were scattered throughout India and did not form close-knit settlements as farmers would. These Moslems became the urban ruling class, military aristocracy, and social elite of India, using Hindus to perform physical and clerical work. Some folk movements did take place and agricultural regions were occupied in the northwest. However, in this large subcontinent, such a restricted immigration movement could do no more than make the Moslems a small but powerful minority in a basically Hindu land.

Progress in converting Hindus to Islam was retarded by poor communications, the insulation of villages from new currents of thought and activity, and the austere and impersonal nature of the new faith. Although success was limited, it should be noted that the majority of Moslems in the subcontinent are of Hindu descent. Forced conversions were only sporadically attempted; pressure in most instances was less obvious, and often a change of religion was voluntary. Many upper-class Hindus were converted for reasons ranging from the religious attraction of Islam to such calculations as the avoidance of heavy taxes and the loss of land, the retention of office, and the desire to join the new elite. Several proudly retained their old names as proof of their Brahmin origin. A number of mass conversions occurred among the lower castes who were attracted by the creed of an equal brotherhood, the relatively few taboos, the simple demands, and the better life promised by Islam. The greatest Moslem success lay in Bengal, which had been the last stronghold of Buddhism; here a militant Hindu dynasty had replaced Buddhist rule shortly before the Moslems arrived. Islam was welcomed as the deliverer from a traditional foe much as it had been earlier in the Middle East by heretical Christians. As a result, central and eastern Bengal, with an adjacent part of Assam to the east, became Moslem strongholds.

Moslem majorities were thus created in two unconnected territorial pockets —one in the east (parts of Bengal and Assam), the other in the northwest (Sind, west Punjab, Baluchistan, and the northwest frontier region). Elsewhere in north and central India there were scattered minority groups. Although the cry for a Moslem state was stridently raised in this century from these exposed elements, it was the geographically compact Moslem sectors that actually formed the physical basis for Pakistan and ultimately made it a reality.

The territorial and political control exercised by the Moslems was far from thorough. Eastern Assam and the extreme south of India (below the Tungabhadra River) never fell to the invader, and, of the areas that were conquered, many did not experience direct Moslem rule. Hindu rulers and administrators often retained considerable power, in return for a promise to contribute armed forces and land-revenue payments to their Moslem overlords. Most of southern India remained independent for centuries after the north fell, and even during the height of Moslem power Hindu principalities retained their identity.

The new conquerors were nonetheless the politically dominant force in India until the eighteenth century, and their influence was widespread, though with varying degrees of intensity. Rigid orthodox treatment of infidels—conversion or death—was obviously impossible, and the Hindu "idolators" were generally tolerated. Nevertheless, persecutions did take place, for Moslem annals gloatingly tell of oppressions and massacres of unbelievers. Hindus also suffered a discriminatory poll tax, as well as heavy exactions designed to keep them from amassing wealth. Moreover, Moslem law replaced Hindu legal practices, with the effect of placing the populace under a strange code and at a severe disadvantage; for the word of an infidel did not hold in a law court against the statement of a believer.

Moslem princes, who ruled on the basis of military strength, destroyed the last theoretical vestiges of dependence on popular support. Except in areas where rule was exercised indirectly, through Hindu chiefs, the gulf between people and ruler widened. The villages alone provided an element of continuity in the management of their own affairs, although a strong ruler could bring the village headman under his control and have his own revenue officers and other agents interfere frequently in local matters. The ruler combined all governing functions within his own person, and the only check on his behavior was the Koran. Yet the absence of over-all order and stability became even more apparent, as the frequency of boundary changes and the recurrent ascents and collapses of petty states indicated. This pattern was further complicated by repeated political assassinations and rebellions within political frontiers. But a general political framework and relations with the Hindu population had been established by 1500.

The Mogul Empire

So rare was political stability in India that a dynasty able to rule a large empire for more than 150 years was a rare phenomenon. The Mogul empire was at its height for that length of time—from the beginning of Akbar's reign (1556) to the death of Aurangzeb (1707)—during which it compiled a remarkable record in political and administrative rule. The Mogul rulers were descendants of the great Mogul warrior, Tamerlane, whose brief three-month invasion of India in 1399 had provided an indelible example of his tremendous destructive power. At the start of the sixteenth century, the Mogul warrior-poet Babur had descended on India from central Asia and defeated the Moslem rulers of the northern regions. His efforts were climaxed by a hard-won victory east of Delhi over the Rajput warrior caste in 1527.

Mogul rule did not take root during the following decades; in fact, the Mogul domain shrank until Babur's grandson Akbar became ruler. He identified himself with Indian interests and undertook a vigorous effort to unite all subjects in a common allegiance. In making toleration of Hindus an instrument of statecraft, Akbar abolished the religious poll tax, accepted Hindus at his court as high officials, declared the slaughter of cows a capital offense, and gave financial support to Hindu temples. He further bolstered Mogul power and reduced the likelihood of organized Hindu opposition by entering into a political alliance with the Rajput warrior princes.

Akbar's tolerance was not based solely on expediency, for he was skeptical of his own faith's orthodox precepts. He later tried to found a synthetic religion composed of the best parts of all the beliefs he encountered, much to the dismay of Islam's religious leaders. His position with his coreligionists was further weakened because he was a Sunni, whereas the great majority belonged to the Shiite sect. His vulnerable status within the Moslem community made an association with Hindu interests all the more valuable in enhancing Mogul power.

Despite Akbar's toleration and wisdom, his main objective was political expansion through military conquest. The Mogul position he inherited found most of north India in Afghan hands or under the rule of Hindu princes. Other states in the Deccan, and Vijayanagar to the south, were as powerful as the Mogul realm. His success in conquering all except the extreme south from this base must be considered a remarkable military achievement. A dynasty with such ambitions could be sustained only by thoroughly despotic rule. As in previous regimes, the power of the king was absolute and there were no popular institutions of protest. Thus the efficient bureaucracy that came into being had no power or will of his own. This administrative apparatus, which raised revenue collection to a fine art, was one of Akbar's most outstanding achievements. The government structure was exercised along military lines and was based on the Persian technique of holding each important official responsible for maintaining and commanding a specified number of troops. Rank in government was determined by the size of one's contingent, and even civilian officials were graded in the military hierarchy.

One unique aspect of Mogul rule was the absence of a hereditary aristocracy. Positions in the court nobility, central bureaucracy, and territorial administration were held at the emperor's pleasure. This aristocracy of office was accompanied by virtual confiscation of a noble's property and wealth on his death; thus his heirs not only failed to inherit his position but also were impoverished by his death. The monarchy's position was in this way protected against a potential threat from the nobility as a class. Nevertheless, in not basing their regime on the support of a stable and loyal upper class, the Moguls dissipated an opportunity to strengthen their rule. The empire thereby came to depend entirely on the personality of the ruler.

Mogul rule reached its zenith under Akbar's three successors, who sustained his creative efforts, maintained the peace, and encouraged cultural activity. The blending of art forms led to outstanding achievements, of which the Taj Mahal is a famous example. Revenue collection expanded so that even in prosperous times taxes rose steeply, for the government's share of agricultural produce mounted. Akbar had raised it to one third of the crop, and in later generations it became one half. The people felt themselves to be mere revenue contributors to Mogul power, lacking rights and owing no real allegiance to a state whose huge apparatus was directed almost exclusively to the service of the ruling class and the grandeur of the empire.

The dynasty's collapse was hastened by a series of weak monarchs in the eighteenth century, but elements of decay had long been evident in the inability of the government to develop a fundamentally constructive program in its golden era. Its public works program, especially in irrigation, water control, and other agricultural matters, was relatively meager. Still worse, the Moguls adopted the pernicious technique of farming out tax-collector rights and selling short-term official positions. These purchasers of course sought to net maximum returns from their brief period of power and squeezed the peasantry unmercifully. The question of dynastic succession proved to be a corrosive factor at the very core of the empire immediately after the death of Akbar. Murder and imprisonment within the family circle accompanied the transfer of power from Akbar's son Jahangir to Shakjahan and Aurangzeb. The empire has been described as an anomaly, comparable to that of Charlemagne's: a highly centralized administration, dependent almost exclusively on the emperor, and lacking a social or popular base of support.

Finally, the policies of Aurangzeb (1659–1707) proved ruinous. His program of expansion led to a reckless attempt to conquer the entire south. This unsuccessful venture overextended Mogul resources and weakened it mortally at the center; ultimately its powerful viceroys in the great provinces broke away from the fragmenting empire. Aurangzeb also revealed an intolerant attitude toward non-Islamic faiths, at great political cost. The policy of toleration had become less pronounced after Akbar's death, and the practices of temple building and cow protection were halted. But Aurangzeb removed the Hindus from government service, reimposed the religious poll tax, doubled the customs duty for Hindu merchants, razed temples built during the previous twelve years, and abolished religious fairs. The Hindus became restive and militant, as the Moguls lost Rajput support and were considerably shaken by an astounding military upsurge of the Mahratta tribes in west-central India. It was at this time that the Sikhs, also persecuted, became bitter foes of the Moslems. Although the empire survived formally until 1857, its wars in central India, defections in the north, and the reappearance of Afghan and Persian invaders, attracted by India's weakness, dealt fatal blows to Delhi's political power in the eighteenth century.

The End of Indian Rule

The sudden rise of Mahratta power was an important manifestation of a widespread Hindu revivalist movement. Under their great military leader Shivaji (1627–1680), the Mahrattas displayed great skill in guerilla and mobile cavalry warfare and won considerable territory in central India during the seventeenth century. Although pushed back by the Moguls, they maintained their position in the region around the city of Poona and reasserted their strength when the empire began to wane. With the aid of a Rajput alliance they almost succeeded in establishing a new dynasty. Blame for their failure has been ascribed to Britain's intervention in the eighteenth century, but the Mahrattas' own inherent defects were at least of equal importance.

Though the Mahratta tribes were organized in a confederacy under a leader —the Peshwa—until 1772, constant quarreling within their own ranks prevented the formation of a unified army for any length of time. This lack of cohesion was so ingrained that any Mahratta leader was liable to side with the enemy at a critical moment. Though powerful enough to undermine Mogul rule, the Mahrattas were so deficient in the arts of government and administration that they had no political system to put in its place. Their primary interest lay in revenue collection, and they often let an area alone if regular payments were made; if a territory's tribute fell into arrears, a large Mahratta raiding party assaulted it as though it were enemy terrain. Finally, in the mid-eighteenth century, the Mahrattas abandoned their mobile combat tactics in favor of the slower mass movements of the Europeans, with disastrous results. Even when allied with the Moguls against Afghan invaders, they were decisively beaten at Panipat in 1761.

By this time, Indian political fragmentation was proceeding with a vengeance, as if to make up for time lost under Mogul rule. The Afghan military victors did not follow the traditional pattern of conquering Delhi and establishing a new empire, but withdrew to their frontiers. The Moguls were left with their shrunken empire in the Delhi region. In the Deccan, the Nizam, ruler of the great Mogul province of Hyderabad, declared his independence. In the extreme south, the kingdom of Mysore was gaining strength. Moreover, the Mahrattas in the west-center, the Rajput in the north-center, and the Sikhs to the northwest were all independent powers. It was in this setting of political chaos that the British made their bid to dominate India. Their most important early successes occurred in the great province of Bengal, whose viceroy enjoyed an almost autonomous position with regard to his Mogul superiors.

The British Empire in India

The Establishment of British Rule

The Western powers arrived in India when the Portuguese Vasco da Gama reached Calicut in 1498. The rest also came from Atlantic and North Sea maritime communities via the sea. This unconventional conquest by hitherto insignificant Europeans had its greatest impact on India and the nearby lands of Southeast Asia; here the subjugation was more complete and the cultural contacts were therefore longer and more intimate than in the Far East. The long-range effects of the phenomenal British conquest of India are still to be analyzed in their proper perspective. Perhaps now that India has achieved its independence and is threading its way in a turbulent world of ideological and power conflicts, the significance of British rule can be more adequately evaluated.

The Portuguese asserted their authority in southern India almost at the same time that the Moguls arrived in the north, at the start of the sixteenth century. Control over trading posts and naval routes sufficed to protect their missionary and commercial activities. Later, the English and Dutch broke Portuguese sea power, and the only remnants of this early incursion are the Portuguese holdings at Goa, Damão, and Diu. The Dutch established themselves in southern India in the seventeenth century, but found that the Mogul conquests severely restricted their trade profits. They then concentrated on the comparatively more lucrative region of the East Indies; the British, unequal to Dutch competition in these islands, were then able to turn to India. There they rivaled France for control of the subcontinent in a contest which ended victoriously in 1763, with the conclusion of the Seven Years' War (1756–1763), a struggle which cost France its empire in Canada as well.

The fact that Westerners were each other's major opponents was in itself very significant. The weak native resistance was not simply a question of technology, for the Indians were able to acquire modern arms and so neutralize this technical handicap. Nor was the national power of the invaders so well developed that they could field overwhelming superior forces. The arrival of two potential conquerors actually gave the Indians an opportunity to gain time and build up their own strength by playing one off against the other. The native political elements, however, were so disorganized that they could not present a unified resistance to this foreign threat; in fact, the Europeans used native princes to further their own plans. The Indian social order at that time could not inspire the national spirit or provide the modern mass discipline required for effective political and military action. In addition, India's backward administrative system and organizational techniques prevented any effective use of the potential available in the numerically superior native elements. Thus Indian military formations, however well-equipped, lacked the discipline and training of their Western opponents, and their system of command remained rudimentary. As a result, small Western armies were able to conquer large, heavily populated regions during the early days of colonial expansion. But the British and French were able to train Indians in their own service, and these soldiers (sepoys) formed valuable complementary units in the conquerors' armies. Before 1750 neither Western force contained more than 2,000 Europeans. At the famous battle of Plassey (1757) a British force under Clive, numbering 3,000 men, defeated a large native force under the Nawab of Bengal, and so won that province. After French power in India was eliminated in the Seven Years' War, Indian resistance and combat skill increased. However, the costs of fighting, the internal disunity that enabled the English to fight their opponents separately, and the relative increase in British fighting strength all meant continued British successes.

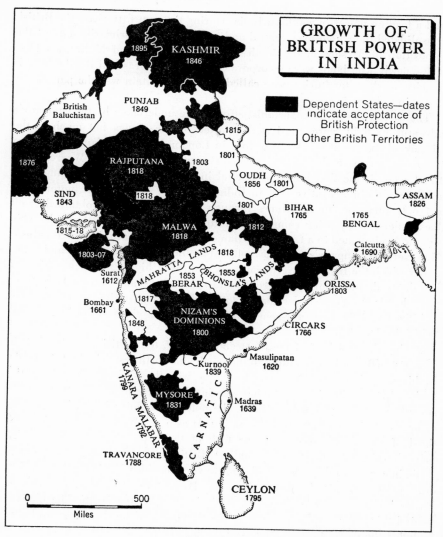

GROWTH OF
BRITISH POWER
IN INDIA

■ Dependent States—dates
indicate acceptance of
British Protection
□ Other British Territories

1895 KASHMIR 1846

British
Baluchistan

PUNJAB
1849

1815

1876

RAJPUTANA
1818

1803

1801

OUDH
1856 1801

ASSAM
1826

SIND
1843

1818

1801

BIHAR
1765

1765
BENGAL

1815-18

MALWA
1818

1812

Calcutta
1690

1803-07

MAHRATTA LANDS 1818

Surat
1612

BERAR
1853

BHONSLA'S LANDS
1853

ORISSA
1803

Bombay
1661

1817

NIZAM'S
DOMINIONS
1800

CIRCARS
1766

1848

Kurnool
1839

Masulipatan
1620

KANARA
1799

MYSORE
1831

CARNATIC

Madras
1639

MALABAR
1792

TRAVANCORE
1788

CEYLON
1795

0   500
Miles

Adapted by permission of George Philip & Son, Ltd.

Actually, the British troops served under the East India Company, a char-
tered commercial organization, founded in 1600, which became titular ruler
of the new realm. The company's main concern was with trade, and for this
purpose three major posts (factories) had been established at Madras (1639),
Bombay (1661), and Calcutta (1690). From these points, British power
fanned out, at first as a protective response to chronic native wars and arbitrary
actions from local rulers, and later as a serious effort to enlarge the realm.
The end of the Seven Years' War found Britain supreme in Bengal Province,

327

and a leading power in southern India. During the next fifty years the British consolidated their hold over central and southern India, primarily against the opposition of Mysore in the south and the now disunited Mahratta tribes. These newly won lands were incorporated into the Madras and Bombay presidencies, as these territories were called. By 1818, Britain was the paramount power in India.

The early successful expansionist efforts were undertaken by the company's adventurous field representatives, supported by the crown, but much to the dismay of the profit-minded directors in London. The most famous of these representatives were Robert Clive, victor over the French, and Warren Hastings, who, as the first governor-general in 1774, established the foundation of Britain's administrative rule in India. Company officials were notoriously corrupt, amassing huge fortunes through tribute or "taxes" obtained from local rulers, or by using company facilities for their own private trade. This situation culminated in a famous parliamentary trial and acquittal of Hastings. However, the company's rule was modified by the India Acts of 1784 and 1786, under which the British government took control of higher policy making and left the trade monopoly, detailed administrative rule, and patronage in company hands. In the decades that followed the administrative system became stabilized and the governor-general in Calcutta was given authority over all British-held territory.

During the first half of the nineteenth century, the British completed their conquest of India by expanding to the north and northwest. The battles fought in this compaign proved to be very arduous, with the Gurkas of Nepal and the Sikhs (1845–1849) in the Punjab offering bitter resistance. As British rule spread over the entire subcontinent, the policy of eliminating and absorbing conquered princely states was discontinued; as a result, an area covering one third of India and containing one fifth of the population remained under princely rule. These states, under indirect British control, were located all over India in a crazy-quilt pattern, and came to vary considerably in level of wealth, degree of modernization, and size. The largest and most important were Hyderabad in the Deccan, and Kashmir in the extreme north. The motives behind this policy of leaving control in the hands of local princes probably included the desire to gain allies and the belief that such indirect rule would be more satisfactory to all concerned. Britain exercised control through a resident, and could even depose a ruler in case of flagrant misgovernment. Generally, the princes' prerogatives were respected and they remained loyal to Britain. In fact, they later posed a serious problem to the nationalist independence movement, siding with the crown against what appeared to be a threat to their survival.

The Administration of British India

The highest official in British India was the viceroy (formerly governor-general), but the realm was subdivided into provinces ruled by governors who had considerable authority. Lesser administrative units called districts were under a collector, deputy commissioner, or district manager, who was the key official in contact with the Indian people. Whatever his title, this officer was a combination magistrate, tax collector, and peace enforcer who personified British rule. An Indian Civil Service was established to staff the higher administrative posts, with recruits drawn from Britain. Indians were admitted at the lower levels, but, beginning with Lord Cornwallis (governor-general in 1786), they were systematically kept out of the higher echelons until the last decades of British rule. Anglo-Indians fared better at first, until the mestizo-led revolts in Latin America against Spain early in the nineteenth century induced the British in India to restrict the role of this interracial group. In the armed forces, the sepoys formed a large percentage of the line troops, but the upper levels of command remained in British hands.

Late in the nineteenth century, the Provincial and Subordinate Civil Services were created in order to encourage the systematic entry of Indians. However, the available posts were those *below* the Indian Civil Service level, as, for example, the deputy to a district magistrate. Later, when certain higher positions were opened, they were too few in number and were reached only at the end of a long career. The effects of this personnel policy in the decades after 1870 was to heighten nationalist fervor among the politically conscious educated classes, whose prestige and chances of employment were so adversely affected. Fortunately, when self-government appeared likely, efforts were made to train Indians for more responsible positions; still, there is a shortage of top-level, experienced personnel today.

The British administrative apparatus made a profound impression on the Indian political scene. Unlike earlier bureaucracies, it was not dependent on the ruler or viceroy, but served as a highly efficient, impersonal arm of the British Raj. It was also able to operate far beyond the scope of earlier bureaucracies, since it made use of modern equipment and organizing techniques. The service continually attracted young Britishers who were willing to serve in rural regions before rising in the ranks. The result was an efficient, honest bureaucracy, which displayed considerable self-respect and a strong *esprit de corps.*

A major accomplishment was the maintenance of law and order, including the elimination of internal political warfare and organized banditry. Equally important, a famine administration was gradually made effective enough to remove this historic threat in the twentieth century. The Bengal famine of 1943 was due to special circumstances—the loss of Burma and its rice supply, a severe drought whose seriousness was underestimated, and a war effort that taxed India's administrative and transport facilities for other purposes. Under normal conditions, careful crop analysis, the development of road and rail networks, and the ability to import food provided effective famine-control measures. In the medical field, remarkable progress was made in stemming fatal epidemic diseases through the introduction of new medical facilities, health education, sewage, vaccinations, and the like. However, the level of health of the average Indian is still well below the Western norm; many millions suffer from malaria, tuberculosis, dysentery, and other diseases which sharply reduce their working effectiveness. Though a basis for further constructive activity has been established, a tremendous medical task remains.

An effect of these British achievements was the remarkable growth of the Indian population. It reached a level of 253 million in 1881, when the first reliable census report was taken; 319 million in 1921; 352 million in 1931; 388 million in 1941; and more than 430 million in 1951 (357 million in India and about 76 million in Pakistan). Agricultural activity was stimulated through better farming techniques, research and education, the establishment of credit societies, and the expansion of irrigation facilities. The new cash crops—cotton in Bombay, jute in Bengal and, for a while, wheat for export in the Punjab— were symbolic of these improvements. Undoubtedly more was accomplished than could have been expected under a native administration, but in view of the scale of population changes, these efforts must be viewed as inadequate. By 1890, India ceased to export food, and each passing decade has accentuated food shortage. India still does not produce its own food requirements but must spend valuable foreign exchange, so essential to its modernization program, for this purpose.

The Agrarian Problem

With industry too small to absorb the mounting labor force, the pressure of people on the land became pronounced. This increase was indicated in the problems of land tenure and debt which began to plague the peasantry, and in the difficulty India encountered in trying to raise, or even maintain, its standard of living. The introduction of a Western legal system further intensified the problem of control over farmland. In pre-British days, land was ample and therefore not too valuable. Moreover, it could not be alienated; since it was not a marketable security, the peasant could not use it as collateral in accumulating debts. The scarcity of money and the self-sufficient nature of the village market economy reinforced this pattern of solvency.

With the appearance of British goods along the coast and then inland as transportation improved, the old artisan class was driven back on the land. The availability of money and goods induced a peasant's "will to borrow" and go into debt. As the population increased, land became relatively scarce and more valuable. The British legal system of contractual obligations allowed the peasants to put up their attractive plots as guarantees on loans, while the judicial process assured the moneylenders of possession in case of default in payment. With interest rates high because capital was scarce, and the peasant both unwise in his borrowings and unaware of the consequences of his new contractual obligations, there developed a vicious cycle of debt, loss of land, and increased tenancy. As the value of land spiraled upward, the "capitalist" would buy land for speculative purposes, rent it on short-term leases to tenants at high rates, and feel under no compulsion to improve the property, let alone embark on such long-range projects as scientific breeding or crop experimentation.

When the end of the American Civil War caused an abrupt fall in agricultural prices, Indian peasants found themselves unable to pay their debts. A series of depressions during the next generation, coupled with a legal system permitting property foreclosures, led to frequent riots in the countryside and a precipitous fall in British prestige. The government maintained a blind adherence to laissez-faire notions then prevalent in Britain, despite the warnings that appeared in many field reports. Peasant indebtedness rose steadly—from £200 million in 1881 to £1,350 million in 1938. Most of this increase can be traced to the free hand given the lender and the unsophisticated, unproductive borrowing of the peasantry. By 1900, disaffection had made the peasant mass a potentially powerful adherent to an anti-British nationalist movement. It remained the task of the middle-class leaders to draw on this source of support and unite the disaffected elements behind an anti-imperialist program.

The British further complicated the situation by conscientiously creating a landlord class, with the objective of establishing a counterpart to the alert rural aristocracy of England. The Cornwallis administration chose the zamindari—hereditary tax collectors who held only restricted powers over the peasantry—to form this new responsible political and economic backbone of the community. Under the Permanent Settlement of Bengal in 1793, the zamindari were given outright ownership of the land from which they had previously collected taxes. Financial conditions favored the new owners, for they were required to pay a fixed sum as a land tax. This amounted in the 1790's to 90 per cent of the annual rent received. Though land values and rents rose during the next century, this sum remained a constant figure, which declined markedly as a percentage of the landlord's intake. The government's share of income from land revenue fell from 90 per cent in 1793 to 25 per cent in 1903–1904. However, when the system was first introduced, the British administration made the novel demand that the landlords make tax payments in cash and by a certain date. The original zamindari found themselves unable to meet these strange stipulations, with the result that the majority of land ownerships fell into the hands of professional moneylenders. The Bengal peasant found his rent rising to one half of the crop, though the landlord's taxes remained fixed. Also, remissions of tax payments by the government in hard times were not passed back to the peasants. The government's over-all tax share of agricultural produce fell from one third in the eighteenth century to one eighth in the twentieth, but most of this difference was siphoned off by the owners.

In other provinces, the government did not repeat this mistake but settled directly with the peasant (ryot), who retained possession of his land. Yet even peasant owners of small tracts would sublease their land at a profit; in fact, the same plot would go through a series of subleases, so great was the demand for land. This hierarchy of exploitation was a symptom of the static nature of India's economy, in which lower consumption per capita accompanied the loss of land ownership. Food consumption, for example, is estimated to have fallen from twenty-four ounces per person per day in 1880 to fourteen in 1936. The 1931 labor census revealed that of the 102 million agricultural workers, about 70 million were landless. Of these, 36 million were tenants and 34 million were farm laborers. Of the 29 million who were cultivating owners, one half owned less than five acres; one half also worked for other owners. Over the years, the landless group had been rising steadily in proportion to the others; British delay in instituting reform legislation made this problem even more acute.

Western Political and Legal Concepts

The basically authoritarian nature of colonial rule tended to obscure the very real effort that the British made to implant Western political ideals, their own system of legal equality, and their respect for personal liberty in the Indian political structure. Senior civil servants continually sought to apply the liberal political and economic doctrines they had learned in Britain as students. This process was retarded by the relatively undemocratic conditions that prevailed in Britain a century ago, and by the repressive measures employed against Indian nationalists in more recent times. Nevertheless, Indians enjoyed considerable freedom under law, and the government observed self-restricting limitations to a degree unheard of under native or earlier alien rule.

In addition to this long exposure to principles of civil and political liberty, the Indians experienced a new sense of administrative unity, which ultimately strengthened the underlying forces of cultural cohesion and spurred the development of modern nationalist sentiment. It is not an exaggeration to say that Britain had a decisive influence in fostering the concept of India as a political unit, the stress on evolution to self-rule, the growth of democratic parliamentary principles, and the use of a competent bureaucracy to give substance to a central governing structure.

However, even a mildly benevolent foreign rule has serious adverse consequences. The apparent omnipotence of British rule and the efficiency of its administrative apparatus had a numbing effect on creative Indian efforts in political and economic affairs. The populace as a whole leaned heavily on the government, especially the district officers. Since Oriental governments were expected to operate in many spheres not usually considered in the public realm in the West, privately sponsored enterprises and welfare activities were rarely found. The tendency to depend on the ruler increased as native institutions, like the panchayat, withered in influence. The long period of British rule, the exclusion of Indians from high levels in the bureaucracy, and the government's failure to encourage self-reliance and self-expression in the mid-nineteenth century all heightened the native sense of inferiority. This feeling led to a hypersensitive Indian insistence on egalitarian principles. The result was that, as India moved closer to self-rule, tension and suspicion between ruler and ruled increased instead of abating.

The judicial system evolved with considerable respect for Hindu and Moslem law, particularly in personal and civil relations. Yet when a uniform judicial code was adopted, even though accompanied by the establishment of a trained judicial hierarchy, it had dislocating effects. The very thought of going to court or otherwise facing the government's enforcement regulations was in itself frightening. The multiple causes for litigation and the principles under which decisions were reached remained beyond the grasp of the average Indian; to him, such justice was capricious, with decisions arrived at by magic formulae. For example, in contracting loans, the peasant did not understand either the binding nature of the contract or the strange legal concepts of private real property and the transfer of possession. Those who, like the moneylender, could master the strange rules of English law stood to profit disproportionately. Moreover, educated Hindus chose to become lawyers in numbers well beyond the profession's needs. In general, legal, bureaucratic, and other white-collar positions had a higher prestige value than more practical professions and skills, including even engineering and medicine. The resultant scarcity of personnel in these and other vital fields involving manual labor has proved the costliness of such vocational prejudice.

Among the positive advantages of the new judicial system was the introduction of the rule of law and its challenge to the historical concept of arbitrary government. In the past, custom and inefficiency had partially shielded the Indian from his ruler, but there was no real defense against the tyranny of a powerful despot. The Western theory of limited rule and circumscribed government took hold in the nineteenth century, as was demonstrated in the strong native reactions to later British violations of the law. Adherence to this concept of government under law, used to Indian advantage under foreign rule, will be a major test of the durability of Indian democracy. Another central concept was equality before the law. Since this signified the absence of privilege based on title, religion, or caste, its introduction had serious repercussions. Up to this time, a Brahmin could not be brought to court by a person of lower caste; nor could evidence from such a source be used against him. The new procedures only gradually came to be accepted in India.

On the whole, the introduction of Western legal ideals strengthened Indian adherence to the concepts of personal liberty and parliamentary government. Britain did not immediately determine to train India for democratic self-rule, but it eventually made this commitment, so astonishing for a colonial power. However, execution of this policy was bound to encounter great difficulty, for it ran counter to many prejudices in the high echelons of the civil service, as well as in the office of the Secretary of State for Indian Affairs in London. The conflicting requirements of maintaining imperial rule and preparing Indians for self-government induced strong emotional reactions and a sense of frustration among the rulers and the ruled. Yet, despite many instances of near-disaster, the British effort remained centered on the development of India self-government.

The Rise of Indian Nationalism

Ironically, rapid change in India's culture or politics was furthest from the desires of the East India Company, especially during its early years of rule. It sought only the minimum adjustments that would consolidate company rule and enable it to operate peacefully and efficiently. Tampering with Indian traditions was considered a dangerous course of action, one that would reduce profits and endanger political stability. Therefore as part of the British stress on tradition and continuity, the hapless Mogul empire was retained as the "sovereign" power in India.

Conservative Reactions and the Sepoy Mutiny

The British conquest in itself, however, was a very unsettling fact, and the relatively few changes made in its wake were sufficient to cause unrest and, later, explosive outbreaks. Despite efforts to let Hindu religious traditions alone, the government found itself embroiled in a controversy with orthodox elements when it halted certain excessive practices. One such custom was suttee, in which a widow was supposed to destroy herself on her husband's funeral pyre. It never won divine sanction in Hindu literature and could therefore be successfully suppressed. However, the law that made suttee a criminal offense in 1829 aroused bitter conservative opposition. The end of female infanticide aroused similar reactions, though to a lesser degree.[2]

The Brahmins also resented the new legal system that placed them under criminal law for the first time, and reduced them, technically at least, to the level of other castes. Moslem landowners were disturbed by new land regulations instituted in the northern and northwestern regions. These were belated and partially successful government efforts to settle directly with the cultivator on equitable terms, in order to encourage security of tenure, increase cultivation, and lighten the peasant's financial burden. Moslem leaders were also antagonized by the late English expansion into their northwestern strongholds. The cultural counterpart of this attitude was a rejection of everything Western as inherently inferior, and a rigid adherence to all Islamic traditions.

Unrest over British rule and reform did not then take the form of modern nationalist opposition, in which the middle class and the peasantry participate. Rather, the traditionalist stand dominated the antigovernment movement in the mid-nineteenth century. In both religious communities, these culturally conservative forces have retained their powerful political influence down to

---

[2] The British also suppressed the widespread practice of thuggee, carried on by the secret thug (deceiver) caste, whose duty it was to murder unsuspecting travelers in the name of the sacred goddess Kali.

the present. Their leadership in the nineteenth century was, however, expended in the brief but furious Sepoy Mutiny of 1857, following which their prestige suffered a temporary eclipse. Their political ambitions at that time were focused on past glories—the Moslems rallying to the old Mogul empire, the Hindus supporting the exiled Peshwa of the Mahrattas. The uprising itself was centered in hitherto loyal Indian military units, where discipline was becoming lax and the alleged challenge to religious traditions stimulated unrest. The mutiny itself was touched off by a rumor that cartridges for a new type of rifle were greased with pig or cow fat; if true, the necessary act of biting the cartridge before loading the gun would in itself be a violation of Hindu and Moslem tenets. Emotions on questions of religious orthodoxy were at a raw edge, and this issue touched off a rebellion among both Hindus and Moslems. The government's political insensitivity and overconfidence were clearly reflected in the original decision to use such greased cartridges and in the fact that the mutiny itself was a complete surprise.

The British military position became especially vulnerable after 1850. A defeat suffered in the Afghan War of 1839–1843 had reduced British prestige in Indian eyes. Later the army's European contingents had been reduced by requirements in the Crimean War (1854–1856) and the Second "Opium War" in China (1856–1860). Since the remaining British units were scattered throughout India, it is not surprising that the unsuspected uprising won several initial victories, although British leaders in the Punjab and elsewhere were alert enough to disarm disloyal regiments on hearing of the outbreaks. The eventual defeat is more astonishing, and can be traced to the lack of popular support behind the mutiny. Many sepoy units remained loyal, and the Nepalese Gurkas, now in the British service, proved their reliability and competence as vital reinforcements that helped quell the mutiny. The ruling elements, who were the leaders of the revolt, could not attract other princes to their cause; the peasantry and the new middle class felt that they had little to gain from the leadership and ideals of such reactionary rebels. Fighting was therefore confined to the area of the Ganges valley, and even there the people were often friendly to the British, or at worst indifferent. An important exception was the principality of Oudh, where a recent land reform had antagonized the ruling class. To Britain's dismay, it also unsettled the intended benefiters, the peasantry, to the extent that they too opposed the government. The revolt was eventually crushed, but only after mutiny, war, and retribution took a heavy toll of human lives. When order was restored, the Mogul empire was officially abolished, company rule was ended, and the British established direct, imperial rule. Queen Victoria was eventually crowned Empress of India, in 1877.

An unfortunate consequence of the Sepoy Mutiny was the deepening of the gulf between the British and the Indians, and the reinforcement of the English attitude of superiority and aloofness. The early years of imperial adventure and freebooting had been characterized by a sense of personal equality, a willingness to intermarry and to mix socially with the Indians. As British settlements grew and wives arrived from England, this type of behavior pattern began to disappear. After the mutiny, the separation of native and ruler became institutionalized, with Indians treated as an inferior, suspect group. The new social and racial atmosphere was symbolized by "No Indians or Dogs Allowed" signs in British social clubs. Accompanying and bolstering this hardened attitude was a change in the Westerners' rationale for their rule. In earlier years it had been based on the acknowledged possession of greater power and organization and superior material advancement. Now, as the concept of the White Man's Burden to uplift the native implied, it was based on a belief in the intrinsic *moral* superiority of the Western rulers.

Such an atmosphere added enormously to the already difficult task of maintaining imperial rule, coping with the new forces of nationalism, and training the Indians for eventual self-government. The controversy over the Ilbert Bill of 1883 was symptomatic of the tenor of the times and intensified the general feeling of hostility. This law proposed to remove an old restriction by permitting Indian judges to try Britons anywhere in India. British civil servants, merchants, lawyers, and planters raised a violent propaganda barrage against this proposal, which logically accompanied the admission of Indians to higher judicial posts. The government backed down and permitted European British subjects to choose a trial by jury, half of which would be Western. This decision provoked a virulent Indian counterreaction and further embittered racial relations.

Origins of Modern Nationalism

The backlash of the Sepoy Mutiny had a numbing effect on the new Indian middle class. Its search for a role in Indian society was hampered and at times frustrated by British social and cultural aloofness, and the imperial display of power. Yet these modernizers were the real revolutionaries of Indian politics. They accepted British rule and tried to adopt the new techniques and concepts of Western life. The enormous difficulty encountered in making this adjustment led some Indians to imitate and accept everything Western to the point of rejecting their own past; this pathetic endeavor resulted in a spiritual vacuum and their failure to gain acceptance at home or abroad. Gradually there developed a movement to reconcile the "best" in both cultures, but even this moderate position meant a fundamental readjustment of one's entire outlook on life. The hostile intellectual environment of the postmutiny era made it all the more difficult to cultivate self-confidence and faith in one's ability to make the proper cultural synthesis.

The political struggle for self-expression did not lie far below the surface of this cultural effort. In fact, the political maturity and self-confidence expressed under Gandhi and Nehru in later generations, though remarkable achievements, had their groundwork in the painful, fumbling trial-and-error activities of the previous century. At first the initiative for political change lay in British hands, especially in the fields of education and legislative training.

The goddess Kali, among whose worshippers were the thugs

(Courtesy Information Service of India)

Kandarya Mahadeva Temple at Khajuraho in central India, a Hindu architectural form of about A.D. *1000*

(Courtesy Government of India Information Services)

Mohammed Ali Jinnah taking the oath of office as Governor-General of Pakistan

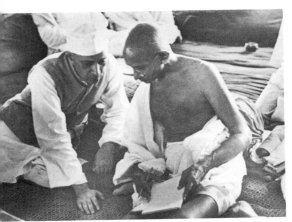

Mahatma Gandhi and Jawaharlal Nehru at the Congress party meeting of August, 1942, in Bombay, when the last "quit India" movement was launched

Moslem refugees arriving in West Pakistan in 1947

A street in Calcutta

The Vishram Ghat at Mathura, one of India's famed holy bathing places

(Courtesy United Nations)

Electrical substation of the Indian Iron and Steel Company plant at Burnpur, receiving its power from the grid of the Damodar Valley project

(Courtesy Information Division, Embassy of Pakistan)

The Adamjee jute mill in East Pakistan, scene of violent disturbances in 1954

The Swedegon Pagoda at Rangoon, Burma

Interior of Swedegon Pagoda — a reclining Buddha

Daw Khin Kyi, widow of the assassinated Burmese revolutionary hero, Aung San, and Director of the Mother and Child Welfare Department

President Diem visiting an area in South Vietnam vacated in 1954 by the Communists under the Geneva settlement

Ho Chi Minh (on right), leader of the Vietminh, and General Nguyen Giap, who directed operations against the French at Dienbienphu

(Courtesy United Nations)

Laundering in a canal in Jakarta, capital of Indonesia

The University of the Philippines in Manila still shows marks of the 1945 campaign

(Courtesy United Nations)

Organized demonstration in Seoul, Korea, protesting the planned reduction of American forces in 1954, and calling for a larger aid program

British forces in the Malayan jungle campaign against the Communist guerrillas

But later these constructive activities were unintentionally complemented by negative stimuli. Racial discrimination, belief in British moral superiority, criticism of Indian customs and traditions, and the grudging manner in which political concessions were granted all served to goad Indians to greater political efforts.

The early modernists found a leader and portent in Ram Mohan Roy (1774–1833), who combined a strong sense of self-respect with a prudent willingness to learn from the West. Roy disapproved of obstructionism, accepted Western rule, and willingly participated in Indian political affairs. A convinced rationalist, he firmly believed that one could remain a Hindu and still accept Western scientific advances and political principles. He strove to reform Hindu culture without betraying its most venerated traditions. His primary efforts at cultural adjustment were focused in the main stream of Hindu interests: an attempt to synthesize a new religious outlook combining the best in the Hindu and Christian faiths. Under Roy's leadership, the Brahma Sabha movement was formed in 1828 for this purpose. In 1845 this led to the formal organization of the Brahma Samaj.

The Brahma Samaj sought to modernize old customs, simplify the basic tenets of faith, and develop a monotheistic doctrine, all within the framework of Hinduism. Though small in number, the group attracted upper-class and intellectual support and reached its peak during the formative decades after 1857. It provided a vitally needed channel through which progressive concepts were introduced into Indian society and served as a transmission belt for the propagation of the liberal political tradition. This achievement would have been far less notable had the group disavowed its Hindu past, for then the modernizers would have been isolated, culturally and intellectually, from their own community. As it was, its concepts were challenged by the traditionalists, who sought to block this modification of Hinduism. A rival group, the Arya Samaj, was founded in 1875 in an attempt to lead Hindu thought back to the ancient scriptures. Though this group believed in social justice and a modification of discriminatory practices, its intellectual outlook provided too narrow a base for modernization. Its heavy reliance on the Vedas as a source of political guidance and its militant "Arya for the Aryans" later found expression within the nationalist political movement and contributed to the Moslems' decision to seek their own political salvation.

The Issue of Education

One of the most important British contributions to the modernization process lay in the field of education. Early in the nineteenth century, Englishmen imbued with the Western missionary spirit were anxious to acquaint India with their civilization. Despite stubborn opposition based on the logical grounds that such action would only encourage the colony to seek its freedom, this program was adhered to with a tenacity not fully appreciated in the modern anti-imperialist era. In retrospect, criticism of Britain's educational policy can be based only on the relative argument that it did not cover a sufficiently wide range of the population.

In 1813, even before it was so committed at home, the government pledged to sponsor higher education in India. The debates then raging over this decision concerned questions of method and purpose. One group, fearful of the effects of a total change and highly impressed with India's historical culture, sought to graft Western scientific and mechanical skills onto the Indian tradition. It can be argued that a nation cannot simply add Western techniques as "armor" to protect itself without leading to inevitable changes in social, political, and religious spheres as well. However, the opponents of this limited approach adopted the positive argument that India should be exposed to the main stream of Western political and philosophical thought. They also advocated the teaching of English language and literature as the means through which this liberal education could be extended. This latter group eventually won out, and their ideas dominated the curriculum at government and Christian mission schools.[3] The educational system proved a strong modernizing force, and English became the language of educated people throughout India. Its great vocational utility in business, law, and the civil service helped to induce native students to undertake Western studies.

Stress was placed on secondary and advanced education, with many students going to England to complete their studies. However, primary education and elementary schools in vernacular tongues did not receive comparable attention. The gap between the mass of the people and this trained elite widened, in terms of political orientation as well as cultural outlook. The upper and middle classes have received during the past century a thorough grounding in Western democratic ideals and traditions, but the peasantry and the new urban laboring class received no training of this sort. Since the democratic faith was implanted in only a fraction of the community, modification of the traditional authoritarian outlook in the lower classes has at best been indirect and weak. It remains to be seen whether this Western tradition can retain its position and gain widespread acceptance by the rest of the population under the trying political and economic conditions of the postindependence period.

Economic Motivations of Nationalism

As the century drew to a close, anticapitalist political and economic doctrines that originated in the West were used to bolster the nationalist position. The arguments against the British were numerous. In terms of physical development, it was clear that Britain was relatively indifferent to the industrial development of India. The state did not plan or direct new industrial or commercial activities on a large scale. Added handicaps to the subcontinent's

---

[3] This view was presented in a famous minute by Thomas Macaulay in 1835. Unfortunately, he revealed such a contemptuous lack of appreciation of Indian culture that the Indians, justifiably angered, have been slow to appreciate the constructive recommendations presented.

development were the Indian disinclination to invest and foreign capital's discouragement at the costs and risks involved. In the decades after 1870 the Indians could compare their situation with that of Japan, where political direction and motivation led to a strenuous program of modernization, despite the expense incurred. The British government in India, by contrast, actually retarded Indian development of light industries in response to pressure from English textile concerns. It failed to protect the new Indian textile industry before the First World War, even though a protective tariff was achieved with the support of British officials in India. British manufacturers then induced the London government to levy a countervailing duty against Indian textile exports that largely canceled this advantage.

Of more immediate appeal was the argument that Britain was exploiting its colony; justifiably or not, poverty and exploitation were linked in the popular mind. The more violent Marxian doctrines, reinforced by Lenin's theory that imperialism was the capitalist system's last stage, found willing disciples in South Asia after 1900. Although the communist and later Soviet versions appeared too extreme, the more moderate socialist ideologies did gain wide currency in India and lands to the east because they challenged, in economic and moral terms, the rule of the capitalist-imperial powers.

Hindu-Moslem Divergences

With each passing decade after 1880 the demand for self-rule mounted in intensity and magnitude until it became the dominant theme in Indian affairs. However, a tragic flaw in this movement was its inability to preserve Hindu-Moslem political unity. As the Indian drive for independence began to show results, Moslem apprehensions increased. It was feared that the political leaders of the predominantly Hindu nationalist movement would be the rulers of the liberated colony. The differences rooted in religious issues became channeled into political antagonisms when nationalism exposed and intensified the existing communal hostilities.

Although in a numerical minority, the Moslems had been the ruling element in central and north India, and the British conquest was looked on as a blow to their position. The bitter wars of conquest of the mid-nineteenth century in the northwest region were still fresh in the minds of the Moslem political elite during the early period of modernization. As a result, antagonism between the British and Moslems, reinforced by the Sepoy Mutiny and the dream of reviving Mogul power, bolstered orthodox Moslem efforts to stay aloof from the conqueror and his ways.

Many Hindus, on the other hand, had been under British rule since the eighteenth century and were able to adjust more gradually to the changed conditions. They did not harbor such deep political animosity, for in many places they would be simply exchanging one non-Hindu ruler for another. The Hindus also proved more adaptable to new cultural concepts; the relatively high degree of flexibility that the Brahmin intellectuals had demonstrated in past epochs of cultural fusion now stood Hinduism in good stead. But this advantage further sharpened the cultural and economic differences between the two religious communities and placed the Moslems under a significant political handicap.

The upper-caste Hindus supplied most of the early students of Western political forms and ideals, literature, and scientific and business skills. The Hindus thus gained a vital early lead in the legal profession, the business world, the government service—important despite its restricted scope—and political affairs. When the Moslems undertook their painful task of adjustment, they found their opponents entrenched in positions of advantage and prestige. They could not fall back on superior organization and skill to compensate in quality for their numerically inferior position. Instead, the distribution of skills simply reinforced the majority Hindu element.

In concluding that the application of Britain's democratic parliamentary ideology would mean Hindu rule, the Moslems, as an irreconcilable minority group, were transplanting cultural and religious differences to the political arena. They feared that the Hindus would make religion the determining political factor and use their majority position to discriminate against the Moslems, individually and as a group, in order to perpetuate their rule. This insecure Moslem community, proud of its past and fearful of reprisals, was easily tempted in coming out of its "cocoon" to seek to insulate itself against such dangers.

It is unfortunate that the Hindus did not appreciate the strength of these fears and act with greater consideration. The British, in turn, have been accused of either underestimating this problem or utilizing it to effect the principle of divide and rule. Actually, this negative attitude toward the Hindu was by no means universally held by the Moslems. However, these fears, fed by a series of events viewed from this suspicion-riddled perspective, came to dominate the Moslem community. This statement is not intended to deny that men of good will in all camps worked for harmonious relations, nor does it argue that the eventual political solution of partition was inevitable. The divisive forces seem in retrospect to have been more purposeful and better organized, and therefore able to carry the day against a bewildered and surprised opposition.

The setting in which the new spirit of nationalism operated was therefore more complex than that of an imperial-colonial rivalry. The Hindu movement embraced such extremes as religious traditionalists and secular reformers, and the methods they advocated ranged from constitutional opposition to violence and terrorism. The Moslems were also of two minds, not only on the question of relations with the Hindus but on the issue of traditionalism and reform as well. To maintain that Britain was the major cause of these splits is to underestimate the vigor of the competing forces at work within the Indian civilization, and the inevitable disagreements that were bound to arise once this tradition was confronted with a dynamic alien culture.

340

Political Self-Expression

An immediate effect of the government's educational policy was to encourage the Indians to demand for themselves the rights and obligations that the British middle class achieved in the nineteenth century. The government did encourage some self-expression in politics, though reforms in this direction were carefully controlled and exasperatingly slow in coming. Beginning in 1861, the British developed a program of "political training" and the gradual transfer of responsibility to Indian political leaders. Legislative and executive councils, with only advisory powers at first, were added to the provincial governments. Membership on these councils consisted of government officials and nonofficial British and native members. After 1900 the nonofficial element, predominantly native, became the majority, and the Indians in these councils were elected. This alteration of membership and the extension of powers beyond the advisory level occurred much more quickly in the legislative councils. The executive councils, in effect fledgling cabinets, gained authority in the provinces very slowly, and did not assume power in the central government until the end of the Second World War.

Indian political self-expression was slow to crystallize in the period following the Sepoy Mutiny; it was not until 1885 that the Indian National Congress was organized. This body, which became the backbone of the national independence movement, was founded by a retired civil servant, Octavian Hume. Its first session was attended by the Viceroy, who gave the organization his blessings. The early years of Congress activity were marked by extreme caution and at least verbal appreciation of British rule. Its members were mostly middle-class Hindus, especially Brahmins, who respresented the new urban elements, plus some landed aristocrats. Mild reforms were suggested in the hope that such reasonable proposals by loyal subjects would bring results. Britain's failure to respond in a generous manner and extend the powers of native self-government more rapidly weakened the disappointed moderate group. This lack of foresight eventually opened the way to power for the more radical and aggressive nationalist elements.

Britain did broaden the base of the central and provincial legislative councils in the Act of 1892, a concession touching on the dual problems of Indian politi-cal freedom and Moslem-Hindu suspicions. The reform was an inadequate concession to Indian claims for increased representation at the center and greater power and authority in the councils. The right to discuss the budget and interrogate the government was granted. More nonofficial members were added to the councils, but they were not yet chosen by election. However, provision was made for designating certain nongovernmental groups—local governmental boards, universities, landholders, and chambers of commerce—to nominate candidates. These nominees would then gain seats on the councils— if the government approved. The absence of territorial elections was in line with Britain's belief that India was not yet prepared for full democratic training. Even this tentative step toward popular choice aroused Moslem concern.

From the first, the National Congress party leaders insisted that their movement was a secular one, with membership open to all Indians. Moslems were willing to join to some extent, and their proportion of the delegates to annual Congress conventions rose from 2 per cent in 1885 to 22 per cent in 1890. However, the majority of the Moslems remained aloof, becoming more apprehensive with each successive British concession toward self-rule. Even the more progressive Moslems, who sought to modernize Islam's culture, hesitated to join the Hindus in a united anti-British front. A most influential reformer was Sir Syed Ahmed Khan, who sought to harmonize Islamic and Western ideals and founded the important Western-oriented Moslem institution of higher learning at Aligarh. Even this great humanist rejected the Hindu call for cooperation and advised his coreligionists not to join the Congress movement. By 1900 the Moslems had overcome their strong anti-British feeling and seemed to prefer Western control to Hindu rule. The rise of the Arya Samaj and other traditionalist Hindu movements led the Moslems to oppose an independence movement until their own security seemed guaranteed, and then to seek a political settlement that would give them their own freedom.

13 *The Struggle*
for Independence

The Indian struggle for freedom after 1900 proved to be one of the most spec-tacular mass movements of political nationalism. When opposition to Britain spread over the entire subcontinent, much of this sentiment was first expressed in terms of local and regional loyalties—in the old Mahratta region around Poona, in Bengal, and among the Sikhs of the Punjab. It was only after considerable effort that the powerful attraction of regional loyalty, expressed in the Bombay and Bengal wings of the Congress party, could be subordinated to a single campaign for independence.

There was also a divergence of views over the method and purpose in this political struggle. Within the Hindu camp itself a wide gulf persisted between the religious traditionalists, who sought to renounce Western culture, and the advocates of a modern secular state. The question of cooperation with the British was also debated. The moderates and Liberals saw in British concessions a basis for the eventual satisfaction of Indian desires. Though influential, they lost political control after 1918 to extremists who demanded immediate self-rule. Also in the picture were practitioners of violence who saw in force and terror important weapons to drive the British out.

The Congress party was remarkably successful in its efforts to fashion a unified political front, retain its beliefs in democratic principles, and acquire a mass base of peasant support, which eventually gave it a majesty and sweep of irresistible proportions. Until 1914 though, there was real danger that its middle-class leadership would dissolve into small warring factions. It took the genius of Mahatma Gandhi to avert this peril. His saintly appearance and appeal to traditional Hindu concepts rallied the peasantry and unified the nationalist movement. However, the political gap between Hindu and Moslem widened and gave rise to a Moslem demand for partition when independence was in sight.

Early Political Currents

The Outburst of Nationalism

The Indian political scene presented three major interrelated strands as the struggle for freedom grew in intensity. In terms of formal structure of government, a direct line can be traced through constitutional reforms—1907, 1919, 1935, and finally 1947—that led to the actual transfer of power. These gave free India a solid political and administrative foundation. But it was the activity of the Congress-led nationalist movement, with its extralegal activities, that dominated events. The third element was the rise of an apprehensive Moslem leadership in earnest search of communal security. Its policy took shape under the influence of the struggles with the Hindu groups and those between Indians and Britain. The interplay of these forces is nowhere better illustrated than in the twenty-year period climaxed by the First World War.

The years after 1896 were marked by political agitation and violence, much of it rooted in the social hostility and aloofness of the previous generation. Tactics of moderation brought so few political and administrative reforms that extremism gained adherents in the Congress party. The spirit of nationalism was further fanned by British difficulties with the Boers in South Africa and the spread of the European concept of self-rule to Asia.

Meanwhile, there arose in Poona a strident cultural nationalism that followed the views of the Arya Samaj and a similar group, the Ramakrishna Mission. This effort to return to pure Hinduism was led by a Brahmin, Bal Gangadhar Tilak, who opposed both Moslems and the British. He lashed out at the "timid" Congress, and justified his journalistic exhortations to violence as saving cherished native traditions. For example, Tilak opposed a government attempt to prevent child marriages under the age of twelve. When famine and plague struck in 1896–1897, he criticized government slowness in aiding distressed areas and called for a no-rent campaign. More serious was his injunction to resist British efforts at epidemic control in Poona to quarantine the diseased; the British troops were required to enter Indian households, in violation of orthodox caste principles. Political murder resulted when two British officers were assassinated. As disease spread through the countryside, agitation for "plague riots" continued among his followers. Tilak was imprisoned for sedition, but in 1901 he led an effort to gain control over the Congress party organization. This attempt was checked in 1905–1907, but it split the nationalist camp and frightened the Moslems.

Tilak's efforts were regional in scope, but the new technique of terror and violence spread to Bengal and its great city of Calcutta, then capital of British India. The intellectuals of this province, who had made great progress in reform and modernization, spearheaded the nationalist movement. Geographically apart from the rest of India, the Bengali retained a strong sense of local patriotism. The Viceroy, Lord Curzon (1899–1905), decided to partition the province for the sake of administrative efficiency, because at that time it included Bengal, Bihar, and Orissa, with a population of 78 million. The Viceroy, for all his success in improving Indian communications, economic diversification, and administrative efficiency, was remarkably insensitive to political feeling. His partition of 1905 made one unit of East Bengal and Assam, and another of Bihar, Orissa, and West Bengal. Since Bengal also contained a large Moslem element, Curzon felt that this division, essentially along religious lines, would enable the Moslems—in the eastern portion—to escape from the shadow of the more advanced and dominant Hindus. The Moslems' response was mixed: the change certainly offered a great opportunity but offended their deep provincial loyalty.

The Hindu reaction was unequivocal and violent, with the partition denounced as an imperial counterattack against India's leading province. Political protest continued incessantly through the viceregency of the Earl of Minto (1906–1911); a widespread series of bombings, gang robberies, and violence created a revolutionary situation. Finally, in 1911, King George V, while in India, announced the reunification of Bengal and the separation of Bihar and Orissa. However, to the dismay of the Bengali, the imperial capital was moved to New Delhi, the old Mogul site.

The cumulative shock effect of these various developments on the Moslems was profound. Sir Syed Ahmed Khan described Tilak's activity as a "civil war without arms." The acts of violence to thwart a reform beneficial to the Moslems and their eventual success reduced Moslem faith in the British as well. During this period, the Moslem community sought to protect its interests by forming a Moslem League in 1906, to act as an effective pressure group on the government. Its first major concern was to avoid the creation of an election system on a pure British model of geographic representation, for this would ensure permanent Hindu domination. The Moslems wanted special representation for themselves as a religious constituency, and on advantageous terms.

The Morley-Minto Reform of 1909

Moslem interest in the electoral system was heightened because a major political reform was in the offing. The new Liberal government in London favored some change, but its own basic confusion was reflected by the Secretary of State for India, Lord Morley, who felt that India was unprepared for democracy. The Viceroy considered representative self-government to be an "impossible ambition." As a result, the reforms were too narrow to satisfy India and literally lacked ideological cohesion. Indians gained wider access to executive posts at the center and in the presidencies of Bombay and Madras; executive councils were established in the other provinces. Major attention was focused on the legislatures, but here the concessions failed to create a system of responsible government. Provincial legislative councils gained nonofficial majorities, to be chosen by an electorate of a little more than 1 million. They were permitted to discuss and pass resolutions on all matters, and so could

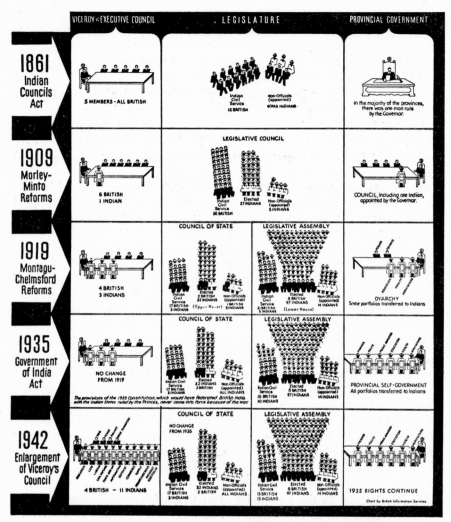

Courtesy: British Information Services.

The Development of Self-Government in British India

bring some pressure to bear on the executive. Unfortunately, this was also an invitation to act irresponsibly, propose popular utopian programs, or criticize the government without having to assume any official burdens. An air of cynicism and unreality resulted, which greatly reduced the benefits of the reform.

More significant were the long-range effects on India's internal political balance. The moderates, led by Gopal Krishna Gokhale, controlled the Congress party, and a real step toward legislative responsibility might have made their position secure. In 1908 Gokhale secured a party pledge to seek reform through

346

peaceful and legal means. When the Morley-Minto reform was first enacted, the moderates entertained high hopes that representative government would be won through persistent legal agitation. Gokhale visited Britain and put the Indian case before the Liberal cabinet, but with the passage of time the moderates became disappointed in their failure to gain results. In 1915 Congress President Sir S. P. Sinha, a high official in the bureaucracy, observed that the 1909 reform was leading up a blind alley.

Another significant result of the Morley-Minto reform was the creation of special communal electorates for the Moslems. Islamic leaders, in a delegation led by the Aga Khan, had demanded that a special number of seats on the legislative councils be reserved for the Moslems alone. Thus in each electoral region there would be a fixed number of contests decided only by qualified Moslem voters. The Moslems refused a compromise offer of reserved seats with joint electorates and eventually won British support for their view. They also gained a larger share of the seats than population figures warranted by arguing for electoral "weightage" because of their importance in the community.

The British have since been accused of consciously applying the imperial tactic of divide and rule. Separate electorates were viewed as a wedge that made political capital out of religious differences and ultimately made the communal problem insoluble. Yet the Moslems were intensely disturbed and required some concessions. Religious antagonism had such deep historical and social roots that its penetration into politics was perhaps inevitable. Britain may well have benefited from the growing Hindu-Moslem antagonisms, and the electoral change certainly violated the territorial principle of representation, but it cannot be considered the central cause of all later trouble. Since the reform of 1907–1909 was not viewed as a step toward parliamentary rule, the British may not have been guilty of ideological hypocrisy. Their failure to think through the problem of self-government was a more grievous error, since its ultimate effect was to strengthen the hand of the extremists when the Gokhale period (1907–1915) came to an end.

The Changing Economic Scene

The onset of a world war quickened the pace of India's political and economic development. The country was undergoing gradual and unspectacular changes that ultimately had a profound effect on its economic and social composition. India had been "opened" to world economic currents by the development of its road, rail, and canal networks. The Suez Canal had made extensive participation in international markets feasible, and foreign trade grew five times between 1858 and 1908. Agricultural output increased under an irrigation system that by 1939 covered more than 50 million acres, or one fifth of the total area cultivated.[1]

---

[1] In 1900–1939 the area cultivated by irrigation rose from 195 million to 228 million acres; forested regions also increased, from 54 to 89 million acres.

The principal cash crops were cotton and jute in the Bombay and Bengal regions, respectively, with mills and processing plants also constructed in these areas. Indigo and tea in Assam, coffee and, temporarily, wheat in the newly irrigated Punjab and Sind regions were additional exports attesting to the increasing diversity of Indian production.

The Indians, stirred by the example of Japan's successes, sought to develop their own industry. They encouraged the teaching of economic and technical courses in colleges, as well as traditional professional studies. One of the most outstanding industrial achievements was the organization of the Tata Steel Works near Bombay, in the face of the free-trade stand of Lord Morley in London and the absence of "infant-industry" tariff protection. The government in India did assist the project with a series of concessions and orders for equipment, including rails and other finished goods.

Economic modernization did not produce tremendous physical changes in this predominantly agrarian society. Rather, it appeared in the increased standardization of price and cost throughout the country, in more frequent use of money, in greater mobility and division of labor, and in the use of impersonal contract-hiring systems. Industrial laborers did not exceed 2,500,000 in 1947, but the country developed the basic substructure in finance and economic organization, as well as in communication facilities, essential for continued industrial growth. Earliest progress was made in steel, textile piece-goods production, coal mining, and such consumer industries as cement, matches, and refined sugar.

A capital market developed more gradually because it was new to Indian commercial traditions and required unfamiliar skills. As foreign capital entered the country in appreciable quantities, the Indians themselves began to form joint stock companies, invest in foreign lands, and support governmental loans. The problem of efficiency in investment and management was partly resolved by the Managing Agency System: British management experts established agencies that invested their clients' funds in varied unrelated industries. The agencies functioned as unofficial centers of liaison for these concerns, and their competence and integrity attracted Indian and foreign capital. Although at times criticized for excessive caution and conservatism regarding innovation and industrial expansion, the Managing Agencies were widely respected and won praise from the Indian Industrial Commission of 1916–1918. By the end of the First World War, India was recognized in the League of Nations as the eighth leading industrial power in the world.[2]

Still, native management was undeveloped, and the country's financial structure remained rudimentary. Business and capital continued to be drawn to the traditional fields of moneylending and land investment, where monetary returns and security were high. Industrial activity remained concentrated primarily in the Bombay and Calcutta regions and a few other cities; thus the new develop-

[2] The number of joint-stock companies in India rose from 1,728 in 1905 to 3,668 in 1919.

ments had a restricted territorial influence. India also suffered during the early stages of modernization because social and economic dislocations loomed large, compared to immediate material returns. It also had to bear the additional burden of a rapidly growing population, which absorbed its increased wealth. The over-all standard of life therefore probably did not change much during the half century after 1890, and not more than 5 to 10 per cent of the total population enjoyed an upper- and middle-class level of well-being.

Symbolic of the link between economic issues and nationalist politics was the increasing popularity of *Swadeshi,* the movement to "buy Indian" goods. The growing tension in Indian-British relations was fed by complaints of imperial exploitation, British control and direction of the economy, and the retarded growth of the Indian industrial and consumer market. Within the nationalist camp there was agreement on the need to protect and guide the development of India's economy, but no consensus as to purpose. Cultural traditionalists argued for a return to the old order, pointing out that the very fabric of India's social structure was being destroyed by modernization and the collapse of native handicraft industries, with little material benefits. The caste system, village society, and family unity, all dependent on inherited and stable vocations, were being undermined. The modernists appreciated these difficulties but envisaged India's salvation through an increased tempo of modernization—in the fields of agriculture and transportation, as well as power and industry. These divergences cut across party lines: many of Gandhi's political followers had little sympathy with his effort to popularize a return to native handicrafts, symbolized by the spinning wheel, and the use of homemade cotton goods. Social reformers like Jawaharlal Nehru, Gandhi's leading disciple, and industrial leaders like his close associate Birla considered these views backward and helped to deny them Congress approval.

By 1919 the Indian effort to gain greater economic freedom from London had become a major issue. At this time the British government in India was given greater latitude to determine economic policy in accordance with Indian needs. A Fiscal Convention was reached whereby India could establish its own tariff policy, without suffering a veto from London, if the government (that is, the British-controlled central executive in New Delhi) and the new Central Legislature were in accord. India immediately eliminated the excise duties on manufactured exports that Britain had imposed in order to neutralize the protection gained by an earlier tariff. For the first time, India gained real tariff protection.

Political Effects of the First World War

The high hopes for political autonomy remained unfulfilled during this period. The war opened on a note of optimism, with the moderates still in command and most Indians demonstrating their loyalty by participating wholeheartedly in Britain's effort. The country raised the Commonwealth's largest volunteer contingent and was of invaluable assistance as a strategic base and source of supply. However, the tide turned steadily against the moderates. After the death of Gokhale in 1915, extremism and its rallying cries of Swaraj (self-rule) and Swadeshi gained prominence. By 1918 the moderates had lost control of the Congress party and a revolutionary situation had developed.

Even the period of moderate control had not been free of violence. Riots and agitation had continued in Bengal. The exclusion of Sikhs and Moslems from Canada in 1914, because of discriminatory immigration laws, had led to terrorism and conspiracy in the Punjab. Further dissatisfaction with the Commonwealth as a whole stemmed from the sweeping discriminatory legislation against Indians passed by South Africa after 1905; an Indian community was originally formed there in 1860, when indentured labor was imported to help alleviate a manpower shortage. The community's leader in this crisis was Mohandas Gandhi, a young lawyer, who sought to gain a compromise through the practice of nonviolent resistance. A settlement reached in 1914 later proved illusory, but the experience was of great importance to Gandhi, who soon returned to India.

The Moslem League became anti-British during the course of the war because the empire was fighting against Turkey and the caliphate, spiritual center of Islam. Some Moslem elements even conspired with the Germans. Common resentment against the British brought Hindu and Moslem leaders closer to agreement than ever before. Both Gandhi, who had at first recruited troops for Britain, and Mohammed Ali, the Moslem leader, had moved from a favorable to an antagonistic stand on the war. An effective leader who brought both sides together was Mohammed Ali Jinnah, a Bombay lawyer and member of both the League and the Congress.

As president of the League Jinnah had it convene simultaneously with the Congress at Lucknow in 1916, where the famous "Lucknow Pact" was concluded. This plan was a political compromise under which the two religious communities agreed to work out a harmonious relationship if Britain yielded to Indian demands for self-rule. In effect, the Hindus accepted the principle of separate electorates—as Britain was later to point out to its critics. The Moslems were to have one third of the elected seats in the central legislature and a fixed proportion, generally under their numerical strength, in the provinces.[3] But no bill affecting a religious community was to become law if opposed by three quarters of the group. The Moslem acceptance of the Congress objectives of dominion status and parliamentary democracy can be credited to the efforts of Jinnah, in whose honor the Congress named its Bombay headquarters. Twenty years later, Jinnah became the moving force in the drive for partition and Pakistan.

All India was keenly awaiting a new reform that would create a responsible democratic national government, and all political elements participated in the

[3] For example, some precentages were, the Punjab, 50; Bengal, 40; United Provinces, 30; Bihar, 25; Madras, 15.

popular exercise of drawing up model constitutions. Interest was centered on the attitudes of the new Secretary of State Montagu and the Viceroy Lord Chelmsford. The latter, with a long service in India, held that self-government within the British Empire was a proper objective. Based on the Viceroy's proposals, Secretary Montagu in 1917 expressed Britain's interest in

> increasing association of Indians in every branch of the administration and the gradual development of self-governing institutions with a view to the progressive realization of responsible government in India as an integral part of the British Empire.

However noble the long-term purpose, the statement clearly reflected the government's caution and stress on gradualism. Britain was making future reform contingent on the behavior of Indians who wanted immediate fundamental changes.

The Government of India Act of 1919

The Montagu-Chelmsford reform of 1919 established parliamentary rule and dominion status as future objectives but made only modest reforms in this direction. The nationalists now doubted Britain's sincerity, and a bitter controversy raged throughout the interwar period.

Under the Act of 1919 the Viceroy retained control over all questions of major importance, but a central legislature was established, consisting of an Assembly and a Council of State. Two thirds of the Assembly was elected—with 7 million persons now voting—but separate communal and special interests retained their representation. The government could override this body with the support of the more conservative Council of State, which had a larger proportion of appointed members. The elected members remained without real power or responsibility and could never force the government's hand on vital issues.

A separate organ at the center was the Chamber of Princes. This consultative body never gained importance because of the aloofness of many princely rulers. However slow British reform appeared to the nationalists, it seemed hasty and dangerous to the princes. The general lag in economic and social modernization in the native states, despite some notable exceptions like Mysore and Travancore-Cochin in the south, made the nationalists anxious to alter this political structure. The largest state, Hyderabad, with a Moslem ruler and a Hindu population, enjoyed a Moslem cultural renaissance at the court but made little economic or political progress. As nationalist agitation increased, the princes became more hostile to the independence movement.

If changes at the center were more a matter of form than substance, real progress was made in provincial affairs. Specific powers were transferred from the center to the provinces in a step toward a federal system, which Britain believed suitable to such a large and diverse country. To support this decision, central and provincial financial powers were clearly demarcated in order to protect the lesser units from central interference. Secondly, the powers given to the provinces were divided between elected Indian officials and the British, under a system called dyarchy. This carefully circumscribed grant of power reflected Britain's belief that this was only a training period for Indian legislators and administrators. Each province was headed by a governor who worked with an executive council, composed of appointed British and Indian members, and a body of Indian ministers selected from the provincial legislature.[4] Certain key powers such as law and order, revenue and finance, were reserved to the governor and his executive council. The other departments were transferred to the Indian ministry responsible to the legislature; these included the "nation-building" functions of education, local government, public health, and economic development. Even though the governor retained reserve and emergency powers to reassert his authority in a crisis, the British felt that they had instituted such a bold and complex change that it would take good faith on all sides to ensure its success.

The Nationalist Response

After some hesitation, Gandhi rejected this British offer as inadequate, a decision that left the moderates in the Congress hopelessly outnumbered. Moslem antagonism had meanwhile been heightened by Britain's acquiescence to Greek and Italian territorial aspirations in Turkey itself. As a result, Congress leaders were able to form an anti-British alliance with the powerful Moslem Khalifat movement, which sought to preserve the caliphate, "the most essential institution for the Muslim community throughout the world."

Nationalists were also aroused by the stern Rowlatt Acts promulgated in 1919 to stem the tide of lawlessness, especially in Bengal. These acts permitted the jailing of suspects without trial, secret trials before three judges, no right of counsel, and no appeal even from capital punishment. In the rioting and agitation against this suspension of British justice, the new laws died still-born. Another crisis occurred in the Punjab, with its discontented Sikhs, angry Khalifat Moslems, and Congress agitators. Since the northwest region was inflamed by tribal struggles and the Third Afghan War, military rule was established to restore order. When a crowd of 10,000 gathered in Amritsar to listen to speeches despite a ban on assembly, General Reginald Dyer ordered the audience machine-gunned in an effort to restore discipline. The official count listed 379 dead and 1,200 wounded. Indians called this a monstrous act of carnage, but General Dyer escaped punishment and even became a hero to Britons in India. This incident shook Britain's confidence in its ability to hold India and strengthened the nationalist cause immeasurably.

All regional and religious groups were fused under the leadership of Gandhi, who even induced the Moslems to accept his doctrine of nonviolent resistance

---

[4] The provincial legislatures were usually single chambers, with a few appointees and a large majority elected—on the territorial, communal, and special-group basis.

as the major tactical weapon. In the anti-British campaign, titles were resigned, students left schools, and lawyers quit their practices. By 1921 the formal civil disobedience campaign reached its peak, spearheaded by a hartal, or economic strike, which stopped all business activity. Unpaid taxes, worker strikes, and the refusal to sell British goods were the peaceful means by which political concessions were to be wrung from Britain. In the political sphere, the Congress boycotted the new constitution, so that the moderate-liberals, determined to give it a fair trial, dominated the legislative elections. Though lacking in prestige and labeled "government men," they did put the 1919 reform into operation.

The disobedience campaign was characterized by disorder and feverish excitement. Gandhi, determined to win self-rule by peaceful extralegal means, had the Congress party constitution amended toward this end. Yet violence during the previous decade and the novelty of Gandhi's strategy made bloodshed inevitable. At the height of the campaign, in February, 1922, a mob at Chauri Chaura in the United Provinces burned to death several policemen. Gandhi abruptly halted the nationalist effort, stating that the people were not yet sufficiently imbued with the spirit of peaceful resistance. He was jailed, and the entire program disintegrated. The Moslems, never enthusiastic about Gandhi's tactics, were left baffled and frustrated. Simultaneously, the Khalifat movement collapsed when Turkish revolutionaries under Mustapha Kemal abolished the caliphate and established a secular state. Moslem-Hindu cooperation, so painstakingly established, was suddenly destroyed; it never regained the degree of success enjoyed in the years following the Lucknow Pact.

Crosscurrents of Nationalist Agitation

Gandhi was released from jail for reasons of health in 1924 as the political scene quieted somewhat, and attention was turned to progress through reform. The moderates who had participated in the 1919 election included C. R. Das and his Swaraj party and Molital Nehru; they now urged the Congress to join in the 1924 contests. This was done despite Gandhi's advice to the contrary, but for the negative purpose of undermining the constitution. The popular Congress won many victories, but its obstructionist tactics upset the delicate system of dyarchy, leading to its temporary abandonment in Bengal and the Central Provinces. Still, an increasing number of Indians gained an understandstanding of democratic processes, and in many instances valuable social and economic legislation was passed.

The Indian provincial ministries were dependent on the British governors for financial support. This awkward situation was further strained by a depressed economic environment. In their desire to maintain budgetary stability, provincial governments generally followed a policy of retrenchment, which cut the nation-building projects sharply. Still worse, the executive councils used their fiscal and tax powers to push through unpopular proposals, including a doubling of the salt tax in 1923, which severely hit the poor. Even the moderates protested against this frustrating constitutional arrangement, but the British persisted in carrying on a planned ten-year trial. The bulk of Indian political opinion had now become revolutionary, in the Gandhian sense of the term, the people believing that independence was there to be seized. The British in turn looked on the Congress as a group of incorrigible and irresponsible agitators, a judgment that they extended to the Swaraj party and other moderate groups.

Meanwhile, Britain faithfully adhered to its program of Indianizing the bureaucracy. In 1917 the government promised to recruit the higher services in India and close some branches to applicants in England. These reforms were carried out in 1924, with the objective of making half the civil service Indian by 1939. Military training of officers proceeded more slowly but was sufficiently advanced to permit rapid Indianization after 1939.

Indian political leadership remained firmly under Gandhi's control during the interwar period. Though of slight physical build, Gandhi possessed an overwhelmingly powerful personality and proved a political-religious philosopher of such importance that he became one of the dominant figures of this century. An ardent nationalist, he was a profound humanitarian who stressed the doctrine of ahimsa, or noninjury of any living being. He denied himself natural comforts, lived unpretentiously in his village retreat, and used the spinning wheel to produce his few garments. He repeatedly endured fasts, long marches, and other great personal sacrifices in order to gain support for the great causes he espoused—Indian independence, a better life for the untouchables, and the preservation of communal peace. These spectacular efforts, undertaken in moments of crisis, further enshrined him as the inspired leader of the Indian people. His political tactics of nonviolent resistance and civil disobedience, called satyagraha—"stubborn adherence to truth" or "soul-force"—signified his belief in positive action against oppressors by spiritual rather than physical power. This philosophy proved dramatically successful in winning peasant support for the Congress party and making it a truly national movement.

The picture and name of Gandhi, as well as those of his younger colleagues Jawaharlal Nehru and Subhas Chandra Bose, became known throughout the land. Whether or not he held an official post, Gandhi represented the strength and authority of the Congress during the recurrent political crises of the interwar period. Though he did not compel the party to follow his advice when its high command (the Working Committee) took a different position, his strategic leadership was supreme. Gandhi's manner at arriving at decisions was somewhat erratic and his critics accused him of being an authoritarian who would brook no opposition within the party. Despite his own religious scepticism and different economic views, Jawaharlal Nehru accepted Gandhi's dominance, and eventually became his political and spiritual successor. Bose, however, an antipacifist Bengali aristocrat, differed with Gandhi on so many points that he eventually broke with the Congress party.

Gandhi's success in linking a modern political movement to traditional Hindu religious and ethical precepts also gave the party the strength it later required to preserve and develop the democratic Western political concepts that were its British heritage. However, the brilliance of this saintly apostle imbued the Congress with a distinctly Hindu flavor, which convinced many Moslem leaders that regardless of Congress' self-portrait as a secular all-Indian body, it was in effect a political-religious movement organized by and for Hindus. Thus the greatest political achievement of Indian nationalism contributed to a further deterioration of communal relations.

Communal tensions existed even during the brief period of Hindu-Moslem cooperation. In 1921, the Moplahs, a fanatical Moslem enclave of Arab descent on the southwest (Malabar) coast, rebelled against the government and conducted a wanton assault on the Hindus. Meanwhile communalist Hindu elements were organizing a dual movement of *suddhi* and *sangathan. Suddhi* was a drive to reconvert those who had left the Hindu faith, while *sangathan* was an effort to give Hinduism a disciplined military spirit. In 1928 communalists, angered by Congress moderation, formed a Hindu Mahasabha party to foster Hindu dominance. The Moslems, especially in Hindu-majority areas, feared crusading assaults by private religious armies. After 1924 communal riots occurred with disheartening frequency all over India, particularly in Bengal, the Punjab, and the United Provinces.[5] In this era of communal and antigovernmental tension, the British passed restrictive legislation and made many summary arrests. Communal unrest was so extensive between 1920 and 1940 that the leader of the Scheduled (untouchables) Castes, Dr. B. R. Ambedkar, described the situation as one continuous civil war.

Efforts at a New Constitution

Preparation for constitutional reform took eight stormy years (1927–1935), during which time all major factions drew further apart. A commission under Sir John Simon (1927–1930) proposed a federal structure, with full ministerial responsibility in the provinces and British domination at the center. The commission had no Indian members, and its chairman was so disappointed by political conditions in India that he doubted the wisdom even of this reform. The Congress was furious at this refusal to grant dominion status and demanded complete independence. By contrast, the Moslems now favored a weak central government, "full autonomy" for the provinces, and legally guaranteed communal representation. A moderate Indian report by an unofficial committee under Molital Nehru favored dominion status, a federal system including democratic princely states, and the end of communal representation. This solution was rejected by all groups concerned.

The Congress then launched another campaign of civil disobedience. In March, 1930, Gandhi touched off the resistance effort with a dramatic march to

---

[5] Among the more spectacular riots were those at Kolat (1924), Calcutta (1926), and Cawnpore (1931).

the sea to make his own salt, in violation of the law and in protest against the high salt tax. This 165-mile walk captured the popular imagination and the number of marching participants increased rapidly. A widespread boycott got under way: government schools and administrative agencies were shunned, taxes remained unpaid, and homespun cotton replaced foreign cloth. Continuous demonstrations at times brought public affairs to a standstill. During 1930 about 50,000 "political offenders," including Gandhi and other leaders, were jailed. The riots and bloodshed accompanying this campaign were looked on by Indians as unfortunate aberrations that did not reduce the grandeur of Gandhi's sacred principles. The British viewed the preaching of nonviolent resistance as a contradiction in terms, for it resorted to inflammatory exhortations and promoted mass hysteria, making the use of force inevitable.

A Round Table Conference in London made some progress in discussing constitutional reform, but it was boycotted by the Congress. The Viceroy, Lord Irwin, induced Gandhi to attend a second conference in 1931, where Gandhi repeated demands for complete independence and the end of communal representation. With the failure of these talks, Gandhi returned to jail and the Congress resumed its campaign of noncooperation.

However, Gandhi did succeed in thwarting a plan to extend communal representation to the Scheduled Castes. One of his main objectives had been the reintegration of untouchables into Indian society, and he threatened a fast to the death in response to this law. Untouchable leaders then accepted a compromise called the Poona pact, which gave the Scheduled Castes some electoral privileges for a period of ten years.

The civil disobedience campaign trailed off in 1934, Gandhi again retired to semiprivacy, and divergent elements began to appear within the Congress party. A left-wing group under Jawaharlal Nehru formed the Congress Socialist party, which remained within the parent body and tried to get Congress to adopt its economic platform. This paralleled the growth of organized labor— by 1938 the All-Indian Trade Unions Congress claimed 325,000 members. The extreme right wing of the Congress party under Subhas Chandra Bose developed an ideology similar to militant fascism, oriented toward violence.

The Extension of Self-Government

The Constitution of 1935

At this critical juncture the British produced a new statute, based on the Simon Report. It made India a federal state and gave the provinces many powers to be exercised free from central supervision. These extensive provincial governing rights were now to come under direct Indian control, for the eleven Governor's Provinces[6] gained full ministerial responsibility. Their British

---

[6] These now were Bengal, Orissa, Bihar, Assam, Madras, Central Provinces, United Provinces, Bombay, Punjab, Sind, and North West Frontier Province.

governors, appointed from the federal center, still had reserve powers of intervention to maintain security, preserve minority rights, and prevent discrimination against British commercial interests. In practice, the governors carefully refrained from interference, so that self-rule at the provincial level became a reality, marking a major change from the Act of 1919.

At the central-government level, however, the new plan was more modest. The Viceroy retained wide powers over defense, foreign affairs, credit, and finance. Otherwise authority was to be shared among the British, the nationalists, and the princes. The federation was to take effect when about half the native states joined, but they refused, in fear of nationalist domination. As a result, the central government continued under the 1919 law, with ruling power in the hands of the Viceroy and his executive council, to be advised but not controlled by an Indian legislature.

Congress leaders warned the princes that when independence came Indian terms would be compulsory and severe. The nationalists launched propaganda campaigns in the native states to hasten democratic reforms, and the largest states, Kashmir and Hyderabad, enlarged their rudimentary legislatures in an ineffectual response. Most princes argued that their authoritarian pattern of rule was more truly in keeping with Indian traditions and popular desires. The problem of accession was not resolved until independence, when the warnings of the nationalists proved most accurate.

The electorate was extended to cover about 35 million people, including 6 million women voters and about 10 per cent of the depressed classes. The Moslems participated in the new system because it established provincial autonomy and retained communal electorates. The Liberals were unenthusiastic but willing to try; it was to prove their last effort for they were soon swamped by the Congress candidates. These candidates agreed to compete in the 1937 elections, despite their opposition to dyarchy at the center and a federalism that might encourage separatist tendencies along territorial lines. The Congress had long been in the political wilderness, and its leaders wanted to take office and direct provincial affairs. They were certain of victory in the provinces after the party's triumph in the 1935 central legislative elections.

The Election of 1937 and Its Effects

The provincial elections of January-February 1937 marked a turning point in nationalist affairs. The Congress won 70 per cent of the popular vote, ample proof of its popularity and organizational skill. Jawaharlal Nehru was party president in 1936–1937 and directed the campaign; yet he did not want the party to take office because of the provincial governors' reserve powers. After Britain promised to avoid undue interference, Congress ministries were formed in provinces where the party gained a majority. Here at last was self-rule, government by a responsible majority party at the climax of a long training period in administration. However, it was followed by the sudden political eruption of the long-standing communal issue.

In communal terms, Sind and the North West Frontier were heavily Moslem; the Punjab (57 per cent) and Bengal (55 per cent) had smaller majorities. A Congress affiliate, the Red Shirt movement, won in the North West Frontier, but in the other three Moslem provinces and distant Assam the Congress did not gain control. Elsewhere it won five majorities and one plurality. The Moslem League at this time was still one of many small middle-class parties that had not even tried to gain a mass following; in Bengal and the Punjab, the Moslem leaders of coalition cabinets were actually not League members. The League had not expected to dominate any provincial cabinet, but its leaders hoped to form coalition governments in provinces where the League captured many Moslem seats. In particular, it ran on a common platform with the Congress in the United Provinces and believed that it received such a promise. However, Congress leaders refused to consider coalitions wherever they had a clear majority. League members were offered cabinet posts only if their group dissolved itself and its members joined the Congress.

The Congress position was constitutionally correct, and membership in it was open to all. There seemed no good reason to single out the communalist League for special political favor. The Congress was at a new height of popularity, claiming that its intense election and membership campaigns had raised its membership from 600,000 in 1936 to more than 3 million in 1938. Moslem adherents, however, were only 3 per cent of this total.

At this stage, communal-political relations were still unsettled. The 1935 law was suspect to the League because Moslems were underrepresented in the Bengal and Punjab legislatures, receiving only 47 and 49 per cent of the seats. The League and Congress adopted similar social and economic election planks and both were anti-British in attitude. The Congress contested only fifty-eight of the Moslem seats, so that little friction occurred during the election. With so little difference in policy, the Moslem League attributed its exclusion from office to the Hindu orientation of the Congress party. The League now became a formal political opponent and sought to increase its own popularity. Moslem League officials in the United Provinces felt betrayed by the Congress, because they were now forced to choose between the two parties after years of fostering communal cooperation.

On taking office, Congress leaders campaigned to win over the Moslem peasantry and absorb the lesser political groups. In response, the League launched a mass membership drive whose success stunned the overconfident Congress. Mohammed Ali Jinnah, permanent League president after 1934, had tried to collaborate with the Congress long after he had rejected Gandhi's principles, with a determination which won him Nehru's approval as "the ambassador of Hindu-Muslim unity." Now, urged by such leaders as the great poet Sir Mohammed Iqbal, Jinnah carried his appeal to the masses in a campaign sparked by the cry that Islam was in danger. Dues were cut to two annas (about two cents) a year, and the League began to win lower-middle-class and peasant support in the Moslem-dominated regions. Until 1938 its greatest attraction had lain in Hindu-majority provinces, but it was now gaining in the Moslem strongholds from which political demands could be made.

The Demand for Pakistan

An important tactic of the Moslem League was to seek out discriminatory behavior in Congress ministries, in order to justify its own communal demands. It established an investigating committee in 1937, which noted complaints: discrimination in civil service promotions and employment; Congress flags over government buildings; the singing of Hindu patriotic songs and the reverence of Gandhi in schools; the discouragement of the use of Urdu; police favoritism to Hindus in communal riots. Jinnah wanted a Royal Commission to investigate these allegations. The Hindus responded by accusing the Bengal and Punjab ministries of favoring Moslems in economic legislation and of fostering communal ill-will. Communal riots increased in number and intensity, involving Moslems and Sikhs in the Punjab and Hindus and Moslems elsewhere.

The Moslem League swiftly dominated the communal elections as it won forty-six of the fifty-six Moslem seats contested in 1938–1942. The premiers of Bengal and the Punjab and their adherents joined the League, which now began to exercise a control over Moslem ministries comparable to that enjoyed by Congress. With power came an increasingly radical attitude. An all-India federation with its Congress majority was considered unacceptable even with weighted, separate electorates. The League urged the abandonment of the 1935 concept of a strong center, and now only moderate Moslems spoke of accepting any federation.

It was in February, 1940, that the League first demanded a separate state of Pakistan. When Iqbal and others had made this proposal a decade earlier it had been dismissed as "chimerical and impracticable" by Indians and British alike. Jinnah now observed that a unified India was the chimera, and he put all his driving force behind the partition movement. The territory claimed for the new state included the *entire* provinces of the Punjab, Sind, and North West Frontier in the west, and Bengal and Assam to the east.

The British and Congress remained incredulous, pointing to the strategic problem of separating the vital and historically vulnerable northern frontier region from the rest of the subcontinent. Critics of partition also challenged the capacity of such a state to survive, for its proposed components were at least 700 miles apart and differed in language, ethnic background, culture, and economic activities. It was also doubted whether the subcontinent as a whole could survive the shock of economic dislocation brought on by partition. Moreover, once political fractionalization started, what was to keep the Sikhs and other groups from demanding political autonomy? Finally, no matter what boundaries were drawn, millions of Hindus and Moslems would remain as minorities in each other's lands, thereby keeping the communal problem alive.

Other Islamic parties and the Moslem community as a whole did not appear enthusiastic at first. But by the end of the Second World War, the League, which had stood squarely on the partition issue, had proved itself in elections as representing Moslem opinion. The community seemed to consider itself Moslem first and Indian second; Jinnah believed that the time was ripe to bring the claim for Pakistan into the political arena. Could he get the British and Congress leaders to accept this extreme communal view?

The Congress in Power (1937–1939)

While Moslem separatism gathered momentum, the Congress party gained experience in provincial administration. Theoretically, each provincial ministry should have been responsible to its own legislature and electorate. Actually, the seven Congress cabinets were closely linked to national party headquarters, which operated as a central source of authority over them. The chain of command in the Congress party had a democratic base in that all who paid their annual dues (four annas) could participate in the nomination of about 2,000 delegates to the annual national convention that chose the party president. The Working Committee of fourteen members had the task of carrying out party policy during the year and was elected annually until 1934. After that date it was chosen by the president, who could thus exercise tighter control over party affairs during his one-year tenure of office. Jawaharlal Nehru was succeeded as president in 1938 by Subhas Chandra Bose, but continued to be the party's most influential political tactician during its period of provincial leadership. Gandhi remained the spiritual leader and "permanent superpresident." The Working Committee exercised direction over the seven Congress provincial ministries, operating through a Parliamentary Board established in 1934 to coordinate such activity. It established the terms for taking office, approved and modified legislative programs, and finally ordered the ministries to resign in 1939. The country clearly looked to this Congress central office for guidance on national policy, and it is significant that Nehru and other leaders remained outside the provincial ministries. The party high command was the closest approximation to a sovereign body under nationalist control in India.

Critics of this system have accused the Congress of distorting and undermining representative democracy. Admittedly, this structure was a departure from British parliamentary technique and it did minimize much of the communal give-and-take that would have been possible under full provincial autonomy. Yet the process was not undemocratic, for the people could always topple this elaborate structure by voting out their Congress representatives and ministries at the next election. India was in the anomalous position of lacking a representative central government but possessing a well-disciplined party that antedated its formal political structure. No process of government as complex as democracy could be transferred from Britain to this environment without undergoing some change in form. Central control had to be exercised through some nongovernmental agency if it were to exist at all. Moreover, the Congress was not so much a party as a national movement encompassing many divergent groups. It was confidently expected that many of these groups would break off and form their own parties after independence. For the moment, the Congress symbolized Indian national aspirations and was bound to dominate new representative institutions.

Central direction was also necessary to strengthen the concept of Indian unity and foster a coherent program of social reform. During their brief tenure of office the provincial ministries enjoyed the substance of power, receiving full cooperation from British governors and loyal obedience from the British-staffed Indian Civil Service. As they grappled with the difficult problems of office, the ministers paid little attention to the abstract notion of fighting the Act of 1935. On the whole, their record in the administration of finance and of law and order was good; the experience and confidence gained here proved of great value when full power was eventually transferred. In the fields of reform, greater success was enjoyed in education and public health than in the more complex matters of agrarian reform and labor legislation. However, a foundation was laid for more sweeping social legislation a decade later.

The End of British Rule

Effects of the Second World War

The British Parliament had reserved for the central Indian government the power to suspend provincial autonomy in time of war. In 1939 the Viceroy declared India a belligerent and suspended political reform for the duration of the Second World War. Lacking a definite promise of future concessions, Congress headquarters ordered its ministries to resign, and the provincial governors assumed power in October, 1939. The Moslem League reacted by organizing a "day of deliverance and thanksgiving." Though demanding Pakistan as their price for cooperation, the Moslem leaders generally gave limited support to the war effort and their ministries continued to function.

The Congress party was in a dilemma because it opposed the British and yet wanted to support the anti-Axis cause, especially in China and Russia. In March, 1940, it refused to support Britain's "imperialist" war effort, demanded a constituent assembly, and threatened another civil-disobedience campaign. Nehru and the Working Committee were adamant on this issue, whereas Mahatma Gandhi advocated a more cautious and cooperative approach. But as fighting neared India, Gandhi too shied away from supporting the war effort.

Under British direction, India became a valuable source of military supplies, a major strategic base, and the contributor of a large volunteer army of 2 million men. The war itself reached the Assam frontier in 1942, as the Japanese swept through all Southeast Asia. The debacle in Malaya cost the British many Commonwealth troops, including a large Indian contingent. Many of its officers and men willingly joined an Indian National Army to fight with the Japanese for Indian independence. Their leader was Subhas Chandra Bose, who had escaped from jail in 1940 after being arrested for sedition. In India itself, Britain did not encounter an organized resistance movement, and the people worked passively under British orders during most of the war. But the Indian National Army caught the popular imagination and played an ambivalent role of enemy-hero during the war.

With the Allied cause at a low ebb, Britain sought to stabilize its suddenly exposed Southeast Asian front by extending political concessions to India. Sir Stafford Cripps, a leading Labor party official and long advocate of Indian freedom, was dispatched by the wartime Coalition cabinet on a mission in 1942 to win Indian support for the war effort. All parties were promised immediate participation in the central government, which would have only two British members, the viceroy and the commander in chief. There would also be an Indian defense minister, but it was made clear that Britain would still direct the war. Congress officials characterized the limited transfer of power as an effort to make India a "supply and commissariat" for British campaigns.

Cripps also extended the promise that India would be given full self-government as a union at the end of hostilities, with freedom to stay within the Commonwealth or leave it. The Congress party rejected his suggestion that the constituent assembly include princely delegates. Nor did it accept his proposal that any provinces might contract out of the Indian Union and form a separate union of equal states. The nationalists wanted immediate self-rule and looked on the British offer, in Gandhi's phrase, as a "postdated check on a bank that is obviously failing."

The Cripps mission failed, Britain was again told to "quit India," and the last and greatest nonviolent resistance campaign got under way. After some hesitation, the central government (fifteen Britons and eleven Indians) took firm action: Congress was outlawed and its leaders were jailed. Gandhi still desired to avoid bloodshed but now observed that if rioting resulted he would consider it unavoidable and not hold himself responsible. Violence did occur on a grand scale, and the disobedience campaign resembled a sudden and vigorous rebellion. Railways were destroyed, the British supply line to the front through Bihar Province was temporarily cut, police stations were destroyed, and civil servants were murdered. By the end of 1942 order was restored as 60,000 Congress leaders were jailed. Restrictions were relaxed as the war progressed, and political prisoners were releasd in 1945. The British promise to reopen negotiations at the end of the war also helped keep the situation in hand.

The Moslem League used the war period to strengthen its position, though Jinnah found it difficult to maintain party control over Moslem ministries. The antipartition Unionist party premier in the Punjab even resigned from the League in 1944. That year Gandhi was released from jail and met with Jinnah to seek a compromise settlement. But the two leaders disagreed on a resolution establishing a single coalition government, to be followed by a plebiscite in the Moslem areas on the question of an autonomous state. Gandhi insisted that the center had to retain control over defense, foreign affairs, commerce, customs duties, and communications. To Jinnah this was the very negation of Pakistan. This basic deadlock was reflected in the failure to form an Indian Executive Council in 1945. Neither Britain nor the Congress would agree to Jinnah's demand that the League nominate all the Moslem members. As a result, no interim government existed when the Labor party took office in Britain in mid-1945.

The Failure to Compromise

The new government decided to hold central and provincial Indian elections and convene a constitutional assembly. The elections sharpened the issue as both the Congress party and the Moslem League won sweeping victories in their constituencies. The League won *all* Moslem seats in the Central Assembly and 446 of the 495 seats in the provinces, failing only in the North West Frontier Province. It now claimed to speak for the entire Moslem community in demanding partition. On the other hand, the communalist Hindu Mahasabha was severely beaten in its extremist anti-Moslem campaign.

The Labor government dispatched a three-man mission under Cripps in March, 1946, to bring about an immediate and peaceful transfer of power in India. Speed was essential, as both the communal and nationalist tensions assumed ominous proportions. Riots occurred in Calcutta, air force units refused to obey orders, and a naval mutiny took place early in 1946. Moderate Congress officials like Sardar Vallabhai Patel were hard-pressed to check widespread armed uprisings. That same winter leaders of the Indian National Army were brought to trial. Though the flamboyant Bose had been killed in an air accident while escaping to Japan, this issue aroused such popular agitation that even the Congress felt compelled to side with the defendants. The British decided not to prosecute, and thus ended an affair which underlined the intensity of Indian nationalist emotions.

The communal question proved insoluble. The Cripps mission was unable to mediate and extract proposals from each side. It therefore published its own plan in May, 1946, an ingenious modification of the 1942 offer, featuring a loose Indian union with three tiers of government. The center was to control only defense, foreign affairs, and communications, and their related finances. At base, the provinces were to enjoy a wide measure of self-government. The novel feature was a middle level of provincial groups voluntarily joined together, with their own executive and legislature. Each provincial grouping was to decide how to divide those powers not vested in the center between the group and the individual provinces. The mission then called for a constituent assembly and again authorized an interim government containing Congress and League officials.

This rational offer of near-Pakistan could not take root in the heated political atmosphere of 1946. Great difficulty was experienced even in organizing an interim cabinet and convening a constituent assembly. The Congress joined the government only when granted six cabinet members to the League's five. Jinnah first refused to participate and that summer, when the Congress took its allotted office, called for "direct action" to achieve Pakistan. Even when the League joined the government in October, 1946, the full cabinet never met but conducted business by correspondence. The Indians were finally committed to responsible positions in the central government, but the direct-action campaign touched off a year of communal rioting. This proved to be the bloodiest period in the independence movement, with Bengal and Bihar provinces alone suffering almost 10,000 fatalities within six months.

The new constitutional proposals were further endangered by Nehru's statement of July, 1946, that "the big probability is that there will be no grouping" and his later observation that the power of the center would inevitably grow. The Moslem League refused to participate in the Constituent Assembly that convened in December, 1946, and ignored the constitutional proposals drawn up by the Congress. In an effort to hasten a solution and compel all parties to act responsibly, the British government declared in February, 1947, that Britain was going to grant India independence no later than June, 1948. A British conference with Nehru, Jinnah, and the Sikh leader, Sardar Baldev Singh, failed to produce a compromise. Terror, violence, and destruction were threatening to sweep across India in catastrophic fashion. The Punjab Unionist coalition cabinet, in power since 1937, had tried to maintain order by banning private armies, but the Moslems responded by a "nonviolence" campaign that the others viewed as an attempt to seize power. With about 5,000 deaths due to rioting early in 1947, the governor had to assume direction of provincial affairs. The Labor government dispatched a new Viceroy, Lord Louis Mountbatten, to seek an immediate settlement of the communal issue.

Agreement on Partition

That spring Mountbatten found a divided cabinet at the center, riots in the great provinces, a dispirited and discouraged civil service, and a British army in the first stages of departure. It became clear that the British would not remain or supply the force to preserve unity. The Congress then made its most vital and statesmanlike concession—that no communal group should be compelled to accept a constitution against its will. Accepting the suggestion of its own provincial parties in the Punjab and Bengal, the Indian National Congress agreed to the partition of India and the division of these two key provinces.

Pakistani adherents had to modify their original demands for all of Bengal, Assam, and the Punjab, which would have limited the Moslem population in the new state to only 52 per cent in the east and 62 per cent in the west. Jinnah accepted what he had earlier described as a "moth-eaten and truncated Pakistan." Even this compromise left over 10 million Hindus in Pakistan and about 40 million Moslems in truncated India.

Lord Mountbatten induced his government to effect this partition immediately. He believed Britain incapable of controlling the situation and hoped that the shock of an immediate transfer of responsibility would avert a calamity. London therefore agreed to grant independence in just two and a half months— on August 15, 1947. The British have been severely criticized for excessive haste in executing what was a most delicate and complex task; by contrast, the separation of Burma from India was staged over a three-year span after 1935. Britain's refusal to exercise paramount authority in enforcing law and order was also condemned as a serious evasion of imperial responsibility. The British maintained that only decisive and rapid change enabled the subcontinent to avoid a major catastrophe at this time. Moreover, Britain itself was in the throes of a strategic and economic crisis and, having decided to withdraw from India, did not possess the energy or motivation to maintain the degree of control required to prevent disorder.

As expected, the Moslem-majority areas voted for partition and formed the new state of Pakistan. It consisted of two parts 1,000 miles apart; West Pakistan—Sind, North West Frontier, Baluchistan, and the western part of the Punjab; and East Pakistan— the eastern part of Bengal, plus the adjoining Sylhet district of Assam. The two new sovereign states of India and Pakistan took their places in the Commonwealth with the right of complete withdrawal. A commission to divide the Punjab and Bengal quickly became deadlocked, and its chairman, Sir Cyril Radcliff, made boundary awards that disappointed both parties.

National assets were to be divided on a ratio of 82.5 to 17.5 per cent in India's favor. The administrative structure and communication facilities had to be rearranged. The advantages lay with India, which was the legal successor state and retained the old imperial apparatus of government. The new state of Pakistan, awkwardly located on the peripheries, faced a much more difficult task of nation building. A sign of trouble was the difficulty Pakistan encountered in acquiring its share of transferrable assets, which it received only after Mahatma Gandhi vigorously insisted that India carry out its part of the agreement. Finally, the fate of the princely states was left open, as these entities faced an uncertain future, suddenly shorn of any protector.

The greatest tragedy was the failure to keep the peace, and the act of partition proved costly in human lives. Bengal, traditional center of violence, remained quiet though restive, thanks to the efforts by Bengali leaders of both communities, ably assisted by Gandhi. To the west, however, rioting and murder occurred in the United Provinces and the Punjab. Moslems, Hindus, and Sikhs on the wrong side of the dividing line were all fair game. Moslem outrages in the North West Frontier Province were matched by Sikh violence when that group passed through Kashmir after leaving West Pakistan. Impartial estimates place the number of deaths through violence at 200,000 and total deaths, caused by the sudden dislocations, at 500,000. The flight of refugees, impelled by fear, reached the staggering total of 12 million, with over 6 million entering and over 5 million leaving West Pakistan. This movement left deep scars on the areas affected and strained relations between the new states even further.

British Rule Reappraised

Independence therefore was finally achieved but at the price of political unity and under conditions that made the security of the region far shakier than anyone had anticipated. Nevertheless, the Labor government's policy to yield power voluntarily was a decision that won for Britain tremendous popularity in India. Despite long years of nationalist antagonism and the difficulty accompanying independence, the popular attitude after partition was pro-British, a fact that made possible the continuation of close ties with the former ruler. Britain's constructive record in the subcontinent now overshadowed the memories of past wrongs to the nationalist cause.

Perhaps the major achievement was the manner in which Indian nationalist efforts remained channeled along political and institutional lines basically similar to Western democratic processes. Fundamentally, India adhered to the ideological principles and administrative rules established by the British Raj, and the temporary recourse to violence, however serious, did not destroy this achievement.

That the rulers could carry on a program of political education and reform while doubting India's ability to absorb these lessons illustrates the strength and weakness of British rule. Consistently obstructive, dubious of successful results, the British government failed to appreciate the intensity of Indian feeling, the scope of nationalist demands, and the ability of its leaders to assume the responsibility of government. As a result, Britain never made the proper concession at the right time, be it 1909, 1919, 1935, or 1942; any one of these reforms would have appeared bold and conciliatory a decade earlier. Instead, the tension of opposition remained at a high level. Yet British control served to stimulate rather than suppress Indian political development, for it did not approach totalitarian ruthlessness. The level of British wisdom and generosity may not have been high by absolute standards, but it was notably superior to other modern imperial regimes, European or Asiatic. When the transfer of power did occur, British rule passed the acid test on two counts: both new states chose to remain within the Commonwealth and both adhered to constitutional, democratic forms of government.

Whether democracy will eventually succeed in India and Pakistan remains a major issue today. British inadequacy on this score may be traced to its failure to develop the Western tradition on a broad enough base, in terms of education and the extension of parliamentary government. On a more current problem, the imperial ruler must share responsibility for the strain that the communal issue placed on the Indian body politic. Nevertheless, the creation of a democratic tradition and the voluntary transfer of power will remain monumental achievements of Britain's empire in India.

14 *India and Pakistan*
after Independence

India

The partition of 1947 added grave difficulties to a subcontinent grappling with the problems of economic progress and political stability. The new order seemed threatened with immediate destruction in the orgy of violence that accompanied independence; it was remarked that the British were a just people—they found India in chaos on their arrival and were leaving it that way. Actually, order was restored and maintained after the frightful summer of 1947, but Indian-Pakistani antagonism remained as a bitter legacy.

Aftermath of Partition

Refugees and Minorities

A most pressing issue was the safety and future of the people directly concerned: refugees in the Punjab, fearful minorities in partitioned Bengal, and the Moslem minorities in the United Provinces and elsewhere in the new Indian Union. There was also a steady flow of evacuees during the uneasy calm following the completion of partition. In mid-1947 there were 56 million Moslems in Pakistan (76.7 per cent of its population) and 38 million in India (12 per cent of India's population). It would have taken a fantastic transfer of tens of millions to end the minority problems. After the migrations of 1947 the Moslem majority in Pakistan reached 85 per cent, but Moslems still comprised about 11 per cent of India's people.

Both states were burdened with great numbers of embittered or dispirited refugees but lacked adequate facilities to care for them. The newcomers were crowded into special camps and confronted with a hostile or indifferent citizenry. Pakistan suffered more than India from this exchange, losing trained Hindu professionals, clerks, and businessmen, while acquiring unskilled peasants who were unable to manage the farms abandoned by the Sikhs. This area depended on a complex irrigation network, much of which the Sikhs had destroyed on departing. Gradual progress has been made in absorbing refugees, but ultimate success in both countries depends on general economic expansion. Evacuees have also demanded that their new homelands recover lost property and wealth, thereby introducing involved questions of legal claims.

An outbreak of violence in Bengal at the start of 1950 again revealed the explosive nature of this problem. Each nation claimed that its coreligionists across the frontier suffered discrimination; riots in the provincial capitals of

Calcutta and Dacca sped up the process of emigration, which had never com‑
pletely ceased. Inflammatory claims and threats in the press, exhortations by
extremists, the bitterness of refugees, and mutual recrimination between govern‑
ments led to a war scare in March, 1950. The next month, however, Prime
Ministers Nehru and Liaquat Ali Khan reached an agreement to protect minori‑
ties, prohibit false and inflammatory propaganda, and set up commissions to
rehabilitate refugees and recover lost property.

There are over 11 million Hindus in East Pakistan, one quarter of its popula‑
tion, and a large-scale migration would be economically ruinous to both parts
of crowded Bengal. J. N. Mandal, an untouchable and the only Hindu in the
Pakistani cabinet, resigned in protest against discrimination against Hindus in
1950. Hindu migrations to West Bengal occurred in 1952 when Pakistan moved
temporarily toward a theocratic state. On the other hand, Moslems continue
to migrate from India to West Pakistan, in an equally disheartening though
less publicized sign of the times. There followed a period of uneasy stability,
though Hindu migration from East Pakistan flared up again in 1956, this time,
however, because of near-famine conditions.

Economic Dislocation

Partition also caused considerable dislocation with regard to transportation
and communication, the distribution of grain and raw-material production,
and the location of industries. East Bengal grows 70 per cent of the world's
jute, but all 100 jute mills were across the border in the Calcutta area. West
Bengal can process 5 million bales a year, but it received only 80 per cent of
this amount in 1949 and much less thereafter, owing to riots and a stoppage
in trade. India is now growing more jute, while Pakistan is constructing its
own mills and processing plants. Similarly, West Pakistan used to send its
surplus wheat and 1 million bales of cotton to India and receive finished goods.
Since partition, India has lost this valuable source of supply. However, India
inherited almost all the industrial plants, together with coal and iron resources.
Pakistan now depends on water power, still another critical issue between the
two states, as a source of industrial energy.

A prepartition standstill agreement to avoid customs duties quickly broke
down as both countries levied export taxes and India raised coal prices. In
September, 1949, Britain devalued its pound from $4.00 to $2.80. India followed
suit, but Pakistan did not. This devaluation ended the equality between their
currencies, raised the value of the Pakistani rupee and commodities by 40 per
cent in terms of Indian rupees, and lowered the cost of India's goods in Pakistan.
India responded with a trade embargo, but Pakistan rode out the storm when
the Korean War sent jute, cotton, and other primary commodity prices soaring.
India then made temporary trade agreements and recognized the level of Paki‑
stan's rupee, but commerce has remained limited in scope and subject to super‑
vision by antagonistic governments. Pakistan eventually brought its rupee to
India's level in 1955, after an adverse shift in world prices, and a new limited

369

trade agreement was reached that year. But the level of trade was only $40 million in 1952–1953, compared to $227 million in 1948–1949, and it will be difficult to regain prewar levels.

The question of water supply pertains to hydroelectric power and irrigation. To Pakistan, a steady flow of water from the Indus River system is absolutely vital to the Punjab-Sind region, which would be parched without its canal-irrigation works. The upper reaches of the Indus and its five tributaries (Jhelum, Chenab, Ravi, Beas, Sutlej) flow through India or Kashmir, a disputed province now controlled by India. In 1948 India agreed not to alter the level of water distribution for five years, but it warned Pakistan to develop its own facilities in the border region. India proceeded with plans to divert the Sutlej for irrigation and power purposes, with a dam at Bhakra and a weir at Nangal, and these went into operation in 1954 despite Pakistani protests. The International Bank for Reconstruction and Development has tried to mediate by proposing that the river basin be developed as a unit. However, in this bitter antagonism, partition again proved the only possible solution: in 1954 it was agreed that Pakistan use the Indus, Jhelum, and Chenab and that India control the other three.

The Princely States

Overshadowing all other disputes is the struggle for Kashmir, the largest princely state. Most states were induced to join India or Pakistan along religious lines, and they were gradually integrated into this new administrative and political structure. Under the direction of Deputy Premier Sardar Patel, India consolidated some 600 states into thirty units by absorbing some, merging others, and leaving a few intact. All received more democratic administrations that deprived their old rulers of power. A similar pattern was followed more slowly in Pakistan, but the decision to form a single province of West Pakistan in 1955 promised to complete the program.

Trouble arose in three states—Junagadh, Hyderabad, and Kashmir. The Junagadh incident, which was quickly settled, bore some resemblance to the Kashmir dispute. This small state of 671,000 people (four-fifths Hindu) was located in Kathiawar and bordered on India. Its Moslem ruler acceded to Pakistan in September, 1947, an act which caused public disorders, an Indian occupation in November, and a plebiscite that resulted in an overwhelming vote to join India.

Hyderabad, largest state in the Deccan, was completely surrounded by Indian territory and also had a Hindu majority; its Moslem ruler, the Nizam, tried to remain independent. The ruling group was Moslem, and Osmania University in Hyderabad was a center of Moslem learning and cultural renaissance. However, the people felt oppressed by an autocratic, unprogressive regime, and the Communists made considerable headway in the Telegu-speaking section adjoining Indian Andhra. When the Nizam refused to institute reform, India responded with an economic blockade. Armed Moslem forces terrorized the populace while the Communists claimed to exercise real power in more than 2,000 villages. Finally, in June, 1948, India launched an invasion (the "hundred-hours war"), turned Hyderabad into an Indian state, and established a more democratic system, though the Nizam was not deposed. However, the political atmosphere was disturbed by acts of violence against Moslems after the invasion.

Kashmir

The case of Kashmir has proved infinitely more complex and perhaps insoluble. Jammu and Kashmir State, as it is officially called, was placed under a Hindu ruling family in the nineteenth century, but three quarters of its 4 million people are Moslem. The Hindus are concentrated primarily in Jammu, but the other populated region, the famed Vale of Kashmir, is overwhelmingly Moslem. The Frontier Districts, which comprise three quarters of its area but contain only 300,000 inhabitants, are also Moslem. The state was governed by Hindu law under a Hindu elite and the people suffered under a backward social code and religious discrimination. The Indian Congress party, however, took the lead in organizing popular opposition to all authoritarian princely states through a State Peoples' Conference; in Kashmir the Conference was led by Sheik Mohammed Abdullah, a noncommunalist Moslem who was in jail in 1947 for reformist agitation. That summer Kashmir signed a standstill agreement with Pakistan but did not join it. Since all Kashmir's lines of communication were with West Pakistan, India immediately began building a road to Jammu. As Hindu and Sikh refugees arrived in Jammu, communal clashes occurred and led to a Moslem uprising. In October, all order collapsed in Kashmir when Moslem tribesmen, with encouragement from Pakistan, invaded Kashmir and moved into the Vale toward its chief city of Srinagar, looting and killing people of all religions. The ruler acceded to India, which flew troops in to save the city and clear the valley of invaders. India thus gained control of Jammu and the Vale, as Azad (Free) Kashmir forces held the large but sparsely settled north. Azad forces were backed by Pakistani supplies and, as was later admitted, regular troops in the spring of 1948.

Lord Mountbatten, who accepted Kashmir's accession as India's Governor-General, stated that the people would ultimately decide their own fate, a position confirmed by Prime Minister Nehru. Sheik Abdullah became Kashmir's prime minister and repressed opponents of his pro-Indian policy. Pakistan agreed to a plebiscite but only if there was international supervision of the vote, a withdrawal of Indian troops, and a coalition government in Kashmir. India rejected this claim, a diplomatic deadlock ensued, and sporadic fighting occurred throughout 1948.

India accused Pakistan of aggression in the United Nations Security Council in January, 1949, but Pakistan replied that the larger issue was India's seizure of the state in violation of the spirit of partition. Its Foreign Minister Zafrullah Khan argued that the case proved India's unwillingness even to tolerate Pakistan's existence. The Security Council succeeded in obtaining a cease-fire at the end of 1949, but it has not been able to arrange a formal truce and the promised plebiscite. India has demanded departure of Pakistani troops, the dissolution of the Azad forces, and the restoration of order by Indian troops. Pakistan feels certain of winning a fair election and wants all troops out of the region. Both governments affirmed their willingness to hold a plebiscite and argued that they would win the vote. The stalemate continued when Kashmir rejected a formal truce, and talks about synchronized troop withdrawals and demilitarization all failed.

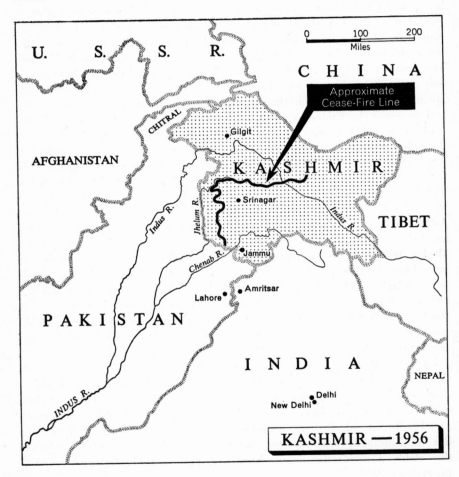

Pakistan contended that India and its submissive Kashmir government were stalling to avoid a vote, and in 1956 Prime Minister Nehru proposed a division of the province along the cease-fire line without any plebiscite. India has been subsidizing Kashmir's economic development in the hope of proving its good intention and winning popular support. Sheik Abdullah, however, displayed separatist tendencies in a desire to keep his state free from a final link with India. He was displaced and jailed during 1954–1956, and the Moslem leaders who replaced him worked to tighten relations with India further. As the dispute wore on, the people of Kashmir developed an evident hostility toward all the major participants.

A new crisis was precipitated when the Constituent Assembly of Kashmir arranged for the state's formal accession to India on Republic Day, January 26, 1957. Pakistan brought the matter before the United Nations Security Council, which on January 24 decided by a vote of 10–0 (the Soviet Union abstaining) that any action taken by Kashmir or either disputant "would not constitute a disposition of the state in accordance with the . . . principle" of free self-determination. India ignored the resolution, declared Kashmir's accession irrevocable, and refused to consider an internationally supervised vote. Pakistan could not get the world body to dispatch troops, but the Security Council did decide "to continue its consideration of the dispute." Partition appears to offer the only possible settlement—Jammu to India, the north to Pakistan, and a plebiscite in the Vale. Prime Minister Nehru, however, would accept a formal partition only along the existing truce line.

The significance of this quarrel cannot be overestimated. For Pakistan, prestige, territory, and its birthright to all contiguous Moslem lands are all at stake. India has the legal claim of accession and defense against aggression. Beyond this, it seeks to prove that a Moslem region can exist harmoniously and prosperously in India and that partition, by inference, was never a valid need. Pakistan argues that India is trying to undermine its basis for existence by this display of force and extremism. Kashmir itself has the rich Vale, its lucrative tourist trade, headwaters of valuable rivers, and a pivotal strategic position in the subcontinent's defense. At present, India and Pakistan have no working defensive agreement, and their forces are in fact pinned down against each other. Military expenses consume from 50 to 60 per cent of each state's regular budget, to the detriment of economic modernization programs. The Kashmir issue also keeps open the opportunity and reason for extremism in Pakistan's domestic affairs and so is the main cause of military tension in the area.

Finally, the incident has impaired the prestige of the British Commonwealth, which failed to provide a solution or the machinery for a settlement. The British may have been wise in remaining impartial, but Pakistan has felt wronged by Mountbatten's action in 1947 and Britain's failure to press India to resolve the dispute. This ill-feeling influenced Pakistan's decision in 1954 to follow India's lead and become a republic within the Commonwealth, although Pakistan realized the value of the crown as a symbol of authority, continuity, and reserve of power—all sorely needed in a country plagued by constitutional difficulties and lack of internal cohesion.

The Death of Gandhi

The greatest victim of the partition was Mahatma Gandhi, who was assassinated on January 30, 1948. All during 1947 he preached against violence and told Sikhs and Hindus that their molestation of Moslems was a discredit to their religions. By December, with refugees flooding into the hungry city of New Delhi, anti-Moslem sentiment reached an ominous level. Gandhi then made an intensive effort to prevent a new outbreak of rioting. Despite warnings from his doctors, he began his final fast in January, 1948, to bring about a "reunion of hearts" among Hindus, Moslems, and Sikhs. The result was a relaxation of tension in the capital and its vicinity. Hindus and Sikhs pledged not to molest their Moslem neighbors. It was during this fast that Gandhi also induced the government to pay Pakistan its share of British India's assets.

His arguments were rejected by Hindu communalists, especially those who had witnessed Moslem atrocities in Pakistan and wished to exact revenge. The nature of Gandhi's philosophy and the success of his fast left them baffled and frustrated. A group of these communalists then planned his death; after a bomb plot failed, one of them shot him at close range at the start of a prayer meeting, killing him instantly. All India was grief-stricken and at the funeral ceremonies, Prime Minister Nehru, in a voice overcome with emotion, lamented the passing of India's great spiritual leader.

The Government of India

With the bitter partition issue behind it, India soon became absorbed in its own massive problems. Kashmir minority difficulties and frontier incidents were of concern primarily to the border regions. The country as a whole turned its attention to the operation of a democratic system, the maintenance of administrative efficiency, the creation of a welfare state, and the task of economic development.

The New Constitutional Order

The Indian venture in democratic self-government is of critical importance in the light of the communist threat in South Asia. Its constitutional structure is as vital a consideration as general political stability and economic reform. Unlike Pakistan, which experienced considerable difficulty in this field, India produced a long, detailed constitution in 1950. First of all, this document of more than 250 printed pages is too detailed and inflexible. It has been criticized for not leaving many matters to the discretion of future governments, acting in the light of practical experience. For example, in 1952 the government sought to alter the size of parliamentary constituencies because of the rapid increase in population, but this required a constitutional amendment and was coolly received.

On the whole, the constitution is a most liberal document, proclaiming the rights of equality, political and civic freedom, and due process under law. There is a formal Bill of Rights, and any law infringing on it is considered invalid. In marked contrast to communist states, India allows and maintains freedom of speech and expression, and peaceful assembly and association, as well as the rights to move freely, live anywhere, own property, and practice any vocation. India enjoys an open society and, considering the problems it faces, has placed amazingly few restrictions on personal liberty. A Preventive Detention Bill was passed in 1950, and extended in 1952, which allowed the government greater leeway in handling arrests than is permitted in the constitution, which required that a prisoner be brought to court within one day of his detention. Prime Minister Nehru defended the need for more stringent procedures because at that time the Communists possessed arms and were a threat to the state in southern India.

The constitution also sums up the progressive aspirations of Indian society in the social and economic sphere. Part IV, "Directive Principles of State Policy," is borrowed from Eire's constitution as a guide to future legislation. The topics range over the field of economic justice and social security. They include broad injunctions against undue concentration of wealth and productive power, while stressing the need for decent working conditions, benefits for the aged, disabled, and unemployed, equal pay for men and women, and the protection of the young against exploitation. These noble aspirations must confront the realities of Indian poverty, the great cost of welfare economies, the power of industrial leaders in the Congress party, and the traditional sanctions of inequality.

Thus the constitution promises to provide free education for all children under fourteen within ten years. An earlier plan had estimated that forty years would be required before universal education and advanced modern facilities could be attained. Before partition, British India had 565 colleges and professional schools, 5,700 secondary schools, 10,300 middle schools, and 187,000 primary schools. The primary schools took 12 million of the country's 40 million children of school age. Even this modest plant, which cost $98 million annually, is a burden for an underdeveloped region. Moreover, almost all schools are in the cities; a vast construction and training program is required if the school plant is to be quadrupled and the constitutional objective met.

The constitution also provides for the protection of minorities, freedom of religion, and the complete abolition of untouchability—here it is to be remembered that India specifically repudiated the concept of political communities that led to partition. The Scheduled Castes and backward Scheduled Tribes were allotted special representation for only ten years, a tacit admission that untouchability could not be eliminated overnight by public order. The Moslems and Sikhs, however, received no special treatment, though the Sikhs are campaigning for provincial autonomy. Anglo-Indians, who held a high proportion of bureaucratic positions, were given preference and protection in this sphere of employment for a limited period.

Social and economic equality for the untouchables is difficult to attain. In fact, in 1951 Dr. B. R. Ambedkar, the Scheduled Caste leader who headed the committee drafting the constitution, resigned as minister of law in protest against the government's inadequate legislation. In a striking move of protest,

375

200,000 untouchables under the leadership of Dr. Ambedkar underwent a mass conversion to Buddhism in the fall of 1956. Nevertheless, some progress was recorded. Even before Indian independence, the untouchables won equality before the law and equal rights in public places. Legally, they could go to school or draw well water with other castes, though social and economic pressures were used to block such activities. Since independence, some states have made it a crime to forbid untouchables to enter hotels or temples. The new federal law of 1955 was a major step forward. It labeled all discrimination against untouchables as crimes, liable to police action. The burden now rests on the accused to prove nondiscrimination in barber shops, temples, schools, and at wells or on the road. The legal position of the Scheduled Castes has improved, but the government cannot compel others to treat them as equals, marry, or eat with them. However, a law of 1956, passed despite orthodox Hindu opposition, permits intercaste marriages. One of its objectives is the eventual absorption of the untouchables into society as a whole.

Efforts are also being made to improve the educational and economic status of the untouchables. Before 1947 the government reserved positions for them in the public service, allotted them part of the public wastelands, encouraged their children to go to school, and established scholarship funds for this purpose. Today there are widespread land-reform programs, larger scholarship funds, more village schools, and compulsory education for these people. As the country industrializes, their economic situation may improve still more rapidly. The untouchables, as the poorest element in the village, are the first to emigrate to the city and work in factories, where there is no discrimination.

Symptomatic of their improved condition was the decision of the All-India Scheduled Castes Federation in 1955 to drop special legislative representation because it was no longer necessary. The educated community recognizes that untouchability is wrong, and the defenders of the status quo are fighting a losing battle against inevitable change.

Structure of Government

The governmental system reflects the extensive research and care that went into its creation. In particular, Anglo-Saxon models were followed in creating a modern parliamentary democracy, an independent judiciary, and a federal structure. The Indians appear confident that they can operate this advanced and complex mechanism successfully.

At the center is a president, the executive head of the state, who is less a political power than a unifying symbol, above the politics of the moment. He is supreme commander of the armed forces and appoints executive officers considered apart from politics—the attorney-general, the chief justice and other supreme and high court justices, the comptroller, and the auditor-general. The president and vice-president are elected for five years by both houses of the federal legislature and the elected members of the state legislatures, whose votes are weighted according to population.

Political power is vested in the council of ministers (cabinet) headed by the prime minister. The latter, chosen by the president, and his cabinet are the leaders of the majority party or coalition and must resign if defeated on a major issue in the lower house. This House of the People has 500 members

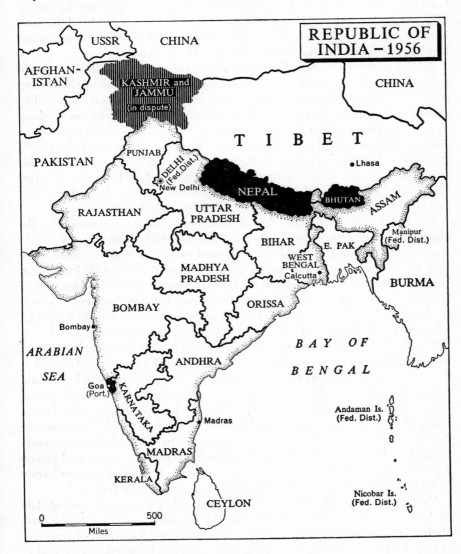

REPUBLIC OF
INDIA – 1956

elected for five years by universal adult suffrage, each member representing a constituency of from 500,000 to 750,000 people. The link to the executive is tightened by the rule that forbids a minister who is not a representative from remaining in the cabinet for more than six months. The upper house, or Council of States, has 250 members, twelve of whom are selected by the president for their outstanding abilities; the others are elected by the lower houses of the state legislatures. As in the U.S. Senate, a term is for six years, with one third of the members running for office every two years. All laws must pass both houses, save that the upper house can only make recommendations on money bills. Otherwise, if the two houses disagree, a joint session is held and the issue is resolved by majority vote. The president may withhold approval or recommend changes, but these need not be acted on by parliament.

With Indian unity assured, a States Reorganization Commission was appointed to study the revision of state boundaries, with a view to eliminating entirely the old princely states and redrawing the map, insofar as it was possible, along linguistic lines. Its report of 1955, as modified by the Congress Working Committee, proposed the creation of sixteen states. The arc of states across northern India remained relatively the same—Rajasthan, Uttar Pradesh (United Provinces), Bengal, and Orissa. In the northern part of the Deccan, within this semicircle, lies the largest state of the Union, Madhya Pradesha (Central Provinces). Thus a formidable bloc of Hindi-speaking states (Rajasthan, Uttar and Madhya Pradesh, and Bihar) is formed in northcentral India.

The two frontier states, the Punjab and Assam, were strengthened by the absorption of the princely states around them. The Sikhs in the Punjab sought a separate state, but this could not be formed on the basis of language, since both Hindi and Punjabi are spoken there. Nor can there be a division along communal lines, since the Sikhs do not hold a majority in any large segment of territory. In the east the small district of Manipur, between Assam and Burma, is placed under federal control. The only other areas made into Federal Districts are the Andaman and Nicobar Islands in the Bay of Bengal.

The Bombay area was first reorganized along linguistic lines for the Gujarati and Marathi-speaking groups. Bombay city was placed under federal control at the request of its Gujarati business community, though it lay within Marathi jurisdiction. The Marathas were angered by this decision and the lack of confidence it implied, and they resorted to riots in Bombay and vicinity late in 1955. The central government then decided to retain a single large state of Bombay, encompassing both linguistic groups. The national Congress party adhered to this decision despite the considerable antagonism it aroused among the Gujarati and in their regional Congress party. The actual reorganization took place in November, 1956, without incident anywhere in India.

Most of the major changes occurred in the south. The recently created state of Andhra was expanded to include the Telegu-speaking part of Hyderabad. Madras state consolidated its Tamil-speaking territory. Two other states, completing the Dravidian language group, were created—Karnataka to the east of Andhra (Konnada-speaking) and the small state of Kerala in the southeastern corner of the peninsula (Malayali-speaking).

The president of the Indian Union appoints the state governors, but he makes these and all other major decisions after consultation with the federal council of ministers. Each state has a council of ministers responsible to a state legislature (or the lower house when there are two chambers).

Unlike the American federal structure, the residual authority of all powers not mentioned in the constitution falls to the federal government, not the states. For the sake of flexibility in social and economic affairs, wide concurrent responsibility is given in welfare planning, monopoly control, social security, and unemployment relief. If India's security is threatened, the president can declare an emergency for two months or longer, with legislative approval. During this time, the Bill of Rights can be suspended, presidential administrative orders for states can be issued, and parliament may legislate in spheres of state authority at any time that two thirds of the Council of State approves. For these reasons, many observers hold that the tone of this federal structure favors centralized power. Yet provincial government has considerable historical prestige in India, for it was the first center of self-rule when "nation-building" authority was granted in 1935. Even today the vital question of agrarian reform is under state auspices. The size of the country, the scope of the problems faced, and the importance of regional differences all make state administration a vital factor in Indian politics.

The judiciary occupies a pivotal role in federal relations, since the Supreme Court exercises jurisdiction over state-state and state-union disputes. There is no separate state judicial system, all courts coming under federal control. Great stress is placed on the independence of the judiciary, now regarded as the defender of the constitutional order and its political safeguards. Freedom from coercion is assured by presidential appointment, respectable salaries, rent-free housing for Supreme Court justices, plus tenure of office. From the first, the courts were overwhelmed with appeals for protection. In response to one of these appeals the Supreme Court, in its first session, compelled the government to amend its press law. Following extremist calls to sedition and violence by the communist and communalist press, the government had prepared a law severely restricting the freedom of the press. When the law encountered bitter opposition in the legislature and the press, it was voided by the court. The government then presented a milder version omitting a precensorship provision, and put the bill through in the form of a constitutional amendment. Many state reform laws aimed at abolishing the zamindari were held up until their constitutional validity was tested. Thus the Indian concept of judicial review resembles the American method of measuring legislative action against a higher, constitutional law. In Britain, by contrast, courts are supposed to determine whether an official action is legal, and not judge the law itself.

The Party System

In a democracy the party system reflects the nature of society and plays an important role in determining the effectiveness of government. The transfer of this peculiarly Western device to India is therefore of the utmost significance.

Undoubtedly the dominant position of the Congress party has been a most important factor in the successful operation of democratic self-government thus far. Its vast popularity as the leader of the struggle for independence, the familiarity of its leaders with democratic methods, and its ability to unite the various state administrations through party control all underline this point. Jawaharlal Nehru has been prime minister of India since independence, and he also served as president of the Congress party (1951–1954), with the power to direct its executive apparatus and policy program. The veteran Congress nationalist, Dr. Rajendra Prasad, is India's first president, with a leading philosopher, Sarvepalli Radhakrishnan, as vice-president. The success of Indian democracy still appears to depend primarily on the leadership of a single party.

The Congress Party

Paradoxically, the Congress party is now on political trial because of its successful campaign for freedom. Fear is expressed that it will degenerate into a party without purpose, living on its past record. After 1949, some critics argued that it would go the way of the Kuomintang, by blocking social reform, and establish a one-party system. Though there is much to criticize, these views proved excessively pessimistic, for the party has thus far adhered to a democratic reformist creed, to the detriment of its communist opponents.

Yet the Congress party is troubled by an absence of fresh personalities, a rather loose party machine, and a need to maintain competent leadership in government and party affairs at the same time. Nation-building tasks are less glamorous than the swaraj movement, for they involve facing a battery of controversial issues that are the essence of politics. Religious traditionalists conflict with those who seek a secular state, while advocates of a planned economy confront opponents of government regulation. The assassination of Mahatma Gandhi in January, 1948, by a Hindu communalist fanatic was a severe national catastrophe that deprived the party of its great spiritual leader.

Shortly after independence, Deputy Premier Patel and the conservative element he represented were criticized for following a do-nothing program that alienated the public. Land reform was muddled and delayed in the states, caste handicaps remained, and an inflation had raised prices to five times their 1939 level by 1950. There was justice in this criticism, but much of it expressed frustration that the millenium had not arrived with independence, and Congress was a convenient scapegoat. The tasks of managing a new democracy, establishing an orderly and honest bureaucracy, and raising the living standard of an agrarian economy whose population had reached 357 million in 1951 are staggering long-term assignments. The people have generally demonstrated that they will patiently accept some reform as a token of future changes.

The Congress party government had proved its administrative competence in absorbing the princely states, maintaining law and order, and continuing the civil service functions established by the British. In its devotion to democracy, it carried out a national election over a six-month period of 1951–1952, staking its future in a fair contest and campaigning on a progressive, reformist platform. Recognizing its earlier weakness in social reform, the Congress, in its Election Manifesto, promised reform in land tenure, expanded production, efficiency in economic affairs, and protection of civil and political rights. At this time the government made preparations for its first five-year plan for economic development.

In preparation for the election, the Congress party also repudiated religious conservatism and communalism. These issues came to a head when a right-wing traditionalist, P. Tandon, was elected party president in September, 1950, over a candidate supported by Prime Minister Nehru. Tandon was anti-Moslem, opposed modern medical practices, and was accused of cultural imperialism. Nehru encountered considerable difficulty with the party's high command and its Central Election Committee. Only when Nehru threatened to resign did Tandon step down, and the prime minister himself became party president. This incident raised the question of how deeply the modern reformist movement had penetrated the party's ranks.

In recent years, the Congress party seems to be losing much of its appeal. Membership dropped alarmingly from 300,000 in 1953 to only 70,000 in 1954. In an effort to relieve the burden on Prime Minister Nehru, a young president was chosen in 1954, U. N. Dhebar. The party also sought to regain the enthusiasm and support of Indian youth, which were slipping away. The prime minister then spoke of retiring from public office completely, to the consternation of his colleagues, who were acutely aware of the party's defects and its dependence on the magic name of Nehru.

The Position of Jawaharlal Nehru

Jawaharlal Nehru stands at the center of India's effort to establish a democratic, secular state that can support long-range economic reforms. A brilliant, emotional nationalist and a democratic socialist, Nehru has undertaken the pivotal job of balancing the divergent elements within the Congress party. His purpose is to retain a parliamentary majority and so gain the necessary support for his cabinet's extensive legislative program. Thus, he refused to join the Socialists when they left the Congress in 1948 because of the parent body's slowness to sponsor reform. In a sense, Nehru's whole career reflects this middle position. Thoroughly trained in the Western way of life and one of the most graceful writers of English prose, he is nevertheless deeply aware of his own country's traditions. He represents the effort of modern India to combine its own culture with Western industrial and democratic ways.

Though still a "leftist," he has remained a practical leader, constantly striving to keep the Congress party on the reformist path. Nehru has also adopted an intermediate policy with regard to Pakistan. But he has proved a difficult negotiator over Kashmir and water rights, and has frequently criticized Pakistan's close alignment with the West in Cold War policy. Nevertheless, he has opposed Hindu communal extremists who want their culture imposed on Moslems still living in India and who have never become reconciled to the existence of Pakistan.

The National Election of 1951–1952

Nehru's leadership was a decisive factor in the Congress electoral victory. This free election was a triumph for democracy because it was faithfully executed and enabled opposing policies to get a fair hearing. The majority party is therefore encouraged to be more responsive to popular demands and more efficient in administering public affairs. Of the 176 million eligible voters, 106 million (60 per cent) participated in elections for the House of the People and almost 102,500,000 voted in state legislative contests. There were eight major parties and forty lesser ones, all using pictorial symbols to identify themselves to the illiterate voters, but the populace as a whole was not any less competent than more literate and experienced electorates. Although it is too early to pass judgment, apparently literacy and a strong middle class may not be as indispensable to democracy as has been believed.

Courtesy: Information Service of India

Party Symbols on Indian Ballots

TOP ROW: 1. Congress   2. Socialist   3. Forward bloc   4. Kizan Mazdoor praja
BOTTOM ROW: 5. Communist   6. Revolutionary   7. Krishikar lok   8. Jan Sangh

In this election Congress received only 45 per cent of the total popular vote, and the Communists made a strong showing in the elections they contested. This fact in itself signifies that the rate of social and economic progress will determine future critical elections. The returns show that, though India is far from a one-party system, it has not yet developed a reliable party system in which the major antagonists are committed to the democratic creed.

Congress ran candidates throughout the country and captured a majority of 367 of the 480 seats contested in the House of the People. The Communists and their allies won 27 seats; the Socialists, 12; the anti-Communist Peasant-Workers Peoples party (K.M.P.), 10; the communalist Jan Sangh (formerly Mahasabha) took only 3 contests (and 3 per cent of the vote); the Scheduled Caste Federation, 2; and the Akali Sikhs, 4. In the state legislative elections, Congress won 42.5 per cent of the total vote and more than 67 per cent of the 3,283 seats contested; this result netted majorities in all except Madras and Orissa and the former princely lands of Pepsu in the Punjab and Travancore-Cochin in the extreme south. As in the national elections, where they polled 10 million votes, the Socialists finished second to the Congress in total votes but gained only 126 seats. By contrast, the Communists concentrated in a few select areas and so won 180 seats with a little over 6 million votes; their coalition fronts in Madras and Travancore-Cochin almost gave them control of these states.

The Parties of the Left

The electorate showed its desire for rapid change by voting for parties advocating reform. The communalist right was repudiated, and major opposition to Congress rule is expected from the left. After the election, the K.M.P. party, which had split off from the Congress because of its alleged conservatism, combined with the Socialists to form the Praja Socialist party. With twenty-two seats and 16 per cent of the popular vote, the new party hopes to unify the democratic left and present the strongest possible non-Communist opposition to the government. In the past, the Socialists were considered a doctrinaire, academic group lacking dynamism and unable to attract confidence in its ability to rule. By adopting Gandhian political and economic concepts and working under the spiritual leadership of Jayaprakash Narayan, the party hopes to gain peasant support.

The Communist party, despite occasional successes, has not developed the native leadership capable of making the most of India's revolutionary situation. In its checkered career, party membership rose from under 5,000 in the 1930's to 25,000 during the Second World War. Since the Communists supported the British war effort, they lost considerable prestige among nationalists. In 1948, following an international communist conference at Calcutta, the party adopted a program of insurrection and violence under its new ultraorthodox leader, B. T. Ranadive. Encouraged by success in Hyderabad and nearby Andhra, Ranadive called for a Democratic Front against imperialism, feudalism, and the middle class, and appealed for mass action. The Indian government responded energetically with a campaign of arrest and repression. By 1950, party membership fell from 80,000 (1946) to 30,000. The party then promised to operate peacefully and, in states where it had not been banned, contested the national election. A. J. Ghosh replaced Ranadive as the party publicly rejected violence as a means to power. An exposure of its secret conferences, however, revealed this change to be a momentary tactic; both Congress and Socialist parties are fully aware that the Communists hope to force their way to dictatorial rule.

In the national election, the Communists assiduously cultivated united fronts with other left groups and unleashed a vigorous propaganda campaign against the Congress. They constantly stressed the "great results" achieved by the new communist regime in China even when it had barely assumed power. A major electoral technique is to organize a coalition through which other left-wing parties can be captured and destroyed, with a view to obtaining a Communist monopoly over antiadministration reformist sentiment. But thus far other left-wing groups have avoided the Communists and have even merged against them. Clearly a major prerequisite for the survival of Indian democracy is the maintenance of an effective *democratic* left opposition to the Congress.

A second communist tactic follows the Maoist approach of a "little Yenan": gain control of a state and its police-administrative apparatus. The Communists will therefore try to use India's federal system to create and expand a territorial base of power. In Madras, it took the skill and prestige of the great Congress patriot, Chakravarti Rajagopalachari, to enable the Congress party to form and maintain a ministry; the Praja Socialists were not tempted by Communist offers of the premiership and other key posts in return for a united front. When the new state of Andhra held its first election in 1955, the Communists fully expected to build their strong position there into a majority, but the Congress campaigned vigorously and won a decisive surprise victory. The second area of Communist electoral strength was Travancore-Cochin, one of the most literate and Christianized of the former princely states. Yet, with Nehru's tireless campaigning in 1951, the voting gave the Congress 1,200,000 votes, the Socialists 500,000, and the Communists and their allies 700,000. This pattern was repeated in 1954: the Socialists formed a government with Congress support, as the Communists tried unsuccessfully to bring the other left groups into their coalition. The difficult economic conditions in these states, the city of Calcutta, and the small state of Pepsu[1] were revealed in sizable Communist votes. The Communists have recently begun to display guerilla strength in the strategic northern kingdom of Nepal, between China and India, thereby increasing the danger to the northern frontier.

In the second national election (1957), the Congress party received nearly half the 115 million votes cast, as it swept three quarters of the central legislature and two thirds of the 3100 provincial contests. The Communist vote went up from 5 to 10 per cent but the Praja Socialist total was halved. Together they won only one third of the Congress total, while the communalist right groups were practically annihilated. Congress failed to win a provincial majority in Orissa, where the Princes' party (Gantatra Parishad) is popular. Its other setback was in Kerala, where the Communists received a majority of two and planned to consolidate their strength by reformist measures. In general, Communist strength was restricted to Kerala and Andhra and the cities of Bombay and Calcutta. The most striking aspect of the voting pattern, when compared to the first election, is the remarkable consistency of the Congress' strength. This stability gives the party grounds for optimism, provided it maintains a good record in reform and development policies.

The Parties of the Right

The national election of 1951–1952 was a bitter blow to the communalist movement. It had been an active cultural and political force for more than

---

[1] Punjab and East Patiala States Union.

a century and its leaders hoped to benefit from the ferment created by partition and independence. The Hindu Mahasabha (General Association), founded in response to the Moslem League, had risen to prominence during the last decade of British rule under V. D. Savarkar. It tried to preserve India for the Hindus and opposed Congress efforts to reconcile religious antagonisms and create a secular state. Like the Communists, it gained ground during the war when Congress was suppressed, and contributed significantly to religious tension and violence at the time of partition. The assassination of Gandhi by a Mahasabha adherent brought the group under a temporary ban and aroused public hostility. One of its leaders, Dr. S. P. Mookerjee of Bengal, resigned from the Cabinet in 1950 because the government did not adopt a sufficiently firm stand toward Pakistan over the Hindu refugee issue. He then founded the Jan Saugh, which campaigned on this issue and stood for a Hindu theocratic state. In 1953 Mookerjee went to Jammu and was jailed because of a disturbance organized there. He died while imprisoned in Srinagar, an incident causing the government some embarrassment.

The R.S.S.[2] (National Volunteer Organization), a totalitarian-style organization led by M. Golwalkar, was associated with the Mahasabha until 1938. It claimed to have only cultural interests, but it too was placed under a one-year ban following Gandhi's death. Narrowly communal, it labeled Pakistan a foe, Indian Moslems a fifth column, and the government too materialistic. Yet it broke with tradition by giving its members military training and treating them as equals regardless of caste. In its new constitution, the R.S.S. claims to be moderate, but the Congress still forbids its own members to join it. Support for the R.S.S. came primarily from the northwest, the area most affected by partition.

Other rightest groups have even smaller followings, and generally express extreme religious views and a desire to return to the "utopian past." The Akali Sikh revivalists, who won thirty-three seats in the state legislatures of Pepsu and the Punjab, have benefited from their campaign for a Sikh state. In general, the communal right is too fragmented and dependent on regional appeals to develop a strong national party. Unless Congress splits and its right wing joins with the communalists, a major political threat from this direction is unlikely.

Economic Conditions and Development Plans

Before it can create an industrialized, literate society with a decent standard of living, India has to avert a *decline* in its economic fortunes threatened by population increases. Systematic planning is therefore essential. Having rejected the tactic of compulsion, India may be unable to accumulate capital or concentrate on heavy industry to the extent followed in China. Moreover, for a variety of reasons, India has discounted private foreign investment and has tentatively given foreign public funds only a marginal position in its over-all

[2] Rashtriva Swayamsevak Sangh.

plan. Only 15 per cent of the second five-year plan (1956–1961) is expected through foreign aid. Still, India seeks to follow a 10 to 15 per cent increase in the national income in the first plan with a 25 per cent rise in the second, without resorting to harsh economic measures. Whether revolutionary results can be achieved through a moderate approach and with minimum foreign assistance remains to be seen.

The poverty of India is evidenced in the very low wages received by those who are fortunate enough to possess professional or industrial skills. In the countryside income is even lower, with only 16 per cent of the populace able to spend more than $750 a year. Half the peasantry make under $300 a year, and a fifth earn less than $150 a year. In industrial Bombay, half of the people earn under $300 a year. This destitution means diets lacking in protein and fats, as well as low caloric content. It also means poor housing and lack of pavement, drainage, and wells; less than 1 per cent of the villages have electricity. In terms of services, only half of the children attend schools and many of these go just for a few years; medical facilities are inadequate in almost every aspect. There is little to tax directly, as only 800,000 have taxable incomes, and two thirds of the revenue collected comes from 5,000 assessees. As a result, there is heavy indirect taxation, yet without such compensation as old-age pensions or a national health service. Taxes collected amount to 7 per cent of the national income and total less than one half of Britain's defense expenditures.

Agricultural Production

India's population has increased by 153 million since 1900, one third of the increase occurring in the decade after 1941. The new Indian Union early faced serious food problems even in maintaining its low daily level of consumption at 1,700 calories. Help was needed in 1945–1946 before independence and again in 1949–1951 as droughts kept production below the level of subsistence. Finally, in 1951, the United States, after an acrimonious debate, enabled India to obtain 4 million tons of wheat through a low-interest loan of $190 million. The need to import food, which continued for a few years, absorbed foreign exchange that could have been used in long-range development projects. Exhortations alone did not improve production, as the failure of the "Grow More Food" campaign indicated by 1952. As long as from 5 to 10 per cent of its food and textile needs had to be imported, India was considered unlikely to make economic progress.

One line of approach was to develop more efficient farming techniques. Experimental stations proved that better seed and fertilizer, simple but improved tools, pest control, and consolidated holdings instead of strips of land could mean a 30 to 40 per cent rise in output. India's land had so deteriorated through erosion, deforestation, and poor irrigation that 183.8 million acres under cereal yielded only 44.2 million tons in 1949–1950, compared to 46.1 million tons from 167 million acres a decade earlier. Japan, for example, produced four times more rice per acre than did India. If India can just reach the Asian average in production per acre it can be fairly certain of self-sufficiency in food. Deep tube wells in North India and expanded use of shallow wells and tanks are important improvements. But the most spectacular effort can be seen in the TVA-like projects going on all over India, with the multiple benefits of irrigation, electric power, and flood control.

The first five-year plan (1951–1956) anticipated an addition of 19 million acres to the 50 million already under irrigation. It is also hoped that these vast projects will control and store rainwater, and thus prevent the cycle of flood and drought. About 95 per cent of India's rain falls in the two-to-three-month monsoon season. There are the Bhakra Dam in the Punjab, which rises to 690 feet (second only to Boulder Dam), and three other major works in the Bengal-Bihar area, Orissa, and Madras-Hyderabad. The Orissa project at Hirakud along the difficult Mahanadi River was completed in 1957. It contains a three-mile dam and sixteen miles of dikes and is expected to irrigate 670,000 acres. The government hopes that this will raise the area's annual production by 400,000 tons and give 123,000 kilowatts, twenty-five times Orissa's present capacity. The federal government plans further projects, and there are seventy irrigation schemes proposed by the states. It is doubtful that funds will be available for all plans, but a vigorous start has been made. Finally, 7 million acres of land that have fallen to Kans grass will be reclaimed by heavy tractors.

The First Five-Year Plan (1951–1956)

The major effort of the first five-year plan, which really took effect in 1953, was in the basic fields of agricultural production, the development of power and transportation, and the growth of textile industries. Industry and social services were given more modest objectives, though the plan sought to lay a basis for rapid expansion in the future. This plan was only the first in a series of four or five scheduled five-year plans. Priorities were set up by a Planning Commission established by Prime Minister Nehru and staffed by economic experts. The commission included important ministers, and all its members were of cabinet rank in order to make its decisions authoritative.

FINAL DRAFT OF THE FIRST FIVE-YEAR PLAN
(IN MILLIONS OF DOLLARS)

	Agriculture; Community Projects	Irrigation and Power	Transport; Communications	Industry	Social Services	Rehabilitation	Others
Amount	756.9	1,179.0	1,043.9	363.4	714.6	178.5	109.2
Per cent of total	17.4	27.2	24.0	8.4	16.4	4.1	2.5

To this public investment of about $4.5 billion was to be added about $1.25 billion in private investment, bringing the total to more than $5.7 billion. However, the government was certain of only two thirds of this amount and was not sure that the rest could be diverted from savings. The plan's objectives were to raise grain production by 9 million tons so that, even with more people, the daily caloric intake would reach 1,850. In addition, a sizable increase in cotton production was sought, to satisfy urgent consumer textile needs.

CROP LEVELS AND TARGETS

In millions		1950–1951	1955–1956	Estimated Production 1955–1956
Food grain	(tons)	54.0	61.6	65.0
Cotton	(bales)	3.0	4.2	4.2
Jute	(bales)	3.3	5.4	4.0
Sugar cane	(tons)	5.6	6.3	5.8
Oil seeds	(tons)	5.1	5.5	5.5

In industrial planning neither communist tactic of a forced pace nor concentration on heavy industry was followed. The plan was a far cry from earlier grandiose schemes, such as the famous Bombay Plan of 1944, drawn up by industrial leaders for rapid modernization. Nevertheless, important advances were sought in steel and mill-cloth production, as well as in the less well-developed categories of aluminum, diesel engines, and commercial fertilizer. Electric power was expected to reach 1,900,000 kilowatts, with the four major projects generating an important part of the total. Private industry was expected to contribute one third of the anticipated investment in industry and expand along with the public sector over a wide range of products. Moreover, more than $60 million was set aside to aid small industries, village crafts, and local workshops in such traditional fields as oil and soap making, hand spinning and weaving, and leatherworking. In a concession to Gandhian economic principles, protection against factory competition was planned for the small producer in these fields.

The plan as a whole absorbed from 5 to 6 per cent of the national income, estimated at a little under $20 billion in 1951. The objective for 1956 was a modest 11 per cent rise in the total national income and an increase of net investment to a level of 7 per cent. The more sweeping objective—to raise the per capita annual income from $50 to $200—will take several more plans.

Evaluation of the Plan

Early results follow a pattern almost directly the reverse of results in communist lands—marked increases in agricultural production and consumer purchases but a serious lag in industrial development. Crop production was a spectacular success, especially after years of near famine. Food grains totaled 65.4 million tons in 1954, though scheduled to reach only 61.6 million in 1956. Cotton production was at 76 per cent of the 1956 objective in 1954. The increase of 11.4 million tons of food was due primarily to two excellent monsoons, but the Planning Commission feels that 4 to 5 million tons stem from permanent improvements: over 7 million acres under irrigation, new interest and better farming methods by the peasants, and increased use of fertilizer. It was optimistically felt that these three factors would mean a 22 per cent rise in food production by 1956, enough to meet population increases and inadequate monsoons. Additional irrigation and fertilizer development under the second five-year plan may mean a 30 per cent rise in food production by 1961. On the debit side, investment in development projects was at only half the monetary levels set by the plan, and many of the schemes were uncoordinated and inefficiently handled. One notable shortcoming was the absence of storage facilities to make the most of the bumper crops. Progress was also slow in creating a system of rural credit, free of moneylender control, that would encourage progressive agricultural techniques still further.

Industrial production rose by 40 per cent over 1950, but it is doubtful whether the rate of investment achieved thus far is sufficient to sustain an upward movement in the economy as a whole. The greatest gains were in cotton cloth, because the agricultural boom meant a widespread increase in purchasing power. But here, as in other fields, increases were derived largely by using existing capacity more fully. There were new industrial plants—textiles, cement, paper, glassworks—in the private sector, and private investments did increase from $56 million in 1951 to $84 million in 1953–1954. Yet over half the money allotted was still to be used by 1954. Government investment was only at the 30 per cent mark, though new steel works by a German consortium were expected to close the gap somewhat. Moreover, production lagged in critical fields. Steel expansion was at 14.9 per cent of its target, and electric power at 42 per cent. Transportation facilities were inadequate, and it is now evident that the targets set in this field were too low. A more systematic and forceful effort in the industrial sector was essential if the rapid rate of growth planned for 1951–1956 was to be achieved.

The Second Five-Year Plan (1956–1961)

This plan is a crucial one, since all sectors of the economy must develop simultaneously at a rapid rate. The cost is to be approximately double the first plan—$11.76 billion as again $5.7 billion. It is hoped that the plan will bring about an 18 per cent rise in per capita income, which will allow people to consume and save at the same time.

As in 1951–1956, almost half the plan must be devoted to transportation, communications, education, and electric power, none of which brings quick returns. Railways will receive $1.68 billion, and roads are to be increased by 25,000 miles. India is planning to develop its heavy industry more rapidly because these products abroad are very expensive, difficult to purchase, and subject to delays in delivery. Industry's share has been raised to about one quarter of the total funds. Of this $3 billion, roughly 80 per cent is allotted to heavy

389

industry and mining, with the main emphasis on steel, cement, coal, lignite, fertilizer, and electrical machinery. Some of the targets are shown in the accompanying table.

INDUSTRIAL LEVELS AND TARGETS

	Units	1955–56	1960–61	Percentage Increase
Cement	(million tons)	4.8	10.0	108
Coal	(million tons)	36.8	60.0	63
Electricity	(million kw.)	3.4	6.8	100
Aluminum	('000 tons)	7.5	25.0	233
Iron ore	(million tons)	4.3	12.5	191
Finished steel	(million tons)	1.3	4.3	231

Since India is the world's cheapest steel producer, it is hoped that the industry will continue to expand and pay its own way. The rest of industry's share allots 7 per cent to factory consumer goods and 13 per cent (a little over $400 million) to hand industry.

It is in agriculture and the cottage industries that India can increase production with relatively little capital expense. Even here, however, irrigation will require $980 million, electricity and transport costs will mount, and capital will have to be advanced for fertilizer, stock, deep wells, and operational costs. Still, agriculture will require only half the capital needed for the new steel mills alone. In fact, agriculture and the village industries will get only one sixth of the total funds. Yet they are expected to account for nearly half of the increase in the national income.

AGRICULTURAL TARGETS, 1956–1961

(In Millions)

	Units	1955–56	1960–61	Percentage Increase
Food grain	(tons)	65.0	75.0	15
Cotton	(bales)	4.2	5.5	31
Jute	(bales)	4.0	5.0	25
Sugar cane	(tons)	5.8	7.4	28
Oil seeds	(tons)	5.5	7.0	27

The Industrial Scene

Industry remains small, absorbing only 20 per cent of the working population, with another 10 per cent operating small enterprises and 70 per cent in agriculture. However, landless laborers form an important segment of the farming group and their only hope is to be absorbed in an expanding industrial economy. The government seeks to create 24 million jobs outside agriculture by 1964. This period of transition will be politically difficult, because the Communists will seek to capitalize on the dislocations, inadequacies, and injustices inevitably accompanying such a change. At present, India's industrial power is concentrated in cotton textiles and jute, with 500 mills employing 1 million workers.

In all there are more than 2,500,000 laborers in industry. Their union affiliations reflect the national political pattern. The Communists captured the All-Indian Trade Union Congress during the Second World War and now claim about 800,000 members. The Congress founded the Indian National Trade Union Congress in 1947; its membership is now 1,400,000. There are several socialist-led movements, including a railway federation, with a total membership of 800,000. Each group undoubtedly has inflated the size of its organization somewhat, but the relative proportions are roughly accurate. Unions are generally impoverished and can do little to aid their members. Still, they contribute to a sense of group unity and have organized strikes for better wages and working conditions. The Congress-affiliated group works closely with the government. At times this cooperation requires the sacrifice of union demands but often it means concessions by the government in return. Industrial relations are generally tense, especially in Calcutta, now developing into a Communist stronghold; though the Communists have gained ground, they have not yet made appreciable inroads in the industrial north. However, the crucial years lie in the near future, and the most critical region may be the industrial heart of India—the Bengal-Orissa-Bihar triangle that is so richly endowed with natural resources.

Programs of Reform

Committed to both the democratic process and a modest program of economic expansion, the government must place great emphasis on economic and social reforms. Only in this way can the present regime be assured of popular political support and a widespread willingness to expand production, especially in agriculture. The peasant is the center of these reforms, which involve his security of land tenure and community-development projects. A related objective, covering the country as a whole, is no less than a relative equalization of existing wealth and property.

Land Reform

The political center of gravity remains in the peasantry, whose security of tenure is an important precondition for the success of the government's economic plans. Relations between the Congress and the peasant masses are somewhat strained, partly because of the countryside's traditional suspicion of all rulers but also because most officials come from an upper-class Westernized environment "ten generations" removed from the primitive countryside. The comparatively high standards of living enjoyed by the bureaucracy and its "night watchman" concept of government inherited from its British mentors increased this sense of apartness. Many adherents of the Congress party itself are landlords, rich tenants, or machine politicians who have consistently opposed a reformist platform.

However, the Congress adopted the slogan "land to the tiller" and fostered a land-reform program in 1937. It gained some security for tenants in Bihar and the United and Central Provinces (Uttar and Madhya Pradesh). But the over-all situation was still characterized by exploitation and inefficiency. The poorest sharecroppers, as in Madras Province, received only 5 to 10 per cent of the crop. Tenants-at-will (those lacking security) fared better but still suffered from lack of tenure. In 1950 the Congress party's Agrarian Reform Committee called for the right of tenants to buy land, an end to the intermediary landholdings and subleases, and ceilings on the size of holdings.

By 1955 some progress was made in eliminating zamindari and other types of intermediary absentee owners, though only five states had abolished them completely. According to the pattern, the peasant pays rent to the government for a number of years and becomes an owner after paying a sum fixed at some multiple of the annual land revenue. Compensation for former landholders is measured in fixed multiples of net rent. Small landholders, who number in the hundreds of thousands, get 3 per cent bonds that assure them the same income as before. The wealthier elements find their income cut to 10 per cent or less in comparison with former rents. Though reforms are slowed down by different conditions in each state and by the high cost of compensation—over $980 million, the trend is to give ownership to the cultivators who were protected tenants under pre-1947 legislation.

Tenancy still covers one quarter of India; in some areas (the Deccan and Punjab) it is even higher, and in others (Pepsu and Nalgonda) has led to violence. Laws to protect tenants also vary, with Bombay having the most comprehensive code, which limits rent to one sixth the crop, minimizes evictions, guarantees leases, compensates tenants for improvements made, and allows tenants to buy the land at prices fixed by tribunals. Yet in Pepsu and the Punjab landlords have resorted to extralegal subterfuges and evasions, altering records, dividing land among relations, and evicting tenants. Rack rents in zamindari private lands and continued exploitation of subleases under the ryotwari system are also common abuses.

There are also the landless, now estimated at one in seven agricultural families, with a high concentration in Travancore-Cochin and Tanjore. Peasant unrest has enabled the Communists to grow strong in Pepsu and Travancore-Cochin. Reclaimed wasteland, gifts (*bhoodan*), and some property from large estates will provide plots for 750,000 families, but only through industrialization can this pressure be adequately reduced. As of 1951, two thirds of the peasants classified themselves as owner-cultivators; by 1960 this catagory may reach four fifths, with adequate protection for the rest. Success in this peaceful revolution appears to depend on how effectively the mass of reform legislation is executed in the near future.

The Community Development Program

The government sought to induce the peasantry to join cooperatives as part of its plan to revitalize the economy, but wisely discarded the plan when it met resistance. Instead, a Community Development Program was launched, with the objective of improving physical conditions in India's 600,000 villages. Training units are dispatched to the villages to teach the peasantry how to improve farming techniques and facilities of health, irrigation, education, and transportation. One of the more heartening aspects of this effort has been the way officials have undertaken manual labor in the villages. In 1952, there were fifty-five development projects, covering 16,000 villages and 11 million people. Projects are selected by the villages themselves, and will be financed by the government for three years, after which they must be self-supporting.

By the end of the first five-year plan, more than 25 per cent of rural India is to be affected. There are 400 projects, covering 100 million people, that will require 30,000 general teachers and several hundred specialists. The government hopes to reach all villages by 1961 through a National Extension Service. The more thorough projects will cover every village by 1966. Experience shows that excellent results are obtained in three years, for villages overcome early suspicion of government intervention and show a keen interest in construction of better cottages, irrigation and farming methods, new schools and roads, health control, and even the creation of local industries.

It is significant that Congress interest in the peasantry has been matched by the Praja Socialist party, which has vigorously sponsored reforms in land tenure and seeks to give the people a democratic alternative to the government. In a related movement, Vinoba Bhave, a saintly follower of Gandhi, has been crusading to have people surrender land voluntarily. It can then be turned over to the landless laborer, who is most often an untouchable. Village reform and political training in democracy can be closely integrated. Grass-roots participation in village decisions concerning projects to be followed, peasant interest in the 1951–1952 election, and village elections at the panchayat level indicate how quickly this can be done. By awakening popular interest in local problems and personalities and giving the villages a voice in concrete issues, the government can instill a respect for the democratic process in rural India.

The Drive for Equality

The prevailing philosophy in India today is a socialism defined in terms of economic equality and security for all. It resembles the Western version of socialism in giving government planning a central place in the economy and in having a steadily expanding sector under public control. However, it seems to seek equality by sponsoring widespread ownership of property on a small scale or, where this is impossible, guaranteeing job security to its citizens. Nationalization as an end in itself is considered outdated dogma and is invoked only when good cause exists, as in commercial airlines or banking.

The Indian economy is centered on the self-employed, who produce more than 60 per cent of the national income. In commerce there are a little over a million employers and four times as many self-employed; there are over 5 million independent handicraftsmen as against half as many in organized labor. In rural areas the landless are only 14 per cent, though this figure varies from a mere 5 per cent in north India to about 50 per cent in Travancore-Cochin. In government and large-scale industry job security makes up for the absence of property rights. A government employee is guaranteed a formal charge, a hearing, and a confrontation of evidence before he can be fired. In business, a tribunal must be convinced that economic loss is involved before retrenchment is allowed, and then there is some severance pay. A modernized industry must retain all its employees.

Tenants in the city as well as on the farm are gaining protection against eviction and high rents. The government's tax policy is manipulated to encourage the middle class to build and keep its own homes. Handicraft industries are receiving considerable protection from the government in five-year-plan allotments, marketing and pricing, tax preferences, and technical aid. Despite some loss in economic efficiency, the state is protecting them against factory competition. Through its tax program, which bears heavily on high incomes, the government is trying to make certain that, if most Indians are to be poor, none will enjoy excessive wealth.

In the social sphere, inheritance rights for women have improved: daughters receive half as much as sons under a new Hindu Succession Bill, and full rather than half-ownership of their own estates. As is true of the untouchables, the effort to better woman's economic and social position remains a long and difficult task of modifying ancient customs.

There is an important element of Gandhi's philosophy in this program—his concern for small property, the peasantry, and the handicraft industries. These social and economic programs are of limited benefit even if ideally carried out. Still, this approach is a measure of the government's good will and earnest intentions. Should the program be carried on effectively, it will do much to counterbalance the slow pace of economic development as long as some steady growth is recorded. This philosophy can do much to ease the shock caused by modernization as India tries to adapt certain Western values to its own modified social system and pattern of beliefs.

Pakistan

Pakistan at its inception lacked the advantages of order and tradition enjoyed by its larger neighbor and therefore encountered considerable difficulty in ordering its public affairs. Though composed of two separate chips off the Indian subcontinent, the new Moslem state is the world's seventh most populous country, with almost 80 million people. It still lives in the shadow of India, whose presence is accentuated by the tense relations between the successor states and the 1,000 miles of Indian territory separating East and West Pakistan. The country was created out of fear that Moslems would remain second-class citizens in a united India—a fear that has been sustained in good part by the continuously hostile attitude of India. But if Pakistan is to justify Jinnah's assertion that it ought to exist by right, it must display a positive program evoking and maintaining the loyalty of its component parts.

The new state has defied predictions that it would soon collapse and be remembered simply as an aberration. Yet it has constantly disappointed its supporters by its slowness to develop a constitutional order, settle relations between its two wings, and determine the place of religion in public affairs. A bewildering turnover of personnel in top government posts, as well as the erosion of the majority enjoyed by the Moslem League, has further complicated the task of nation building. These difficulties quickly became intensified and fed on each other to such a degree that the state's ability to survive became a critical issue before a decade had elapsed.

The country is overwhelmingly agricultural; almost 90 per cent of the people lived in villages at the time of partition. Both the major ports, Karachi in the west and Chittagong in the east, required extensive improvements to serve Pakistan's needs. Railway lines were meager and road networks were geared to the military defense of the northwest frontier. No jute was processed, and only 10 per cent of the 1,500,000 bales of cotton produced in Pakistan was milled at home. High world prices for jute, cotton, and wheat after 1947 gave Pakistan a strong international monetary position and enabled it to start many long-range development projects. But this prosperity brought a false sense of economic security, which was rudely shattered when prices fell after 1952. A severe foreign-exchange crisis and a food shortage seriously endangered the modernization program and intensified the existing political crisis.

The Political Setting

Organizing a New State

The enthusiasm generated by the birth of Pakistan contributed to the new state's ability to overcome immediate handicaps and establish its machinery of government. This task absorbed most of the country's energy, because Pakistan lacked the personnel and physical plant around which a new regime could be immediately organized. Moslem civil servants were hampered in their movement from India to the new capital of Karachi by riots and transportation difficulties; moreover, all administrative files and records were in New Delhi. Lahore was Pakistan's first city and cultural center but was located near the Indian frontier. Though Karachi lacked facilities, it expanded rapidly, and its population of 360,000 in 1941 grew to more than a million by 1951. Dacca, an historic center of Moslem culture, became the capital of the new state of East Bengal.

The new bureaucracy has been one of the brightest aspects of Pakistan's first years. Civilian and military officials have remained loyal to the regime and to the objective of creating a democratic order. The public services created by

Britain have been maintained. Law and order were upheld even along the frontiers, and the serious refugee problem was kept under control.

The country has been on a near-war footing since its birth, and its military competence has been a source of national pride. Pakistan has also undertaken a vigorous foreign policy. It retained old connections by remaining in the Commonwealth and participating in the Colombo Plan, but joined with its neighbors as one of the five Colombo Powers stressing the independence of Southeast Asia. Pakistan also made an important alliance—the Baghdad Pact— with its Turkish and Iraqi coreligionists to the west and joined the American-sponsored Southeast Asian defense system. This policy has further enhanced national self-confidence, but it has proved to be an economic burden. Though the nation's financial affairs have been skillfully handled the public debt still mounts. Treasury bills and loans are required to support a capital budget that, unlike the regular budget, cannot be balanced by receipts.

Pakistan's constitutional structure remained temporarily under the Act of 1935. A Constituent Assembly was chosen in 1947 to serve as a federal legislature until it prepared a new constitution. Delegates were selected by provincial legislatures at a ratio of one per million inhabitants and the Moslem League enjoyed an overwhelming majority of the seats. A cabinet responsible to the Assembly and a governor-general, nominated by the cabinet and acting on its advice, formed the executive. The 1935 pattern of central-provincial relations was also retained on a temporary basis; the main provinces (called governor's provinces) were West Punjab, Sind, and the North West Frontier in West Pakistan, and East Bengal on the other wing. The western half of the country also retained additional subdivisions, six princely states and tribal areas inherited from the British. Each province had a legislature-cabinet system, and a governor appointed by the governor-general, with power to assume control in exceptional circumstances.

Weakness of Provincial Government

Critical observers pointed out that West Pakistan contained fewer districts— the basic administrative subdivision under British rule—than had existed in the undivided Punjab. Such elaborate provincial administrations were inefficient and quickly proved to be centers of corruption. The difficulties that arose in the provinces immediately after partition revealed that these political units were sources of grave weakness.

The Punjab came under Moslem League control in 1947 after a decade of rule by an antipartition Unionist ministry. The new administration's incompetence obliged Governor Mudie, under orders from the governor-general, to dissolve the legislature and hold new elections. The governor, a retired British official, had handled the refugee problem well and had also exposed corruption in the refugee property allocations. In 1949, the Punjab Moslem League successfully demanded Mudie's recall, labeling him a "foreign dictator." In Sind, the first chief minister was dismissed for maladministration and the second for electoral misconduct. These dismissals led to a long and bitter struggle within the provincial Moslem League organization. In the North West Frontier Province, the pro-Congress Moslem Red Shirt Organization was banned, and its leaders, including Dr. M. L. A. Khan Sahib, were jailed. Energetic industrial and social-service programs, though, enabled the region to make considerable progress after 1947, as its 2,500,000 tribesmen showed signs of becoming more pacified. But even then disaffection persisted among its political leaders.

The Problem of East Pakistan

The "balkanized" structure of West Pakistan assumed critical importance when East Pakistan (East Bengal plus the Sylhet section of Assam) regarded this structure as a device to keep Bengal in a permanent minority in the federal legislature. History has shown how difficult it is to create and maintain federations even under favorable circumstances. East Pakistan, in this case, felt isolated from the west, resented an apparent monopoly of federal posts by Punjabis, and was incensed when Urdu was proclaimed an official language, whereas Bengali was not. Export profits came from East Bengal's jute trade but were utilized to develop West Pakistan. The condescending attitude of these western countrymen further added to the irritation. Bengal had, in fact, long been famous for a provincialism that had led some of its Moslem leaders like H. S. Suhrawardy, the last premier of united Bengal, to favor an autonomous united province instead of partition.

East Pakistan, with only 54,000 square miles, has over 42 million inhabitants or more than half the nation's population. It has 800 people per square mile, in contrast to 109 in West Pakistan, with its 306,000 square miles. Rainfall ranges from 75 to 160 inches a year in the east but only from 10 to 20 inches in the west. Bengali Moslems accepted partition because it freed them from the cultural and political domination of their Hindu neighbors, but they were extremely sensitive about becoming a colony of their coreligionists in the west. As a result, representation at the center became a vital constitutional question. Bengal demanded, in the name of good government and fair play, that West Pakistan be consolidated into a single province, with each wing given equal representation. There also developed a more radical demand for autonomy, control over its own finances, and language parity. More ominous was the threat of a separatist movement that could destroy the precarious unity of the new nation.

The Religious Question and the Constitution

Bengal is also the home of 11 million Hindus, a fact intensifying the need to settle the role of the Moslem religion in public affairs. Creation of a religious state might have undermined national unity further and made the tension in Indian-Pakistan relations literally unbearable.

In its Aims and Objects Resolution of March, 1948, the Constituent Assembly emphasized the Islamic faith, invoked its deity, and upheld the right to live according to the Koran and Sunna (religious traditions). The statement also guaranteed fundamental political, social, and economic rights to all and promised to protect minority rights. The non-Moslems remained fearful of being treated as second-class citizens and were not satisfied with Prime Minister Liaquat Ali Khan's assurances that all rights would be protected and anyone would be welcome into the government service. Other Moslem leaders added that the Koran called for tolerance, not compulsion, and that Islam would point the way to a democratic society with economic and social justice based on "Islamic socialism."

The years after 1949 were anxious ones for the Hindus, and their sporadic migrations to India were a measure of this uncertainty. In December, 1950, the Basic Principles Committee on the Constitution presented an imposing array of fundamental rights, promising all equality before the law and protection against arbitrary state action. Religious freedom was guaranteed, with other political and civil rights. But the worries of the minority groups and the modernists were soon justified by a fierce attack on the Basic Principles Committee by the mullahs, the orthodox priesthood. When they demanded a fully Islamic constitution, a new report of January, 1953, made important concessions to their position. It provided for boards of religious leaders to advise the legislatures on new laws and to be available for consultation on laws considered repugnant to the scriptures. Also, a bill had to receive a majority of Moslem votes to become law if a religious board found fault with it. Minority and reformist groups, including feminist leaders, countered with a vigorous attack against the report, as a grant of veto power to the mullahs. By the end of 1953 the proposal was discarded. Thus the fight for a secular state was won, though Islamic overtones remained. The minorities were not appeased by separate representation for minority religious communities.

A Confused Party System

The Moslem League revealed both the strength and weakness of the new state. Unlike the Indian Congress party, the League fell into disuse shortly after partition. Its leaders held that parties should not influence the affairs of state. They believed in the democratic process but apparently did not envisage a party system as the means of channeling power and responsibility. The League's historic role had been that of a revolutionary communalist body and not a party in the Western sense. Only when biting criticism from religious extremists, regionalists, and other opponents of the government became serious did Moslem League officials reorganize their party. Its leaders still believed that the League should monopolize political power and serve as a semiofficial body to strengthen national unity and stability. The creation of new opposition parties was denounced as an act of enmity destructive to national security. The League and Pakistan were linked together as indissoluble in the minds of the country's political leaders.

This attitude, as well as the peculiar structure of Pakistan, gave substance to League fear that political rivals might destroy Pakistan's precarious unity. The parties that grew most rapidly were regional, communal, and separatist. Though H. S. Suhrawardy tried to build his Awami League on a national basis by winning refugee support and exploiting the Kashmir issue, his base of power remained in Bengal. Another Bengali ex-premier, Fazlul Huq, formed a United Front that aimed at provincial autonomy; he combined with Suhrawardy in a coalition against the governing Moslem League to contest the Bengal provincial election of 1954. Political opposition in the North West Frontier Province also had a regional coloration, with a leadership still not reconciled to the concept of Pakistan.

The Socialist party has remained a minor force, and the Azad Pakistan party appears to be a small Communist-front group. The Communists themselves are less active than in India, though they have found influential supporters like Iftikhar ud-Din, publisher of the *Pakistan Times*. A sensational development in 1951 was the government's discovery of a communist-inspired plot to assassinate the leaders of the state and create a military dictatorship. The plotters were motivated by personal ambition and frustration over relations with India. Fifteen people, including the army chief of staff, were jailed after being found guilty of conspiring against the state. Clearly Islam was not an absolute guarantee against the penetration of communist influence.

The identification of the League with the government was most marked in the Constituent Assembly where, under a system of communal representation, it held all except one of the Moslem seats until 1954. The League has tried to remain a mass organization open to all Moslems over eighteen, with dues at two annas a year. Its provincial organizations choose delegates to the All-Pakistan Moslem League Council of about 450 members, which then elects a president each year. The president in turn appoints his own Working Committee. The All-Pakistan and Provincial League Councils are also responsible for the choice of League candidates in legislative elections. Since the positions of federal prime minister and League president went together until 1956, government and party were easily identified as one in the popular mind. This fact left both open to criticism for any difficulty the nation encountered. With some justice, the League could be blamed for corruption, the slowness of economic reform, delays in forming a new constitution or holding national elections, and the trouble over religious and regional issues.

The Turbulence of National Politics

Since partition, the national administration has suffered from a large number of shocks. These were both symptoms of a difficult situation and important contributions to Pakistan's duress. Major political developments included the decline of the Moslem League, a continuous change in the nation's political leadership, and grave difficulties in devising proper constitutional means for dealing with a series of crises.

The Crisis of Leadership

The first governor-general was the great Jinnah, who also held the difficult positions of League President and head of the Constituent Assembly. His death in 1948 deprived the country of its revered leader and symbol of unity. His successor as governor-general was Kwaja Nazimudden, a moderate, religious League member from Bengal. The country was fortunate in having Liaquat Ali Khan as prime minister. He had been League Secretary (1936–1947) and Jinnah's first assistant in negotiations for independence. He was a progressive modernist who asserted the authority of the central government, followed a cautious policy with regard to India, and was respected by his countrymen. It was therefore a great shock when he was assassinated by a Moslem communal extremist in 1951. A leader of his caliber was difficult to find, and Governor-General Nazimudden became prime minister. He in turn nominated a career civil servant, the capable Finance Minister Ghulam Mohammed, as governor-general.

But in the years 1951–1953 many grave issues arose to tax the new cabinet beyond its capacity. It was Nazimudden who temporarily yielded the power of legislative veto to the mullahs, to the dismay of the modernists. And he was not successful in resolving the issue of legislative representation between the country's two wings. In 1952 a proposal to give both wings equal representation in both houses angered West Pakistan, for it made Bengal the equal of all the rest. Student riots in West Pakistan added to the tension as antagonism mounted.

Meanwhile the country suffered a staggering economic blow when its windfall profits from agricultural exports ended. The Korean War had brought high prices and also enabled Pakistan to collect heavy export duties on jute, cotton, hides, and tea. This revenue covered extensive commitments in national defense and development programs in power, irrigation, and industry. By 1953 prices had fallen and the tea industry, with plantations located in the Sylhet section of East Pakistan, was endangered. Wool, hides, and skins lost their competitive market position. Even cotton and jute, which comprised 90 per cent of the exports, faced stagnant markets. The sudden shortage of foreign exchange was serious enough, but 70 per cent of Pakistan's revenue was derived from import and export duties. As exports fell, imports had to be curtailed, the regular budget was upset, and this loss of revenue plunged the country further into debt. The cruelest blow was a food shortage in 1952–1953 in a country that had been the breadbasket of the subcontinent. More than 1.5 million tons of grain had to be imported in 1953.

The governor-general suddenly dismissed the cabinet in April, 1953, and appointed another Bengali, Mohammed Ali, Ambassador to the United States, as premier. The new cabinet was more modernist and checked the mullahs' power. It also promised vigorous economic action, especially in food production, which had been neglected in favor of industrial projects. Nazimudden challenged the governor-general's action as unconstitutional, but he finally resigned as head of the Moslem League and retired from public life on a pension.

The Bengal Crisis

The cabinet of Mohammed Ali also lasted for two years (1953–1955) and, like its predecessor, was buffeted by political storms. In 1953 it tried to settle the regional question by making the total membership of the two wings equal in the central legislature. It also gave a virtual veto on legislation concerning regional affairs to each wing. The head of the state and the prime minister were to come from different parts of the country. Widespread relief greeted this constitutional settlement, but the agreement was suddenly rendered meaningless by the Bengal provincial election of April, 1954.

This was Pakistan's first major election, forerunner of a national election to be held after the constitution was ratified. Fazlul Huq had succeeded in gathering all dissident elements under his United Front and campaigned with an openly provincial appeal. The Moslem League ministry in Dacca was a poor one, and appeared indifferent to public opinion. Above all, the vote was a protest against the Karachi government of the west. The League suffered an utter rout, winning but ten of the 309 contested seats. The new United Front government now demanded that Bengali be treated as a national language; that the central government be limited to foreign affairs, defense, and currency; that East Pakistan be given control over the profitable jute trade; and that East Pakistan have its own ordnance plant and be militarily self-sufficient.

Within a month, however, the province was swept by riots and disorder. These began as labor unrest in factories, but soon West Pakistan officials and technicians were assaulted and murdered. Near-anarchy reigned, but the provincial administration failed to act, either through inertia or because it wanted to force the hand of the center. Again Governor-General Ghulam Mohammed moved swiftly; he declared an emergency in East Pakistan, suspended the legislature, dismissed the cabinet, and appointed Defense Minister General Iskander Mirza as governor with full powers. Order was restored, but the problem could not be resolved by denouncing Fazlul Huq or blaming the communists. Bengal's demands had to be met in a manner that satisfied the demand for autonomy yet preserved the federal structure.

One important concession was the elevation of Bengali to an equal status with Urdu and English as a language to be spoken in parliament. English is to be used officially for twenty years after the constitution goes into effect, while a common national language is being fostered. Jinnah had maintained that this should be Urdu, but only 1 per cent of East Pakistan's population claimed to know that language in 1947. English is the most convenient bridge between the two regions, but it is doubtful whether national pride will permit its retention.

The End of League Dominance

As a consequence of poor leadership and organization, the League lost support in the west as well as in Bengal. Party discipline, never very strong, now threatened to collapse, and one observer remarked that "at times it seems as if everybody is in the Opposition." The Moslem League representatives from East Pakistan in the Constituent Assembly offered to resign after their party's defeat, but this suggestion was rejected, in the hope that this "Long Parliament" would finally finish its constitutional duties in 1954. However, with the League discredited and the government unrepresentative, there seemed little chance that a constitution could be acted on.

To bolster the government, Ghulam Mohammed hurled another of his thunderbolts. He pardoned Dr. Khan and his colleagues in the North West Frontier Province and brought him and H. S. Suhrawardy into Mohammed Ali's reshuffled cabinet in a search for greater stability. The Constituent Assembly had opposed Ghulam Mohammed after Nazimudden was ousted. When it refused to make one state out of West Pakistan and sought to curtail his powers, the governor-general dissolved the legislature and declared a state of emergency in October, 1954. The Assembly denounced his action as unconstitutional, but Ghulam pointed to the governor-general's responsibility for the nation's welfare under the 1935 Act and his powers under Section 9 of the India Independence Act of 1947.

Law Minister Suhrawardy formulated the provision for a unified West Pakistan and a single legislature with equal representation for both wings. A new Constituent Assembly was chosen in 1955 by indirect elections in provincial legislatures, the emergency having been ended in East Pakistan. The Moslem League was still the largest party in parliament, but it was now a minority element. The other major groups were the United Front and the Awami League, both from Bengal. This new body was authorized to validate all earlier laws declared illegal by a Federal Court on a technicality, and form a new constitution within six months. In April, 1955, it was given the old powers of the Constituent Assembly to act as a federal legislature. It had eighty members, half from each wing of the country.

The state did not collapse during its long ordeal because the civil and military bureaucracy remained loyal to its task and faithful to the democratic heritage, although it had ample opportunity to establish a dictatorship and perpetuate its own power. Ghulam Mohammed and his colleagues scrupulously obeyed all decisions of the judiciary and worked for a constitutional settlement in 1955. The situation in East Pakistan became stabilized when the United Front was again allowed to direct provincial affairs. A new ministry was formed under Abu Hossain Sarkar, for whom the former leader, Fazlul Huq, stepped aside. The question of making West Pakistan a single unit was submitted to the new Assembly, though at first Ghulam Mohammed wanted to proclaim this as an order. The new Constituent Assembly finally passed this act of integration by a vote of 43 to 13, with 24 abstentions, in September, 1955, and Dr. Khan was appointed the first Chief Minister of West Pakistan.

During this time, the position of Mohammed Ali was weakened and his cabinet fell. Moslem League and United Front opposition kept H. S. Suhrawardy from becoming prime minister; and another veteran civil servant, Chaudhri Mohammed Ali succeeded Mohammed Ali. He formed a cabinet balanced evenly between eastern and western members. In August, 1955, General Mirza became governor-general when the ailing Ghulam Mohammed retired.

The New Constitution of 1956

The way was now cleared for this coalition cabinet to produce a constitution that would satisfy both wings of the country. A new government draft was placed before the legislature in January, 1956. Though many problems had been cleared away, there were still certain major issues outstanding: what level of provincial autonomy to allow? to have joint or separate electorates? to have the Republic "Islamic" in character?

The second and third questions were of great concern to the Hindu minority who wished to have a secular constitution and joint electorates. It considered separate electorates the basis of a Moslem communal state and an obstacle to the creation of a truly homogeneous nation. Orthodox advocates of communal electorates threatened violence if they did not get their way; proponents of joint electorates repeatedly walked out of the legislative debates and were adamant in their stand. The constitution-makers parried this question by leaving it up to the future parliament to decide how national and provincial elections would be conducted.

Minority efforts to secularize the constitution failed, because a motion to eliminate the term "Islamic" from the basic document was defeated. Moreover, the president of the republic has to be a Moslem. Thus in March, 1956, Pakistan was declared to be an Islamic Republic, and Iskander Mirza was chosen as its first president by the Moslem League—United Front Coalition. The consitution directs the state to discourage all forms of discrimination and to protect all minority groups. Both the president and the prime minister have averred that they will work earnestly toward these objectives.

The question of central vs. provincial power was decided in favor of the provinces. East Pakistan consistently advocated provincial autonomy, and, after its influence at the center rose in 1955, West Pakistan also adopted this view in order to avoid dominance from the east. The central government has therefore been given control over defense and all measures connected with its foreign affairs, currency, and communications. All powers not reserved to the center are vested in the provinces. The law creating the unit of West Pakistan had carefully balanced allocations of power in order to allay fears in Sind and the frontier region concerning Punjabi domination.

The central government consists of a single-house National Assembly and a president and vice-president, elected jointly by the members of the central and provincial legislatures. This federal legislature is to have 300 members, half from each wing, elected by adult suffrage. For ten years there are to be ten additional seats for women. The form of government is a parliamentary democracy with the president selecting a prime minister who has the confidence of the legislature. The rest of the cabinet is chosen in accordance with the prime minister's recommendations. The cabinet is to be collectively responsible to the National Assembly. Parliament is to meet for two sessions each year, one of them to be held in Dacca. The Assembly can amend the constitution by a two-thirds majority of those present and voting, provided that this is also a simple majority of all members of the legislature. In this way it is hoped that the balance between East and West Pakistan will be maintained. The opposition was critical of the wide powers that could be inferred in the constitution for both the president and the provincial governors. Mindful of this and of the governor-general's act of dissolution in 1954, the Constituent Assembly cancelled a provision allowing the president to dismiss the legislature arbitrarily. National elections under this new system were expected early in 1957.

The National Assembly continued as a provisional legislature but changes in the party pattern continued unabated. A new Republican party replaced the Moslem League as the dominant party of West Pakistan. Led by Dr. Khan Sahib and supported by President Mirza and the influential governor of West Pakistan, Mushtaq Ahmed Gurmani, it won the following of most Moslem League leaders. In September, 1956, the League, now holding only ten seats in the central legislature, split with Prime Minister Chaudhri Mohammed Ali and sought to censure him. The latter promptly resigned and was succeeded by H. S. Suhrawardy, who headed a Republican-Awami cabinet. This two-party coalition reflected current national sentiment since it contained the dominant element in each half of the country. Prime Minister Suhrawardy and President Mirza set aside their long-standing antagonism and agreed to work together to attain that elusive objective, a stable central government.

In the light of Pakistan's stormy political history, the relationship among president, cabinet, and National Assembly remains to be worked out. The ability of the state to operate with a weak center also remains to be proved, for it is a radical experiment in modern federalism. It is interesting to note that such a structure was recommended in the Lahore resolution of 1940, which originally demanded a Moslem state. Nevertheless, as an underdeveloped country, Pakistan needs a central authority that can plan and perhaps direct the country's economic growth.

The Economic Situation

Chaudhri Mohammed Ali did much to bring the economic situation under control while he was finance minister. The country now enjoys a grain surplus and is no longer haunted by the threat of famine. Its development projects are more realistic and methodical and can make use of the natural gas discovered at Sui, Baluchistan. These projects can revitalize West Pakistan's economy by reducing its dependence on costly foreign sources of power.

The country also seeks to attain self-sufficiency in textiles and will no longer gamble its economic security on cash-crop exports. In August, 1955, the Pakistani rupee was realistically devalued to India's level; this act ended an overvaluation that had hurt exports and reduced revenue. It may also ease trade relations with India, especially with regard to East Pakistan's jute. Meanwhile, if India and Pakistan adhere to their agreement on water supply from the Indus River system, a major cause of insecurity can be eliminated.

As in the political field, India was quicker and more systematic in its economic planning, though Pakistan formulated several early projects that were coordinated under the Commonwealth Colombo Plan. Under its six-year program, Pakistan was to spend about $700 million, of which more than half was to come from abroad. The government soon expressed disappointment at the limited scope of this plan. Power development had, in fact, absorbed a great share of the money. However, when the years of prosperity suddenly ended, the Karachi government had to delay the fulfillment of even these modest plans.

Two major power projects are in the North West Frontier Province, where the Kabul River enters the Peshawar plain, and on the Indus River. These will enable the rich coal-starved Punjab area to draw benefits from the northwest mountain regions that until now have been an economic burden. There are at least three additional power stations being developed in West Pakistan. The most important agricultural extension projects are the Lower Sind Barrage scheme to open 1,600,000 acres of land for cultivation, and the spectacular Thal project, where the Jinnah Barrage is to use Indus River waters to feed canals in the Thal desert of northwest Punjab. About 1,500,000 acres of this 4-million-acre desert are being reclaimed and used to settle refugees from India.

In East Pakistan, most problems revolve around jute. Ports for export and mills for processing were prime requirements. Chakra harbor was improved and facilities at Chittagong were expanded fivefold so that it could handle 2,500,000 tons of cargo annually. East Bengal has 2,000 miles of water channels, the chief means of transportation; this is to be doubled and new types of river craft are being developed. There are about a million small jute cultivators and a small number of mill owners. The government is hurriedly constructing four new processing mills, but fear of nationalization and memories of costly crop surpluses at the end of the Korean War have unsettled the industry. The Dacca government defends its plan to nationalize the jute industry by arguing that profits are going to speculators and non-Bengali traders.

East Bengal is also interested in re-establishing its traditional trade relations with India and is quick to blame Karachi for failing to resolve differences with India. A new trade agreement in 1953 did provide for the export of 1,800,000 bales a year to India for a three-year period, but even this amount was below the 2,500,000 that Pakistan can export.

Improvements can have their full impact only if agrarian reforms are diligently pursued. Land-tenure conditions in the Punjab were satisfactory in comparison with the zamindari system of Bengal or absentee ownership in Sind. Even so, further reforms were needed to give the tenant security and even ownership. A Punjab Moslem League manifesto in 1950 called for a ceiling of 100 acres on land ownership and a rent ceiling at 40 per cent of the crop. A bill was passed abolishing the *jagir* (land gift) system, under which beneficiaries exercised landlord rights. Critics observed that laws were delayed, giving landlords a chance to take evasive action. More significant were the difficulties encountered in Sind and Bengal, where the need for reform was much greater. Moslem League officials and provincial legislators were often landowners who sought to block reforms. Since 1955 the new administration in East Pakistan has made some progress. In land reform it has abolished the zamindari system and has been distributing land in accordance with the principle of leveling economic conditions. In the field of education, Bengal has made important advances in primary school training; in fact, it is ahead of West Pakistan in this respect. However, at the university level, its two institutions are of a lower caliber and it therefore lacks the professional and technical administrators found in West Pakistan.

The Five-Year Plan of 1956

The country's first comprehensive development plan was presented to the legislature by the Planning Commission in May, 1956. It reduced the emphasis on industrialization found in earlier programs, and recognized that a shortage of skilled personnel would restrict the plan's scope. Nevertheless, the Commission aimed at a 20 per cent rise in the national income, or a 12 per cent increase in per capita income despite an expected population growth of 7.5 per cent. Public spending on development was set at 8,000 million rupees ($1.5 billion), as against 3,600 million ($700 million) from private sources.

Main emphasis is placed on agriculture, which receives one third of the public funds. Much of this money is to go into village-aid programs. These are to reach one quarter of Pakistan's villages by 1960 and all of them by 1965. Three million acres of new land are to be cultivated as part of the over-all effort to expand production of rice by 11 per cent, wheat 17 per cent, jute 15 per cent, and cotton 38 per cent. Power and transport facilities are each allotted about 20 per cent of public spending, since they are essential to agriculture and lay the groundwork for industrialization.

Power output is to be tripled, but there is still a great shortage for the purpose of industrial development. Public funds for manufacturing are restricted to about 10 per cent of the total outlay, though this sector is expected to gain a larger share of private capital investment. The planners anticipate a 75 per cent rise in industrial output, for Pakistan has made good progress since 1952, when it had practically no manufacturing facilities. Fertilizers and sugar, two costly imports, are to be produced domestically, and jute processing is to be expanded. In addition, efforts will be concentrated on such basic commodities as cement, steel, caustic soda, and sulphuric acid.

The rest of the public development funds are devoted to health and other social services. The commission has planned for 250,000 houses, 40 per cent of which are for refugees. The government is to prepare building sites but encourage individual owners to build their own homes. Education, especially at the secondary level, and the training of technicians and teachers form an integral part of the program, as the chief means of overcoming the bottleneck in skilled personnel.

Since the country is endowed by nature with adequate food and cloth, it can attain self-sufficiency under competent management. However, the road to industrialization is a long one for a land with practically no industrial base and meager power resources. Progress can be made eventually only if the political situation allows for consistent long-range planning.

Bibliography

INDIA AND PAKISTAN

General

SMITH, V. A., *The Oxford History of India.* Oxford: Clarendon Press, 1920.

DODWELL, H. H. (ed.), *The Cambridge History of India.* New York: Macmillan, 1934.

The Cambridge History of India. 5 vols.; London: Cambridge Univ. Press, 1922-1937.

MORELAND, W. H., and A. C. CHATTERJEE, *A Shorter History of India.* 2d ed.; New York: Longmans, Green, 1945.

SPEAR, P., *India, Pakistan and the West.* New York: Oxford, 1949.

RAWLINSON, H. A., *India: A Short Cultural History.* New York: Appleton-Century-Crofts, 1938.

SPATE, O. K., *India and Pakistan.* New York: Dutton, 1954.

MORRISON, C., *A New Geography of the Indian Empire and Ceylon.* London: Nelson, 1926.

BROWN, W. N., *The United States and India and Pakistan.* Cambridge: Harvard Univ. Press, 1953.

Indian Civilization

MAJUMDAR, R. C., and A. D. PUSALKER (eds.), *The Vedic Age.* London: Allen & Unwin, 1951.

MACDONELL, A. A., *India's Past.* New York: Oxford, 1927.

GARRATT, G. T. (ed.), *The Legacy of India.* New York: Oxford, 1937.

MOOKERJI, R. K., *Hindu Civilization.* London: Probsthain, 1951.

BLOOMFIELD, M., *The Religion of the Veda.* New York: Putnam's, 1908.

KEITH, A. B., *The Religion and Philosophy of the Veda and Upanishads.* 2 vols.; Cambridge: Harvard Univ. Press, 1925.

EDGERTON, F., *The Bhagavad-Gita.* 2 vols.; Cambridge: Harvard Univ. Press, 1944.

BOUQUET, A. C., *Hinduism*. New York: Longmans, Green, 1950.

BARNETT, L. D., *Hinduism*. London: Constable, 1913.

RHYS DAVIDS, T. W., *Buddhism: Its History and Literature*. New York: Putnam's, 1918.

ZIMMER, H. (ed. by J. Campbell), *Philosophies of India*. New York: Pantheon, 1951.

MORGAN, K. W. (ed.), *The Religion of the Hindus*. New York: Ronald, 1953.

RADHAKRISHNAN, S., *The Hindu View of Life*. New York: Macmillan, 1927.

STEVENSON, M. S., *The Heart of Jainism*. London: Milford, 1915.

BARTH, A., *The Religions of India*. London: Truebner's, 1881.

FARQUHAR, J. N., *A Primer of Hinduism*. 2d ed.; New York: Oxford, 1912.

O'MALLEY, L. S. S., *Popular Hinduism*. New York: Macmillan, 1935.

WHITEHEAD, H., *The Village Gods of South India*. 2 vols.; New York: Oxford, 1924.

ARCHER, J. C., *The Sikhs*. Princeton: Princeton Univ. Press, 1946.

SINGH, K., *The Sikhs*. London: Allen & Unwin. 1953.

Early History

PIGGOTT, S., *Prehistoric India to 1000 B.C.* London: Penguin, 1950.

MACKAY, E. J. H., *Early Indus Civilizations*. London: Luzac, 1948.

WHEELER, R. E. M., *5000 Years of Pakistan*. London: Royal India and Pakistan Society, 1950.

MOOKERJI, R., *Asoka*. London: Macmillan, 1928.

SMITH, V. A., *Asoka: The Buddhist Emperor of India*. Oxford: Clarendon Press, 1909.

TARN, W. W., *The Greeks in Bactria and India*. London: Cambridge Univ. Press, 1938.

LANE-POOLE, S., *Medieval India*. London: Allen & Unwin, 1903.

ELPHINSTONE, M., *History of India*. 9th ed.; London: Murray, 1905.

LANE-POOLE, S., *Babar*. Oxford: Clarendon Press, 1909.

MALLESON, G. B., *Akbar and the Rise of the Mughal Empire*. Oxford: Clarendon Press, 1908.

SMITH, V. A., *Akbar: The Great Mogul Emperor*. Oxford: Clarendon Press, 1917.

MORELAND, W. H., *India at the Death of Akbar*. London: Macmillan, 1920.

MORELAND, W. H., *From Akbar to Aurangzeb*. London: Macmillan, 1923.

IRVINE, W., *The Later Mughals*. 2 vols.; London: Luzac, 1921–1922.

British Rule in India

WILBUR, M. C., *The East India Company*. New York: Smith, 1945.

FURBER, H., *John Company at Work*. Cambridge: Harvard Univ. Press, 1950.

GRIFFITHS, P., *The British Impact on India*. New York: Macmillan, 1952.

THOMPSON, E., and G. T. GARRATT, *Rise and Fulfillment of British Rule in India*. New York: Macmillan, 1934.

WINT, G., *The British in India*. London: Faber & Faber, 1954.

WOODRUFF, P., *The Men Who Ruled India: The Founders*. New York: St. Martin's Press, 1953.

WOODRUFF, P., *The Men Who Ruled India: The Guardians*. New York: St. Martin's Press, 1954.

O'MALLEY, L. S. S. (ed.), *Modern India and the West*. 5th ed.; London: Oxford, 1941.

LYALL, A., *The Rise and Expansion of the British Dominion in India*. 5th ed.; London: Murray, 1910.

CUMMINGS, J., *Political India: 1832–1932*. London: Oxford Univ. Press, 1932.

KEITH, A. B., *Constitutional History of India*. London: Methuen, 1936.

MATTHAI, J., *Village Government in India*. London: Allen & Unwin, 1915.

DUNBAR, G., *India and the Passing of Empire*. New York: Philosophical Lib., 1952.

KNIGHT, H., *Food Administration in India: 1939–1947*. Stanford: Stanford Univ. Press, 1954.

India and Pakistan after Independence

Nationalism and Partition

PARKIN, R., *India Today: An Introduction to Indian Politics.* New York: John Day, 1946.

DESAI, A. R., *Social Background of Indian Nationalism.* Bombay: Oxford Univ. Press, 1948.

SMITH, W. R., *Nationalism and Reform in India.* New Haven: Yale Univ. Press, 1938.

COUPLAND, R., *The Indian Problem.* New York: Oxford, 1944.

COUPLAND, R., *India: A Restatement.* New York: Oxford, 1945.

SITARAMAYYA, B. PATTABHI (ed.), *History of the Indian National Congress.* 2 vols.; Madras: Law Printing House, 1935, 1947.

SMITH, W. C., *Modern Islam in India.* 3rd ed.; London: Gollancz, 1946.

BIRDWOOD, C. A., *A Continent Decides.* New York: Praeger, 1954.

LUMBY, E. W. R., *The Transfer of Power in India.* New York: Praeger, 1954.

TUKER, F., *While Memory Serves.* London: Cassell, 1950.

PRASAD, R., *India Divided.* 3rd ed.; Bombay: Hind Kitabs, 1947.

CAMPBELL-JOHNSON, A., *Mission with Mountbatten.* London: Hale, 1951.

ANDREWS, C. R. (ed.), *Mahatma Gandhi: His Own Story.* New York: Macmillan, 1930.

ANDREWS, C. R. (ed.), *Mahatma Gandhi: His Own Story Continued.* New York: Macmillan, 1931.

ANDREWS, C. R., *Mahatma Gandhi's India.* New York: Macmillan, 1930.

GANDHI, M. K., *Gandhi's Autobiography.* Washington: Public Affairs Press, 1948.

FISHER, L., *The Life of Mahatma Gandhi.* New York: Harper, 1950.

SHEEAN, V., *Mahatma Gandhi.* New York: Knopf, 1955.

BIRLA, G. D., *In the Shadow of the Mahatma.* Calcutta: Orient Longmans, 1953.

NEHRU, J., *Toward Freedom.* New York: John Day, 1941.

NEHRU, J., *The Discovery of India.* New York: John Day, 1946.

BOLITHO, H., *Jinnah: Creator of Pakistan.* New York: Macmillan, 1954.

JINNAH, M., *Some Recent Speeches and Writings.* 2 vols.; Lahore: Ashraf, 1947.

TAGORE, R., *Reminiscences.* London: Macmillan, 1940.

CHANDHURI, N. C., *An Unknown Indian.* New York: Macmillan, 1951.

AMBEDKAR, B. R., *Pakistan, or The Partition of India.* 3rd ed.; Bombay: Thacker, 1946.

Politics since Freedom

ALL-INDIA CONGRESS COMMITTEE, *1st Year of Freedom.* New Delhi: 1947, and annually thereafter.

WALLBANK, T. W., *India in the New Era.* Chicago: Scott, Foresman, 1951.

BOWLES, C., *Ambassador's Report.* New York: Harper, 1953.

MELLOR, A., *India since Partition.* New York: Praeger, 1951.

WOFFORD, C., and H. WOFFORD, JR., *India Afire.* New York: John Day, 1951.

KARAKA, D., *Betrayal in India.* London: Gollancz, 1950.

NEHRU, J., *Independence and After.* Cambridge: Harvard Univ. Press, 1951.

GLEDHILL, A., *Fundamental Rights in India.* London: Stevens, 1956.

SYMONDS, R., *The Making of Pakistan.* London: Faber & Faber, 1950.

KHAN, LIAQUAT ALI, *Pakistan: The Heart of Asia.* Cambridge: Harvard Univ. Press, 1950.

FELDMAN, H., *A Constitution for Pakistan.* London: Oxford, 1956.

JENNINGS, I., *The Commonwealth in Asia.* New York: Oxford, 1951.

MASANI, M. R., *The Communist Party of India.* New York: Macmillan, 1954.

KAUTSKY, J. H., *Moscow and the Communist Party of India.* New York: Wiley, 1956.

RAMA RAU, S., *This Is India.* New York: Harper, 1954.

LADY HARTOG, *India: New Pattern.* London: Allen & Unwin, 1955.

TRUMBULL, R., *As I See India.* New York: Sloan, 1956.

MUEHL, J. F., *Interview with India.* New York: John Day, 1950.

KORBEL, J., *Danger in Kashmir.* Princeton: Princeton Univ. Press, 1954.

BRECHER, M., *The Struggle for Kashmir.* Toronto: Ryerson, 1953.

MURPHY, G., *In the Minds of Men.* New York: Basic Books, 1953.

TINKER, H., *The Foundations of Local Self-Government in India, Pakistan and Burma.* New York: De Graff, 1954.

KARUNAKARANAN, K. P., *India in World Affairs: 1947–1950.* New York: Oxford, 1953 and annually thereafter.

ALEXANDROWICZ, C. H. (ed.), *Indian Yearbook of International Affairs.* Madras: Univ. of Madras, 1952 and annually thereafter.

KOTHARI, S., *India's Emerging Foreign Policy.* Bombay: Vora, 1951.

MERTI, B., *Nehru's Foreign Policy.* New Delhi: Beacon, 1953.

COUSINS, N., *Talks with Nehru.* New York: John Day, 1951.

REDDING, S., *An American in India.* Indianapolis: Bobbs-Merrill, 1954.

SELIGMAN, E., *What the United States Can Do about India.* New York: New York Univ. Press, 1956.

LEVI, W., *Free India in Asia.* Minneapolis: Univ. of Minnesota Press, 1952.

Social and Economic Conditions

HUTTON, J. H., *Caste in India.* New York: Macmillan, 1946.

FUCHS, S., *The Children of Hari.* New York: Praeger, 1951.

SINGH, M., *The Depressed Classes.* Bombay: Hind Kitabs, 1947.

EMERSON, G., *Voiceless India.* 2d ed; New York: John Day, 1930.

FARQUHAR, J. N., *Modern Religious Movements in India.* 2d ed.; New York: Macmillan, 1931.

ROLLAND, R., *Prophets of the New India.* New York: Liveright, 1930.

ZELLNER, A. A., *Education in India.* New York: Bookman Associates, 1951.

INDIAN MINISTRY OF EDUCATION, *Gandhian Outlook and Techniques.* New Delhi: 1953.

KONDAPI, C., *Indians Overseas: 1838–1949.* New York: Oxford, 1951.

DAVIS, K., *The Population of India and Pakistan.* Princeton: Princeton Univ. Press, 1951.

PATWARDHAN, V. N., *Nutrition in India.* New York: Heinman, 1952.

REED, M., *The Indian Peasant Uprooted.* New York: Longmans, Green, 1931.

DARLING, M., *The Punjab Peasantry in Prosperity and Debt.* 4th ed.; London: Oxford Univ. Press, 1947.

MAYER, A. C., *Land and Society in Malabar.* London: Oxford Univ. Press, 1952.

PATEL, G. D., *Agrarian Reform in Bombay.* Bombay: The Author, 1950.

PATEL, G. D., *The Indian Land Problem and Legislation.* London: Sweet, 1954.

THIRUMALI, S., *Postwar Agricultural Problems and Policies in India.* New York: Inst. of Pacific Relations, 1954.

SHARMA, T. R., *Location of Industries in India.* Rev. ed.; Bombay: Hind Kitabs, 1954.

THOMAS, P. J., *India's Basic Industries.* Calcutta: Orient Longmans, 1948.

VAKIL, C. N., *Economic Consequence of Divided India.* Bombay: Vora, 1950.

VAKIL, C. N., and P. R. BRAHMANANDA, *Planning for Shortage Economy.* Bombay: Vora, 1952.

GADGIL, D. R., *Economic Policy and Development.* Poona: Gokhale Inst. of Politics and Economies, 1955.

ANSTEY, V., *Economic Development of India.* 4th ed.; New York: Longmans, Green, 1952.

KELMAN, J. H., *Labour in India: A Study of the Conditions of Indian Woman under Modern Industry.* London: Allen & Unwin, 1923.

BUCHANAN, D. H., *The Development of Capitalistic Enterprise in India.* New York: Macmillan, 1934.

PLANNING COMMISSION, *The First Five Year Plan* and *The First Five Year Plan: A Summary.* New Delhi, 1952.

PLANNING COMMISSION, *Second Five Year Plan: A Draft Outline.* New Delhi, 1956.

Five Year Plan Progress Report for 1953–54.
New Delhi: Manager of Publications,
1954.

CEYLON

BAILEY, S. D., *Ceylon.* New York: Longmans, Green, 1952.
JENNINGS, W. L., and L. H. W. TAMBIA,
The Dominion of Ceylon. London: Stevens, 1952.

JENNINGS, W. I., *The Economy of Ceylon.*
2d. ed.; Madras: Oxford Univ. Press,
1951.
COLLINS, C., *Public Administration in
Ceylon.* New York: Royal Inst. of Int.
Affairs, 1951.
NAMASIVAYAM, S., *The Legislature of Cey-
lon: 1928–1948.* London: Faber & Faber,
1951.
RYAN, B., *Caste in Modern Ceylon.* New
Brunswick: Rutgers Univ. Press, 1953.

PART FIVE **Southeast Asia**

General Introduction

to Part Five,

Southeast Asia

The world of Southeast Asia is bounded by China and Japan to the north, India and Pakistan to the west, the island continent of Australia to the south, and the waters of the Pacific, now dominated by the United States, to the east. But, despite its proximity to the great Asian states, in recent centuries this area was dominated by the great Western maritime powers. Spain and then the United States ruled the Philippines, Britain held Burma and Malaya, Holland controlled Indonesia, and France conquered the states of Indochina. Only Siam, located as a buffer between Burma and Indochina, remained free from colonial rule. A related factor was the high degree of security enjoyed by Southeast Asia in international affairs until the late 1930's. Its existence was placid enough to earn a description as a "quiet corner" of the world. Yet within a brief span of fifteen years, beginning in 1940, this entire order was shattered. The Western overlords, fighting a bitter war against Germany, could not resist Japanese aggression or stem the tide of nationalism that came in its wake.

The nationalist movement had been gaining momentum since the turn of the century. Japan's victory over Russia in 1904–1905, the Chinese Revolution of 1911 and the principles of Sun Yet-sen, the stirrings of democracy and self-determination that were Allied rallying cries late in the First World War, and the rise of Gandhian nationalism in India all sparked nationalist sentiment in Southeast Asia. The Japanese conquests of 1941–1942 smashed the myth of the invulnerable West, reduced its prestige, and critically impaired its ability to re-establish the old order after 1945. The abrupt onset of the Cold War on the heels of the victory over the Axis also kept Western political and military power off balance. By 1955 all states except Malaya were free, and that land was soon to gain its independence. But the pace and direction of these vast changes proved impossible to control. After the Chinese Communist victory over the Nationalists, Southeast Asia became a center of attraction for nearly all the major powers. In short, the area came to feel the dual effects of nationalist and social revolutions, and so became a primary concern in the diplomacy of the great powers.

Political Divergences

A cursory examination of the political units in Southeast Asia leaves one with the feeling that they have little in common. A wide variety of languages exists, and, even before the advent of European rule, cultural divergences and political animosities were quite marked. Each imperial power established its own form of rule and legal code, adopted its own policy toward native customs, and followed its own bent on the question of independence. The Americans taught the Filipinos English, established American political institutions, and carried out a promised grant of freedom under relatively stable conditions. In Burma, Britain established its own legal system and let native forms of authority disintegrate; it had not progressed far in political reform when it precipitously gave in to Burma's demand for freedom. France brought to the component parts of Indochina—Tonkin, Annam, Cochinchina, Laos, and Cambodia—its Napoleonic Code, its culture, and a vague promise of equality within the French Union, but stubbornly refused to transfer any real power until a full-scale rebellion got under way. Confusion over the meaning of cultural assimilation and the meaning of the French Union, plus the attempt to maintain colonial rule, led to a Communist triumph in the northern part of Indochina. The Dutch tried to strike a balance between the Anglo-American and French approaches by combining respect for Indonesian customs with strict paternalistic rule; after 1945 Dutch promises of a future partnership were sharply rebuffed and a nationalist rebellion led to a clean break between the two lands.

Actually, the claim that each land represents a compact nation-state in the modern sense of the term may in itself be an overstatement. Burma's constitution officially recognizes that Burma is a union of different peoples, but it is still debatable whether even a loose federation will enable the dominant Burmese people to keep the allegiance of the other groups. Indochina has already been shattered into the large state of Vietnam (Tonkin, Annam, and Cochinchina) and two small kingdoms of Laos and Cambodia. Vietnam itself was partitioned between north and south as a consequence of a colonial war and the Cold War, and the two kingdoms are wedged between it and Thailand (Siam) to the west. The Thai people are fairly homogeneous, but even here the picture is clouded by the presence of an unassimilable minority of 3 million Chinese. A further complication is that eastern Burma, Laos, and Cambodia, as well as the nearby border regions of China, are all peopled by Thais. Thailand made territorial claims against its small neighbors after 1940, but had to disgorge them in 1945; today, a similar device may be used by its powerful northern neighbor to further Chinese expansion. Malaya presents a different problem. The peninsula is organized into a federation of sultanates and is dominated by Malays.

There are, however, almost as many Chinese as Malays, as well as a considerable number of Indians, so that the original inhabitants now form less than half the population. The great island port of Singapore is overwhelmingly Chinese in population. The Philippine Islands have enjoyed a strong sense of historic unity and separate indentity. However, the Indonesian archipelago has experienced considerable difficulty in forging a cohesive state. This nation extends over 3,000 miles and is peopled by divergent ethnic and linguistic groups that have enjoyed separatist traditions. The creation of a unitary state instead of a federal structure was one consequence of the struggle for independence against Holland, but how well it will operate in this context remains to be seen.

Considerations of Security and Strategy

Despite these significant divergences, there are features common to the region as a whole. The sudden turn of events since 1940 revealed how vulnerable the area is to foreign pressure. The Japanese invasion and the Cold War have demonstrated that the 160-odd million people of Southeast Asia (approximately half living in Indonesia) cannot at their present state of organization and development protect themselves against a strong neighbor or even a distant determined power. The area can survive politically only as a buffer zone that depends on a continued balance of power among larger Asian states and the major participants in the Cold War. Prior to 1940, the region's security rested on a series of fortunate accidents. The Western imperial powers, with sufficient strength to police the area, worked in relative harmony with one another. Modest military commitments were enough, since there was no great threat from Asia itself. The major colonial powers—Britain, France, and Holland—enjoyed friendly relations and operated as informal allies. The region's security was based on British naval strength and the great colony of India, the essential military underpinning of British interests in Asia. The rise of Japan, two major wars, the surge of nationalism, and the emergence of a powerful Communist China swept away this protective apparatus. Today the security of Southeast Asia is one of the most sensitive problems of Eastern Asia and world politics as a whole.

To the West, Southeast Asia is more than an important territory to be held against communist pressures. The Malay Peninsula and the Republic of Indonesia have great strategic importance, for they lie athwart the sea routes linking India to Australia and the western Pacific. Loss of the Straits of Malacca off Singapore and the Strait of Sundra through Indonesia during the Second World War created great difficulty for the (British) Commonwealth and American forces. In terms of continental strategy, Burma, Thailand, and Indochina form a buffer area as well as line of convergence for India and China. The Japanese invasion of 1942 came eastward across these lands and petered out at the Indian frontier; this route might be more successfully utilized by a more powerful aggressor who enjoys a shorter line of communication. Southeast Asia is thus a strategically vital area in the defense of both Australia and India, two major bastions of the free world.

A related consideration is the strategic value of many products grown in the region, though this potential is reduced by the substitutes and synthetics developed in industrialized states. These products remain, however, invaluable military resources. Tin, rubber, and oil were important inducements in Japan's decision to launch a war of conquest, as part of a larger scheme to form an economically well-knit Greater East Asia Co-Prosperity Sphere.

Economic Considerations

The economic importance of Southeast Asia was built on its cash crops and mineral resources—rubber, tin, oil, copra, hemp, teak, tea, quinine, and rice. Before 1940 the region played a vital role in the pattern of international trade. A far larger share of its income was involved in foreign trade than was the case in the larger continental states. It formed a vital corner of the triangular trade pattern, in which a favorable American balance of trade with Europe was evened out through a favorable European balance with Southeast Asia, and a similar advantage on the part of Southeast Asia with regard to the United States. Much of Europe's famous "dollar gap" after 1945 can be traced to the disruption of this sequence. The recovery of Southeast Asia's economy from the dislocations of war and revolution, and its resumption of its role in world trade are matters of global importance.

Some of the states of Southeast Asia—Burma, Thailand, and southern Indochina—also produced rice for export to neighboring states. Political strife before and after 1945 played havoc with this production, an inflationary spiral set in, and the governments of Burma and Thailand took over control of rice exports. The price of rice jumped temporarily, and this commodity was brought directly into the field of politics. Since rice is the basis of Southeast Asia's economy, its higher value caused a general rise in prices, particularly in the restive urban areas. The peasantry still lives on a subsistence economy, operating small plots, consuming the rice it needs, and selling only the surplus. Thus the old economic structure has been only slightly modified and over-all modernization is impeded. Still, it is worth noting that the areas responsible for these rice surpluses were settled and cultivated late in the nineteenth century. This achievement in the great delta regions of lower Burma, southern Siam, and Cochinchina indicates what can be done with modern methods in other unsettled river and flat coastal lands of Southeast Asia.

The economic relations between the new states and their former rulers remain close, partly because of the trade patterns noted above but also because these countries require foreign aid. A further complication stems from the considerable amount of money invested by Western nationals during the period of colonial rule; a large part of it was retained by these investors, despite the transfers of power, usually as part of the political settlement. Thus the Dutch suffered a diplomatic-political defeat in Indonesia during 1949–1950 but managed to protect their centuries-old economic interests. And the Americans insisted on equality with Filipinos in economic affairs before granting independence. This stipulation caused heated debates in Manila and required an amendment to the Philippine constitution.

"Plural Societies"

Another striking feature of Southeast Asia's economy was the rise of a "plural society." Each category of economic activity is fairly closely identified with a single ethnic group, so that cultural and racial differences within a country become further intensified, as lines of economic cleavage. When Southeast Asia became a land of opportunity during the nineteenth century, many Chinese and some Indians migrated there. The Chinese proved hard-working, thrifty and far more competent to deal with a money economy than were the natives. They quickly dominated middle-class operations as businessmen, traders, retail store owners, and moneylenders—and kept the less sophisticated native communities in perpetual debt. A major variation on this theme occurred in Burma, where the *chettyar* subcaste of moneylenders arrived from India to assume this function. Agricultural workers also went from India to Burma, where they would work for low wages, earn their money, and return home with enough funds to support their families. The Burmese were at a disadvantage in competing with such frugal immigrants.

Throughout Southeast Asia, natives, Chinese, and Indians would engage in their own fields of specialization. In Malaya, for example, Chinese worked the tin mines, whereas Malays raised rubber. In general, a stratified class pattern developed, with the Western community holding the top governing and business positions, the Chinese predominating in the middle-class group, and the natives almost exclusively in the field of agriculture. The new urban laboring force usually included native and foreign Asian elements with little mixing in any one field of occupation.

It is difficult to assess the effects of this development. The Chinese contributed useful skills and hard work to the region's economic development, but they were also accused of taking unfair advantage of the native community. Racial prejudice and bitter antagonism developed among the Asians. When the war ended in 1945, Indonesians and Malays celebrated by assaulting and killing Chinese before law and order were restored. Also, Burma, after becoming independent in 1948, was quick to put pressure on the Indians to leave. An aggravating factor was the unassimilable nature of the Chinese, who retained their old customs, family ties, and language in foreign lands. They established their own schools and sought to preserve their cherished traditions. Even their political allegiance was doubtful, for all Chinese governments insisted that the Overseas Chinese remain citizens of their homeland. With the rise of Chinese power, these settlers pose a security problem for Southeast Asian states. On the other hand, repressive action could bring reprisals from China, and the dispossession of this wealthy middle class would be a costly and dislocating activity. Yet the existence of "two Chinas"—one on the mainland and one on Formosa—can neutralize the loyalty of the Overseas Chinese and so may offer a basis for stability. However, statecraft of the highest order is required to resolve this dilemma. It exists most acutely in Malaya, but is also felt in Indonesia and in traditionally independent Thailand, where nationalism has assumed a strong anti-Chinese tone.

OVERSEAS CHINESE

	Chinese	Percentage of Total Population
Malaya & Singapore	3,000,000	50.8
British Borneo	220,000	25.0
Thailand	3,000,000	15.8
Indochina	1,000,000	3.7
Indonesia	2,000,000	2.6
Burma	300,000	1.7
Philippines	150,000	0.7
Total	9,670,000	5.7

SOURCE: W. H. Mallory, "Chinese Minorities in Southeast Asia," *Foreign Affairs,* XXXIV, No. 2 (January, 1956), 259.

The existence of these plural societies presents a serious problem for self-governing democracies. Racial antagonism and socio-economic fragmentation of society can strain even a mature political order, but when the middle class, because it is alien, is in conflict with the rest of the community, the difficulty is compounded. Only in the Philippines is the middle class firmly rooted in the native political order; here mestizo descendants of Spanish-native or Chinese-native intermarriages have taken part in commercial activities. Of the attempts elsewhere to integrate Chinese and Indians into the political community, the success of a Malay-Chinese-Indian political alliance in the 1955 Malayan election is the most hopeful sign.

Foreign Cultural and Ideological Influences

India, China, and the West have all had an impact on the region's culture. Chinese influence was greatest in Annam and Tonkin, whose inhabitants adopted Confucian beliefs and the Chinese moral ethic. However, these Indochinese retained a sense of separate identity and proved hostile toward their aggressive northern neighbor. India's influence is most marked by the spread of Buddhism, which is the religion of Ceylon, Burma, Thailand, Laos, and Cambodia. The Moslem religion also spread eastward from India to Malaya, Indonesia and the island of Mindanao in the southern Philippines. Although in the sixteenth century the Spaniards conquered and Christianized the Filipinos, this Moslem element, dubbed Moros, remained. These higher religions throughout Southeast Asia were imposed on a much simpler animism and belief in primitive spirits that still pervades the region. In general, the people of this region have displayed a high degree of tolerance toward new religions. The Islamic code in Indonesia, for example, is not adhered to as rigidly as in Southwest Asia; the earlier animistic customs as well as the Hindu and Buddhist traditions are still evident in the East Indies. The Annamese, an industrious people, could easily adapt themselves to Confucianism. Elsewhere Buddhism proved a suitable faith, in lands where life was relatively placid, conducted in harmony with nature, with little concern for material progress or change.

The advent of the West changed the region's economy by introducing material progress, cash crops, a monetary exchange, and large commercial entrepôts. Also, the Western philosophy of man as a being apart from nature, able to master his physical environment, implied a dichotomy and perhaps a conflict with one's surroundings. Western legal codes, the cycles of prosperity and depression, and the absence of political protection, save in Indonesia and Malaya, brought landlessness and debt to the peasant and further undermined the old order. Better food production, health facilities, and communications led to phenomenal population increases, especially in Java. In this revolutionary environment, communism, with its emphasis on class warfare, struggle, and material progress was no longer out of place. Yet, except for Indochina, the rapid disappearance of imperial rule kept it from riding to power as the champion of national self-determination. The struggle now is continued within these new and fairly weak states.

Nationalism and Regionalism

The spread of nationalism to Southeast Asia, with its political concomitant, the small nation-state, has been greeted with mixed feelings by sympathetic analysts. On the one hand, it has meant liberation and a chance for independent cultural development for many divergent ethnic groups. However, these new states are relatively small, insecure, and self-centered. Fiercely conscious of their new independence, the governments of Southeast Asia are determined to avoid any political combination that ties them too closely with India or China. Nor are they willing to submerge themselves in a regional federation, however loosely drawn. Opponents of such a move have argued that six weak states with identical needs and competing economies would derive little benefit from political union. The lack of administrative experience, the need for technical experts, the shortage of foreign capital, and their military vulnerability would indeed persist under any circumstances. Union might bring some cohesion, a greater sense of confidence, and a stronger belief in Southeast Asia's chance to survive among the world powers. However, the cold facts of modern politics reveal that there is little sentiment for federation and no prospect of its coming to pass in the near future.

Almost every state in the region is confronted with a problem of maintaining its own political cohesion in the face of challenges from minority ethnic groups, regional separatists, or communist rebels. Communism seeks to undermine the political stability of individual states and opposes constructive efforts toward regional cooperation under any auspices other than its own. In this struggle it faces opposition from noncommunist nationalists, the (British) Commonwealth, and American interests and policies in the region. Area-wide developments as well as external influences continue to play an important role in Southeast Asian politics, and will be reviewed later. These considerations must be kept in mind while we consider the political record of the individual states.

15 *Burma, Thailand,*

Indochina

Burma

Burma is an extreme example of a traditional order and culture disintegrating under the impact of Western domination. The British conquerors treated the country as a vast economic plant to be worked on efficiently and rationally under a laissez-faire doctrine. The dislocations that resulted were keenly felt by the Burmese, as most of the benefits accrued to British and Indian newcomers. This ill-will in turn bred a fierce antiforeign sentiment that became the central theme of Burma's nationalist movement.

The country is about the size of Texas and is strategically located on India's eastern frontier, though a dense jungle makes contact somewhat difficult. To the north lies China, to the east Laos and Thailand. Of Burma's 17 million inhabitants, 11 million are Burmese, located primarily in the rich river valleys in the center and south. Other native elements are culturally and politically behind the Burmese and occupy the 40 per cent of the land that is hilly and less fertile. Of these, the Shan, related to the Thai, total 1 million, as do the Kachins and Chins. The Karens, originally from the Karenni Hills, are slightly more numerous; they were freed from Burmese domination by the British, and a minority of this group became Christianized. Many settled in the plains and river areas among the Burmese but retained their own identity. They played an important role in the community as a source of military manpower. There was constant friction between Karens and Burmese. Karens were used to suppress a Burmese revolt in the nineteenth century, and the Burmese assaulted the Karens in 1942 on the heels of the Japanese invasion. Since independence, it has been very difficult to establish harmonious relations between the two peoples. Finally, there are over 1 million Indians—merchants, bankers, and workers—and about 200,000 Chinese.

The geographic division of the land into Upper and Lower Burma reflects these ethnic demarcations. Lower Burma consists of the delta regions of the Irrawaddy, Sittang, and Salween rivers, plus the coastal plains of Arakan to the west and Tenasserim to the east of this river complex. Here are grown the great rice crops that made Burma a leading exporter before 1940. But, aside from

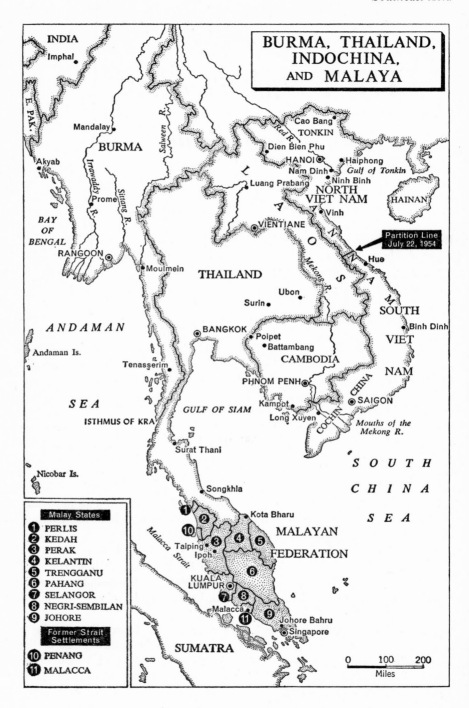

BURMA, THAILAND, INDOCHINA, AND MALAYA

INDIA

Imphal

E. PAK.

Mandalay

BURMA

Salween R.

Akyab

Irrawaddy R.

Prome

Sittang R.

BAY
OF
BENGAL

RANGOON

Moulmein

Cao Bang
TONKIN

Dien Bien Phu

Red R.

HANOI • Haiphong
Nam Dinh • *Gulf of Tonkin*
Ninh Binh

Luang Prabang

L A O S

NORTH
VIET NAM

Vinh

HAINAN

VIENTIANE

Mekong R.

Partition Line
July 22, 1954

Hue

THAILAND

Ubon

Surin

A N D A M A N

Andaman Is.

Tenasserim

S E A

GULF OF SIAM

ISTHMUS OF KRA

BANGKOK
Poipet
• Battambang

CAMBODIA

PHNOM PENH

Kampot

Long Xuyen

COCHIN CHINA

SOUTH

VIET

NAM

Binh Dinh

SAIGON

*Mouths of the
Mekong R.*

S O U T H

C H I N A

S E A

Surat Thani

Nicobar Is.

Songkhla

Kota Bharu

Malacca Strait

Malay States

① PERLIS
② KEDAH
③ PERAK
④ KELANTIN
⑤ TRENGGANU
⑥ PAHANG
⑦ SELANGOR
⑧ NEGRI-SEMBILAN
⑨ JOHORE

Former Strait Settlements

⑩ PENANG
⑪ MALACCA

① ② ⑩
Taiping ③ ④ ⑤
Ipoh

MALAYAN

FEDERATION

⑥

KUALA
LUMPUR ⑦ ⑧

Malacca ⑪ ⑨

Johore Bahru
Singapore

SUMATRA

0   100   200
Miles

tin and oil, most of the mineral wealth is located in the north—in the mountains and narrow upper reaches of the river valleys. Actually, the historical center of Burmese culture lies in the country's central rolling plains, about 300 to 400 miles inland up the rivers. Within this region there are no obstacles to the east-west communication lines bisecting the great rivers. With geographic barriers around this central pocket assuring them relative isolation, the Burmese were able to develop their own independent culture.

Historic Burma

The Burmese and other native groups actually originated in China but brought very little of this culture in their migrations. Their first and perhaps greatest Burmese dynasty, the Pagan (1044–1287), was destroyed in an invasion by the Mongol rulers of China. Later, when the Manchus sent brief expeditions to Burma in the seventeenth and the eighteenth centuries, a tenuous vassal relationship was established. But political relations remained strained and cultural contacts were sparse. By contrast, cultural ties with the racially unrelated Indians to the west proved more fruitful. Contact came primarily through Indian merchant colonies along the Burmese coast, at some distance from Burma's "heartland." The Burmese, Shan, and Mon peoples adopted Buddhism in the Hinayana, or "Lesser Vehicle," version as practiced in Ceylon. This taught that each person must work out his own salvation, in the Buddhist sense, and find enlightenment for himself. (By contrast, the Mahayana, or "Greater Vehicle," version of Buddhism, which went from India northward to China and Japan, stressed *bodhisattra*—the person who postpones his entrance into nirvana until all living beings are saved, partly through his efforts.) When Hinduism swept Buddhism out of India, it proved too particularist to gain a following in Burma. The Burmese continued to borrow heavily from India, as exemplified in their architectural form and the use of Pali (the sacred script of Buddhism). Yet there was no intermarriage with the caste-bound Hindus, though marriages with male Moslem Indians occurred later.

Burma's political history seemed to veer from virtual political chaos to strong expansionist dynasties. Under its three powerful dynasties, the country produced a vigorous military record.[1] The rise of British rule in India was paralleled, around 1750, by the reunification of Burma under its last great dynasty. It enjoyed military successes against Chinese invaders and in its own campaigns of conquest in Siam and Assam. These adventures brought Britain into contact with a Burma whose isolated rulers underestimated Western military strength. Frontier incidents touched off a series of Burmese wars (1824, 1852, and 1885) that ended in the British conquest and annexation of 1886.

The traditional Burmese political system that was overthrown included a socially static order and an unproductive economy. In theory, the center of

[1] Besides the Pagan, there was the Pegu period in the fourteenth and fifteenth centuries, and the final Konbaungset dynasty in the mid-eighteenth century.

authority was a despotic royalty, but the monarchs exercised real power only sporadically and were mercifully inefficient even on those occasions. Provincial rule was loosely administered, and government at the local level was based on near-feudal concepts. Military forces were raised by feudal levies of chieftains who retained control of their followers. Hereditary headmen carried on the functions of local government, each acting as a squire for a "circle," or group of fifteen to twenty villages. India's caste system was never adopted, and ordinary citizens worked the same fields as the headmen and feudal retainers. Women enjoyed a large measure of freedom, Buddhist educational facilities were widespread, and the country enjoyed some degree of literacy. The close harmony between church and state contributed to this development and was related to the vigorous growth of the Buddhist monastic system. Though too loosely organized to be a strong political force, monks were venerated and played an important role in Burma's culture. All males could rise in the social order through a religious career and all youths were expected to serve as monks for a brief period. In general, the sanctions of Buddhism operated as a disciplinary and cohesive force in society.

An elaborate central administration existed but did not come into direct contact with the people, as the state still depended on the hereditary local chiefs. The king, however, did exercise some authority over the hill people, who were gradually being absorbed into Burmese civilization. Thus the circle of villages, Buddhism, and the monarchy all had stabilizing influences, and society operated with a minimum of sanctions. In this context, custom backed by religious authority was a powerful social regulator. Civil and religious laws were not sharply differentiated, and settlements were reached primarily through arbitration. Disputants would reach an agreement with the help of a paid referee, with social pressure and even expulsion from the community as penalties for recalcitrance. In general, then, the social order was stable, but it depended on intangibles—political authority based on personal ties, and social obligations regulated by custom and religious sanctions.

British Rule

The annexation of 1886 touched off a rebellion that took several years to quell, following which British rule became security-oriented. The Burmese were disarmed, Indian troops were stationed in the country, and British and Indian administrators took over direction of public affairs, with Burmese restricted to subordinate posts. Under British rule of law, foreign peoples and investments poured into Burma. The country had become a vast economic plant whose operators had only the profit motive in common.

The settlement of Lower Burma led to the commercialized production of rice for overseas markets. This enterprise was manned by the Burmese themselves, who increased the area under cultivation by 150,000 acres each year until 1930. But fluctuations in world market conditions, unfamiliarity with Western law, and the superior business competence of the *chettyar* moneylenders led the peasants into debt and deprived them of control over the land. The *chettyars* saw in the ricelands an excellent opportunity for investment, and by 1930 they had £50 million tied up in Burma, a stake more valuable than all British invest‐ ments. Furthermore, timber, oil, and minerals also brought profit to the foreign‐ ers, and foreign labor was used in all nonagricultural activities except oil extraction. The economic picture was exceedingly frustrating to the Burmese. They hardly benefited from the high rate of dividends or the phenomenal rise in exports, which doubled between 1890 and 1914 and then rose by another 50 per cent in the 1920's.

The British also dismantled the traditional political order by abolishing the hereditary chieftainships and the historic circle of villages. The individual village became the basic administrative unit and its new chief official, the village headman, served as police officer, magistrate, and tax collector. He was respon‐ sible to the British district officer and not to his fellow townsmen. As the new centralized government became more remote from the people, the political order no longer served as a check on impersonal economic forces, and political leadership passed into extremist nationalist hands. Another factor contributing to the disintegration of the social fabric was the decline in the moral and edu‐ cational leadership of the monastic orders. Western education offered a good chance of advancement in the civil service, and Britain instituted lay schools because of popular demand. This well-intentioned educational system was capped by a national University of Rangoon in 1923. However, the Western and monastic systems remained separate, and it was inevitable that the old order should decline in prestige and use. Moreover, as the government did not give official support to the Buddhist orders, their discipline fell alarmingly. The revered yellow-robed monks became a disruptive force; monasteries served as centers of operation for lawless gangs, and banditry (dacoitry) became wide‐ spread. Militant nationalists also used the immunity of the yellow robe to cover their vigorous activities.

In this environment the drive for self-government added to the general chaos. British concessions never satisfied the nationalists but were sufficient to weaken the executive agencies. Economic depression, the beginnings of self-rule, and communal tension characterized the 1930's. The British government still con‐ ceived of its task as the maintenance of law and order, giving free play to social and economic forces. This attitude further embittered the Burmese, especially when no action was taken against mortgage foreclosures and continued Indian immigration. Such policies helped cause bitter anti-Indian race riots in 1930 and 1938.

Burmese Nationalism and British Reform

British political reform gave Burma more self-rule than any other South Asian colony except the Philippines. Yet Burma refused to stay in the Common‐ wealth after independence. The British political order enjoyed little prestige, and the liberal ethic proved an inadequate basis for social cohesion. Burma's modern nationalists soon discarded liberal economic theory and stressed the need for central control over economic affairs. They turned to socialism and to the totalitarian ideologies of the Axis and Communist powers. Any assistance, Japanese or Russian, was welcomed in the struggle to be rid of Britain, alien residents, and the colonial order.

Since Britain failed to transfer decisive executive power to the Burmese, its political concessions were poorly received. The Burmese constantly presented extreme demands and rejected anything short of home rule. Finally, when a major reform was instituted in 1937, it came in an atmosphere of intense suspicion and ill-will, and had little time to establish itself before the Japanese invasion of 1942. In general, Burma's constitutional development paralleled that of India, to which it was administratively attached until 1937. A small legislative council on which Burmese were represented was created in 1897. After the First World War a semidemocratic form of government was introduced, with about 17 per cent of the people gaining the right to vote. The Burmese were given control only of the "nation-building" ministries—agriculture, forestry, health, education, local government—which were responsible to a legislature. The British still administered defense, foreign affairs, justice, finance, and communications. This infuriated the Burmese in the legislature and they refused all ministerial posts; this dual system (dyarchy) survived only because the non-Burmese native elements were willing to participate.

The suspicious Burmese opposed separation from India after 1930 for fear that their political reform would be allowed to lag, and an Anti-Separation party won a smashing electoral victory in 1932. However, Burma received a new constitution of 1935, which granted near-autonomy, though the governor still retained the power to veto legislation, enforce vital regulations rejected by the legislature, and take charge in an emergency. There were also Excluded Areas—the Shan states, Karenni, and Chin lands—which remained under the governor's control. These regions were treated differently from the rest of Burma, retaining their own traditional system with only indirect control from above. The use of hill tribesmen in military police formations further intensified the sense of separateness among the peoples of Burma.

The Burmese participated in the 1937 elections and finally assumed control over the ministries. However, their performance was inadequate. Personal bickering and jockeying for position took precedence over the formation of party alignments with set policies. Administrative competence suffered in the early years of self-rule, which were marked by bribery and corruption. The political leaders during the years 1937–1941 were Ba Maw and his Sinyetha (Poor Man's) party and U Saw, who led the Myochit (Patriotic) party. Had the system functioned for a while, a more competent party might have evolved and proved the worth of constitutional channels. At the start, however, revolutionary fervor and instability remained the dominant features of Burmese politics. These considerations are illustrated by the history of the Thakins, a youthful group organized at Rangoon University in the late 1930's as the *Dobama*

Asiayone (We Burmans Association). Members addressed each other as Thakin, or Master, in mocking imitation of an earlier form for addressing the British rulers. They held Buddhism to be essential to Burmese culture but also accepted Western skills and education, thus pointing the way to an effective national regeneration. Unlike other groups in parliament, they won widespread popular support because of their intellectual competence, disinterested patriotism, and opposition to corruption. In 1941 thirty of their leaders fled Burma at Japan's invitation and received collaborationist training on Formosa. They returned with the invader in 1942 and some participated in the Ba Maw cabinet set up during the Japanese occupation.

The Effects of War and Liberation

The Burmese either welcomed and aided the Japanese forces or sat idly by during the conquest of 1942; only the hill people assisted the British. Japanese rule, as in other lands, served as a catalyst that sped the process of Burma's political maturation, yet exercised little influence of its own. Japan used anti-Western slogans and gave Burma the trappings of self-rule, but the word of Japanese "advisers" was law. Burmese labor was harshly exploited, and totalitarian rule angered a people accustomed to a more lenient British authority. The Burmese came to despise the fascism of Japan, and many who were first inclined to cooperate with the Japanese later supported the Allied cause. They worked with the Western armies when the tide of battle turned in 1943–1944 and organized guerilla formations that harassed the Japanese.

However, Japan had granted Burma independence under its own president in 1943. Burmese officials had not fled with the British but retained their posts and maintained law and order with Japanese help. The country gained a foreign ministry and an army manned by Burmese rather than hill people. Toward the end of the war, the government began to exercise the substance as well as the form of self-rule and was determined not to return to the old order. As the war had caused Indian economic overlords to evacuate, the Burmese could reassert their control over the land in defiance of their creditors. Many Communists had been jailed at the start of the war, though they urged resistance to Japan. As the country swung around to this view, the Communists' early stand and notable underground efforts earned them widespread prestige and considerable political-military influence by the end of the war. At that time they sought to capitalize on nationalist sentiment by adopting an extreme anti-British position.

The returning British administration added to its own difficulties by misreading popular sentiment. This government-in-exile returned from Simla, India, believing that the people were still unprepared for freedom, and sought to re-create the prewar system. It even expected Burmese cooperation because independence was promised in the future. The Burmese were angered to see old officials and their inexperienced subordinates take over posts that they themselves had administered under the Japanese. Britain's plans for economic rehabilitation were also suspected as part of a scheme to re-establish enterprises for foreign exploitation, although these efforts did have productive value. What could not be tolerated was the attempt to reinstate absentee landlords and moneylenders with their prewar legal claims and rights. The country was on the brink of rebellion, a mood encouraged by the fact that thousands of young men who served in the guerilla forces were not disarmed, disbanded, or given immediate employment. Instead, they continued in their habit of drift and violence, joined the Communists, or prepared to fight the British purely as nationalists.

The nationalist leader was the popular hero Aung San, a Thakin and wartime resistance leader. He headed the dominant Anti-Fascist People's Freedom League (AFPFL), which included the Socialists, Communists, and various nationalist groups. Other leading non-Communists besides Aung San were Thakin Mya, head of the peasant organization and leader of the Socialist party, and Thakin Nu, a contemplative Buddhist intellectual. In April, 1946, the non-Communist leaders of the AFPFL reached an agreement with the British Governor Rance to take positions in the executive council of the government. The Communists, excluded from high AFPFL offices, continued to agitate for a strike and were ejected from the league. Aung San now sought to prevent the disorders that his own threats and nationalist exhortations of the past two years had made possible. His extralegal Patriotic Volunteer Organization (PVO), composed of guerilla veterans, proved difficult to control. Revolutionary disorders swept the country and Communist agitation for freedom mounted. Aung San was obliged to seek a definitive settlement with Britain granting a complete break from the Commonwealth. In an agreement of January, 1947, Britain promised Burma its freedom within a year under a constitution of its own choice. Defense and financial matters still had to be arranged, but Aung San's prestige assured support for this settlement. His AFPFL won 190 of the 220 seats contested in the April, 1947, election of a constituent assembly.

Independence and Civil War

Aung San and his colleagues might have effected a peaceful transfer of power despite widespread anarchy, Communist intransigence, and the diffusion of military authority, but he, Thakin Mya, and five other cabinet members were assassinated by gunmen hired by U Saw, the prewar political leader. The prompt appointment by Governor Rance of Thakin Nu, vice-president of the AFPFL, to be premier prevented total chaos. With independence guaranteed and the country's leader dead, there was nothing to hold the nationalist forces together.

The Nu-Attlee Agreement of October, 1947, recognized the Republic of the Union of Burma as independent in January, 1948. It also precipitated the final break between the Communists and the government. In this settlement, Burma gained some financial concessions and, in return, recognized the validity of unexpired business contracts conferring rights on foreign citizens. Burma also acknowledged an obligation to pay compensation for contracts or property taken over by the government. There was, in addition, a three-year defense arrangement, including British training missions and permission for Britain to come to Burma's aid if needed. The Communists declared this independence to be a sham and laid plans for rebellion; when the government discovered this, it outlawed the party in March, 1948. This act touched off a civil war in which the Rangoon regime lacked sufficient power to crush the rebels. When a majority of the PVO defected to the Communists, the situation became grim.

The desertion of two battalions of Burmese troops left the government heavily dependent on its Karen contingents; the army's leader, in fact, was a Karen. However, a rebellion broke out among the Karenni, thereby removing another region from central authority and undermining the government's confidence in the army. In the years following 1948, the government held only Rangoon and its immediate vicinity, as the country was reduced to a condition of near-anarchy. The majority of the PVO, the Communists (themselves split into Red Flag and—the majority—Stalinist White Flag groups), the Karens, and an alarming number of bandits (dacoits) all defied central authority. The rebellious forces were at odds with one another and could not coordinate their activities effectively. Gradually the regime rebuilt its military strength, pushed the Communists into the hills, and gained control over most Karenni territory. These opponents still exist but do not now menace the government's existence. Order is not completely restored and dacoitry is prevalent, but the government is now in effective control of the country.

The New Political Order

The constitution of the new state was approved before Aung San's death in 1947. It established a federal union of Burma Proper with the Shan, Kachin, and Karenni states. These minority elements were given considerable autonomy in order to keep them from seeking Britain's protection. Karen leaders wanted full control over their own peoples, even those living among the Burmese; rejection of this claim had much to do with their resort to violence. Non-Burmese hold seventy-two of the 125 seats in the upper house, the Chamber of Nationalities. The premier and cabinet are responsible to a Chamber of Deputies of 250 members, elected from single-member districts. Legislation must pass both houses and, in case of differences, by a majority vote in which both houses sit together. There is also a president, elected for five years by both houses, and an independent judiciary to enforce the laws, interpret the constitution, and assure the protection guaranteed under a liberal bill of rights.

The government has gained considerable power since 1949. Then only 15 per cent of the land tax could be collected, and rice exports were the only reliable source of revenue. A Commonwealth loan for the rice crop of 1950 helped tide the government over its most difficult period. Elections were held in 1951, with the AFPFL coalition winning 220 of the 250 seats in the lower house. The strongest member in this dominant coalition group is the Socialist party, a forceful minority element in the cabinet. Its president is U Ba Swe and its secretary is U Kyaw Nyein, the minister of industries. As a party within a party it receives special treatment from Premier U (formerly Thakin) Nu, who is more assertive in controlling the rest of the cabinet. An All-Burman Peasants Organization under Thakin Tin, a Socialist, is an important semi-independent component of the AFPFL. It controls agricultural loans, influences the implementation of land reform, and has its own force of Peace Guerillas. Another is the Trade Union Congress, which was successfully purged of Communists without suffering disruption, although a rival Workers and Peasants party was formed. The Trade Union Congress is under U Ba Swe and has about 40,000 members. Communal organizations representing various minority elements complete the AFPFL coalition.

Despite a complex and inefficient national structure, and some popular discontent, the AFPFL continues to dominate Burma's politics. It won 33 of the 35 seats in the Rangoon elections of February, 1955, and captured 169 of the legislature's 250 seats in the national election of 1956. However, the opposition, National United Front, which had Communist support, showed surprising strength. Complaints arose that, with power, the AFPFL officials became arrogant and corrupt. They compared unfavorably with devoted underground Communists who attracted the idealistic students. Premier U Nu is still Burma's most popular political figure and a mainstay of the AFPFL. He is a socialist but not a formal member of that party; nor is he as doctrinaire as his colleagues who seek to end the mixed economy and introduce a pure Marxian socialist system.

Economic Conditions and Reforms

The effort to create a welfare state was complicated by the dual needs to repair war damages and evolve a modern economy. Considerable damage was caused by such defensive tactics as the destruction of rail lines by the retreating British in 1942. Land cultivation and extractive industries both suffered during the war, and over 2 million acres under rice reverted to semijungle. Burma has still not regained its old annual export levels of $3\frac{1}{2}$ million tons of rice, 250,000 tons of timber, 100,000 tons of minerals, and 250 million gallons of oil. Production in 1951–1952 reached only 70 per cent of the 1938–1939 level; wolfram mines in Karenni territory and tin mines in the Tenasserim region could not be worked. Large-scale projects suffered from political chaos, lack of skilled personnel, and a hostile attitude toward foreign capital. Socialist aspirations to nationalize all industries, expropriation of foreign firms, and a constitutional requirement that Burmans own 60 per cent of the stock in many extractive concerns frightened off foreign investors. Aid from the World Bank has been sought, but American assistance was angrily renounced for reasons of foreign policy in 1953. Help from the Commonwealth Colombo Plan is of some value but hardly enough. A reparations settlement with Japan for $200 million in capital goods and services, plus $50 million to be invested in joint enterprises, may be of great importance. Japan's contribution was expected to amount to one third or one quarter of Burma's public capital formation in 1955–1956.

Rice was the mainstay that kept the government afloat despite the ravages of war and rebellion. The government, which exercises a trade monopoly through the State Agricultural Marketing Board, took advantage of world demands to raise the price from £40 a ton in 1949 to £60 to £70 in 1953. The cultivator received only £22, the government taking the rest. When the world market broke in 1953, Burma was slow in lowering its price to about £45. It was left with considerable quantities of stored rice and faced the greater problem of finding markets for future crops. This is a most vital issue, since export profits were expected to finance the welfare program and industrial expansion.

The years before 1952 were devoted to planning, and the program was surveyed that year by an American group of experts. The costly construction phase was undertaken in 1952, but many schemes will be slow to yield productive results. Other programs, such as schools and hospitals, are social investments that cannot bring monetary returns. This program was optimistically described as one of self-help, called *pyidawtha* by the Burmese. Its objective was to build a sturdy nation in a socio-economic revolution carried out by Burmese methods. Certain early successes resulted from a village-township development scheme in which modest projects for road, bridge, school, and reservoir construction are subsidized by government allowances.

On the national level, the 1952 plan sought to double the national income of $700 million by 1959. Such a goal called for an investment of almost $1.5 billion over this period, or about $200 million a year. This sum was well above the pre-1940 annual rate of capital accumulation, which was about $60 million. All this was predicated on a rice-export price of £55 ($154) per ton. High priority was given to postal, telephone, and transport facilities, especially railways, whose mileage fell from 2,000 to 1,500 as a result of the war. Industry received only modest emphasis at first, though mining, hydroelectric machinery, and a few manufacturing plants were stressed. Burma hopes to double rice production and raise other crops to new levels by 1957, mainly by reclaiming old lands and by clearing an additional half-million acres. In the light of the unfavorable turn in foreign trade, the projects can be cut somewhat, especially where foreign currency is essential, but the government is committed to carry on the core of its program. Other objectives are the revival of traditional religious values and universal education, to further the cultural assimilation of the hill people. The monastic orders, Buddhist missionary work, and the study of scriptures were all given public support. On the land-tenure question, legislation in 1948 permitted the government to distribute large estates, on adequate compensation, among tenants and farm laborers. Some pilot projects were undertaken during the civil war; on the whole, this policy has allayed much of the peasantry's traditional suspicion of government.

433

Foreign-Policy Attitudes

In its foreign relations, Burma has followed a strong neutralist line, similar to that of India and Indonesia in the years after 1948. In its anti-Western xenophobic mood of 1947–1948, it even chose to leave the Commonwealth in order to enjoy complete independence. However, its policy is also rooted in a realistic fear of antagonizing its Chinese neighbor, which is considered an ever-present threat. In 1953 Burma rejected sorely needed American technical and economic assistance, in a gesture motivated by all these considerations. The immediate cause of this break was the pressure of Chinese Nationalist troops in the Shan state just below the Chinese border, where they had fled in 1949. Burma had recognized the Peking regime at the end of 1949 and later agreed to a border rectification demanded by China; it did not want foreign troops on its soil, especially if they gave Communist China a chance to intervene. After considerable negotiation, many Nationalists were flown to Formosa and others were routed in a battle by Burmese troops. The sudden temporary appearance of Chinese Communist forces inside Burma's northern frontier in 1956, as a result of a still unsettled boundary dispute, amply justified Rangoon's cautious attitude.

Burma's military agreement with Britain was allowed to lapse and a much looser arrangement has been made. The country remains devoted to democratic ideals and has been fighting communism at home vigorously, since it is the regime's mortal enemy. Yet it continues to have normal relations with Russia and China, and in its quest for rice markets may establish economic links with the Soviet bloc, if it cannot earn sufficient foreign currency in dealing with the West. What to do if foreign and internal communist thrusts become acute is a continuous problem for this vulnerable state. During 1955–1956, U Nu was reported to have been dismayed by the activities of foreign communist embassies in Rangoon and to have pronounced neutralism a failure. However, Burma will have no part in any alliance network, such as the Southeast Asian treaty system based on American support.

Thailand (Siam)

A History of Independence

The small kingdom of Siam, unlike its neighbors, remained independent throughout the period of Western imperialism. Symbolically, a treaty of commerce between the United States and Siam in 1833 was the first agreement of this type made by the Americans in the Far East. Diplomatic skill and good fortune enabled the Siamese to suffer no more than small border losses to their powerful French and British imperial neighbors. China, to the north, was generally too weak to be a menace, though, at the height of its power, the Manchu dynasty treated Siamese traders as the bearers of tribute. The British, in Malaya to the south and Burma to the west, were very sensitive to French threats at Siam from Indochina to the east. The kingdom served admirably as a buffer zone separating the two European powers and preserving a political balance.

Before the Europeans arrived in force, Siam had experienced turbulent relations with Burma and Cambodia. It suffered from their attacks late in the eighteenth century but gradually cleared out the invaders and, in the following century, gained control over Cambodia. When the French arrived to establish a protectorate over that principality, they were welcomed as a relief from Siamese domination. At the turn of this century, Siam was compelled to yield small border lands to the two French protectorates of Laos and Cambodia and to Malaya in the south. In return for these frontier concessions, Siam gained jurisdiction over French and British subjects residing on its soil. It enacted a modern legal code and after 1918 was able to end extraterritoriality, imposed in the previous century. Thus the foreign menace brushed lightly against Siam, which did not suffer unduly even after siding with Japan in 1941. As a result, the country has enjoyed a more placid history and now bears few of the ravages of war and civil strife. It has been relatively successful in preserving traditional institutions and maintaining a high level of social cohesion and stability.

Problems of Modernization

Despite this relative calm and prosperity, Siam encountered the same problems as its neighbors—nationality and nationalism, economic reform and welfare services, political democracy and adjustment to Western ideals. Of its 18 million inhabitants, one sixth are Chinese and 700,000 are Moslem Malays. Neither minority could be assimilated in terms of religion, language, or custom. Although the Malays are a lesser problem, they are located just above the Malayan border and their demands for autonomy arouse suspicions of separatism in the capital city of Bangkok.

The country is slightly smaller than Burma and has one big river—the Menam —within its border. The Mekong River, which plays an important role in the economy of Cochinchina, forms part of its eastern frontier. Bangkok lies in the southern delta and plains region, the most fertile area in Siam and the heart of its rice culture. It is here that the Chinese are concentrated, as tradesmen and merchants. Doubtful of their political loyalty, jealous of their economic power, and fearful of China itself, the Siamese embarked on a program of forceful assimilation and tried to halt further immigration. Independent Siam proved to be more narrowly nationalistic than any of its former colonial neighbors.

The country's economic resources are plentiful and there is no problem of overpopulation. A rice surplus is produced annually for export. However, there are technical problems of getting better crop yields and raising the nation's standard of living. The country lacks trained technical personnel, a competent modern bureaucracy, and adequate social services. Health facilities are inadequate and about 70 per cent of the people are illiterate. The desire to industrialize has also gained momentum, posing difficult questions of competence and efficient use of available skills and resources.

Political Reform

In the political sphere, the Siamese tried to fashion a modern nation-state and then a democratic constitutional order. This effort, inspired by Western ideals and pressures, has been going on for over a century, but progress has been limited and erratic. The Siamese developed a modern administrative system but are still some distance from truly representative government. In recent times, the political order resembled that of a Latin American oligarchy: Westernized military and civilian leaders vying for power, frequent palace coups, and an indifferent majority in the countryside untouched by these events. This experience once again demonstrates how sweeping is the change to a democratic order and how difficult it is to reorient a culture without external guidance or control.

The monarchy was the original source of the reform program. Two competent absolute monarchs of the Chakri dynasty, Mongkut (1851–1868) and his son Chulalongkorn (1868–1910) undertook a farsighted program of modernization. Their absolute power and control over administrative affairs ensured the acceptance of all changes without effective protest. They abolished slavery and the old feudal order, introduced a modern judicial system, and replaced the rudimentary method of farming taxes with a modern system of collection. They also organized a civil service along Western lines and introduced some basic functions of state administration, including railway and postal services.

These changes created a new class of civil administrators and military leaders who challenged the principles of monarchial rule. Some sought democratic reform, but all wanted a share of governing power commensurate with their official positions. In 1932 this Westernized group seized power through a bloodless coup that deprived the monarchy of real authority. It called itself the People's party though the masses were hardly involved in this action or in the struggles for power that continued within this ruling clique. The new masters of Siam did not tolerate an open competitive party system but sought to perpetuate their own power.

There were three main groups within the ruling oligarchy. These were the civilian liberals, led by a commoner, Pridi Banomyong; another civilian group close to the throne, which sought to revive the power of the monarchy; and the military leaders who executed the 1932 coup. Pibul Songgram rose to prominence in the military group by thwarting a royalist counterstroke in 1933. Until 1937 the new oligarchy operated in an uneasy balance between Pridi and Pibul under a nationally popular premier, Colonel Phya Bahol. In 1938 Pibul became prime minister, and military dominance was assured. However, even before he assumed power, the government refused to permit rival parties to form and cemented its power by arresting and even executing political opponents. In 1940 a bill was brought before the Assembly, created under the 1932 constitution, to permit political parties. However, the rise of Japan, which now dominated Indochina, created a situation unfavorable to democratic reforms. The dominance of the revolutionary group, permitted for one decade in the constitution, was now extended for ten more years.

The War Period and Intensive Nationalism

Pibul's first period of rule (1938–1944) was featured by an intensive outburst of nationalism and an alliance with Japan. Symbolically, the country's name was changed from Siam to Thailand; the government hoped to rule over all Thai-speaking peoples. For this purpose, an alliance with the Japanese enemy of the West was essential. Even in 1933, Siam had refrained from voting in the League of Nations when Japan's aggression in Manchuria was condemned. Trade relations with Tokyo had become closer as Siamese purchases quintupled between 1925 and 1935 (from \$2.25 million to \$12.15 million). By 1941 Japan was the country's most important customer for rice, tin, and rubber. Closer ties were evident in 1940, when Japan agreed to Siam's demand for a frontier rectification with Indochina. Despite a neutrality agreement, which it signed in 1940 with Britain, Pibul's regime declared war on the Anglo-American powers in January, 1942. The following year it acquired territory inhabited by the Shan (Thai) people of Burma as well as four Malay states previously ceded to Britain along the southern border.

Despite its anti-Western foreign policy, the government sought to modernize the country along Western lines. It fostered Western dress, simplified its language, and, by imitating Western social practices, sought to give the country a more civilized and dignified appearance. It also attempted to give the country a greater degree of political cohesion, similar to that enjoyed by the Western nation-states, and crystallize loyalty around the state. The drive for cultural, ethnic, and social unity led the regime to intervene in religious affairs; it made the practice of Buddhism a patriotic duty and cast doubts on the loyalty of followers of other faiths. Discrimination in favor of Buddhists and pressures on Moslems and Christians were maintained until Pibul was ousted in 1944, and then reintroduced on his return to power in 1947.

The education system was revised in an effort to heighten popular loyalty to the state and the ruling clique. The Ministry of Education exercised tight controls over teaching personnel, educational methods, and subject matter. The number of schools increased as compulsory education was introduced, but the motivation remained intensely nationalistic, in a manner reminiscent of Japan after the Restoration of 1868. The government also hoped to assimilate Chinese and Malay children through school training. The Chinese had established their own schools, with only one or two Siamese on each staff; an attempt was now made to install Siamese faculties at these institutions, with

Chinese taught as a foreign language. The Chinese then resorted to evasive tactics and the government closed down schools violating the education laws. Conditions have been uncomfortable for the Chinese since 1938, but the regime has failed to assimilate the young Chinese with regard to the Siamese language or culture patterns. Under parental instruction, the Moslem Malay children refused to cooperate in Siamese schools and learned their own language at home; nor would these followers of Islam bow to the idol of Buddha even as a duty to the state. An education law in 1948 made Siamese the major part of the curriculum and allotted only a small amount of time for Malay. This action served only to increase Malay antagonism to the policy of assimilation.

Attempts to control Chinese immigration also encountered grave difficulties even after Thailand and China signed their first modern treaty in 1946. Bangkok established an annual quota of 10,000 for Chinese immigrants, which brought a protest from China. As the civil war in China intensified, this official number was drastically reduced and a tough program of control and deportation was followed. Still, the illegal flow of immigrants continued at an alarming rate. With the rise of a Chinese Communist power, this problem merged into the larger question of Thailand's national security.

The Politics of Peace

When Japan lost control of the military situation in 1943, Pibul's position became untenable. He had aligned the country diplomatically and economically with Tokyo and had also sought to emulate Japan's ideological and political system. His government fell shortly after Tojo lost power in 1944. His opponents had formed an underground Free Thai movement under Pridi, who had been made regent at the start of the Pacific War. Pridi now became the power behind a series of cabinets that held office from 1944 to 1947. During the last year of the war the Thai government gave clandestine help to the Western military forces.

Since he enjoyed Allied favor, Pridi won easy terms for his country. He annulled the declaration of war, restored territory seized under Japanese protection, and signed a treaty with Britain in 1946. This agreement placed the country's economy temporarily under foreign control and allotted 1,500,000 tons of rice to Britain as a peace offering. The United States, which had never recognized Pibul's declaration of war, induced Britain to settle on milder terms. This was most fortunate, since Thailand could not deliver the rice as promised. Conditions later returned to normal, and the country again became an exporter of rice and other raw materials. Thus it acquired a strong position in foreign trade, since these commodities were in high demand after the war.

In domestic affairs Pridi's leadership proved far less effective. Frequent cabinet changes deprived the government of adequate continuity of policy. It could not cope with the difficult problems of economic rehabilitation and was guilty of gross mismanagement and corruption. Pibul had been arrested as a war criminal but was not brought to trial, since he had not violated laws existing in 1942. He then regrouped his political forces, gained the army's support, and held a far stronger position than did his opponents. Pridi, who lacked a firm base of power, could not unite the liberal and civilian groups under his leadership to confront Pibul's threat. Pibul bided his time only because of his unpopularity with the Western allies, but in 1947 he engineered a bloodless coup and regained power. Pridi fled into exile as an outlaw, accused of complicity in the mysterious death of the king in 1946.

In his second period of rule Pibul continued his efforts to develop a homogeneous, modern nation-state. To the policy of cultural assimilation, he added an extremely costly campaign to "nationalize" the middle class by expropriating the Chinese and replacing them with Siamese. The monetary expense, loss of skills, and dislocation of the economy slowed down this program and led to efforts at reaching a compromise. In the long run, political tensions and problems of economic development can be resolved only if the Chinese community is accepted and in turn believes itself to be an integral element in the Siamese political community.

Economic Programs

To a certain degree, the policy of expropriation was linked to the program of economic modernization. Public corporations were formed prior to 1940 when the government owned and operated paper, sugar, tobacco and canning factories, and planned to branch into other consumer industries. Siamese were placed in charge of operations, but, as they lacked the skill and drive of the Chinese, these ventures did not fare too well. However, the government continued along this line after the war in such fields of production as textiles, cement, wine, cigarettes, hides, and rubber. The administration also established a monopoly over rice exports, reducing the peasant's share of the export price below the prewar level of 60 per cent. Moreover, the middleman's share fell from 40 to 10 per cent after the war. The result was a lucrative income for the government, which enabled it to finance many projects until 1953. As was true of Burma, the end of a seller's market for raw materials posed problems for future development and economic stability. This issue is highlighted by a law requiring 51 per cent of all stock in economic enterprises to be native-owned. Though some controls were relaxed, as in the Fuel Oil Act, which allowed British and American firms to return under old terms, the trend is toward control over foreign concerns.

The regime has moved cautiously in the field of reform, though it has spurred a village development program similar to the more ambitious projects in India and Burma. Water, rail, and road networks have been given high priority; these works were begun before 1940 but were set back by the war. A social insurance program for employees has been promised, together with cooperative societies for rice production and consumption. The government has also undertaken to raise living standards, improve health facilities, and develop the country's irrigation system.

Alignment with the West and Political Reform

In the atmosphere of the Cold War, Thailand's wartime collaboration with Japan was forgotten and the country moved quite rapidly into the Western camp. Under Marshal Pibul it became the first state in that region to associate itself with the American cause and express a willingness to join in an anti-Communist alliance. It supported the United Nations action in Korea with a small contingent. Thailand has received foreign aid in the form of economic and military assistance from the United States, and a substantial loan from the International Bank for Reconstruction and Development. In 1954 Bangkok adhered to the Southeast Asia Treaty defense organization and pressed for an even firmer military commitment than the United States finally undertook. The members of this treaty organization held their first important meeting in Bangkok early in 1955 and decided to make that city the headquarters of the alliance. There are Thai adherents of the neutralist line adopted by Burma, but thus far they have been unable to influence policy or gain much propular support for this view.

Pibul's dictatorship has depended heavily on military support. Though there has been a scramble for power among the police, army, and navy, these elements have held together well enough to maintain the regime. There has been a series of realignments within the government as well as occasional use of force, but Pibul has remained firmly entrenched in power. His former rival, Pridi, was heard over Radio Peking in 1955 calling for a revolutionary change to oust this regime. However, the real threat from China lies in its military power and the use of an "autonomous" Thai-speaking province just across the border as a center of subversion.

In 1955 the government took tentative steps to introduce more democracy without upsetting political stability. Reforms have been slow because a sudden change might arouse the military leaders on whom Pibul depends. Moreover, the people themselves appear uninterested in democratic forms, and the government's own record has made political opponents suspicious of its good intentions. It permitted free speech, allowing the Royal Cremation Grounds to be used for political talks, including antigovernment harangues. Political parties were allowed to form, provided they were registered with the government, in preparation for the 1957 election. Pibul's regime still retained the privilege of nominating, in the King's name, half the House of Assembly. Consequently many former leaders remained in retirement and the first opposition groups were weak. When the election was held, the government controlled the ballots and declared itself the winner. Opposition electioneering was permitted during the campaign and was also allowed to be expressed in futile protests over the tabulation of results.

Many advocates of reform fear that the government is interested only in "half-hearted, formalistic" change that goes no further than allowing parties to be organized. Thus a progovernment party has been formed, with Pibul as its head, the commanders of the army and air force as deputy leaders, police

general Phao as secretary-general, and a civilian with important financial connections as treasurer. On the other hand, a former prime minister, Nai Khuang
Aphaiwongse, decided to head the re-created Democratic party, a moderate liberal organization. Two major problems are the evident reluctance of the government to yield its monopoly of power in the near future and the apparent lack of
popular demand for party government. After 1940, Pibul tried to copy Japan's
political system; fifteen years later he seemed equally interested in introducing
some form of democracy, however cautiously, into this independent kingdom.
The government may sincerely be interested in such reforms, but in 1956 it
again withdrew many of these freedoms, evidently in fear that its authority
might be undermined.

Indochina

Indochina, a land that bears the name of two great Asian states, was a center
of violence for almost a decade after 1945. Here intense nationalism came under
communist domination as the French imperial rulers waged a desperate war
to retain their power. The French people, however, were unwilling to support
an all-out effort; for example, they permitted regular troops but no conscripts
to fight in this "dirty jungle war." Rebel skill increased, Communist China
arrived at Indochina's northern frontier, and France could not rally nationalist
anti-Communist support. A military collapse threatened, and, in the face of
crumbling French defensive bastions, the Communists won a decisive diplomatic triumph at Geneva in 1954. This gave them immediate control over much
of the northern half of the country and a good opportunity to extend their
power below the dividing line of latitude 17°. It was now left to the anti-
Communist nationalists in southern Vietnam, Laos, and Cambodia to bear the
burden of competing with the Communists in the struggle for Indochina.

The Historical Setting

This dramatic political struggle is taking place in the southeast corner of
Asia. Like Burma, Indochina is partially insulated from its northern Chinese
neighbor by a mountain range; communications to the west are impeded also
by jungle and swamps. Within Indochina itself, land routes are few and difficult to use, and most contacts are made by sea. This method has proved satisfactory because most people live near the coast or near major inland waterways.

The political subdivisions of Indochina reflect a profusion of cultural and
ethnic groups. The Annamese form the largest element—more than 70 per cent
—of the 29 million inhabitants. They inhabit the three parts of Vietnam—
Tonkin in the north, the long and narrow state of Annam, which runs along
the coast, and Cochinchina in the south. The Annamese first settled in the Red
River delta region of Tonkin, where they developed an intensive subsistence
rice culture. Population pressure induced them to settle scattered parts of
Annam and then Cochinchina, where a second great rice culture was developed
along the Mekong River. In modern times economic necessity led the Anna-

mese to push inland toward Cambodia in the southwest. But they were too tradition-bound to leave their homeland in large numbers.

This Annamese, or Vietnamese, civilization was strongly influenced by China, which ruled the country from 181 B.C. to 939 A.D., and again held it temporarily under the Ming dynasty. Family ties are very important, and the father holds a dominant position as priest of the ancestral cult. An elaborate governmental structure and imperial system were developed on the Chinese model, but the Annamese kingdom was split into two states—Tonkin and Cochinchina—late in the seventeenth century. Dynastic quarrels marked the next 200 years and facilitated the French conquest.

The village was the main organizational unit, enjoying a self-sufficiency in both economic and social affairs until modern times. More than one fifth of the villages in north and central Vietnam organized irrigation, grain storage, and even land ownership on a commercial basis. The people of the north gained a reputation for industriousness and efficiency, but overpopulation in the Red River delta and a heavy dependence on farming kept them impoverished. This area is still the most populous region of Vietnam, and the Red River delta, with the major city of Hanoi and the port of Haiphong, remains the country's political center of gravity.

In their migration southward the Annamese encountered an Indic civilization which they pushed back to Cambodia. The Cambodians adopted both Buddhist and Brahmin faiths, and possessed a proud historical tradition of their own. The great ruined city of Angkor still reflects their powerful empire, which lasted from 800 to about 1400. At present they number approximately 4 million people and possess a more highly developed social structure than their neighbor state of Laos to the north, for the Thai people there still live in a tribal state of organization. This little kingdom of Laos is sparsely settled, with only 1 million inhabitants, but it is strategically located between Communist-held North Vietnam and its western neighbors, Burma and Thailand.

The Red and Mekong valleys are the economic centers of Vietnam. In the north the land is carved into very small units, generally owned by the peasants farming them. Before 1940, about 60 per cent of the farmers owned less than an acre of land each, and a good number had nothing at all. By contrast, the more recently settled south operates on a plantation-tenancy system largely developed by the French. Cochinchina produced an important rice surplus for export, but much of it had to go to Tonkin, which suffered a chronic deficit. This was in part due to the population rise in Indochina under French rule, from 15 million in 1910 to 24 million in 1940. During this time, emigration was at a minimum and France did not foster an industrialization program of the magnitude needed to meet the situation.

French Political Rule

France had conquered Indochina in the later half of the nineteenth century. It began with Cochinchina, extended its rule to Cambodia after 1859, and then embarked on the subjugation of the north in 1867. The conquest was completed in 1893, despite strong Chinese objections and periodic wars against Annamese and Chinese forces. During the following decade, France even acquired a sphere of influence over China's three southern provinces north of the Tonkin border. Saigon in the south became the colony's capital. A governor-general exercised complete authority over Cochinchina and the four protectorates of Tonkin, Annam, Cambodia, and Laos. No real power was delegated to local assemblies. The French were even reluctant to allow Western-trained Vietnamese into high posts in the colonial bureaucracy.

The French proved extremely efficient in crushing the rising tide of nationalism before 1940. One effect of this domination was that the nationalists failed to develop a mass patriotic movement strong enough to compete with the Communists for leadership of the liberation movement. Nationalist-Communist friction was apparent in the 1920's and precipitated the disintegration of the Revolutionary party of Young Annam. A Nationalist Annamite party patterned after the Kuomintang never succeeded in becoming well organized, and it too collapsed when the Yen Bay revolt of 1930 was crushed. Thus the field was left open to the more persistent Communists, who were capable of surviving in the hostile environment created by the French in the interwar period. Under Ho Chi Minh (Nguyen Ai Quoc) and General Vo Nguyen Giap, the party became the strongest native force, ready to lead a nationalist revolution at the first opportunity.

The French were even more reluctant than other Western rulers to train and develop native administrators. This attitude was in harmony with their concept of colonial rule, which was not geared to prepare a dependent people for self-government. France extended its system of centralized administration to its colonies, ruling them through a highly organized bureaucracy directed by permanent officials in Paris and overseas. Nor did the French envisage freedom for their domains. Instead, they conceived of their empire (later the French Union) as an integral unit in which the colonies assimilated Gallic culture and eventually reached France's higher standard of living and civilization. This was expected to bind the subject peoples even closer to Paris politically. Such a philosophy ran counter to the spirit of nationalism and infuriated the Vietnamese because it was so restrictive, compared to policies of other imperial powers. The French air of condescension, the history of a conquest by force, the absence of real cultural assimilation, economic poverty, and exploitation all strengthened the will to freedom that burst forth in 1945.

France's Economic Record

The French made several contributions to the Vietnamese economy, including the development of a modern rail and road network and the extension of a complex canal-irrigation system in Tonkin. In Cochinchina France can be credited with spearheading the intensive cultivation of the Mekong delta, draining the land and establishing large canal works for irrigation and transportation. Despite a lack of secondary canals, the area under crops quadrupled here between 1890 and 1940. Rice exports rose to 200,000 tons annually. Coal from the north, rubber, and corn were also sent abroad in appreciable quantities, almost exclusively to France. An educational system, including a University of Hanoi, a small number of high schools, and grammar schools for 500,000 children, was created. Medical facilities were improved, and a fair labor code was gradually introduced to ease working conditions.

Nationalist agitators stressed the exceedingly low wages paid to both rural and urban laborers, especially on the rubber plantations in the south. The Vietnamese peasant suffered from usurious interest rates, an indirect tax system accounting for two thirds of the government's budget, and a poverty so severe that it caused chronic and widespread undernourishment. Population increases and dependence on world market conditions made the situation even more difficult and uncertain. Society was becoming modernized to the extent of weakening family and communal ties and undermining village self-sufficiency. The Vietnamese were at a dangerous stage of development under French rule, for these dislocations overshadowed any benefits that might be gained in the long run.

More immediate was the complaint that the economy was organized exclusively for the benefit of the imperial rulers or, rather, a well-knit group of French concerns. France did little to develop new methods of food cultivation, improve the quality of rice, or create adequate marketing and credit facilities. The ubiquitous Chinese, located primarily in the south, monopolized rice purchases and were partly responsible for the uneven quality of a finished product, which could not compete with Burmese or Siamese rice. Only corn was developed as an alternate food crop, and this was exported mainly to France as cattle food. Rubber exports increased from 10,000 tons in 1909 to 70,000 tons in 1939, but again, the French plantation owners rather than the Vietnamese benefited. Yet the investments entailed capital risks: efforts to grow tea and coffee on plantations were not too successful, and the experiment in cotton proved a total failure.

Vietnam is well provided with minerals, but the extractive industries lay in French hands. Two firms had a virtual monopoly of the 2,500,000 tons produced in 1939. Though Indochina possessed fuel, iron ore, and nonferrous metals, France blocked the growth of processing industries based on these products. Rice- and sugar-processing plants were developed, and there was some manufacturing of cement, cotton yarn, and tobacco. But industrialization as a whole was retarded in order to provide a ready market for French textile, steel, and machine products. Indochina was given a high protective tariff with preferential treatment for French goods. It was thus deprived of inexpensive commodities from Japan and other states, yet did not acquire a protective wall behind which it could develop its own industries. The country did not realize the economic potential of its available industrial power, resources, and skills. Even the technical training of Vietnamese was approached cautiously, despite the opinion of many colonial administrators that this hard-working people would produce excellent results if properly guided.

Effects of Japanese Occupation

French invulnerability was suddenly destroyed in 1940 when Germany conquered Western Europe and Japan took control of the northern half of Indochina. The following year the rest of the colony was occupied, as a springboard for Japan's 1941–1942 offensives. The French colonial administration was allowed to remain in office for reasons of expediency and because its Vichy (Pétainist) superiors in Europe were cooperating with the Axis powers. The colonial government was placed in a difficult position, because it opposed the Japanese. Yet it also feared that even secret cooperation with an anti-Japanese Vietnamese resistance movement would strengthen the nationalist cause. In fact, most French activity during the war was devoted to the suppression of nationalist uprisings. The critical moment came toward the end of the war, when French officers prepared to lead their forces against the Japanese in support of Allied landings. The Japanese, though, became aware of this plan, captured and jailed the entire French garrison, and in March, 1945, declared an end to the "colonial status of Indochina." With this sudden elimination of French power, resistance leadership fell to the Vietminh League (League for the Independence of Vietnam) under Ho Chi Minh, who thereby gained a position of real power as the war ended.

Ho's forces received aid from the United States late in the war and were given sympathetic support by the anticolonial Chinese Nationalist government. The Vietnamese nationalists now sought complete independence. The Vietminh had controlled a portion of Tonkin even before Japan surrendered; at war's end it gained a firm hold in the north and occupied Saigon in the south. A provisional government was formed under Ho in Hanoi and a Declaration of Independence of Vietnam (Land of the South: Tonkin, Annam, and Cochinchina) was proclaimed. The emperor of Annam, Bao Dai, who had already issued a similar declaration for his kingdom, then resigned in favor of Ho.

Britain and China drew the assignment to disarm the Japanese and restore order in Indochina. In their sphere (below latitude 16°) the British, who would not deal with the nationalists in Saigon, helped the French regain control of the government. After French reinforcements arrived, the British departed early in 1946; the French controlled the cities, but Vietminh guerillas dominated a considerable part of the southern countryside. In the north, the Chinese let the Vietminh regime alone and would not permit French troops to enter until February, 1946, and then only after China gained railway concessions and a special status for its nationals in Indochina. When the French landed at Haiphong, they encountered a confident native government enjoying widespread popular support. By contrast, the little kingdoms of Laos and

Cambodia agreed to stay in the French Union and accept French advisers, in return for a wide grant of autonomy in domestic affairs.

The Failure of Negotiations

The Second World War had a devastating effect on France's international position, so that the French now looked to their empire to help sustain them as a world power. They therefore felt that to retain control of all possessions was a matter of vital national interest. Because Indochina was the richest prize of all, its loss would seriously reduce the value of the empire and perhaps start a chain reaction in other territories. Unlike the British Commonwealth, the French Union did not extend much autonomy to the colonies; nor did it allow the free choice of staying within the Union or severing relations. These points became major issues in French-Vietnamese negotiations. Another problem was the fate of Cochinchina, which Ho insisted was part of Vietnam and which the French wished to keep "autonomous." Nevertheless, an agreement to end hostilities was reached in March, 1946, and France was able to occupy Tonkin. In return, it recognized the Republic of Vietnam as a free state, which remained in the Indochinese Federation (Vietnam, Laos, Cambodia) and the French Union. A referendum was to determine the future of Cochinchina. The questions of diplomatic relations and French interests in Indochina were to be settled by negotiation.

However, the French governor-general, Admiral d'Argenlieu, tried to detach Cochinchina from Vietnam in order to ensure French control of this rich area. On the issue of political alignment, conferences held in 1946 failed to bring a settlement. The Vietnamese insisted on complete freedom and looked on the ambiguous phrase of independence "within the framework of the French Union" as a face-saving statement for France. To the French, this was a binding commitment to remain in the Union. The Vietnam regime enjoyed the support of the nationalist movement throughout 1946. In a national election that January, before the French returned to Tonkin, 90 per cent of the people had voted for and supported Ho overwhelmingly. His government soft-pedaled its communist orientation and increased its prestige, promising sweeping reforms, developing a native administration and army, and drafting a new liberal constitution.

The French failure to make concessions with regard to Cochinchina and Union membership led to a bitter and disastrous war. It has been argued that a timely concession in 1946 would have preserved French economic and cultural interests, avoided war, and blocked Communist rule. Yet Ho and his colleagues were devoted Communists of long standing and they did control the Vietminh movement, even though they depended heavily on non-Communist nationalist support. By this time French concessions would simply have meant turning all of Vietnam over to the Communists. Even while the March, 1946, agreement was still in effect, the Communists were planning to assert their authority through use of coercion and force. They developed a plan to drive the French out within two years by tactics of boycott and sabotage, even if a moderate agreement was reached. The situation in Vietnam, in fine, was unique in Southeast Asia. The quality of native Communist leadership and France's effective suppression of nationalist movements meant that a peaceful settlement here would have insured Communist rule. In any event, war was the path chosen when hostilities opened in the Hanoi-Haiphong region late in 1946.

The French Defeat in War

France drifted into war without a fixed purpose or will to bear the high cost of colonialism. Consequently, its policy proved a diplomatic and military failure. As an imperial power, France could not rally popular Indochinese support against the Communist-led Vietminh rebels. In order to break Ho's monopoly of nationalist prestige, France had to sponsor a rival nationalist regime that could inspire patriotic support. The logic of this move required a really free anti-Communist regime, in which case France would be fighting to create a free state without benefit to itself. In practice, France tried the half-way measure of creating a nationalist regime over which it could retain considerable influence. Its head was Emperor Bao Dai, who agreed to return in 1948–1949 after hard bargaining that won for Vietnam the province of Cochinchina and a promise of independence. Though recognized by America and Britain in 1950, Vietnam lived in the shadow of French power and failed to gain the support of the anti-Communist Catholics or the Cao Dai sect. A further hardship was Bao Dai's incompetence and indifference to affairs of state. The Vietnamese army could not carry its share of the military burden, for the French did not give it the vigorous training that the South Koreans received under American guidance after 1950. Important political concessions to Vietnam, such as autonomy in currency, treasury policy, and navigation were made reluctantly in piecemeal fashion and brought no political benefits to France. A grant of full independence, coming after the military situation had deteriorated, naturally did little to raise French prestige.

French regulars, African units, and foreign legionnaires battled an ever-growing rebel army in Tonkin. Guerilla tactics enabled the Vietminh to survive against a superior opponent in 1947–1950. Then, with Chinese assistance, the rebels turned the tide, after capturing the frontier posts that the French hoped would seal off the Chinese border. Neither a system of blockhouses in the countryside nor the creation of mobile units could check the rise of rebel power. When the hinterland was lost, the French forces fell back to a defense of the Red River delta area. In a final effort to defeat the bulk of the Vietminh forces in a field engagement, paratroopers were sent to occupy the interior strongpoint of Dienbienphu, located in a valley. The result was a costly but successful assault by General Giap's Communist forces and the loss of the entire garrison of 15,000 men in 1954. The French army's failure to relieve the defenders, who had held out for two months, revealed the desperate nature of the military situation in the north. The entire delta region was now heavily infiltrated and in danger of falling to rebel armies.

The Geneva Settlement and After

Lesser defeats in Tonkin had overturned a French cabinet in the nineteenth century. The disaster at Dienbienphu had a similar effect, and it brought Pierre Mendès-France to power. He was willing to accept the loss of northern Vietnam as the price of peace. His agreement, reached at Geneva in July, 1954, partitioned the country at latitude 17° but gave the French several months to evacuate the north. They took with them an appreciable quantity of American miliary supplies and many Vietnamese who wanted to migrate to the south. It was also agreed that, as a step toward reunification, a national election would be held in two years. The Vietnamese Communists believed that they would have gained control over the whole country without a settlement, but they were induced to follow a moderate line by their Russian and Chinese colleagues. However, they pursued their ultimate objective as energetically as ever, urging Tonkinese not to evacuate and planning a vigorous propaganda campaign for the elections. Vietminh leaders were certain that they would win this vote and thus gain control over the south in a matter of time. In 1954 their military victory, powerful army, and great prestige among nationalists made them appear far superior to the confused Vietnam administration in Saigon. Moreover, antagonism between the southern nationalists and France continued to mount, and it was exceedingly doubtful whether France would fight to protect the non-Communist portion of Vietnam.

THE VIETMINH REGIME

The northern regime of the Vietminh controlled a population of 14 million as against 11 million under the Vietnam government in the south. It possessed coal and other mineral resources but lacked sufficient food. Its Communist rulers now set about creating their totalitarian state, though their policies were influenced by the need to maintain popularity in the south. The Communists asserted their dominance over all nationalist elements that had cooperated with the Vietminh forces in order to defeat the French. They quickly rooted out sources of potential opposition among landowners and merchants, as well as officials. A system known as *phat-dong* was used to dominate the countryside. A team of cadres entered a village, isolated the property owners, collected unfavorable dossiers on them, and explained to the poorer villagers how they had been exploited. A "people's court" composed of poor villagers then tried the property owners; the latter were punished and their land was distributed among the villagers. To cement its hold, the Communist regime placed the poorer peasants in dominant positions on village administrative councils. The army has also been systematically purged of unreliable elements, with new recruits drawn from loyal regions that completed *phat-dong* operations. There are also peasant militia forces trained to act as local defense units in their home regions. In the cities, low prices in government cooperative stores, currency reform, and oppressive taxes served to ruin most private business concerns.

The Chinese Communist technique of mass indoctrination is also being followed. Pictures of "Uncle Ho" are everywhere. Everybody must join some association—of women, agricultural workers, students, and the like. These groups expose their members to propaganda for such long periods of time that all thought of active opposition is literally extinguished. Since civil servants under the old regime refused to serve the new masters, the Vietminh has had to depend on large numbers of Chinese technicians while they train new administrative cadres. The regime is also dependent on foreign economic aid because Tonkin has an annual deficit of from 100,000 to 150,000 tons of rice. In mid-1955 Ho Chi Minh went to China and Russia for assistance and received from Peking a promise of more than $300 million, which, together with a smaller Russian grant, would be much more than South Vietnam is receiving. It is questionable whether assistance on this scale will actually be given, but the Russians did send 150 tons of purchased Burmese rice to carry the country through 1956. Food, foreign exchange to build its trade, textiles, and machinery are the area's major economic needs.

Changes in the Vietminh top command in 1955 led to speculation that Ho was becoming an honorary leader and figurehead, while his younger colleagues assumed real power. Ho yielded the premiership to Pham Van Dong, who retained the post of foreign minister, at which he excelled in the 1954 Geneva conference. Dong, who is also the party theoretician, shares top leadership with party secretary Truong Chinh and General Giap. Another interesting change was the creation of a Communist-dominated Fatherland Front, similar to East European satellite coalitions in practice and name. It is filled with innocent-sounding names representing socialists, democrats, and various sects, and is evidently a device for camouflaging Communist supremacy and gaining nationalist support in the scheduled all-Vietnam election. Despite this "coalition" policy and a temporary elimination of brutality, the Vietminh has lost much of its earlier popularity. In the fall of 1956, the government admitted that peasant uprisings had occurred in predominantly Roman Catholic regions. These were caused by opposition to a harsh land policy and came at a time when political reforms and an election were being promised in an effort to revive the Communists' waning prestige.

THE SOUTH VIETNAM REGIME

The major threat to Vietnamese communism is an effective, democratic government in the south. This area's greater wealth and easier living conditions added to the Communists' difficulty. However, the political situation in the Saigon region was so chaotic that in 1954–1955 it seemed doubtful that South Vietnam could survive. Ngo Dinh Diem, an ardent nationalist who refused to hold public office under French tutelage, became premier in 1954. Under his vigorous anti-Communist leadership, South Vietnam refused to sign the Geneva accord. His attempts to create a cohesive social and political order ran into several obstacles. The French, who still held many key posts as advisers, especially in military affairs, were antagonistic to his leadership. However, he received firm American support, in the form of a military advisory team, supplies, and economic assistance amounting to a few hundred million dollars.

Another cause of difficulty was Bao Dai's failure to provide the nationalist leadership required in this revolutionary crisis. The chief of state, in fact, spent his time shooting tigers near Dalat, Indochina, but was more frequently in the resort town of Cannes on the Riviera. The corruption, inefficiency, and low morale of the country could be traced in good part to this ineffective ruler who owed his throne to the French. Finally, the police and military power of the South were weak. Leading army officials were disdainful of Premier Diem. Two semi-independent sects, the Hoa Hao and the Cao Dai, retained their own military formations and territorial bases of rule. A bandit group, the Binh Xuyen, had purchased from Bao Dai control of the Saigon police duties as well as gambling and similar concessions in the capital district.

Premier Diem proved himself a fervent, incorruptible nationalist leader who won a widespread popular following, to the surprise of his opponents and foreign observers. A showdown occurred in 1955 when he launched a military assault against the Binh Xuyen that featured spectacular street battles in Saigon itself. He simultaneously asserted control over the army, removed its recalcitrant leaders, and gained firm control of Saigon. No longer a "virtual prisoner in his residence," the premier endeavored to reduce the power of the other sects. The Hoa Hao group has resisted efforts to destroy its autonomy, but it has been restricted to a small area of the country. The Cao Dai sect is cooperating with the government, and its private armies are being integrated into the national force.

Meanwhile, from 800,000 to 1,000,000 people, including many Roman Catholics, took advantage of the free travel permitted under the armistice to flee from Tonkin. These refugees gathered in the Saigon region, where they were quartered in squalid tent camps and lived on government aid. The problems created by such a mass movement cannot be immediately resolved, but substantial progress has been made in resettling refugees on land taken from the feudal sects.

The Vietnamese army developed into a competent force during 1955–1956. The Americans suggested that an expert force of from 80,000 to 100,000 men be kept under arms, but the government rejected this advice and kept its force at about 220,000 men. In part this decision was motivated by political reasons —to make room for the troops of cooperative southern sects. The French steadily reduced the size of their forces, and all were evacuated by 1956. Paris could no longer be expected to extend infantry support in defense of the south against its northern foe. The United States is now South Vietnam's chief source of foreign help, but it too has not made any precise commitment, even though

Indochina was brought under the Southeast Asian Treaty arrangement of 1954–1955. Both Vietnamese regimes were committed to free elections in 1956, but Premier Diem refused to negotiate with the Vietminh, even though the Communists might use this as grounds for launching an assault. His position was strengthened in 1956 when Britain and Russia, recognizing the overriding importance of maintaining peace, did not press for an election at the scheduled date. The southern leader claims that the Vietminh would never allow free elections or permit independent candidates to run for office. The Communists have, in fact, violated the Geneva accord by increasing their military stockpile and divisional strength from seven in 1954 to twenty in 1956, blocking the exodus of many would-be refugees to the south, and using intimidation against political opponents. Thus the uneasy partition continues, while the south tries to strengthen its army, set its political house in order, and become a sovereign independent state.

South Vietnam has succeeded in this effort to a greater degree than seemed possible at first. When the premier was certain of his control over the police and military forces, he moved to oust Bao Dai from all offices. Late in 1955, a popular referendum was held that gave Premier Diem an overwhelming victory, following which he deposed Bao Dai and became chief of state in his place. A pro-Diem Assembly was elected in March, 1956, to approve a new constitution. It cannot be inferred, however, that South Vietnam will become a democratic state in the immediate future. The siege conditions in which it finds itself and the political approach of Ngo Dinh Diem point toward a semi-authoritarian order. He used some degree of coercion in the public ballots held in 1955–1956, but in retrospect these victories accurately reflected popular acceptance of his leadership. His critics in Britain and France complained of his authoritarian tendencies and argued that the new constitution would merely give a legal covering to his dominant position. More significant are complaints about inefficiency and corruption leveled against the chief of state's relatives and friends, who obtained important positions of power. Also, it was alleged that the Communists still enjoyed a considerable following in the south. Regardless of how accurate these criticisms are, it is clear that only competent long-range reforms and the development of democracy will enable South Vietnam to maintain itself in competition with the north.

The constitution approved by the Constituent Assembly in 1956 was influenced by the country's difficult security problem and by President Diem's belief that the executive branch needed broad powers during this emergency. Freedom of speech, thought, press, assembly, and association are granted, but the president is given the right until 1959 to suspend them temporarily, if so required by security considerations. The government is divided into executive, legislative, and judicial branches but "the President of the Republic assumes the leadership of the nation," and he has the power to proclaim laws when the National Assembly is not in session. However, these acts are subject to later legislative review; the parliament can also pass laws over a presidential veto, with a three quarters majority. An early draft of the constitution gave the president the right to dissolve the legislature in case of a serious disagreement between the two branches. This was modified to provide for a national referendum to be called by the president in such a crisis. The president's term is for five years and the National Assembly, now composed of the 123-man Constituent Assembly, serves for three years.

The document is a realistic portrait of the present government, and is somewhat more liberal than was first expected. Considering that the 1956 legislative election was the country's first, it appears to have been successfully handled, and the institutions created by the constitution do provide a setting for the growth of democracy. The Diem regime can be credited with the creation of an orderly government, substantial enough to impress foreign observers with its durability. It remains to be seen whether it will also prove sufficiently progressive and democratic to attract the loyal support of the Vietnamese people.

LAOS AND CAMBODIA

Laos was supposed to be completely evacuated by the Communists in 1954. Instead, the Vietminh supported a Pathet Lao (Communist) effort to hold two provinces—Phongsaly and Samneva—and negotiations for a political settlement broke down. The little kingdom asserted its complete independence and held a national election in December, 1955. The anti-Communist parties won handily, but royal troops were forcibly kept from asserting their authority in the two Communist-held provinces. Undoubtedly Vietminh leadership and equipment were behind this added violation of the Geneva accord.

Cambodia fared better than all other parts of Indochina, because it was left completely intact by the truce. Its vigorous ruler, King Norodom Sihanouk, had disbanded the Assembly for three years in 1952 and tried to put through constitutional reforms that would have barred from office those who had recently fought for the Communists. The Indochinese Armistice Commission (India, Canada, and Poland) ruled that this reform would have violated provisions of the truce. Sihanouk promptly abdicated in favor of his father, formed a Popular Socialist Rally, and in September, 1955, won an overwhelming victory at the polls, capturing all ninety-one Assembly seats. Cambodia has severed all ties with the French Union, and follows an anti-Communist policy at home, but is neutralist and critical of the United States. It signed a military-aid agreement with the United States that did not bind it to the West on policy matters and so was accepted by the Armistice Commission. Adhering to an independent neutralism, Cambodia's leaders announced that their country would avoid military alignments but would seek American help if attacked. Together with Laos, Cambodia became a member of the United Nations in December, 1955.

16 *Malaya, Indonesia,*

the Philippines

Malaya

British Rule

The Malay Peninsula, somewhat smaller than Florida, was a quiet backwater of Asia in 1880. It consisted of nine small states ruled by local sultans. The land was still unaffected by the European political-economic sweep across Asia, though Britain had been in this vicinity during the nineteenth century. The British possessed three port cities—the island of Singapore off the peninsula's southern tip, Penang off the west coast, and Malacca on the west coast. These cities were eventually grouped as a crown colony, the Straits Settlements. Singapore was the personal triumph of Sir Stamford Raffles, who acquired this natural harbor early in the nineteenth century so that the East India Company could challenge Holland's trade monopoly in the Indies. A policy of low taxes and free trade made Singapore a great entrepôt in regional trade and in Southeast Asia's commerce with the West. Storage, processing enterprises, merchandise grading, and other auxiliary activities were developed in the great port. Its only industry was tin smelting, based on the valuable mines of Malaya. The British followed an isolationist policy in their Straits Settlements, maintaining commercial relations with the peninsula, rejecting a policy of territorial expansion, and staying out of Malaya's internal affairs.

The situation changed, however, in the last quarter of the nineteenth century. There was a sudden outburst of European imperial expansion, coupled with the rise in value of Malaya's tin and rubber resources and the collapse of order on the peninsula. The sultans warred constantly against one another and could not even check the quarrels of their nominal subordinates. In addition, Chinese tin miners engaged in their own feuds, and offshore piracy flourished. The British therefore intervened and assumed control of the nine Malay States by 1909. The sultans agreed by treaty to follow the advice of a British resident on all matters except Malayan customs and the Moslem religion. The country now experienced considerable economic growth, for its potential wealth attracted British and Chinese capital investments and Chinese and Indian workers.

Britain at first planned to assert its authority only indirectly, through advice and persuasion. As conditions became more complex, however, it assumed direct political leadership, especially in the four southern Federated Malay States. The governor of the Straits Settlements was also the high commissioner for the nine states; he was assisted by advisory councils in the colony and a federal council in the Federated States. Though legally an absolute ruler, the high commissioner still depended on compromise and persuasion, and rarely insisted on a measure opposed by unofficial members of a council.

The loss of effective political power did not trouble the Malays, for their sultans retained formal sovereignty, and most of their customs were undisturbed. Aside from a small, Western-trained group oriented toward democracy and nationalism, the people accepted a benevolent authoritarian regime as a natural order. British rule, moreover, had been established by request rather than conquest.

The population of Malaya is relatively concentrated, because only 15 per cent of the land is under cultivation. Of the rest, 72 per cent is jungle and 11 per cent is swampland. Since the center is a mountain chain sloping down to the sea on both sides, the peninsula's coasts are the centers of most economic activity. Malaya led the world in tin and rubber production before 1941, and was also an important source of gums, spices, copra, and other tropical products. However, it was not self-sufficient in rice, producing only 36 per cent of its consumption needs.

Chinese immigration reached a high level in the half century before the Second World War. By 1947, 728,000 of Singapore's 938,000 inhabitants were Chinese; Malays barely outnumbered the Chinese, 2,400,000 to 1,900,000, on the mainland. The Chinese settled primarily on the west coast and controlled about one third of the tin production. They also accounted for one seventh of the rubber output, compared to 46 per cent from British estates and 41 per cent from Malay small holdings.

The Malay people were barely emerging from a semiprimitive tribal society and lacked the social discipline, economic skill, and business sense to compete with the Chinese. Because Britain followed a laissez-faire policy in economic affairs as well as immigration, the Chinese quickly established their ascendancy in the commercial field. The Malays followed the relatively simple pursuits of growing the country's rice and all the rubber produced by small farmers. Many fell into debt to Chinese or Indian moneylenders, while others were at the mercy of Chinese retailers or produce buyers. Since Malays generally did not like to put in regular hours, Chinese labor dominated the tin mines and Indians worked on British-held rubber plantations. Both foreign groups performed most of the urban labor required by business and industry.

Nevertheless, the imperial rulers protected the Malay political position by making only Malays or Britons eligible for civil service posts. The Malays were suspicious of any form of democracy that might give political power to the numerically large Chinese community. The British decided that democratic reforms could come only after the Malays mastered their abrupt cultural transition from feudal to modern times and were able to cope with the more advanced Chinese.

The Malays accused the Chinese of coming—with the sole purpose of making money and then leaving—only after Britain had created favorable economic conditions. These immigrants were also suspected of remaining loyal to China. It is true that only one third of the Chinese considered Malaya their permanent home. Even the Straits Settlements Chinese who became British subjects retained a strong affection for China. The Kuomintang regime did its best to maintain this tradition, and its Malayan branch worked hard to increase its membership and sustain loyalty to the homeland. Chinese vernacular schools also fostered a patriotism that the British were unable to curtail.

Economic and political differences were reinforced by religious and racial conflicts. Malay Moslems looked down on both Indians and Chinese for their sacrilegious idolatry and ritualistic impurity. The Chinese in turn proved clannish and confident in the superiority of their culture. Intermarriage was abhorrent to both groups, and racial tension mounted as Malay nationalism asserted itself.

The British have been accused of failing to prepare Malaya for self-rule or create the proper atmosphere for communal tolerance. However, by pre-1940 standards, their rule was tolerably successful, since the various races lived together with at least surface harmony under British authority. The government established fairly decent health standards in a country that had been one of the world's worst malarial regions. Public education facilities were established for Indian Tamils as well as Chinese and Malays, and since 1945 all three groups have received equal treatment. Also, a University of Malaya was formed by reorganizing the old liberal arts and medical colleges. More recently, in the early 1950's, the Chinese tried to establish a University of Singapore, but, owing to communist pressure and sabotage, they abandoned this project. Britain also improved the country's tin and rubber production, but Malaya still depended heavily on the volatile world-commodity markets for its prosperity.

Effects of the War

The Japanese invasion of 1941–1942 dealt a blow to British prestige from which it never fully recovered. Postwar analyses indicate that Britain lost a race against time by about six weeks in its effort to stabilize the Malayan front in 1942. Allied defeats elsewhere in Asia, the difficult situation in Europe, and the invader's skillful tactics led to this swift conquest. The Japanese landed on the northern portion of the peninsula and moved southward to Singapore, using overland and coastal water routes. The guns of the great base pointed menacingly but harmlessly out to sea as the Japanese entered from the rear. Japanese rule was harsh and the impressment of labor on the Burma-Siam railway aroused popular hatred. The allegedly pro-Asian Japanese ironically succeeded in stirring anti-Chinese sentiment but could not foster antagonism to the British. However, Britain's military failure and Japan's misrule created a wider audience for those anxious to preach the doctrine of self-government; this environment also intensified racial hostility and narrow ethnic nationalism.

Another dark shadow of future events was cast by the Communist party of Malaya, an almost exclusively Chinese group that led the underground activity against Japan. Aided by British arms and paratroopers, these 6,000 Communists harassed the occupiers and prepared to assist a planned British assault. The sudden end of warfare and Britain's return in 1945 caused the Communists to modify their ambitious plan to gain immediate control over the country. Instead, they cooperated temporarily with Britain but hid their arms and retained their combat organizations in preparation for a renewed thrust.

The returning British forces received a joyous welcome from large crowds, a phenomenon not matched elsewhere in Southeast Asia. The imperial rulers were faced with three major problems in the postwar period: economic rehabilitation and long-range development, the military menace posed by the Communists, and the thorny issue of establishing self-government in a land split into three ethnic groups. Under Japanese rule the public services, especially health and education, had deteriorated rapidly; and the flow of battle had caused great destruction, especially to transportation facilities. Much of the land under rubber was overgrown, and, though careful tending brought production back to prewar levels by 1948, the industry found its very foundations menaced by the development of synthetics. Chinese tin miners could resume work quickly because they depended on hand labor, but the British mines were operated by dredges in need of repair. Tin production was still at half its prewar level in 1948, and the country was short of cotton cloth and rice. Though Singapore regained its position as commercial entrepôt and tin smelter, rice remained scarce because of chaotic conditions in Burma and Indochina. The Korean War brought temporary relief by creating a sellers' market in Malaya's cash crops, but the long-term problem of economic development again came to the fore when this boom ended.

The Communist Menace

Early postwar economic difficulties, especially high food prices, brought turbulent protests from the relatively new trade unions. The Communists had gained considerable influence in these bodies and used them to foment unrest, discredit Britain, and disrupt the economy further. They hoped to gain power during the resulting chaos. In June, 1948, the Malaya Communist party, still overwhelmingly Chinese in membership, opened an assault on the government that soon evolved into a long guerilla war. Just prior to this military uprising, Malay and Indian labor leaders had split with the Chinese, thereby depriving the Communists of effective union support. This break also kept the uprising from assuming an all-Malayan appearance.

The Communists expected to drive the British out but soon realized that they had overestimated their own strength: a guerilla force composed of 5,000 men, mainly young Chinese immigrants trained during the war. They then resorted to violence against Kuomintang Chinese and European rubber and tin producers who were relatively isolated in a countryside surrounded by jungle. The terrain was admirably suited for these tactics. The rebels at first extended their operations to urban areas, terrorized selected victims, and alternately threatened and befriended villagers in rural areas. When a British assault was launched, the smaller units simply dissolved in populous regions and larger formations hid in the jungles. The economy was sorely taxed, Britain's resources were drained, and the people were kept in a state of confusion and terror. Gradually Britain built up its own forces, developed a Malayan police force, and pushed the Communists into the jungle.

Here the insurgents depended on communities of Chinese squatters who had fled to jungle clearings during the Japanese occupation to practice subsistence farming. Distrustful of government and vulnerable to guerilla attacks, the settlements offered an excellent base of supply and formation. The government therefore decided on a bold policy of relocating these people compulsorily in new villages that could be protected and controlled. This enormous task of resettling 500,000 people was completed by 1954 under the direction of General Gerald Templar, the High Commissioner. The Communists were then driven deeper into the jungle and lost much of their effectiveness, for a good deal of their effort now had to be expended in collecting food for survival. The emergency was therefore considered to be under control by 1955, but the self-styled Malay Races Liberation Army survived and kept in contact with China. Should southern Indochina come into communist hands, the danger may again become acute. Even in isolation, it took 40,000 British regulars, 60,000 Malay policemen, and a home guard of 200,000 Malays and Chinese to restore order against a foe numbering from 4,000 to 6,000. Following Malaya's first national election in 1955, the new native government earnestly sought to reach a truce settlement with the rebels, and threatened a war of extermination should resistance continue. Communist leader Chin Peng would not surrender and agreed to negotiate only after Britain withdrew completely from Malaya. Negotiations were broken off early in 1956 when the Malay government would not grant an unconditional amnesty, and the grim struggle was resumed. In 1956, only 42 per cent of Malaya was judged to be completely cleared of Communist penetration.

A political settlement between Malays and Chinese appears an essential counterpart to the task of checking communism. The issues are most clearly joined in the problem of squatter resettlement. Unless these Chinese, totaling 10 per cent of the population, become loyal, responsible citizens, they may develop into new centers of unrest and communist recruitment. The government has therefore fostered community projects and built hospitals, schools, and welfare centers. It has also trained elected local councils to assume the duties of local government, relieving the district officer of this function. Village home guards have been organized to protect the settlements against Communist raiders; these units have freed regular forces for other duties and given the former squatters a sense of confidence. Such measures may prove satisfactory provided the communist military menace remains under control and the problems of self-government are resolved.

Community Relations

The future of Malaya depends on the ability of its Malay and Chinese communities to live together. Malay resentment of the Chinese was expressed in many ways after 1945. There was strong opposition to recruiting Chinese home guards or allowing them to enter the police and military services. Malays also criticized the high cost of servicing relocated Chinese communities, and it is debatable whether an independent Malaya would continue all these essential activities. During the emergency years the loyal Chinese formed a Malayan Chinese Association (MCA), which grew so rapidly that the Malays at first feared its latent political influence. The Malay dilemma lies in the fact that Chinese political loyalty and monetary support are essential if the country is to avoid strife and make economic progress. Yet political concessions to a group that cannot be assimilated and that enjoys economic supremacy may give the Chinese a position of dominance in Malayan affairs. Evidently mutual confidence must be carefully nurtured if political reform is to be meaningful.

Britain's first major political reform after 1945 aroused Malay antagonism because it reduced the sultans' formal rights and made broad concessions to the Chinese. Britain had the sultans yield their sovereignty, divested them of all remaining powers, and proposed a Malayan Union with a powerful center. Union citizenship, a key issue in race relations, was to be open to all born in Malaya or Singapore, or who had lived there during ten of the past fifteen years; thereafter five years of residence would suffice. The Malays accepted the notion of federation and of citizenship for all *loyal* residents but were angry over the poor treatment of the sultans and these lenient citizenship provisions. A political movement arose, led by the aristocratic English-trained Dato Onn bin Jafar, then premier of Johore state. He headed the United Malay National Organization (UMNO), which rose rapidly to political prominence and established branches throughout the land.

Britain yielded in 1947 and recognized the formal power of the sultans. A Malayan Federation of all nine states was created under the joint sponsorship of Britain and the sultans. British advisers still directed defense and foreign affairs, and the sultans remained obliged to follow their advice. In addition, the power of each state was to be limited in favor of federal authority. The central government was under a high commissioner who, at UMNO insistence, had the duty of protecting Malay interests. He exercised authority with the assistance of an executive council composed of official and unofficial members representing all races. A ninety-six member legislative council was created to pass on all laws and financial matters. It had fifteen official and sixty-one unofficial members, with Malays comprising at least thirty-one of the total. Malayan citizenship was restricted to Malays, and to Indian and Chinese

British subjects born in federal territory. Immigrants could be naturalized only after fifteen years of residence, provided they intended to remain in Malaya; however, they could retain their allegiance to their former homeland. This reform was opposed by the Chinese, who protested against discrimination. A minority of Malays wanted full democratic reform and hoped for a union with Indonesia. However, most Malays supported this constitution, which went into effect in 1948.

In an effort to integrate the Chinese into the political community, the government allowed them to compete for civil service posts and later eased the citizenship laws. All Indians and Chinese born in Malacca and Penang were made citizens; the same treatment was accorded those born in a Malay state if one parent was also born there. The British still did not follow a policy of *jus soli*—the granting of citizenship to all who were born in Malaya. However, these new rules and reforms of the naturalization laws raised the number of citizens from below half to 72 per cent of Malaya's adult residents.

Self-Government

Political agitation increased for an elected federal legislature, which was considered a vital step on the road to self-rule. In order to hasten this process, the UMNO and the MCA, later joined by the Malayan Indian Congress, formed an Alliance coalition. After considerable discussion, General Templar decided to hold an election in 1955 for a slight majority (fifty-two) of the legislature's ninety-six seats.[1] The Alliance stressed interracial cooperation and presented an election slate of thirty-five Malays, fifteen Chinese, and two Indians. Under MCA pressure it moved toward a citizenship policy of *jus soli*. This moderate racial policy was opposed by Dato Onn, who resigned as president of the UMNO. He was succeeded by Tengku (Prince) Abdul Rahman, who also became leader of the Alliance.

Dato Onn resigned as home minister in the federal government and formed a rival Party Negara, composed of the Malay elite—senior officials, lawyers, and commercial leaders. He earnestly sought to re-establish his popularity with the peasantry and appealed to old traditions, suspicion of other races, and local loyalty to one's individual state. The Party Negara demanded a curb on immigration, stricter citizenship requirements, a Malay civil service, Malay as the national language, and complete independence by 1960.

The Alliance was disturbed by this campaign, despite its own great prestige, ample funds from Chinese sources, and a record of 226 victories in 268 contests in municipal and state elections. It no longer talked of *jus soli*, but stressed the need for immigration controls. It demanded a new constitution, *Merdeka* (freedom) by 1959, with Malay as the national language in ten years. The Chinese were perturbed by this shift of policy but patiently supported the

---

[1] The other forty-four members remained British appointees, representing the government, the sultans, and a variety of interest groups.

459

Alliance, since this was their sole path to political influence. Because of citizen- ship problems and political apathy, only 180,000 of the 1,280,000 voters in the 1955 election were Chinese. Nevertheless, they were cheered by the fact that Tengku Abdul Rahman would not yield to pressure from within the UMNO to scrap the multiracial Alliance slate. He was completely vindicated when the Alliance won a smashing victory, because its entire slate, save one Malay candi- date, was elected.

The Alliance now enjoyed a clear legislative majority (51/96), and Tengku Abdul Rahman became Malaya's chief minister. He renewed demands for im- mediate self-rule, and early in 1956 was promised dominion status within the Commonwealth by August, 1957. In this transitional period, the chief minister was given a greater voice in government affairs and Malayan ministers were promised immediate control over internal defense, security, finance, and com- merce and industry. A commission was appointed to draft a new constitution for this independent Federation of Malaya. Following the formal acceptance of the agreement by the nine sultans and the British government, British advisers are to be withdrawn from these states. Britain, however, promised to continue its economic and military aid to Malay in its fight against the Communists, and the new Malayan government has agreed to have British forces remain in the peninsula. The chief minister, expecting Communist and perhaps extreme na- tionalist criticism of this policy, has frankly acknowledged that Malayan forces alone could not maintain security against the approximately 3,000 Communist rebels still at large.

A similar agreement regarding Singapore's self-rule was planned for April, 1956, with Britain retaining control over defense and foreign affairs. The 1955 election in this city was dominated by left-wing groups. The Labor Front, led by David Marshall, won control of the twenty-nine member assembly. It has stood by the principles of democracy against the pressure of the communist- inspired People's Action party. The latter endeavored to embarrass the Mar- shall administration by fomenting riots and strikes, especially among Chinese students, infiltrating the Labor Front, and making extremist demands. The responsibility of office led the Labor Front to curb these politically-inspired acts of violence, but Singapore's democratic structure is much less securely rooted than Malay's. Its large Chinese population, political inexperience, and uncertainty about the future all increased its vulnerability to the communist menace. An impasse was reached in London in 1956 when Britain insisted that it have the right to decide when to intervene in order to prevent a breakdown of law and order. Negotiations collapsed; Chief Minister Marshall resigned and was succeeded by Lim Yew Hock, also of the Labor Front.

The new chief minister was equally determined to gain freedom for Singapore but he realized that the grave communist menace had to be brought under con- trol. He observed that the Communists had infiltrated many unions, private Chinese schools, and civic organizations, and were threatening the future of the colony's democratic government. In the fall of 1956 he suddenly arrested subversive elements including union officials, dissolved communist-front groups, detained many Chinese for deportation, and barred a Chinese students' union as a communist organization. The effort to weed out communist agitators from private Chinese schools led to student riots, financed by communist unions, in October, 1956. With the aid of Malayan troop reinforcements, the government took firm action in suppressing violence. It also moved against unions, linked to the People's Action party, which were believed responsible for riots in May, 1956. Singapore emerged from this turmoil in a more stable political condition than it had enjoyed for years, and Chief Minister Lim planned to press Britain for self-rule at his first opportunity.

A wider foundation encompassing Malaya, Singapore, and British Borneo has been considered by leading officials, and it may prove the most practical course to follow. The Singapore government appears to prefer only a link between the city and the mainland. However, the Malayan government has opposed a simple link with the great port. It would like to balance an addition of Singapore's Chinese population with Borneo's Moslem Malays and Dyaks. This wider union, moreover, would probably mean a transfer of the federation's capital from its present location of Kuala Lampur on the peninsula, to Singapore. Whether Singapore would be willing to become the Chinese center of a predominantly Moslem state is a critical question.

The Economic Future

Meanwhile the International Bank for Reconstruction and Development surveyed the economies of Malaya and Singapore and in 1955 recommended a long-term economic program. With a rising population and an aging rubber economy, Malaya is encountering great difficulty in attracting foreign investment. Only by modernizing its rubber industry, diversifying crops, improving transportation, and cultivating more land can the economy as a whole expand. Such a program in turn would make an asset of the country's larger population. Expansion of the rubber industry is advised despite competition from synthetic products, because of increased world demand. This goal would cost $125 million over a five-year period; other recommended expenses are transportation, $94 million; electric power, $71 million; and drainage and irrigation, $55 million. This program, if successful, would insure income from rubber exports while other cash crops are going through the costly developing stage. On the other hand, self-sufficiency in rice is considered too costly to be worth the effort.

Singapore must diversify both its types of industry and form of business organization. At present, the small family is the major unit of operation, a situation severely restricting economic growth. The Bank suggested that a variety of industries be developed for domestic and regional markets, as was done in Hong Kong. Both Malaya and Singapore are in need of a higher tax policy, efficient administration, and skillful political leadership to guide these programs.

Thus economic development takes its place alongside the communal problem, the communist menace, and the transition to self-rule as a major problem confronting the Malay Peninsula.

Indonesia

The great Indonesian archipelago lies across 3,000 miles of equatorial waters between Malaya and Australia. It is a barrier between the Indian Ocean on the west and the South China Sea and Pacific Ocean on the east. Formerly called the East Indies, it was famed for its seas and straits and was likened to the Mediterranean and Caribbean regions, which also lie between two continents. The area is a strategic gateway to India and Australia, both of which were exposed to Japanese pressure when Indonesia fell in 1942. The islands are rich in natural resources, and the eastern sector, a backwater today, was called the Treasure Islands in the early days of Western expansion because of its valuable spices. In modern times, oil, rubber, quinine, nonferrous metals, and sugar made this colony most profitable to its Dutch rulers. Indonesia is also the most populous of the lands of Southeast Asia, with 80 million inhabitants. Its political center is in Java and nearby Madura, the most densely settled territory in the world, with a population of 52 million. Nearby Sumatra, to the northwest, has 12 million.[2] It was in these islands that the greatest political and cultural progress was made. The development of the archipelago as a whole was most uneven, with variations ranging from extensive urbanization on Java to primitive tribalism on Borneo and other outer islands.

Evolution of Dutch Rule

The Dutch gained control of the East Indies as part of a maritime expansion that netted a series of outposts from the southern tip of Africa to Japan. Holland lost South Africa and Ceylon to Britain but managed to retain the Indies, though these came under London's control during the Napoleonic War. The Dutch East India Company, which spearheaded this expansion, was primarily interested in trade and profits, and only reluctantly did it establish a territorial-political base of rule in the eighteenth century. It then found that the burden of running a government was a great handicap to profit making. By 1800 the Dutch government had assumed political control and had taken over the agreements made with native rulers. However, as Holland did not desire to exercise thorough control over the entire archipelago, attention was centered on Java and its environs. Only after 1900 was Dutch authority extended over all the outer islands. The move, motivated by fear of foreign intervention in this last feverish phase of European colonial expansion, required vigorous military campaigns. But Holland gave the islands a unified rule and a central adminis-

---

[2] The rest are Celebes, 6 million; Lesser Sundas, 5 million; Borneo, 4 million; the Moluccas, 2 million; others, 500,000.

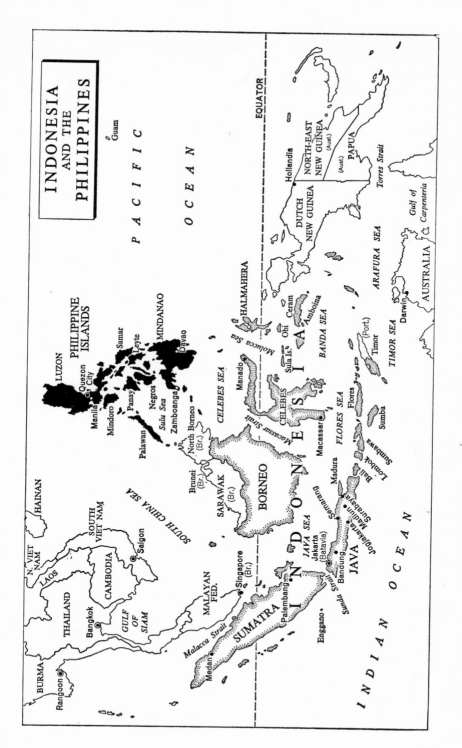

INDONESIA
AND THE
PHILIPPINES

PACIFIC

OCEAN

Guam

EQUATOR

Hollandia

NORTH-EAST
NEW GUINEA
(Aust.)

PAPUA
(Aust.)

Torres Strait

DUTCH
NEW GUINEA

Gulf of
Carpenteria

PHILIPPINE
ISLANDS

LUZON

Quezon
City

Manila

Mindoro

Palawan

Panay

Negros

MINDANAO

Samar

Leyte

Davao

Zamboanga

Sulu Sea

North Borneo
(Br.)

Brunei
(Br.)

SARAWAK
(Br.)

BORNEO

CELEBES SEA

Manado

Macassar Strait

CELEBES

HALMAHERA

Molucca Sea

Obi

Ceram

Amboina

Sula Is.

BANDA SEA

ARAFURA SEA

AUSTRALIA

Darwin

TIMOR SEA

Timor
(Port.)

I   N   D   O   N   E   S   I   A

FLORES SEA

Macassar

Flores

Sumba

Sumbawa

Lombok

Bali

Madura

Surabaja

Madiun

Jogjakarta

Bandung

Semarang

JAVA

Jakarta
(Batavia)

JAVA SEA

Sunda Strait

Palembang

SUMATRA

Enggano

Medan

Malacca Strait

MALAYAN
FED.

Singapore
(Br.)

SOUTH CHINA SEA

Saigon

SOUTH
VIET NAM

N. VIET
NAM

LAOS

HAINAN

CAMBODIA

THAILAND

Bangkok

GULF
OF
SIAM

BURMA

Rangoon

INDIAN   OCEAN

tration around which a spirit of nationalism and ambition for self-rule could crystallize.

When the government assumed full power it sought to end the budgetary deficits suffered by its predecessor. The Dutch East India Company used to receive a percentage of the peasant's crop as rent or tax payment. The Dutch now instituted the more profitable Culture System, requiring the peasants to place a certain part of their land and its produce at the government's disposal. The farmers then had to devote a specified number of days at labor, growing crops that the government exported for profit. This system proved a financial success, but it exposed the vulnerable peasants to grave abuses and had the further effect of closing the country to private enterprise and economic modernization. The Dutch middle class at home campaigned so vigorously for a more liberal program that late in the nineteenth century the government permitted modern trade and industry to develop in the Indies. The mother country also recognized its responsibility to protect the native people and their customs and guard them from exploitation. This Ethical Policy became the official creed by 1900. Such paternalistic rule, motivated by good intentions, had many admirable results. Unlike the British in Burma, Holland shielded its colony from the full dislocating impact of Western economic political and legal systems. Customary (*adat*) law was preserved where possible and the administration operated by means of indirect rule, governing through a native aristocracy. Thus Java and Madura were under a regency and contained four princely states, while the other islands had petty sultanates and other forms of local rule. The peasantry was protected from the Western legal system and the plagues of contracts, legal foreclosures, and the alienation of property through debt. As a result, landlessness and tenancy did not become major issues in Indonesia.

This method of rule has won high praise from observers like J. S. Furnival, who saw a marked contrast between the integrated society of the Indies and the social decomposition that afflicted Burma before 1941. Yet it can be argued that Indonesia was too thoroughly insulated from the West and was bound to suffer from the inevitable dislocations that followed independence and continued modernization. Indonesia's difficulty in organizing itself after 1950 can be traced in part to this background. For example, much political energy has been expended in debating whether, in the intellectual and conceptual sense, free Indonesia ought to have any Western orientation. A more specific criticism of Dutch rule is that indirect control was simply a façade. The general operations of colonial affairs were transacted under a heavily centralized administration completely dominated by the Dutch. Moreover, within this framework native authorities gained a power over the peasantry that the customs of precolonial days denied them. A further consequence of this system was a split within the numerically small native elite, for when a middle class developed, its nationalist fervor and cultural orientation brought it into conflict with most of the aristocracy.

Nor was Dutch rule a perfect model in the realm of economic welfare. Modern health measures, internal security, and stable economic conditions, beneficial ends in themselves, led to a tremendous population rise on Java and Madura: from 5 million in 1815 to 40 million in 1930 and almost 50 million in 1940. This increase meant exceedingly small holdings for the peasantry. It is even argued that mounting population pressure, with increased taxes and debts, caused a gradual impoverishment of the people in the generations after 1918. There was no significant effort at large-scale resettlement in the less crowded outer islands, nor was a vigorous program of industrialization undertaken to raise living standards. When the nationalist fever began to sweep the country, there was little in the government's record of economic achievement, however well-intentioned its paternalistic policy, to keep the peasantry loyal to the imperial regime.

The Rise of Nationalism

As in other Asian lands, the nationalist movement, which began about 1900, was centered in the new middle class. Young Asian students in Holland were impressed with the theory of democratic self-rule and quickly noted the difference between the authoritarian system at home and the self-government enjoyed by the Dutch people. This educational process also gave rise to other difficulties. Too few Indonesians received proper modern training, and those who did failed to win positions in Indonesian government and business commensurate with their skills. The staff of the Indonesian civil service was 79 per cent native, but this was primarily in the lowest ranks. Natives occupied 99 per cent of the lowest positions and only 6.9 per cent of the highest level of government posts.

Economic unrest was not confined to this "intellectual proletariat" alone. The first important Indonesian political party was the Sarekat Islam, founded in 1913 by Java business leaders who sought greater opportunity for native enterprises. Then, in the 1920's, the newly organized labor unions were the center of vigorous political activity against the Dutch. Also, the depression of the 1930's seriously reduced Indonesia's exports and compelled the Dutch to institute tariff barriers, thereby blocking peasant access to cheap Japanese goods. In addition, European and Chinese business elements held a favored position with regard to income and tax requirements, a condition that strengthened the economic bases of the nationalist movement. The Chinese in particular had assumed many middle-class functions; they controlled trade, dominated the capital market, and had the peasantry in their debt.

Indonesian nationalism before 1940, for all its vigor, lacked effective leadership and a sense of cohesion. The Sarekat Islam movement lost its early dominance when an internal struggle developed between moderates and radicals. After losing this contest, the radicals provoked violence and bitter strikes in the labor movement. This disturbance culminated in an armed uprising in 1926–1927, which was crushed by the government. The Dutch then instituted a system of tight political controls, enforced by rigorous police activity and an elaborate network of informants. The persistent strength of nationalism was reflected in the growth of "wild schools," where native youths were educated in an environment free from Dutch influence. Political study clubs also developed in the 1920's, and an Indonesian Nationalist party emerged under the fiery leadership of Achmed Sukarno. He called for noncooperation and sought to overthrow the Dutch by mass revolutionary action. Other important nationalists, including Mohammed Hatta and the socialist leader Sutan Sjahrir, disagreed with this concept of a mass political base. Instead, they sought to create a dedicated cadre around which an enduring movement could be built. In any event, the Dutch smashed all these groups in 1929–1930, sending their leaders into exile for the rest of the interwar period. Dutch rule appeared supreme, and only the most moderate nationalist movements were tolerated.

The ease with which nationalist movements were suppressed gave the regime a false sense of confidence. Secure in the illusion that its power was impregnable and that the Indonesians were loyal after 300 years of close ties with Holland, the government moved very slowly to initiate political reform. It therefore lost an opportunity to secure its political position on the islands before nationalism resumed its march to power. The Dutch did not consider their colony to be politically mature or adequately integrated to warrant self-rule. Actually, the area contained a variety of races and cultures, though the Malay tongue and Moslem religion were common unifying factors. The Netherlands government did envisage a future movement toward self-rule but conceived of it in very gradual, evolutionary terms. The objective was not independence but a binding union or confederation with Holland.

When some autonomy was extended to the East Indies in the 1920's it was of little value to the natives. A *Volksraad*, or legislature, was established, but it had to share power with a governor-general responsible to the Dutch government. Only the wealthy could vote, and even then one third of the *Volksraad* was appointed. Representation was along communal lines, and Indonesians received only half the seats. Reserve powers for both the governor-general and the Dutch government completed this restrictive system. The *Volksraad* was more influential in practice than might be inferred from this description, for its appointed and European members displayed an independent attitude. After the German conquest of Holland in 1940 most moderate nationalists were eager to cooperate with the Dutch, offering to establish a lasting commonwealth tie in return for responsible parliamentary self-government. However, the Netherlands government-in-exile at London was less important at this time than the Dutch colonial officials in the colony. These administrators were unsympathetic, rebuffed such offers, and even forbade the use of the term "Indonesia."

War and Revolution

The Japanese invaders of 1942 found the inhabitants antagonistic or indifferent to the Dutch, whose prestige was demolished by military defeat. The conquerors played on these anti-Western sentiments and sought Indonesian assistance in the war. They even permitted a native government to be organized under Sukarno and Hatta, who were brought back from exile. Other banished leaders also returned, but some chose to work underground against Japan in the struggle for freedom. Though Japan did not grant real power to the native regime, the establishment of this formal authority had an electrifying effect on the internal political situation. Possession of office raised nationalist prestige in peasant eyes and gave the Indonesians a psychological lift and feeling of confidence. The Sukarno regime organized a centrally controlled political apparatus on Java and Sumatra and established an administrative system loyal to the revolutionary cause. Every device of public office was used to spread nationalist propaganda among the people. An even more important achievement was the creation of a loyal and disciplined nationalist army.

When the war ended in 1945, Japan planted a "political time bomb" by quickly proclaiming an independent Republic of Indonesia. The British contingents that arrived to maintain order and demobilize the Japanese had to rely on the Republic, because it commanded popular loyalty and their own strength was insufficient to cope with the situation. The Dutch, indignant at both the Japanese and British, denounced these acts as giving substance to a "house of cards"—the nationalist Republic.

The next four years were marked by extensive but futile efforts by Holland to re-establish its power in Indonesia. As soon as Dutch troops arrived late in 1945, resistance developed on a full-fledged military scale. British forces succeeded in taking the naval and port city of Surabaya at the end of the year, but the extent of native opposition convinced them that a political settlement was more advisable than a forcible reoccupation of Java. The Dutch, however, grimly endeavored to reassert their paramountcy, and during 1946 they gained control of most of the Java coast. The Republic remained powerful on Sumatra and in the interior of Java, moving its capital from Jakarta (Batavia) inland to Jogjakarta. Meanwhile the Dutch succeeded in dominating the outer islands and establishing friendly regimes there. They planned to use these governments as units in a new Indonesian federal structure to insure the "political containment" of the Republic.

During the years 1946–1948 the Netherlands government vacillated between this type of political arrangement and forceful attempts (police actions) to eliminate the Republic entirely. A Conservative victory at home in the first postwar election pointed toward an attempt at a forceful reassertion of Dutch authority. A temporary settlement, the Linggadjati Agreement, was reached in November, 1946, providing for a free and democratic United States of Indonesia, composed of the Republic, Borneo, and East Indonesia. This federated state was to join in a Union with the Netherlands as an equal partner. Then, in 1947, the Dutch launched their first police action, which reduced Republican territory to a small segment of central Java. Despite this act, another compromise was arranged under the auspices of the United Nations, which had come into the picture when hostilities broke out in 1947. This second settlement, the Renville Agreement of January, 1948, was even more favorable to the Dutch. It carved new states out of the Republican territory and raised the number of federal units to sixteen. However, hoping to smash the Republic completely, the

Dutch launched an air-land assault in December, 1948, captured Jogjakarta, and overran all Republican territory.

Then the Dutch position disintegrated, just as it appeared to carry the day. Militarily, the Republic's army avoided capture, infiltrated the Dutch lines with its units intact, and brought pressure on the occupiers of Jogjakarta. The likelihood of a full-scale destructive war disturbed the civilian Dutch officials and businessmen in the colony. Holland's diplomatic position also suffered, for this second assault aligned the United Nations squarely against it—including the United States, which hitherto was hesitant to oppose its Dutch ally. The Asian nations held a special conference at New Delhi in January, 1949, demanding the transfer of sovereignty to Indonesia. Within Indonesia, the native federalist allies of the Dutch from the outer islands were alarmed by Holland's display of violence. They had been fearful of Javanese-Republican domination in a free state. The federalists now joined forces with the nationalists and demanded that the Netherlands honor a promise given in 1946 to create a United States of Indonesia by 1949. In their political isolation, the Dutch agreed to negotiate with the Indonesians at Round Table Conferences held at The Hague in 1949. The federalist-nationalist alignment held firm, and an agreement was reached in November, 1949, that established the United States of Indonesia.

The Form of Independence

An elaborate federal structure was created, but it lasted less than one year. The accompanying Netherlands-Indonesia Union, on which the Dutch pinned such high hopes, was dissolved in five years. Holland's proposal for a binding union was rejected by all native factions, who would accept only a loose tie that stressed national independence and had absolutely no status under international law. The ruler of the Netherlands was recognized as the head of the union, but the only regular agencies created were a secretariat and a court of arbitration. The turning point was Indonesia's refusal to accept any formal machinery for cooperation in defense, foreign policy, or economic affairs. Dutch civil servants and military advisers stayed during the transitional period, and Holland loaned the new state $52 million. Nevertheless, relations deteriorated rapidly between 1950 and 1955. A major source of friction was the nationalist claim that Dutch New Guinea (West Irian) should be transferred to Indonesia as part of the new state's birthright. The Netherlands refused to yield this backward territory because its inhabitants were ethnically unrelated to the Indonesians.

Another difficulty stemmed from the Indonesian guarantee of 1949 to safeguard and respect Dutch investments and property. This settlement secured a privileged position for the fairly extensive holdings of Dutch nationals. As a continuing symbol of imperial rule, it was bound to cause tension in a newly independent state. The extremely bitter feeling against Holland that persisted after independence fed on this alleged inequity. Indonesia tried repeatedly to renegotiate a settlement, arguing that the guarantee retarded the country's economic growth. The nationalists claimed that the agreement was in derogation of their parliament's sovereign right to have jurisdiction over the economic concessions to be made to foreigners. The Dutch refused to yield to the claims that all foreigners should receive equal treatment. Nor were they impressed by the moderate nature of Indonesia's proposed legislation on this problem, for without treaty safeguards there was no guarantee that an extreme nationalist cabinet would respect these laws. The weak Netherlands-Indonesian Union could not survive in this hostile environment and, under Indonesian insistence, was formally dissolved in 1954. Two years later the Indonesians unilaterally declared the economic settlement of 1949 was no longer in effect.

The federated United States of Indonesia created under Dutch influence was even shorter-lived. It took only from November, 1949, to August, 1950, for the Republic to absorb all other fifteen states. The Republic had been the spearhead of the revolution and the other units lacked its dynamism and prestige. The dual governments (federal at Jakarta and republican at Jogjakarta) proved an awkward system as well as a heavy drain on personnel. The Republic quickly regained the regions carved from its domain by the "police actions," and by August, 1950, even the outer island states ceded their authority. A unitary Republic of Indonesia was created with a capital at Jakarta under its original leaders, President Sukarno and Vice-President Hatta.

The Problems of Government

The new state of Indonesia began operations under a provisional constitution that provided for a parliamentary form of government. As a result, the executive was directed by a premier and his cabinet who were responsible to the national assembly, but the formal relationship between the premier and the president was not clearly defined. President Sukarno was an ambitious leader with tremendous popular appeal, who supported the extreme nationalist position against the Dutch. He did not conceive his role as a ceremonial chief of state. Instead, he intervened in party struggles, frequently in a decisive manner.

The first parliament, which served until 1955, was an appointed one, with a membership roughly proportional to the estimated strengths of existing political groups. As a consequence, no party enjoyed a clear majority and the country was governed by a series of coalition cabinets. The two leading parties, the Nationalist and Masjumi (Moslem) found it difficult to work together, and hostility between them increased annually. Personal rivalries, the prevalence of cliques, a dependence on splinter parties, and a rapid turnover of cabinets came to characterize the Indonesian scene. Vice-President Hatta headed the first post-independent cabinet (1949–1950), but he soon resigned as premier in order to stay out of the immediate political struggle. The Masjumi then dominated the government between 1950 and 1952, with Mohammed Natsir, the party's chief and leader of its reformist wing, in office in 1950–1951. He was followed by the Sukiman Cabinet (1951–1952), whose leader represented the Masjumi's more conservative, orthodox wing. Significantly, this government was overthrown in 1952 because it accepted American aid under the Mutual Security Program, which required all recipients to pledge to maintain their independence and strengthen the free world. This relatively harmless statement involved no alliance commitment or political obligation, but the Nationalists were able to appeal to the country's neutralist sentiment and overturn the mildly pro-Western Masjumi cabinet.

Another moderate cabinet under Premier Wipolo held office in 1952–1953, but it too fell under Nationalist pressure. The Nationalists finally took office, without Masjumi support and with the blessings of President Sukarno. This cabinet, headed by Ali Sastroamidjojo, depended on the Communists for its parliamentary majority. It followed a firmly neutralist line in foreign policy, was vigorously anti-Dutch, and joined with President Sukarno in frequent demands for the "return" of Irian. The Ali government tried to stay in office in the hope of dominating the first national election, scheduled for 1955. The Masjumi denounced the Nationalists as a party without a program that was behaving in a cynical and opportunistic manner by collaborating with the Communists. The complaint was also made that Premier Ali was a mere figurehead through whom President Sukarno was exercising real authority without being accountable to the legislature. It was during this administration that President Sukarno became estranged from other major political leaders. A marked rift has even developed between the president and Vice-President Hatta, to whom the Moslem political groups looked for leadership.

Another important development was the rise in prestige of the Communist party during the Ali administration. Both the Nationalists and the Communists hoped to use the other to their own advantage in this collaboration. Though the Indonesian Communist party held no ministerial posts, it exercised some influence over policy. This was a sharp rise from the depths to which the party sank in 1948. In September of that critical year the Communists launched a revolt at Maduin against the Republican government but were crushed by Republican forces under Colonel Nasution. The party began operating in a legal manner after 1950 and, with the rise in prestige of Communist China and the growing influence of its embassy in Jakarta, it began to make up lost ground. The Communists were particularly successful in infiltrating and dominating SOBSI, the country's largest labor federation. The sympathetic government of 1953–1955 helped the party to complete its political comeback.

The Army and Politics

The fall of the Ali cabinet in 1955 brought to a climax still another facet of Indonesia's political problems, the role of the armed forces. The army had been loyal to the united revolutionary leaders during the war against the Netherlands and was a factor of growing importance in the unstable political environment that came with freedom. However, there had been some friction within the army over the question of reorganization. In 1952 the defense minister, the Sultan of Jogjakarta, who was one of the heroes of the revolution, presented a plan to modernize the armed forces, reduce their size, and improve military efficiency. This problem had significant political overtones, because the sultan and many professional military leaders were friendly with Socialist party leader Sutan

Sjahrir and were intellectually if not politically oriented toward the West. These officials also worked closely with the Netherlands Military Mission, established for three years in 1951. The proposed reforms were challenged by the leaders of irregular troop units whose power was now jeopardized. They in turn were backed by the Nationalists who, supported by President Sukarno, accused the modernists of being unable to think in a "proper Indonesian manner." As a result of this conflict, the Dutch mission was terminated, the reform failed, and the defense minister resigned at the end of 1952. It was shortly after this that the Nationalists took office.

By 1955, however, the political tide had turned somewhat against the Nationalists, as their administration came under fire for corruption and excessive concessions to the Communists. The army opposed the cabinet's nominee for a new chief of staff and had its revenge when the cabinet fell during the ensuing ministerial crisis. President Sukarno was abroad at this time and Vice-President Hatta handled the negotiations that led to the formation of a moderate, Masjumi-led coalition under Premier Burnanuddin Harahap. Colonel Nasution, who had a reputation of being a firm anti-Communist, became the new chief of staff. In any event, it is questionable whether military subordination to civilian rule can be perpetuated if cabinet instability, a rising Communist menace, and political recourse to military support continue.

The Election of 1955

The Harahap government assumed the role of caretaker administration to conduct the elections and stayed in office until the new parliament assembled in the spring of 1956. A complex system of proportional representation was used to elect the new legislature, as well as a separate constituent assembly in a second election held shortly after the first. On the whole, the election was a fair one, with a second ballot held where legitimate complaints were registered. The Harahap cabinet achieved a good record of weeding out the corruption inherited from the previous regime and bringing some order out of the chaotic situation it inherited with regard to the budget and foreign exchange. The Masjumi party had been most persistent in calling for this long-delayed election because it was confident of victory, an opinion generally seconded by most foreign observers in Indonesia.

However, the election brought surprising results, generally confirming the stalemate that had been reflected in the political maneuverings of recent years. The Masjumi party was thwarted in its quest for a majority by the unexpected success of another Islamic group, the Moslem Teachers party (Nahdatul Ulama), which had broken off from the Masjumi in 1951 because the latter was too conservative. The Communists also scored heavily, whereas the Socialist party won fewer than 5 per cent of the total vote. The Communists and Nationalists did well in Central Java as well as in their acknowledged stronghold of East Java, while the Masjumi made its strongest showing in the outlying islands. The Nationalists (8,434,653 votes) finished slightly ahead of the Masjumi (7,903,886), though each won fifty-seven seats in the legislature. The Moslem

Teachers, also called the Moslem Orthodox Radicals, received 6,955,141 votes and forty-five seats. The Communists, with 6,176,914 votes, netted thirty-nine seats. President Sukarno declared after the election that he favored Communist participation in a coalition government. Both Moslem parties, though they could not cooperate with each other, were firm in their refusal to deal with the Communists. They agreed to join a Nationalist cabinet headed by Ali Sastro-amidjojo, and this three-party coalition government was formed in March, 1956. Premier Ali, who also has expressed his desire for Communist participation, seeks to bring about a "united front" coalition of Communist-Nationalist-Moslem Teachers that will exclude the Masjumi from office.

The Problem of Order and National Cohesion

The unitary state had been formed in the heat of nationalist anger at Holland in 1950. The absence of an adequate public service to administer such a wide area raises questions about the efficiency of this structure. The state's cohesion is also threatened by fears of "Javanese imperialism" in the outer islands. To a certain extent these problems are related to the government's inability to exer-cise a true monopoly of violence. The habit of violence, acquired during the political turmoil of the 1940's, has been difficult to suppress and banditry has existed in Java since Japan gave arms to native elements in 1945. During the ensuing years of revolution, robbery and looting became so widespread that many sections of Java were considered unsafe for travel. This situation gradu-ally improved, but in 1955 road and rail lines were still not fully secured. There has also been continuous, large-scale pilfering from ships in Indonesian harbors.

Guerilla activity has been a recurrent phenomenon, frequently resorted to by groups who are opposed to the government on political grounds. Foremost of these is the Dar-ul-Islam, a right-wing religious movement that seeks to overturn the constitutional order and establish a theocratic state. It has used fanatical terrorist tacts in pursuit of this objective. The Dar-ul-Islam operates from a strong base in West Java, but it is influential elsewhere on the island and has successfully kept the government from establishing firm control over these areas. A lesser and briefer menace shortly after 1949 was a force of irregulars led by a Dutchman, Captain Westerling, which caused considerable trouble before it was eliminated. This incident further strengthened persistent Indonesian fears that Holland was still a threat to the country's freedom.

Fear of Javanese domination of the outer islands revived after the departure of Dutch rule. On the other hand, Republican leaders remained suspicious of the federalist concept, since it was a device employed against them by the Dutch. To this political issue are added, as obstacles to national unity, the poor lines of communication and a low literacy rate. A particularly difficult situation flared up in the eastern islands—the Moluccas, Macassar, and Amboina—where insurrections took place in 1950–1951 and again in 1954–1955. Political oppor-tunism, regionalist loyalties, and the desire for autonomy were important causes of unrest. In addition, this region, especially Amboina, was a traditional source of manpower for the Dutch colonial army. When the Indonesian government reduced and eliminated these formations, anti-Javanese sentiment found expression in military and popular uprisings. Another sore spot has been Achin, the extreme northwest section of Sumatra, long known for its localist sentiment. Agitation against the regime in 1954 became intertwined with the struggle for land reform. The Jakarta government was particularly embarrassed because certain squatter settlements were located on Dutch estates and so were in direct conflict with foreign economic interests, which the central authorities were under treaty obligations to protect.

Before the Ali cabinet could complete one year in office it was plagued by further rebellions in Sumatra, corruption, scandals, and a constitutional crisis. Popular discontent with the government's failure to establish a sound political order was seconded by a keen disappointment over its inability to sustain an economic development program. This discontent found expression in an unsuccessful coup of November, 1956, the resignation of Vice-President Hatta, and an army-led rebellion in Sumatra just as the year ended.

The Sumatra rebels demanded more autonomy in domestic island affairs and the expenditure of more government funds on local projects. Rebels and officials in the central and southern parts of the island withheld provincial revenues derived from customs duties, excise taxes, government services, and public enterprises. This was particularly significant, since oil and rubber exports from Sumatra accounted for 71 per cent of Indonesia's foreign exchange.

The weak coalition government lost Masjumi support but, sustained by President Sukarno, it managed to hold power despite a series of scandals which exposed some high officials as embezzlers and manipulators of the exchange rate. Masjumi efforts to topple the cabinet involved a plan to have a Hatta-led government replace it, but the votes for this maneuver were lacking. Vice-President Hatta resigned in protest against the government's inadequacy and the positions taken by President Sukarno on many issues. A confirmed democrat and neutralist, Hatta believed that only a government on the American model could resolve Indonesia's dilemma. By this he meant a strong presidential-cabinet system and a federal structure with autonomy for the state governments. He was perturbed by the president's willingness to cooperate with the Communist party, his toleration of the Nationalist-led cabinet, and his theory that Indonesia had to gain West Irian to complete its revolution. Since President Sukarno had already stated his belief that parties should be "buried," Masjumi and other factional leaders feared that he would use the existing crisis to scrap all political groups and assume dictatorial rule.

For his part, President Sukarno disavowed such intentions but held that Western parliamentary democracy, suitable enough in prosperous and literate communities, was too complex for Indonesia. To preserve democracy he proposed to break the existing pattern and create an authoritative advisory council under presidential chairmanship, composed of representatives of military and religious groups. It would act as his consultative agency but with power to pass on all major decisions taken by the parliament. Mohammed Natsir described this proposal for "guided democracy" as a threat to the republic's survival.

Conclusion

The Constituent Assembly, meeting since November, 1956, was thus confronted with an embittered continuation of the Masjumi-Nationalist conflict, now extended to differing views about the nation's basic organization. The communist menace, if anything, was intensified by this development. The other questions still remain—what to do about regional autonomy and how to appease the adherents of an Islamic state. Finally, Indonesia must still create an effective public administration service if it is to proceed systematically with plans to realize its great economic potential.

The Philippines

In 1898 the United States gained control of the Philippine Islands as a totally unanticipated consequence of the Spanish-American War and, in one long leap, found itself enmeshed in the power politics of the Far East. The colony was to become an important factor in United States diplomacy and military strategy, but America's attitude toward this distant possession was one of indifference. After the exuberance aroused by Admiral Dewey's conquest of Manila, popular interest declined precipitously. The government was left to grapple with the novel problem of ruling a people who could not be incorporated into the federal union for reasons of race, culture, and geography. Opposition to this annexation was strong from the first, and the peace treaty with Spain was barely passed by the Senate. With the onset of an agricultural depression after 1919, pressure mounted to put a tariff on Philippine exports to America. There was also considerable agitation against the admission of 5,000 Filipino immigrants a year. In the 1930's, American idealists who wanted the island to be free combined with these special economic interests to have a pledge of independence given in 1934, a promise that was honored in 1946.

How effective was American rule in assisting the islands' evolution toward democracy, economic well-being, and social stability? This question must be studied in terms of America's impact on a Malay people occupying a subtropical archipelago. But we must also consider the three centuries of Spanish rule that had a profound impact of its own. Personal and place names, the Catholic faith, and the economic and administrative structures all bear evidence of a Spanish legacy that made the Philippines resemble Latin America in many ways. It is not surprising that only limited changes in the Filipino political culture should occur during the two generations of American rule.

The Philippine and Spanish Background

Centuries of foreign rule have given the Philippines a high degree of unity and political cohesion, despite the great cultural diversity reflected in a variety of ethnic and linguistic groups. Christianity is the religion of 90 per cent of the people (80 per cent are Catholic) ; there are one million Moros (Moslems) in the southern island of Mindanao and an equal number of pagans throughout the islands. The land itself is rich in resources and fertile soil, but only one quarter of the arable land was cultivated before 1941. The mass of the people did not enjoy a decent standard of living and suffered the poor conditions of life experienced throughout East Asia. The rice bowl of central Luzon, the main island, is the most heavily populated section, the scene of direst poverty, and the source of most political unrest. Under Spanish rule, a sharp class divergency between aristocrat and peasant occurred. However, a native middle class of considerable size developed, especially after 1900, and almost one third of the population lived in cities of 15,000 or more. Spanish-Filipino and Chinese-Filipino mestizos form the core of this class, and their mixed ancestry is a symbol of social prestige. As in nearby countries, the population of the Philippines has risen markedly, from 7 million in 1900 to 21,440,000 in 1954.

The major Spanish achievements since their conquest of the islands during the sixteenth century were in religious conversion and in administration. By contrast, economic development was hindered and an oppressive political and social system was introduced. Before the Spaniards arrived the Filipinos had a loose system of village government in which the basic unit was a group of fifty or more families. The new rulers inaugurated a heavily centralized rule whose effects are still felt today. At the center was the governor-general to whom all administrators of provinces, districts, and lesser units were responsible. The landholding system resembled Europe's feudal order. Spanish nobles were awarded large tracts of land and as caciques, or political masters, of these estates they exercised almost full control over their serfs. A parallel authority was the Church, whose clergy often served to mitigate the impersonal and harsh rule of the political authorities and landlords. The Church was also instrumental in having slavery abolished as a legal practice, though the problem of human bondage has persisted here as elsewhere in Southeast Asia.

The friars of the Church gained control over vast tracts of land and proved an important influence in political and social affairs. By the nineteenth century, both the nobles and friars were considered unbearably oppressive by a large segment of the native population. After 1850, when the China trade opened and Spain's prestige suffered accordingly, Manila's importance as a seaport declined sharply. The ideals of nationalism and democracy that were causing unrest and disturbances in Spain soon spread to the island colony. Late in the century, intellectual reformers like Marcelo del Pilar and José Rizal popularized these novel doctrines, and there arose a revolutionary group, the Katipernan, led by Andres Bonifacio and Emilio Aguinaldo. A revolt in 1896 was suppressed, Rizal was killed and so martyred, and other leaders went into exile. When the United States declared war against Spain in 1898, it destroyed the Spanish fleet in Manila Bay and landed forces on Luzon. Filipino cooperation in the encirclement of Manila was most valuable. The Americans collaborated with the insurrectionists, bringing Aguinaldo back from exile, and the nationalists in turn assisted the invaders in their capture of Manila. The native leaders who then declared their independence were shocked to learn that the United States had replaced the weak Spanish regime. Their response was another rebellion under the militant Aguinaldo, but American troops quelled this uprising after a short but violent campaign.

American Colonial Policy

A Commission headed by J. G. Schurman investigated the political situation and reported that the Philippines were unprepared for self-rule. This belief formed the basis for American policy, which was to tutor the Filipinos in the light of their own customs and so train them for eventual independence. The early period of rule under Republican administrations (1900–1913) bore the mark of the islands' first civilian chief, William Howard Taft, who called the Filipinos "our little brown brothers" and strove to implant a moderate, paternalistic rule. He asserted the primacy of civilian rule over American military administrators and, though no promise of independence was given, planned to increase native participation in governmental affairs as the Filipinos gained experience. American colonial policy followed the great traditions of the rule of law and self-limitation on administrative powers. The Philippine people were given all the civil rights enjoyed by Americans, except trial by jury and the right to bear arms.

In the first years of American rule, the Filipinos formed a Federalist party, favoring autonomy within the American union. But the doctrine of complete independence soon predominated, and the Nationalist party, founded in 1907, spearheaded the drive for freedom. It so dominated Filipino politics, including the legislative assembly, also established in 1907, that a virtual one-party system developed. The great Nationalist leader, Manuel Quezon, proved a devoted patriot, a competent party boss, and a popular figure among the masses. Though some independents like Tomas Confesor were popular in their own right, Quezon's control over the nationalist movement proved unshakable.

American tutelege failed to produce a competitive party system or give the Filipinos adequate administrative experience. Policy toward the colony inevitably became an issue in domestic American politics. The Democratic triumph of 1912 led to a rapid Filipinization of the public service and the establishment of a native majority in the country's executive body, the Philippine Commission. A definite promise of independence was made, to take effect when a "stable government" was established. Meanwhile the Jones Bill of 1916 granted broader autonomy to the Filipinos. Republican critics of this sweeping program argued that corruption and inefficiency were undermining the colonial administration and that the native government was far from competent. When they returned to power in 1921, the Republicans reintroduced tighter American controls. The Filipinos strongly resented this move, as well as the high moralistic tone adopted by the colonial administration. Clearly, the path toward self-rule was decidedly uneven and beset with frustrations for ruler and colony alike. There was also justice on both sides—the Americans proved insensitive to the impact of nationalism, and the Filipinos did not exhibit the level of administrative competence required for self-government.

By 1930 the combination of idealism, economic pressure by groups opposed to Filipino competition, and colonial nationalism led to a precipitous drive to grant freedom. In spite of a veto by President Herbert Hoover, Congress passed an independence bill, based on an agreement with a Filipino Commission headed by Sergio Osmeña and Manuel Roxas. The act provided for independence in ten years, allowed American military bases, established strict control over Filipino immigration, and placed quota limits and tariffs on Philippine goods. Quezon opposed this settlement for reasons of personal prestige and because some of the clauses were too harsh. He had the Philippine Assembly reject this act and in 1934 personally negotiated a new agreement—the Tydings-McDuffie Act. It left the question of bases to be settled later and won better import quotas on sugar and coconut oil, but little else was changed. The Filipinos still owed allegiance to the United States during the ten-year transitional period, and Washington retained the right to interfere in native affairs. The agreement contained provisions for a quota on free-trade goods and a tariff schedule that was to be gradually intensified. In 1939 the period of favorable treatment for Philippine goods was extended beyond the proposed date of independence (1946) in order to prevent economic dislocations.

Economic Problems

These complex arrangements indicated that serious economic problems were involved in the separation of the colony from the United States. Paradoxically, while the United States was guiding the Philippines toward political freedom it was, perhaps unwittingly, undermining the islands' chances of maintaining economic independence. In the first place, the American regime did not systematically plan the development of the nation's economy. Investment and trade were geared to private-profit motives, and little attention was paid to broadening the nation's industrial base or expanding its productivity in an orderly manner. Production lagged in both consumer and producer goods, and only extractive industries and processing mills were developed to any extent. Americans accounted for 60 per cent of all foreign investment, but this amounted to a relatively slight $258 million. Most efforts were centered in mining, electric power, and export industries. Sugar production—primarily for export—was the major industry, involving 2 million people. Manufacturing assets in 1938 were only $178 million; other totals were mining, $100 million; utilities, $28 million; and lumber, $18 million. Philippine capital accounted for 35 per cent of the manufacturing and 48 per cent of the mining investments. In agriculture, the archaic Spanish land-tenure system had hardly been touched, since American authorities respected these early grants.

A second major issue was the close integration of this economy with the lucrative American consumer market. Spain retained special trading privileges with the Philippines until 1908; when these expired the rights of other powers, under the most-favored-nation clause, also lapsed. Free trade between the Philippines and the United States was established between 1909 and 1913, thus giving the colony a great advantage over all other foreign competitors in the American market. Sugar was the largest cash crop developed under this stimulus; other products were coconut, tobacco, manila hemp (abaca) and copra. Total trade rose from $34 million in 1899 to $250 million in 1940, and the American share rose from 16 to 75 per cent. With such great stress on plantation crops, the Philippines resembled other countries specializing in raw materials. Yet its very foundation rested on American tariff policy. The economy became distorted in the sense that it could not compete in world markets if it had to face the same American customs barrier that confronted all other states. In stressing these exports the country failed to maintain self-sufficiency in rice production, though it could easily have achieved this objective. Moreover, those who profited from these sales of cash crops did little to modernize the economy or build up its productive capacity. Even with a cushion of gradual tariffs and free-trade quotas on certain items, many Filipinos came to see the value of a commonwealth tie to America as an alternative to complete independence. Military-strategic considerations reinforced this view when the Japanese menace began to loom large in 1940.

The Need for Reform

A new constitutional system was put into effect in 1935 following the Tydings-McDuffie Act. It included a six-year term for the president and a unicameral legislature; in 1940 the constitution was amended to resemble the American system of a four-year executive period and two legislative bodies. President Quezon remained in firm control of the government; in fact, when he stood for re-election in 1941 he won 90 per cent of the vote without even campaigning. The opposition accused the legislature of subservience to the president and described it as a center of corruption and opportunism. The civil service continued to operate with a certain degree of efficiency, though not at the level enjoyed under the American-controlled merit system. Thus the country's political and administrative structure encountered some difficulty in making the transition to democratic self-government, but the Philippine record was not markedly different from the experiences of the older Western democracies in their early phases of development.

The government left more to be desired in the realm of social and economic reform. The American rulers had made considerable progress in public health, which at one time had been so poor that the Philippines suffered the highest infant death rate in the world. Manila was made into a modern city with an improved harbor, and a transportation network was developed on Luzon and the other islands. A public education program that included the teaching of English was introduced, but despite its wide scope almost half the children of school age did not receive the prescribed training. The average peasant could not spare his children's labor even though schooling was free. It is significant that the poor had little chance to vote, for literacy qualifications restricted the franchise to 14 per cent of the population. The educational system was centralized and its services were curtailed in 1940 in economy moves that further limited the value of the program.

The economic system as a whole operated for the benefit of the few. The distribution of income was highly unequal, with landlords and, to some extent, the urban centers profiting at the peasants' expense. In addition, there developed an excessive concentration of people in central Luzon. Tenancy abuses in this rice bowl of the Philippines were most flagrant, and the region actually became overpopulated, though the country as a whole was not densely settled. The government, because it was intimately related to the economic ruling class, proved unable to legislate major reforms. The Quezon administration's response to these grave problems was a relatively ineffective "social justice program." Its primary objectives were to protect farm tenants and urban workers, assure better wage rates and fairer rents, and encourage peasant migration from Luzon to the less sparsely settled island of Mindanao. Very little legislation was actually passed, and even this was not adequately enforced.

Unrest spread throughout the countryside in the 1930's, though Quezon's personal popularity remained undiminished. However, the privileged class, in effect protected by the aura of his prestige, controlled the apparatus of government and prevented any effective protest from being registered through constitutional channels. There was a series of weak revolts against authority, the most important being the Sakdal uprising of 1935, but these were crushed by government forces. Efforts were also made to form a party representing the underprivileged, but such attempts failed for lack of funds, adequate leadership, and organizational skill. By 1940 the temper of the opposition was such that when the president was given emergency powers, primarily because of the Japanese threat, it accused the administration of imitating fascist Spain. In the years just preceding the Japanese invasion the socialists and Communists began to lead the agitation for greater democracy and economic reform. Labor unrest mounted and peasant-tenant riots in central Luzon became more frequent. These were portents of the intensive troubles which were to confront the Philippines in the chaotic period of the 1940's.

War, Independence, and American Relations

The Filipinos were shocked by Japan's successful invasion and conquest of their homeland in 1941–1942. The Americans had failed in their trust to protect the islands, defense preparations were inadequate, and organized resistance collapsed after a valiant defensive stand on Bataan Peninsula, Luzon, early in 1942. This disaster was used as a rationalization by those who collaborated with the Japanese occupation force. President Quezon and Vice-President Sergio Osmeña established their government-in-exile in America, but many die-hard anti-Americans, including the aging Aguinaldo, supported a pro-Japanese policy. A republic created by Japan in 1942 was headed by President Jose

Laurel, but the collaborationist issue became blurred when those accused of helping Japan pleaded hidden patriotic motives or the expediency of self-preservation.

Filipino units fought loyally with the American forces in the early campaigns of 1942, undertaking widespread guerilla and intelligence operations against the Japanese during the occupation. Native troops also cooperated with the American counterinvasion of 1944–1945, when Leyte (1944), Luzon (1945), and the rest of the islands were liberated. This record of military collaboration with the West was unequalled elsewhere in Southeast Asia. The promise of independence, the permeation of Western ideals, and a bond of Philippine-American friendship contributed to this war record. With the removal of the Japanese, the prewar government returned, with Sergio Osmeña as president following the death of Quezon late in the war. The formal transfer of sovereignty was completed as scheduled, on July 4, 1946, despite the dislocations caused by the war, for democratic traditions were considered sufficiently secure to warrant such quick action.

American economic aid during 1944–1946 was essential because the country had suffered severely from the harsh Japanese rule and from the loss of trade and inflation accompanying it. Japan's resistance to the American assaults of 1944–1945 had also resulted in widespread damage and destruction. American aid, which was generous—about $1 billion—was extended in the form of soldier and veteran pay, wages for labor, war damages, and surplus property grants. Unfortunately, this assistance under the Tyding Rehabilitation Act was not used constructively or prudently by the recipients to strengthen the economy.

Moreover, the benefits of the act were all but forgotten in the light of the economic agreement that the American Congress passed as a supplement to Philippine independence. This agreement—the Bell Trade Act—barely got through the Philippine legislature, where it was denounced as a humiliating vestige of economic colonialism that would keep the country dependent on the United States. The Act provided for free trade until 1954 and limited tariff duties for twenty years thereafter, but many Philippine export items were to be limited by quotas. What rankled most was a provision giving Americans preferential treatment over other foreigners, by allowing them the same rights Filipinos enjoyed to possess land and exploit natural resources. To carry out this provision, the Philippine constitution had to be amended, for it placed all foreigners at an equal disadvantage in these matters. Filipino antagonism to this agreement led to repeated demands for its revision.

Poor management of economic affairs after 1945 was reflected in the Philippines' inability to maintain exports, unwise expenditure of valuable foreign currency on luxury imports, and continued importation of food and other products that actually could have been produced at home. By 1950 the trade balance was so precarious that import and currency restrictions had to be introduced. When chronic budgetary deficits led to further requests for American aid, the United States dispatched the Bell Economic Survey Mission in 1950 to make an intensive investigation of the situation. It recommended a modest five-year-aid plan costing $250 million, with both governments providing technical missions to improve conditions in the Philippines. But the Filipinos had sought aid on a grand scale, similar to that of the Marshall Plan for Europe; they were also upset by the unfavorable American comments on government fiscal policy and the inefficiency, corruption, and swollen size of the bureaucracy. The Bell Mission, like other study groups before it, deplored the feudal conditions prevailing in most villages and emphasized the need for immediate agrarian reform. The Philippine government challenged this "interference in internal affairs." It considered these criticisms gratuitous, since they came from a government that had done little to alter the situation for almost half a century. Nonetheless, the aid program was put into effect and the economy made gradual, if unspectacular, progress. It developed a more balanced and diversified structure and moved closer to a competitive position in the world market. As in other aspects of Filipino-American relations, tensions and differences over the aid program were widely publicized, but they were of minor importance, compared with constructive achievements.

This latter generalization applies to political relations between the two countries. In 1948 the Philippines granted military bases to the United States, despite a flurry of nationalist, anti-American sentiment leading to protest demonstrations. In 1956 the United States yielded to Filipino desires by transferring ownership of the bases to the Philippines while continuing to utilize them. The main Philippine concern was that the islands would be unprotected. Since even colonial status proved an inadequate guarantee in 1941, verbal assurances of American support after independence were considered insufficient. In order to overcome Filipino anxiety over a resurgent Japan and win Manila's approval of the 1951 peace treaty, the United States signed a defense treaty with the Philippines, pledging its aid against an attack. In general, Philippine foreign policy has avoided extreme nationalism, stressed cooperation with the United States, and avoided neutralism in the Cold War. Yet it has not been simply a handmaiden of American foreign policy and has had in Carlos Romulo a diplomat of international stature. The country has vigorously supported other colonial efforts at independence and has participated in many cultural and political activities of Southeast Asia. It vainly fostered regional political solidarity in 1949–1950 and has seen its earlier hopes of becoming a political leader of Southeast Asia treated as quixotic and unrealistic. Since 1950, the Philippines have taken a firm anti-Communist stand, extended military support to the United States–United Nations operations in Korea, and served as host nation to the treaty conference that established the Southeast Asia defense organization (Manila Pact) in 1954.

The Party System

Philippine politics after the war was featured by the development of a two-party system, with the Liberals challenging the Nationalists and capturing the presidency in the years 1946–1953. The constitutional order proved strong enough to withstand the shock of postwar dislocations, violence and fraud in elections, and a serious Communist-led rebellion. The party system featured cliques, rapid transfers of allegiance, and stress on personalities rather than issues. It has been somewhat volatile, resembling that of Japan in its early stages of democratic self-rule. Yet in 1953 a fair election was held, and since that time the legal channels of government have proved broad enough to enable the passage of long-range reform legislation.

The death of Manuel Quezon was a serious blow to the Nationalists, for President Osmeña could not keep this party united in the confused period following military liberation. He was defeated in the 1946 election by the Liberal candidate, Manuel Roxas, a more dynamic personality. Roxas claimed to be on better terms with the Americans, despite the fact that he was an official in the Laurel regime and was accused of collaboration with the Japanese. He had married into a cacique family, and, despite promises of reform, his administration did little to challenge the privileged positions of the landlords in the countryside. Nor did the upper class suffer when Roxas died unexpectedly in 1948 and was succeeded by Vice-President Elpidio Quirino; he too failed to induce his party to carry out a reform program. His Nationalist opponents also came from this same privileged class, and did not differ from the Liberals in fundamental policy. However, the Nationalists claimed greater competence in fostering economic development and promised to renegotiate the economic agreement with the United States. Ironically, this party of Quezon now turned to the still-popular Jose Laurel for its leadership and nominated him to run against the Liberal Quirino in the 1949 election.

The campaign centered on the issue of corruption in government and the personalities of the candidates. Like the 1946 election, which was marked by bitterness and brutality, this contest produced a high degree of violence and fraud. Quirino and the Liberals won, but many argued that a fair tabulation would have given the victory to Laurel. During the next four years, the administration was mercilessly criticized as corrupt, and incompetent in its dealings with the United States. Laurel and other old-guard anti-Americans wanted to loosen ties with America. Quirino himself was constantly at odds with Washington over the foreign-trade issue, the Japanese peace treaty and reparations, the need for greater aid, and American criticisms of conditions in the Philippines. The Bell Mission of 1950 provided ammunition for Quirino's opponents by listing a wide variety of reforms that were essential counterparts to an effective aid program. These included a more efficient and honest tax collection, paring down of swollen bureaucratic staffs, an end to the extensive practice of using public offices as sinecures for political friends and relations, and the introduction of a comprehensive land reform program.

Another major problem was the government's inability to maintain law and order in the face of a major Communist revolt and widespread banditry. Only after 1950, when Ramon Magsaysay became the minister of defense, was systematic progress made along these lines. Magsaysay's popularity rose suddenly because of his proved competence, and he soon rivaled President Quirino as the government's leading figure. As a contest between the two took shape, Magsaysay resigned from the government early in 1953. He argued that the program to maintain law and order was not being pursued with sufficient vigor and, moreover, could not succeed without widespread reforms that would reduce the communist appeal. He then became the Nationalist candidate for president and was strongly supported by Laurel, despite his own extremely pro-American outlook. The 1953 election proved a fair and comparatively orderly one, and Magsaysay defeated Quirino by a smashing two-to-one margin.

The Problem of Internal Security

Under Magsaysay, as defense minister and president, internal peace became firmly secured. After 1945, with many people possessing rifles and accustomed to guerilla fighting, banditry spread though the islands on a large scale. One shocking incident in 1949 was the highway murder of the widow of Manuel Quezon and most of her party while traveling in northern Luzon. The Communist menace became most acute at this time. For a while even the country-side around Manila and the capital itself were endangered. As in nearby lands, the Communists thrived on the chaos caused by Japan's invasion and the inability of the peasantry to obtain adequate reforms through legal channels. The party had been outlawed before 1940, but it operated a secret underground movement, maintained a popular front with the socialists, and had an established territorial base in central Luzon. During the Japanese occupation, the Communists and other groups formed the Hukbalahap (Huks), or People's Anti-Japanese Army. They gained control of sections of central Luzon and developed an effective guerilla force that kept much of the rice from Japanese hands. The Huks also administered territory under their control; here they confiscated large estates, ended the semifeudal power of the caciques, and established local self-government. At the end of the war they resisted the return of landlords and tried to maintain their wartime regime. The Roxas government was correct in its contention that the Huks engaged in violence and were led by Communists whose ultimate objectives were contrary to peasant wishes. But the Manila authorities were sympathetic to the old order, and the reforms that they did pass were forced on them by rebel pressure. Without any hope that either major party would espouse their cause, the peasants were driven to support the Huks, and the Communists gained complete domination of the Hukbalahap apparatus after 1945.

Most Huk peasants were willing to stop fighting, receive guerilla combat pay after Japan was beaten, and resume their activities as peaceful farmers. But determined Communist leadership, the antipeasant orientation of the government, and the general absence of law and order thwarted a peaceful settlement. The Huks won seven Congressional seats in 1946 on a platform of land reform and "real freedom" from the United States, but were barred from Congress. In the violence that followed, the rebels were guilty of excesses and the constabulary rightly gained an unsavory reputation for cruelty and corruption.

When Quirino took power in 1948, he stressed his own humble origin, promised amnesty, and proposed an ameliorative land-reform welfare program. The Huks, led by the Communist Luis Taruc, called for more sweeping reforms, an end to the American ties, and, finally, the overthrow of the regime.

The Communist movement spread over Luzon, Mindanao, and other islands and extended its support among peasants, laborers, and Chinese residents. The bulk of the people, however, did not rally to the rebel cause. When Magsaysay became defense minister in 1950, he revamped the constabulary and depended primarily on the army to carry out the antiguerilla campaign. The army protected the peasants and treated them with respect; in the past the constabulary had acted as adjuncts to the landlords' private forces in suppressing the peasantry. When Magsaysay resigned in February, 1953, to campaign against Quirino, he promised more vigorous military operations against the Communists and sweeping land reforms. His election victory that year was hailed as proof that a victory for the "common man" over the vested interests and aristocratic cliques could be achieved through the orderly process of government.

The Magsaysay Administration

Actually, the Nationalist party was still a coalition of reformers, old guard anti-Americans, and the landed gentry. President Magsaysay thus had to struggle to gain control over his own party in order to muster Congressional support for his policies. In this he was handicapped by his own inexperience and the entrenched position of his opponents in both parties. Satisfactory progress maintained against the Huks led to the surrender of many rebel leaders, including Taruc, who was given a relatively mild ten-year sentence. Yet not until August, 1955, did Magsaysay get a land reform program through the legislature, and only after considerable presidential pressure. The new law granted him the power to break up large landed estates for distribution among the peasants, and even expropriate property if necessary. The Magsaysay administration also sought to improve the position of farm tenants by protecting them against landlord exploitation, teaching new agricultural techniques, and establishing cooperatives to finance credit on reasonable terms. At the start of 1957, the president claimed that the economy's productivity as a whole increased by 30 per cent between 1953 and 1956. It will take several years to determine whether an adequate reform program has finally become a reality.

In foreign policy, President Magsaysay rejected a policy of neutralism in favor of retaining close relations with the United States. The American request to negotiate for new bases on the islands was granted, and the Philippines participated in SEATO maneuvers with the United States and Thailand in the latter state during February, 1956. The president won a significant vote of confidence in the senatorial election of November, 1955, conducted with foreign policy as a major issue, when Nationalist candidates. all but one selected by Magsaysay, won six of the nine seats at stake.

Undoubtedly, Magsaysay's hand was strengthened by a favorable revision of the Trade Agreement Act with the United States, completed in September, 1955, and effective January 1, 1956. This accord reduced the rate at which American tariffs would be applied to Philippine products[3] and increased the tariff schedule on American exports to the Philippines. The United States dropped its quota on rice and eased the quota arrangement on other products. The new agreement also removed limitations on Manila's freedom to alter the Philippine exchange rate and permitted it to impose an export tax if it so desired. Finally, in the matter of using natural resources and operating public utilities, each signatory agreed to treat the other's citizens as it did its own. American political leaders favored this bill because of their confidence that President Magsaysay could defeat the communist menace in the Philippines and at the same time give the country the high-caliber leadership it so clearly needs if it is to realize its democratic heritage.

The accidental death of Ramon Magsaysay in 1957 again threw Philippine politics into a factional turmoil. Vice-President Carlos Garcia succeeded to the presidency and later won the general election held that year.

Bibliography

SOUTHEAST ASIA

General

HALL, D. G. E., *A History of South-East Asia*. New York: St. Martin's Press, 1955.

HARRISON, B., *Southeast Asia: A Short History*. New York: St. Martin's Press, 1954.

LEMAY, R., *The Culture of Southeast Asia*. London: Allen & Unwin, 1954.

MILLS, L. (ed.), *The New World of Southeast Asia*. Minneapolis: Univ. of Minnesota Press, 1949.

TALBOT, P. (ed.), *South Asia in the World Today*. Chicago: Univ. of Chicago Press, 1950.

THAYER, P. W. (ed.), *Southeast Asia in the Coming World*. Baltimore: Johns Hopkins Press, 1953.

THAYER, P. W. (ed.), *Nationalism and Progress in Free Asia*. Baltimore: Johns Hopkins Press, 1956.

MENDE, T., *Southeast Asia between Two Worlds*. London: Turnstile Press, 1955.

HOPKINS, H., *New World Arising*. London: Hamish Hamilton, 1952.

[3] For example, percentage of customs duties to be applied under the 1946 accord were, 1956—15; 1963—50; 1970—85; 1974—100. Under the new accord, percentages for these years are 5, 20, 60, 100.

HOLLAND, W. L. (ed.), *Asian Nationalism and the West*. New York: Macmillan, 1953.

DOBBY, E. H. G., *Southeast Asia*. New York: Wiley, 1951.

LANDON, K. P., *Southeast Asia: Crossroads of Religion*. Chicago: Univ. of Chicago Press, 1949.

DUBOIS, C., *Social Forces in Southeast Asia*. Minneapolis: Univ. of Minnesota Press, 1949.

LASKER, B., *People of Southeast Asia*. New York: Knopf, 1944.

LASKER, B., *Human Bondage in Southeast Asia*. Chapel Hill: Univ. of N. C. Press, 1950.

EMERSON, R., L. MILLS, and V. THOMPSON, *Government and Nationalism in Southeast Asia*. New York: Prentice-Hall, 1948.

THOMPSON, V., and R. ADLOFF, *The Left Wing in Southeast Asia*. New York: Sloane, 1950.

THOMPSON, V., and R. ADLOFF, *Minority Problems in Southeast Asia*. Stanford: Stanford Univ. Press, 1955.

MOOK, H. J. VAN, *The Stakes of Democracy in Southeast Asia*. New York: Norton, 1950.

EMERSON, R., *Representative Government in Southeast Asia*. Cambridge: Harvard Univ. Press, 1955.

PURCELL, V., *The Chinese in Southeast Asia*. London: Oxford Univ. Press, 1951.

ROBEQUAIN, C., *Malay, Indonesia, Borneo, and the Philippines*. New York: Longmans, 1954.

FURNIVALL, J. S., *Colonial Policy and Practice*. New York: Cambridge Univ. Press, 1948.

MILLS, L. A., *British Rule in Eastern Asia*. Minneapolis: Univ. of Minnesota Press, 1942.

BURMA

HALL, D. G. C., *Burma*. New York: Longmans, Green, 1925.

HARVEY, G. E., *History of Burma*. London: Longmans, Green, 1925.

HARVEY, G. E., *British Rule in Burma*. London: Faber & Faber, 1946.

CHRISTIAN, J. L., *Modern Burma*. Berkeley: Univ. of California Press, 1942.

CHRISTIAN, J. L., *Burma and the Japanese Invader*. Bombay: Thacker, 1945.

APPLETON, G., *Buddhism in Burma*. Calcutta: Longmans, Green, 1943.

STEVENSON, H. N. C., *The Hill People of Burma*. Calcutta: Longmans, Green, 1945.

MARSHALL, H., *The Karens of Burma*. Calcutta: Longmans, Green, 1945.

LEACH, E. R., *Political Systems in Highland Burma*. Cambridge: Harvard Univ. Press, 1954.

NU, THAKIN, *Burma under the Japanese*. New York: St. Martin's Press, 1954.

LEWIS, N., *Golden Path*. New York: Scribner's, 1952.

DONNISON, F., *Public Administration in Burma*. New York: Royal Inst. of Int. Affairs, 1953.

Knappen Tippetts Abbet Engineering Co., *Preliminary Report on Economic and Engineering: Survey of Burma, for Burma Economic Council*. Washington: Burmese Embassy, 1952.

ANDRUS, J. R., *Burmese Economic Life*. Stanford: Stanford Univ. Press, 1947.

UNION OF BURMA ECONOMIC AND SOCIAL BOARD, *Pyidawtha: The New Burma*. Rangoon, 1954.

THAILAND

WOOD, W. A. R., *History of Siam from the Earliest Times to the Year 1781*. London: Allen & Unwin, 1926.

LANDON, M., *Anna and the King of Siam*. New York: John Day, 1944.

LANDON, K. P., *Siam in Transition*. Chicago: Univ. of Chicago Press, 1939.

THOMPSON, V., *Thailand: The New Siam*. New York: Macmillan, 1942.

DE YOUNG, J. E., *Village Life in Modern Thailand*. Berkeley: Univ. of California Press, 1955.

INGRAM, J. C., *Economic Changes in Thailand since 1850*. Stanford: Stanford Univ. Press, 1955.

REEVE, W. D., *Public Administration in Siam*. New York: Royal Inst. of Int. Affairs, 1952.

MACDONALD, A., *Bangkok Editor*. New York: Macmillan, 1949.

INDOCHINA

BRODRICK, A. H., *Little China: The Annamese Lands.* New York: Oxford Univ. Press, 1942.

CADY, J. F., *The Roots of French Imperialism in Eastern Asia.* Ithaca: Cornell Univ. Press, 1954.

THOMPSON, V., *French Indo-China.* New York: Macmillan, 1937.

ROBEQUAIN, C., *Economic Development of French Indo-China.* New York: Oxford Univ. Press, 1944.

ENNIS, T. E., *French Policy and Development in Indochina.* Chicago: Univ. of Chicago Press, 1936.

ROBERTS, S. H., *History of French Colonial Policy: 1870–1925.* 2 vols.; London: King, 1929.

LEWIS, N., *A Dragon Apparent.* New York: Scribner's, 1951.

NEWMAN, B., *Report on Indochina.* New York: Praeger, 1954.

FALL, B. D., *The Viet Minh Regime.* Ithaca: Cornell Univ. Press, 1954.

HAMMER, E., *The Struggle for Indochina.* Stanford: Stanford Univ. Press, 1954.

HAMMER, E., *The Struggle for Indochina Continues.* Stanford: Stanford Univ. Press, 1955.

DOOLEY, T. A., *Deliver Us from Evil.* New York: Farrar, Straus, & Cudahy, 1956.

BILODEAU, C., and others, *Compulsory Education in Cambodia, Laos and Viet-Nam.* Paris: UNESCO, 1955.

MALAYA

WINSTEDT, R., *Britain and Malaya: 1786–1941.* London: Longmans, Green, 1941.

WINSTEDT, R., *The Malays: A Cultural History.* Rev. ed.; London: Routledge & Kegan Paul, 1950.

DOBBY, E. H. G., *Malaya and the Malays.* London: Univ. of London Press, 1947.

THOMPSON, V., *Postmortem on Malaya.* New York: Macmillan, 1943.

COLONY OF SINGAPORE, *Annual Reports.* London.

FEDERATION OF MALAYA, *Annual Reports.* Kuala Lumpur.

SMITH, T. E., *Population Growth in Malaya.* London: Royal Inst. of Int. Affairs, 1952.

JONES, S. W., *Public Administration in Malaya.* New York: Royal Inst. of Int. Affairs, 1953.

INTERNATIONAL BANK FOR RECONSTRUCTION AND DEVELOPMENT, *The Economic Development of Malaya,* 1955.

BARTLETT, V., *Report from Malaya.* New York: Criterion Bks., 1955.

PURCELL, V., *The Chinese in Malaya.* New York: Oxford Univ. Press, 1948.

PURCELL, V., *Malaya: Communist or Free?* Stanford: Stanford Univ. Press, 1954.

MILLER, H., *The Communist Menace in Malaya.* New York: Praeger, 1954.

HANRAHAN, G. Z., *The Communist Struggle in Malaya.* New York: Inst. of Pacific Relations, 1954.

INDONESIA

KENNEDY, R., *The Ageless Indies.* New York: John Day, 1942.

VANDERBOSCH, A., *The Dutch East Indies.* Berkeley: Univ. of California Press, 1942.

BOUSQUET, G. H., *A French View of the Netherlands Indies.* New York: Oxford Univ. Press, 1941.

TER HAAR, B., *Adat Law in Indonesia.* New York: Inst. of Pacific Relations, 1948.

DuBois, C., *The People of Alor: A Socio-Psychological Study of an East Indian Island.* Minneapolis: Univ. of Minnesota Press, 1944.

METCALF, J. E., *The Agricultural Economy of Indonesia.* Washington: Department of Agriculture, 1952.

BOEKE, J. H., *The Structure of the Netherlands Indies Economy.* New York: Inst. of Pacific Relations, 1942.

BOEKE, J. H., *The Evolution of the Netherlands Indies Economy.* New York: Inst. of Pacific Relations, 1946.

FURNIVALL, J. S., *The Netherlands Indies: A Study in Plural Economy.* London: Cambridge Univ. Press, 1939.

MOOK, H. J. VAN, *The Netherlands Indies and Japan.* New York: Norton, 1944.

SJAHRIR, S., *Out of Exile.* New York: John Day, 1949.

WOLF, C., JR., *The Indonesia Story.* New York: John Day, 1948.

SCHILLER, A. A., *The Formation of Federal Indonesia.* The Hague: Van Hoeve, 1955.

KAHIN, G. McT., *Nationalism and Revolution in Indonesia*. Ithaca: Cornell Univ. Press, 1952.

BRO, M. H., *Indonesia, Land of Challenge*. New York: Harper, 1954.

HUTASOIT, M., *Compulsory Education in Indonesia*. Paris: UNESCO, 1954.

WESTERLING, R., *Challenge to Terrorism* London: Kimber, 1952.

WOODMAN, D., *The Republic of Indonesia*. New York: Philosophical Lib., 1955.

THE PHILIPPINES

BENITEZ, C., *History of the Philippines*. Boston: Ginn, 1940.

HAYDEN, J. R., *The Philippines: A Study in National Development*. New York: Macmillan, 1942.

U.S. HIGH COMMISSIONER TO THE PHILIPPINES, *Annual Reports*.

GRUNDER, G. A., and W. E., LIVEZEY, *The Philippines and the United States*. Norman: Univ. of Oklahoma Press, 1951.

JENKINS, S., *American Economic Policy toward the Philippines*. Stanford: Stanford Univ. Press, 1954.

SPENCER, J. E., *Land and People in the Philippines*. Berkeley: Univ. of California Press, 1955.

MALCOLM, G. A., *First Malayan Republic: The Story of the Philippines*. Boston: Christopher, 1951.

BERNSTEIN, D., *The Philippine Story*. New York: Farrar, Straus & Cudahy, 1947.

ABAYA, H. J., *Betrayal in the Philippines*. New York: Wyn, 1946.

TARUC, L., *Born of the People*. New York: Int. Pubs., 1953.

ROMULO, C. P., *Crusade in Asia: Philippines Victory*. New York: John Day, 1955.

SCOFF, A. H., *The Philippine Answer to Communism*. Stanford: Stanford Univ. Press, 1952.

ZAFRA, U. A., *Philippine Economic Handbook*. Silver Spring, Md.: Westland, 1955.

PART SIX

International Relations
in the Far East

17 *Russia in the Far East*

The Russian record in Asia in the past century has, in retrospect, been far more successful than that of other Western powers. The policies and objectives of both Czarist and Soviet regimes and Russia's relations with the great states of China and Japan have constantly bewildered Western observers. One source of uniqueness was Russia's ability to pursue expansionist tactics without much interference from other Western states. During the nineteenth century there was friction with Britain north of the Indian border, but by then Russia had overrun vast territories inhabited by Moslem tribes in Central Asia and reached the borders of Afghanistan, Tibet, and China's Sinkiang Province. In the north, the Russian frontiers reached Mongolia and Manchuria and extended down the Pacific coast to Korea. Westerners have described the Czars and their Soviet successors as expansionists, motivated by territorial and ideological imperialist ambitions.

Yet the Chinese have generally considered the Russians to be friendlier than the Western maritime powers. Posing as protectors of the Chinese against foreign encroachments, Czarist regimes were able to amass vast tracts of land and still retain Chinese good will. Perhaps overland colonial expansion was less obvious than conquest made by sea. Then, too, the Russians, to bolster their argument, often assured their Oriental neighbors that they were really Asiatics and pointed to their geographic location, Mongol rule in the Middle Ages, and a culture different from the West. And, despite their expansionist policy, they did not treat the Chinese or Japanese as inferior representatives of an alien culture; rather, they operated without that infuriating air of moral superiority so often assumed by the West.

By contrast, the West could claim that Russia under its last Czar, Nicholas II (1895–1917), was avidly expansionist in the Far East and that Soviet Russia has tirelessly sought to subvert allegedly sovereign, independent states to Communism by every available device. The Russians in this century were guilty of many specific acts of hostility, ranging from an insistence on a large indemnity following the Boxer uprising of 1900 to a cynical disregard of neutrality treaty obligations with Japan undertaken in 1941 and 1944. Yet even the traditionally wary Japan, which had always based its policy toward Russia on "realism" and force, was shocked by Stalin's declaration of war in 1945. Japan had gone so far as to request Moscow in 1943–1944 to act as a go-between in arranging an honorable peace.

An important strand of modern Asian intellectual opinion places Soviet Russia in a separate category, superior to the Western states. This point of view is contained in a study by the Indian publicist and diplomat, K. M. Panikkar, whose views have generally mirrored the attitudes of his contemporaries.[1] It may be that to a South Asian, Western imperialism at home is more loathsome than the more distant activities of the Russians. Though the American record in Asia was hardly one of full-fledged conquest and the United States promised freedom to its only colony well before the Pacific War of 1941, South Asians point to the United States as the actual or potential kin to the West European tradition of imperialism. And though the present Chinese-Russian alliance can of course be explained in terms of ideological affinity, it is also true that this decision was reached voluntarily by Peking in 1949, despite a long record of Russian aggression against China and a poor showing by Moscow in the Chinese civil war. Even Japanese neutralists today are not gravely handicapped when they imply that Russia can be treated on a basis of reciprocity, despite its historical position as Tokyo's "natural enemy" and propagator of an abhorrent ideology.

Communism as a creed has also been used to advantage by the Russians in dealing with their Asian neighbors—as a doctrine that would bring industry and modernity, power, and well-being to backward agrarian lands. Thus the Russians boast of their own rise to a great industrial power within two generations, while the Chinese promise "socialism" (a modern industrial economy) in fifteen years and complete modernization in fifty years. The appeal of these programs and achievements is deeply felt, even in Japan. To the failure of the West to foster modernization during the period of imperial rule is added the greater accusation of having purposely kept Asia's economies in a colonial state so that its raw materials, resources, and markets could be profitably exploited. In the first official visit by Soviet leaders to India and Burma late in 1955, Nikita Khrushchev and Premier Nicolai Bulganin made broad use of such accusations and boasts in their outright propaganda attack against the West.

However, we must not conclude that the Russians are above suspicion today, or that free Asians regard them as the major champions of peace, friendship, and economic progress. Communist political methods, although too often minimized, arouse considerable antagonism in the new democracies of Asia as well as in Japan. Also, the struggle against native communist political and military challenges has alerted many Asian public officials to the purposes and nature of this totalitarian movement. The North Korean aggression of 1950 had a profound moral effect on Asians. At the very least, it served to check the uncritical acclaim with which many publicists discussed communist intentions

---

[1] Panikkar, K. M., *Asian and Western Dominance* (London: G. Allen & Unwin, 1953).

and ethical purposes. The moral appeal of communism also suffered to the extent that Communist China is feared as a menace to Southeast Asian security. Nevertheless, Russia today possesses a strong territorial strategic base, directs a persuasive and effective communist movement and, with its Chinese ally, is in a position to menace all of East Asia. We must now examine Russian policy, trace its course of development, and note the frequent setbacks as well as the successes that it has recorded.

Expansion under the Czars

Early Russian Expansion

Though Russia overthrew its Mongol rulers in 1480, the great advances east of the Urals were not begun till 1581, when a fur-hunting expedition, led by Yermak, defeated the Sibir tribes in battle. In 1638, following the east-west tributaries of the great Siberian rivers, the Russians reached the Pacific. Since the vast north Asian stretches were only sparsely settled in the following centuries, the Russian provinces on the Pacific were somewhat vulnerable. Though they served at times as springboards for further advances, their inherent weakness and distance from Russian centers of power exposed them to Japanese and, potentially, Chinese thrusts.

Russia's early contacts with China succeeded in fixing boundaries and regulating relations between the two states. Following some border clashes, the Treaty of Nerchinsk (1689) established peace between the two powers. It also provided for trade, as Russia wished, and set the Manchurian-Siberian boundary at the northern *watershed* of the Amur River. A similar trade-boundary Treaty of Kiakhta (1729) fixed the Siberian-Mongolian borders and permitted Russia to open a legation at Peking. China dispatched diplomatic missions to St. Petersburg in 1730 and 1733. Yet it refused to treat other Western envoys on a basis of equality for another century and sent no missions to the West until 1870.

To the north, Russian explorers pushed on to the Kamchatka Peninsula and into the New World. Under the energetic Governor-General Nicolai Muraviev, Russia strengthened its hold on its eastern provinces, built a naval base at Petropavlovsk, and strengthened its claim to Sakhalin Island opposite the mouth of the Amur River.

In the 1850's the Russians took advantage of the fact that Britain and France attacked China in the Second Opium War (1856–1860). In May, 1858, Muraviev induced the Manchu dynasty to move the Siberian frontier southward from the Amur watershed to the river itself. This was a very extensive concession and Peking was slow to ratify it—until Britain and France renewed their assault on China in 1859–1860 and occupied Peking. The Russians urged the Western powers to take a firm line with China, meanwhile presenting themselves to Peking as China's indispensable friend, the only one who could intervene

493

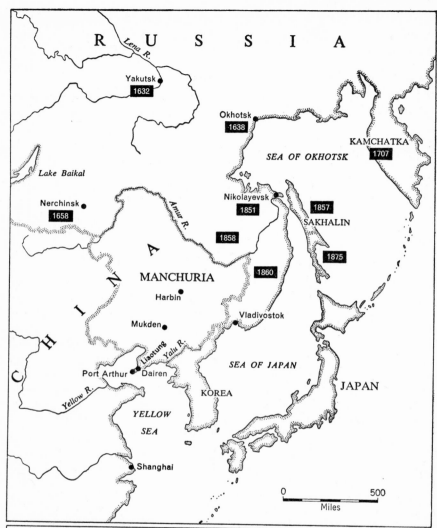

RUSSIAN EXPANSION IN THE FAR EAST
17th – 19th CENTURIES

and prevent the depredations allegedly planned by the West. Actually, the Western allies had already determined to quit Peking; the Russians themselves were annexing land, for they had simply moved the boundary markers down to the Amur River and, along the coast, all the way to Korea. Yet China yielded these territories in the Treaty of Peking (1860), making the Amur River the frontier and giving Russia a coastal strip between Manchuria and the Pacific. At the southern tip of this new Maritime Province the great base of Vladivostok

494

was built. Thus the West exerted diplomatic and military pressure against the Manchus and won only Chinese enmity; Russia used this clash to net extensive territorial gains while strengthening its reputation as China's friend.

Expansion in Manchuria and Korea (1894–1904)

The Trans-Siberian Railroad was the great symbol of Russia's expansion to the east after 1890. By 1895 its contruction had made considerable progress under the direction of Finance Minister Sergei Witte. He wished to concentrate on economic penetration of the Orient and opposed saber-rattling and war as costly, dangerous projects. The new ruler, Nicholas II, at first supported this approach, which again turned China's difficulty to Russian advantage. This time it was the harsh Japanese peace treaty of 1895, which extracted the Liaotung Peninsula on Manchuria from China. Russia induced Germany and France to intervene, voided this treaty clause, and then loaned China the money it required to pay a war indemnity to Japan. Russia and China then signed a fifteen-year defensive alliance (Li-Lobanov Treaty) in 1896, promising to help each other if attacked in China or Korea. Chinese ports were to be open to Russia in time of war, and the Russians were allowed to construct railways in China in order to fulfill these military obligations. China did not wish the Russian government to build the railway, even though loans from Russia paid for it. Instead, the Russian-Chinese Bank, first created by Witte to handle the indemnity loans, was to direct its construction. Thus the famous Chinese Eastern Railway was built, running from Chita in Siberia across Manchuria to Vladivostok. The line's management was restricted to Chinese and Russians, with China responsible for the railroad's security but the construction company in control of the land. China could repurchase the railroad in thirty-eight years or receive it without charge in eighty.

It was at this point that the Czar came under the influence of adventurous advisers, and Russia's ambitions took an ominous turn toward territorial aggrandizement. The wild scramble for concessions in China was launched in 1898 and Russia gained a lease, over Witte's objections, to the very territory in southern Manchuria denied to Japan in 1895. Thus the Russians modernized the Port of Dairen, developed a naval base at Port Arthur, and gained permission to establish a railroad link between their leasehold and the Chinese Eastern to the north. When the antiforeign Boxer Uprising occurred in Peking during 1900, Russian troops occupied all of Manchuria, while a force of 4,000 was sent to the Chinese capital. The Russians continued to behave in a friendly manner toward China, distributing relief supplies and calling for an early evacuation of foreign troops. However, Russia also demanded the largest indemnity and did not evacuate Manchuria. Under Japanese pressure, a withdrawal was promised in 1902, but the troops were merely kept in the railway zone as "guards." By 1903 the Chinese Eastern was completed and its link to Dairen was begun.

Since Britain was not willing to challenge this threat, only Japan, with its defensive-offensive aspirations, stood in Russia's path. The two powers had reached an agreement in 1875 recognizing Russian control of Sakhalin and Japan's claim to the Kuriles. Moreover, the Japanese at that time were honored because the treaty was signed under terms of diplomatic equality. But by 1900, relations between the two countries were strained.

Even more than Manchuria, the Japanese were concerned about Korea, where Tokyo was seeking to establish its hegemony. In 1885 the Koreans were anxious to have a third power as a makeweight in what was then a Chinese-Japanese dispute. They therefore agreed to have Russia train their troops. However, the war of 1894–1895 ended Chinese influence, and Japan now sought to consolidate its position. Korean opposition to this threat led the Japanese to indulge in court intrigue at Seoul, during which the queen was murdered and the king of Korea was obliged to seek asylum in the Russian legation during 1896. The Russians then gained important timber and mining concessions in northern Korea, and their French allies were allowed to build a railway from Seoul northward to the Manchurian border.

Japan was willing to divide Korea into spheres of influence at latitude 38°, but Russia was not satisfied with the northern half. The two major powers reached agreements (1896–1898) to recognize Korea's sovereignty and help the country establish internal order; in addition, each promised, before intervening in Korea, to mark out its respective zones and undertake joint consultations. Russia tacitly recognized Japan's economic primacy in southern Korea, as well as its right to build a Pusan-Seoul railway. However, Czarist troops now appeared in northern Korea in the guise of lumber workers, and all Japanese attempts to reach a definite diplomatic settlement before 1904 proved fruitless. Russia appeared determined to hold Manchuria and infiltrate Korea even at the cost of war; its Far Eastern leaders even seemed eager for a military showdown.

War, Defeat, and Stability (1905–1917)

Tokyo responded by launching a war and carrying the fight into Manchuria, the main theater of land combat. Though the Russians were defeated in infantry battles and all but annihilated at sea in 1904–1905, Japan was too exhausted to follow up its victories or invade Siberia. At the Treaty of Portsmouth (1905) Russia yielded the southern half of Sakhalin, granted Japan fishing rights off Siberia, gave it a free hand in Korea, and recognized its economic primacy in southern Manchuria. In 1910 Japan formally annexed Korea, which it held as a colony until 1945.

After 1905 Russia and Japan remained wary neighbors who lived in peace until the Bolshevik Revolution of 1917. They were induced to cooperate in order to protect their economic spheres of influence against American efforts to establish free trade and internationalized railway direction in Manchuria. The two states made three agreements (1907, 1912, 1916) all paying lip-service to China's integrity and the concept of economic equality for all states. Actually, these treaties recognized Russian predominance in northern Manchuria and

Outer Mongolia, and Japan's primacy in southern Manchuria, Korea, and Eastern Inner Mongolia. As wartime allies in 1916, they agreed not to make a separate peace or enter into political agreements against each other.

Thus, by 1917, Russia still held important interests in the Far East. These included the Chinese Eastern Railway through Manchuria, as well as the great semicircular Trans-Siberian route around Manchuria's jagged northern border. Its economic sphere in Manchuria after 1905 was still four times as large as Japan's. Russia made considerable use of its rights to build factories, schools, and churches; it also developed mines, forest industries, and river shipping, and constructed telegraph routes. There were more than 100,000 settlers and 30,000 soldiers in Manchuria, and the Russians were in effective control of Harbin and other important urban centers.

Sinkiang and Outer Mongolia

Progress in Central Asia was substantial and less costly. Russia gained special trade concessions in Sinkiang in 1851 and, after 1860, occupied the region of Ili in that area in the course of suppressing a Moslem uprising. Instead of regaining this territory, an incompetent Chinese envoy yielded most of Ili to Russia, granted special trading rights, and promised an indemnity payment. This ill-fated Treaty of Livadia (1879) was set aside, however, by the Treaty of St. Petersburg (1881), which returned most of Ili to China in exchange for an indemnity, allowed Russian consuls in Sinkiang and Mongolia, and gave Russia building and free-trade rights in these border regions.

Russian economic penetration of Sinkiang proceeded apace, but no efforts were made at political subversion even when the Chinese Revolution of 1911 weakened Peking's hold over the border regions. Outer Mongolia was a different matter, for here the populace was antagonized by a recent influx of Chinese settlers. When it declared its independence in 1911, Russia recognized the new state, sent it arms, and offered its services as a mediator. In return for continued political support, it received commercial rights in this region. In 1913 Russia adopted a "compromise" position, recognizing Chinese suzerainty over Outer Mongolia, provided that Peking did not send troops there or interfere with Mongolian self-rule. A Russian-Chinese treaty in 1915 formalized this status of suzerainty and autonomy; it forbade Outer Mongolia to have foreign relations but required that Russia be consulted on all territorial or political issues. This treaty meant that a joint protectorate was established, an important step in Russian efforts to detach Outer Mongolia completely from China.

Soviet Policy between World Wars

Early Soviet Policy

The Bolsheviks managed to retain much of this Czarist inheritance, despite the weakened power of Russia in the 1920's and Japan's expansion in the 1930's. The Communist regime adopted new tactics and pursued more subtle and complex goals than its Czarist predecessor. It can be argued that imperial Russia had apparently reached the physical limits of national expansion. The new Soviet government sought to convert other states to communism but was also concerned with Russian territory while this was being done. For the most part, the communist movement and its international agency, the Comintern, were used primarily to protect or advance the interests of the new "Socialist Fatherland" during the early, vulnerable period of its existence.

The first task confronting the new regime in the Far East was self-preservation in the face of an Allied intervention in Siberia late in the First World War. The Japanese army sent a large contingent and gave secret help to White Russian counterrevolutionaries in their effort to gain control over eastern Siberia. However, American opposition, the hostility of the Russian people, and war-weariness in Japan served to make this project abortive. As foreign troops withdrew, the Russians created a Far Eastern Republic but reincorporated this region into the Russian Soviet Republic in 1923.

War, revolution, and civil strife all weakened Russian power. The new regime sought stability and recognition but also wished to keep its self-defined "capitalist enemies" off balance. The Soviets therefore agitated against imperialism and promised to sacrifice Russian privileges in neighboring lands. A Congress of Eastern Peoples was held at Baku in the Caucasus during 1920, and it issued a call, which proved to be premature, for the "toiling masses" of Asia and Africa to revolt. In 1922, when excluded from the Washington Conference, the Soviet Union organized a Congress of Toilers of the Far East and again urged Asians to emancipate themselves, under the leadership of their proletariat.

The creation of Communist parties subject to Moscow's control in alien lands was another lever in Russian hands. These could serve to foment communist uprisings or support anti-European nationalist movements in colonial lands. Communist parties were created in Japan, India, and elsewhere, but the focal point of this policy was China, which was already in a revolutionary ferment. Communist ideology, Russian diplomacy, and Soviet interference in domestic affairs made deeper and more lasting penetrations in China than anywhere else.

Intervention in China

In 1918–1919 the Russians proclaimed a new policy toward China, with a revolutionary flourish. They renounced Czarist encroachments in Manchuria, formally ended the Boxer indemnities, and canceled all special privileges for Russians, including extraterritoriality. They even promised to return territory seized by the Czars, the Chinese Eastern Railway, and various mines and forests without compensation. The hostile Peking regime did not take up these offers at first. Meanwhile Russia dispatched agents to China in 1921 to organize a Communist party, a move symbolic of the Soviet ability to operate on many levels. The intellectuals in the north, who were to form the original core of the Communist party, were impressed with these offers and contrasted them sharply with the shabby treatment of China by the Western powers at Versailles.

Rebuffed in Peking, the Russians sought to deal with Sun Yat-sen. They hoped to gain diplomatic recognition while assisting and perhaps molding the course of China's revolution. However, early Soviet promises appeared less generous when specific negotiations were begun. Russia now explained that it simply meant to recognize China's political sovereignty in Manchuria—which the Czars never claimed had been surrendered—but not to yield any Russian *property* rights. However, Sun was satisfied with the promise of the Soviet envoy, Adolf Joffe, that Russia would not try to communize China because conditions were not suitable. Joffe claimed that Russia sought only to create a strong nationalist state that could shake off its "semicolonial" subservience to the West.

These preliminary negotiations led to the Koo-Karakhan Treaty of 1924. It established diplomatic relations, ended old Czarist treaties, and placed all future relations on a basis of justice, equality, and reciprocity. Each agreed to prohibit subversive activity and propaganda against the other's political order. Moscow formally renounced its concessions in Chinese cities, extraterritoriality, and the Boxer payments. Outer Mongolia's status as autonomous was reaffirmed, and the Russians retained their property rights in the Chinese Eastern Railway for eighty years.

The Soviet Union then gave invaluable aid to the Nationalist revolutionary cause and used its disciplinary power to have the Chinese Communists support the Kuomintang. As this phase of the revolution reached a climax under the leadership of Chiang Kai-shek in 1926–1927, Soviet policy became submerged in confusion and contradiction and ended in a debacle. The Chinese Communists hoped to seize power through cooperation with the Left Kuomintang, which they expected to control. Only Russian guidance and support could make this gamble work, but such aid was not forthcoming. Instead, until 1927 Moscow steadfastly insisted on Communist cooperation with the Nationalists.

Stalin encouraged revolutionary agitation among the peasants, but when agrarian uprisings occurred in 1926 he would not support them because these attacks were directed against the landlord class, a bulwark of Kuomintang support. He therefore ordered the Chinese Communists to assist the Left Kuomintang government at Hankow to suppress such uprisings. By June, 1927, with the split within the Kuomintang apparent, Stalin still favored a coalition but now believed the Communists could be the dominant partner. His advisers in China correctly warned that this would mean a break in the Hankow government, leading to the Communists' ejection. When the Left Kuomintang did precisely that and came to terms with Chiang Kai-shek, the Chinese Communist party suffered a crushing defeat and the Russian advisers were forced to leave the country. This disaster was then compounded by new orders to the Chinese Communist remnants from Moscow in the period of 1927–1930, calling for a combined urban-rural uprising. These were dutifully attempted and were crushed. The Comintern also kept shuffling the Chinese party's leadership and so destroyed what was left of its effectiveness. Only after the rise of Mao Tse-tung did the Chinese Communist party again become a major political force.

During this unsuccessful intervention in the Chinese Revolution, the Russians also encountered difficulties in the north. In 1924, following his treaty with the Nationalists, Lev Karakhan reached an understanding about the Chinese Eastern Railway with the Peking government and later with Chang Tso-lin, the Manchurian warlord. By these terms, only Russia and China could operate the line or decide its future status; moreover, Chang Tso-lin won China the right to the railroad in sixty years. In 1929 his son and successor, Chang Hsueh-liang, in an attempt to eliminate foreign privileges, arrested Soviet consular officials in Manchuria, closed lines of communication, and interned Russian railway employees. An undeclared war followed, but his force was no match for the regular Soviet troops under General Galens, former military adviser to the Nationalists. At the end of the year, the Russians regained their earlier rights, but the Manchurian picture was to undergo drastic changes with the Japanese invasion of 1931.

Outer Mongolia and Sinkiang

Anarchy and terror afflicted Outer Mongolia until Soviet forces arrived in 1921 and installed a pro-Russian government. In 1923–1924 the Kuomintang accepted this Soviet occupation in return for a Russian disavowal of imperialist designs. However, "sovietization" continued under Russian instructors who remained after the army withdrew, and a Mongolian People's Republic was proclaimed. This pattern of a "people's democracy," which the Russians were to impose on their satellites after 1945, was first developed in the primitive Mongolian environment. The capital, Urga, was renamed Ulan Bator (Red Hero), other foreign influences were excluded, and aliens could enter only with Soviet permission. Physical improvements were undertaken, but collective farming and industrialization were approached cautiously because of the economy's pastoral backward nature. The Russians fostered Mongol educational and cultural development within a communist framework, emphasizing Mongol nationalism and its strong anti-Chinese bias. As Japanese pressure mounted in 1935, with an abortive thrust into Eastern Inner Mongolia, the Soviet Union signed a defensive alliance with Outer Mongolia in 1936, promising to fight for its territorial integrity just as though it were part of the Soviet Union. China in turn protested that this agreement violated its own sovereign rights, which Russia was still legally committed to recognize.

In Sinkiang, the cautious policy of the Czars was continued. The Chinese-appointed governors of Sinkiang made certain that the questions of border relations, refugees, and trade were handled with due consideration for Russian interests. As the economic development of Soviet Asia progressed, its political and commercial attraction increased. China's third postrevolution governor, Sheng Shih-tsai, came under Russian influence. His reform programs proved so radical that his rule had to be sustained by Russian arms against several rebellions. Soviet financial and technical aid was extended in developing Sinkiang's mining and oil industries and transportation facilities. The Russians repeatedly avowed their respect for China's sovereignty and territorial integrity, and Chinese influence remained a potent force in Sinkiang. As German and Japanese pressures absorbed Russian attention and Nationalist China was driven into the interior after the Japanese invasion of 1937, Sinkiang officials tried to reorient the province toward China. However, as the Nationalist regime was too weak to assert its dominance, Russian pressure was renewed after 1943. The local bureaucracy was divided in its allegiance and revolts occurred until 1945, when the Kuomintang and Russians negotiated a new settlement.

A Cautious Policy toward Japan

The rise of Japanese imperialism in Asia caused the Soviet Union to readjust its policies toward the border regions and China. Constantly alert against an assault on its European frontier, Russia followed a very cautious defensive policy in the Orient. When Nazi Germany attacked Russia in 1941, a Japanese assault from the east might have destroyed the Communist state. Hence the wariness that had marked Czarist relations with Japan continued under Stalin's regime.

The first issue between the two powers was the liquidation of Japan's Siberian venture, which was finally completed in 1923. Only in 1925 did Japan recognize the new regime and establish diplomatic relations with Moscow. In return, Russia recognized the validity of the 1905 peace treaty. Each promised to accord the other most-favored-nation treatment and to refrain from propagandizing or in any way subverting the other's internal political order—a promise the Bolsheviks apparently never tired of making or breaking. Supplementary economic agreements gave Japan timber concessions in Siberia, plus mining and timber rights on the Russian half of Sakhalin Island. A fishing convention in 1928 made an important economic concession to the Japanese, allowing them to fish and to manufacture maritime products off the coast of Siberia.

The long-range Russian plan was to create an adequate army in Siberia that could be sustained in supplies and equipment by regional industries. Meanwhile Russia was severely taxed to develop a force that could defend its own frontier. Just as Japan was passive during the Soviet-Manchurian railway imbroglio of 1929, the Soviet Union stood by during Japan's assault on Manchuria in 1931. Commissar of Foreign Affairs Maxim Litvinov did criticize Japan's aggression, China's failure to resist, and the ineffectiveness of the League of Nations. Yet he also assured Japan of Russia's strict neutrality and refused to cooperate even with the League's mild efforts in 1932. The Russians even proposed to Tokyo a nonaggression pact, similar to the types Moscow was concluding with its European and West Asian neighbors. The Japan of 1932 was in no mood for such limiting commitments, and its more flamboyant orators threatened deep advances into Siberia.

An immediate diplomatic issue was the future of Russian economic rights in Manchuria. The Soviet government continued to operate the Chinese Eastern Railway while Japan endeavored to end this intrusion in an area it hoped to develop industrially. Following "bandit" assaults, the loss of rolling stock and the like, Russia decided in 1934 to sell the railway to Japan, and a financial settlement was reached in 1936.

At this time the Soviet Union temporarily abandoned its policy of isolation, joined the League of Nations (1934), and made defensive alliances with France and Czechoslovakia (1935–1936). It propagandized against Japanese aggression and publicly announced its protection of Outer Mongolia. Russia refused to give Japan another fishing agreement on a long-term basis when the old convention expired in 1935. Instead, it allowed only annual renewals, following elaborate and difficult negotiations. The Russians had already planned to increase their share of the catch purchased in Siberian ports and to develop fish canneries to compete with the Japanese.

When Japan joined Germany in the Anti-Comintern Pact in 1936, Russia sought to bolster its security in Asia by fostering Chinese unity. This meant diplomatic support for Chiang Kai-shek and instructions to the Chinese Communists to join in a united front with the Nationalists. After Japan attacked China in 1937, Russia and China concluded a nonaggression pact. Each promised not to attack the other, refrain from aiding an aggressor, and make no treaty that would ease the attacker's task. The Russians reinforced their diplomacy with military aid in 1937–1941, for which the Chinese made partial payment in metals and tea. Moscow also loaned the Nationalists $250 million and developed road networks across Sinkiang and Mongolia. Military instruction units were also dispatched as Germany withdrew its advisers.

Japan supplemented its thrust against China with a series of assaults on the Soviet Union along the Manchurian and Mongolian frontiers. The struggles centering about disputed border regions were brief ones, but it is likely that Japan would have undertaken extensive campaigns had these engagements succeeded. In 1937 Japan sank two Russian gunboats and occupied two Amur River islands without a fight. However, in mid-1938 Japan tried to seize a key hill at Changkufeng, overlooking the rail approach to Vladivostok, but this divisional assault was beaten off. Early in 1939 there were further inconclusive hostilities near Manchouli on the Argun River. Finally, in the late summer of 1939, as the European crisis reached a war stage, Russia and Japan clashed at the junction of the Outer Mongolian-Manchurian borders in the Nomohan district near the Khalka River. A small war ensued on a thirty-five-mile front for several weeks, but the Japanese withdrew after heavy losses.

The Russo-German Nonaggression Pact of August, 1939, was a further inducement to Japan to stabilize the Siberian front. The Axis Pact of 1940 specifically excluded the Soviet Union as a target, and Japan went ahead to seek a status quo settlement with Russia. In retrospect, it seems that such an agreement depended on stable Nazi-Soviet relations. To the Russians in early 1941, a neutrality treaty with Japan was a godsend, enabling them to avert a two-front war. Yet it was Japan that made the diplomatic concessions for the five-year neutrality pact of April, 1941, yielding its economic concessions in Northern Sakhalin. Promises to respect the integrity of Manchukuo and Outer

Mongolia were also exchanged. This agreement violated the Soviet promise made in the 1937 nonaggression treaty with China. Stalin was so delighted with this settlement that he not only saw Foreign Minister Matsuoko off at the Moscow station but embraced and kissed him in a farewell gesture.

Japan adhered to its agreement when the Russians did not collapse under the German onslaught that followed. There was also a competent communist spy ring at work in Tokyo under Victor Sorge in the German Embassy, so that the Russians were fully aware of Japan's decision and planned their military campaign accordingly. Since the German onslaught was barely checked in 1941–1943, the success of Soviet diplomacy and espionage in reducing a military threat from Japan was of vital importance.

The Dawn of Victory

As early as 1943, the Russians regained the diplomatic initiative in East Asia. They reasserted their economic claims in Sinkiang, criticized the Chinese Nationalist war effort while acknowledging Chiang as the country's leader, and called on the Chinese to form a new popular front against Japan. With the defeat of Germany evident in 1944, the Americans began pressing Russia to enter the Pacific War. Nationalist China was also anxious to reach a political settlement with the Soviet Union in order to enhance its own authority once Japan was beaten. As a result, Stalin could extract concessions from the United States at the Yalta Conference of February, 1945. He appears to have sought recognition of definite but limited Russian rights in the Far East. Neither this settlement nor subsequent Russian actions foreshadowed the amazing events that were to occur in China.

The Yalta accord guaranteed the status quo of Outer Mongolia, and the transfer of Southern Sakhalin and the Kurile Islands to Russia. The Soviet Union promised to respect China's sovereignty in Manchuria in return for regaining operational control of its railroads. It also obtained a lease on the naval base at Port Arthur, while Dairen was to be internationalized. Stalin acted the patriot, spoke of reversing the results of the inglorious war of 1904–1905. He was also careful to inject vague terms into the agreement, subject to later Russian distortion, stating that the "pre-eminent interests" of the Soviet Union in Dairen and the railway zones should be safeguarded. He then promised to enter the war within three months of Germany's defeat.

The Japanese, meanwhile, unaware of Russian intentions, were fruitlessly asking Ambassador Jacob Malik and even Stalin and Foreign Minister Molotov to negotiate a peace for them. Stalin had already branded Japan as an aggressor in 1944, and in 1945 Molotov belatedly renounced the neutrality pact of 1941 on the grounds that Japan was an enemy of Russia's allies. Finally, the Soviet government announced its support of the surrender terms drafted at the Big Three Potsdam Conference in July, 1945. Still the Japanese were amazed when the Soviet Union declared war on August 8, 1945, two days after the atomic bombing of Hiroshima. Major offensives were launched in Manchuria and northern Korea, the areas roughly delimited as Russian spheres of military operations by the military staffs at Potsdam. Red Army veteran forces quickly smashed the Japanese defenders, whose strength had been depleted during the war, in little more than a week of fighting. This vigorous Soviet assault probably contributed to Japan's decision to surrender in mid-August. The Red Army claimed that 600,000 prisoners were taken and 80,000 Japanese soldiers were killed. However, in the fantastic propaganda claims of the Cold War, Moscow held that Russia brought Japan to its knees almost singlehandedly.

The Aftermath of Victory

The occupation of Japan proved to be an almost exclusively American affair, as Russia failed to get its own zone in Hokkaido or a military commander with power equal to General MacArthur's at SCAP. Nor was Russia successful at obtaining large-scale reparations or a sizable portion of Japan's commercial fleet. The Soviet Union, having gotten the Kuriles and Southern Sakhalin, could only agitate against the American occupation, demand more drastic reform, and call for a trial of the emperor as a war criminal. Soviet officials also charged that Japan was not being truly democratized but was becoming an economic colony of the United States as well as a military base for future American aggression in the Far East.

The China Question

Matters progressed more favorably for Soviet Russia on the Asian mainland. China reluctantly reached an accord with Russia based on the Yalta agreement, but only after the Soviet army had entered the war. This Sino-Soviet Treaty of August, 1945, actually granted Russia broader rights in Manchuria than envisaged by the Americans in February. In addition, the independence of Outer Mongolia was recognized, following a plebiscite. Russia then violated its treaty promises in Manchuria, aiding the Communists and handicapping the Nationalists where it could. The Soviet government refused the Nationalists permission to debark troops at Dairen but allowed the Communists to filter into Manchuria at will and take over Japanese military equipment. Meanwhile, anticipating Kuomintang domination of Manchuria, the Russians, before leaving in the spring of 1946, despoiled the heavy industries built up by Japan. This device served the double purpose of seizing reparations and weakening a potentially powerful Chinese base near Russia's vulnerable eastern provinces.

The Russian pattern of economic control in Manchuria following the military evacuation was reminiscent of Czarist penetration. The Russians established a Far Eastern Bank, a Far Eastern Trading Company, and a Far Eastern Transportation and Warehouse Company. Soviet officers and soldiers were "discharged" from the army and remained in important civilian posts or as guards of Russian property. The Soviet government also dominated the railroad and ports, kept the Americans out, and hamstrung Nationalist efforts to gain control over these facilities. Such precautions, like the looting of Manchuria, indicate that the Russians expected the Nationalists to control this region.

Despite the treaty violations, the Soviet position on the internal Chinese political situation seems to have been one of cautious noncommitment. In 1945 Moscow probably would have been satisfied if the Chinese Communists had been able simply to hold out in the northern part of Manchuria, above the Sungari River. There they could have been sustained by the Russians while serving as a buffer to protect Russian territory. In 1945 Stalin maintained that Chiang Kai-shek was too powerful to be dislodged and advised his "Chinese comrades" to accept limited representation in a central government as proposed by the Nationalists. Ironically, the limited assistance Soviet Russia did extend to the Chinese Communists enabled the rebels to undermine the weakened Kuomintang. Yet even in 1948, when the Communists dominated Manchuria and made important inroads into North China, there are reports that the Russians still advised caution and a consolidation of gains already won. As in 1945, the Chinese Communists followed their own line of reasoning and attacked before the international situation changed or the Americans decided to intervene with large military forces.

Russia and the "New China"

From 1946 to 1948 the Russians maintained formal diplomatic correctness in their relations with Nationalist China, though they stressed the extensive nature of the crisis and tried to have it discussed in the Council of the Foreign Ministers.[2] By 1948, Soviet propaganda was hammering away at Kuomintang tyranny and "American aggressiveness" in China. The collapse of the Nationalists in 1949 was marked by a wild flight of its government from Nanking to Chungking with various intermediary stops. The Soviet Ambassador followed along, in a move symbolic of the grim joke of formal recognition. On October 1, 1949, the Communists proclaimed their People's Republic of China, and Russia transferred its diplomatic recognition to the new regime the next day. Red China was welcomed into the Soviet camp with much pomp and ceremony. Chinese labor and cultural delegations to Moscow were given special treatment. When Mao Tse-tung and his entourage arrived to adjust treaty relations at the end of 1949, they were greeted with a fanfare and Stalin himself conducted the negotiations.

A basic problem still confronted Soviet Russia in its Far Eastern policy. It could retain its rights and privileges, which were tangible assets, or turn them over to its new ideological ally. The latter policy involved a short-term gamble on the durability of the Chinese Communist regime. Eventually it meant that Russia's Far Eastern territory might become a hostage to a China made powerful with considerable Russian assistance. The Sino-Soviet Treaty of February,

---

[2] This was a postwar agency on which the United States, Russia, Britain, and France were represented.

1950, was a compromise arrangement in the form of limited Russian concessions. It abrogated the old treaties and established a new defensive alliance, to fight together against any future aggression by Japan or any other state collaborating with Japan. Like other postwar Soviet pacts, this treaty was based on Article 107 of the United Nations Charter, which permitted alliances against a former Axis enemy. In this way, the Russians could undertake widespread commitments against the West without violating the letter of the Charter. Both China and Russia promised to consult on matters of common interest, pursue the objectives of "peace and security," and work toward an early peace treaty with Japan.

The Russians agreed to restore to China without compensation control of Manchuria's railroads, now called the Chinese-Changchun Railway, with all its property, when peace was made with Japan or by the end of 1952. At that time Soviet troops would leave Port Arthur, but Russia could have use of that base, at China's request, should a military crisis arise. The future of Dairen was left for later negotiations. An economic accord produced a $300 million Russian loan at 1 per cent interest to aid Chinese reconstruction and industrialization. Such loans, modest by American standards, were quite costly to the Russians; as Chinese needs mounted, this problem became a major issue in Russia's domestic economic planning. Soviet technical missions began arriving in China and, though large in number, kept generally to themselves and did not intrude openly in Chinese affairs. In March, 1950, another economic agreement was reached: joint stock companies were to exploit oil and nonferrous metals in Sinkiang and operate civilian airlines from Peking to points in Soviet Asia. Plans were also laid to intensify overland trade and communications networks. Though many of these economic arrangements were delayed by the Korean War, they were resumed with surprising vigor after 1953.

Soviet policy in the Far East after 1950 operated from these basic treaty arrangements with China. When the United States held that Russian imperialism still prevailed along the great Chinese border lands, the two communist allies angrily denounced this view and held that the alliance was between equals. Moscow undertook an intensive campaign to gain diplomatic recognition for Red China and particularly sought to have the Peking regime replace the routed Nationalist, now on Formosa, at the United Nations. Its campaign was adamant and included a boycott of all United Nations functions at the start of 1950. Russia and China jointly denounced the United States for keeping Formosa from the "rightful owners," blocking Peking's acceptance at the United Nations, and planning aggression in Asia.

The Korean War

Aggression, of course, was planned and executed by the communists when North Korea attacked South Korea on June 25, 1950. It was a peculiar struggle in that the Russians prudently held aloof from direct official participation. The Soviet Union had gained control of North Korea above latitude 38° when an

Allied military decision was reached in 1945 to divide military occupation zones at this line. Both America and Russia were committed to a free, united, democratic Korea, but the Russians immediately sealed off their part of the land. This section held one third of Korea's 29 million people and most of its heavy industry, mining, and electric power. North Korea was a strategically valuable land whose control was safely and inexpensively assured through a loyal native Communist government. All American and United Nations Assembly efforts to sponsor a free election that would lead to national unification were rejected. Undoubtedly the vigorous anti-Communist regime under Syngman Rhee in South Korea, plus a likelihood that a united Korea would be a non-Communist state, accounted for Russia's attitude. If the Russians considered North Korea essential to their territorial security, South Korea was equally vital to preserve Japanese independence and the American position in the Far East, especially after the Communist victory in China. Had the assault of 1950 succeeded, it would have upset the balance of power in Northeast Asia, with serious repercussions all along the Soviet perimeter. The stage for this high drama was set in 1949 when the Russians withdrew their army at the start of the year and the Americans later pulled back to Japan, leaving only a military training mission in South Korea.

Russian culpability in this assault stemmed from the fact that Moscow trained, advised, and equipped the North Korean army, giving it tanks and other offensive weapons. Moreover, Russia did not act to prevent the attack, as it could easily have done; on the other hand, since there is no clear evidence that the Soviet government ordered the attack, the initiative for triggering the war may have rested with the North Koreans. Once combat was joined, the Russians apparently worked to keep the war in bounds and avoid a general holocaust. Thus they did not permit North Korea to have its own air force, which could widen the zone of combat by attacking United Nations bases in Japan. Nor did Soviet submarines molest the American transport force which landed at Inchon, just below latitude 38° in September, 1950, though this move broke the North Korean offensive and shattered its army. More mystifying still was Russia's absence from the United Nations Security Council when that agency branded North Korea as an aggressor in June, 1950, and recommended that United Nations members give military aid to the South Korean defenders. Russia could easily have used its veto power; it was certainly not swayed by world public opinion, for when Jacob Malik returned to the Security Council in August, he paralyzed its operations and blithely held that South Korea was the aggressor. Nor did Russia support any effort to get North Korea to withdraw its forces from South Korea that summer. Premier Stalin showed little interest in the mediation proposals that Prime Minister Nehru of India set forth after the outbreak of hostilities.

In the fall of 1950, the American–South Korean forces followed up their victory over the aggressor with a rapid movement across North Korea, up to China's frontier along the Yalu River. The Chinese Communist forces, which had been marshaling strength since the war began, then entered the war and forced the Allied armies back into South Korea. However, Chinese assaults in turn were hurled back in severe combat early in 1951, and the American-led United Nations forces (including some troops from sixteen other nations) pushed the front north to latitude 38°. There the battle line became stabilized, though bitter fighting continued. Russia was now committed to building up the Chinese army and air force, supplying modern arms, and yet keeping the war in bounds. The war was a strain on China's economy, and its leaders complained that their country bore the brunt of the fighting but never received enough military equipment.

A suggestion that a truce could be arranged was made in 1951 by Jacob Malik in an offhand manner at the conclusion of a long speech which was typically vitriolic against the United States and other Western powers. The enthusiastic Western reaction may have caught the Russians unawares; nonetheless, truce talks were soon begun between the warring sides. Negotiations dragged on for two years before their successful conclusion. During this time, combat remained restricted to Korea, where fighting was bitter though limited along a fairly stable front.

Evolution of Relations with China

Meanwhile Sino-Soviet relations continued to evolve along the lines set in 1950. Neither power signed the Japanese Peace Treaty of 1951. At the end of 1952 Russia yielded the Chinese-Changchun Railway and the port of Dairen as well. The Chinese requested the Russians to remain a while longer at Port Arthur. An impasse was reached in 1952–1953 over economic aid, and a Chinese mission to Moscow remained long after the political delegation departed. During this time negotiations for a Korean truce were held up at one major point—the voluntary repatriation of prisoners. The United Nations Command insisted on this right for the approximately 25,000 Chinese prisoners who did not want to be sent home. The Peking government insisted that all captives be exchanged.

The log-jam broke in 1953, following the death of Stalin that March. There followed China's acceptance of voluntary repatriation of prisoners, the end of the Korean War in mid-1953, and new Soviet promises of aid to China in 1953–1954. The 1953 agreements called for Russian economic and technical aid to construct ninety-one new enterprises and rebuild fifty existing ones. In October, 1954, Communist party Secretary Nikita Khrushchev and Marshal Bulganin came to Peking to celebrate that regime's fifth anniversary. They promised additional funds for these 141 plants and support for fifteen more enterprises. The projects covered a wide variety of industries and included iron, steel, and nonferrous metallurgical plants; factories which produced heavy machinery so that China could make its own finished goods; oil plants, chemical industries, coal mines, and power stations. Additional loans amounting to about $230 million were extended, but the Chinese had to pay for all aid, aside from technical assistance, with food and exports of raw material.

508

Also, the Russians liquidated four joint-stock companies created in 1950–1951: oil and metal concerns in Sinkiang, the civil airlines, and a shipbuilding and repair concern in Dairen. The value of the Soviet share was to be paid by China over a period of years, with raw-material exports required by Russia. The Russians finally withdrew from Port Arthur by 1955 and transferred its installations to China without compensation. Scientific links were regularized by a five-year agreement to exchange technical data and specialists, which could be extended another five years. Overland rail, road, and air routes were also expanded and were expected to mount in importance as these interior regions were developed.

Soviet controls in China have thus loosened to the extent that Russia's only major lever of influence is the economic assistance program administered from Moscow. Even this is a disappearing asset, since its very success reduces China's dependence on Soviet guidance. China today is clearly a full-fledged partner in what the Russians call the "world camp of socialism and democracy."

A further sequel to the Korean War was the rehabilitation of North Korea. A Russian aid program of 1953 was aimed at restoring the hydroelectric, steel, oil, and chemical plants ruined in the war. With a Chinese army there and Peking's promise of economic assistance, the degree of control exercised there by China and Russia is not clear, but it appears that North Korea may be coming under China's sphere of responsibility.

Russian Policy since Korea

With communist rule firmly entrenched in China and North Korea, the Soviet bloc of powers could now turn its full attention to Southeast Asia, India, and Japan. Undoubtedly the Russians and Chinese are working in close cooperation. China's geographic position and military power, its industrial revolution and overseas nationals all point to Peking's importance in pressing communist expansion in Asia. Nevertheless, Russia remains China's protector and its opposition must be taken into account by anyone challenging Peking; for Soviet diplomacy and military might lie behind China's foreign policy toward Formosa, Korea, and Southeast Asia.

The Russians, however, have not been relegated to a secondary role in Asian affairs. Moscow still exercises control over the Communist parties of Japan and India and has asserted itself in formal diplomatic relations with these two powers. It is unrealistic to conclude that specific zones of operation are marked out or that China's area of action is limited to Southeast Asia. China is leading the communist effort to induce Japan to orient its foreign-trade policy and diplomacy away from the West. Also, Peking appears to be the major political and military threat to Nepal and northern India. On the other hand, Russia has recently become active in Southeast Asia and has extended promises of aid in that region.

On the whole, Soviet policy toward Asia has become more subtle and flexible since 1945. At that time Russia not only challenged the entire system of Western colonialism but also bitterly criticized the trend toward independence as a sham.

It supported the Indonesian independence effort but appeared irritated when a political settlement was finally reached through United Nations efforts. It doubted the reality of Burmese freedom, calling Aung San a puppet during his lifetime, and did not establish diplomatic relations with Rangoon until 1951. Philippine freedom was branded a fiction, recognition was refused when the Americans were granted bases, and the regime was labeled fascist. Indian independence was described as incomplete, and both Gandhi and Nehru were severely criticized. Russian policy began to change with the Korean settlement in 1953. Soviet Foreign Minister Molotov conducted intensive negotiations with the French and Chinese at Geneva in 1954, following which a compromise truce was reached in the Indochinese war. Molotov and Foreign Minister Eden of Britain served as cochairmen of signatories of this agreement. Russia is therefore able to raise the issue of free elections in Vietnam called for in the accord. In 1955, however, Moscow did not press this matter; moreover, it recognized the independence of Laos and Cambodia and did not oppose their entry into the United Nations.

The immediate objectives of Soviet foreign policy are to undermine the diplomatic and military ties formed by the United States in East Asia and to encourage neutralism in non-Communist lands. The main weapons in this campaign have been the use of diplomacy, promises of aid to neutralists, and vilification of American allies. Pakistan, an adherent of the Baghdad and Manila defense pacts, has been subjected to strenuous Russian criticism; yet it was also offered considerable Soviet financial assistance. The Soviet government has praised neutralist India, asserted India's right to Kashmir, and offered extensive economic aid. Russia even supported the outlandish Afghan claims that a large part of West Pakistan be transformed into an independent state for that land's Pathan tribesmen.

Japan, with its American alliances and bases, has been dealt with most severely in negotiations over a peace treaty. Russia has ignored Tokyo's request for a return of the Kuriles or part of Sakhalin, and blandly denies that it still holds 100,000 Japanese war prisoners. It did sign a peace accord in 1956, regularizing diplomatic and economic relations, but did not yield to any significant Japanese territorial demands.

Russia may be able to exercise even greater political influence in Northeast Asia when its own plans to create a great industrial complex in the Lake Baikal region reach fruition. It is expected that this area will produce 15 to 20 million tons of pig iron a year within two decades and become the third largest industrial center in the Soviet Union.

In 1955–1956 Russian diplomacy moved into high gear, with loans to India totaling $226 million to build a large steel mill, an oil refinery, and fertilizer and heavy machinery factories. Western observers ruefully noted that this "monument type" of aid can make a better impression on the recipients than a larger aid program geared to bolster the entire economy. In 1955 Prime Minister Nehru visited Moscow and became the first non-Communist since 1917 to address a large public audience. Premier Bulganin and party-leader Nikita

Khrushchev visited India at the end of the year and were given large receptions, the most spontaneous and enthusiastic being that in Calcutta. The occasion was used to spread vicious anti-Western propaganda, extend offers of more aid to India, and indicate that the Nehru administration was considered eminently suitable in Russian eyes. Like other foreign Communist groups, the Indian Communist party was placed at a disadvantage by this visit. Khrushchev is reported to have told a local Communist—with more guile than honesty—that he was concerned primarily with the man's Indian nationality and only incidentally with his party affiliation. To a Westerner, this strikes a familiar chord —Stalin's emphasis of interest in and support of the Chinese Nationalists, as long as this suited the temporary objectives of Russian foreign policy. At this stage of the Cold War, the Russians were satisfied with a joint declaration stressing the value of neutralism, mutual friendship, the abolition of hydrogen and other atomic weapons, the Soviet "solution" of the German problem, and the maintenance of peace. Given the peculiar Soviet definition of these terms, this agreement was well tailored to Russian foreign-policy objectives.

A similar performance was accomplished by Bulganin and Khrushchev when they afterward visited Burma. They praised the land's neutralism, condemned the Western "imperialists," and offered to purchase Burmese surplus rice. In 1956 the Russians signed a three-year pact with Burma, exchanging Soviet machinery, goods, and services for 400,000 tons of rice.[3] It is difficult for Westerners to conceive that a South Asian state like Burma could be lulled into friendship for the Soviet Union after the bitter military-political experiences it endured from native communist uprisings. Yet there is ingrained in the present political order a degree of hostility to the West, a willingness to trust professed Soviet objectives, and a desire to maintain peace. As a result, this novel Soviet use of traditional devices of diplomacy has undoubtedly benefited Russian policy. It remains the hope of Western diplomats that continued internal communist pressures, the persistence of a Sino-Soviet military menace, and the basically aggressive nature of international communism will have a counterbalancing effect.

Russian efforts meanwhile remain focused on dividing the free world by setting Asians against Westerners, intensifying existing conflicts between Asian states, and, over the long haul, supporting native communist efforts to undermine democratic regimes. American policy makers fear that the division of free Asia into neutralists and Western allies may weaken the non-Communist position and encourage Soviet or Chinese aggression.

Yet the United States cannot simply repudiate neutralist states, for this could increase the danger of internal communist subversion in these lands. American foreign policy has undertaken a global effort to contain communist power, a self-imposed assignment of staggering proportions. The problems raised in Asia represent one of the greatest challenges to this policy of containment.

[3] The neutralist Burmese balanced this agreement by obtaining two loans, totaling about $20 million, from the Western-oriented International Bank for Reconstruction and Development, for railway and harbor improvement.

18 *United States Policy*

in Eastern Asia

There is a paradox in the historical relations between the United States and the two continents of Europe and Asia. Despite America's cultural and family ties to Europe, its political attitude in the century after 1815 was one of isolation and a conscious effort to keep out of the Old World's wars. Yet when two major wars occurred there in this century, the Americans found themselves compelled to participate and, on each occasion, provided the decisive influence that tipped the scales from defeat to victory. The Far East, twice as distant from Europe and inhabited by alien peoples of exotic cultures, was a region in which American interest and participation mounted steadily during the nineteenth century. There was no built-in antagonism to taking part in the affairs of China, Japan, Korea, and the Philippines as American influence expanded across the Pacific Ocean. America became a colonial power, created important missionary works, extended its commercial relations, and eventually engaged in complex diplomatic undertakings and political commitments. Nevertheless, the government and its sovereign public were unwilling to support this position with the treasure and military sacrifices required. In this sense the American policy in Asia was even more limited than in Europe, despite the superficially more intimate diplomatic activity in the Far East that occurred in time of peace.

It is true that a Japanese assault on Pearl Harbor brought the United States into the Second World War. But it is also a fact that Japan and the United States first reached an irreconcilable conflict over the security of Britain's possessions in Southeast Asia. Once the struggle was joined, top priority was given to the defeat of the more powerful and important German enemy, and the Pacific War was relegated to a secondary position. Again, once Japan was beaten, East Asia was given a low military-diplomatic priority during the years 1945–1950. It was Europe that was shored up with economic assistance under the Marshall Plan, a NATO defense agreement, and a military assistance program. Though considerable help was given to China, Japan, and the Philippines, there was no integrated policy, no alliances were formed, and a program of military disengagement was apparently undertaken.

512

Only when the global threat of communism was clearly recognized did the United States reverse this trend, and then it made only a partial commitment to the defense of East Asia. Moreover, the Communist victory in China and a North Korean assault on South Korea were necessary to achieve this much. America undertook military action to save South Korea, and in 1951–1955 concluded a series of limited treaties from Japan to Pakistan, which formed an incomplete arc around China.

A major theme in this story of diplomatic ties and commitments is the great tragedy of American-Chinese relations. Despite Peking's current propaganda, which depicts the United States as the great conspirator directing a world imperialist plot against China, the United States had been the most sympathetic and helpful of all Western powers. Its diplomacy adhered steadfastly to the principle of supporting Chinese sovereignty, though little material assistance was extended before 1940. The fate of China was closely related to America's entry into the Second World War, and the diplomacy of President Franklin Roosevelt was directed toward maintaining its security and enhancing its international prestige. The astounding collapse of the Nationalists (1946–1949) was a bitter blow to Americans, many of whom had personal ties in China. The domestic American political situation became intensely and emotionally embittered over this issue. As a consequence, to sift the facts and make an impartial appraisal of American policy in East Asia after 1945 has been more difficult than any other aspect of foreign policy.

It is our task to survey the development of American policy in the Far East and examine the basis of its course of action. We must see whether commitments undertaken were recognized as vital to American interests and what steps were taken to honor them. Finally, we must examine the present American security policy in the light of the lessons of the past, in our quest for a solution to the difficulties confronting us today.

Early Contacts with Asia

Early Commercial Relations

The basic stimulus for American activities was commerce, the dream of great Chinese and Japanese markets. Even the acquisition of California and Oregon in the 1840's was partly justified by the claim that it would enhance the Asian trade. America's first commercial ties were established with the Orient when the "Empress of China" sailed from New York to Canton in 1785. Though trade gradually increased in other Asian lands, Canton remained the central port. Fur and, later, agricultural and mineral products were exchanged for spices, tea, and the like. The American diplomatic and consular services were rudimentary, and the United States possessed no naval bases or colonies early in the nineteenth century; thus American nationals were left to shift for themselves. After 1800 the foreign residents generally presented a unified front to their antagonistic Chinese host at Canton, but the Americans stopped short of cooperating when force was used. They were more conciliatory and strove to get along with the Chinese, though they insisted on being treated equally with the other foreigners, who had gained certain rights and privileges through the use or threat of force.

The first formal American treaty of commerce and friendship was made with Siam in 1833, following a British agreement there in 1826. The first major agreement in Asia was the Treaty of Wanghsia (1844), negotiated with China by Caleb Cushing. He sought trading rights similar to those gained by the British in the Treaty of Nanking, though this agreement did not extend to territorial concessions or legalized trade in opium. The Chinese were anxious to treat all foreigners equally, for their own protection, and so allowed the United States full trading rights and consulates in the five treaty ports of Canton, Amoy, Ningpo, Foochow, and Shanghai, together with the right to rent land and enjoy extraterritoriality. The United States also benefited from the treaty concessions gained by Britain and France in the Second Opium War, which opened more ports and set tariffs at 5 per cent. The first American Minister to Peking was Anson Burlingame, sent in 1861. His moral suasion was so great that the Chinese made him their first minister to the West, and in 1867 he won for China a treaty with the United States that opened America to Chinese immigration.

A Japanese treaty rounded out this flurry of mid-century diplomacy. America's first interest was to safeguard shipwrecked sailors who were harshly treated by the Tokugawa rulers; later the desire for coaling stations and trade were added incentives. Commodore Matthew Perry arrived at Tokyo in 1853 with these demands; told to wait at Nagasaki, he bluntly retorted that he would return the following spring for an answer. He then occupied the Bonin Islands, established a coaling station in the Ryukyus, and made a trade agreement with their ruler. Perry was a great imperialist visionary who wished to hold these islands, take Formosa, and create bases in the Far East to sustain American maritime rights in competition with the Europeans. In 1854 the Japanese agreed to a restricted trade settlement that permitted some commerce but no permanent residence. In 1858 Townsend Harris negotiated a comprehensive settlement by pointing out that the United States sought no land but that other Western powers might seize bases there if Japan did not regularize its foreign relations. The treaty provided for an exchange of diplomats and the right to trade. America was allowed consulates, land leases in treaty ports, a fixed tariff, and a most-favored-nation clause.

The more grandiose dreams of territory and empire, however, were thwarted by popular American opposition to such ventures. The United States was content to have even Hawaii remain independent. It had successfully pressed Britain and France, in 1843 and 1849, to disavow seizures of these islands. In fact, the Fillmore administration rejected an offer of Hawaii's ruler to cede his lands to America in 1851, an attempt at annexation was vetoed by President Pierce in 1854, and a reciprocity treaty was defeated in 1855. Though Secretary of State

Seward, in the 1860's, viewed the Pacific as the center of future world affairs and wished to foster a great American maritime empire, his only success was the widely opposed purchase of Alaska from Russia in 1867. He failed to gain a foothold in China or even establish a treaty with Hawaii.

A commercial treaty with Hawaii was finally concluded in 1875. It provided that no territory should be leased or sold to a third power. On its renewal in 1884, America gained the right to establish a fortified naval base at Pearl Harbor, near Honolulu, on Oahu Island. During this time American traders and planters came to dominate the Hawaiian economy. Oriental immigrants arrived in large numbers, and the Japanese became the majority element on the islands. Elsewhere, the Samoan Islands, near Australia and New Zealand, also interested the Americans because of a fine harbor at Pago-Pago. In 1878 a commercial treaty was signed with the Samoans, partly to block expansionist German ambitions. This issue was settled with the establishment of a codominium of Britain, America, and Germany in 1889.

The Expansion of the 1890's

The last decade of the century witnessed a revival of expansionist ideology. It briefly occupied a dominant position, especially during the Spanish-American War of 1898. It netted only modest territorial gains, however, for by the turn of the century American possessions in the Pacific included only Alaska and the Aleutians (1867), Midway Islands (1867), Hawaii (1898), Samoa and Wake (1899), Guam (1899), and the Philippines (1899). Nor did this imperialist spirit survive after 1900. Still, it had far-reaching consequences because it involved the United States intimately in Far Eastern affairs as a major power.

Events in Hawaii indicated how strongly the trend toward expansion was resisted. In 1893 the American settlers, using an American ship and marines stationed there, carried out a coup against the queen, and immediately signed a treaty of accession to the United States. The Cleveland administration took office, however, before the treaty passed the Senate. The President rejected it, tried unsuccessfully to undo the revolution, and ended by recognizing the new republic established by the rebels. When William McKinley took office in 1897, he negotiated a new treaty of annexation but could not get it through the Senate in the face of Democratic and anti-imperialist Republican opposition. He then resorted to a joint resolution, which needed only a majority vote in each house, compared to the two-thirds vote a treaty required in the Senate. But even this resolution lagged in Congress during 1898, until the patriotic momentum generated by the war against Spain ensured its passage.

The surge of imperialist interest coincided with the end of continental expansion and the closing of the last land frontiers. It was spurred on by the erroneous economic belief that American markets were becoming saturated and that foreign customers were therefore needed to absorb the produce of the country's growing industrial plant. Finally, there was a revival of the belief that America had a mission to propagate its democratic and republican beliefs abroad. This attitude was linked to the prevalent notion that the Anglo-Saxon "race" was a superior one, with a religious-educational mission to perform overseas. A strategic underpinning was provided by Captain Arthur Mahan, naval officer and publicist, whose brilliant studies illuminated the role of sea power as a major force in shaping world history. He saw in a large navy and strategic bases the means to enhance American power and security and bring about a great empire. His views were seconded by such important Republican leaders as Senator Henry Cabot Lodge and Theodore Roosevelt. The American navy increased from a small force in the 1890's to one of the three largest in the world by 1914. Other objectives of the expansionists were the creation of a canal to link the Atlantic and Pacific, control of the Caribbean and Hawaiian approaches to this link, and penetration of the western Pacific. A stimulus was provided by Germany's sudden quest for empire, reflected in its effort to purchase the Spanish colonies of Cuba, the Philippines, and the mid-Pacific islands.

The war with Spain over Cuban independence gave the expansionists their opportunity. As Assistant Secretary of the Navy, Theodore Roosevelt ordered Admiral Dewey to attack the Spanish fleet in the Philippines; thus the war was extended from Cuba to the Far Pacific. When the Philippines were captured, the imperialists campaigned vigorously to hold this unexpected gain. The annexation of Hawaii occurred at this time and, though it could be justified on defensive grounds, it set a precedent for similar actions. The expansionists sought to gain the support of the business community, which was at best lukewarm. They pointed out that all European powers had bases in or near China and that Manila would provide an entry into the potentially vast China market. President McKinley, who only gradually came to support the annexation of the Philippines, had this provision incorporated into the 1899 peace treaty with Spain.

The anti-imperialists fought hard against annexation of an alien land whose people would not be allowed to join the American Union. They failed to defeat the treaty in the Senate by only two votes. Moreover, a resolution definitely promising independence to the Filipinos ended in a deadlock and was defeated only when Vice-President Garett Hobart cast his negative vote. The insurrection on the islands (1899–1902) strengthened the anti-imperialist argument; even the most ardent expansionists were badly shaken. However, they insisted on keeping the Philippines under American tutelage, though the colony was not made an incorporated territory, as were Hawaii and Alaska, in preparation for statehood.

Throughout this burst of expansionism, isolationism retained its powerful hold on American political thought. This was the political doctrine of retaining a completely free hand in world affairs, unencumbered by any alliances or obligations to help any other power. A more sweeping type of isolationism—total noninvolvement in world affairs—was difficult to practice, for the nation had already become a world power. America now faced new and difficult questions: What were its vital interests? What involvements, if any, should be undertaken in their behalf? Was the policy of no alliances adequate to meet this situation? How would the United States honor its commitments in a crisis?

The Open Door and the Chinese Puzzle

These queries can serve to introduce the problem of China's territorial integrity and America's stand on the issue. During the years bounded by the Open Door notes (1899–1900) and the attack on Pearl Harbor (1941), the United States became increasingly involved in Chinese affairs. Was this essential to American interests, and, if so, were the policies adopted suitable to the objectives sought? Or was the undertaking an aberration that warranted no sacrifice because it was a pointless commitment? Whatever one's view, the policy adopted by the United States appears in retrospect to have been an untenable combination of both. America undertook to support China's integrity but never committed itself to act, use force, or conclude enabling alliances. In fact, such considerations were frequently denounced during this period.

The Open Door Notes and After

The very origins of the Open Door notes reflected the improvisation and imprecision that characterized American Far Eastern policy. In the 1890's the major advocate of the Open Door, or equal trade opportunity for all, was Great Britain, the economic leader that stood to gain the most from an unrestricted China trade. However, by 1898, with other European powers establishing spheres of influence, Britain abandoned this concept as impractical and sought to protect its own paramount position in the Yangtze valley. Meanwhile the Americans had just acquired the Philippines and were hoping to expand their China trade. Secretary of State John Hay and his adviser, W. W. Rockhill, were influenced by an Englishman, Alfred E. Hippisley, a veteran of the Imperial Maritime Customs Service, which collected tariff duties for the Manchu government. Rockhill and Hippisley drew up a statement that simply called for nondiscrimination in tariff rates, railroad charges, harbor fees, and port dues. The note did not ask for the end of spheres of influence or request that capital investments and industrial activity be given impartial treatment. It was in the American tradition of simply seeking equal trading rights.

The matter took on a more serious tone in the aftermath of the Boxer Rebellion of 1900. The American government sought to reduce foreign pressure on China, and so Hay issued a second note stating that it was the policy of the United States to support China's territorial integrity and administrative entity. This was a unilateral undertaking that no other power supported. Nor was the United States ready to give substance to this position. When the Japanese, deeply concerned over Russian penetration of Manchuria in 1900–1901, asked if America would join with it in a diplomatic front against St. Petersburg, Secretary Hay responded that the United States would not act "singly, or in concert with other powers to enforce these views in the east. . . ."

517

The American public, nevertheless, sympathized with Japan in its war with Russia, for the Asians seemed to represent progress and Westernization. The Roosevelt administration felt that a Japanese victory would redress the balance of power in Asia, but, as the war brought impressive Japanese triumphs, the President feared that the scales would tip too far the other way. His role as a mediator in working out a peace treaty during 1905 was a useful application of his limited power to maintain a political equipoise in the Far East.

Ironically, at this stage, possession of the Philippines became a source of weakness rather than strength, because President Roosevelt realized that the American people were against using force to maintain the colony. Since a military alliance toward this end was out of the question, he fell back on requests for larger naval appropriations. He also reached a settlement with Japan in the form of two executive agreements. The Taft-Katsura agreement of 1905 recognized Japan's primacy in Korea in return for a disavowal of aggressive interest in the Philippines. In the Root-Takahira agreement of 1908, both parties announced their respect for each others' territories and for the Open Door in China, and then went on to note that Japan had special economic interests in Manchuria. This was in effect an admission that a "closed door" existed in Korea and Manchuria. The concessions stemmed from Roosevelt's calculations that these lands lay outside America's zone of vital interests. He also realized that only diplomacy could be used, and in a very restricted way, to preserve the Open Door in China Proper.

The succeeding administration of President William Taft and Secretary of State Philander Knox, which was unwilling to accept these limitations, sought to re-establish the Open Door for all of China. But an attempt to equalize trade rights and internationalize railroads in Manchuria met with no success, as Japan and Russia cooperated to protect their respective spheres against all outside interference. Secretary Knox did succeed in establishing a consortium to control the activities of all alien capital in China, but when President Wilson took office in 1913 he rejected American participation in this program because it interfered in China's internal affairs.

Effects of the First World War

The European War of 1914 removed the "invisible hand" that had kept the Chinese situation in delicate balance. Only the United States, with its insistence on the Open Door, stood in Japan's way, but Washington had no intention of resorting to force. Secretary of State William Bryan continued along the well-worn path of yielding ground. In 1915 he stated that the United States would not acknowledge Japanese control over China as envisaged in the Twenty-one Demands. However, he did recognize that territorial *contiguity* created special relations between Japan and districts near its possessions—Shantung, Southern Manchuria, and Eastern Inner Mongolia. This statement left the Japanese uncertain as to American intentions. When the United States entered the European war, Japan sought American recognition of its paramount interests in China, but the United States hedged and the Lansing-Ishii agreement of 1917 proved to be a vague, unsatisfactory compromise. As a concession to Japan, the United States recognized the importance of territorial *propinquity* and Japan's special interest in Chinese territory contiguous to its own. However, it also supported China's territorial integrity and sovereignty, as well as the Open Door in trade. As translated into Chinese by Japan, this document stated that America recognized Tokyo's paramount interests. The United States quickly responded that it recognized only special interests of an economic nature and denied that any political rights were involved.

The Washington Conference and settlement of 1921–1922 resolved this issue by providing for a holiday in expensive naval construction, the famous 5:5:3 ratio in capital ships, a general treaty of friendship (Britain, France, America, and Japan), and a nine-power recognition of the principle of the Open Door in China.[1] This compromise settlement gave Japan security in the western Pacific in return for a promise to respect Chinese sovereignty. The Harding administration, so isolationist with regard to Europe, was continuing the Republican party's policy of greater participation in Pacific affairs. The United States, however, made no commitments to act in the future should these treaties be violated. President Harding strongly asserted that no entangling alliances of any kind were formed, and Senator Lodge stressed that the only obligation undertaken was one of consultation, not enforcement. Typical of America's attitude was the failure to keep the navy up to the battleship limits (525,000 tons) established by the agreement. The London Naval Treaty of 1930 projected the capital ship agreement to 1936 and extended the limitations to auxiliary ships. This action appeared to strengthen the original settlement, but the entire structure still depended on Japanese prudence and Tokyo's willingness to abide by its formal promises.

The general difficulty of implementing an idealistic policy without force in the Far East was underlined in 1929 when a Russian-Chinese struggle developed over railway rights in Manchuria. The Soviet Union, as well as America and Japan, had signed the Kellogg-Briand Pact of 1928, which outlawed war as an instrument of national policy. The American appeal to Russia to halt hostilities was rejected with the observation that this issue did not concern the United States, which had not even recognized the U.S.S.R.

The Problem of Aggression (1931–1937)

When Japan launched its invasion of Manchuria in violation of its 1922 and 1928 treaty agreements, it presented an acid test of the Open Door policy. In all fairness it should be noted that Britain and France were not interested in taking action against Japan even though they were committed, under the League Covenant and the Washington treaty, to oppose aggression. Eastern Asia did not directly involve their own security interests, France was troubled by a

[1] Details are described in Chapter 8, pages 226–227.

threatened resurgence of German power, and Western Europe was in the throes of a strong pacifist movement. The American Secretary of State, Henry Stimson, favored a vigorous policy and had the American Consul at Geneva attend meetings of the League Council when collective measures to meet the crisis were discussed. However, American participation was limited to arousing world public opinion against war and aggression.

The Secretary of State repeatedly stressed the immoral and illegal nature of Japan's action. He proposed bold steps, such as economic sanctions and cooperation with the League should it decide to act. President Herbert Hoover, however, effectively vetoed such a policy. His major contention was that the Japanese invasion of Manchuria did not imperil the freedom or the economic or moral future of the American people. He was willing to cooperate with the League only where it proposed negotiation or conciliation. He held that sanctions of any sort were the road to war, that the treaties of 1922 and 1928 were not military alliances, and that their strength lay in the fact that they were enforceable only by the world's moral opinions. He evidently concluded that the preservation of China's integrity was not vital to the national interest; yet he quite sincerely believed that a great moral issue was involved, in which America had an important stake. The President therefore suggested that America refuse to recognize any territorial changes in East Asia that were achieved by force or in violation of treaty obligations. This policy became known as the Stimson Doctrine of Nonrecognition (1932), when the Secretary of State informed Japan that the United States would not recognize the legality of the situation created by Japan or accept any arrangement that impaired American treaty rights or China's integrity.

This stand had no immediate effect, for Japan completed its Manchurian campaign and in 1937 attacked China Proper. It is a matter of judgment whether these attacks impaired American interests, but the crisis made painfully clear the discrepancy between an avowed American position and the unwillingness to make sacrifices necessary to maintain it. Finally, the Hoover administration, though it chose to avoid coercion, did not break with past commitments or resolve this dilemma. Instead, it bound America more firmly to China in a moral sense: America refused to recognize the legality of an attack just as it had tried to prevent one in the past. This tangled heritage remained with President Franklin Roosevelt and Secretary of State Cordell Hull when Japan invaded China and the threat of world war loomed again late in the 1930's.

During the years 1935–1937 America had become more isolationist than ever, and Congress passed a series of Neutrality Acts designed to eliminate American trade and maritime activity in areas involved in war. The President, however, was authorized to decide when a war was in progress. Consequently, when Japan launched its "China Incident," President Roosevelt did not recognize it as a war and so permitted American ships to carry essential goods to

China; such trade would have been impossible had the neutrality laws been invoked. The United States then licensed the export of arms to China via Hong Kong and, together with Britain, extended credit to the Nationalists to stabilize their currency and pay for supplies.

In a bold attempt to challenge isolationism, President Roosevelt made his famous "quarantine speech" in October, 1937. He called for the peace-loving nations to work together against the aggressors and noted that isolation or neutrality offered no escape. The response was overwhelming disapproval of his stand, and isolationist sentiment was expressed with great intensity. This reaction discouraged the President, who decided to move with greater circumspection, an attitude seconded by the extremely cautious Secretary Hull, who felt that the speech set back the internationalist cause. Advocates of a more active policy disagreed and felt that a sustained campaign against isolationism would be fruitful. However, talk of sanctions and of convening a world peace conference was dropped, and the administration followed a passive line in diplomacy.

The League again found Japan guilty of treaty violations and called on the signatories of the Nine Power Treaty of 1922 to confer, with the objective of ending the war. By now the European situation had become so tense that none of the major powers would even consent to be host nation, and the conference was convened by Belgium at Brussels in 1937. Once again the American delegate was limited to discussing a peaceful settlement through negotiation. The Japanese envoy stated that his government would not tolerate any outside interference in this dispute. While Japan was tearing Chinese territorial integrity to shreds, the Brussels Conference ended on a pathetic note—a reaffirmation of the Open Door but no commitment by anyone to undertake effective counteraction.

The Pacific War

The Road to War

We must now consider why the United States, which avoided any action against Japan in 1937, was willing to face a conflict in 1941, even as part of a two-front war. The China front, stabilized in 1939, did not impell this radical change in policy. Rather, the new American position must be evaluated in the light of the war in Europe, Germany's victories in 1940, and the mortal danger to Britain in 1940–1941. Until these events occurred, America remained a relatively passive, if interested, observer of world politics. The sinking of the "Panay" in December, 1937, brought no public desire for vengeance. Nor were the people greatly aroused by Japanese violations of American economic rights; they supported diplomatic protests and demands for damages but would not allow these issues to lead to a major conflict. On the other hand, once Japan began its systematic air attacks on Chungking and other cities in 1939, a move to embargo shipments of oil, high octane gasoline, and scrap iron to Japan gained widespread support. Since these embargoes would have violated the Treaty of Commerce of 1911, Secretary Hull notified Japan on July 26, 1939, that the treaty would be abrogated as of January, 1940. No embargo was imposed at that time, but the threat of economic sanctions now became more evident.

The basic American position from 1939 to mid-1941 was that Nazi Germany was the primary menace and that Britain had to be supported at all costs. Since the United States was militarily unprepared, the State Department and the military leaders pressed all the more vigorously for a cautious policy in the Orient. As long as there were moderates in the Japanese government, such as the Yonai Cabinet of 1940, Washington had an added incentive to move with care in the Pacific. Unfortunately, the imbalance in Europe that riveted American attention on Britain was also the lure that attracted Japan to try to expand in Southeast Asia, to the detriment of British security interests. During the two years before the attack on Pearl Harbor, American policy in the Far East was a mixture of caution and increasing resistance to Japanese expansionist efforts. Only in the latter half of 1941 was the clear-cut issue of peace or war drawn.

The weapons available to the United States in 1940–1941 were trade restrictions, used very carefully and gradually, manipulation of its main fleet, and continued assistance to China. In 1940 the fleet, normally stationed at San Diego, was in Pacific waters on maneuvers. The British requested that an American naval force be dispatched to Singapore. American naval authorities, however, argued that the fleet was not ready for a war and that they wished to return it to the West Coast for additional preparation. The Administration, in a compromise measure, decided to keep it at Pearl Harbor and later sent some ships to the Philippines. Similarly, an intermediary position was taken on economic sanctions. Secretary of War Henry Stimson and others urged a total embargo on all key strategic items, but Secretary Hull warned that this would drive the Japanese to invade the Dutch Indies and so go to war with Britain. Therefore it was decided to restrict the shipment of some items to Japan but to do this tactfully, by establishing a licensing system on the justifiable grounds that the American defense effort required such regulation of exports. By September, 1940, when Japan occupied northern Indochina, the embargo was extended to all scrap iron and steel, aviation gasoline, and some other petroleum products. With regard to China, America extended loans in ever-increasing amounts and firmly rejected any possibility of recognizing the puppet government established at Nanking in March, 1940.

Japan made its first serious diplomatic foray against American interests in Europe by signing the Tripartite Pact of October, 1940; for it was now committed on paper to fight the United States in the Pacific should America go to war against Germany. Though the following months brought further economic restrictions through the licensing program, the State and Navy Departments were more anxious than ever to avoid direct pressure on Japan. Admiral Stark had presented a war plan early in 1941 that stressed avoiding a conflict with Japan because it was the Atlantic that held the key to Britain's fate.

The Japanese occupation of Southern Indochina in July, 1941, brought the issue to a head, because this move was clearly in preparation for an assault on Southeast Asia. Coupled with the Tripartite Pact, it constituted a grave menace to the West's defensive position against Germany. As Admiral Richard Turner told Japanese negotiators later in the year, Japan's actions in undermining Britain's position in Asia weakened it seriously in the vital Atlantic theater and so necessitated an American response to counter this threat. America's position now became more uncompromising. Late in July all Japanese assets in the United States were frozen, and on August 1 an embargo was placed on many types of oil shipments and several other items. Though this was not a total embargo and the United States delivered no ultimatum, the Japanese soon decided that their only recourse lay in war. The American lend-lease program of aid to China also went into effect in August, and shortly thereafter American planes and volunteer aviators began to serve China in an effort to protect the Burma road from bombing attacks.

We have already seen that Premier Konoye was anxious to negotiate with President Roosevelt that summer and had his army's agreement to evacuate Southern Indochina and render the Tripartite Pact meaningless.[2] The militarists, however, demanded, in return, recognition of Japan's political-economic hold over North China and the right to retain troops there. The United States could never accept this demand. But could it have settled the other issues, while keeping the question of China in abeyance, as suggested by Ambassador Joseph Grew? The British vehemently opposed any appeasement of Japan, and the Chinese adamantly insisted that any settlement short of Japanese evacuation would undermine their will to resist. Nor would the American Congress and public tolerate such a compromise. On no other grounds, though, were the Japanese militarists likely to agree to dissolve their German alliance and leave Indochina without receiving a reward. If they did stand idly by while America aided Britain and Russia to defeat Germany, they would later have to evacuate China under Allied pressure. In the last analysis, it was the militarist urge for expansion, now cutting across American strategic interest in Britain's safety, that led to the Pacific war.

We may also conclude that in a deeper sense there could be no half-way settlement on China and that this was the issue on which all peace talks foundered. Yet had Britain not been endangered when the Japanese moved south in July, 1941, the United States would in all likelihood not have become involved in a war in the Pacific. An illusion arose during the war years that America

[2] See Chapter 9, pages 247–248.

523

went to war in order to save China and so gave rise to an unwarranted assumption that the doctrine of the Open Door was a valid one; that is, that America was willing to back this commitment with force.

The Chinese Military Theater

American policy toward China between 1942 and 1949 has generally been judged from the perspective of the Cold War. Actually, decisions made through 1945 were based on strategic objectives of a different sort, conceived in the heat of a difficult two-front war. The wartime objectives proved to be a logically consistent continuation of prewar diplomatic priorities. The war in Europe came first, followed by the ocean-island campaigns against Japan; the Chinese theater on the Asian mainland came last.

Even the effort against Japan lacked the ground and air strength American commanders in the Pacific sought. But by 1945 there were fourteen divisions assigned to this campaign, as well as the largest and most powerful fleet ever assembled. Two major campaigns were waged toward the Japanese home islands, westward from Hawaii and northward from Australia. When they merged with the liberation of the Philippines and the occupation of Okinawa and Iwo Jima early in 1945, Japan itself was open to invasion.[3]

By contrast, the United States could not spare even the two or three divisions sought by China early in 1942. American military leaders felt that the Chinese theater of operations was peripheral to the major war effort. They did see the value of using Chinese air bases to bomb Japan, but in mid-1944, with the capture of Saipan and Tinian in the Marianna Islands, alternate bases were created in the Pacific. Therefore the army plan of campaign did not include any landings on China until the very end of the war. At that time it prepared a secondary thrust at Canton to link up with Nationalist forces, while the main attack was launched against Japan. Tokyo's capitulation in August, 1945, made these efforts unnecessary.

Nor could much material aid be given to China. The needs of other theaters always took priority, even when this meant denying to Chungking equipment that was already promised. Moreover, the physical problem of supply became almost impossible when Japan conquered Burma in 1942, for thereafter all goods had to be flown over the Himalaya Mountains at great effort and expense. For example, China was supposed to receive a monthly supply of 11,000 tons by September, 1943; yet that February it totaled only 3,200 tons and fell to 2,500 in April.

Numerous other issues underlining this problem quickly arose in the China theater. A military mission was dispatched to China under General Stilwell (1942–1944). He operated without a clear line of authority and lacked political finesse in dealing with the British and Chinese, but he was a strong advocate of military reform and vigorous campaigns against the Japanese by the

[3] See Chapter 9, pages 249–252, 256–259, for description of the war.

Nationalists. Chiang Kai-shek proved dangerously irresolute on these points, but on the other hand, he could not tolerate Stilwell's failure to see that the Chinese Communists were a grave menace to his regime. A further rift developed with the American camp between the advocates of air power and those who wanted to build a modern Chinese army. Since supplies were entirely inadequate, neither program made sufficient progress to hold the Japanese in check. Finally, the British in Southeast Asia were quite dubious about the competence of the Chinese forces and were opposed, for reasons of political prestige as well as on military grounds, to their participation in combined operations in Burma. However, such a campaign was finally launched in 1944, clearing northern Burma, although a land supply route to China was still not constructed by the end of the year. Meanwhile, in China itself, the Japanese railway offensive of 1944 advanced with devastating effect. Even when American victories in the Pacific caused the Japanese to withdraw from the region of Chungking toward the coast late in 1944, the Chinese were left in terribly battered condition and could not be assured of any direct ground support.

American Diplomacy and China

The American government, realizing that it could give the Nationalists only limited military assistance, tried to bolster them in other ways. It advanced China's claim to great power status in the face of British skepticism and Soviet indifference. It also sought to regularize Sino-Soviet relations, a problem very much in Chiang's mind as the war drew to a close. Finally, in its hope to strengthen China's internal order, the United States tried to end the debilitating civil war and foster administrative and political reform.

Though China was never given an equal share in the conduct of the war, America supported it at all major conferences. In October, 1943, the Chinese were invited to sign the declaration of general principles drawn up at the Big Three Moscow conference. President Roosevelt and Prime Minister Winston Churchill met with Chiang Kai-shek at Cairo in November, 1943, and promised to return Manchuria, Formosa, and the Pescadores to the Republic of China. This Cairo Declaration of December 1, 1943, was an earnest effort to bolster Chinese morale. Prime Minister Churchill was somewhat annoyed at the intrusion of these issues, which he considered to be of little consequence, into the great power talks then occurring with Stalin at Teheran. It was also in keeping with American policy that China was made one of the five sponsoring powers of the United Nations at the San Francisco conference of April, 1945, and was given a permanent seat, with the power of veto, on the Security Council. In this spirit of stressing China's freedom and equality, Secretary Hull had negotiated a treaty with China earlier in the war (January, 1943) that yielded America's right of extraterritoriality, a privilege long resented by the Nationalists.

The United States agreed to Chiang Kai-shek's repeated requests in 1943–1944 to arrange a Chinese-Russian settlement. Washington itself was anxious to have the Russians enter the Pacific war. This Stalin agreed to do at Teheran in 1943. He also promised air bases in Siberia but never actually allowed them. Late in 1944 the American Joint Chiefs of Staff estimated that it would take eighteen months after Germany fell to defeat Japan. They therefore favored a Russian attack on Manchuria to relieve America's burden; as a result, in October, 1944, tentative military plans were laid for a Soviet encircling movement in that region.

The Yalta agreement of February, 1945, was a comprehensive arrangement for (1) Russia's entry into the war three months after the defeat of Germany, (2) a Soviet promise to reach an agreement with China respecting its territorial integrity and recognizing Nationalist control, (3) in return for railway and port concessions in Manchuria and Soviet acquisition of Southern Sakhalin and the Kuriles.[4] The failure to inform Chiang Kai-shek of this settlement because of poor security conditions in Chungking has been sharply criticized as an act of bad faith. In retrospect it seems that if Japan did learn of Russia's plans, its peace party might have held an even stronger position. Still more damaging was the fact that Russian obligations toward China were all promisory notes to be honored after the Soviet received its reward.

On the other hand, this diplomatic settlement may have been too *optimistic* an interpretation of the Asian power situation at the start of 1945. In the final demarcation of war zones that year, Russia was restricted to Manchuria and northern Korea. The United States was given as its military sphere the Japanese home islands, part of Korea, and all of China below Manchuria. For this demarcation to be militarily realistic, either Japan had to be knocked out immediately, or, if an invasion was required, the Nationalists would have to play a vigorous role in regaining Chinese territory and restricting the Soviet forces to their assigned zones.

The Situation in China

Yet in 1944 the Nationalist military position was at its lowest point. In addition, the government's failure to enact reforms or reach a settlement with the Chinese Communists threatened to ruin all its chances for a useful war effort against Japan. Many Americans in China urged that a coalition of Nationalists and Communists be formed. It may be that they made a primary error in failing to recognize the fanatical zeal and purpose of the communist revolutionary effort. Many American press correspondents in Chungking, thoroughly discouraged by the Kuomintang's lack of competence, were impressed by the Communists and their allegedly democratic outlook as "agrarian reformers." Some foreign-service officials in the Embassy and at Stilwell's headquarters reasoned that the Communists were bound to win out and that America should set its policy accordingly. Ambassador Clarence Gauss concluded that only through reform could the Kuomintang gain the political strength required to cope with

[4] For details see Chapter 6, page 147, and Chapter 17, pages 504–505.

the great burden that was to come with victory, but he was pessimistic about the government's intentions and capacity to survive. The *official* American approach was to exhort the Nationalists to a greater war effort, a broad social reform program, and a party reorganization that would revitalize the Kuomintang.

An important mission to Chungking was dispatched under Vice-President Henry Wallace in June, 1944. Wallace reported that Chiang Kai-shek would continue the war at all costs and should be given as much assistance as possible. Chiang told Wallace that he favored a sweeping reform program but was postponing it to the safer atmosphere of the postwar period. Wallace, observing that Chiang was sorely troubled over the internal political situation, recommended that Stilwell be replaced, a coalition be formed of the Kuomintang and *non*-Communist democratic parties, and that a special envoy be sent to China. The envoy chosen was Patrick Hurley, who first stopped at Moscow in August, 1944, where he was promised that Russia would not aid the Chinese Communists. Later, when he became Ambassador to China (December, 1944), he worked for a Communist-Nationalist coalition, but he made little progress before Japan surrendered. Hurley was a staunch supporter of Chiang Kai-shek. Yet he was slow to understand the nature of Communist purposes or Soviet intentions. By contrast, Ambassador Averell Harriman and George Kennan in Moscow repeatedly warned of Russian duplicity, the ambitions of the Chinese Communists, and the danger of collusion between the two in Manchuria and North China. As the war drew to a close, the question of internal unity remained unsettled.

The War's End

Within the American command in 1945 there was a sharp disagreement over Japan's will to resist. Admiral Ernest King presented the navy's opinion that Russian assistance was unnecessary and that an assault against the home islands could be averted, for a blockade and air assaults would bring Japan to its knees. Perhaps this policy would have worked, even without an atomic bombardment. Certainly Russia's occupation of Manchuria and the horrified Asian reaction to atomic attack had adverse effects on America's position in the Cold War that followed. Yet it is highly questionable whether Japan would have surrendered *when* it did without these multiple shocks. A war of attrition would have taken many months, during which time it would have been difficult to limit Soviet military penetration to Manchuria and North Korea. Without the atomic attacks, it is probable that the invasion of Japan would have occurred as planned: at Kagoshima Bay (November, 1945) and the Tokyo Plain, Honshu (February, 1946). The Japanese had massed their main defensive forces at these points and were prepared to hurl their airplanes at the invader, kamikaze-fashion, as on Okinawa. It is in the light of this military problem and the difficult situation on the mainland that the atomic bombing of Hiroshima and Nagasaki must be evaluated.

Japan capitulated formally on September 2, 1945. Suddenly the United States found itself with a large military force in the Far East, free of burdensome combat obligations. At this juncture American policy adhered with surprising fidelity to the tradition of limited involvement and began a process of disengagement from the Asian mainland. The major military task was the occupation of Japan, which was allotted fourteen divisions. By contrast, three American divisions went to South Korea in September, 1945, and only two to China, still last on the military priority list. These forces in the Pacific were soon sharply reduced as the army underwent a rapid general demobilization.

This restriction of interest had its gravest effect in China, where General Albert Wedemeyer, who had replaced Stilwell in October, 1944, was given conflicting directives. He was told to help the Nationalists regain control over the country below Manchuria but to refrain from becoming involved in a civil war. With American transport aid, United States Marines in the northern port cities, and the Japanese surrendering only to the Kuomintang, the Nationalists gained control of central China and had penetrated into North China in the fall of 1945. However, by now it was evident that any further aid to the Nationalists would involve American troops in a land campaign. This fact was clear from the Communist threat to resist an American landing at Chefoo, on the northern shore of Shantung Peninsula, preparatory to moving into Manchuria.

Until October, 1945, the United States government hoped to liquidate its China commitment by withdrawing all troops, completing the task of equipping the thirty-nine Chinese divisions it had trained late in the war, and promising more aid later. With conditions in North China now getting out of hand, a small American force was kept there. That fall General Wedemeyer cogently observed that China could not be unified without involving American forces on a scale far larger than was available or planned for the entire Far East. At the time Japan surrendered, General MacArthur felt that he could not spare any of his occupation forces for duty in China; by the end of 1945 there were no forces in the Pacific capable of handling such a large task. To compound the difficulty, Chiang Kai-shek planned to push on to Manchuria when it was evacuated by the Russians, and requested additional American help for this purpose. Since Wedemeyer was concerned about the Nationalists' ability to hold even North China, he vainly urged Chiang to consolidate his position in China Proper, strengthen his armies, and institute a reform program before extending his commitments. Meanwhile, the United States government was still banking on a political settlement to resolve the Chinese problem. It therefore left some troops in China and sent supplies to the Nationalists, but was determined to avoid a large-scale commitment on the mainland.

Climax in China

Ambassador Hurley continued to mediate between the Nationalists and Communists until he resigned in November, 1945. His successor as mediator was

General George Marshall, wartime Army Chief of Staff. Marshall achieved a temporary truce in February, 1946, but it broke down by mid-year. In January, 1947, the civil war was in full swing, and Marshall departed, blaming both sides for their failure to compromise. During 1946 an embargo was placed on arms shipments to the Nationalists in order to bring pressure on them to negotiate. This was lifted in 1947, once the fighting resumed, and it is the testimony of American military observers in China that the disaster that soon followed stemmed from poor strategy and a lack of will-to-fight, rather than a shortage of matériel. Although American assistance may not have been sufficient to help the Nationalists against a well-equipped foe like Japan, it was adequate compared to the level of military strength attained by Chinese Communists.

With Chiang Kai-shek dangerously committed to an offensive against the Communists in 1947, George Marshall, then Secretary of State, dispatched a mission under General Wedemeyer on a fact-finding tour of China. Wedemeyer was appalled at Nationalist corruption and incompetence, which he blamed for the rise of the communist menace. However, he believed it absolutely urgent that the Communists be checked, and toward this end urged that large-scale American military assistance be sent to China. He recognized the need for widespread social reforms if any aid was to be helpful. He was also concerned that Chiang, though sincere, lacked the determination to overrule the cliques surrounding him and implement such a program. In order to insure effective administration of the aid program, Wedemeyer recommended American direction of operations in China, and asked that 10,000 officers and men be sent to put these sweeping plans into effect.

The Defense and State Departments turned down the plan, for they were doubtful of Nationalist capabilities. Also, there were only one and a half uncommitted divisions stationed in the United States in 1947. In 1948 Congress earmarked economic assistance under the Marshall Plan for China. But this type of help could not save the Nationalist cause. Only the Wedemeyer solution, involving massive intervention, appears to have been adequate, and it went the way of all plans for large-scale aid to China. In 1947 the situation in Europe had deteriorated dangerously, and large funds were required to stabilize matters. The Truman administration concluded that to press for assistance for China and Europe simultaneously would have imperiled both programs in Congress. It chose to save Europe, because it was strategically more important and appeared more likely to use the aid effectively. In the end, Nationalist incompetence and the absence of a sweeping American intervention ended in Chiang's flight to Formosa in 1949.

It is misleading to argue that the United States "caused" the fall of Chiang's China in the years 1944–1948. Pressure for a coalition there may have been, but coalitions had been formed with the Communists throughout free Europe in 1945–1947. This device worked to the advantage of the democratic parties, for coalition cabinets brought national stability and enabled Europe to survive the wartime shock of dislocation. Once the Cold War began, the Communists were successfully ousted from government, even in vulnerable lands like Italy and Finland. It may be that more aid might have been sent to China in 1946–1948, but only help of an enormous magnitude and military intervention would have sufficed. It is unfortunate that neither the administration nor the opposition faced up to this issue squarely. There is no way of knowing whether such American operations would have been supported by domestic public opinion, or, for that matter, tolerated by the Chinese people, but this question was never brought to a head. The Open Door was closed with surprising suddenness and firmness by the Communists in 1949.

The policy of diplomatic support for the Open Door and China's integrity thus lasted for exactly fifty years, 1899–1949. It cannot be held that this was a sound policy in the sense that the United States was willing to make the sacrifices required to sustain it. Moral commitments to the doctrine and false optimism as to its feasibility clouded the issue further. One interpretation of this long frustrating record is that the American government and people decided, wisely or not, that China's integrity as a democratic state was not a vital American interest. A different conclusion might have been drawn by following the logical argument that a balance of power in East Asia depended on a secure and independent China. With China free of foreign domination, not aligned with its Japanese or Russian neighbors, and not extending its own power beyond its frontiers, the region could not come under the control of a single power complex. A comparison might be made with Western Europe, which the United States has striven to keep free from an aggressor's grip. Of course this region is closer to America and possesses great industrial power, so that its loss would create an immediate challenge to American security. China may have been essential to American security in a parallel manner, but East Asian politics were not considered from this perspective in Washington. From the time of Russia's thrust into Manchuria in 1900 down to the Wedemeyer Report of 1947, no responsible political leader ever seriously proposed a major military commitment to this area.

A Policy of Containment

When American military strength was reduced in 1945, Army officials decided that the United States had no vital stake in Korea. They were even wavering with regard to Japan. After 1949 this outlook was modified as a consequence of Peking's foreign policy and the North Korean assault on South Korea. We must therefore turn to a consideration of Korean affairs and see how events on that peninsula influenced American Far Eastern policy.

America and Korea (1945–1950)

In the summer of 1945, American and Russian staff officers established latitude 38° as the demarcation line of their military zones of occupation. Both governments were committed to the unification of Korea. However, the Russians

occupied their zone in August, 1945, and soon established a Communist government under Kim Il Sung. The Americans moved cautiously on occupying South
Korea in September. They refused to recognize a left-wing People's Republic
that had just been proclaimed in Seoul. A rival rightest faction was led by
Syngman Rhee, who had established himself as a political leader on his return
from a long period of exile. The United States placed his Korean Provisional
Government in power. Though this regime frequently resorted to coercive
tactics and pressures to maintain its dominant position, rival groups formed
their own parties and prepared to compete in the promised national elections.

The military demarcation line hardened into a permanent frontier as the
United States and Russia could not agree to any formula that would allow
unification by means of a free election. The south held two thirds of the country's 29 million inhabitants, and the Rhee government was vigorously anti-
Communist. The Russians therefore rejected any formula that would not guarantee the Communists a secure position in a unified Korea. With the collapse
of Russian-American talks in 1947, the United States turned to the United
Nations General Assembly to break the deadlock. In November, 1947, the
General Assembly called for a nation-wide election of a legislature that would
set up a provisional government, after which all foreign troops would withdraw.
A United Nations Temporary Commission on Korea came to Seoul but was
barred from visiting North Korea. It cooperated with the United States in preparing South Korea for its first free election in May, 1948. The voting was
preceded by a disorderly campaign, and many left-wing groups refused to
participate for fear that the election would widen the split between north and
south. Nevertheless, the United Nations Commission recognized the right-wing
victory in the south as a valid expression of the popular will. A Republic of
Korea was formally constituted in August, 1948, with Syngman Rhee as its first
president. The next month the Communists established the Democratic People's
Republic of Korea. In the next legislative election (May, 1950), the pro-Rhee
candidates were unsuccessful and their total fell from 81 to 48. Though the
formal opposition also declined, from 65 to 22, the number of independents
rose from 64 to 140.

In determining its basic policy toward Korea during 1945–1950, the American government was guided by (1) the steadily growing nature of its commitments as the Cold War unfolded and (2) the limitation on its available power.
In the late 1940's the Defense Department was limited to an annual budget of
$15 billion, contrasted to the $35 to $40 billion level averaged in the mid-
1950's. The country was committed to a "twenty-division foreign policy," with
only fourteen divisions in being. The basic recommendation was formulated
in a note by the Joint Chiefs of Staff in September, 1947, submitted by Secretary
of Defense James Forrestal. His position, concurred in by Army Chief of Staff
General Dwight Eisenhower, was that the maintenance of troops in Korea was
an overcommitment. The military leaders did not consider the peninsula
essential to American security. In their view, a garrison in Korea would be a

liability in time of war, since major operations in Asia would bypass the penin-sula. Consequently, American forces were withdrawn in June, 1949, following a Russian evacuation of the north at the end of 1948. However, the United States had given South Korea economic aid and in 1949 established a military mission to train a native security force. It was hoped that these formations could cope with the frequent internal disturbances and border assaults per-petuated by the Communists.

By contrast, the United States worked strenuously to strengthen Europe's position in 1948–1950. Marshall Plan aid was sent at the rate of about $5 billion a year to repair the European economies, the North Atlantic Treaty was ratified in 1949, and a military assistance program was planned shortly there-after. In Asia, the trend toward disengagement continued through 1949–1950, even though China fell to the Communists. The Nationalists on Formosa were offered no protection as they girded themselves for a Communist attack early in 1950. Nor was America interested in Australian, Philippine, or Thai sugges-tions for a Southeast Asian security pact. Army ground forces in the Far East were reduced to four occupation divisions stationed in Japan. Secretary of State Dean Acheson summed up the government's basic policy in January, 1950. He stated that the United States would fight without consulting other powers if any attack were made on the island perimeter defense of the Aleu-tians, Japan, the Ryukyus, the Philippines. He added that aggression elsewhere would be met by going to the United Nations and acting through that body, but he gave no firm commitment of unilateral American action. There matters stood on June 24, 1950, when North Korea launched a carefully prepared assault on South Korea.

The Korean War

The South Korean army was no match for the mechanized force of the attackers. Seoul fell in a few days, and the defensive forces quickly disinte-grated. Confronted with this imminent disaster, the United States committed itself to defend South Korea and took the case to the United Nations Security Council. The United Nations Commission, still in Korea, reported that the North Koreans were clearly guilty of aggression. On June 25, the Security Council, with Russia still boycotting it because the United Nations had not seated Communist China, called on North Korea to withdraw its forces. On being rebuffed, the Security Council branded North Korea an aggressor on June 27 and recommended (but did not order) that United Nations members give South Korea the support it needed to repel the attack.

President Truman ordered ground units to join the navy and air force already participating in the defense of South Korea. He also instructed the Seventh Fleet to prevent any attack on Formosa, in order to "neutralize" that island for the remainder of the Korean War. As American forces arrived in Korea, the invader slowed down his drive. In the tense summer of 1950 a front became stabilized in the southeast corner of the peninsula. As other nations (eventually sixteen in all) contributed forces to the Korean front, an international United Nations command was established in July, 1950, under General Douglas MacArthur. The United States, though, still furnished seven divisions, or 90 per cent of all foreign troops, and shared about an equal burden with the reorganized South Korean army. On September 15, 1950, General MacArthur directed a brilliantly executed landing at Inchon, just below latitude 38°, which encircled and effectively smashed the North Korean army. American and South Korean troops quickly reached the old demarcation line without encountering opposition.

At this point President Rhee and General MacArthur sought to occupy all of Korea and unify the country. The General Assembly in this hour of success gave its permission for such an advance on October 7, 1950, by recommending that steps be taken to assure a unified, democratic Korea and to assist in the country's rehabilitation. The American government was told by its field command that the Chinese would not intervene. It nonetheless publicly disavowed any aggressive intention against China and ordered that only Korean troops be sent to the Manchurian and Siberian frontiers. Just as United Nations troops neared the Manchurian border in November, the Chinese intervened in full force, as the Indian Ambassador to Peking had warned. One American unit had actually reached the Yalu River boundary when a general retreat was ordered. The Chinese almost overwhelmed their opponents, who barely escaped intact and retreated into South Korea during the winter of 1950–1951. The Chinese Communists, in turn, then tried to sweep through South Korea but were sharply checked and suffered great losses. They were then pushed back to latitude 38°, where the front became stabilized in the spring of 1951.

The American government at this juncture decided against a major effort to break the apparent stalemate, despite the proposal of General MacArthur that the war be expanded in an effort to achieve total victory. He recommended air reconnaissance over the China coast and Manchuria, the bombing of Manchuria as well as Chinese coastal cities and supply lines, a blockade of China, and the use of Nationalist troops from Formosa in the Korean campaign. (Chiang Kai-shek's offer of Nationalist troops at the start of the war had been rejected on military grounds and to avoid merging the Chinese civil war with the Korean conflict.) When the Truman administration did not accept MacArthur's views but sought to keep the war limited, the general publicized his position outside regular military channels in an effort to muster popular support for his program. For this he was abruptly removed from command in April, 1951, and was replaced by General Matthew Ridgway. The utmost the Truman administration would do outside Korea was maintain the neutralization of Formosa, sponsor a resolution in the General Assembly denouncing Communist China as an aggressor (passed February 1, 1951), and induce the General Assembly to place a rigid embargo on all arms and war material shipments to China (passed May 18, 1951).

Why did the United States intervene in Korea? And once this involved a war

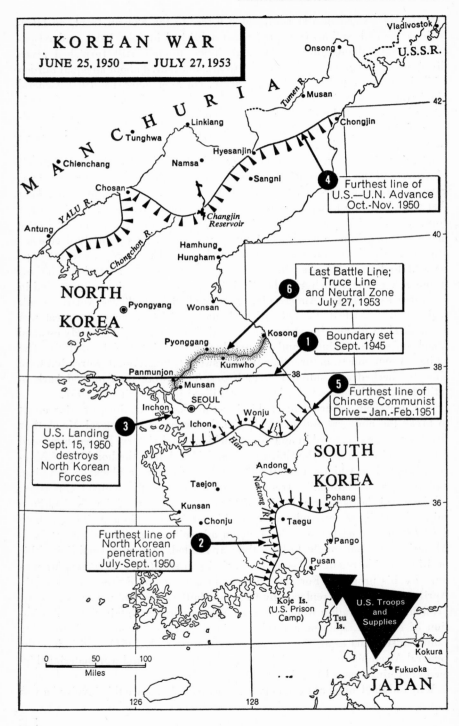

KOREAN WAR
JUNE 25, 1950 —— JULY 27, 1953

U.S.S.R.

Vladivostok

Onsong

M A N C H U R I A

Tumen R.

Musan

Chongjin

42

Linkiang

Tunghwa

Hyesanjin

Chienchang

Namsa

Sangni

4 Furthest line of
U.S.—U.N. Advance
Oct.-Nov. 1950

Chosan

YALU R.

Changjin
Reservoir

40

Antung

Chongchon R.

Hamhung
Hungham

NORTH
KOREA

Pyongyang

Wonsan

6 Last Battle Line;
Truce Line
and Neutral Zone
July 27, 1953

Pyonggang

Kosong

1 Boundary set
Sept. 1945

Kumwho

Panmunjon

38

Munsan

38

SEOUL

5 Furthest line of
Chinese Communist
Drive – Jan.-Feb. 1951

Inchon

Wonju

3

Ichon

Han

**U.S. Landing
Sept. 15, 1950
destroys
North Korean
Forces**

SOUTH

Andong

KOREA

Taejon

Naktong R.

Pohang

36

Kunsan

Chonju

Taegu

Pango

**Furthest line of
North Korean
penetration
July-Sept. 1950**

2

Pusan

Koje Is.
(U.S. Prison
Camp)

Tsu
Is.

U.S. Troops
and
Supplies

Kokura

0   50   100
Miles

Fukuoka

JAPAN

126

128

534

with China, why did the American government restrict the conflict, even though this meant only the protection of South Korea? To begin with, it should be noted that the intervention took the form it did because America had four divisions in nearby Japan, Russia was still boycotting the Security Council and so interposed no veto, and a United Nations Commission was in Korea and so gave an immediate authoritative assessment of war guilt. Once the attack occurred, the United States was compelled to respond, in order to check the seemingly unstoppable communist steamroller and to justify the principle of collective security against naked aggression.

By 1950, the Communist victory in China was merely the most recent and awesome achievement of this global movement. Communism purported to be the wave of the future—with a doctrine, an explanation of history, a well-knit organization, and devoted servants to back its claim. The Soviet expansion of 1945–1948 in Europe, the ideology's sudden prominence in Asia, the finality with which any one country was taken into the communist fold, and the grave nature of the Russian menace had all served to unnerve the free world. Now, after long denouncing aggression when they were weak, the communists were resorting to force to expand their realm. Had this aggression succeeded, it would have terrorized all states around the entire communist perimeter and perhaps destroyed their will to resist. The danger was heightened by a depressing comparison with the 1930's, when totalitarian aggression raged unchecked and undermined the League of Nations and the balance of power as well, while war-weary democracies stood by. Had this disaster been repeated in 1950, all chance for stabilizing a political-military front against communism might have been destroyed.

Moreover, Korea itself was a strategically vital territory which, despite the earlier opinion of the Joint Chiefs of Staff, had an intrinsic importance of its own at the center of Northeast Asia's power balance. Modern Japan has consistently held that the fate of at least southern Korea was linked to its own security. It is difficult to envisage Japan as an effective ally of the United States with this area controlled by an opposing power bloc. Had South Korea fallen, the greatest industrial state in Asia would have been under unbearable military and psychological pressure to follow at least a neutralist course in foreign policy. America's vigorous action in defending Tokyo's vital security interests has enabled a more favorable policy to prevail in the difficult Japanese political scene. The decisive American commitment in Korea may also have deterred the communists from using or displaying force elsewhere.

The Korean War was well suited to limited combat in the physical sense. The United States, with superior fire power and control of the seas, was able to hold a delimited front against a numerically larger opponent. As Manchuria was a privileged sanctuary, so were Japan and the sea lanes protected from enemy air attacks. A larger American military effort might have cleared the enemy from North Korea. Beyond this was the possibility of overthrowing the Communist Chinese regime. This task, however, would have required a full-scale war, perhaps involving Russian participation. To attain these objectives,

America would have had to reverse its traditional military policy and commit the bulk of its forces to the East Asian mainland. As a consequence of the Korean War, America was galvanized into accelerating its program to defend Europe. Its army there was increased from two divisions to six in 1951, and air units on Britain and the continent were expanded. Europe was urged to undertake large-scale rearmament, and the United States campaigned for a new German army.

Had America failed to act in Korea, Europe would have been paralyzed with fear; on the other hand, a full commitment in Asia might have undermined Europe's vulnerable security position. The question was not one of deferring to the Europeans, who had little direct interest in Asia, but of deciding from the American viewpoint that it was essential to strengthen the security of Europe with the power that was then at Washington's disposal. It was for this reason that the Joint Chiefs of Staff held, in the words of its chairman, General Omar Bradley, that an enlarged struggle in the Far East was "the wrong war in the wrong place at the wrong time."

In sum, the act of aggression in 1950 and the spread of communism across Eurasia induced the United States to fight in Korea. But it fought a territorially limited war, extending it to North Korea only when this did not appear to be a costly venture. Once China was in the war, the United States government, remarkably consistent with earlier American attitudes toward the Far East, decided that it would not undertake a major effort to alter the status quo in North Korea or China. It did, however, hold on grimly to South Korea during two more years (1951–1953) of combat.

Treaty Commitments in 1951

The United States made its first treaty commitments in Asia in the aftermath of the Korean aggression. Like the military policy on the peninsula, these steps were definite but limited. Their purpose was to bolster the American security network in the western Pacific.[5] The primary arrangement was a security treaty with Japan, to supplement the carefully drawn peace settlement in September, 1951. It permitted the United States to dispose forces in Japan and establish bases there. Its purpose was to maintain Japanese and Far Eastern security in case of armed assault and also against large-scale internal riots and disturbances. No other foreign power was to receive the right to have bases in Japan during the treaty's life. This was to last until both signatories agreed that alternate arrangements which effectively satisfied Japan's security needs had come into being.

Only by entering into direct defensive treaties with the Philippines (August

---

[5] An earlier arrangement in this region was the United States–United Nations Trust Agreement of April, 1947, which made Japan's former mandates trust territories, administered by the United States as a strategic area. This agreement gave America the right to use these islands as military bases, but it also meant that the United States had the obligation to assist in their economic and political development.

30, 1951) and Australia and New Zealand (September 1, 1951) could the United States induce these powers to accept a political settlement with Japan. As the Australians had lost confidence in the security value of the Commonwealth as a result of the 1942 campaigns, they depended on American support. Yet they were not certain of American assistance and their fears were centered about Japan in two different ways. First they were concerned lest Japan gain freedom of maneuver by establishing a strong diplomatic bargaining position between the two major power blocs. Secondly, if a choice of priorities had to be made in a crisis, there was a danger that the United States would place the defense of Japan ahead of that of Australia. In addition to a longer tradition of involvement in North Asia, America also had bases and forces stationed there. The 1951 treaties therefore guaranteed defensive assistance to these three island states. Even so, the signatories lacked many benefits enjoyed in Europe under NATO: a treaty organization, defense forces, and the certainty of quick action. The only diplomatic machinery provided was the bare agreement to hold yearly consultations. Nor would the United States guarantee the island barriers to the north of Australia as the Canberra government requested. Consequently, the Pacific signatories sought a firmer defense arrangement for Southeast Asia after 1951.

The same cautious broadening of American interests took place with regard to Formosa. Economic assistance again increased, military aid was resumed, and a military mission totaling almost 1,000 men by 1952 trained the Nationalist forces. The Truman administration kept the island neutralized through 1952. This kept the Nationalists from launching a major attack on the mainland, but they were not equipped for such a venture at this time. Admittedly, Kuomintang morale suffered from neutralization, since its political reason-for-being was predicated on a return to the homeland. In military terms, though, the act of neutralization served to protect the Nationalists and was so evaluated by the rest of the world.

The Korean Peace

In Korea the stalemate continued, as peace discussions began in July, 1951, and were conducted for two harrowing years. Negotiations were extensive on all major points, but all issues were soon resolved except that of prisoner repatriation. When the Eisenhower administration took office in January, 1953, it carried on the basic Korean policies of its predecessor. In fact, the new Democratic approach of carefully delimited commitments in East Asia was carried to its logical conclusion by the first Republican government in Washington since 1932. The focal point of this remarkable continuity in policy was the achievement of a peace in Korea. Following the death of Josef Stalin in March, 1953, the Chinese Communists agreed to accept the principle of voluntary repatriation. India accepted the difficult task of administering this important settlement. As a truce became likely that spring, President Rhee endeavored to continue the war in the hope of achieving Korean unification and, if possible, eliminating the communist menace. He was also fearful of being left without allies, though by this time the Republic of Korea army had a well-knit force of 600,000 men. The United States, anxious for an armistice, told the Koreans that it would discuss a defense treaty, the problem of Korean unification, and the departure of Chinese troops from North Korea after peace was restored. President Rhee then grudgingly acquiesced, but only after defiantly releasing 25,000 North Korean prisoners taken in the war.

The truce of July 27, 1953, called for a cease fire, a neutral zone at the battlefront, no reinforcements for either side, a four-member Neutral Nations Supervisory Commission (NNSC) (Sweden, Switzerland, and the communist states of Poland and Czechoslovakia), and a political conference to discuss a general settlement of Korean and related problems. Though the Chinese then reduced their strength, the North Korean army was built up; the communists violated the armistice by constructing air fields, and stationing more than 200 jet planes in North Korea. In 1954 the Swiss and Swedish members acknowledged that they were effectively prevented from exercising adequate supervisory powers in North Korea. This fact, plus the unneutral behavior of the Polish and Czech members induced the United Nations to remove the NNSC from South Korea in 1956. General political conferences and bilateral American-Chinese talks made no progress, in the years after 1953, toward reunifying Korea or reducing Sino-American tensions.

Meanwhile the United States and United Nations undertook to finance the reconstruction of South Korea. American aid alone totaled $5 billion over a five-year period; the Koreans were given a voice in the import and construction programs, which began to have salutary effects in 1955. President Rhee, however, remained a difficult negotiator who was antagonistic to Japan, levied high taxes on American businessmen, appealed to his countrymen to support a militant reunification program, and debated strenuously with the United States government over monetary exchange rates. He also had the constitution amended to provide for a popular, rather than legislative, election of the president, and won the first such contest handily in 1952. South Korea was by no means a democratic state. Like South Vietnam, it had experienced a long authoritarian colonial rule, had little preparation for democracy, and underwent harrowing experiences after 1945. However, in the presidential election of May, 1956, the victorious eighty-year old president found his majority sharply cut and the Democratic opposition candidate Chang Myun defeated Rhee's vice-presidential running mate. The fairness of the election, the desire to foster democracy, and the avoidance of extremism were all hopeful signs accompanying this contest.

In its foreign relations, South Korea benefited from the joint declaration issued by the sixteen United Nations powers that fought in its defense.[6] They promised on July 27, 1953, to resist any renewed attack and added, ominously,

[6] In addition to the United States, these were Australia, Belgium, Canada, Colombia, Ethiopia, France, Greece, Luxembourg, the Netherlands, New Zealand, the Philippines, Thailand, Turkey, South Africa, and the United Kingdom.

that the response to such aggression would not be confined to Korea. Thus the United States became committed to an expanded war over Korea, but it did so to defend the status quo and preserve the peace. South Korea also received its promised American alliance in October, 1953. It provided for consultation if either was threatened and a commitment to act in case of attack, "in accordance with [the signatory's] constitutional processes." The treaty was worded to cover all Korea, provided that unification was attained by lawful means; in effect, this was another restraint on South Korea's militant leaders, in return for a reaffirmation of American support of the quest for unity.

President Rhee did not lightly yield his bellicose views. In November, 1953, while visiting Formosa, he joined the Chinese Nationalists in asserting a determination to destroy aggressors and march to the Yalu. The following spring he offered to send two divisions to Indochina when that war was at its climax. That summer he came to America and preached a militant call for action but, whatever antiappeasement sentiment there may have been in Washington, he received absolutely no backing from any responsible political faction. The Korean leader has been sharply criticized by Asian neutralists for his militant outlook and authoritarian tactics. Yet when these governments demanded that America keep him in line, the United States repeated with truth and irony that he was no puppet of the State Department, which he so repeatedly harassed.

The Dilemma of Indochina

The truce in Korea did not bring peace in Asia. The Peking regime was now free to help the Vietminh rebels and build up military pressure against Formosa. The situation in Indochina proved the more critical, for the French position in Tonkin collapsed during 1953–1954. This occurred despite American material aid, which had begun in 1950 and had reached an annual level of $800 million by 1954. The United States faced a thankless political task in Indochina. During the war it supported the French, who were intensely disliked throughout the region. Washington's efforts to win French concessions for the Vietnam nationalists were met with dismay in Paris and Saigon. When the United States supported the anti-French Diem regime after the truce settlement of 1954, the former imperial ruler accused the Americans of trying to "replace" it in Vietnam. Nor were other Asian neutralists satisfied with the militantly anti-Communist Diem government, which displayed authoritarian tendencies and refused to discuss reunification with the Vietminh regime.

But the most critical problem was that of military intervention in 1954. In the fall of 1953, Secretary of State John Foster Dulles warned China that if it entered the Indochinese war, the United States would consider this act an aggression and might not confine its response to that front. However, unlike the Korean statement, this was a unilateral position, assumed in a nationalist-Communist rebellion. This warning did not stop the Chinese from sending technical and material aid in increasing volume and effectiveness. The United States then dispatched Air Force technicians to Vietnam. But with Dienbienphu besieged and all Tonkin endangered in 1954, the question became one of "another Korea." That spring, the American government faced the issue of intervention squarely and decided against it. Secretary Dulles blamed this failure on Britain because it had backed down on an earlier promise to take joint military action. London replied that it had never committed itself and added that American Congressmen themselves had objected to assuming military obligations.

President Eisenhower was already on record as being "bitterly opposed" to military participation in this war. Moreover, the moral-political issues in the conflict were far less clear-cut than in Korea, which involved the spirit of the United Nations Charter and the problem of aggression. Hence, the United States told the French, who called for at least an air strike to relieve Dienbienphu, that it could act only under certain conditions. These included a consideration of Asian aspirations, an invitation by Asians to participate, clarification of the moral issues by the United Nations, American Congressional approval (which was not given), and collective action. This reply amounted to a clear refusal of military assistance, leaving France no alternative but the Geneva settlement of July 21, 1954. The United States was present at these negotiations, though it tried vainly to disassociate itself from the loss of North Vietnam by refusing to sign the agreement. However, it did promise to refrain from using force to upset the understanding, but added that a new aggression in violation of this settlement would be a threat to international peace and security. The settlement still does not meet the main problem of securing the South Vietnam regime against its more powerful Vietminh neighbor. The Communists in essence argue that they can legally use force to unite the country if the free national elections promised at Geneva are blocked by Saigon's intransigence.

The Disposition of Formosa

The remainder of 1954 was devoted to negotiating a pair of treaties covering Formosa and a segment of Southeast Asia. These were important extensions of the effort to contain communism, but they were carefully restricted in scope. In the case of Formosa, the treaty formally restricted American obligations to the preservation of the status quo. This limitation marked a sharp reversal by the Republican party which had stridently advocated a vigorous China policy between 1947 and 1953. In his inaugural address of January, 1953, President Eisenhower continued his predecessor's defense of Formosa but removed all restrictions on Chiang Kai-shek's assaults against the mainland. Actually, Nationalist units had been undertaking small forays before 1953 and, since these forces were not capable of doing much more, this celebrated "unleashing" of Chiang Kai-shek had no appreciable significance.

By mid-1954, the Communists began a steady bombardment of Nationalist-held islands located just off the port of Amoy and nearby regions along the China coast. Would the United States protect these offshore islands as well as Formosa and the Pescadores, which were about ninety miles out to sea? Washington was willing to sign a treaty covering Formosa and the Pescadores, but to include the offshore islands, especially Quemoy and Matsu, might have em-broiled it in a war. The Nationalists evacuated the Tachen Island group near the China coast in 1954 but would not yield the other islands without a fight.

The upshot was the treaty of December, 1954, ratified February, 1955, which extended limited security guarantees to the Chinese Nationalists. The United States promised to defend only Formosa and the Pescadores against a foreign assault and internal subversion, taking action in accordance with its constitu-tional processes. In addition, the Senate Foreign Relations Committee attached three "understandings" that qualified and limited American obligations. The first concerned the confused legal tangle in which both Chinese camps claim clear title to Formosa and the Pescadores. The Senate noted that the treaty in no way modified their legal status, thereby leaving the United States uncom-mitted on the question of ultimate sovereignty. Secondly, Senate approval was made a precondition for any future widening of the area covered by the treaty. Finally, America was to act only if the Nationalists had to fight in self-defense. This last was a warning that the United States would not become involved in a war caused by a Nationalist assault on the mainland. Yet when the problem of the offshore islands became critical in 1955, Congress resolved to give President Eisenhower standby powers to commit American forces if he deemed it neces-sary. This move was temporary, however, and did not signify a long-term military obligation.

The future of Formosa remains a puzzling issue. Its international position has depended on the determined American policy not to recognize Communist China or acknowledge it as China's representative at the United Nations. The United States had wide support for this stand while the Korean War was in progress, but it lost much of its backing after 1953. When Nationalist China vetoed the admission of Outer Mongolia to the United Nations in December, 1955, despite American requests that it abstain, considerable foreign opposition mounted against its position on the Security Council. A possible compromise might be the acceptance by Communist China of Nationalist-China-on-Formosa as a separate state, which would be admitted to the United Nations and protected under its auspices. In return, Communist China could gain admission to the United Nations and the Security Council as the regular Chinese delegation. Thus far none of the protagonists has accepted the "two Chinas" solution.

Bilateral American-Chinese negotiations at Geneva during 1955–1956 foun-dered on the issue of Formosa. The United States favored a general understand-ing that allowed each side to pursue its own objectives by peaceful means without yielding the inherent right of self-defense. With regard to Formosa and other outstanding issues, the Americans sought an agreement to settle disputes through peaceful negotiations without resorting to the threat or use of force. This proposal was rejected by Chou En-lai, who viewed it as an effort to tie Peking to an acceptance of the status quo. He has repeatedly claimed that the Formosa issue was an internal Chinese affair and that the island would undergo "peaceful liberation."

If no settlement is reached, what policy can America follow should the

Communists muster a large invasion force and strike at Formosa? According to Peking, the Nationalists are a menace to the new Chinese regime. Therefore a delayed end to the civil war would actually not be an act of aggression. This view can gain widespread support in Asia, where Peking's claim to Formosa is generally recognized. To maintain its present policy, the United States may be required to act in diplomatic isolation and eventually commit a larger force to protect Formosa than was required in the early years of Communist rule.

Finally, how are the Nationalists to perpetuate their regime if America's purpose is to maintain the status quo? The United States mission on Formosa has risen to 8,000 people, to administer an annual aid program of $350 million. Most of this is military—$250 million directly and $47 million as "direct forces support." The economy is also being developed, but any hope of making it self-sufficient rests on cutting down the military program and the large twenty-one division Nationalist army. Though the emergency remains, the Kuomintang now realizes that there is only the remotest possibility of realizing the great objective of "returning to the mainland." Under such conditions the blandishments of Peking's propaganda, calling on the Nationalists to give up the fight, pose as great a threat as Communist military might.

The Defense of Southeast Asia

In 1954 the United States also undertook the difficult task of organizing a defense arrangement for Southeast Asia. An agreement was reached at Manila in September, 1954, which was ratified early in 1955. This achievement was limited in respect to the number of Asian members, the territorial scope of the treaty, and the extent of America's military commitment. The signatories included the United States, Britain and France, the old Commonwealth powers of Australia and New Zealand, the Philippines, and only Thailand and Pakistan on the mainland. The hard core of the "Seato" Manila Pact was the statement that armed aggression in the treaty area against any signatory menaced the safety of all and that the others would act against this common danger in accordance with their constitutional processes. The United States made an important qualification by stating that it was committing itself only against communist aggression.

The treaty area was defined as extending from West Pakistan to the Pacific Ocean, going northward to latitude 21° 30′N. The Indochinese states were brought under the treaty's protective mantle by special protocol, but this demarcation line excluded both Formosa and Hong Kong. Thus Secretary Dulles failed in his effort to weld the "three fronts" of South Korea–Japan, Formosa, and Southeast Asia in a firm anti-Communist commitment that would activate all sectors should aggression occur at any point.

The Manila Pact also called for economic cooperation for social progress, the peaceful settlement of disputes, and the maintenance of free institutions. On the initiative of President Ramon Magsaysay, a Pacific Charter was simultaneously adopted, stressing the principle of equal rights and self-determination. It included a promise to promote self-government and independence where desired and when the people were prepared to undertake the responsibilities that came with freedom. Secretary Dulles had proposed an unequivocal stand favoring the end of colonialism, but this milder statement was adopted at the insistence of the Commonwealth members.

Protection against subversion was also stressed, with consultation provided for in case a member's inviolability was threatened by means other than a foreign attack. To avert unwarranted intervention, it was agreed that the call for such help had to come from the government concerned. Finally, a Seato Council of Foreign Ministers was created to undertake annual consultation, handle military planning, and implement the treaty.

Some organizational progress was made at the first two Council meetings, held at Bangkok (February, 1955) and Karachi (March, 1956). Bangkok was made headquarters of the alliance, and a permanent political representative was assigned to this body from each member state. A full-time executive secretariat was created in 1956 and the representatives' staff was expanded. A training center and information clearing house were established to cope with the problem of internal communist subversion and the tactics of insurrection. Such police training in detection and combat is useful to the extent that communist strength is based on conspiratorial effectiveness and use of violence. A research center was also created in Bangkok under the staff of Council representatives to produce reports on current developments in communist activities. Offices for public and cultural relations were set up and the Seato organization established a common budget to finance its various agencies.

These efforts at integration have added substance to the Seato system, but it remains a pale reflection of NATO. It functions as a political agency, rather than as a center of military might; for its major achievement is the stated determination of its members to resist communist aggression. The signatories have depicted communism as the major threat to their security, whether it uses military force or political-economic tactics of infiltration. This is the fundamental difference in outlook that distinguishes the Seato group from the neutralist powers.

Yet the limited military obligations assumed under Seato's auspices seriously restrict its effectiveness. The commitment to go to war in the event of an attack is not as "automatic" or binding as under NATO. Nor has the United States made a specific commitment of troops to the region or agreed to establish an international military command there. America opposed tying troops down to a fixed military base, and favored a "mobile reserve" that could be sent anywhere. Nevertheless, United States military policy after 1953 called for fewer infantry divisions and, when two divisions were withdrawn from Korea, they were sent home. A strong ground reserve was not readied for quick action in Southeast Asia. Nor has large-scale military aid been sent to the Asian members; Pakistani officers have described American assistance as a "nuts and bolts" type of program. A combined military exercise was held in Thailand in February, 1956, including American, Filipino, and Thai forces. It was so hastily called that Pakistan was not given time to participate and, though useful, did not reveal any great combat strength in the region. Nevertheless, these Seato activities have aroused the vigorous opposition of neutralist powers who are antagonistic to military alliance blocs. Western explanations that Seato and other defense arrangements are really responses to the Sino-Soviet alliance bloc created in 1950 go unheeded in these circles.

This problem reflects a weakness in Seato that stems from its lack of more Asian participants. Because of this want, the non-Asian members are reluctant to emphasize the importance of the organization. A specific instance was the decision not to funnel economic assistance to Asia through the Seato structure, though the treaty stresses welfare and economic progress. The Asian Seato powers seek preferential economic treatment, but America and Britain have constantly stated that they will not grant needed economic assistance to Asia on the basis of military and political ties. This disturbs their Seato partners, who are told, somewhat irrelevantly, that there are other agencies for transmitting aid to the Orient. Obviously the West is anxious not to antagonize powerful neutralist states, who are highly critical of any type of "tied assistance."

The diplomatic problems confronting Pakistan illustrate the divergent problems related to Seato membership. India maintains that Karachi seeks military strength, with Kashmir as an objective, and is not concerned with communist aggression. Though India's army is three times stronger than its neighbor's, the United States had to assure New Delhi of Seato's peaceful intent and of its own determination to side with any power defending itself against aggression. In an effort to keep its military superiority, India bought sixty medium jet bombers from Britain in 1956. This led Pakistan to protest that London was acting in violation of its Seato obligations. On the other hand, Karachi sought Seato's support against Afghan agitation for the dismemberment of West Pakistan and the creation of a Pushtu tribal state along its western frontiers, with an outlet to the sea. At the 1956 Council meeting, all Seato powers stressed their support of the existing frontier (the Durand Line) and promised to aid in case of Afghan aggression. The United States, however, again restricted this promise to communist aggression, offering to consult in other cases. Britain was particularly disturbed by this equivocal American stand as well as Washington's refusal to join the Baghdad Pact for Middle Eastern security. By contrast, Britain did not want Seato to discuss the Kashmir question, whereas America was willing to have it on the Seato Council agenda in 1956. Even a mild Seato appeal to India and Pakistan to settle the issue peacefully was resented in New Delhi, for India considers Seato, by its very existence, to be an instrument of pressure in Pakistan's hands.

Finally, the French have lost strategic interest in Southeast Asia as a consequence of their defeat and virtual exodus from Indochina. Paris is always absorbed in the problem of European security, and after 1954 there were colonial revolutions in North Africa to consume the bulk of its military strength. The Socialist-dominated government of Guy Mollet believed that the threat of communist military expansion was ended by 1956 and that considerations of welfare economies would form the major battle ground of the Cold War.

Conclusion

When Communist China entered the Korean War in 1950, its leaders called the United States a "paper tiger." America did not bomb Chinese cities as the Peking government anticipated, but it did fight a war in Korea. Its long shadow may have also induced the Indochina settlement of 1954. By mid-century the United States had definitely turned its back on the tremendous obligations implied in an Open Door policy. However, it did not retreat to a purely island defense chain. Instead, it committed itself to the Asian mainland, in Korea and Southeast Asia, for the first time. This policy immediately raises new and difficult questions. What forces (type and strength) are required to honor these obligations? Is American security dependent on holding all or parts of these treaty fronts? Is it essential that these disjointed Asian fronts be linked, even if this adds Hong Kong and perhaps other areas to America's obligations? Has the American decision to retract or hold back its infantry strength after 1953 undermined its ability to assist anti-Communist defenses on the Asian mainland?

This last issue touches on Seato's failure to develop into a tightly knit, powerful military command. Yet this very factor may have made it less objectionable to the neutralists, whose support is essential if a real balance of power is to be established in East Asia. As it is, many specific points of friction developed between these powers and the United States. They did not fight in Korea, they opposed the counterinvasion of North Korea, and they criticized the United Nations condemnation of China as an aggressor and the subsequent strategic embargo. Since 1954 they have called for the normalization of trade and diplomatic relations with Peking. In order to evaluate American policy from a more general perspective, we must now turn to a broader consideration of Asian international politics and the neutralist position in this setting.

19 *The Pattern*

of International

Relations

Political change and violence have become recurrent phenomena in eastern and southern Asia. When Japan was defeated, the Western democracies appeared to be the only major powers with any direct influence in East Asia, and they gave the area a relatively low priority of attention even after the Cold War began. Since Europe and the Middle East were held to be in mortal danger, attention was riveted there. Britain was liquidating its imperial responsibility in southern Asia and was anxious to cut its commitments drastically. With Japan defeated, no other Asian power appeared capable of exercising a dominant role. The United States looked on China as a friendly and nonaggressive power that, despite its relative weakness, could effectively represent the region on the United Nations Security Council. The Far East, thus stabilized, was expected to enjoy a respite during which the colonial lands could gain their independence and adjust themselves to a new pattern of international relations.

Problems that appeared isolated in 1945—Japan under American occupation, the former colonies and their new freedom, the Indonesian and Indochinese struggles, the Civil War in China—merged into an area-wide pattern by 1948. That year, for example, there were communist-led civil wars and uprisings in Burma, Malaya, Indonesia, and India. The major turning point was the communist victory in China, for this increased the tempo of change and insecurity. Now, for the first time, there was a real possibility that the Communist bloc could muster enough force and ideological appeal to overrun all Asia. The North Korean attack and the Vietminh victory against the French would probably not have occurred had the Kuomintang remained in control of China.

The Korean and Indochinese truces brought a halt to major acts of force. However, the tension over Formosa and Nationalist-held islands off the China coast still has serious military overtones. The struggle for Asia continues, though diplomacy, economic competition, and propaganda may have supplanted violence as the primary means used.

546

Asian and Western Divergencies

The Nature and Strength of Neutralism

America's consideration of Asian political problems from the perspective of the Cold War is understandable, in the light of United States security problems and domestic American politics. Large-scale expenses and military sacrifices to maintain the balance in Asia can be justified if Soviet communism is a major enemy whose further expansion would spell disaster. Yet this point of view raises a great dilemma for American policy in the Far East because many of the free nations of Asia look at the situation from quite a different angle. Thus, all noncommunists can aver with honesty that they seek a strong Asia that is independent and democratic. But neutralists do not regard American intervention as a blessing. They do not consider United States foreign policy a protective shield for their vulnerable homelands or agree that American might is staving off ruthless communist penetration and conquest. Instead, the neutralists hold that the Cold War is a source of concern primarily to the Western world, and is sucking Asia into its vortex. The Americans are pictured as the prime agents of this unfortunate development, acting against the interest and wishes of the Asian peoples. Neutralists argue that all Asians, including the Chinese, want peace, that communism is not as great a menace to political stability as is poverty, and that the white imperialists and their American successors must still be watched with suspicion. The American stress on order and self-defense is looked on as either a dark plot to instill indirect Western rule or a foolish preoccupation with a menace whose importance is terribly exaggerated. Such policies, if pursued with the fervor of a crusade, the neutralists conclude, might even precipitate the general struggle they avowedly seek to prevent.

The fundamental policy of the neutralists is nonalignment with any power bloc, particularly those led by the Americans or Russians. This position is dominant in India, Indonesia, Burma, and, since the election of 1956, in Ceylon. There are strong minority currents favoring this view in Japan and Pakistan. Tokyo's Socialists are committed to a policy of nonalignment, and many of the right-wing nationalists still favor a less precisely defined foreign policy independent of American influence. In Pakistan, Bengali political leaders, underrepresented at the center until 1955, have challenged many policies adopted at Karachi, including the Seato and Baghdad Pact alliances. To a lesser extent, neutralism has some support in Thailand, where a cabinet minister resigned when Bangkok adhered to Seato, and the press adopted an anti-American tone. Neutralism also had a sizable following in the Philippines until submerged by the pro-American approach of its remarkably popular President Ramon Magsaysay. On the other hand, in the states where the leadership and general public are neutralist, there are minority elements of varying strength that favor closer ties to the West.

In criticizing Washington's stress on military as against economic aid, neutralists also complain of America's favoritism toward its treaty allies. They argue that Asian states should be assisted on the basis of equality, mutual respect, and their record in economic improvement. America, it is claimed, seeks to "dictate" and prod, instead of letting Asians decide what they need. The United States, which has often agreed that economic and social development are vital, realizes that it places greater stress on security matters. Washington held that it would like to reverse this proportionate emphasis but dares not do so for fear that the entire region's defenses would collapse.

From this basic conflict are derived many other divergences. Americans are particularly upset because many democratic Asians act as apologists for communism and the Peking government in particular. There are glowing reports on peace, prosperity, and progress in the "New China" by cultural delegations from India and other lands. Communist truce violations in Korea and Vietnam are played down or ignored, especially the increased communist military strength in North Korea and the restraints against travel and political freedom in Vietnam. Another instance was India's attitude toward Chinese prisoners taken by the United Nations forces in Korea. India is alleged to have urged them to return to their homeland and has, in general, acted in the belief that these men were somehow forced by America to choose to remain abroad. Equally appalling to the West is the equation of neutralism with respectable government in Asia, whereas the states that are American allies are generally denounced as quasi-colonial, fascist, or American puppets. The duly elected Philippine government was considered in New Delhi to be less democratic than the strongly neutralist Indonesian cabinet of 1953–1955, though that country had still not held a national election and was beset by corruption and internal unrest. Many doubts were even raised about the origins of the Korean War, though it was a clear case of communist aggression. For those who did blame North Korea, including Prime Minister Nehru, this act was more than balanced by America's counteroffensive above latitude 38°, which brought China into the war. Nor can Americans comprehend why Asians should be impressed by such palpable frauds as the Moscow-sponsored "Stockholm" Peace Petition, against the use of atomic weapons in war, when Russia is fully armed in every category of weapons. Still worse was the willingness of some to believe China's totally unsubstantiated charge that the United States used germ warfare in Korea. Even the former Indian Ambassador to Washington, Mme Pandit (Prime Minister Nehru's sister) observed equivocally that people are driven to do strange things in time of war.

Asians in turn are constantly at pains to criticize the nature of the race problem in the United States and South Africa, in contrast to alleged equality in the Soviet Union. American "support" of colonialism, actually a cautious disapproval of the policies of its Dutch and French allies, is an even greater source of Asian despair. Especially discouraging to Asians was the large-scale American help given to the despised French in Indochina as the war there went against the Europeans. The Americans of course constantly urged the French to give wider self-governing powers to Vietnam. But Washington's argument that this was an anticommunist struggle backfired because Asians retorted that, if Ho the communist was driving out the French, then communism is an acceptable creed in Asia.

In a positive sense, neutralists hold to the theory that, by remaining uncommitted, Asia can best promote the cause of world peace. Coexistence is their watchword, not in the communist sense of a temporary lull in the struggle against capitalism, but as the only feasible long-term alternative to mutual destruction. An unaligned Asia is held to be a stabilizing element in the world, especially when it diligently seeks to prevent wars or mediates a restoration of peace at every opportunity. India's obsession against blocs or alliances of any sort has led it to oppose even a neutralist bloc. Suspicion of the West and of military alliances is evident in the antagonism displayed toward NATO. Only in Asia does the communist argument that NATO is an instrument of potential aggression carry any weight; it is even pictured in some extreme circles as a grouping of old colonial powers, supported by the United States, who still seek to exploit Asia. A similar antagonism was expressed toward the Southeast Asia Defense Treaty when it was proposed in 1954. Indonesia even advocated as a countermeasure that India and Burma join with it in signing a nonaggression treaty with China.

An anti-Western neutralist bias was clearly expressed at the Asian Socialist Conference held in Rangoon in January, 1953. Suspicion of Europe was profound enough for the Asian socialists to form a separate organization of their own rather than join formally with European socialist parties, which are generally anticommunist and pro-American in their orientation. World peace, the conferees decided, was threatened primarily by colonialism, economic disequilibrium, and the politics of spheres of influence. A committee report on the tensions in Asia that could lead to general war completely ignored the dangers created by world communism and its expansionist tendencies. Even the issue of poverty and exploitation of people by their fellow Asians was omitted. Instead, the conference committee stressed the dangers emanating from the presence of foreign troops, Asian alignments with Western powers, and the existence of colonial remnants like Goa. The Socialist Conference recognized that the neutral states, stretching from Egypt to Indonesia, were weak in that they lacked internal cohesion and defensive power, but salvation was declared to rest in firmer neutralism.

The Role of India

The future of Asian neutralism is largely dependent on Indian leadership, for India is the leading advocate of such a policy and is the strongest of the uncommitted powers. Indian policy, however, is not based wholly on such idealistic pacifist lines, for one of its main tenets is to be strong and self-reliant. It has maintained an efficient army, with the help of British training and Anglo-American equipment, and has strengthened its hold over the small northern border kingdoms of Sikkim and Bhutan. New Delhi also intervened in Nepal, just below Tibet, in order to modernize this state and so check communist infiltration and domination of a revolution. A progressive pro-Indian government of the Nepal Congress party was aided and the authority of the king was revived. The situation in Nepal, though, is by no means stabilized and, with democracy an untried form of rule, there is still considerable fear that political instability may lead to communist rule. Indian concern about communist assaults from within and across its borders remains a persistent if minor theme in its foreign policy.

Meanwhile, to the north, Tibet is being turned into a well-populated Chinese province. Peking settled 500,000 Chinese there in 1954–1956 and plans to bring this total to 3 million by 1963, in contrast to 1948 when only 1 million Tibetans occupied the area. The development of a large road network, running east to China and south to India, strengthens the idea that in the future the Himalayan region might cease to be a quiet buffer area and become a source of danger.

Primary emphasis and publicity, however, are given to such basic ideals as complete freedom for all dependent peoples, the end to all European rule in Asia, and the elimination of racial discrimination. Prime Minister Nehru has often claimed that India is too weak a power to affect international affairs and therefore cannot become involved in issues beyond its immediate national interests. Yet the facts argue otherwise on both counts. India is the strongest power in free Asia and, despite some suspicion of domination in Ceylon and Pakistan, has enjoyed considerable prestige. It raised the largest volunteer army, more than 2 million men, in 1939–1945, and its troops fought well on several fronts. Many Americans see India as a rallying point around which the free nations can build a real balance of power and attain stability in Asia.

Indian foreign policy since 1950 has covered a very broad field, often plunging boldly into the unknown to further the cause of peace. Prime Minister Nehru unsuccessfully appealed to Stalin to bring about a truce in the Korean War shortly after it began. Later, India served as an intermediary in the truce negotiations and carried out the thankless job of supervising the exchange of prisoners. India also participated in the Indochina truce talks and again served, with Canada and Poland, as supervisers of the truce terms. It has repeatedly proposed a major power conference on Asian affairs and called on the United States and Red China to settle their difference through diplomacy. Indians have condemned the Manila Pact and other defense alliances for reversing the trend toward conciliation. They cite the Geneva settlement on Indochina as an example of this wiser approach and as proof of the value of India's independent foreign policy. Conciliation was also behind the Prime Minister's acceptance of the Five Principles of Coexistence in a joint statement with Premier Chou En-lai of China in mid-1954. To the criticism that these were mere words that did not guarantee Chinese compliance, Nehru responded that even if Peking was insincere, the pact made for a peaceful atmosphere and for noninterference in the internal affairs of other states.

550

It is difficult to judge the neutralist approach and particularly its Indian manifestation. India refused to sign the Japanese Peace Treaty because it aligned a defenseless Japan with the United States. An American military aid program to Pakistan in 1954 was denounced by Prime Minister Nehru, who called it a hostile act that spread the climate of uncertainty and war, and made a settlement in Kashmir impossible. Nehru also proved sensitive to foreign decisions affecting Asia that were taken without due consideration of Asian views. Two examples are the United Nations General Assembly resolution condemning China as an aggressor in February, 1951, in which few Asian states concurred, and the Manila Pact itself, in which only three of the eight signatories were Asian states.

Yet India has taken firm steps to prevent internal subversion. New Delhi's argument that economic and social reform is the best way to combat communism also finds a certain response in American thought that recognizes the negative orientation of military defense. The United States can be criticized for fostering a Seato arrangement that has organizational value but lacks effective military power, at a price of antagonizing the dominant (neutralist) attitude in Asia. India, on the other hand, may be unwarranted in adopting a tone of moral superiority because it "works for peace" between the two blocs. For this policy depends on the existence of a power bloc that can stalemate communist pressure and so make India's moderate compromise position a realistic one. The United States still holds the view that it is shoring up the free world's position in Asia, a thankless task carried on under withering criticism from the major beneficiaries.

A meeting in Washington between President Eisenhower and Prime Minister Nehru in December, 1956, contributed to a better and more sympathetic understanding of the motives behind each government's policies. However, in January, 1957, a foreign policy resolution of the Congress party Working Committee revealed that India still had a fundamental distrust of military alliances advocated by the United States, considering them as part of the cycle leading to war. On the other hand, this resolution also expressed India's first straightforward criticism of Soviet intervention in Hungary. The Anglo-French action in Suez was coupled with the Hungarian affair to show the inadequacy of armed force as an instrument of diplomacy or ideology. The Western withdrawal was noted with approval in contrast to Soviet action in Hungary, and the resolution further regretted the check this affair administered to the democratization of central Europe. This stand marked a major split with China, which had tried to induce India to accept Soviet policy toward Hungary.

China and the Communist Bloc

The great communist crisis of 1956, in which Poland sought to assert its independence and revolts swept Hungary, revealed how influential Red China had become in international affairs. The unity of the Communist bloc, already endangered by Yugoslavia's defection in 1948, was close to being completely shattered. That Soviet Russia needed and received help from China is as significant as the line of action adopted in Peking. Its influence as an independent force in the communist movement was dramatically revealed during Chou En-lai's tour through East Europe during the winter of 1956–1957, when each visit to a capital city resulted in a major policy declaration.

Basically, the Chinese government strove to keep the international communist front intact, while preserving Poland's internal sovereignty and assuring its own Asian neighbors that it would not resort to violence as Russia had in Hungary. China came out against "great nation chauvinism" and reaffirmed its adherence to the basic principles of coexistence, as for example in a joint communiqué with Cambodia in November, 1956. However, the highest organ of the Chinese Communist party strongly defended the Soviet Union the following month, supporting its intervention in Hungary as a move necessary to thwart what Premier Chou later called a "crazy subversive movement." China also reaffirmed its view that Russia remained at the head of the "socialist camp," around whom all communist states had to rally against the American-led "imperialist camp." In this vein, Titoism was denounced as a divisive influence, Josef Stalin was highly praised, and Stalinism was defended as "primarily communism."

Within this framework, the Chinese were anxious to assist the Poles, whose fate was the critical issue at this time. In fact, Peking had pointed to Poland's newly won freedom as evidence that communist states could get along as true equals even though differences might arise, because they had no basic conflicts of purpose. Actually the Poles were living in fear of Soviet diplomatic and military pressure, isolated geographically and ideologically from the West. They avidly sought Chinese support and were gratified by Chou's sympathetic attitude during his stay in Warsaw in January, 1957. Poland was ready to listen to his warnings against adopting Yugoslavia's ideological position or establishing close ties with that government. On January 16, 1957, a joint Chinese-Polish policy statement accepted "proletarian internationalism," i.e. Soviet leadership, as the basis of relations among communist powers. Poland also gave its support to the puppet Hungarian government, though it had markedly different views about that crisis from those expressed in Peking and Moscow. China then placed itself squarely in support of Poland's effort to liberalize its own political and economic affairs, free of Moscow's overbearing influence, noting that relations between communist states had to be based on "non-interference in their internal affairs, equality and mutual benefits."

China was successful in carrying out its self-appointed task of mediator because it was respected by all parties. The Russians had admired their record of self-reliance and achievement and were now pleased by this contribution to communist solidarity. As a result, China's prestige in Moscow rose further and the alliance was consequently strengthened. Meanwhile, Peking's helpful attitude toward Poland enhanced China's position in East Europe and won support for its call to unity. The satellites admired China for its independence, and regarded it as a distant, friendly power which could serve as a counterweight to the Soviet Union within the communist camp. Hence it was a major achievement and a measure of China's great influence that this Asiatic power could intervene in European affairs, assist Russia, and ease Poland out of its isolation.

The Level of Regional Unity

In terms of the Cold War, it might be said that there are three groups of states in Asia—communist, anticommunist, and neutralist. This classification is, however, a grave oversimplification, for relations are too complex to be reduced to such orbits. For one thing, there is a general agreement throughout the region on certain principles, even if different meanings are read into them. These include "Asia for the Asians," the end to imperialism everywhere, and the drive for economic well-being. Yet there is no grouping of Asian states that can be termed stable or that can serve as a unifying force in the search for these objectives. A closer examination of efforts to achieve some sort of regional unity reveals a crosscurrent of competing interests and antagonisms that add to the divergences represented in the Cold War.

Thus South Korea is bitterly hostile to Japan, though both are American allies and, geographically at least, appear to have identical strategic interests. Nor is the Japanese shadow completely erased in Southeast Asian lands. Pakistan remains a hostile critic of India and is involved in a dispute with its western neighbor, Afghanistan, because of the latter's efforts to detach at least the frontier regions of West Pakistan. Ceylon, too, is suspicious of India, and relations are further strained by the problem of Indian Tamil immigrants. Thailand's historical difficulties with its neighbors make close cooperation in that area a difficult, though not insuperable, obstacle.

Even Cold War politics has many variations. The South Koreans and the Chinese Nationalists on Formosa both adhere to an extremist view and wish for war to defeat their communist opponents. President Rhee of South Korea was even willing to add Soviet Russia to the list of military antagonists. By contrast, Japan and the Asian Seato members are far more cautious. Though they agree that a posture of strength is essential, their objective is to maintain peace. Neutralism also is adhered to, in varying degrees of intensity, with Burma taking a less insistent stand than India or Indonesia. Ceylon, which had been only mildly neutralist, adopted a policy similar to India's when the opposition party led by Mr. Bandaranaike won the election of 1956. Finally, there are beleaguered noncommunist states of Indochina, protected by Seato yet not in that organization, anticommunist but not aligned with the West under the Geneva truce terms.

The mutual wariness of Asian states is revealed in their regional conferences. The first was an unofficial Inter-Asian Relations Conference at New Delhi, attended by twenty-eight states in March, 1947. It was a spectacular demonstration, allowing some new states to display their newly gained sovereignty. All participants stressed their common interest in political freedom, women's

ASIAN CONFERENCE PARTICIPANTS, 1947–1955

Country	Asian Relations 1947	Re Indonesia 1949	Baguio 1950	Colombo Powers 1954	Seato 1954	Bandung 1955
Burma	X	X		X		X
Cambodia	X					X
Ceylon	X	X	X	X		X
Comm. China						X
Nat. China	X	*				
India	X	X	X	X		X
Indonesia	X		X	X		X
Japan						X
S. Korea	X					
Laos	X					X
Malaya	X					
Pakistan		X	X	X	X	X
Philippines	X		X		X	X
Thailand	X	*	X		X	X

Other participants:

1947: Afghanistan, Bhutan, Cochinchina, Egypt, Iran, Jewish group (Israel), Mongolia, Nepal, Tibet, Turkey, and eight Soviet republics.

1949: Australia, Afghanistan, Egypt, Ethiopia, Iran, Iraq, Lebanon, Nepal,* New Zealand,* Saudi Arabia, Syria, Yeman.

1950: Australia.

1954 (Seato): Australia, France, New Zealand, United Kingdom, United States.

1955 Asian: Afghanistan, Iran, Iraq, Jordan, Lebanon, Nepal, Saudi Arabia, Syria, Turkey, Yemen.

African: Egypt, Ethiopia, Gold Coast, Liberia, Libya, Sudan.

* Observer.

rights, better living conditions, and closer cultural contacts with each other. However, the dream of even a loose Asian Union was rejected by the Arab states. Moreover, the East Asian states were not in harmony. Nationalist China defended its nationals abroad and reaffirmed its right to protect them; it also was jealous of Indian aspirations to Asian leadership. The lesser states generally sought to preserve their newly acquired freedom from any encroachments by larger powers. They were even suspicious of one another and developed no broad Southeast Asian political or economic agreements.

In January, 1949, India called a second conference, this time an official meeting of nineteen governments to champion the cause of Indonesia. Rebellion against Dutch rule was reaching a climax, for Holland's second "police action" was threatening to destroy the entire independence movement. A unanimous resolution supporting the Indonesians was adopted. It was strikingly moderate in tone and contributed to the successful effort of the United Nations Security Council to reopen the negotiations that soon led to the end of Dutch rule. In August, 1949, still another conference was sponsored from New Delhi, this time by the Indian Council of Cultural Cooperation.

At this time, the Philippine government tried to gain the initiative when President Quirino sponsored a tighter organization of Asian states. In 1949 Korea's Syngman Rhee called for a military alliance of free Asia without which, he observed, any agreements would be worthless. He was seconded by Chiang Kai-shek, who had by now, however, been driven to Formosa and lacked prestige in Asia. These efforts were rejected by the neutralist governments. Foreign Minister Carlos Romulo of the Philippines then soft-pedaled the military theme and toured Asia in an appeal for political, cultural, and economic unity. The result was a conference held at Baguio, Luzon, in May, 1950. Since the neutralists opposed any formal arrangement, the conference simply stressed the need to end colonialism and preserve the integrity of new states. It took no stand on relations with the West but declared its adherence to the principles of the United Nations, and emphasized economic-cultural affairs rather than political relations among states. Both the Philippines and Australia proposed military cooperation, but this item was not even placed on the agenda for discussion. The communist issue was handled in a "compromise" resolution, which described it as an internal problem that each state could best handle by bettering living conditions. No permanent secretariat or other intergovernmental machinery was established, and India, which had not wished to see any conference held, blocked efforts to arrange a subsequent session. There Asia stood on the eve of the Korean War, and no significant changes have occurred on this front since 1950.

More recent meetings have underlined this tendency to drift apart. In 1954, there were two important conferences, but only one state, Pakistan, attended both. The first was held at Colombo, Ceylon, and the five participants—Burma, Ceylon, India, Indonesia, and Pakistan—became known as the Colombo Powers. They met while the great power conference at Geneva was considering the Korean and Indochinese questions. The Colombo Powers were united in calling for a cease-fire in Indochina and a commitment by France to end its rule there. In addition, they stressed the importance of controlling all weapons of mass destruction, the value of having Peking represented at the United Nations, the need to end all colonialism, and the justice of Moroccan and Tunisian demands for self-rule. There was an announced determination to resist alien ideologies, plus an affirmation of faith in democracy. These were coupled with a promise to resist internal interference by "external Communists, anti-Communists, or other agencies." Though only India and Indonesia still held colonialism to be a greater threat than communism, this conference proved a qualified victory for their neutralist position.[1] When the American-sponsored conference for a Southeast Asian treaty organization convened that September in Manila, Ceylon disappointed the West by deciding not to join Pakistan, the Philippines, and Thailand in attending.

---

[1] In November, 1956, the Colombo Powers, except for Pakistan, met in New Delhi to denounce both the Anglo-French intervention in Egypt and the Soviet repression of Hungary.

The Bandung Conference of 1955

The final major assembly of the first postwar decade was the historic Bandung Conference sponsored by the Colombo Powers. It was held in April, 1955, with almost all the states of Asia and Africa invited. Indicative of the tactical considerations behind even so grandiose a project was India's desire to bolster the prestige of the host country, Indonesia, whose neutralist cabinet was in danger of falling. The conference was conducted smoothly as Bandung, Java, was placed under heavy military protection. Among the absent were South Africa, Nigeria, Nationalist China, and the two Koreas, as well as Israel, omitted to appease the Arab bloc. Chou En-lai led an impressive delegation from Peking and proved a most attractive figure. He took a moderate, friendly tone toward all present and even offered to negotiate the question of Formosa, though insisting that it had to go to China. However, even this was a welcome relief from the propaganda threats and artillery exchanges that preceded the meeting, and were resumed before the year ended.

The Conference was not the sweeping communist success that the Americans had feared. There were some spectacular denunciations of communist imperialism, though these came from West Asian states like Iraq. More important was the general refusal to follow Chou's racist call for antagonism against the whites or to adopt an anti-Western tone. Neutralists supported certain of China's demands, including United Nations representation and control of Formosa, but they would not follow it into an anti-Western front.

Premier Nehru of India was anxious to keep the discussion on broad principles that would evoke unanimous agreements. However, many controversial issues were raised and vigorously debated before a compromise communiqué was issued. This final statement stressed the authority of the United Nations and generally adhered to the ideals of political liberalism and democracy. No reference was made to the favorite communist theme of coexistence, but neither was communism called a new form of colonialism, as some delegates demanded. Instead, the ten principles of good neighborliness included warnings against aggression, threats of force, and racial discrimination. Also emphasized were the rights of small nations, the principle of peaceful settlement of disputes, and the importance of respecting human rights and international obligations. The freedom of all states to join any arrangement for collective self-defense was recognized, provided these were not made in the "private interests" of any great power. All colonial rule was again roundly condemned, though some delegates had Soviet Moslem territories and Eastern Europe in mind when they supported this plank. However, only the following were given explicit support: Indonesia's claim to Western New Guinea; Yemen in its conflict with Britain over Aden Tunisia and Morocco in their quest for self-rule; and the Palestine Arabs. In all instances, fresh negotiations and peaceful settlements were urged. Finally, world disarmament was endorsed, including India's appeal for an end to atomic-weapon tests.

The conference was clearly a prestige triumph for the newly arrived political states of Asia and Africa, conducted with sobriety and moderation. Yet the political alignments remained unchanged, though each side could claim partial success. China made a good impression, India believed that it served as a restraining influence, and the anticommunist forces were satisfied that their impact was felt. Through it all there persisted the thread of reasoning that Asia could really be an area of peace, that its nationalism was less virulent than the West's, and that aggression and imperialism would not be generated from this source. In the light of communist intentions (as interpreted in the West) and the imbalance that threatens the eastern half of the continent, this contention remains to be proved. In any event, the conference trumpeted the arrival of Asia as a force to be reckoned with in world politics, one which would play a greater role in determining policies affecting its fate.

The United Nations

The General Assembly provided a valuable forum from which a resurgent Asia could express its views and extend its influence. India used the United Nations as a center in which to strengthen the neutralist camp when the Cold War began, and took part in organizing a group of uncommitted states. This Arab-Asian bloc, formed in 1950, has become an important pressure group that seeks to sponsor common policies. It holds regular caucuses and has achieved considerable success in fields where common interests are deeply rooted. These are primarily race relations and colonialism, important issues in United Nations affairs. This bloc successfully sponsored Libya's freedom, as well as that of Eritrea in East Africa, and thus fanned the flames of nationalism in French North African territories. It is also pressing for the freedom of trust territories like Tanganyika and is even trying to make imperial powers accountable to the United Nations for policies in colonial lands not under United Nations jurisdiction.

The bloc has been less united on Cold War issues. Divisions arose over the question of seating Communist China, Burma's complaint in 1953 against the pressure of Nationalist Chinese troops on its territory, and Thailand's request in 1954 for a border observation team to prevent Vietminh penetration of its frontiers. Still, if the Arab-Asian bloc presents a united front, it can control many votes in the Assembly, an organ whose prestige increased when the Security Council became veto-bound. Certainly the neutralist element in the Arab and Asian states is increasing in power. During the Korean War, for example, the General Assembly passed the resolution of October, 1950, allowing United Nations forces to cross latitude 38°, but thereafter the Arab-Asian states fostered a policy of moderation, limited war, and a negotiated settlement. Generally these nations advocate the neutralist position in Assembly debates: China intends no aggressive action, mediation can lead to a settlement of major issues, and communism can be effectively checked only through vigorous social and economic policies. Yet a question remains, what will the neutralists do if communism subverts Burma, overruns the tiny state of Laos, or menaces Thailand through the "Thai Autonomous People's Government" in China? At present, however, Western efforts to detach Burma and Ceylon from this neutralist orbit, broaden alliances under the Baghdad and Seato pacts, or establish bases on Asian soil are bitterly resented by many Arab-Asian states.

The Commonwealth

One of the strangest paradoxes in this political setting is the high regard in which Britain is held in India and other former colonies, despite its long history as an imperial power and its close American alignment in the Cold War. Much of this is explained by the post-1945 policy of granting independence to the Asian colonies and preparing others in Africa and Latin America for self-rule. In addition, the United States is now the dominant power of the West, bearing the largest share of the responsibility for decision making. As a result, Washington has drawn much of the fire of neutralist criticism and London has benefited thereby.

The Commonwealth organization, a loose and informal "holding company" of Britain and its former colonies, is both a contributor to this phenomenon and a major consequence of this friendly attitude. Only Burma among the former Asian colonies chose to exercise its right to leave the Commonwealth, but the rest voluntarily remained. Even Burma retained British military advisers at first and accepted a Commonwealth loan in 1950 valued at £7.5 million, half of which was contributed by Britain.

The Commonwealth was attractive to its new members because of its very informal structure. Its loose organization emphasized meetings that explored member attitudes on various topics without leading to any official agreements or decisions. These restrained discussions were matched by the absence of a permanent secretariat. There is some method and order to this system, with premiers meeting every year or two, and foreign ministries conferring between these sessions. Finance ministers also hold periodic sessions, and other high officials frequently exchange views. But there is no binding foreign policy, and the Commonwealth would collapse if it tried to assume such a burden. Complete independence was insisted on by Canada and Australia in 1918, and the new Asian members have simply reinforced this view. Decisions are taken individually, though each state has a moral obligation to consider the views of other members.

The Asian members were both relieved and impressed by the value and flexibility of this system, which did not impair their newly gained sovereignty. This arrangement also had the positive advantage of assuring these new, somewhat insecure states of a close link to more prosperous nations that have at least a moral duty to render economic and even military aid in time of crisis. Furthermore, in these frequent exchanges of views, the new members could profit from the dependable Western civil services in managing such complex international mechanisms as foreign trade and finance. In more recent years, the Western members have also benefited from the general exchanges of information occurring within the Commonwealth, especially with regard to soundings in the Cold War.

The effort to clear away suspicions that thrived on the intense nationalism of the past generation was fairly successful. Symbolic of the problem raised was India's willingness to join the Commonwealth, but only as a republic that owed no allegiance to the crown. According to the Statute of Westminster of 1931, the three cardinal principles of the Commonwealth were the crown, the voluntary nature of the association, and equality of all members. The Indian problem was considered at a meeting of prime ministers in October, 1948, and resolved at a later meeting in April, 1949. India accepted the king (or queen) as the symbol of this free association—as Head of the Commonwealth; but it pledged no allegiance to the monarchy and gave it no place in its formal structure of government. Pakistan retained its dominion status at first, but in 1956 became an Islamic republic within the Commonwealth. This decision was due to internal nationalist pressures and antagonism at India's superior moral tone, as well as the failure of the Commonwealth to help Pakistan in the Kashmir dispute.

To the extent that there is a "Commonwealth approach" to foreign policy, it was set at the January, 1950, foreign ministers' conference at Colombo, Ceylon. The site was chosen to highlight the growing importance of Asia and yet avoid involvement in the India-Pakistan controversy. It was at Colombo that a joint proposal by Australia and Ceylon to link the Commonwealth together in a military pact or a common front against communism was defeated. Even Britain's proposals for consultative machinery for joint defense and joint military staff arrangements were turned down. India again stressed its aversion to military blocs and repeated its argument that the main front was in social and economic reform. The older members then accepted this emphasis and agreed to concentrate on efforts to raise living standards. Under the joint sponsorship of Australia and Ceylon, a proposal was adopted to work out a long-term program for economic development. Eventually labeled the Colombo Plan, this project was modest in scope and was based on the initiative and good faith of the Commonwealth powers for its success. It was the first comprehensive effort to work out a general development program for South Asia and as such had an important psychological impact.

The Colombo Plan

The program was first planned for 1951–1957 and later extended to 1961. It was based on the separate plans for economic development drawn up individually by Asian member states. Like the Commonwealth itself, the Colombo Plan arrangements were voluntary and flexible, with one member giving technical and capital aid to another through bilateral arrangements. It had no detailed scheme or over-all blueprint and therefore established no central directing agency. Its first purposes were to find out the area's needs, estimate its resources, focus attention on the development problem, and provide a framework for international cooperation. Since only India had worked out a complete plan by 1951, the coordination of other state projects was rudimentary at first. Yet even at this early stage, the Asian states stressed certain common development needs (especially irrigation, railways, and power), as well as social welfare programs. By undertaking surveys of needs and capacities, the Colombo Plan spurred the other Asian states to develop their own projects more quickly.

Central machinery for advice and mutual consultation was provided through the Consultative Conference. Here each nation's over-all plans and specific projects were examined and criticized by the other members. The Consultative Conference was given no administrative authority or decision-making power, but it helped with joint consultations, discussions, and analyses of major projects. Both the International Bank for Reconstruction and Development and the United Nations Economic Commission for Asia and the Far East attend its annual meetings and maintain close liaison at other times. The Consultative Council issues reports on the area's over-all growth as well as on the progress of each individual country.

Originally all the independent Commonwealth states, except South Africa, were members of the Consultative Council, along with Malaya, Singapore, and British Borneo. The original target of aid was set at approximately $5 billion, of which Britain promised $840 million. Internal financing and loans from both public and private foreign sources were anticipated, but major interest was centered in American assistance. Some of the projects could be internally financed, but in terms of foreign currencies the program revealed a need for $3 billion. Of the total amount, India was scheduled to receive the largest share —$3.86 billion; Pakistan was next, with $740 million; Ceylon had $285 million, and the rest all totaled $300 million. Targets were to raise acreage by 13 million, add 17 per cent (another 13 million acres) to land under irrigation, increase food production by 10 per cent, and electricity by two thirds. In all, 34 per cent of the funds were marked for transportation and commerce, 32 per cent for agriculture (including river development), 18 per cent for housing and social welfare, 10 per cent for industry and mining, and 6 per cent for fuel.

Other countries were invited to work with the Consultative Council and join in preparing plans for international action. Nonmember observers appeared in 1951, and membership grew over a four-year span to include all of free Southeast Asia, Japan, and the United States. The aid target was raised to $8 billion as development plans were expanded. Of this $1 billion came from the Commonwealth by 1954, with another $500 million assured. In 1955, it was estimated that 80 per cent of the cost would come from local resources, but foreign assistance was still of critical value. Some aid was given in the form of essential goods, ranging from wheat to steel, with the recipient states earmarking equivalent (counterpart) funds in their own currency for development projects. In all, $5.6 billion had been spent by 1957.

In addition to a shortage of capital, most Asian states also lacked sufficient technical personnel. It was estimated that 1,411 high-ranking specialists were needed, of which India sought 638 and Pakistan 460. There was also a great need for second-line experts, who were not being supplied in sufficient numbers through the American and United Nations technical aid programs. Therefore a Commonwealth Technical Assistance Scheme was established, with all participants contributing to its $22.4 million total. A Council was created to provide foreign experts, necessary equipment, and the training of local personnel. Again no central agency controlled the funds; contributor and recipient had to decide how to use the money through bilateral arrangements. By mid-1954 half the funds had been allocated, and the rate of achievement was accelerating. There were 502 requests for experts and 263 appointments made; training facilities for 2,293 were sought and 1,653 provided. The United Nations and its specialized agencies supplied almost 1,500 experts to this region in 1950–1954; and the United States, through its Point Four Program, sent 786 experts. Yet both foreign experts and trained natives are in short supply, and it has proved difficult to coordinate these international technical aid programs efficiently.

The Colombo Plan, because of its limited financial scope, has been dubbed "Asia's Watering Can," and indeed it is but a pioneer effort in a region that needs long-term, large-scale development programs. Nevertheless, an important beginning has been made. The plan operates in a democratic fashion, for it is based on projects developed by free governments that must justify their policies at home and abroad. Though each participant works out its own sources of assistance, it is still committed to some degree of international economic planning. Even more important, the older Commonwealth states have shown that Asian views on development problems and the Cold War are listened to and respected.

The British Position

The Commonwealth links its Asian members to Britain, a pivotal state in the Western defense system. But their alignment is based on tradition and involves no binding commitment. Britain hopes that it will provide an unobtrusive incentive for these states to follow a Western orientation. At present Britain is allied with Pakistan in the Seato and Baghdad Pacts. Its only bilateral military accord was with Ceylon, which agreed to a naval base at Trincomalee and an air base at Katunayaka. This agreement contributed to Ceylon's security and served as a link to the other major naval base at Singapore. However, in 1956 the new Ceylonese government successfully insisted that this agreement with London be terminated. Britain then decided to reopen an air base in the Maldive Islands just below Ceylon, but British over-all strength is a far cry from the dominating force of earlier days. Britain's moral prestige in South Asia also suffered a severe blow as a result of its ill-fated military venture against Egypt in the Suez region in the fall of 1956.

India's refusal to join in defense planning has ended an era in which that subcontinent and Australia served as the strategic strongholds of a southern

Asian security system. Britain may retain defense and security positions in Malaya and Singapore after its political control ends. Yet these areas, plus other islands, now under a High Commissioner for Southeast Asia, form a very limited power base. Britain therefore cannot depend on territory and military strength to regain the authority and prestige it enjoyed before 1939. It is only through the Commonwealth framework, with its stress on self-rule and voluntary association, that British influence and leadership in Asia can be effectively asserted. Hence it is willing to stress economic and technical aid and even give assurances of political-military aid without reciprocal commitments.

India, for example, is not committed to aid Britain and generally looks on Europe as a distant world whose security problems bear no relation to Asian affairs. Nor is it obliged to act if Malaya, Singapore, Hong Kong, Borneo, or other parts of the old empire are endangered. British critics of the Commonwealth bitterly observe that this organization has no real value and simply means that high commissioners instead of ambassadors are exchanged between members. And, in fact, the Commonwealth has not acted as a cohesive force in world politics; it has not even resolved or mitigated many of its intramural problems. These include the India-Pakistan dispute, the most serious one in South Asia, Ceylon's uneasy relations with its large neighbor, and South Africa's racial segregation program, which has dismayed all other Commonwealth members. In addition, there is Australia's white immigration policy, regulating settlement in a sparsely inhabited land of 11 million. Australia has tried to follow a constructive and friendly policy in Asia by supporting Indonesia's bid for freedom (though not for Western New Guinea) and a program of economic and technical aid. However, it fears being swamped by colored immigrants from the north and adheres firmly to its restrictive immigration program.

On balance, though, the Commonwealth is a great pioneer effort in the field of international organization and politics. It has global significance as a laboratory for training modern democratic states, in Africa and Latin America as well as Asia. The importance of its new Asian members lies less in population weights than in the knowledge that these are the Commonwealth's first non-white, non-Western members. The eventual outcome of this attempt to establish close links between the West and the "underdeveloped, uncommitted" areas may vitally affect the political and ideological orientation of much of the world.

Other International Considerations

The relationship between the Colombo Plan and other organizations reflects the wide range of international agencies concerned with economic affairs. There are numerous specialized bodies associated with the United Nations dealing with food, health, education, labor, and the like that operate on a global basis. A Technical Assistance Board has been established, with funds of its own, to extend expert aid and train personnel under United Nations auspices. This technical assistance program is limited in funds, operating on an annual budget of $20-odd million. Its long-term goal is to double this relatively modest sum.

At the regional level there is the United Nations Economic Commission for Asia and the Far East (ECAFE), established in 1947, which has parallel organizations in Europe and Latin America. It has a central machinery, including a permanent secretariat, thereby insuring continuous activity at a regional level. It conducts research into development problems, evaluates policies, and makes suggestions. Yet it is not an executive or directing agency and has no power to carry out its own recommendations. Its strength lies in creating a climate of opinion and getting governments to respect its views. Its annual conference has an important impact, since its member states are represented by leading economic and public officials. At these meetings the Asian economic situation is discussed on the basis of an impartial survey made annually by the commission. The agency also issues quarterly bulletins and other special studies. Its prestige, like its level of competence, has risen steadily in recent years.

The Position of Japan

A common aspiration running through all Asian plans is the attainment of industrialized, diversified economies. It is here that Japan enters with hopes of serving as Asia's workshop and in this way stabilizing its own precarious economic structure. The Japanese see in Southeast Asia a possible replacement for the loss of pre-1941 markets, which were after all rooted in their political control of Manchuria, Formosa, and North China. However, even with American support, this effort is beset with serious economic and political problems. Southeast Asia is now interested primarily in capital goods rather than the consumer items that used to be the mainstay of Japanese exports. Like India, these Asian states now manufacture their own textiles and may actually compete with Japan in exporting such products. A further difficulty is Britain's reluctance to face uncontrolled Japanese competition, for fear that lower labor and transport costs will harm its own vital export drive. Britain first objected to allowing Japan to join G.A.T.T. (General Agreement on Trade and Tariffs), an international undertaking to liberalize trade. After Japan was accepted, Britain and other states invoked certain restrictive qualifications against the Japanese, which were legally permitted under the agreement.

Japan's future in Asia depends on an alleviation of trade rivalries, as well as its own economic efficiency and development of capital-goods exports. But another important element here is Japan's political strength. This is bound to reassert itself after having been suppressed in the first postwar decade by the pressure of American power, the rise of China and India, and Japan's own paralyzing feeling of uncertainty. There is considerable apprehension in Asia concerning the future course of Tokyo's foreign policy. Japan's neighbors, whatever additional fears they may harbor, are on guard against being drawn into Tokyo's orbit through the device of economic penetration.

The question of Japanese reparations for war damages brought both the

563

economic and political aspects of this question into focus. This reminder of past aggressions was also a possible way of healing old scars and creating a better atmosphere for future relations. Japan recognized the need to offer goods, services, and technical aid as well as money as reparations payment, but the wide gap between what was offered and what was demanded reflected emotional antagonism as well as different economic estimates. The log-jam was broken in 1954, when Burma accepted $220 million and a Japanese commitment of $50 million in capital investments. This move might have important long-term effects on Burma's pattern of trade and its traditional association with the British sterling bloc. Soon after, Thailand accepted $66 million in reparations.

Negotiations with the Philippines proved more difficult, but a settlement was reached in 1956, when Tokyo accepted a claim for $800 million. Of this, $250 million were to be in loans, with the rest in goods and services. Japan hopes that this settlement will facilitate an agreement with Indonesia, whose claim for a few billion dollars in reparations is considered far too extravagant. If settlements are made with all other states, Indonesia may be induced to follow suit. Then Japan has an excellent opportunity to establish strong commercial ties with Southeast Asia, but much of its export trade will have already been "paid for" by war damages. If Tokyo is to stand this strain of unrequited exports, it must follow a careful program of industrial rationalization, planned expansion of capacity, and austerity in domestic spending.

The American Perspective

The questions of military and political security continue to weigh heavily on free Asia. Britain and, for the first time, Australia have committed military forces to Malaya, but even this situation may be modified after Malaya gains self-rule. Elsewhere it is the United States that has assumed the major burden. America has guaranteed the rest of free Asia against a renewed Japanese assault, while simultaneously shielding Japan from continental pressures. Finally, the United States has committed itself to the defense of South Korea, Formosa, and Southeast Asia. It is part of the logic of America's containment policy that the United States is admirably situated, on a global scale, to support coalitions of free states on the peripheries of Eurasia. This concept, however, depends on the desire of the exposed nations to secure themselves against the communist menace.

The ideal situation for Asia's military security, from an American perspective, would be a coalition led by Japan and India and supported by the United States. This would bear a plausible resemblance to NATO and give the area a certain protection against aggression. Unfortunately, such an objective is painfully distant from the hard facts of Asian politics. An Asian People's Anti-Communist League was organized in 1954, but it is an unofficial grouping, lacks an established policy, and shows no indication of offering adequate resistance to communism. Its original membership was composed of delegates from Hong Kong, Macao, the Ryukyus, South Korea, Nationalist China, Thailand, the Philippines, and Vietnam, a grouping of states that represent very little power. A Nationalist Chinese invitation to have Japan join the group was blocked by South Korea. The United States has had little success in bringing together, in any sort of cohesive coalition, even the countries that are its allies.

In this uncertain environment, economic assistance may be more fruitful than a purely political-military approach. Yet it has proved difficult to extend aid effectively with the desired political results. Unlike Western Europe at the time of the Marshall Plan, the Asian states have been unable to work together. The United States tentatively considered a $200 million program for Asia in 1955, similar in concept if not in size to the 1948 European aid program. The Asian states held a meeting at Simla, India, after the great Bandung Conference, to discuss a coordinated effort to implement this policy, and it proved a fiasco. Ceylon suspected Indian domination and would not even attend. Japan and India favored a joint effort, but the others shied away from Japanese leadership and feared that these two states would enjoy unfair advantage. A final communiqué announced that there was no need for a special Asian organization to handle American aid, a stand that drew widespread criticism in Asia and the West and had much to do with America's failure to produce a long-range capital aid program at that time.

For their part, Asians have been upset over the fact that American assistance to the Orient followed the course of Washington's political and military commitments. In 1945–1949, the lion's share went to China ($1.515 billion), Japan ($1.478 billion), the Philippines ($555 million) and South Korea ($341 million), in sharp contrast to aid extended to India ($14 million) and Indonesia ($130 million). The scales were only slightly redressed in 1950–1952.[2] To July, 1953, Europe received in postwar aid $34.3 billion, compared to East Asia's $8.3 billion. Most of this latter sum went for military aid and defense support that centered on Japan, the Philippines, South Korea, and Nationalist China. This pattern continued in 1953–1954, when large expenditures were devoted to bolstering the French Vietnam position in Indochina. Only by 1955 did the Far East receive a greater share than Europe, with the emphasis on economic rather than military assistance. For example, American aid to Pakistan totaled $300 million in 1951–1955.

India received $88.7 million in 1954 and $77.3 million in 1955, and it is possible that an annual level of $100 million may be reached and sustained for some time. The American aid program to India appears to have been continued in spite of political antagonisms created by foreign policy differences. During 1952–1956 direct government aid totaled $326 million, or about 7 per cent of India's first five-year plan. When an earlier food loan and private aid program are added, the over-all total reaches about $1 billion, with primary emphasis on agriculture and community development projects. By 1957, the impact of the program was felt in almost all branches of Indian economic affairs, as expressed in sixty-three operational agreements between the two countries.

[2] Aid was, in millions of dollars: India, 203; Indonesia, 68; Burma, 9; Pakistan, 8; by contrast, South Korea received 363; the Philippines, 508; Japan, 223; and Nationalist China, 156.

The sudden appearance of Russia in the mid-1950's as a source of capital aid for Asia and other underdeveloped areas first caused consternation in the West. However, there is no reason why the Soviets should not share the moral burden of assisting these states to develop their economies. From the Western vantage point, anything that helps these states prosper is to be welcomed, at least in theory. It would also be useful to have Soviet boasts and promises matched against achievement in technical aid, capital loans, and delivery of materials. When the novelty of Russian help wears off, should such aid actually materialize, intelligent comparisons with Western assistance programs in Asia can be undertaken. The essential element to keep in mind is the preservation and strengthening of the democratic form of government in Asia. Should Russian aid not be a source of subversion but actual help in the economic development of Free Asia, it might be turned to the advantage of the West.

Conclusion

In the present climate of political opinion, it appears impossible to organize a comprehensive military defense of free Asia. Where a military alignment is impossible, it remains the task of the West to prove that it seeks only what the free Asians seek—the independence and stability of all democratic nations. Western political and economic policy must be directed toward the attainment of this more realistic objective. The continued faith of Asian intellectuals in the democratic ethic is a primary aspect of this problem. It may be that the internal struggle over ideology rather than foreign aggression or subversion will determine the future of Asian politics. In determining a course of political action, the West must balance its own security requirements with a policy that gives the free states of Asia a maximum opportunity to develop along democratic lines.

Bibliography

INTERNATIONAL RELATIONS IN THE FAR EAST

KOREA

HULBERT, H. B., *History of Korea.* 2 vols.; London: Routledge & Kegan Paul, 1906.

LONGFORD, J. H., *The Story of Korea.* London: Allen & Unwin, 1911.

OSGOOD, C., *The Koreans and Their Culture.* New York: Ronald, 1951.

NELSON, M. F., *Korea and the Old Order in Eastern Asia.* Baton Rouge: Louisiana State Univ. Press, 1945.

KEITH, E., and E. SCOTT, *Old Korea.* New York: Philosophical Lib. 1947.

GRAJDANZEV, A. J., *Modern Korea.* New York: John Day, 1944.

McCune, G. M., *Korea Today*. Cambridge: Harvard Univ. Press, 1950.

Meade, E. G., *American Military Government in Korea*. New York: King's Crown Press, 1951.

Oliver, R. T., *Syngman Rhee*. New York: Dodd, Mead, 1954.

Chung Kyung Cho, *Korea Tomorrow*. New York: Macmillan, 1950.

Taylor, G. D., *Korea: A Geographic Appreciation*. Ottawa: Department of Mines and Technical Surveys, 1951.

Lee, H. K., *Land Utilization and Rural Economy in Korea*. Chicago: Univ. of Chicago Press, 1936.

Robert Nathan Associates, *An Economic Program for Korean Reconstruction*. New York: Columbia Univ. Press, 1954.

Report of the UNESCO-UNKRA, *Educational Planning Mission to Korea: Rebuilding Education in the Republic of Korea*. Paris: UNESCO, 1954.

RUSSIA IN THE FAR EAST

Kolarz, W., *The People of the Soviet Far East*. New York: Praeger, 1954.

Shabad, T., *Geography of the USSR: A Regional Survey*. New York: Columbia Univ. Press, 1951.

Dallin, D., *The Rise of Russia in Asia*. New Haven: Yale Univ. Press: 1949.

Golder, F., *Russian Expansion on the Pacific: 1641–1850*. Cleveland: Clark, 1914.

Lensen, G. A., *Russia's Japan Exposition 1852–1855*. Gainesville: Univ. of Florida Press, 1955.

Lobanov-Rostovsky, A., *Russia and Asia*. New York: Macmillan, 1933.

Pasvolsky, L., *Russia in the Far East*. New York: Macmillan, 1922.

Witte, Count (ed. and trans. by A. Yarmolinsky), *The Memoirs of Count Witte*. New York: Doubleday, 1921.

Price, E. B., *The Russo-Japanese Treaties of 1907–1916*. Baltimore: Johns Hopkins Press, 1933.

Norton, H. K., *The Far Eastern Republic of Siberia*. London: Allen & Unwin, 1923.

Yakhantov, *Russia and the Soviet Union in the Far East*. New York: Coward McCann, 1931.

Whiting, A. S., *Soviet Policies in Asia: 1917–1924*. New York: Columbia Univ. Press, 1954.

Fischer, L., *The Soviets in World Affairs*. 2 vols., 2d ed.; Princeton: Princeton Univ. Press, 1951.

Dallin, D., *Soviet Russia and the Far East*. New Haven: Yale Univ. Press, 1948.

Moore, H. L., *Soviet Far Eastern Policy: 1931–1945*. Princeton: Princeton Univ. Press, 1945.

Beloff, M., *Foreign Policy of Soviet Russia*. 2 vols.; New York: Oxford Univ. Press, 1947–1949.

Hindus, M., *Russia and Japan*. Garden City: Doubleday, 1942.

Mandel, W., *The Soviet Far East and Central Asia*. New York: Dial Press, 1944.

Creel, G., *Russia's Race for Asia*. Indianapolis: Bobbs-Merrill, 1949.

Tompkins, P., *American-Russian Relations in the Far East*. New York: Macmillan, 1949.

Pavlovsky, M. N., *Chinese-Russian Relations*. New York: Philosophical Lib., 1949.

Wu, Ai-chen K., *China and the Soviet Union*. New York: John Day, 1950.

Degras, J. (ed.), *Soviet Documents on Foreign Policy*. 3 vols.; New York: Royal Inst. of Int. Affairs, 1951-1953.

Beloff, M., *Soviet Policy in the Far East: 1944–1951*. New York: Oxford Univ. Press, 1953.

Haines, C. G. (ed.), *The Threat of Soviet Imperialism*. Baltimore: Johns Hopkins Press, 1954.

Wei, H., *China and Soviet Russia*. New York: Van Nostrand, 1956.

THE UNITED STATES AND EAST ASIA

U.S. Dept. of State, *Foreign Relations of the United States* (yearly coverage). Washington: Government Printing Office.

The United States and World Affairs (annual since 1938–1939). (World Peace Foundation; Council on Foreign Relations since 1951.)

Documents on American Foreign Policy (annual since 1934) (Council on Foreign Relations).

Texts and Surveys

BEMIS, S. F., *A Diplomatic History of the United States.* 3rd ed.; New York: Holt, 1950.

BAILEY, T. A., *A Diplomatic History of the American People.* 4th ed.; New York: Appleton-Century-Crofts, 1950.

BATTISTINI, L. H., *The United States and Asia.* New York: Praeger, 1955.

DULLES, F. R., *America's Rise to World Power: 1899–1954.* New York: Harper, 1955.

PRATT, J. W., *A History of United States Foreign Policy.* New York: Prentice-Hall, 1955.

Relations to 1941

DULLES, F. R., *China and America: The Story of Their Relations since 1781.* Princeton: Princeton Univ. Press, 1946.

DENNETT, T., *Americans in Eastern Asia.* New York: Macmillan, 1922.

TREAT, P. J., *Diplomatic Relations between the United States and Japan.* 3 vols.; Stanford: Stanford Univ. Press, 1932.

TREAT, P. J., *Japan and the United States: 1853–1921* (revised and continued to 1928). Stanford: Stanford Univ. Press, 1928.

FOSTER, J. W., *American Diplomacy in the Orient.* Boston: Houghton Mifflin, 1903.

SWISHER, E., *China's Management of the American Barbarians.* New Haven: Yale Univ. Press, 1953.

PRATT, J. W., *Expansionists of 1898.* Baltimore: Johns Hopkins Press, 1936.

DENNETT, T., *Roosevelt and the Russo-Japanese War.* Garden City: Doubleday, 1935.

ZABRISKIE, E. H., *American-Russian Rivalry in the Far East: 1895–1914.* Philadelphia: Univ. of Pennsylvania Press, 1946.

GRISWOLD, A. W., *The Far Eastern Policy of the United States.* New York: Harcourt, Brace, 1938.

FIFIELD, R. H., *Woodrow Wilson and the Far East.* New York: Crowell, 1952.

LI TIEN-YI, *Woodrow Wilson's China Policy.* New York: Twayne, 1952.

GRAVES, W. S., *America's Siberian Venture: 1918–1920.* New York: Jonathan Cape, 1931.

WHITE, J., *The Siberian Intervention.* Princeton: Princeton Univ. Press, 1950.

MANNING, C. A., *The Siberian Fiasco.* New York: Library Pubs., 1952.

BORG, D., *American Policy and the Chinese Revolution: 1925–1928.* New York: Macmillan, 1947.

STIMSON, H. L., *The Far Eastern Crisis.* New York: Harper, 1936.

PAN, S., *American Diplomacy Concerning Manchuria.* New York: Humphries, 1939.

BISSON, T. A., *American Policy in the Far East: 1931–1941.* New York: Inst. of Pacific Relations, 1941.

GREW, J., *Turbulent Era.* Boston: Houghton Mifflin, 1952, Vol. II.

HORNBECK, S. K., *The United States and the Far East.* Boston: World Peace Foundation, 1942.

JOHNSTONE, W. C., *The United States and Japan's New Order.* New York: Oxford Univ. Press, 1941.

FEIS, H., *The Road to Pearl Harbor.* Princeton: Princeton Univ. Press, 1950.

LANGER, W. L., and S. E. GLEASON, *The Challenge to Isolation: 1937-1940.* New York: Harper, 1952.

LANGER, W. L., and S. E. GLEASON, *The Undeclared War: 1940–1941.* New York: Harper, 1953.

U.S. DEPT. OF STATE, *Foreign Relations of the United States, Japan: 1931–1941.* 2 vols.; Washington: Government Printing Office, 1943.

U.S. CONGRESS, *Events Leading up to World War II* (H. R. Doc. No. 541, 78th Cong., 2d Sess.) Washington, 1942.

Pearl Harbor Attack, Hearings before the Joint Committee on the Investigation of the Pearl Harbor Attack, 79th Cong., 1st & 2d. Sess. pursuant to S. Con. Res. 27 as extended by S. Con. Res. 49, Nov. 15, 1945, to May 31, 1946. 11 parts; Washington, 1946.

HULL, C., *The Memoirs of Cordell Hull.* 2 vols.; New York: Macmillan, 1948.

The Pacific War and Its Aftermath

GREENFIELD, K. R. (gen. ed.), *The United States Army in World War II: The War in the Pacific.* See, among others, C. F. ROMANUS and R. SUTHERLAND, *Stilwell's Mission to China* (Washington: Government Printing Office, 1952) in this series.

MORISON, S. E., *History of the United States Naval Operations in World War II.* 10 vols.; Boston: Little, Brown, 1947-1956.

LEAHY, W. D., *I Was There.* New York: Whittlesey House, 1950.

SHERWOOD, R. E., *Roosevelt and Hopkins.* New York: Harper, 1948.

FEIS, H., *The China Tangle.* Princeton: Princeton Univ. Press, 1953.

STUART, H. L., *Fifty Years in China.* New York: Random House, 1954.

STIMSON, H. L., and McG. BUNDY, *On Active Service in Peace and War.* New York: Harper, 1948.

KING, E., and W. M. WHITEHILL, *Fleet Admiral King.* New York: Morton, 1952.

MILLIS, W. (ed.), *The Forrestal Diaries.* New York: Viking, 1951.

PEFFER, N., *Basis for Peace in the Far East.* New York: Harper, 1942.

LATTIMORE, O., *Solution in Asia.* Boston: Little, Brown, 1943.

ISAACS, H., *No Peace for Asia.* New York: Macmillan, 1947.

LAUTERBACH, R. E., *Danger from the East.* New York: Harper, 1947.

VINACKE, H. M., *The United States and the Far East.* Stanford: Stanford Univ. Press, 1952.

LATOURETTE, K. S., *The American Record in the Far East.* New York: Macmillan, 1952.

U.S. DEPARTMENT OF STATE, *United States Relations with China: with Special Reference to the Period 1944-1949.* Washington, 1949.

UTLEY, F., *The China Story.* Chicago: Regnery, 1951.

U.S. CONGRESS, *The United States and the Korean Problem: Documents 1943-1953* (Sen. Doc. No. 74, 83d Cong., 1st Sess.). Washington, 1953.

U.S. SENATE, *Military Situation in the Far East.* Hearings before the Committee on the Armed Services and the Committee on Foreign Relations (U.S. Senate, 82d Cong., 1st Sess.). 5 parts; Washington, 1951.

TRUMAN, H. S., *Memoirs.* 2 vols.; Garden City: Doubleday, 1955-1956.

BUNDY, McG. (ed.), *Pattern of Responsibility.* Boston: Houghton Mifflin, 1952.

DULLES, J. F., *War or Peace.* New York: Macmillan, 1950.

DEAN, W. F., *General Dean's Story.* New York: Viking, 1954.

POATS, R. M., *Decision in Korea.* New York: McBride, 1954.

MARSHALL, S. L. A., *The River and the Gauntlet.* New York: Morrow, 1953.

OLIVER, R. T., *Verdict in Korea.* Pennsylvania State College: Bald Eagle Press, 1952.

CALDWELL, J. C., *The Korea Story.* Chicago: Regnery, 1952.

KAHN, E. J., *The Peculiar War.* New York: Random House, 1952.

KENNEDY, E. J., *Mission to Korea.* London: Verschoyle, 1952.

CLARK, M. W., *From the Danube to the Yalu.* New York: Harper, 1954.

JOY, C. T., *How the Communists Negotiate.* New York: Macmillan, 1955.

BARTLETT, N. (ed.), *With the Australians in Korea.* Canberra: Australian War Memorial, 1954.

WHITNEY, C., *MacArthur: His Rendezvous with Destiny.* New York: Knopf, 1956.

ROVERE, R., and A. SCHLESINGER, *The General and the President.* New York: Farrar, Straus and Cudahy, 1951.

DILLE, J., *Substitute for Victory.* New York: Viking, 1954.

DEWEY, T. E., *Journey to the Far Pacific.* Garden City: Doubleday, 1952.

STANTON, E. F., *Brief Authority.* New York: Harper, 1956.

FARLEY, M. S., *United States Relations with Southeast Asia.* New York: Inst. of Pacific Relations, 1955.

ROSTOW, W. W., with R. W. HATCH, *An American Policy in Asia.* New York: Wiley, 1955.

SCHWANTES, R., *Japanese and Americans: A Century of Cultural Relations.* New York: Harper 1955.

BOWLES, C., *The New Dimensions of Peace.* New York: Harper, 1955.

The Southeast Asia Collective Defense Treaty, Hearings before the Committee on Foreign Relations, Senate, 83d-84th Cong., on Executive K, November 11, 1954, Jan. 19, 1955. 2 pts.; Washington, 1955.

Mutual Defense Treaty with Korea, Hearings before the Committee on Foreign Relations, Senate, 83d Cong. 2d Sess. on Executive A, Jan. 13-14, 1954.

Mutual Defense Treaty with the Republic of China, Report of the Committee on Foreign Relations, Senate, 84th Cong., 1st Sess., on Executive A, Feb. 8, 1955. Washington, 1955.

ASIAN INTERNATIONAL RELATIONS

JONES, F. C., H. BORTON, and B. R. PEARN, *The Far East: 1942–1946.* New York: Oxford Univ. Press, 1955.

ROYAL INSTITUTE OF INTERNATIONAL AFFAIRS, *Political and Strategic Interests of the United Kingdom.* London: Oxford Univ. Press, 1939.

KAHIN, G. McT, *The Asian African Conference.* Ithaca: Cornell Univ. Press, 1956.

WRIGHT, R., *The Color Curtain.* Cleveland: World Pub., 1956.

FISHER, M. W., and J. V. BONDURANT, *Indian Views of Sino-Indian Relations.* Berkeley: Univ. of California Press, 1956.

Documents Relating to the Discussion of Korea and Indo-China at the Geneva Conference, April 27-June 15, 1954. London, 1954 (Cmd. 9186).

Further Documents Relating to the Discussion of Indo-China at the Geneva Conference, June 16-July 21, 1954. London, 1954 (Cmd. 9239).

The Korean Problem at the Geneva Conference, April 26-June 15, 1954. Washington, 1954. (Dept. of State, International Organization and Conference Series II, Far Eastern.)

CONSULTATIVE COMMITTEE ON ECONOMIC DEVELOPMENT IN SOUTH AND SOUTHEAST ASIA, *The Colombo Plan for Co-operative Economic Development in South and Southeast Asia.* Annual since 1952.

GREAT BRITAIN. COMMONWEALTH RELATIONS OFFICE. COUNCIL FOR TECHNICAL COOPERATION IN SOUTH AND SOUTH-EAST ASIA. *The Colombo Plan: Technical Cooperative Scheme.* Annual Report.

LOW, F., *The Struggle for Asia.* New York: Praeger, 1956.

MICHENER, J. A., *The Voice of Asia.* New York: Random House, 1951.

ABEGG, L., *The Mind of Asia.* New York: Thomas, 1952.

BALL, W., *Nationalism and Communism in East Asia.* New York: Cambridge Univ. Press, 1952.

COOKE, D., *There Is No Asia.* Garden City: Doubleday, 1954.

TAYLOR, E. L., *Richer by Asia.* Boston: Houghton Mifflin, 1949.

LATTIMORE, O., *Situation in Asia.* Boston: Little, Brown, 1949.

VAN DE VLUGHT, *Asia Aflame.* New York: Devin-Adair, 1953.

CALDWELL, J. C., *Still the Rice Grows Green.* Chicago: Regnery, 1955.

WINT, G., *Spotlight on Asia.* London: Penguin, 1956.

Index